EDUCATING YOUNG HANDICAPPED CHILDREN

A Developmental Approach

Second Edition

Contributors

Paul A. Alberto, Ph.D.
Kevin Cole, M.S.
Rebecca R. Fewell, Ph.D.
Kathleen Gradel, Ed.D.
James M. Kauffman, Ph.D.
Jean F. Kelly, Ph.D.
M. Beth Langley, M.A.
David Page, Ph.D.
Milton Seligman, Ph.D.
Robert Sheehan, Ph.D.

EDUCATING YOUNG HANDICAPPED CHILDREN

A Developmental Approach

Second Edition

S. Gray Garwood

Tulane University
New Orleans, Louisiana

AN ASPEN PUBLICATION®
Aspen Systems Corporation
Rockville, Maryland
London
1983

Library of Congress Cataloging in Publication Data

Garwood, S. Gray.
Educating young handicapped children.

"An Aspen publication."
Includes bibliographies and index.
1. Handicapped children—Education. 2. Developmental psychology. 3. Child development. I. Title.
LC4015.G34 1983 371.9 82-20726
ISBN: 0-89443-929-4

Publisher: John Marozsan
Editorial Director: R. Curtis Whitesel
Managing Editor: Margot Raphael
Editorial Services: Eileen Higgins
Printing and Manufacturing: Debbie Collins

Library of Congress Catalog Card Number: 82-20726
ISBN: 0-89443-929-4

Printed in the United States of America

1 2 3 4 5

This edition is dedicated to my mother, *Ida,* to my grandmother, *Lucile,* to my father, *Sam,* and to my aunt, *Cena.*

Table of Contents

Preface to the First Edition

This book represents our belief that the intense interest in early childhood special education, which is reflected in PL 94-142, will necessitate a meld between programs that educate young children and programs that educate young handicapped children. Specifically, it seems most likely that professionals who work with young handicapped children will do so comparatively. That is, attempts to intervene in and facilitate the development of young handicapped children will probably be based strongly on knowledge of how normal or general development progresses. Also, it is not unfeasible that demands for a less restrictive environment for optimum development will lead to provision of public educational services for *all* preschool-aged children. If this happens, then certainly all professionals working with children will need to base their intervention efforts on developmental milestones in all areas of growth, especially the physical, cognitive, and social domains.

These three growth domains serve as markers in this book to isolate material significant to an eventual comprehensive view of the young child. Part I offers a special perspective. Part II discusses normal physical development and congenital and other conditions that result in physical and multiple handicaps as well as ways of working with physically handicapped preschool children. Part III focuses on cognitive development as well as on handicapping conditions that affect overall cognitive promise: sensory handicaps, learning disorders, and mental retardation. Finally, Part IV discusses social development, factors that affect it, and emotional disorders in early childhood. In each unit, the special contributions by leading special educators focus specifically on ways of working with handicapped children. Reference material in the appendixes helps select specific assessment and curriculum materials pertinent to early childhood. In addition, the appendixes contain suggested forms to assist in preparing individualized education programs as well as general guidelines for assessing developmental progress in young children.

I hope this book helps you help young children grow.

S. Gray Garwood, Ph.D.
Tulane University
New Orleans, Louisiana

Preface to the Second Edition

The original edition of this book was published at a time of great optimism regarding the educational future of young handicapped children. Today, that optimism is somewhat dampened. Not only does a basic shift in federal funding and social policy planning appear to be under way, but also several recent Supreme Court decisions may dilute efforts by states, local educational agencies, and citizens' groups to ensure that young handicapped children receive optimal assistance in realizing their developmental potential. In spite of these developments, or because of them, those of us who are concerned with child growth and development must intensify our efforts to foster growth by creating innovative but workable behavior change strategies, by continuing to provide quality and appropriate training to students entering the field, and by urging parental, community, state, and federal support for our efforts.

It is not easy to accomplish these goals; greater sophistication and more elaborate skills will be required than have been required of us in the past. For this reason, this revised edition contains much that is new. Each of the chapters that has been retained from the original edition has been completely revised to include current research pertinent to the area being discussed, in addition to practical, applied information. Three completely new chapters have been added: one on curriculum issues, one on working with families, and one on program development and evaluation. The appendixes have also been completely revised and updated.

We are still optimistic about the educational future of young handicapped children. This new book reflects that optimism, but also provides a ''practical reality'' approach that should help early childhood special education continue to develop as a useful career field, one that helps young children grow.

S. Gray Garwood, Ph.D.
March, 1983

Acknowledgment

While a great many people have contributed to this book, I especially want to acknowledge the help of Nelda Clements, whose careful reading and excellent typing make writing much easier.

Part I

Early Childhood Special Education

Chapter 1

Special Education and Child Development: A New Perspective

S. Gray Garwood

The roots of American psychology lie in education; because of psychologists' initial emphasis on the study of the learning process, psychology was naturally partnered with education. For many psychologists, this was an uneasy relationship. They were seeking to establish psychology, a relatively new discipline, as a science, resting on empirically collected data, theory, rigor, and control. These aims were, for many, incompatible with the naturally occurring process of education. Furthermore, education was deemed an inappropriate bedfellow because, in the early part of the twentieth century, education was considered neither a science nor an art. The two disciplines split. Psychology was relocated to liberal arts colleges and was called either a natural or a social science. Since those times, both disciplines have become multifaceted areas, dotted with subfields such as regular, special, vocational, administrative education, and developmental, social, school, and educational psychology.

In recent times, the two disciplines have begun to form a new alliance. Psychology has moved into the schools both for research (e.g., educational psychology) and for applied practice (e.g., school psychology, counseling and guidance, testing), and education has again become a natural laboratory for studying child behavior. Both fields have clearly benefited from this renewed collaboration. Most recently, the medical specialty of pediatrics has joined this alliance. The participation of pediatricians is a result of conclusions reached by the Task Force on Pediatrics (1978), which pointed out four key areas in which pediatric training was deficient: (1) developmental, behavioral, and biosocial pediatrics; (2) handicapping conditions and chronic illness; (3) nutrition; and (4) adolescent medicine. In addition, Bennett (1982) attributes this involvement to the dramatic growth of knowledge stemming from child development research, especially data relating to the value of early identification and intervention for subsequent behavioral outcomes.

One very obvious outgrowth of this renewed cooperation can be seen in the specialties of developmental psychology and early childhood education, especially early childhood special education (ECSE). Itself a new subfield within education, ECSE is concerned with providing meaningful and appropriate educational experiences to preschool children who, because of some handicapping condition, are not likely to benefit from regular preschool educational experiences as much as nonhandicapped children benefit. To ensure the maximum educational benefit for such children, ECSE specialists have enlisted the support of those in various other disciplines, such as developmental psychology. Together, these professionals are creating effective ways to facilitate development in young handicapped or exceptional children. The key role of the developmental psychologist is to provide information about how development occurs, which factors facilitate developmental progress, and which factors interfere with that progress. In turn, early childhood special educators use this information to develop intervention strategies and to structure learning environments that will give preschool exceptional children the best possible chance of fulfilling their potential. The results of these applied efforts, of course, provide important feedback as to the accuracy of developmental research findings.

THE DEVELOPMENTAL PERSPECTIVE: MECHANISTIC AND ORGANISMIC VIEWPOINTS

Developmental psychology is a special perspective within psychology; it involves the study of human development from conception to death. Specifically, developmental psychologists are concerned with those physical and psychological processes that enable the individual to adapt continuously to the world throughout the life span. Recently, this concern has been expanded to include those factors that are external to the individual but affect the rate and nature of developmental progress. For example, the February 1982 issue of *Child Development* contains research reports dealing with such diverse topics as the effects of the father's prolonged absence on youngsters' cognitive development, effects of social class on ratings of infant temperament, effects of motor activity on memory, the development of map-reading skills, and changes in children's understanding of the mind and brain.

The mechanisms or processes used to explain developmental phenomena are tied to theoretical conceptions of development. In psychology, two global views have dominated scientific thinking about the nature of developmental or behavioral change: the mechanistic and the organismic.

The Mechanistic Viewpoint

Following Descartes' "man as machine" model, the mechanistic model describes behavior in terms of a one-to-one relationship between environmental stimuli and behavioral responses. The individual is viewed as the passive object of environmental actions. This view is the basis for traditional behaviorism and reinforcement theory. Specifically, proponents of such a view argue that (1) behavior change results from forces external to the individual so that development is not a consequence of internally mediated restructuring; (2) the same principles govern behavior change in all organisms at all ages; and (3) complex behaviors result from linkages among less complex behaviors (chaining). Consequently, development is seen as essentially quantitative and continuous, because complex behavior represents only an accumulation of more and varied responses. "The developing child may be adequately regarded, in conceptual terms, as a cluster of interrelated responses interacting with stimuli" (Bijou & Baer, 1961, pp. 14-15).

Mechanistic theory is best expressed in the work of Skinner and his colleagues. Because B.F. Skinner's operant model focuses on the effects that environmental reinforcers have on behavior, learning is seen as heavily dependent on reinforcement. Skinner's views have been translated into practice in the early intervention program for Down's syndrome children that operates at the University of Washington in Seattle.

> Teaching techniques that are used routinely include modeling, cuing, prompting and physically helping an infant make the desired response . . . [and] . . . reinforcement of desired behaviors is stressed. At the infant level, reinforcement is mainly adult praise and attention. The infant is smiled at, talked to, patted, stroked and generally given a great deal of enthusiastic affection. . . . Occasionally a primary reinforcer . . . is used when a particularly difficult task is required. (Dmitriev, 1979, pp. 205-206)

Clunies-Ross (1979) has described a similar Down's syndrome program in Australia; the entire curriculum of this program is based on the "concepts, principles, and techniques of applied behavior analysis." (p. 170).

The Organismic Viewpoint

Those who adhere to the organismic viewpoint see development as initiated from within the child. Thus, development is marked by continuous change as lower levels of behavior are restructured into higher levels of behavior. Individuals are instrumental in bringing about their own development since they actively reach out to make contact with the environment and, in so doing, generate new experiences that are subsequently used to restructure earlier and simpler behaviors. The development of more efficient behaviors permits more effective environmental interactions, and this transactional process results in a continuous process of developmental change.

Development, thus viewed, is a series of sequential stages, each of which gives way to a higher order stage of functioning. The characteristics of the previous stage are altered, then integrated into the characteristics of the next higher stage of functioning. Because of this process, each stage of development is unique. Consequently, development is described by qualitative changes in behavior. The theory of Jean Piaget illustrates the organismic viewpoint. In his cognitive-developmental theory, Piaget seeks to explain how the individual acquires and organizes knowledge; he describes four major stages of cognitive development, each succeeding stage characterized by the acquisition of more differentiated and more complex mental skills (see Chapter 10, Emotional Disturbance). Table 1-1 shows the significant components of both mechanistic and organismic views.

Changing Scientific Orientation

Within the past 15 years, there has been a significant shift in theoretical emphasis. The mechanistic orientation has, to a large extent, been replaced by the more process-oriented organismic viewpoint. Several factors have contributed to this change. Advances in the biological and physiological sciences, for example, have helped to bring about a shift in emphasis from external determinants of development (e.g., home environment or quality of mothering) to ways in which organisms contribute to their own development. Such advances include an increased methodological sophistication in studying genetic contributions to behav-

Table 1-1 Comparative Summary of Mechanistic and Organismic Models

Feature	*Mechanistic Model*	*Organismic Model*
Behavioral analysis focus	Overt behavior	Internal processes
Nature of behavioral elements	Discrete and autonomous	Organized into wholes or structures that determine meaning
Control over behavior	External stimuli	Active and selective determination of behavioral interactions
Major characteristic of knowledge acquisition	Additive/quantitative	Interactive/qualitative
Behavioral continuity	Continuous	Discontinuous

ior, as well as a greater knowledge of how neurophysiological, endocrine, and neurotransmitter processes interact with the environment and affect the organization of behavior. Ainsworth, whose work on attachment processes typifies this changing orientation, describes it this way: "these influences have tended to shift the attention of many developmental psychologists from an almost exclusive concern with environmental control to increased interest in what is inside the organism to start with, how this inner programming affects the response to environmental input, and how it becomes transformed as a consequence of organism-environmental transactions" (1972, p. 99).

Contributions of Mechanistic and Organismic Viewpoints

Both theoretical conceptions of development have provided important insights into human development. The mechanistic approach has fostered experimental and theoretical rigor and has increased our knowledge of the socialization process and the role of social learning and reinforcement mechanisms in altering behavior. In education, this knowledge has been useful in structuring behavior modification techniques that encourage children to develop self-help skills and behavior controls, in developing task analysis procedures and programmed instruction, and in helping children acquire language and communication skills, to name but a few.

Likewise, the organismic approach has made significant contributions to psychological knowledge and to applied educational practices by demonstrating the importance of environmental stimulation and early intervention to enhance learning, as well as the importance of communication to learning. Perhaps its most influential contribution has been its emphasis on individual-environment transactions and the effect of these interactions on development, which has led to a resurgence of collaboration between educational practitioners and developmental researchers in such varied projects as infant stimulation programs, preschool enrichment programs, and cognitive and social skills training efforts.

Applications of Mechanistic and Organismic Viewpoints

Both mechanistic and organismic views of development offer a theoretical rationale for ECSE intervention efforts, including program philosophy, structure, operation, assessment, and evaluation. The mechanistic approach has generated the operant or behavioral model that is based on traditional learning and reinforcement theory. Very briefly, according to such a model, programmatic intervention efforts focus on

1. defining the nature of the child's problems and establishing priorities about the order in which these problems are to be dealt with

2. conducting task analyses
3. defining target behaviors
4. maintaining accurate records of the frequency with which target behaviors occur
5. selecting appropriate times and places for intervention and instruction
6. determining reinforcers, negative consequences, and instructional aides and procedures
7. testing for generalization or transfer
8. ensuring that behavioral gains are maintained.

Lancioni (1980) has reviewed evidence of the effectiveness of operant techniques with young children and concludes that the data support the incorporation of such procedures into early intervention programs. He identifies several reasons that operant practices seem feasible:

- Experimental evidence supports the use of operant techniques to strengthen or weaken behaviors.
- Operant procedures can be implemented across diverse settings and behaviors.
- Behaviors resulting from conditioning strategies can be maintained after intervention is terminated.
- Parents and teachers with minimal training can reliably carry out the necessary conditioning strategies.
- The main techniques used are well enough developed that step-by-step planning is possible.
- Implementation of operant conditioning techniques does not require costly or sophisticated materials.
- The vast body of literature on child and adult operant conditioning outcomes offers guidelines to useful combinations of behavior change strategies.
- The immediate feedback received by intervenors can serve as a reinforcer to encourage them to continue and to broaden their efforts.

(For a more thorough discussion of operant procedures, see Chapter 8, The Young Mildly Retarded Child, and Sameroff & Cavanaugh, 1979.)

Classical conditioning procedures based on the work of Pavlov and Watson have not been as well studied as have operant ones (Fitzgerald & Brackbill, 1976). It is clear, however, that these procedures can be used effectively to alter behavior; they have been especially useful in altering deviant behaviors in young children (Graziano, DeGiovanni, & Garcia, 1979).

Because the cognitive-developmental model stems from organismic theory, such an approach focuses on

1. identifying sequences of cognitive growth (e.g., visually directed reaching, object permanence, causality, imitation)
2. translating these sequences into curriculum (see Dunst, 1981, for a model of this process)
3. assessing a child's current status with respect to these sequences
4. determining where in a particular sequence to intervene
5. providing experiences deemed relevant to facilitate the desired behaviors
6. reassessing a child's status after exposure to these experiences to determine how to proceed

The Infant, Toddler, and Preschool Research and Intervention Project (Bricker & Bricker, 1976) illustrates how the cognitive-developmental model is interpreted in program philosophy and practice. According to the Brickers,

> Actions of the infant produce consequences that are associated with a rapid increase in the rate or intensity of the actions. . . . As the action-reaction system continues to operate, the child learns to make discriminations about which objects are suckable, graspable, shakable, bangable, and throwable. As these action-object relationships increase in number and become coordinated, . . . the infant's action system moves out of the involuntary mode into one that can be considered voluntary, deliberate, or intentional. (p. 549)

Likewise, Dunst's work illustrates how this approach can be used in assessment (1980) and in structuring curriculum (1981).

HISTORICAL OVERVIEW OF SPECIAL EDUCATION

Just as professionals in general education attempt to provide appropriate instruction to children who function within the normal social and intellectual range, those in special education seek to ensure that children who are exceptional in some way receive instruction appropriate to their capabilities and needs. It is only recently, however, that special educational services have become available on a widespread basis and have been expanded to encompass the needs of *all* exceptional children.

Before the eighteenth century, individuals with handicaps were regarded with hostility, fear, and superstition. They were thought to be somehow "cursed" and not to deserve the rights due other human beings. The handicapping conditions recognized at the time were usually gross physical, mental, or sensory handicaps that were very apparent to others; the typical handicapped individual was one who might look something like the one-eyed hunchback of Notre Dame. Conditions such as mild mental retardation, emotional disorders, learning disorders, or giftedness were not yet recognized as exceptional conditions.

By the nineteenth century, advances in science and changes in the philosophical views of human nature began to alter views of the handicapped. John Locke, who saw the human being as a blank slate at birth, argued that people learn through their senses and that knowledge comes from experience, not from God. In *Origin of Species,* Charles Darwin also attacked the notion of divine creation. Another significant event was the attempt by Itard, a consulting physician to the National Institute for Deaf-Mutes in Paris, to train the Wild Boy of Aveyron. Itard was familiar with Locke's views, and, when the Wild Boy was brought to the institute for care, Itard asked permission to work with the boy, whom he named Victor.

Victor had apparently been abandoned as a small child and grew up as an animal. He was truly wild. He could not speak; he selected food only by smell; and he displayed no affection or concern for other humans. He also walked with a swaying, animal-like gait; frequently had convulsions; and would bite and scratch others if threatened. Itard started Victor on a sensory training program. By 1801, Victor ate and slept normally and was able to keep himself clean. He had become sensitive to touch, taste, and smell. He showed affection for, and dependence on, his governess. And he had learned a few crude symbolic skills, such as arranging letters to spell out the word *milk* and producing monosyllabic sounds to indicate his desire for some item.

Five years later, in 1806, Victor could distinguish gross sound differences, such as the difference between a drum and a bell. He could respond to differences in the tones of the human voice and could distinguish colors and letters, but he still could not "think" as we know it. When puberty occurred, many of these training gains were lost as Victor again became unmanageable, and the training program was terminated. Despite this negative ending, Itard's work had shown that it was possible, through education and training, for retarded individuals to develop self-help skills. This was also made clear in the United States by the work of one special teacher, Anne Sullivan, who worked with one special child, Helen Keller. Miss Keller, with the help of her teacher, was able to break through her blindness and deafness to become an important symbol for the value of special education.

It was not until the twentieth century, however, that special education became an organized and recognized profession. Several separate organizations had been formed to help individuals with specific handicapping conditions, such as the Convention of American Instructors of the Deaf, the American Association of Instructors of the Blind, and the American Association on Mental Deficiency. There was little communication among these organizations, however, and their numbers were too small to have any great national impact. It might be said that

Alexander Graham Bell, who was actively involved in training the deaf, was responsible for organizing special education because he twice petitioned the National Education Association (NEA) to create a new multidisciplinary division within the NEA to deal with the educational needs of the handicapped. Bell suggested that this new division be called the Department for the Education of Classes Requiring Special Methods of Instruction. Unfortunately, when the NEA responded to Bell's petition, in 1897, they named the new division the Department of Education of the Deaf, Blind, and the Feebleminded, after the three major handicapping conditions involved. Eventually, this department became known as the Department of Special Education.

With the organization of special education forces within the NEA, public schools began to hold classes for handicapped children. By 1911, there were special education classes in 99 American cities. World War I and the Great Depression interfered with the growth of this movement, however, and these classes decreased in number until after World War II.

The effect of World War II on education in general was phenomenal, but its effect on special education was of paramount importance. During the war, nearly 1 million men were rejected for military service because intelligence testing revealed some degree of mental incompetency. Yet many of these men were able to return home and *visibly* lead productive and useful lives. This helped to reduce the stigma associated with mental handicaps. But it was the aftermath of the war that really brought the handicapped to public attention. Among the returning veterans were many thousands of men who were now physically, intellectually, or emotionally impaired. Their presence in such large numbers called for both social rehabilitation programs and research programs to develop effective treatment procedures. For the first time, the handicapped became a visible minority, and attitudes toward them began to change. Parents were no longer made to feel ashamed of their handicapped children, and they began to organize pressure groups, such as the United Cerebral Palsy Association, to demand access to educational resources that did not require institutionalization of their children. These parent groups were joined by special education professional groups, such as the Council for Exceptional Children.

Efforts to seek better educational services for the handicapped minority were furthered by the historic Supreme Court decision in *Brown v. Board of Education of Topeka*. In this decision, the Court ruled that state laws permitting or requiring segregated public schools violated the Fourteenth Amendment's "equal protection under the law" clause. Recognizing that what applied to one minority group would also apply to another minority group, the special education pressure groups exerted sufficient legal and social pressure to bring about changes in federal law regarding the education of all handicapped children and youth (Tables 1-2 and 1-3).

Table 1-2 Significant Court Decisions Affecting Special Education

Case	*Decision*
Hobson v. Nathan (1967)	Schools cannot assign children to special education classes on the basis of culturally discriminatory standardized test data.
Mills v. Board of Education of the District of Columbia (1971)	All children previously excluded from public schools must have equal opportunity for a public education, regardless of the degree of severity of their handicap.
Pennsylvania Association for Retarded Children v. the Commonwealth of Pennsylvania (1971)	All mentally retarded children have a right to an education at public expense, and parents have a right to due process before a child's status in school can be altered in any way.
Lori Case v. State of California (1973)	Handicapped children cannot be assigned to self-contained classrooms when it is possible to educate them in the same classrooms that "normal" children attend.

Effects of Public Legislation on Special Education

Twenty-five years ago, only about 40 colleges and universities offered courses on mental retardation. Only 15 of these institutions offered doctoral training in special education. In fact, in 1953, only 4 such doctorates and 130 master's degrees were awarded in the United States (Burke, 1976). Clearly, in spite of special education's long history, it had few professionals at this time. This rather bleak picture was changed by the massive financial support that resulted from federal legislation (see Table 1-3). In 1960, nearly 1 million dollars was authorized for federally assisted special education programs. Four years later, that figure had risen to 13 million dollars; by 1976, over 40 million dollars had been allocated to special education programs (Burke, 1976). In 1979, the amount allocated under PL 94-142 was 465 million dollars (Sabatino, 1981), and by 1982, 969 million dollars had been appropriated (Children's Defense Fund, 1982). Today, more than 250,000 people work in this field in some capacity.

PL 94-142

In 1975, despite the nearly 20 years of federal support, almost 2 million handicapped children were being excluded from public education. Furthermore, many of the estimated 8 million exceptional children receiving some form of special education were not receiving "appropriate" services. Many handicapped children were being placed in inappropriate educational settings because their

Table 1-3 Significant Federal Legislation Affecting Special Education

Public Law	*Purpose*
PL 83-531 (1957)	Provided the first research support for the study of handicapping conditions
PL 85-926 (1958)	Authorized grants to colleges and universities for the training of special education leadership personnel, as well as payment of funds to states for training teachers to work with the mentally retarded
PL 88-164 (1963)	Expanded categories of handicapped children to include not only the mentally retarded but also hard-of-hearing, deaf, speech-impaired, visually impaired, seriously emotionally disturbed, crippled, or other health-impaired children needing special education as a result of their impairment
PL 89-750 (1966)	Amended the Elementary and Secondary Education Act of 1965 by adding Title VI, which authorized funds to initiate, improve, and expand programs for the handicapped; also created the Bureau of Education for the Handicapped and the National Advisory Committee on Handicapped Children
PL 90-170 (1967)	Authorized programs in physical education and recreation for the handicapped and the training of leadership personnel, supervisors, and researchers
PL 90-576 (1968)	Authorized agencies other than colleges and universities or states to apply for training grants
PL 91-230 (1970)	Authorized funds for the inclusion of learning disabilities and reinforced the federal government's role in educating handicapped children
PL 94-142 (1975)	Incorporated previous benefits from legislative and judicial action into one legislative act reflecting national policy regarding the education of handicapped individuals.

handicaps had not been detected (Abeson & Zettel, 1977). It became clear that a greater effort was needed. Congress responded to this need by enacting PL 94-142, and President Gerald Ford signed it into law on November 29, 1975. Under this law, Congress clarified national policy regarding the education of the handicapped:

> It is the purpose of this Act to assure that all handicapped children have available to them, within the time periods specified, a free appropriate public education which emphasizes special education and related services designed to meet their unique needs. (PL 94-142, 1975, Section 3, c)

Therefore, in September 1978, all elementary and secondary school handicapped children became eligible for a free public education. In 1980, this age range was extended upward to age 21. The law also provided for an incentive grant program to encourage states to provide educational services to handicapped preschoolers (ages 3 to 5). To date, approximately 20 states have made such services available to handicapped preschoolers.

PL 94-142 has been called the handicapped child's Bill of Rights. Under the law, each exceptional child eligible for services has a right to

1. *education:* No longer can handicapped children be regarded as too severely handicapped to benefit from some form of education at public expense. Furthermore, handicapped children are now eligible to participate in *all* programs provided by public schools for nonhandicapped children.
2. *nondiscriminatory evaluation:* Testing and evaluation materials and procedures used must not be culturally discriminatory. They are to be in the child's native language or mode of communication, and no one test can be the basis for a decision regarding the placement of a child or a change in the child's status.
3. *appropriate education:* Each handicapped child must be provided with a written individualized education program (IEP), stating which educational services will be provided to the child and why. It must be acceptable to parents or legal guardians, and the school systems are legally responsible for providing the services described in each IEP. Furthermore, IEPs must be updated periodically, usually at least once a year.
4. *due process:* In order to ensure that all the child's legal rights are satisfied, due process requires written notice before any change is made in the child's status and an opportunity for the child's parents or legal guardians to object to any change, to obtain an independent evaluation of the child, to examine all relevant records, to request a hearing, and to appeal any decision.
5. *placement in the "least restrictive environment":* A handicapped child must now be placed in the educational environment that is least restrictive of the child's development.

These are significant rights, and ensuring that they are met means dramatic changes in both regular and special education facilities, practices, personnel requirements, and training.

It is still too early to make strong statements about the effectiveness of PL 94-142. As would be expected, the implementation of this law has not been without problems, and its results have been studied for the most part only by individuals with highly specific concerns or interests. Consequently, PL 94-142 is currently the object of much fragmented debate. There are arguments over the effects of mainstreaming (e.g., Hauser, 1979; Larrivee & Cook, 1979; Safford & Rosen, 1981; Vincent, Brown, & Getz-Sheftel, 1981), assessment practices (e.g., Hamilton & Swann, 1981; Harber 1981; Orlando, 1981; Smith & Knoff, 1981), parental participation (e.g., Foster, Berger, & McLean, 1981; Goldstein & Turnbull, 1982; Winton & Turnbull, 1981), the IEP (e.g., Kaye & Aserling, 1979; Pugach, 1982; Sabatino, 1981; Tymitz, 1981), awareness of the law's contents (e.g., Joiner & Sabatino, 1981), and due process (e.g., Smith, 1981), to mention only a few.

It may be that PL 94-142 will not survive the 1980s. Already it has become tremendously costly and critics argue that it entails much unnecessary intervention by the federal government on states' prerogatives and responsibilities. At this writing, the Department of Education has issued proposed new regulations to replace those already in effect for PL 94-142. These new regulations if adopted would drastically change current requirements, reducing considerably any state's involvement in the education of handicapped individuals. While the proposed new regulations are not likely to be totally accepted by the public or the Congress, the changes contained in the current set of regulations would:

- delete current requirement for holding an IEP meeting within 30 days after the time a child has been shown to be in need of special education; instead of the set time period, states would be required to hold such a meeting within a reasonable time period
- delete current requirement of obtaining parental consent before having a child evaluated or placed in an educational program
- change the least restrictive environment stipulation so that schools could decide against mainstreaming a particular child if mainstreaming would lead to substantial and ascertainable disruption of educational services to other students
- weaken requirements for multidisciplinary evaluations of children
- weaken requirements for providing related services to handicapped children
- increase costs charged to parents of handicapped children
- weaken requirements that schools offering programs to nonhandicapped children make such programs available to handicapped children also
- weaken assessment procedures for determining whether a child has a specific learning disability
- reduce protections afforded children and their parents under "due process" provisions.

In addition to diluting the effectiveness of legislative gains such as those contained in PL 94-142 through regulatory actions, attempts by the Reagan government to combine handicapped funds in general block grants will also affect a state's ability to provide quality educational services to handicapped individuals. Block grants are federal dollars provided to state or local governments in accordance with a statutory formula for use in a broad functional area, largely at the recipient's discretion. These funds might be used to provide services for the handicapped, but they might not. Much would depend on the community and the strength of local and state lobbying groups.

Between 1960 and 1970, the number of categorically funded programs rose from 100 (funded at 7 billion dollars) to over 530 (funded at more than 30 billion dollars). Strong criticisms were made in Congress and elsewhere that categorical grants have become too complex and too piecemeal, do not properly consider local needs, are not effective in dealing with national problems, and are too costly. In fact, Sabatino (1981) seems to support this position when he argues that "appropriate special education service-delivery systems and their curricula cannot be mandated. Special education should be a continuum of programs and services that are consonant with local conditions; for locally is where special education happens" (p. 21).

Currently, the Department of Education operates about 160 categorically funded programs. In 1982, Congress agreed to merge 28 of these, but the Reagan administration clearly wants more of these categorical programs merged into block grants. Current plans call for 80% of a state's block grant for education to flow through to local levels, with the amount given to each school district determined by school enrollment data. Ideally, local needs will determine how these dollars are spent.

WHO ARE EXCEPTIONAL CHILDREN?

Traditionally, exceptional children have been categorized, on the basis of their major characteristic, into eight groups:

1. *Emotionally disturbed children* exhibit learned behaviors that are consistently maladaptive or inappropriate.
2. *Learning disabled children* exhibit a disorder in one or more of the basic psychological processes involved in understanding or in using spoken or written language.
3. *Mentally retarded children* exhibit subaverage general intellectual functioning that begins during the developmental period and is associated with impaired adaptive behavior.
4. *Visually handicapped children* either are blind or have only partial sight.
5. *Hearing impaired children* are hard of hearing or deaf.

6. *Children with speech disorders* speak in a way that deviates so much from that of others that it calls attention to itself, interferes with communication, or causes maladaptive behavior.
7. *Physically handicapped children* are crippled as a result of neurological, orthopedic, or chronic health disorders.
8. *Gifted children* exhibit outstanding ability or achievement; giftedness is often defined as an IQ of more than 120 points.

Handicapped children may suffer from more than one handicapping condition, and some professionals consider "multiple handicapping conditions" a separate category. Table 1-4 compares the frequency with which various handicaps occur with the percent of such children who received services in 1980-1981.

Even though the behaviors associated with one type of handicap often resemble those associated with another sufficiently to make accurate diagnosis a major problem, these separate categories of exceptionality were created by federal legislation. PL 85-926 authorized funds to provide services for the mentally retarded. Later, PL 88-164 created several more categories of exceptionality. The category of learning disability was added by PL 91-230. These and similar laws set up separate administrative budgets and procedures for those with various handicapping conditions, thus solidifying the categorical approach to handicapped children. Under PL 94-142, this categorical approach has been maintained.

Other methods for classifying handicapping conditions have been proposed in order to avoid separating handicapped children into discrete groups. One approach

Table 1-4 Comparison of Children Aged 3-21 Served by Special Education in 1980-1981 with Estimated Prevalence Rates

Handicap	*Percent of Children Served*	*Range of Estimated Rates*	
		Low	*High*
Mental Retardation	1.74	1.30	2.30
Hard of Hearing	0.08	0.30	0.50
Deaf	0.08	0.08	0.19
Speech Impairment	2.40	2.40	4.00
Visual Impairment	0.06	0.05	0.16
Emotional Disturbance	0.72	1.20	2.00
Orthopedic Impairment	0.13	0.10	0.75
Other Health Impairment	0.21	0.10	0.75
Learning Disability	2.93	1.00	3.00
TOTAL	8.35	6.53	13.65

Note: Based on data supplied by the United States General Accounting Office in a report entitled *Report to the Chairman, Subcommittee on Select Education, Committee on Education and Labor, House of Representatives,* IPE-81-1, September 30, 1981.

has been to cluster children into only five groups on the basis of type of deviation (Kirk, 1972): (1) communication disorders, including learning disorders and speech handicaps; (2) mental deviations, including giftedness and retardation; (3) sensory handicaps, including auditory and visual handicaps; (4) neurological and orthopedic conditions, including brain or physical damage; and (5) behavior disorders.

Quay (1973) has proposed a three-group classification: process dysfunctions, experience defects, and experience deficits. Process dysfunctions include handicaps related to sensory, motor, or neurological problems of the child; experience defects are environmental traumas that produce behavior disorders; and experience deficits refer to handicaps caused by insufficient experience or inadequate training. Of course, child psychiatrists, who are frequently responsible for determining a child's diagnostic category, use still another system. This rather elaborate system is detailed in the American Psychiatric Association's diagnostic manual, the *DSM-III* (1980).

One problem with all categorical approaches is that they tend to cause confusion in educational approaches to exceptional children. Different labels (e.g., learning disabled, mentally retarded) tend to imply that different educational settings and instructional approaches are required. While this may be true with some older children who have certain disabilities (e.g., autism), it is not always true with preschool children whose exceptionalities may not be easily classified and whose developmental variability is still likely to be high. Therefore, recent efforts to cluster exceptionalities by degree of severity, regardless of etiology, make good sense for ECSE.

Handicapping conditions may be classified as mild, moderate, and severe. According to such a taxonomy, mildly handicapped children can be included in regular educational settings for the most part. Children with mild forms of retardation, behavioral disturbance, or sensory loss, for example, can be dealt with in the same educational environment, one that includes children free of handicapping conditions. All such children could benefit from the same or similar instructional techniques, modified according to the needs of each child. Such an approach to preschool special education is termed *noncategorical*. Children with moderate degrees of exceptionality can probably benefit more from being placed in separate classrooms within the same public school that children in the mild category attend. Finally, severely handicapped children may require educational strategies that are used in institution-like settings.

Unfortunately, teacher preparation and certification has typically been categorically based. As late as 1977, most state certification was by category. At this writing, however, about 20 states have adopted or are considering a noncategorical or generic certification approach. This change is, in part, due to the growing recognition that categorical preparation and certification are inefficient. Blackhurst (1981) has identified five problems that illustrate this inefficiency:

1. Handicap categories provide few helpful instructional guidelines; essentially, they are educationally irrelevant.
2. There is a great deal of overlap across the categories. Handicapped children exhibit a wide range of behaviors, many of which do not fit neatly into a single diagnostic category.
3. Categories label the child as defective and imply the defect rests within the child; this leads to stereotyping and negative expectations.
4. Instructional materials are not category-specific.
5. Categorical teacher preparation results in redundancy in training and perpetuates professional barriers.

DEVELOPING HUMAN COMPETENCIES: THE ALLIANCE BETWEEN SPECIAL EDUCATION AND DEVELOPMENTAL PSYCHOLOGY

There is a natural alliance between special education and developmental psychology, as mentioned earlier, because the two professions complement one another in a unique way. Developmental psychologists study the processes that govern the development of behavioral sequences, while special educators apply the discoveries of the developmental psychologists to help handicapped children maximize their potential. Special educators develop educational strategies based on their understanding of normal developmental processes. Not only is this a valuable service to the handicapped, but also it is an important bridge that connects theory, research, and practice. By applying psychological findings, special educators help further our knowledge of human nature and provide the necessary feedback loop between research findings and applied practices.

If this feedback loop is to be fully effective, psychologists and educators must have a common conception about the end-state of the developmental process. Such a common point of view can be found in the recently expressed concern over the development of human competencies. *Competence* has been defined as the ultimate direction of human growth, that is, every person seeks to become a competent, fully functioning human. According to several psychologists (Ainsworth & Bell, 1973; Anderson & Messick, 1974; Connolly & Bruner, 1973), the notion of competence includes three essential components:

1. the ability to select and use information from the environment in developing appropriate strategies for action
2. the ability to initiate the behavioral activities necessary to carry out these plans
3. the ability to learn from one's successes and failures by developing new strategies for action

In other words, competence describes the development of the individual's overall effectiveness in dealing with the world. In order to become competent, children must develop

- cognitive skills for processing information about the world
- behavior to satisfy needs, desires, and goals
- emotional attitudes to guide behavior
- awareness of self and of others within the framework of a complex social network

Given these general guidelines, McDavid and Garwood (1978) have proposed a model for the development of human competencies that includes the development of a number of important "survival" skills. These survival components of the human competency model are

1. physical-motor skills to allow the child to manipulate and interact efficiently with the environment
2. cognitive or intellectual skills to enable the child to interpret and use information available through the senses
3. social and interpersonal skills to facilitate the child's effective interaction with other people and provide an accurate understanding of the world and the people within it
4. recognition of personal feelings or attitudes to allow the child to develop an accurate conception of his or her own abilities and position in the world

The specific examples of each of the four categories of human competencies given in Table 1-5 reflect cultural values regarding what is desirable. They provide a sense of direction in terms of the desired outcomes of education and indicate the kinds of skills that are needed to achieve competence in our society. Finally, this model suggests the skills needed by anyone who plans to work with children, exceptional or otherwise. Professionals who work with children must be able to

1. analyze the developmental processes associated with any growth area
2. evaluate the status of a child at any point along the developmental continuum in order to determine how far the child must go to become competent
3. separate the required behaviors in any competency area into segments that handicapped children can confront and master

Developing competence in handicapped children thus involves understanding, analyzing, and evaluating their status; it also involves the application of specific skills of judgment and action.

Table 1-5 A Model for the Development of Human Competencies

Attribute or Competence	*Example*
Physical Development	
Large muscle motor skills	"I can run and I can skip rope."
Small muscle motor skills	"I can button my coat and cut paper with my scissors."
Perceptual-motor skills	"I can pick all the blue beads out of a box of mixed beads."
Efficient coordination of behavioral responses	"I can walk a balance beam by putting one foot in front of the other and by using my arms for balance."
Cognitive or Intellectual Development	
Curiosity and exploration	"I like to go different places and try different things."
Control of attention and selective perception	"I can pay attention to the teacher even when others are talking."
Perceptual skills of discrimination, detecting a pattern, etc.	"I can find hidden figures in a picture puzzle."
Language and communication skills	"I know the alphabet, I can read, and I can write."
Cognitive categorization: concept formation	"I know the difference between a baseball and a softball."
Memory and information retrieval skills	"I can do my multiplication tables up to the 4's."
Critical thinking: analysis	"If the sun is in front of me and it is afternoon, I must be walking west."
Creative thinking: synthesis	"I can draw a square and then make it into a car or a boat."
Problem solving: deductive application	"If I want to build a tree house, I need nails, wood, a hammer, and a saw."
Flexibility in information-processing strategies	"Since it didn't work that way, I'll try it this way to make it work."
Qualitative and relational concepts (logical operations)	"5 + 3 = 4 + 4"
Social and Interpersonal Development and Societal Orientation	
Sensitivity in social relationships	"I know how my brother felt when he broke his favorite toy."
Positive affect in interpersonal relationships	"I feel happy because I think you care for me."
Appreciation of social roles	"He acts that way because he is the group leader today."
Regulation of antisocial behavior	"I won't steal anything because I might get into trouble."
Prosocial morality (altruism)	"I can't eat all of these cookies so I'll share with my friends."
Acculturation: general reserve of information about one's culture	"I know what time it is; I can name the days of the week, the months of the year, and all the seasons."

Table 1-5 continued

Attribute or Competence	*Example*
Facility in using resources for acquiring information	"I know how to work the tape recorder and the record player and how to use the dictionary."
Positive attitudes toward education, school, and learning	"I like to learn about math and people and animals."
Enjoyment of humor, play, and fantasy	"I like to play make-believe and make up funny stories."
Attitudes toward Self	
A consolidated sense of identity, differentiating oneself from the rest of the world	"I am Pat, and no one else is exactly like me."
A concept of the self as an agent to initiate and control	"If I work at it, I can do lots of things."
Realistic appraisal of the self with realistic positive self-regard	"I can ride a skateboard as well as anyone I know."
Awareness and recognition of feelings	"Sometimes I get scared and I'm always glad when my parents come home."
Motivation to seek competence, not only for the consequences, but also for success for its own sake	"I like to work puzzles; it makes me feel good to know I can do it by myself."

Note: Adapted from *Understanding Children: Promoting Human Growth* by John W. McDavid and S. Gray Garwood. Copyright © 1978 by D.C. Heath and Company. Reprinted by permission of the publisher.

ECSE: ISSUES FOR THE 1980s

As a discipline, ECSE seems to be in an enviable position for the decade of the eighties. It is a young field and, therefore, relatively unencumbered by potentially harmful long-standing traditions. The fact that it is multidisciplinary by nature facilitates the provision of more varied and more appropriate services to young children who are handicapped or who are at risk. Furthermore, ECSE has the support of federal and state legislation that, though not always mandating services, generates a positive climate in which such services may be consistently provided. Its professionals use a variety of theoretical paradigms, and the interactions of these professionals are likely to produce new and potentially more meaningful models, strategies, or treatment modalities for helping young children acquire self-enhancing behaviors. Finally, its research orientation leads to data-based programming.

For all these reasons, professionals in ECSE seem to be especially qualified to begin dealing with a number of significant issues confronting their field today.

Screening and Assessment

Special educators have reason to be particularly concerned with the assessment process. The process of systematically assessing behavior plays a prominent role in special education, because the individuals whose behavior is being assessed are exceptional (or suspected of being so). Special educators have a very clear need as well as an obligation to see that the assessment process does not ultimately work against the overall best interests of the exceptional children involved. For example, the norms of many currently used assessment instruments (e.g., the Bayley Scales) were established by testing only normal or typical children; atypical children were deliberately excluded. Special educators must be concerned about the adequacy and accuracy of assessing exceptional behaviors by using an instrument composed of items that may not sample the range of behaviors encountered in the atypical or exceptional child.

Another important problem is that the developmental schedules used to assess change may not include a fair and sufficient number of behavioral items at any general age range and within any particular behavioral domain. Many assessment instruments contain few items that measure specific behaviors in very young children. This lack is not a particular problem when the task is to assess change in a normal child, because the normal child's rate of growth is relatively rapid and the child ultimately "grows into" areas of more complex behavior where assessment can be made more meaningful. For many young handicapped children, however, the rate of change is not nearly so rapid. All too often, handicapped children never develop the degree of behavioral complexity or competency that characterizes normal development. There is almost always some degree of change, but, with present systems of assessment, these circumstantial changes may go unrecorded. Such insensitivity to developmental gains works against the exceptional child, for the gains often not only go unrecorded but also tend to go unnoted by child caregivers. Frequently, this failure helps relegate the more severely handicapped to an even more diminished status, leading to a very unfortunate and serious form of labeling behavior.

Several issues are becoming increasingly important factors in assessing behavior. Assumptions underlying the assessment process—those of the assessor as well as those of the persons who created the assessment instruments and procedures—must be identified. For example, differing assumptions are possible about the nature of developmental change; those who believe it is prompted by biology or environment might argue that change is due to maturation or to experience, while those who believe it is prompted by biology *and* environment in continuous interaction would hold that developmental change results from a child's interactions, using a variety of behavioral competencies, with various environmental circumstances.

One logical assumption derived from the transactional view is that individual differences in development result from differences in both environmental opportunities and constitutional makeup. This assumption is widely accepted. Assessments of developmental level generally make it possible to determine whether development is advanced or delayed, although always in terms of normal or typical growth or developmental change. *If* normal developmental change results from the interactions of a typical child with a given set of competencies in a given environmental situation, it is also logical to assume that alternate sequences could lead to the acquisition of a behavioral competency, given differences in environmental circumstances or constitutional makeup. This second assumption has received very little attention; however, as a result of the day-to-day experiences of many special educators who test children in classrooms and find sets of splinter skills or even a behavioral competency full-blown, increasing scientific attention is being given to the possibility that developmental change need not occur as the emergence of behavior *A* at 13 months, behavior *B* at 18 months, and behavior *C* at 36 months.

Feuerstein and his colleagues have proposed a more process-oriented approach to assessment (Feuerstein, Miller, Hoffman, Rand, Mintzker, & Jensen, 1981; Feuerstein, Miller, Rand, & Jensen, 1981). With this approach, termed the Learning Potential Assessment Device (LPAD), assessment itself is used to teach children tasks, and the children's resulting behavior is used as the basis for decision making on their problem-solving ability and potential. Obviously, such an approach to assessment is more time-consuming, but the data indicate that it provides a more accurate picture of a child's current and future developmental status. Even though a change in the focus of developmental assessment from chronological age to the interrelationships of behaviors comprising emerging sequences would have serious implications in many areas of special education (e.g., teacher training, curriculum development, assessment with respect to the individual, program evaluation, integration of typical and atypical children into the same educational setting), such a change seems worthy of serious consideration.

The Family and the Young Handicapped Child

Today professionals are becoming more comfortable studying child behavior as it occurs naturally, for example, in interaction with significant others in the child's daily life. This change has given rise to some very interesting and fruitful investigations of the ways in which child behavior is affected by transactions with others, such as the mother (Clarke-Stewart & Hevey, 1981), the father (Parke, 1979), parents (Masur & Gleason, 1980), siblings (Rowe, 1981), and peers (Cooper, 1980), as well as the ways in which others' behavior is affected by children (Bell, 1979; Bell & Harper, 1977; Patterson, 1980).

One positive byproduct of these new views and methodologies has been the increasing concern about the family's effect on behavior. The family has long been recognized as a critical socialization force. As Framo (1979) points out, "The family . . . has survived through history as the most workable . . . unit for mediating the culture" (p. 988). Since the first world war, however, concurrent social and economic forces seem to be having an escalating effect on family structure. The extended family has been reduced to the nuclear family, and the nuclear family is rapidly becoming the single parent family, especially among the poor. Hetherington (1979) has noted that nearly half of current marriages end in divorce. Furthermore, the parent in the single parent family (usually the mother and the primary socialization agent) is increasingly more often employed outside the home (Hoffman, 1979). Clearly, not only are these structural changes decreasing the availability of family members to provide needed emotional and other critical support services to each other, but also such changes are harbingers of stress and turmoil that do not bode well for families or family members. A number of studies have documented the impact of stress on family functioning and child care (see Schaefer, 1976, for a brief review).

Stress can reduce family flexibility and efficiency, increase family conflicts, alter family coalitions, and decrease coping ability, all of which can, in turn, contribute to the development of disturbed or deviant behavior in children as well as in adults. Furthermore, especially among low-income populations, such stresses can impair a child's developing cognitive and social competencies (Field, Widmayer, Stringer, & Ignatoff, 1980). For example,

- Infants of parents who provide low levels of auditory, visual, tactile, and kinesthetic stimulation and who do not make the stimulation contingent upon the infants' responses may develop less than optimal general intellectual and social competencies.
- Toddlers of parents who are overly restrictive and who also direct hostility toward the child may develop adult-directed emotional dependency.
- Young children of parents who do not provide consistent external rewards for appropriate self-control behaviors, who fail to model self-control behaviors themselves, and who do not provide the young child with meaningful cognitive structuring (mediated cognitions) surrounding the application of rewards and punishments may fail to internalize self-control strategies.
- Children of parents who fail to demand age-appropriate behavior; to enforce rules firmly and consistently; and to encourage, listen to, and heed their children's communications may not develop appropriate levels of independence and autonomy.
- Children of parents who are punitive and nonaccepting of their children consistently display aggressiveness. Parental nonacceptance is also clearly

related to withdrawn-neurotic behaviors and to psychosomatic disorders in children. (See Martin, 1975, for a more thorough review of these effects.)

While some of these parental behaviors may be due to ignorance or adherence to an inappropriate child care model, it is likely that stress within the family caused by such factors as divorce, death, economic deprivation, the mismatch of child and adult personalities, or the presence of a handicapped child contributes to the parental use of these unfortunate child care behaviors. Framo (1979) writes, "Whatever is human in people . . . comes from their family relationships. [But] . . . family living can also . . . provide the context for tragedy and anguish . . . —the cruel rejections, marital discord or emptiness, murderous hostility, the child unloved or discriminated against, 'parentification' of the child, jealousy, hatred, unrealized fulfillments, and outrages against the human spirit" (p. 988).

Clearly, there is a need to focus attention on the family, not only because it is so important in providing appropriate care to children, our most valued resource, but also because it is the crucible from which children emerge. Thus, "the whole child" can only be understood by studying the child in this real context. Unfortunately, at a time when it is scientifically feasible to study child development in this way and when, more than ever, the family needs assistance, interest in research and intervention in the family milieu is waning. As Gray and Wandersman (1980) point out, the results are frequently modest, and researchers are required to make many decisions regarding "goals, sampling, comparison groups, design, measures, and analyses" (p. 993) that may compromise meaningful interpretations of their data. While these difficulties can be overcome, the current political and economic climate may not tolerate the costs of the kinds of careful, systematic, and long-term investigations of families that are needed.

Program Evaluation: Determining Intervention Effects

Intervention efforts with infants and young children who are either at risk or are already handicapped have increased to the point that early intervention now involves thousands of diverse professional and paraprofessional individuals, many of whom are engaged in determining if such programs are effective. In the United States, many millions of tax dollars are being spent to support such early intervention efforts. The results have not been all that promising, but there appears to have been relatively little pressure to base future funding of similar efforts on evaluation outcomes. Given the tenor of the times, such largesse is not likely to be continued.

There are two general classes of at risk or handicapped infants and children served by intervention programs. One class consists of individuals whose developmental progress is likely to be negatively affected or depressed by a host of environmental conditions (e.g., poverty, single parent family, low socioeconomic status, maternal age), singly or in combination. The second class consists of individuals who have a biological impairment (e.g., Down's syndrome). Individuals affected by the interaction of environmental and biological factors (e.g., those with fetal alcohol syndrome) may be considered a third general class, but these individuals are classed with the biologically impaired group for the purposes of this discussion.

Research to evaluate intervention efforts with environmentally deprived young children has generally indicated that these programs have a positive effect (Miller, 1981). As Beller (1979) notes in his comprehensive review of programs for children from birth to age 3, "most disadvantaged children . . . gained substantially from the infant intervention programs" (p. 887). Beller, however, qualifies this interpretation by stating that little is known about the effect of variations in age at treatment onset, length of treatment, or type of treatment.

Biologically impaired young children are much fewer in number than the environmentally deprived, they are a much more heterogeneous population, and they are much more likely to experience severe neurological or physical impairment. Intervention efforts for the biologically impaired are likely to be aimed not so much at "normalizing" the child but instead at preventing deterioration of the child's existing, although limited, intellectual potential (i.e., maximizing the child's limited capacity) or at slowing the rate of natural, predictable deterioration. Of course, there are exceptions, such as intervention efforts designed to help the physically impaired but mentally intact child learn effective compensatory strategies.

Because the number of biologically impaired young children available to participate in an intervention program at any point in time is relatively small, because biologically impaired groups are so varied with respect to etiology and prognosis, and because the range of intellectual ability among such a group can be quite wide (Hayden & Haring, 1976), intervention efforts are very likely to be highly individualized (see Bryk & Light, 1981, for a discussion of this problem with respect to evaluation design). Furthermore, intervention programs for the biologically impaired are likely to vary from site to site, making generalizations about treatment effects very difficult. For example, some programs have concentrated on neurodevelopmental therapy, which consists of a series of exercises designed to reduce the control that the child's primitive reflexes have on developing motor patterns (Gillette, 1969). Other programs have concentrated on various theoretically derived curriculums designed to foster combinations of general cognitive, emotional, social, or self-help competencies (Aronson & Fällström, 1977). Still others have focused on training parents to intervene with their children (Piper & Pless, 1980; Shearer & Shearer, 1976).

All intervention approaches differ further in the use of staff, in the behavior reinforcement strategies employed, and in the accuracy with which they adhere to their stated model. Additionally, as Bricker, Carlson, and Schwarz (1981) have pointed out, attempts to determine the efficacy of infant intervention programs are hampered both by lack of suitable instrumentation and by the inability to use true scientific methodology in setting up intervention programs for subsequent evaluation (based on child change data usually).

Although all these arguments can be used to qualify evaluation outcome, will they continue to mollify the growing doubts of practitioners and researchers working in the area of early intervention? For example, Ferry (1981) argues against infant intervention efforts from a practitioner's viewpoint, and Piper and Pless (1980) argue against the efficacy of infant intervention from a researcher's point of view. Bricker and co-workers (1981) and Denhoff (1981) have opposing viewpoints. Perhaps it is time to consider other ways of evaluating the efficacy of such programs. Many of the factors that make evaluation of early intervention programs so difficult are not going to disappear, even if appropriate designs or sufficiently sensitive, reliable, and valid instruments are developed. Therefore, while it is certainly useful to draw on resources such as those contained in Berk's (1981) *Educational Evaluation Methodology: The State of the Art,* it may be time to begin thinking about alternative but equally valid outcome measures as a basis for determining program impact.

One suggestion is to focus more on parent change data. Denhoff (1981) lists four specific benefits of parent-infant intervention efforts:

> (1) They provide the infant and his/her parents with opportunities . . . to develop to full potential. (2) Strengthening of the natural interactions between infant and parents that these programs provide is fundamental to . . . family development. (3) . . . Problems that produce parent guilt, anger, and frustration are lessened in a supportive milieu. (4) Constant reinforcement between infant and parents . . . may lay the groundwork for the eventual emergence of positive developmental patterns. (p. 35)

If these are reasonable outcomes, and they seem to be, it would make sense for evaluators to collect family change data, in addition to child change data, for use in determining program efficacy. After all, there is no reason to believe that intervention is any less valid if only parents (and perhaps siblings) are *measurably* affected by it. Furthermore, these outcomes could easily be tied to a theoretical framework that would generate evaluation research hypotheses.

Educational Programming

There is growing and welcome concern that early intervention efforts should seek to coordinate curriculum planning and implementation more closely with the needs of individual handicapped children. Specifically, this seems to entail a variation of Hunt's (1961) ''problem of the match''—providing a child with educational experiences that are appropriate for the child's developmental status. The development of educational programming that is flexible enough to be matched reasonably with individual learning or behavioral characteristics will require a concerted effort. Standardized curriculum packages that ignore characteristics of a particular subpopulation of handicapped children (e.g., the blind, the physically impaired) or that do not allow for matching a particular child's unique learning or behavioral strengths with appropriate curriculum alternatives should be used only reluctantly. This suggests that a better means is needed to evaluate the effectiveness of various curriculums in promoting change among different subpopulations of handicapped children.

Redefinition of Learning

Currently, learning is regarded by many as the result of either cognitive-developmental processes (an organismic approach) or the accumulation of stimulus-response associations (a mechanistic approach). In the cognitive-developmental model, the child is considered a discoverer, a knowledge seeker, an active inventor of reality. Unfortunately, many handicapped youngsters lack the requisite abilities to initiate environmental exploration and must be taught how to explore the environment. Therefore, the two theoretical approaches must be combined in order to utilize the technology of behaviorism with the individual's attempts at cognitive mastery. Also, processes associated with learning that are not typically contained within a developmental framework per se (i.e., attention and memory processes) must be considered.

Bandura's (1977) reformulation of social learning theory makes it possible to include behavioral change strategies, cognitive-developmental variables, and information-processing variables, thus providing what may be termed a cognitive learning model. In Bandura's reformulation, learning may be described as the outcome of essentially four processes:

1. *attentional,* which includes aspects of both the child's physical and experiential state and of the event to which the child is attending
2. *retentional,* which includes developing cognitive abilities
3. *motor reproduction,* which includes the impact of the child's developing physical abilities on learning
4. *motivational,* which includes the child's previous reinforcement history

Table 1-6 shows how an intervention program could theoretically and pragmatically include components of both the mechanistic and organismic theoretical approaches, thereby utilizing the best of each in early childhood intervention.

Table 1-6 Component Processes Governing Learning in Cognitive Learning Model

Attentional Processes	*Retentional Processes*	*Motor Reproduction*	*Motivational Processes*
Characteristics of event	Symbolic coding	Physical capabilities	External reinforcement
Distinctiveness	Cognitive organization	Availability of component responses	Vicarious reinforcement
Affective valence	Symbolic rehearsal	Self-observation of reproductions	Self-reinforcement
Prevalence	Motor rehearsal	Accuracy feedback	
Complexity			
Functional Value			
Child characteristics			
Sensory capacities			
Arousal level			
Perceptual set			
Past reinforcement			

Note: Adapted from Bandura, 1977.

REFERENCES

Abeson, A., & Zettel, J. The end of the quiet revolution: The Education for All Handicapped Children Act of 1975. *Exceptional Children,* 1977, *44,* 114-130.

Ainsworth, M.D.S. Attachment and dependency: A comparison. In J.L. Gewirtz (Ed.), *Attachment and dependency.* New York: Wiley, 1972.

Ainsworth, M., & Bell, S. Mother-infant interaction and the development of competence. In K. Connolly & J. Bruner (Eds.), *The growth of competence.* New York: Academic Press, 1973.

American Psychiatric Association. *Diagnostic and statistical manual (DSM-III).* Washington, D.C.: Author, 1980.

Anderson, S., & Messick, S. Social competency in young children. *Developmental Psychology,* 1974, *10,* 282-293.

Aronson, M., & Fällström, K. Immediate and long-term effects of developmental training in children with Down's syndrome. *Developmental Medicine and Child Neurology,* 1977, *19,* 489-494.

Bandura, A. *Social learning theory.* Englewood Cliffs, N.J.: Prentice Hall, 1977.

Bell, R.Q. Parent, child, and reciprocal influences. *American Psychologist,* 1979, *34,* 821-826.

Bell, R.Q., & Harper, L.V. *The effect of children on parents.* Hillsdale, N.J.: Erlbaum, 1977.

Beller, E.K. Early intervention programs. In J. Osofsky (Ed.), *Handbook of infant development.* New York: Wiley, 1979.

Bennett, F.C. The pediatrician and the interdisciplinary process. *Exceptional Children,* 1982, *48,* 306-314.

Berk, R.A. *Educational evaluation methodology: The state of the art.* Baltimore: Johns Hopkins Press, 1981.

Bijou, S.W., & Baer, D.M. *Child Development,* New York: Appleton-Century-Crofts, 1961.

Blackhurst, A.E. Noncategorical teacher preparation: Problems and promises. *Exceptional Children,* 1981, *48,* 197-205.

Bricker, W.A., & Bricker, D.D. The Infant, Toddler, and Preschool Research and Intervention Project. In T.D. Tjossem (Ed.), *Intervention strategies for high risk infants and young children.* Baltimore: University Park Press, 1976.

Bricker, D., Carlson, L., & Schwarz, R. A discussion of early intervention for infants with Down's syndrome. *Pediatrics,* 1981, *67,* 45-46.

Bryk, A.S., & Light, R.J. Designing evaluations for different program environments. In R.A. Berk (Ed.), *Educational evaluation methodology: The state of the art.* Baltimore: Johns Hopkins Press, 1981.

Burke, P.J. Personnel preparation: Historical perspective. *Exceptional Children,* 1976, *43,* 144-147.

Children's Defense Fund. *A children's defense budget: An analysis of the President's budget and children.* Washington, D.C., 1982.

Clarke-Stewart, K.A., & Hevey, C.M. Longitudinal relations in repeated observations of mother-child interaction from 1 to 2½ years. *Developmental Psychology,* 1981, *17,* 127-145.

Clunies-Ross, G.G. Accelerating the development of Down's syndrome infants and young children. *The Journal of Special Education,* 1979, *13,* 169-178.

Connolly, K., & Bruner, J. (Eds.). *The growth of competence.* New York: Academic Press, 1973.

Cooper, C.R. Development of collaborative problem solving among preschool children. *Developmental Psychology,* 1980, *16,* 433-440.

Denhoff, E. Current status of infant stimulation or enrichment programs for children with developmental disabilities. *Pediatrics,* 1981, *67,* 32-37.

Dmitriev, V. Infant learning program for Down's syndrome. In B.L. Darby & M.J. May (Eds.), *Infant assessment: Issues and applications.* Seattle: Western States Technical Assistance Resource, 1979.

Dunst, C.J. *A clinical and educational manual for use with the Uzgiris and Hunt Scales of Infant Psychological Development.* Baltimore: University Park Press, 1980.

Dunst, C.J. *Infant learning: A cognitive-linguistic intervention strategy.* Hingham, Mass.: Teaching Resources, 1981.

Ferry, P.C. On growing new neurons: Are early intervention programs effective? *Pediatrics,* 1981, *67,* 38-41.

Feuerstein, R., Miller, R., Hoffman, M., Rand, Y., Mintzker, Y., & Jensen, M.R. Cognitive modifiability in adolescence: Cognitive structure and the effects of intervention. *The Journal of Special Education,* 1981, *15,* 269-288.

Feuerstein, R., Miller, R., Rand, Y., & Jensen, M.R. Can evolving techniques better measure cognitive change? *The Journal of Special Education,* 1981, *15,* 201-220.

Field, T.M., Widmayer, S.M., Stringer, S., & Ignatoff, E. Teenage, lower-class, black mothers and their preterm infants: An intervention and developmental follow-up. *Child Development,* 1980, *51,* 426-436.

Fitzgerald, H.E., & Brackbill, Y. Classical conditioning in infancy: Development and constraints. *Psychological Bulletin,* 1976, *83,* 353-376.

Foster, M., Berger, M., & McLean, M. Rethinking a good idea: A reassessment of parent involvement. *Topics in Early Childhood Special Education,* 1981, *1*(3), 55-66.

Framo, J.L. Family theory and therapy. *American Psychologist,* 1979, *34,* 988-992.

Gillette, H.E. *Systems of therapy in cerebral palsy.* Springfield, Ill.: Charles C. Thomas, 1969.

Goldstein, S., & Turnbull, A.P. Strategies to increase parent participation in IEP conferences. *Exceptional Children,* 1982, *48,* 360-361.

Gray, S.W., & Wandersman, L.P. The methodology of home-base intervention studies: Problems and promising strategies. *Child Development,* 1980, *51,* 993-1009.

Graziano, A.M., DeGiovanni, I.S., & Garcia, K.A. Behavioral treatment of children's fears: A review. *Psychological Bulletin,* 1979, *86,* 804-830.

Hamilton, J.L., & Swann, W.W. Measurement references in the assessment of preschool handicapped children. *Topics in Early Childhood Special Education,* 1981, *1*(2), 41-48.

Harber, J.R. Assessing the quality of decision making in special education. *The Journal of Special Education,* 1981, *15,* 77-90.

Hauser, C. Evaluating mainstream programs: Capitalizing on a victory. *The Journal of Special Education,* 1979, *13,* 107-130.

Hayden, A., & Haring, N. Early intervention for high risk infants and young children: Programs for Down's syndrome children. In T.D. Tjossem (Ed.), *Intervention strategies for high risk infants and young children.* Baltimore: University Park Press, 1976.

Hetherington, E.M. Divorce: A child's perspective. *American Psychologist,* 1979, *34,* 851-858.

Hoffman, L.W. Maternal employment: 1979. *American Psychologist,* 1979, *34,* 859-865.

Hunt, J. McV. *Intelligence and experience.* New York: Ronald, 1961.

Joiner, L.M., & Sabatino, D.A. A policy study of P.L. 94-142. *Exceptional Children,* 1981, *48,* 24-33.

Kaye, N.L., & Aserling, R. The IEP: The ultimate process. *The Journal of Special Education,* 1979, *13,* 137-144.

Kirk, S.A. *Educating exceptional children* (2nd ed.). Boston: Houghton-Mifflin, 1972.

Lancioni, G.E. Infant operant conditioning and its implications for early intervention. *Psychological Bulletin,* 1980, *88,* 516-534.

Larrivee, B., & Cook, L. Mainstreaming: A study of the variables affecting teacher attitude. *The Journal of Special Education,* 1979, *13,* 315-324.

Martin, B. Parent-child relations. In F. Horowitz (Ed.), *Review of child development research* (Vol. 4). Chicago: The University of Chicago Press, 1975.

Masur, E.F., & Gleason, J.B. Parent-child interaction and the acquisition of lexical information during play. *Developmental Psychology,* 1980, *16,* 203-208.

McDavid, J.W., & Garwood, S.G. *Understanding children.* Lexington, Mass.: D.C. Heath, 1978.

Miller, L.B. Prevention through early intervention: Effectiveness of selected components. In M.J. Begab, H.C. Haywood, & H.L. Garber (Eds.), *Psychosocial influences in retarded performance* (Vol. 2). Baltimore: University Park Press, 1981.

Orlando, C. Multidisciplinary team approaches in the assessment of handicapped children. *Topics in Early Childhood Special Education,* 1981, *1*(2), 23-30.

Parke, R. Perspectives on father-infant interaction. In J.D. Osofsky (Ed.), *Handbook of infant development.* New York: Wiley, 1979.

Patterson, G.R. Mothers: The unacknowledged victims. *Monographs of The Society for Research in Child Development,* 1980, *45*(5).

Piper, M.C., & Pless, I.B. Early intervention for infants with Down's syndrome: A controlled clinical trial. *Pediatrics,* 1980, *66,* 83-89.

Pugach, M.C. Regular classroom teacher involvement in the development and utilization of IEP's. *Exceptional Children,* 1982, *48,* 371-374.

Quay, H. Special education: Assumptions, techniques, and evaluative criteria. *Exceptional Children,* 1973, *40,* 165-170.

Rowe, D.C. Environmental and genetic influences on dimensions of perceived parenting: A twin study. *Developmental Psychology,* 1981, *17,* 203-208.

Sabatino, D.A. Are appropriate educational programs operationally achievable under mandated promises of P.L. 94-142? *The Journal of Special Education,* 1981, *15,* 9-24.

Safford, P.L., & Rosen, L.A. Mainstreaming: Application of a philosophical perspective in an integrated kindergarten program. *Topics in Early Childhood Special Education,* 1981, *1*(1), 1-10.

Sameroff, A.J., & Cavanaugh, P.J. Learning in infancy: A developmental perspective. In J. Osofsky (Ed.), *Handbook of infant development.* New York: Wiley, 1979.

Schaefer, E.S. Scope and focus of research relevant to intervention: A socioecological perspective. In T.D. Tjossem (Ed.), *Intervention strategies for high risk infants and young children.* Baltimore: University Park Press, 1976.

Shearer, D.E., & Shearer, M.S. The Portage Project: A model for early childhood intervention. In T.D. Tjossem (Ed.), *Intervention strategies for high risk infants and young children.* Baltimore: University Park Press, 1976.

Smith, C.R., & Knoff, H.M. School psychology and special education students' placement decisions: IQ still tips the scale. *The Journal of Special Education,* 1981, *15,* 55-64.

Smith, T. Status of due process hearings. *Exceptional Children,* 1981, *48,* 232-237.

Tymitz, B.L. Teacher performance on IEP instructional planning tasks. *Exceptional Children,* 1981, *48,* 258-259.

Vincent, L.J., Brown, L., & Getz-Sheftel, M. Integrating handicapped and typical children during the preschool years: The definition of best educational practice. *Topics in Early Childhood Special Education,* 1981, *1*(1), 17-24.

Winton, P.J., & Turnbull, A.P. Parent involvement as viewed by parents of preschool handicapped children. *Topics in Early Childhood Special Education,* 1981, *1*(3), 11-20.

Part II

Physical Development

Chapter 2

Physical Development: The Young Child's Growing Body

S. Gray Garwood

It is important to understand the processes related to physical development because appropriate physical development is the key to intellectual, personal, and social development. Just as the sensory organs take in information about the world, the motor system facilitates contact with that world. The nervous system guides an individual's responses to this world, and its efficiency and integrity determine that individual's ability to profit intellectually from these interactions. Thus, a child's body is the mechanism through which the child interacts with the physical and social world. It is also an important symbol of the child's personality because it is the basis for comparison of self with others. For these reasons, a child's physical growth cannot be separated from his or her overall development.

The process of development begins when a male and a female germ cell combine to form a fertilized egg. This fertilized egg, too small for the naked eye to observe, immediately begins a growth process that culminates in a human being characterized by a host of complex behaviors, such as talking, walking, thinking, loving, and evaluating. Two factors are critical in shaping the course of development: the child inherits a unique biological makeup, and the child exists in a dynamic environment. The biological component contributes a genetic plan for the development of body structures, and scientists refer to this factor as the *nature* factor. The second factor, called the *nurture* factor, refers to environmental events that facilitate or retard the normal course of development.

Because biologically determined behaviors cannot be examined outside an environmental context, it makes little sense to debate which of these two factors is more critical to development. Most people concerned with human development accept this natural limitation on the scientific study of growth and have come to regard human behavior as a dynamic system that includes both biological and environmental determinants. Most recently, development has been viewed as the outcome of the continual interplay between the individual and the environment. This model is called the transactional model and is discussed in detail by Sameroff and Chandler (1975).

GENETIC INFLUENCES ON DEVELOPMENT

Although a fertilized egg, or zygote, is an incredibly small organism, it usually contains the necessary material to generate the full range of human complexity: the ability to move, think, feel, and act purposefully. Various aspects of development, such as when, where, and how it is to occur (e.g., when limbs are to appear, where they are to appear, and how they are to be formed), are initially controlled by combinations of genetic material. The environment is also a factor critical to development, however; it can be propitious, allowing for full expression of genetic potential, or it can be harmful, interfering with or altering the course of typical development.

Genetic Transmission

Genetics is the study of biological inheritance and of environmental factors that influence this inheritance. Charles Darwin's investigations led him to propose that, given the hostile nature of the environment, only those members of a species with the best adaptive characteristics are likely to survive to reproduce offspring. Darwin called this process natural selection. He argued that survival traits were initially structural changes that occurred by accident but were then passed on within a species because they facilitated survival. Mendel, who knew of Darwin's views, grew and carefully observed many varieties of the garden pea, a self-pollinating plant. Based on these observations, Mendel concluded:

1. Heritable characteristics are transmitted by genes.
2. Mature organisms have two of each type of gene.
3. When these genes mix, one will be dominant and one recessive.
4. In reproductive cells, genes divide to give each new reproductive cell only one of each pair of genes.
5. Random mating of male and female reproductive cells results in the large numbers of individual variations within a species.

Mendel's conclusions provide the basis of modern views of genetics.

It was the work of Watson and Crick that clarified not only how cells could reproduce themselves but also how these cells could form so many different body components. In 1953, they built a model for the structure of the molecule deoxyribonucleic acid (DNA), which they claimed explained "the mystery of life" (Watson, 1968). They conceived of the DNA molecule as a double helix, two long strands of chemical material wound around each other and connected by complementary pairs of nitrogenous bases, creating a twisted ladder effect. The two long chains (or sides of the ladder) consist of phosphate and deoxyribose sugar groups, and the cross pieces (or rungs) consist of adenine paired with thymine, and cytosine paired with guanine. These cross pieces are held together by a loose chemical bond. Self-replication of cells occurs when this bond is broken, allowing the double helix structure to unwind (Figure 2-1). The separated halves collect and organize new cellular material into the needed nitrogenous bases tied to a segment of the sugar phosphate material. This material then aligns with one of the existing but now split halves of the double helix to form complementary adenine-thymine and cytosine-guanine pairs; the newly combined segments then rewind into the double helix structure, creating new double-chained molecules that are identical to the original (Watson, 1976).

Hereditary information that directs development is stored in genes in this way. The four nitrogenous bases are responsible for genetic transmission of hereditary material. These bases form triplet sequences called codons, and the genetic code is contained in the many possible combinations of these triplet sequences. Each codon specifies a different amino acid, a combination of carbon, hydrogen, oxygen, and nitrogen joined together to form protein. Amino acids, in turn, determine the production of part or all of different proteins. (For a more thorough review of this process, see Keeton, 1972). In essence, then, a gene is a segment of DNA that encodes a particular protein or part of one.

Genes are contained in units called chromosomes. The human fertilized egg has 23 pairs of chromosomes, half contributed by each parent; this results in a unique combination of chromosomes that explains most of the variations among individuals. The randomness with which a particular chromosome from a pair ends up in a particular sex cell and the exchange of genetic material between chromosomes

Figure 2-1 DNA—The Transmission of Genetic Information

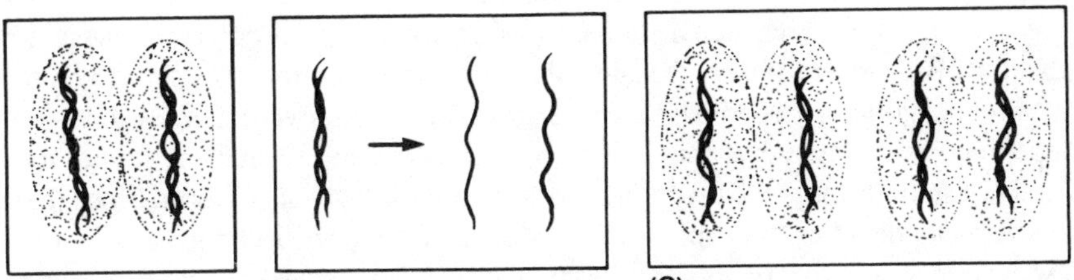

(A) (B) (C)

Key: *A*, A chromosome pair within a cell, which contains genetic information inherited from the parents. This information, consisting of chemical substances called deoxyribonucleic acid (DNA) arranged in the spiral forms, is located in each chromosome. *B*, DNA creates duplicate spirals in new cells by unwinding to collect and organize new materials so they match the existing spiral, and then rewinding the existing spiral with the newly created duplicate. *C*, The original cell multiplies into two and the DNA spirals rewind themselves. This process of cell division creates new but identical chromosome pairs containing the individual's genetic code.

lying next to each other when cell division occurs account for additional variations.

Mitosis is the process by which exact copies of all but reproductive cells are produced. In the mitotic process, chromosome material becomes arranged in double strands; the two members of each pair split lengthwise, separate from each other, and move to opposite cell walls. The cell pinches in at the middle and ultimately splits into two, each with 23 pairs of chromosomes. These two daughter cells reproduce, creating others that reproduce in a continuing process until the designated structure is completed. Completion, as well as maintenance of the completed structure, is under the control of the various arrangements of the codons located along segments of DNA contained in the various chromosomes.

Sex cells are not formed in this manner. Instead, they are formed through a process termed meiosis, which involves two division processes. When male or female sex cells are formed, they also contain 23 pairs of chromosomes. Upon reaching maturity, however, they separate and move toward the opposite cell wall. Eventually, 23 chromosomes are lined up along one wall, 23 along the other; the cell now splits down the middle, creating two cells, each with half the total number of chromosomes needed (23 instead of 46). When fertilized, the cell has the full complement of 46 chromosomes, half contributed by each parent. (For a more thorough review of mitosis and meiosis, see Moore, 1977.)

An infant's sex is determined by one of the 23 pairs of chromosomes, the sex chromosomes. In males, this chromosome pair is structured differently from all others. One of the pair is a large chromosome with many genes (X chromosome); the other is small and contains only a few genes (Y chromosome). In contrast, female sex cells contain two X chromosomes. When male sex cells split during meiosis, the resulting reproductive cells have one X and one Y chromosome. If the male sex cell with the X chromosome fertilizes a female sex cell, the infant will be female (X,X); if fertilization occurs with the male Y chromosome, the infant will be male (X,Y). Certain characteristics, such as red-green color blindness and hemophilia, are sex-linked, because they are carried on the sex chromosome.

Monozygotic or identical twins develop from one ovum fertilized by one spermatozoon. Instead of remaining together as one mass, after the first mitotic cell division, the new cells separate and two individuals begin to form. Since these individuals develop from the same zygote, they have the same genetic history. Dizygotic or fraternal twins simply share the same uterus; two ova are fertilized by two spermatozoa at the same time. The offspring have a different assortment of genes, and they can be of either sex or can occur in combination. Multiple births of more than two occur in the same manner. The study of differences between twins, either monozygotic or dizygotic, has helped to increase current understanding of the nature of genetic control over development (Fulker, 1981).

As noted earlier, chromosomes occur in matched pairs, half contributed by each parent. These are termed homologous chromosomes. Genes also occur in matched pairs, and those located at the same place on homologous chromosomes are likely to contain similar codon groupings. Different forms of the same gene are possible, however, and these variations are called alleles. If an infant inherits different alleles for a particular location, the infant is said to be heterozygous for the trait or structure determined by this piece of genetic material (e.g., eye color, blood type, or body chemical). The infant who inherits identical alleles is said to be homozygous with respect to that trait or structure. For example, phenylketonuria (PKU) is an enzymatic disorder that can lead to mental retardation if not treated very early in life, usually within the first 6 months. The allele that produces the necessary enzyme is noted as a P,P pair. The allele that results in a failure to produce the needed enzyme is noted as a p,p pair. Within each of these pairs, the alleles are identical, so both individuals are homozygous for their respective pairings and both have the same respective genotype or genetic makeup. Infants who inherit a P,p pairing are heterozygous for this allele. Like the P,P infants, those with P,p have the needed enzyme. Thus, the behavior of the two groups, the P,P and the P,p, is outwardly similar—they have the same phenotype—but they are still genetically different. The P allele is said to be dominant over the p allele. Dominant alleles mask the effects of other alleles (in this case, the p allele) and have genetic dominance over recessive alleles. Recessive genetic traits can appear only when both parents contribute identical recessive alleles, as in the p,p pair.

Now that scientists understand more about the way in which genes interact, it is possible to make predictions about a person's phenotypes and genotypes, and genetic counseling has lately become available to prospective parents. This service can provide information to couples about genetic trait combinations that result in abnormality or early death, allowing prospective parents to make realistic decisions.

How Genes Direct Development

It is not yet clear exactly how a single cell develops into a complex human being, although the discovery of the role played by DNA has contributed enormously to the field of developmental genetics. In addition, much more is now understood about the interaction of the organism and the environment. For example, it is known that the embryo's surface cells can more readily participate in gaseous exchange than can the deeper inner cells, which suggests a chemical interaction process in development (McClearn & DeFries, 1973). Work with the larvae of certain insects has also been instructive. Chromosomal "puffing," that is, transient swellings of particular chromosome regions, has been observed. In those areas where puffing occurs, production of DNA's messenger, ribonucleic acid (RNA), is intensified.

Jacob and Monod (1961) have presented a useful model of the way in which genes create and control the biochemical levels needed to produce various proteins required for growth. They have postulated several types of genes: structural genes, which contain the hereditary blueprint, as well as operator and regulator genes, which act together to control the activity of structural genes. Their operon model is useful in illustrating how genes are regulated to control both timing and growth in developmental sequences.

Waddington (1957) has also described a model, "the epigenetic landscape," which depicts gene-environment interaction in development. This contoured landscape contains hills and valleys; the individual's genotype determines the degree of contour. Waddington visualizes a ball, representing the individual's phenotype, on this landscape. As development proceeds, the ball rolls forward along a genetically determined valley or pathway. Environmental events, varying in intensity and duration, can displace the ball from its pathway, however. Its return to its original path is a function of the steepness of the valley's walls (the degree of genetic control). Waddington also suggests that there are "critical periods when a lateral excursion will direct the ball into one of two or more alternative pathways which represent distinct pathways of development" (McClearn & DeFries, 1973, p. 163). This model is useful for understanding not only individual differences in the course of development but also gene-environment interactions that affect development.

OVERVIEW OF PHYSICAL GROWTH

Physical growth may be divided into three stages for the purposes of studying risk factors associated with development: (1) prenatal development, including embryonic (the first 3 months of pregnancy) and fetal (the remaining months until birth) development; (2) perinatal development (from birth until about 1 month after); and (3) postnatal development (after the 1st month).

Prenatal Development

The first 7 to 10 days following fertilization is called the period of the zygote. During this time, the fertilized egg (zygote) develops into the embryo. After the egg has been fertilized, it begins to divide as the zygote travels down a fallopian tube toward the uterus. By the 3rd day, enough cells have been formed so that a solid mass (the morula) is evident. This mass enters the uterine cavity on approximately the 4th day, and uterine fluids collect between its cells, forcing it to separate into an outer and an inner cell mass. The outer cell mass (trophoblast) develops into the amnion, a membranous sac surrounding the embryo and protecting it from stress, and the placenta, a spongy network of blood vessels and tissues. The inner cell mass (embryoblast) develops into the embryo, beginning with the differentiation of endodermic, ectodermic, and mesodermic tissues and the appearance of the embryonic disk, a thin, platelike mass of tissues. This occurs about the 8th day. By day 10, the embryo and its membrane are fully embedded in the upper portion of the uterus.

The amnion is filled with a fluid that aids development in several ways. According to Moore (1977), amniotic fluid prevents the embryo (and later the fetus) from adhering to the amnion, helps to maintain symmetrical growth as well as skeletal-muscular growth, maintains a relatively constant body temperature, and cushions the embryo against jolts. This fluid is derived from both the mother's blood and infant excretions; because the embryo normally swallows amniotic fluid and urinates into this fluid medium, the fluid contains many substances that are used to diagnose genetic disorders and fetal maturity (Battaglia & Simmons, 1978).

During the prenatal period, amniocentesis may be performed. In this procedure, the physician collects amniotic fluid by inserting a needle through the mother's abdomen into the amnion. The fluid is analyzed to detect a variety of genetic disorders long before birth (Fuchs, 1980). The list of disorders that can be detected in this way includes aminoacidopathies; chromosomal abnormalities; galactosemias; Hunter's, Hurler's, and Down's syndromes; maple syrup urine disease; muscular dystrophies; and Tay-Sachs disease. Fetal sex and some early neurological defects can also be determined (U.S. DHEW, 1979). In addition, the volume of amniotic fluid may indicate various handicapping conditions. For example, too little fluid is associated with an absence of kidneys or urethral obstruction, and too much fluid is associated with central nervous system dysfunction (Moore, 1977).

Usually, amniocentesis is done at 16 to 17 weeks' postmenstrual age (age counted from the 1st day of the mother's last menstrual period, averaging 2 weeks before fertilization). Fuchs points out two hazards to this procedure, both associated with increased risk of miscarriage. Amniocentesis could lead to spontaneous abortion, or it could cause an immunological reaction in the mother if, as a result of the procedure, fetal blood enters the mother's bloodstream. North American studies conclude the risk from performing amniocentesis to be less than 0.5%, but British researchers estimate the risk to be between 1% and 2% (U.S. DHEW, 1979).

The placenta is a temporary organ that differentiates and grows out of embryonic tissues. It is an active and selective organ that separates the circulatory systems of the fetus and mother, forces an exchange of materials, and provides alimentary, pulmonary, renal, hepatic, and endocrine services for the fetus; it is capable of regulating many of the mother's body functions and can synthesize hormones needed for development. Thus, the placenta is a complex multiple organ system, not just a passive filter (Beaconsfield, Birdwood, & Beaconsfield, 1980). A less than optimum placenta, either in positioning or size, may have a deleterious effect on the developing organism (Adamsons, 1978).

When the period of the zygote ends, approximately 10 days after fertilization, the developing organism is referred to as an embryo until about the beginning of the 4th month of pregnancy. This time period is critical in the development of physical structures, especially the 4th through the 7th weeks when about 95% of the embryo's body parts appear (Table 2-1). Any interference during this time period could result in death or abnormal development.

Noxious or harmful environmental events, such as maternal ingestion of drugs or excessive use of alcohol and other stimulants, can interfere with normal growth processes. Generally, three critical periods for physical development are recognized. The first is the 2 weeks after the ovum is fertilized, when environmental disturbances can prevent the zygote from implanting in the uterine lining or result in spontaneous abortion. The second period extends approximately from day 13 to day 60, when all body tissues and organs are developing. This is perhaps the most

Table 2-1 Characteristics of Embryonic Development

Day	*Event*
1	Fertilization occurs and cell division begins.
3-6	The zygote passes through a fallopian tube and enters the uterine cavity, where it attaches itself to the uterine wall.
7	Endodermic tissue begins to appear; this tissue is important in the formation of the liver, pancreas, bladder, trachea, bronchi, lungs, pharynx, middle ear, tonsils, parathyroids, and urethra.
8	Ectodermic tissue begins to appear; this tissue is important in the subsequent development of skin, hair, nails, mammary glands, anterior pituitary gland, tooth enamel, inner ear, eye lens, central and peripheral nervous system tissue, adrenal gland, retina, pineal body, and sweat glands. The embryonic disk is formed at this time.
10	The zygote is completely embedded in uterine lining, and period of zygote ends.
11	Placental circulation appears.
16	Mesodermic tissue begins to appear; this tissue contributes to the formation of the skull, muscles and connective tissue, dentine, skin, blood and blood vessels, spleen, adrenal cortex, kidneys, and reproductive organs.
18	The neural plate, the primitive central nervous system, appears.
19	The brain begins to form, and the thyroid gland begins to develop.
21	The heart tubes begin to fuse to form the primitive heart.
22	The primitive heart begins to beat.
26	Arm buds begin to appear.
27	Leg buds begin to appear.
30	Eye and nose structures form.
31	The mouth begins to form.
31	Hand structures begin to appear.
34	Foot structures begin to appear.
40	The palate begins to develop.
48	All essential and external physical structures have begun to develop, and the embryo is about 30 mm in length.

critical period, because serious but not terminal deformities can occur. During the third period, which includes events that occur after the 2nd month, environmental disturbances can result in physiological defects, minor morphological abnormalities, and functional disturbances of the central nervous system. The abnormalities that can occur in these critical periods are summarized in Table 2-2.

Developing Physical Systems

As Table 2-1 indicates, the body's many specialized organs and structures develop from the three primary tissues: endodermic, ectodermic, and mesodermic.

Cardiovascular System. Embryonic development requires nourishment and oxygen, as well as a method for disposing of wastes. For these reasons, the cardiovascular system, composed of the heart and blood vessels, becomes functional first. Early in the 3rd week, blood vessels and a primitive heart begin to form. By the end of that week, the two are linked into a functional, although primitive, cardiovascular system. The primitive heart contains only two chambers at first; between the 4th and 5th week, it takes on its adult appearance by developing four chambers: two upper (atria) and two lower (ventricles).

The embryo's initial blood supply comes from the mother via the placenta. By the 2nd month, self-production of blood begins, first in the liver, then in the spleen, in bone marrow, and in lymph nodes. At birth, important circulatory changes are caused by the cessation of fetal blood circulation through the placenta and the onset of lung functioning.

Urogenital System. The body's reproductive and elimination systems are closely associated. Parts of one system overlap and function as parts of the other system. The urinary system begins to develop during the 4th week and includes the

Table 2-2 Abnormalities That Can Occur in Critical Periods of Prenatal Development

Developing Structures	*Weeks during Which Major Damage Can Occur*	*Weeks during Which Minor Damage Can Occur*
Central nervous system	3 to 5½	5½ to 38
Heart	3½ to 6½	6½ to 8
Arms	4½ to 7	8
Eyes	4½ to 8½	8½ to 38
Legs	4½ to 7	8
Teeth	6½ to 8	8 to 16
Palate	6½ to 12	12 to 16
External genitalia	7½ to 15	15 to 38
Ears	4 to 13	

- kidneys, a filter that collects body fluid wastes in the form of urine
- ureter, a tube that carries urine away from the kidneys
- urethra, the urine-eliminating canal connecting the bladder with the outside
- adrenal gland, a hormone-producing body.

The reproductive system includes the internal reproductive organs, genital ducts, and male or female external genitalia. Genetic sex is determined at fertilization, but sexual differentiation does not begin until about the 6th or 7th week. At this time, gonadal development begins in the male child; this process is believed to be under the control of one small part of the Y chromosome (Ohno, 1976). About 6 weeks later, embryonic gonadal tissue in the female child forms ovaries containing all ova that she will ever have. Further reproductive development, the differentiation of internal organs, begins at 12 weeks also. In males, the wolffian ducts enlarge and the mullerian ducts atrophy; in females, the reverse occurs. Finally, external genitalia are formed. If the hormone testosterone, which is present in the fetal testis as early as 8 to 10 weeks after conception (Reinisch, 1976), is present, male genitalia are formed; if not, female genitalia develop.

Respiratory System. During the 4th week, the respiratory system begins to emerge. A primitive pharynx develops, followed by the larynx, trachea, and the esophagus. Beginning with the 5th week, lung buds appear and begin to differentiate into the bronchi, the lungs, the pleural cavities, and the pleura, a membrane that surrounds the lungs. Normally, by 26 weeks, the lungs are sufficiently developed to permit survival if the infant should be born prematurely. Around this time, surfactant, a chemical substance that covers the surface of the air cells lining the lungs prior to birth, is produced. At birth, the lungs are about half-filled with fluids. These fluids must be rapidly replaced with air, and, in this process, the birth cry (air being rapidly forced over the vocal cords) occurs.

Digestive System. The primitive digestive system begins to emerge during the 4th week. It consists of three parts:

1. the foregut, which contributes to the development of the pharynx and the lower respiratory system, the esophagus, stomach, duodenum, liver, and pancreas
2. the midgut, which contributes to the development of the duodenum, jejunum, ileum, cecum, appendix, and the colon
3. the hindgut, which contributes to the development of the colon, the rectum, and the upper portion of the anal canal

During the 5th week, embryonic development is so rapid that the abdomen becomes overcrowded. Therefore, the midgut moves into the umbilical cord and remains there until about the 10th week, when it moves back into the abdomen.

Branchial Apparatus. The branchial arches, clefts (grooves), and muscles that form the face, tongue, palate, pharynx, and the neck make up the branchial apparatus. The arches appear as ridges on the site of the future head and neck; they are separated by grooves, or clefts. During the 4th week, face, ear, and neck structures begin to emerge. The roof of the mouth or palate begins to develop during the next week.

Skeletal and Muscular Systems. Mesodermic tissue begins to form into the body's skeletal and muscular systems during the 4th week. Arm, and then leg buds, also appear at this time. During the 5th week, extensive head growth occurs because of the rapid growth of the brain. The elbows and wrists become visible, and primitive fingers begin to emerge. By the 6th week, the head has become visibly larger than the body's trunk, and primitive fingers and toes begin to develop. Thus, by the end of the first 2 months, the embryo has begun to look human. The head is now round; a neck exists; eyelids have emerged; and the limbs are well developed, with well differentiated fingers and toes.

Nervous System and Sensory Organs. Many millions of nerve cells (neurons), elaborately interlaced with each other and connecting all parts of the body, comprise the nervous system. This system has two major divisions: the central nervous system (CNS), which consists of the brain and spinal cord, and the peripheral nervous system, which includes neural pathways throughout the body. The nervous system regulates and coordinates body activities by means of three types of nerve cells: sensory, motor, and association neurons. Sensory neurons transmit information (electrical pulses) from the body's senses (e.g., eyes, ears, nose) to the brain. Motor neurons enable the body to respond to stimuli by conveying messages to muscles in the body. Association neurons provide the needed connection of sensory stimuli and motor actions through the integrative aspects of the CNS so that purposeful and appropriate responses can be produced.

The brain is a large collection of nerve cells and fibers that are hierarchically organized. The lowest levels of the brain, which evolve first, are responsible for controlling basic survival behaviors, whereas the higher levels make these lower level behaviors more goal-oriented. The CNS is contained in three layers of meninges, nonnerve tissue that physically supports the CNS. The outside layer, the dura mater, contains the blood vessels that supply the CNS. The inner layer, the pia mater, makes contact with the neuron tissue of the CNS. In between is the arachnoid layer. Cerebrospinal fluid, which has a nutrient function, circulates between the pia mater and the arachnoid. When cerebrospinal circulation or absorption is disrupted, excess fluid accumulates. This forces the developing head bones apart, increasing head size and resulting in hydrocephalus, a condition that can produce mental retardation if the brain becomes severely compressed. This condition can be relieved by inserting a pressure-sensitive valve (shunt) that automatically opens to drain these excess fluids into either the amnion (in the unborn infant) or into the bladder.

The nervous system contains literally billions of neurons, arranged systematically throughout the body, that are linked together to form nerves. Each neuron contains a cell body from which extend many hairlike branches called dendrites and one longer structure termed the axon (Figure 2-2). Neurons do not touch each other; if they did, behavioral options would be sorely reduced. Instead, there is a small gap, a synapse, between each neuron. When an individual acts or reacts, neurons are excited and begin to transmit information in the form of electrical energy down to the end of the axon where a chemical transmitter substance (e.g., acetylcholine, noradrenalin, serotonin, dopamine) is stored. Once triggered by the information impulse, the transmitter diffuses across the gap between the neurons and makes contact with particular receptors located in the dendrites of the adjacent neuron (the postsynaptic site). If a sufficient amount of transmitter substance is received, this neuron fires an electrical impulse down its axon; this process of transmitting information continues to the desired endpoint.

If these excitatory transmitter substances were allowed to accumulate at the postsynaptic site, there would be constant excitation of the neuron involved, and appropriate behavior would be unlikely. Consequently, soon after a transmitter substance has arrived at a postsynaptic receptor site, enzymes at this site break down the transmitter substance so that the neuron returns to its resting state. As this occurs, energy is expended, and glucose is oxidized.

The nervous system begins to form during the 3rd week when ectodermic tissue forms the neural plate. From the neural plate, the neural tube and the neural crest are formed. The neural tube then differentiates into the CNS during the 4th week, and the neural crest begins to differentiate into the peripheral nervous system. The end of the neural tube nearest the head develops into the brain (Figure 2-3). It consists of three primary areas, the hindbrain, the midbrain, and the forebrain, and five secondary areas: (a) myelencephalon and metencephalon (hindbrain), (b) mesencephalon (midbrain), and (c) diencephalon and telencephalon (forebrain).

The myelencephalon region contains the medulla oblongata and the reticular formation. The medulla oblongata contains ascending sensory and descending motor nerve fibers. These fibers consist, in part, of neurons of cranial nerves that control sensory and motor functions of the head, as well as survival responses such as respiration, heart action, and gastrointestinal functioning. The reticular formation contains ascending neurons that are part of the extrapyramidal system, which mediates motor action, and descending neurons that are part of the behavioral arousal system, the reticular activating system, which mediates sleep and waking states.

The metencephalon contains the cerebellum and the pons. The cerebellum is the first brain region to become specialized; it coordinates sensory-motor activity by

Figure 2-2 Outline of a Motor Neuron

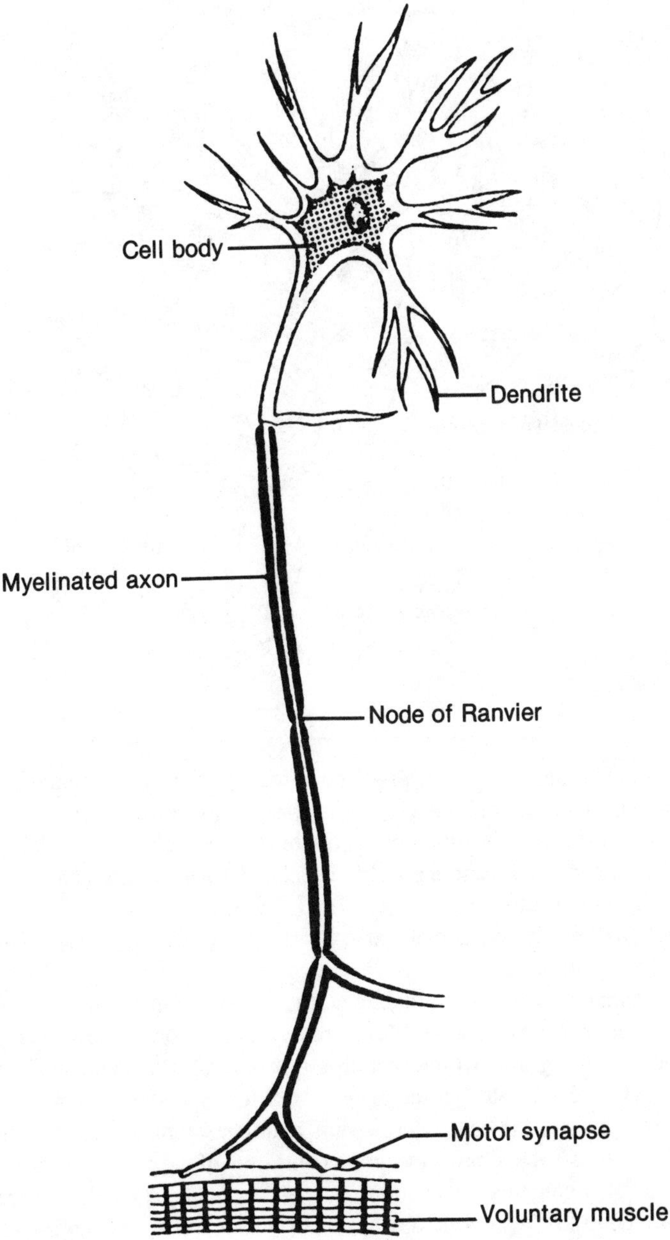

Figure 2-3 Diagram of Brain Areas and Interconnections

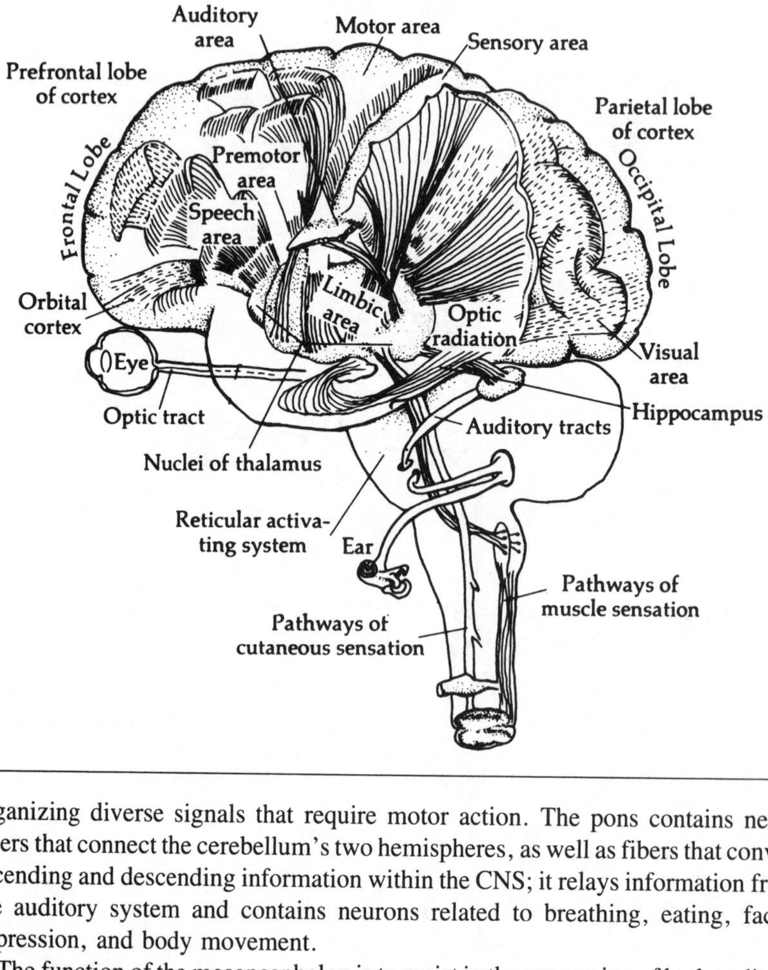

organizing diverse signals that require motor action. The pons contains nerve fibers that connect the cerebellum's two hemispheres, as well as fibers that convey ascending and descending information within the CNS; it relays information from the auditory system and contains neurons related to breathing, eating, facial expression, and body movement.

The function of the mesencephalon is to assist in the processing of both auditory and visual information.

The diencephalon contains the thalamus, the hypothalamus, and the subthalamus. The thalamus acts generally as a relay station for sensory and motor information, receiving data from ascending sensory pathways and sending it to specific sensory areas located in the neocortex. More specifically, these cortical relay nuclei are involved in processing visual, auditory, somatesthetic (perception of heat, pressure, pain), and proprioception (sensation of movement) information. The thalamus also contains association nuclei (i.e., nuclei related to processing higher, more complex behaviors) and subcortical nuclei (i.e., nuclei involved in controlling shifts in attention and in mediating impulses arising from the viscera). The hypothalamus is involved in regulating the expression of basic drives, as well as related survival behaviors (e.g., flight or fight). The subthalamus is connected by neurons to the extrapyramidal system located in the myelencephalon and, thus, is involved in controlling movement.

The telencephalon has three parts: basal ganglia, rhinencephalon, and neocortex. Basal ganglia are believed to be involved in controlling gross motor movements, such as walking, and in inhibiting muscle tone, the degree of tension or contraction needed to maintain body posture; changes in tone produce movement. The rhinencephalon is part of the limbic system, which is involved in controlling emotional states and processing information received through the sense of smell. The neocortex, the last brain region to evolve, is the brain's most complex structure, consisting of six distinct cell layers that make up the two hemispheres. Each hemisphere is divided into four lobes:

1. frontal, containing the primary motor area and involved in controlling fine and gross movement
2. parietal, containing association cortex areas and somatosensory projection areas, also involved in perceiving taste, connected by nerve fiber to the thalamus
3. occipital, containing primary vision projection area and association cortex
4. temporal, containing primary auditory projections and association areas

Myelination of the CNS begins in midfetal life and continues for several years after birth. Myelination is a process whereby the nerve fibers become coated with a fatlike substance, called the myelin sheath. This sheath forms around portions of nerve tissue and enables information to be transmitted through the nervous system much more efficiently and quickly. It acts like insulation, preventing diffuse neuronal discharge.

Development of eyes and ears begins in the 4th week. Eye development is first evident when a pair of optic grooves appears in the neural fold. As these grooves develop, optic vesicles form, connect with the forebrain, and become the optic stalks. At the same time, the lens, retina, iris, and cornea are forming. Between the 3rd and 6th week, eye development is in a critical period and can be seriously affected by environmental agents. The ears are also forming during the 4th week. The inner ear develops from ectoderm tissue, the middle ear from the cartilage of the first two branchial arches, and the external ear from the first branchial arch.

Fetal Development

By the end of the embryonic period, the developing embryo has experienced phenomenal growth and differentiation when the simplicity and size of the fertilized egg 3 months earlier are considered. It is now about 25.4 mm long; has well-formed arms, legs, fingers, and toes; and a human face containing eyes, ears, nose, and mouth. Its heart beats, and its nervous system is functioning.

During the second and third trimesters of prenatal development, the embryo is termed a fetus. In the fetal period, the remaining body parts appear and embryonic development is refined (Table 2-3). (See Moore, 1977, for more detail.)

At birth, the condition of the neonate (newborn) is typically evaluated by delivery room personnel. One commonly used standardized system is the Apgar Scale, by which the general health status of the neonate is scored at 1 minute and again at 5 minutes after birth (Apgar and Beck, 1973). Other neonatal assessment procedures include a neurological assessment (Prechtl & Beintema, 1964) and a behavioral assessment (Brazelton, 1973). (For a more thorough discussion of these and other neonatal status examination procedures, see Brazelton, Als, Tronick, & Lester, 1979; Fewell, 1983; Rosenblith, 1979; and Self & Horowitz, 1979.)

Influence of Obstetrical Medicines on the Neonate

Brackbill (1979) reviewed empirical evidence of the effects of perinatally administered drugs (e.g., uterine muscle stimulants, inhalant anesthetics, local

Table 2-3 Fetal Development

Week	*Characteristics of Fetal Development*
12	Crown-rump length (from head to seat) is about 87 mm, and weight is about 45 g; the fetus is human in appearance; muscles are developing and spontaneous movements begin to occur; external genitalia begin to appear; fingernails and toenails begin to form; eyelids begin to form; head growth, which made up approximately half of the fetus at week 8, slows; growth in body length becomes rapid; upper limbs have reached their final relative length.
16	Crown-rump length is about 140 mm, and weight is about 200 g; eyelids begin to blink; mouth is capable of opening; hair begins to appear on head and body; hands are now capable of grasping; legs have lengthened.
20	Crown-rump length is about 190 mm, and weight is about 460 g; sweat glands emerge; skin takes on adult form; hair and eyebrows are visible.
24	Crown-rump length is about 230 mm, and weight is about 820 g; body is lean but well proportioned; taste buds appear on tongue; fetus is capable of making crying sound and of inhaling and exhaling.
28	Crown-rump length is about 270 mm, and weight is about 1,300 g; eyes are open; fetus can survive outside the womb if born before term but mortality rate is high; fetus moves into upside-down position for birth.
38	Crown-rump length is about 360 mm, and weight is about 3,400 g; birth normally occurs.

anesthetics) on subsequent infant behavior. She summarized her interpretations of these data as follows:

1. Obstetrical medicines have a subsequent negative effect on infant behavior.
2. These effects are dose-related, that is, the infants of mothers who received higher doses or stronger drugs are more affected.
3. These effects are not short-lived.
4. These effects are strongest in cognitive and motor areas.

Recently, Murray, Dolby, Nation, and Thomas (1981) have expanded Brackbill's interpretation of drug effects to include expectancy effects as well. These researchers compared neonates born to mothers who received little or no medication during delivery with two groups of neonates whose mothers received various combinations of obstetrical medications. Their findings indicated that direct drug effects were present immediately after birth but tended to disappear after approximately 1 month. At 1 month after birth, however, mothers who had received little or no medication more often reported their babies to be sociable, easy to take care of, and rewarding to interact with; these mothers also were more responsive to their babies' cries. Murray and co-workers interpret their findings as consistent with the view "that early encounters with a 'drugged' and disorganized baby may build up a false picture that can interfere with the development of a reciprocal relationship" (p. 81). Such findings are disturbing and bear replication. If these interpretations are correct, it seems reasonable to conclude that some of the mild, and perhaps even moderate, handicapping conditions observed in children may be related to delivery room medication procedures, inappropriate expectancies, or both.

Perinatal and Postnatal Growth and Development

Physical Growth

At birth, neonates must make a number of transitions if they are to survive and thrive. As Timiras (1972) has pointed out, the infant moves at birth from a fluid to a gaseous environment characterized by fluctuating temperatures and is subject to a great variety of stimuli rather than the primarily vibratory stimuli of the womb. Oxygen is no longer received from the mother's blood, but from the natural environment, and nutritional needs important for growth and development now depend on the vagaries of food availability and digestive sufficiency.

During the 1st year, growth is quite rapid. Infants typically weigh about 3400 g at birth, 6800 g at 5 months, and 9979 g by the end of their 1st year. Similarly, neonates are about 508 mm long; by 6 months, they are 660 mm long, and by the end of their 1st year, they are about 762 mm in length (Wasserman & Gromisch, 1981). The growth data from a sample of middle-class Finnish infants illustrate this; these infants showed average increases of 50% to 55% in length and 180% to 200% in weight during their 1st year (Kanters & Tiisala, 1971). These data are likely to reflect growth patterns in the United States as well. As Eichorn (1979) has pointed out, during the first 6 months or so, length and weight growth patterns are typically uniform, regardless of the family's socioeconomic status or the country's level of industrialization. After about 6 months, however, social class and technology do affect physical growth patterns.

Infants also increase rapidly in size of specific body parts during their 1st year. Data from the Denver Child Research Council (Hansman, 1970) show that average increases in overall body length, hip breadth, and shoulder breadth were 55% for boys and 54% for girls. Average increases in crown-rump (head to buttocks) length were 45% in boys and 42% in girls. Similarly, for head circumference, average increases of 39% for boys and 35% for girls were recorded.

Despite the rapid increase in size, rate of growth declines in the child's early years. In the Finnish sample, the rate at which boys were growing lengthwise fell from 45.8 cm/year between birth and 3 months to 14.4 cm/year during the last 3 months of the first year. Similarly, their rate of weight gain decreased from 10.3 to 3.4 kg for the same two comparison periods. Sex differences were apparent in these data only for the first 3 months; female growth velocities were about 14% less for length and weight. After the 1st year, physical growth slows, and the pattern across the childhood years is steady and linear. Recently, the longitudinal data from the Fels Research Institute, the National Center for Health Statistics, and the Center for Disease Control have been combined to develop physical growth norms for boys and girls between the ages of birth and 18 years. These growth charts include normative data on length and weight for age, head circumference for age, and weight for length (Zaichkowsky, Zaichkowsky, & Martinek, 1980).

Neurological Development

The development of the nervous system is obviously critical to physical development, since the nervous system coordinates and regulates body actions. The behavioral differences between a neurologically intact, physically normal infant and one who is brain-damaged demonstrate how significant the nervous system is to physical, particularly motor, development. At birth, the brain is about 25% of its adult weight; at 6 months, 50%; and at 2½ years, about 75%. In contrast, the infant's body weight at birth is about 5% of its adult weight and only reaches 50% of its adult weight by age 10. The nervous system does not grow uniformly. Different parts reach maturity at different times, which explains why infants are not very behaviorally organized or efficient early in life. The spinal cord, midbrain, and portions of the hindbrain mature before the front brain, but the cerebellum, which is part of the hindbrain, reaches maturity after the front brain (Tanner, 1978).

Just as different portions of the nervous system mature at different times, functional areas of the brain also develop in a specific order. The first to mature is the primary motor area, followed by the primary sensory, visual, and auditory areas, in that order. By the time the infant is 3 months old, these primary areas are relatively mature, and most of the neural fibers entering the neocortex have been myelinated to some extent. The association areas, which are used to organize and interpret neural impulses, thus making behavior more efficient and organized, are slower to develop. The process of myelination parallels continued integration of association and primary cortical regions. For example, fibers linking the cerebellum and the neocortex do not become fully myelinated until about age 4 (which, of course, affects the child's ability to exercise fine control over voluntary motor behavior), and the reticular formation is probably not completely myelinated until puberty (Tanner, 1978).

Despite differences in maturity gradients, all the sensory organs are fully developed and ready for use in the neurologically intact full-term infant. The eyes are open and the pupillary reflex, which controls the amount of light admitted, is intact. Because infants are not usually able to focus both eyes until at least several hours after birth and may not be able to do so for several days, coordinated focus may be irregular and inconsistent for some weeks. Visual tracking (coordinated movement of the two eyes) is typically not possible until about the 2nd week; this is more likely a function of neuromuscular practice, however, rather than structural inadequacy. The auditory system also seems to be well developed at normal birth; that is, infants can hear, although it is not known how well they can hear. It seems likely that detection of subtle sound distinctions requires experience. Newborns also respond to touch, vibration, smell, and taste.

Endocrine Development

The endocrine system produces chemical substances called hormones, which continually regulate and integrate body functions (Table 2-4). These glands develop early, and their secretions play an important role in tissue and organ development. Hormone production varies at different stages of development. For example, the amount of growth hormone found in the fetal anterior pituitary changes dramatically. At 68 days of gestational age, it is approximately 0.04 μg; at 25 to 29 weeks, approximately 225 μg; and at 35 to 40 weeks, approximately 675 μg. The growth hormone level increases right after birth, but, by the end of the 1st month, it drops to its adult values (Sizonenki & Aubert, 1978).

Motor Development

Since motor activity depends on neurological functioning, motor development (i.e., the process by which the infant acquires voluntary control over movement) parallels maturation of the nervous system over the first few years after birth.

Table 2-4 Endocrine System Glands and Hormones

Gland	*Hormone*	*Function*
Pituitary (master gland)	Growth activating hormone and stimulating hormones for thyroid, adrenals, and ovaries	Acts with thymus to regulate growth, with thyroid to regulate metabolism, with ovaries to regulate female ovulation
Thyroid	Thyroxine	Regulates general metabolic rate
Parathyroid	Parathormone	Regulates metabolism of specific chemicals that affect muscle tone, fatigue, and bone growth
Adrenal	Adrenaline, epinephrine, norepinephrine	Assists with stress and demands for activity
Pancreas	Insulin	Regulates sugar metabolism in body tissues and storage of sugar in blood
Gonads (male)	Androsterone	Regulates secondary sex characteristics (e.g., beard, hair) and sexual arousal
Ovaries (female)	Estrogen	Regulates secondary sex characteristics (e.g., breasts) and sexual arousal

Because of this relationship, motor activity, especially during infancy, has diagnostic value in determining neurological intactness.

The midbrain, which is the most developed at birth, is also the center of reflex activity. Since the neocortex is not fully mature at birth, infant survival depends to a large extent on a number of primitive reflexes that involuntarily control behavior. These reflexes include such survival behaviors as eye blinking, salivating, gagging, and urinating, as well as reflexes such as rooting, sucking, and grasping (Table 2-5).

As the neocortex matures and association areas become integrated, the infant gradually acquires voluntary control over movement. At birth, for example, the primary motor area of the neocortex is the most mature area, and this allows some control of hands, arms, and the upper trunk. Motor development in the lower trunk and lower extremities occurs more slowly, however, and children typically do not have complete control over leg movement until the 2nd year. This developmental lag reflects the sequence of the child's interactions with the world. Soon after birth, environmental interactions occur primarily through the senses. Later, as motor skills emerge, the child interacts with the environment by turning and lifting the head, lifting the trunk, grasping, and eventually by crawling and then walking. This pattern of development is illustrated by the ages at which the typical infant

Table 2-5 Primitive Reflexes

Reflex	*Description*
Moro	When infant's head is extended backward, arms move into an embracing position; usually present from birth until about 5 to 6 months; absence at birth or presence after 5 to 6 months is taken as evidence of neurological dysfunction.
Asymmetrical tonic neck reflex	If infant's head is turned to one side, body adopts the traditional fencer's position; usually disappears by 5 to 6 months, although it has been known to persist as late as 9 months in some normal infants.
Tonic labyrinthine reflex	Response depends on position of infant's head—if infant is lying in supine position, posture is characterized by legs straightened, shoulders retracted, neck arched, and head pressed against the surface; if infant is in a prone position, arms and legs become bent under body and neck and head become flexed toward the surface; usually loses its influence over voluntary control of behavior at 1 to 3 months; at 1 month, infant can lift head from prone position; at 2 to 3 months can lift head from supine position.
Positive supporting reflex	If infant's feet are placed on hard surface, infant reacts by stiffening leg muscles, causing legs to straighten to support body's weight; neonatal form present from birth to about 6 to 8 weeks then wanes; infantile form reappears between 6 to 9 months and can, if strong, interfere with walking since it forces legs apart, scissors-like; reflex must lose its influence before walking can begin.
Placing reflex	When top of infant's hands or feet touch surface, hands or feet move over and above stimulus; present in newborn and gradually becomes a part of voluntary motor activity over 1st year.
Stepping reflex	If infant is supported in standing position, legs alternate in a walking motion; present soon after birth until end of first 3 to 4 months.
Landau reflex	When infant is held in horizontal prone position, infant automatically lifts head up, and this increased muscle tone causes legs to extend and back to arch; typically present by 6 months and becomes incorporated into voluntary motor activity during 2nd year.
Symmetrical tonic neck reflex	If infant is in hands-knees kneeling position with head extended, arms extend and hips bend; if infant's head is bent down, arms bend at the elbows and hips extend; if reflex appears, does so between ages 6 to 9 months.

Table 2-5 continued

Reflex	*Description*
Rooting reflex	Light pressure on infant's cheek near mouth causes infant to turn in direction of stimulation; usually present from birth to about the 3rd postnatal month.
Sucking reflex	If infant's lips or gums are lightly touched, sucking starts; usually present from birth to about the 3rd postnatal month.
Grasp reflex	If pressure is applied to infant's palm, four fingers automatically and tightly close over object that is causing pressure; usually present from birth to 5 to 6 months.

moves through the following (abbreviated) series of stages in acquiring control over walking:

- sits alone, 8 months
- stands by holding on, 10 months
- stands alone, 15 months
- walks alone, 16 months

Developing motor behavior is thus characterized by two concurrent patterns: cephalocaudal, in which development proceeds from head to tail region, and proximodistal, in which development proceeds from the body's inner regions to its extremities. Following these patterns, as discussed earlier, muscles of the upper trunk develop before those of the lower trunk, and the large inner muscles develop before the smaller muscles in the hands and feet. This explains why infants and young children usually develop large muscle skills (gross motor behavior) earlier than they develop small muscle skills (fine motor behavior).

Primitive and Automatic Reflexes. Control over motor development is tied to two classes of reflexes, primitive and automatic. Although primitive reflexes are important for initial survival, they would interfere with normal growth and development if they persisted. For example, if the grasp reflex persisted beyond the first 6 months, it would limit an infant's access to valuable sensory input through tactile stimulation. Likewise, the tonic labyrinthine reflex, if continuously present, would make it difficult for the infant to lift the head and straighten the arms and legs. This, of course, would seriously reduce the infant's sensory stimulation and exploratory activity.

Automatic reflexes, in contrast, augment motor development. These postural reflexes, which are critical to maintaining balance, consist mainly of righting, supporting, and equilibrium responses to changes in muscle tone (i.e., increases or decreases in muscle tension that affect body position). Automatic reflexes are not present at birth; they appear over the first 2 years of life, paralleling maturation and integration of the brain's primary and association areas. As they are acquired, they signal a reduction of lower brain reflexive control over behavior and an integration of these primitive reflexes into the infant's ability to execute purposeful, integrated, and voluntary behaviors.

Automatic reflexes include the head-righting reflex, which keeps the head in an upright position in spite of changes in body posture; derotative reactions, which set up sequential movement of body parts needed for such motor activities as rolling over; protective reflexes, which enable the body to react to rapid changes in position, as in a fall; and equilibrium reactions, which make it possible to maintain a given posture in the face of subtle changes in body position. The relationship between these automatic reflexes and the early development of motor skills is summarized in Table 2-6.

Motor Developmental Milestones. During infancy, many important motor milestones are reached (Table 2-7). These acquisitions provide the infant with the necessary motor substrate for developing cognitive and social skills. (For a more thorough review of motor milestones in infancy and early childhood, see Chandler, 1979.)

The Development of Prehension. Not just grasping activity, but controlled, visually directed reaching is prehension. Its development is important because it gives the infant control over the environment that is critical to subsequent cognitive and social development. The emergence of prehension indicates the beginnings of the infant's attempts to coordinate visual and motor systems (e.g., eye-hand coordination). Piaget (1952) and White (1971) have investigated the emergence of visually directed reaching, and their findings are summarized in Table 2-8.

Sex Differences

Very early in development, sex chromosomes and prenatal hormones induce sexual differentiation; prenatal hormones also affect brain development. It has

Table 2-6 Relationship of Automatic Reflexes to Motor Skills

Automatic Reflex	*Motor Skill Acquired*
Head righting	Early prone and supine head lift, reaching, sitting up
Derotation	Rolling over, coming to a sitting position
Protective equilibrium	Stable sitting, stable standing, walking
Equilibrium	Crawling, cruising

Table 2-7 Age at Which Motor Milestones Are Reached

Behavior	*Approximate Age at Onset (Months)*
Walking	
Sits alone for 1 minute	8
Crawls	9
Stands by holding on	10
Creeps	11
Stands alone	15
Walks alone	16
Walks backward	18 to 21
Manipulation	
Reaching movement	4
Contact and primitive squeeze	5
Squeeze grasp	6
Hand/palm grasp	7
Superior palm grasp	8
Superior forefinger grip	10

Table 2-8 Sequence of Behaviors in Prehension Development

Age (Months)	*Behaviors*
1 to 2	Objects being sucked are not grasped by hand; the hand is an object to be sucked; the infant does not look at what is being grasped.
2 to 3	Eyes follow hand's motions, but the hand does not try to grasp what the eyes see; this is a "swiping" behavior.
3 to 4	The hand grasps the object being sucked; the grasped object is brought to the mouth to be sucked.
4 to 5	The hand reaches and grasps the seen object.
5 to 6	True visually directed reaching occurs; the infant reaches for an object and examines it before bringing it to the mouth to be sucked.

been suggested that many sex differences result from the influence of prenatal androgens on brain development. For example, the presence of prenatal androgens can alter the cyclical reproductive biorhythms of female rodents in adulthood. It is not clear, however, if this same effect occurs among human females who were exposed to excessive levels of prenatal androgens. Prenatal androgens can affect the display of other behaviors (e.g., sexual preference behaviors, fear responses, aggression levels, eating behavior, activity levels, and rough-and-tumble play). With the exception of rough and tumble play, these effects have been found only in rodents, not in humans. It is not yet known if sex differences in rough-and-tumble play result from hormones or from socialization.

Other sex differences include (1) the more advanced developmental status of girls, a difference that is usually maintained until adulthood and is typically reflected in other maturational areas, such as motor coordination (Tanner, 1978); (2) the typically shorter stature of girls (except during early adolescence); and (3) the weight differential—girls tend to weigh less at birth, and this difference normally is maintained except during puberty (Archer, 1981).

Another interesting sex difference relates to cerebral hemisphere specialization. Whitelson (1976) has reported that girls' brains may not become specialized as early as do boys' brains. Her study involved 200 right-handed children, aged 6 to 13 years, who were all normal with respect to IQ, school achievement, and health status. She asked the children to palpate two meaningless shapes, one with each hand, that they could not see. Afterward, they were to select the two shapes from a visual display. This requires tactile shape discriminative ability, which is a right hemisphere function. Whitelson found left-right hand differences for boys at all ages, but no differences for girls; overall accuracy did not differ by sex. She interpreted these findings as an indication that boys' brains become specialized for spatial processing early, whereas bilateral representation continues in girls at least until adolescence. She concluded that these data may reflect a sex difference in the neural organization of cognitive skills.

Diet, Nutrition, and Medical Care

In the United States, dramatically undernourished infants or children are rarely seen. More moderate forms of malnutrition do occur in the U.S. population, however, not merely because of poverty, but because of careless planning, personal family tastes, superstitions, and habits. Infants and small children may suffer a shortage of iron, which can lead to anemia, or a shortage of iodine, which can cause thyroid problems. Protein deficiencies are associated with sensory, perceptual, and mental lethargy (while mild); with dwarfing and immobility (when severe). Parasitic infections, such as pinworms, are more common than many people think, and their effects can be similar to those of protein deficiencies.

While nature typically performs very well to ensure the survival and development of the fetus and infant, much can be done to help nature. Public health departments, welfare departments, and home economics extension services can help families improve diet and health care. Most middle-class families, especially in urban areas, are able to provide rather good diets and medical care for their children. Among the economically disadvantaged, however, such attention is often seriously inadequate or totally lacking. The greatest tragedy occurs when a condition that could be easily remedied if diagnosed early is allowed to progress to its later stages, when it becomes partially or totally irreversible. Middle-class children typically have the benefit of continuing medical attention, so the rate of birth defects is much lower among these children as compared with the rate of birth defects among the children of minority groups and the poor. Within these populations, poor diet and health conditions often go unrecognized until the child enters school—or even later—when it is frequently too late for total remediation. Middle-class teachers, expecting that any such conditions have been detected in the preschool years, frequently deal with the behavioral manifestations of such problems (e.g., inattentiveness, disobedience, distractibility, shyness) as problems of social adjustment rather than as medical ones. Thus, early and regular diagnostic medical attention for all infants can contribute significantly to individual physical, cognitive, and social growth and development.

REFERENCES

Adamsons, K. Fetal growth: Obstetric implications. In F. Falkner & J.M. Tanner (Eds.), *Human growth* (Vol. 1). London: Bailliere Tindall, 1978.

Apgar, V., & Beck, J. *Is my baby all right?* New York: Trident Press, 1973.

Archer, J. Sex differences in maturation. In K.J. Connolly & H.R. Prechtl (Eds.), *Maturation and development*. London: Heinemann, 1981.

Battaglia, F.C., & Simmons, M.A. The low-birth-weight infant. In F. Falkner & J.M. Tanner (Eds.), *Human growth* (Vol. 2). London: Bailliere Tindall, 1978.

Beaconsfield, P., Birdwood, G., & Beaconsfield, R. The placenta. *Scientific American*, 1980, *243*, 94-103.

Brackbill, Y. Obstetric medication and infant behavior. In J. Osofsky (Ed.), *Handbook of infant development*. New York: Wiley, 1979.

Brazelton, T.B. Neonatal Behavioral Assessment Scale. *Clinics in Developmental Medicine* (No. 50). London: Spastics International Medical Publications with Heinemann Medical Books, 1973.

Brazelton, T.B., Als, H., Tronick, E., & Lester, B.M. Specific neonatal measure: The Brazelton Neonatal Behavior Assessment Scale. In J. Osofsky (Ed.), *Handbook of infant development*. New York: Wiley, 1979.

Chandler, L. Gross and fine motor development. In M. Cohen & P. Gross (Eds.), *The developmental resource*. New York: Grune & Stratton, 1979.

Eichorne, D.H. Physical development: Current foci of research. In J. Osofsky (Ed.), *Handbook of infant development*. New York: Wiley, 1979.

Fewell, R. Infant assessment. In S.G. Garwood & R. Fewell (Eds.), *Educating handicapped infants: Issues in development and intervention*. Rockville, Md.: Aspen Systems Corporation, 1983.

Fuchs, F. Genetic amniocentesis. *Scientific American*, 1980, *242*, 47-53.

Fulker, D.W. Genetics and behavioral development. In K.J. Connolly & H.R. Prechtl (Eds.), *Maturation and development*. London: Heinemann, 1981.

Hansman, C. Anthropometry and related data, anthropometry skinfold thickness measurements. In R.W. McCamonon (Ed.), *Human growth and development*, Springfield, Ill.: Charles C Thomas, 1970.

Jacob, F., & Monod, J. On the regulation of gene activity. *Cold Spring Harbor Symposia on Quantitative Biology*, 1961, *26*, 193-209.

Kanters, R., & Tiisala, R. Height, weight and sitting height increments for children from birth to 10 years. *Acta Paediatrica Scandinavica, Supplement*, 1971, 220.

Keeton, W.T. *Biological science*. New York: Norton, 1972.

McClearn, G., & DeFries, J. *Introduction to behavioral genetics*. San Francisco: W.H. Freeman, 1973.

Moore, K.L. *The developing human*. Philadelphia: Saunders, 1977.

Murray, A., Dolby, R., Nation, R., & Thomas D. Effects of epidural anesthesia on newborns and their mothers. *Child Development*, 1981, *52*, 71-82.

Ohno, S. The development of sexual reproduction. In C.R. Austin & R.V. Short (Eds.), *Reproduction in mammals 6: The evolution of reproduction*. Cambridge: Cambridge University Press, 1976.

Piaget, J. *The origins of intelligence in children*. New York: International Universities Press, 1952.

Prechtl, H., & Beintema, D. *Neurological examination of the full-term newborn infant*. London: Heinemann, 1964.

Reinisch, J.M. Effects of prenatal hormone exposure on physical and psychosocial development in humans and animals. In E.J. Sachar (Ed.), *Hormones, behavior and psychopathology*. New York: Raven Press, 1976.

Rosenblith, J. The Graham/Rosenblith Behavioral Examination for Newborns: Prognostic value and procedural issues. In J. Osofsky (Ed.), *Handbook of infant development*. New York: Wiley, 1979.

Sameroff, A.J., & Chandler, M.J. Reproductive risk and the continuum of caretaking causality. In F.D. Horowitz (Ed.), *Review of Child Development Research* (Vol. 4). Chicago: University of Chicago Press, 1975.

Self, P., & Horowitz, F. The behavioral assessment of the neonate: An overview. In J. Osofsky (Ed.), *Handbook of infant development*. New York: Wiley, 1979.

Sizonenki, P.C., & Aubert, M.L. Pre- and perinatal endocrinology. In F. Falkner & J.M. Tanner (Eds.), *Human growth (Vol. 1)*. London: Bailliere Tindall, 1978.

Tanner, J. *Foetus into man*. Cambridge, Mass.: Harvard University Press, 1978.

Timiras, P.S. *Developmental physiology and aging*. New York: Macmillan, 1972.

U.S. Department of Health, Education and Welfare, Public Health Service, National Institutes of Health. *Antenatal Diagnosis*. 1979.

Waddington, C.H. *The strategy of genes*. New York: Macmillan, 1957.

Wasserman, E., & Gromisch, D. *Survey of clinical pediatrics*. New York: McGraw-Hill, 1981.

Watson, J.D. *The double helix*. New York: Atheneum, 1968.

Watson, J.D. *The molecular biology of the gene*. New York: Benjamin-Cummings, 1976.

White, B. *Human infants: Experience and psychological development*. Englewood Cliffs, N.J.: Prentice-Hall, 1971.

Whitelson, S.F. Sex and the single hemisphere: Specialization of the right hemisphere for spatial processing. *Science*, 1976, *193*, 425-427.

Zaichkowsky, L.D., Zaichkowsky, L.A., & Martinek, T.J. *Growth and development*. St. Louis: Mosby, 1980.

Chapter 3

Physical Bases of Handicapping Conditions

S. Gray Garwood

Physical growth is under the control of the individual's genetic blueprint, which regulates both the rate and the nature of physical development; however, environmental events or factors can alter nature's intent. Under optimal conditions, genetic and environmental factors interact for normal conception and prenatal growth, birth, and subsequent development. When conditions are not optimal, either as a result of a genetic accident or because of environmental interactions that prevent normal development, one or more handicapping conditions can occur. Most handicapping conditions are the result of congenital malformations, physical malformations that are present at birth. They may be large or small; they may be inside the body or on its surface; and they cause about 15% of newborn deaths and are the major source for severe illness and death during childhood. In addition, postnatal diseases and injuries can give rise to handicaps in children.

CHROMOSOMAL ABNORMALITIES

Gene-based malformations as a result of chromosomal abnormalities most frequently cause developmental abnormalities (Polani, 1981). Chromosomes, which contain genetic information, are arranged in pairs called autosomes and sex chromosomes. Normal growth occurs when the 22 autosomal pairs divide by mitosis and the sex chromosome pair divides by meiosis. Sometimes these processes are flawed, and numerical errors or rearrangements result in fewer than the normal number of chromosomes (hypodiploidy), more than the normal number (hyperdiploidy), or transfer of part of one chromosome to another. When a single chromosome occurs where there is normally a pair, it is a monosomy; when more than a pair are present, it is usually a trisomy or a mosaic or multisomy. Polani (1981) has classified chromosomal abnormalities as (1) developmental anomalies, ranging from gross to subtle variations in structure or behavior (e.g.,

Down's syndrome); (2) chromosomal instability disorders, which result from defects of deoxyribonucleic acid (DNA) synthesis or repair; and (3) chromosomal variants, which had been considered relatively unimportant, but are now thought to have detrimental phenotypic effects in some cases.

Monosomies that result from improper mitotic division are rarely encountered, since an embryo with fewer than the normal supply of autosomes does not usually survive. Survival is possible, however, if a monosomy results from improper meiotic cell division. This rare occurrence produces Turner's syndrome, in which the infant is a female with only one X chromosome. Such a child has a short webbed neck, short fingers, low-set ears, a triangular mouth, and little sexual differentiation. Mental retardation is not commonly associated with this syndrome.

Trisomies are more frequent and can occur in either autosomes or the sex chromosome. Klinefelter's syndrome is caused by a sex chromosome trisomy; this XXY pattern results in a male with female characteristics, both in body shape and in glandular development. Usually, such children are mentally retarded and sterile. Autosomal trisomies include a variety of syndromes. The most common is Down's syndrome, which is a trisomy of the 21st chromosome. The extra chromosome originates from one of three different errors of chromosome distribution during meiosis or mitosis. Nondysjunction, which accounts for 90% to 95% of children with Down's syndrome, occurs when the sperm's or the egg's 21st chromosomal pair fails to separate during the meiotic process, producing a fertilized egg with 47 chromosomes, three on the 21st pair. Down's syndrome can also result from an abnormal fusing of chromosome pairs in which the extra number 21 chromosome is translocated to another chromosome. This translocation form accounts for approximately 3% to 4% of individuals with Down's syndrome. In the least common form, some cells have 46 chromosomes and some have 47 chromosomes because of an error in one of the divisions of the fertilized egg. This mosaic form of Down's syndrome accounts for about 1% of Down's syndrome individuals.

Regardless of the type of chromosomal error, children with Down's syndrome have the same physical, mental, and social characteristics: poor muscle tone; slanting eyes; folds of skin at the inner corners of the eyes; small, low-set ears; short neck; small hands and short fingers; and shorter than average stature. Heart defects are present in about 40% of Down's syndrome children, and hearing losses are also often observed. Children with Down's syndrome are retarded in varying degrees.

Deletions of chromosomal material also cause structural abnormalities. Arrangement of chromosomal material within the normal 23 pairs may be defective, for example, because part of the necessary chromosomal material has accidentally been deleted during cell division. The partial deletion of a portion of the 18th chromosomal pair results in the birth of a severely mentally retarded infant with microcephaly (abnormally small head) and other gross congenital anomalies.

Another such defect is associated with the cri du chat syndrome, which occurs when part of number 5 chromosomal pair is incomplete. The infant with this syndrome is severely mentally retarded, and, in about half the cases, the infant's cry sounds like a cat mewing, owing to abnormal larynx development.

Approximately 10% to 15% of congenital abnormalities are caused by genetic mutations. Such conditions include achondroplasia (short limbs, large head, and abdominal protrusion) and polydactyly (extra, often incompletely formed fingers or toes). (For more detail on this topic, see McClearn & DeFries, 1973; Boyce, 1975; Smith, 1976; or Wasserman & Gromisch, 1981.)

Hertig (1967) and Alberman and Creasy (1975) have estimated that only about one-third of successful fertilizations lead to the birth of a surviving infant. More graphically, of 100 successfully established pregnancies, about 25 will be aborted; of these 25, some 40% to 60% of fetuses will have a major chromosomal anomaly. Two infants will die during or immediately after birth. Approximately 73 will survive, some (about 0.5%) suffering from conditions caused by chromosomal abnormalities. Of the chromosomal abnormalities that occur, approximately one-half are trisomies for one of the 22 autosomes; only a few of these are compatible with survival (e.g., trisomies 13, 18, and 21; Table 3-1). Currently, nearly 50 chromosomal syndromes have been identified (Polani, 1981).

Using amniocentesis, scientists are now able to determine early in pregnancy whether chromosomal structures in the fetus are normal. The physician can extract a sample of amniotic fluid and analyze it for chromosome composition. If abnormalities are found, parents may then decide if abortion is warranted. Robinson (1979) offers a thought-provoking review of these techniques. Genetic engineering technology, although certainly controversial, may in the future permit the correction of genetic mistakes that today account for more than 2,000 diseases. Once safe techniques are developed, it may be possible to modify genetic defects either by correcting the mistake in DNA structure or by transferring a normal gene into a dysfunctional cell (Anderson & Diacumakos, 1981).

TERATOGENS

Exposure of the developing fetus to certain environmental agents can interfere with normal growth processes, especially if such exposure occurs during a critical period of structural development. Some teratogenic chemicals and their effects on the developing organism are outlined in Table 3-2. Infectious agents also can alter normal development, depending on the time of exposure. Such agents include cytomegalovirus, rubella virus, *Toxoplasma gondii*, and herpesvirus (Table 3-3). Embryonic and fetal development can also be hampered by certain environmental events, such as exposure to irradiation or to maternal consumption of alcohol and

Table 3-1 Chromosomal Abnormalities

Chromosome Arrangement	*Sex*	*Risk Factor*	*Characteristics*
Sex Chromosome trisomies			
47, XXX	Female phenotype	1:1,000	Normal in appearance; fertile; may be retarded
47, XXY	Male	1:500	Klinefelter's syndrome; small testes; hyalinization of seminiferous tubules; aspermatogenesis; may be retarded
47, XYY	Male	1:1,000	Normal in appearance; often tall; may have personality disorder
Autosome trisomies			
Down's syndrome (Trisomy 21)		1:600	Mental retardation; flat nasal bridge; slant to eyelids; protruding tongue; simian crease in palm; congenital heart defects
E Syndrome (Pairs 17-18)		1:3,300	Mental retardation; growth retardation; prominent skull (back); short sternum; ventricular septal defect; micrognathia; low-set, malformed ears; flexed fingers
D syndrome (Pairs 13-15)		1:5,500	Mental deficiency; sloping forehead; malformed ears; microphthalamous bilateral cleft lip or palate; polydactyly; rocker heels; short-lived

tobacco (Table 3-4). For the reader who wishes to pursue this topic in more depth, much of the information contained in these tables was derived from Moore (1977); Smith (1977); Wasserman and Gromisch (1981); Wright, Schaefer, and Solomons (1979); and the 1981 edition of the *Physician's Desk Reference (PDR)*.

EFFECTS OF CONGENITAL MALFORMATION ON THE DEVELOPING CHILD

Cardiovascular System

Rapid embryonic development requires nourishment and oxygen, as well as a method of waste disposal. For these reasons, the cardiovascular system (heart and

Table 3-2 Teratogenic Effects of Some Chemicals

Drug or Chemical	*Effects on Development*
Androgenic agents	Use of synthetic progestogens to prevent natural abortion has contributed to virilization of female fetuses.
Antibiotics	Maternal use of tetracycline during the second and third trimesters can cause subsequent minor damage to an infant's teeth (e.g., discoloration). Penicillin is thought to be harmless.
Antitumor agents	Such drugs as busulfan have been known to contribute to fetal death, congenital skeletal and other malformations, intrauterine growth retardation, central nervous system damage, and damage to developing gonads.
Thyroid drugs	Potassium iodides in cough mixtures (e.g., Quadrinal) and radioactive iodine can cause congenital goiter. Propylthiouracil, which inhibits synthesis of thyroid hormones, can cause goiter and even cretinism in developing fetuses.
Lysergic acid diethylamide (LSD) and marijuana	There are conflicting views about both. To date, the evidence that either is a teratogenic agent is sparse, but reports of both limb and central nervous system malformations have been reported following use of one or both.

blood vessels) is first to become functional, early in the third week. The complexity of the cardiovascular system makes congenital malformations rather common (about 0.7% of all live births). Three such malformations are patent foramen ovale, patent ductus arteriosus, and ventricular septal defects. Patent foramen ovale results when the foramen ovale, the opening between the left and right atria, fails to close. Patent ductus arteriosus, the most common cardiac malformation associated with maternal rubella infection, during the first trimester, occurs when the opening between the aorta and the ductus arteriosus fails to close as it should, usually by the 2nd week after birth. Patent ductus arteriosus occurs two to three times more often in females. A ventricular septal defect, which is the most frequently reported cardiac defect, results from inadequate tissue growth and fusion of the dividing wall between the two ventricles.

Urogenital System

Reproduction and elimination systems are closely associated; parts of one overlap and function as parts of the other. The urinary system, which begins to develop during the fourth week, includes: (1) kidneys, which filter and collect body fluid wastes in the form of urine; (2) the ureter, a tube which carries urine away from the kidneys; (3) the bladder, which stores urine; (4) the urethra, the urine-eliminating canal connecting the bladder with the outside; and (5) the adrenal gland, a hormone-producing body.

Table 3-3 Teratogenic Effects of Some Viral Infections

Infection	*Effects on Development*
Rubella	The probability of a rubella syndrome child being born to a woman exposed to infectious German measles during pregnancy is between 1:40 and 1:50. Exposure is most likely to result in a rubella syndrome child if the exposure occurs during the first trimester, but this is not always the case; 12% of rubella syndrome infants are born to mothers infected during the second, and 1% are born to mothers infected during the third. There is even a possibility that exposure just before pregnancy can result in a rubella syndrome child. Of the defects that can occur, hearing problems are most common (25%), followed by heart (2%), nervous system (2%), and vision (2%) defects; multiple defects are also possible. Rubella infants typically have a low birth weight, and many experience some motor development delay. Furthermore, there is some evidence of a higher than normal number of emotional or behavioral problems and of slight to moderate intellectual impairment. Treatment is prevention, by means of either a massive injection of immune serum globulin or injection of live virus before pregnancy.
Syphilis (Treponema pallidum)	After about the 4th month, syphilis can cross the placenta. It causes fetal death in about 25% of all maternal infections. The infected child appears normal at birth, but within a few weeks begins to show typical signs of syphilis (e.g., moist skin lesions, and a rash on palms and soles). If untreated, the child develops physical anomalies, such as cranial frontal bossing and saddle nose; deafness could ensue. Treatment involves injections of penicillin either to the mother prior to the birth or to the infant after birth.
Toxoplasmosis (Toxoplasma gondii)	Parasites from certain foods or possibly from cats can infect the pregnant mother, cross the placental barrier, and cause prematurity, severe neonatal disease, or fetal death. The fetus is most susceptible during the second trimester. Chorioretinitis (retinal inflammation) is the most common feature and typically involves both eyes.
Cytomegalic inclusion disease	Cytomegalovirus has been found to exist, or to have existed, in the majority of women of childbearing age. This virus is probably most harmful to the fetus during the first and second trimesters, and effects on the infant vary from severe mental retardation with seizures and deafness to no noticeable effects. There is no specific treatment for neonatal cytomegalovirus, but preventive measures for pregnant mothers are currently under study.
Herpesvirus	Herpes simplex can cross the placental barrier or infect the neonate at birth. Signs of infection usually appear between 3 and 7 days following birth and include temperature instability, lethargy, respiratory distress, jaundice, encephalitis, retinal infection, and microcephaly.
Erythroblastosis fetalis	Not truly an infection, erythroblastosis fetalis is caused by genetically determined differences between maternal and fetal blood. If the embryo inherits a protein substance, the Rh factor, from the father, and the mother lacks this substance, consequences to the unborn

Table 3-3 continued

	child can be serious if any of its blood accidentally mixes with maternal blood. If this happens (usually during birth), the mother's body treats fetal blood as a virus and generates antibodies to fight this "infection." These antibodies pass into the fetal bloodstream and destroy large numbers of fetal red blood cells. Death is one consequence, but severe anemia, jaundice, and mental retardation may also occur. This problem has been reduced by immediately treating new Rh-negative mothers with RhoGAM if their infant is Rh-positive; RhoGAM helps destroy Rh-positive antigens and blocks formation of antibodies in the mother, thus protecting her future children.

Table 3-4 Teratogenic Effects of Some Environmental Events

Environmental Event	*Influence on Development*
Alcohol consumption	Fetal alcohol syndrome infants are born to mothers who regularly consume alcohol; about 89 ml (3 oz)/day is sufficient to place the fetus at risk for this syndrome. Clinical features include prenatal and postnatal growth deficiency, as well as physical anomalies of the ear, mouth, heart, kidneys, bones, and especially the face. Distinctive facial features include short palpebral fissures of the eye, short upturned nose, and a thin upturned upper lip. Mental retardation is quite common, as is hyperactivity and poor fine motor coordination. Current conservative incidence figures place the number of fetal alcohol syndrome infants at 1 or 2 per 1,000 live births, or about 4,000 to 5,000 affected infants per year in the United States (Abel, 1980; Wasserman & Gromisch, 1981).
Cigarette consumption	There is evidence of an association between maternal smoking and increased neonatal mortality, low birth weight, retarded postnatal growth, increased childhood pulmonary disorders, and mental retardation (Abel, 1980).
Maternal emotional state	Emotional changes in the mother that cause an increase in the levels of certain body chemicals (e.g., adrenalin) appear also to influence fetal development. Mothers who are irritable, anxious, and emotional during later pregnancy are more likely to produce infants who are hyperactive, irritable, and prone to sleeping and eating problems.
Exposure to irradiation	Use of x-rays as a treatment procedure can cause microcephaly, mental retardation, and skeletal malformations. It is not clear whether diagnostic x-rays cause such abnormalities, but caution is advised, especially during the first trimester.
Maternal age	The age range 20 to 35 seems to be best for childbearing. Mothers below or above this age range have a disproportionate number of mortalities and a higher incidence of mentally retarded children.

The reproductive or genital system includes internal reproductive organs, genital ducts, and male and female external genitalia. Although the infant's sex is determined at fertilization, sexual differentiation does not begin until about the seventh week. (For a more detailed discussion of the genital system, the reader is referred to McDavid and Garwood (1978) or to Moore (1977).)

Congenital malformations of the urinary system are relatively common. Kidney and ureter abnormalities, such as duplication of the upper urinary tract, absence of one kidney, and abnormally positioned kidney(s), occur in 3% to 4% of the population. Reproductive abnormalities are less common, but they do occur. Gonadal sex is controlled by the Y chromosome. If a Y chromosome is present, testes develop and male hormones are produced to stimulate development of the male genital system; if no Y chromosome is present, female genitalia develop. Cases of true hermaphroditism are very rare. The true hermaphrodite has both ovarian and testicular tissue, the individual may appear as male or female, but external genitalia are ambiguous. More common are errors in sex determination (male or female pseudohermaphroditism and testicular feminization). (For a more complete discussion, see Money & Ehrhardt, 1972.)

The Respiratory System

During the fourth week a primitive pharynx develops, followed by the larynx, trachea, and the esophagus. By the fifth week, lung buds appear and begin to differentiate into the bronchi, the lungs, the pleural cavities, and the pleura, a membrane which surrounds the lungs. By 26 weeks, the lungs are typically sufficiently developed to permit survival if the fetus is born before term.

Major congenital malformations of the lower respiratory system are rare. The most common of such malformations is tracheoesophageal fistula, an abnormal passage most frequently connecting the trachea and the upper portion of the esophagus, which occurs in about 1:2,500 births. Infants with this condition choke when they are fed, causing food to pass into the respiratory tract. Hyaline membrane disease, or respiratory distress syndrome, is the most common serious disease affecting newborns. Infants with this disease do not produce enough of a chemical substance called surfactant, and a thin membrane that interferes with breathing forms inside the lung. This disease is responsible for about 12,000 neonatal deaths each year and occurs in about 10:1,000 to 20:1,000 live births or 350:1,000 low-birth-weight infants (Wasserman & Gromisch, 1981).

Branchial Apparatus

This structure in the embryo is comprised of branchial arches, clefts or grooves, and muscles which will ultimately form the face, tongue, palate, pharynx, and neck. The arches appear as ridges, separated by grooves or clefts, on the site where the future head and neck will be. During the fourth week, face, ear, and neck structures begin to emerge. The roof of the mouth or palate begins to develop during the fifth week. Congenital malformation of the branchial apparatus probably originates when the head structures begin to develop. The most common congenital malformations of the face are probably cleft lip and cleft palate. Cleft lip occurs in approximately 1:900 births, with or without cleft palate. Cleft palate occurs in approximately 1:2,500 births (Moore, 1977). Clefts are either genetically or environmentally induced and result from faulty tissue fusion; they may be totally or partially corrected by surgery.

Digestive System

Three general parts (the foregut, midgut, and hindgut) comprise the primitive digestive system. The foregut contributes to the development of the pharynx, lower respiratory system, esophagus, stomach, duodenum, liver, and pancreas. The midgut contributes to the duodenum, jejunum, ileum, cecum, appendix, and colon. The hindgut contributes to the development of the colon, rectum, and upper portion of the anal canal. Congenital malformations of the digestive system include such common conditions as pyloric stenosis, a narrowing of the opening between the stomach and the duodenum, which occurs in approximately 1:200 male births and 1:1,000 female births (Moore, 1977). Its etiology appears to be genetically based, and it is usually treated by surgery (Smith, 1977). Intestinal and anal malformations may also occur.

Skeletal and Muscular Systems

Mesodermic tissue begins to form skeletal and muscle systems during the fourth week. Arms and leg buds also appear at this time. During the fifth week, rapid brain development results in extensive head growth. By the sixth week the head is visibly larger than the trunk, and primitive fingers and toes have begun to develop. Most skeletal and muscular malformations are genetically induced, but a number result from gene-environment interactions. These malformations include acrania (partial to total absence of the cranium) and spina bifida occulta (lack of vertebral closure in the spine). Major limb malformations are normally rare, the recent exception being the severe limb malformations that occurred in infants whose mothers took thalidomide during pregnancy. [Scientists have only recently discovered why tests of the drug failed to indicate its teratogenic effect. Apparently, the livers of fetal rats, which were used to test thalidomide's effects, did not metabolize it as human livers do.] Minor limb malformations are more frequent. They include such conditions as polydactyly (extra fingers or toes), syndactyly (fusion of fingers or toes), and clubfoot (talipes equinovarus), which occurs with a 2:1 ratio favoring males (Moore, 1977).

The Nervous System

Disorders of the nervous system may take several forms. Congenital malformations are fairly common and are caused most often by defective closing of the neural tubes during the 3rd and 4th weeks. Such defects may affect the nervous system alone, or they may include surrounding bone or muscle tissue. Spina bifida, for example, is a developmental defect of the spinal cord caused by a fusion failure; the resulting gap allows the spinal cord to protrude, and defects range from relatively minor (e.g., spina bifida occulta) to serious (e.g., myelomeningocele). Other nervous system problems stem from genetic disorders, such as phenylketonuria (PKU), which are caused by inadequate production of needed enzymes or hormones; demyelinating diseases, such as multiple sclerosis, which involve the progressive destruction of the axon's myelin sheaths; viral or bacterial infections, such as polio or meningitis; lack of sufficient oxygen or glucose, which can cause destruction of greater or lesser areas of the brain; and lesions that can affect motor or sensory processing.

The two most frequently encountered eye abnormalities are cataracts and glaucoma, both resulting from maternal rubella infection. Inherited recessive genes, rubella, and syphilis are common causes of congenital deafness.

METABOLIC DISORDERS

In 1934, Folling reported the association between phenylketones in the urine and mental retardation, thus giving credence to Garrod's (1909) early statement that inborn metabolic errors could be responsible for structural or behavioral deficits. Metabolism involves physical and chemical changes within the body that alter the nature of biochemical substances and transform foods into energy. The major components are carbohydrates, proteins, and fats. Carbohydrates are chemical elements found in the form of sugars and starches. Proteins are chemical substances that produce amino acids, the body's building blocks, which are essential for tissue growth and repair. Fats, or lipids, are chemical elements that break down into acid and alcohol substances to aid in body development and to maintain function. All these components are necessary for normal development and, with the endocrine glands, comprise the body's chemical system.

Carbohydrate Disorders

Carbohydrates are the brain's major energy source; thus, carbohydrate abnormalities affect nervous system development. Such disorders include:

- hypoglycemia (low blood sugar levels), characterized by mental retardation, seizures, respiratory problems, low blood sugar levels, low birth weight: TREATABLE.
- glycogen storage diseases, characterized by abnormal accumulations of glycogen in body organs, absence of enzyme needed for carbohydrate metabolism: Type I and III are TREATABLE; Type II infants usually die before 1 year of age.
- Galactosemia, characterized by inability to digest milk, jaundice, retardation if untreated: TREATABLE by removing milk from diet.

These carbohydrate disorders can all lead to varying degrees of mental retardation if undetected. Because nearly all are treatable if detected in time, early diagnosis is critical.

Protein (Amino Acid) Disorders

Although protein disorders are not believed to result from a specific synthesis deficit of brain protein, three categories have been described: (1) overflow aminoacidurias, in which an amino acid overflows into the urine as a result of an abnormal concentration of that amino acid in the blood; (2) no-threshold aminoacidurias, which are characterized by enzyme deficiencies without abnormal concentrations in the blood; and (3) transport aminoacidurias, which are caused by faulty mechanisms for reabsorbing amino acids into the kidneys.

1. overflow aminoacidurias
   - phenylketonuria
   - tyrosinosis
   - maple syrup urine disease
   - hypervalinemia
   - isovaleric acidemia
   - hyperlysinemia
   - citrullinemia
   - hydroxyprolinemia
   - hyperprolinemia
   - histidinemia
   - oasthouse urine disease
   - hyper-β-alaninemia
   - carnosinemia
   - hypersarcosinemia
2. No-threshold aminoacidurias
   - homocystinuria
   - argininosuccinicacidurias
   - cystathioninuria
3. Transport aminoacidurias
   - Hartnup disease
   - Joseph's syndrome
   - methionine malabsorption

The following are examples of these three types.

Phenylketonuria

Phenylalanine hydroxylase is an enzyme (i.e., a chemical substance produced by the body to break down substances in other parts of the body) that is involved in changing phenylalanine to tyrosine. When faulty enzyme action inhibits this transformation, phenylalanine accumulates in the blood and overflows in the urine, resulting in PKU. If undetected, PKU can cause mental retardation and associated disorders. It can be prevented if a diet containing only small amounts of phenylalanine is begun within the first 6 months. As children on this restricted diet grow older and are exposed to a greater variety of foods, it may be difficult to maintain them on a phenylalanine-free diet, however. Furthermore, there is some disagreement about when the special diet can be discontinued. Some argue that the diet can be abandoned when brain growth is complete, but others argue that continuing the diet beyond the preschool years may reduce the risk of learning or behavior problems (Wright et al., 1979).

Homocystinuria

A no-threshold disorder, homocystinuria is associated with mild to severe mental retardation, seizures, sparse hair, some spasticity, and abnormal lenses. The cause is believed to be a defective enzyme usually found in the brain and liver tissue. This disorder can be detected at birth by urinalysis, and a therapeutic diet of restricted protein can alleviate the problems associated with this deficiency.

Hartnup Disease

When certain chemical agents are not transported to the stomach and kidneys, the transport disorder Hartnup disease results. This disease is characterized by mental retardation, as well as skin rash, spastic behavior, and tumors. Hartnup disease can be treated by administration of nicotinic acid, which improves the skin condition and relieves most of the motor-neurological disorders.

Lipid Disorders

Recently, many diseases have been shown to be associated with an accumulation of lipids, which are a major chemical component of the brain. All can result in mental retardation.

Amaurotic family idiocy (Tay-Sachs disease) begins during the 1st year and is related to an enzymatic defect in the metabolism of certain lipids involved in brain development. The term *amaurotic* refers to progressive degeneration; in Tay-Sachs disease, brain deterioration is so rapid that the infant usually dies before age 2. Approximately 80% of infants with this disease are of Jewish ancestry. This disease has other forms that differ in age of onset, such as Bielschowsky-Jansky disease (late infancy), Vogt-Spielmeyer disease (juvenile years), and Kufs' disease (adult years).

Like Tay-Sachs disease, Niemann-Pick disease occurs in infancy and mostly affects Jewish children. The symptoms (e.g., jaundice, diarrhea, and eventual mental and physical deterioration) appear about halfway through the 1st year, although variations of this disease can occur late in life. Death usually occurs between 12 and 20 years.

Other lipid disorders are

- Gaucher's disease. Central nervous system development is abnormal in infancy; death occurs by age 2. There is no adequate treatment.
- sulfatide lipidosis. After 1 to 1½ years, mental deterioration sets in. Absence of deep tendon reflexes is characteristic. There is no adequate treatment.
- Hurler's syndrome. Short stature, skeletal deformities, deafness, heart trouble, and mental retardation are characteristics.
- Hurler group. Although the clinical picture is similar to Hurler's syndrome, these conditions are not associated with mental and motor retardation. Deterioration sometimes occurs between 2nd and 4th years. Disease is seen only in males.
- Sanfilippo's syndrome. Mild early retardation is followed by rapid deterioration between 2nd and 4th years.

ENDOCRINE DISORDERS

Endocrine system malfunctioning can affect physical development in a number of ways. Pituitary disorders, for example, include (1) growth hormone deficiency, which usually becomes evident during the first 2 years, affects males more than females, and is characterized more by height than weight retardation; (2) giantism or acromegaly, which is marked by excessive height increases, usually in adolescence; (3) tumors or adenomas; and (4) diabetes insipidus, which is caused by vasopressin deficiency and is characterized by high concentrations of blood sugar (hyperglycemia) and sugar in the urine (glycosuria). Diabetes is fairly common, occurring in about 2% of the population, and accounts for 0.04% of children's hospital admissions (Wright et al., 1979).

Hypothyroidism can be either congenital (approximately 1:4,500 live births) or acquired (usually after age 6). Congenital hypothyroidism, or congenital cretinism, can be apparent by 2 to 3 months after birth and is marked by prolonged jaundice, poor feeding, constipation, inactivity, and delayed motor development.

Hyperthyroidism, which is rare, usually occurs in early adolescence and is more common among females. Thyrotoxicosis, an autoimmune disorder, occurs rarely in the neonate but does occur in young children; it is characterized by excessive activity, emotional instability, fine tremors of the hand, accelerated growth, weight loss, and frequent vomiting (Wasserman & Gromisch, 1981).

Congenital short stature refers to the normally occurring short height of children from families in whom short stature is common. In addition, short stature can also be attributed to (1) primary skeletal growth deficiency, a genetically based bone growth disorder (e.g., achondroplasia); secondary growth deficiency with prenatal onset (e.g., fetal alcohol syndrome); and secondary growth deficiency with postnatal onset (e.g., malnutrition) can result in short stature (Smith, 1977).

Other endocrine-based disorders include sexual development disorders such as sexual infantilism (e.g., Turner's or Klinefelter's syndromes) and sexual precocity or accelerated pubertal onset (typically before age 8 for females and before age 9 for males). Congenital adrenal hyperplasia is a genetically based steroid production error that causes varying degrees of masculinization of female genitalia; males can also suffer from this disorder. Without treatment, both sexes experience early epiphyseal fusion and corresponding short stature. (For a more complete discussion, see Money & Ehrhardt, 1972, or Wasserman & Gromisch, 1981.)

POSTNATAL HANDICAPPING CONDITIONS

A number of handicapping conditions are not present at birth but develop later in infancy and childhood. These include a variety of dysfunctions, such as blindness and heart disease.

Physical Injury at Birth

Bone damage, bleeding, bruising, or other physical injuries at birth may affect the child's development. Because bleeding affects the infant's supply of oxygen, excessive bleeding can be especially harmful. The consequences of oxygen deprivation for even a few minutes can be mild to severe brain damage.

Blindness

Most frequently, blindness results from prenatal causes, including infectious diseases (e.g., meningitis, rubella), trauma, and fetal exposure to harmful substances. With retrolental fibroplasia, which is most commonly observed in the preterm or low-birth-weight infant, severe vision loss or blindness is caused by the infant's exposure to an excessively high oxygen concentration. Phelps (1981) estimates that 546 infants were affected in 1979. In congenitally blind children, motor development is not likely to be affected in the first few months, but developmental lags become apparent after that time, especially in areas that involve orientation to the external environment (Warren, 1977).

Deafness

An individual is said to be deaf when hearing ability is impaired to the extent that linguistic information cannot be processed through the auditory system (Report of the Ad Hoc Committee to Define Deaf and Hard of Hearing, 1975). It is estimated that 1 of every 1,000 individuals is deaf and that approximately 1.2 of 1,000 school-aged children have a profound hearing loss (Wright et al., 1979). Causes of hearing problems vary. Known causes include inherited recessive deafness, meningitis, serous otitis media, blood incompatibility, intrauterine infection, and lack of oxygen during delivery. In about 50% of the cases of hearing loss, however, the cause is unknown.

Heart Disease

There are two major categories of childhood heart disease: disease caused by infections and disease resulting from congenital heart disorders. By far the most common cause of childhood heart disease is rheumatic fever, which usually occurs after age 5. This disease may affect many other body tissues at the same time, such as the joints, the skin, and the brain. Rheumatic fever leaves scar tissue in the heart, and this tissue can interfere with normal functioning, leading to permanent heart disease.

Muscular Dystrophy

A neurologically based disease, muscular dystrophy is characterized by the progressive deterioration of muscle tissue and is thought to be a hereditary disorder, probably resulting from a biochemical defect. Motor neuron cell bodies degenerate, causing atrophy of the nerves that connect the motor system to muscle tissue. The result is paralysis of the muscles. The affected child gradually becomes weaker and weaker until death ensues, usually by the third decade, because of pulmonary infections, cardiac arrhythmia, and respiratory distress (Smith, 1977).

Cerebral Palsy

Damage to the brain's motor control system results in cerebral palsy, which is generally characterized by paralysis, weakness, and poor coordination. These characteristics are considered nonprogressive and nontransient. The causes of cerebral palsy are complex and include the following: (a) birth injury, including anoxia and hemorrhage; (b) congenital cerebral defect; (c) postnatal head injury; (d) infection; and (e) unidentified or other causes. Proper diagnosis includes consideration of the following seven subcategories:

1. spastic (jerky motor movements)
2. athetoid (excessive involuntary movement)
3. rigidity (either continuous or discontinuous)
4. ataxic (incoordination due to kinesthetic or balance disturbances)
5. tremor
6. atonia
7. mixed

In addition, proper classification includes consideration of the brain and body regions involved, as well as sensory impairment, intelligence, and emotional development. Approximately 3 of each 1,000 U.S. children are affected by cerebral palsy. About one-third of those affected die before age 6; one-third are only minimally affected, and the remaining one-third are moderately affected. Cerebral palsy is frequently accompanied by mental retardation, speech difficulties, and emotional problems, all of which interfere with learning (Denhoff, 1981; Ferry, 1981; Wright et al., 1979).

Minimal Brain Dysfunction

The clinical utility of the term *minimal brain dysfunction* is not clear; alternate labels include the terms *learning disability, brain-injured child, dyslexia, slow learner,* and *hyperactive syndrome*, to name but a few. Recently, in the third revision of the *Diagnostic and Statistical Manual (DSM III),* the American Psychiatric Association (1980) changed the term to "attention deficit disorder," reflecting a growing concern for the cognitive aspects of the disorder. The diagnostic signs used to identify a child affected by minimal brain dysfunction or attention deficit disorder include

- abnormal motor functions, usually indicated by high levels of activity (hyperkinesis) and impaired coordination. The hyperactive child is a restless and active infant who walks early, stands early, and is meddlesome as a toddler. In school, these children do not adjust well, irritate teachers, and have difficulty learning. They have short attention spans, are easily distracted, and verbally overactive.
- perceptual-cognitive abnormalities associated with distractibility and short attention spans. These children are not alert to visual detail; their memory for what they have seen is very brief; they are poor listeners; they do not

comprehend instructions readily; and they are often seen as disobedient because of this failure to carry out instructions.

- poor impulse control and low tolerance for frustrations. The impulsiveness of these children interferes with their ability to wait for gratification of their needs or desires. The result is often aggressive and destructive behavior. These children appear to be poor planners; they seldom think far ahead; they are often reckless and act with little regard for their own or others' safety; they wear everything out rapidly; they appear stubborn, selfish, bossy, disobedient, and negativistic. Yet just as readily, this same impulsiveness may reveal their needs for love and affection in the form of extraordinary dependence and attention seeking.
- abnormal emotionality. In some children, rapid mood changes are characteristic. Either these children lack the capacity to experience and display emotions of all sorts, or this insensitivity is merely the consequence of their rapid shifts of attention and mood.

This syndrome is more prevalent in males than in females. Males often show only soft signs of behavioral disorders; females are more likely to show signs of a well-defined neurological disorder accompanying behavioral disorders. The reason for these sex differences is not clearly understood, but it is likely that early oxygen deprivation may be one cause. Males show more signs of slight anoxia at birth (e.g., bluish color, lethargy, lack of appetite, inactivity) than do females. Also, several established physiological differences imply that males are more vulnerable to interference with oxygen distribution to neural tissue: they are larger and heavier at birth; they are muscularly more active, which requires more oxygen; they have a larger head (although less dense brain tissue) at birth, and they typically have a smaller carotid artery, which is the main source of blood to the brain.

Treatment is difficult because the physiological base of this disorder is obscure and because the pattern of behavioral disorders can easily be confused with other conditions. Hyperactivity, for example, is not restricted to children with minimal brain dysfunction; it may be a child's response to tension, anxiety, stress, or overstimulation. Amphetamines have been effective in treating hyperactivity. Although these drugs normally elevate sensory and motor activity levels, they apparently have a tranquilizing effect in hyperactive children. Methylphenidate hydrochloride (Ritalin) is the most commonly used of these drugs; unfortunately, it must be administered to the child frequently, and it has some side-effects that must be considered. Ritalin can arrest the child's rate of growth somewhat, and there is some risk of arresting the child's growth altogether. Ritalin also produces a very unstable and erratic sense of body awareness, and this can interfere with stabilization of the child's self-concept. A newer drug, pemoline (Cylert), appears to be free of these undesirable effects.

Postnatal Infections

Encephalitis is an inflammation of the brain tissue caused by a virus transmitted through the bloodstream. There are many types of viral encephalitis, but almost all are associated with headache, fever, lethargy, vomiting, seizures, and alterations of consciousness. Physically, these diseases result in neck stiffening, increased intracranial pressure, reflexive contraction and pain in the hamstring muscles when any attempt is made to extend the leg, and indications of upper motor neuron disease. Some of the more severe forms of encephalitis are

- eastern equine encephalitis (east of Appalachian Mountains) and western equine encephalitis (west of the Appalachian Mountains). Virus is transmitted by mosquitoes. Paralysis; emotional, language, visual, and intellectual disturbances; and seizures may result.
- Japanese encephalitis. Virus is transmitted by mosquitoes. Infection can (although it rarely does) result in paralysis, intellectual retardation, and personality changes.
- poliomyelitis. The disease is caused by three different viruses. Usually affecting children, it results in motor, but not sensory paralysis. Polio has been greatly reduced by preventive vaccines.
- subacute sclerosing encephalitis. The disease is characterized by early mood, personality, and intellectual regression. Seizures increase in frequency, and the child becomes progressively demented; death follows.

Meningitis is a bacterial infection, and most cases occur in children below age 5. Only a few types of bacteria cause this disease; of these, *Hemophilus influenzae* is the most common causative organism in infancy and childhood. This bacterial organism is found in respiratory infections that lead to influenza and to influenzal meningitis. The symptoms are lethargy, fever, meningeal signs, and seizures. Children who recover fully from this disease can be left with spastic motor behavior, paralysis, deafness, intellectual and motor retardation, or hydrocephaly (water on the brain).

Poisons

Homes are filled with many chemical agents that are toxic to children; if ingested, these toxins can affect CNS functioning. They may be classified as drugs, household poisons, and agricultural chemicals:

1. drugs
    analgesics, such as aspirin
    antihistamines

anticonvulsants
amphetamines
corticosteroids
sedatives
tranquilizers

2. household poisons
   carbon tetrachloride
   methyl alcohol
   ethyl alcohol
   gasoline
   kerosene
   toluene (airplane glue)
   naphthalene (moth balls)
   lead-based paint
   home permanent neutralizing fluid
   carbon monoxide
3. agricultural chemicals (e.g., pesticides)

Epilepsy

A convulsive disorder, epilepsy is caused by excessive neuronal discharge within the brain, followed by seizures that range from massive convulsions and loss of consciousness (grand mal) to very brief losses of consciousness and few or no outward signs of behavioral disturbance (petit mal). Approximately 0.5% of all children with epilepsy experience a repetitive sequence pattern.

A petit mal version of epilepsy occurs frequently in early childhood, and the high incidence is probably related to brain damage that occurred at, or prior to, birth. This early childhood form of epilepsy, characterized by minor motor seizures (twitching), usually begins either between 3 and 6 months of age or after age 2 (mostly between ages 3 and 5); it is nearly always associated with some degree of mental retardation. Infants with this form of epilepsy may have as many as 100 attacks per day, usually in the early morning hours and always of very brief duration.

Hypsorhythmia is a term used to describe an abnormal spike pattern appearing on an electroencephalogram. In hypsorhythmia the number and voltage of the spikes increases slowly or rapidly; when the seizure is fully developed, normal cortical activity is replaced by random high-voltage slow waves and spikes. This seizure pattern is commonly associated with mental retardation.

Treatment for seizures includes therapy for the cause if it is known (e.g., insulin if the child is diabetic) and administration of the appropriate drug (Wasserman & Gromisch, 1981).

LOW BIRTH WEIGHT

Premature babies, those who weigh less than 2,500 g, are more appropriately labeled low-birth-weight babies. This term is a summary index; it does not indicate whether the full gestation period has been completed, but, instead, whether the infant has the degree of physical and neurological maturity necessary for survival. It is an imprecise description, however, for some low-birth-weight infants are born before the expected time but possess appropriate weight for their gestational age (i.e., infants delivered before 32 weeks' gestation), and others are born either at term but below the expected weight or preterm and below their expected weight for gestational age (small-for-dates infants or those whose birth weight falls below the 10th percentile). Consequently, low-birth-weight infants represent a heterogeneous group. Some are healthy enough to cope well with birth and other perinatal stressors; others are so stressed by their physical condition at birth that they do not cope well with perinatal stressors. The development of infants in this latter category is most likely to differ from normal development, depending on the number, duration, and strength of stressors present.

This percentage of infants with a low birth weight increases as the level of industrial technology decreases. For example, low birth weight is a risk factor affecting 7% of infants born in the United States. In rural Guatemala, 20% to 40% of the infants born have a low birth weight (Martorell, 1980). Correlates of low birth weight show (1) a higher incidence among the least privileged, (2) a rate of occurrence five times as high in less prosperous nations, and (3) a higher incidence among mothers who are older or younger than average, who smoke, who are single, and who have histories of reproductive failures.

Low-birth-weight infants frequently have perinatal and postnatal health complications and a greater tendency to be neurologically abnormal, both in terms of motor (e.g., cerebral palsy) and sensory (e.g., vision or hearing defects) development (Davies & Stewart, 1975). Lipper, Kwang-sun, Gartner, and Grellong (1981), for example, found that the incidence of abnormal neurobehavioral outcomes (as indexed by Bayley Developmental Scale scores and the result of a neurological exam) increased when birth weight, gestational age, and head circumference were decreased. Among a group of 127 low-birth-weight infants, examined at 7 months, 45 had moderate to severe neurological abnormalities and low Bayley scores (Mental Development Index less than 80). Also, a gestational age of less than 30 weeks and a small head circumference (less than 26 cm) were associated with high frequency of neurological abnormalities in these infants.

The results of a longitudinal investigation of small-for-dates infants are also instructive. Fancourt, Campbell, Harvey, and Norman (1976) reported follow-up data on 60 infants who had been identified in utero as small-for-dates by using ultrasound cephalometry to measure rate of head growth. Fancourt and co-workers found that those infants whose head growth had begun to slow before 34 weeks of menstrual age were more likely to be below average in height and weight at age 4.

Parkinson, Wallis, and Harvey (1981) followed 45 of the 60 infants examined by Fancourt and associates. When these children were between 5 and 9 years of age (average age was 7), their teachers were asked to assess their abilities in reading, writing, arithmetic, drawing, music, games, creative activities, and activities requiring reasoning ability, independence, and imagination; teachers also rated the children on 16 behavior ranges (e.g., from fussy to easy to please, from cries frequently to never cries, from adaptable to upset by new situations). An analysis of these data revealed that those children who had experienced longer periods of intrauterine growth retardation (i.e., were small-for-dates) had significantly lower ratings on many of these measures than did children whose growth retardation started late in pregnancy or who experienced no apparent growth retardation.

As Davies and Stewart (1975) and Sameroff and Chandler (1975) have pointed out, social class is a very significant predictor of birth weight. Sameroff and Chandler summarized their review of risk factors affecting development by stating that "behavioral deviation found in children who have complicated births may not be caused by the complications themselves but rather by a third factor. . . . Low socioeconomic status appears to be such a variable" (pp. 209-210). With respect to both social class and attitude effects, Field, Widmayer, Stringer, and Ignatoff (1980) found, for example, that lower class teen-age mothers of preterm infants held "less realistic developmental expectations, less desirable child-rearing attitudes, and less optimal evaluation of their [child's] temperament" (p. 433), and these factors appeared to contribute to the risk status of the preterm infant, along with social class and age.

NUTRITIONAL EFFECTS

Physical growth results from an increase in cell number, an increase in cell size, or both acting together (Winick & Noble, 1966). Such growth is maintained by energy that is generated from proteins. Appropriate growth, therefore, depends on consumption of sufficient amounts of nutrients for the synthesis of proteins that, in turn, are metabolized to create the energy needed for growth.

Energy is required not only for physical development, but also for maintenance of developing structures, and the amount needed for each function varies with age. For example, the total energy cost of a normal pregnancy is approximately 80,000 kcal. This figure represents maternal consumption of an extra 150 kcal/day during embryonic development and consumption of an extra 350 kcal/day during fetal development (Martorell, 1980). Similarly, in the first 3 postnatal months, the ratio of energy (in caloric form) required for maintenance over growth is 3:1. By the end of the 1st year (recall that rate of growth declines rapidly over the 1st year), an infant needs 13 times as many calories for maintenance as for growth; by the end of the 2nd year, 34 times as many calories are needed to maintain normal physical development (Johnston, 1980). Obviously, then, the importance of appropriate and sufficient nutritional intake for both prenatal and postnatal development cannot be overstated.

Undernutrition, whether it occurs prenatally or postnatally, can have deleterious effects on both physical growth and mental development, usually by affecting production of either ribonucleic acid (RNA) or DNA (Deo, Bijlani, & Ramalingaswami, 1975). A reduction in RNA, for example, can decrease protein synthesis, which, in turn, can cause atypical anatomical changes; it can also delay developmental maturation, which, in turn, is likely to delay mental development (Deo et al., 1975). Similarly, a reduction in the synthesis of DNA can reduce the total cell mass in organs, affecting CNS growth and leading to mental retardation; it can also reduce bone growth, resulting in physical growth retardation.

The influence of malnutrition on mental development is pervasive. For example, malnutrition can reduce skull size and brain weight by interfering with the growth of brain cells in sufficient numbers and of adequate size (Zemenhof, van Marthens, & Margolis, 1968). Similarly, malnutrition can influence the biochemistry of the brain. It has been shown that malnutrition can influence the excitatory and inhibitory capacity of the nervous system by affecting neurotransmitter development (Bourgeois, Schmidt, & Bourgeois, 1973). Finally, the brain's electrophysiological activity can be influenced by nutrition. Coursin (1974) has shown that malnutrition can result in prolonged neural impulse conduction time, delays in information-processing ability, increased latency times, and abnormalities in response patterns. Based on these findings, it seems logical that development of more observable indexes of mental development would also be affected by malnutrition, and this appears to be true (Cravioto, De Licardie, & Birch, 1966; Hertzig, Birch, Richardson, & Tizard, 1972; Pollitt, 1972).

Like low birth weight, malnutrition is associated with lower socioeconomic conditions. The Ten-State Nutrition Survey, in which anthropometric, dietary, and biochemical data were collected on over 40,000 individuals, revealed that several socioeconomic status variables (e.g., per capita income, household income, and income relative to needs) were good predictors of height, weight, and head circumference in children; in general, more typical physical development was associated with higher socioeconomic status (Garn & Clark, 1975). Researchers have concluded from these and similar data that U.S. pregnant women, infants, and young children who are living near, at, or below the poverty level are at risk: "Considering the extremely high incidence of severe undernutrition among pregnant women, it is quite possible that most of the infants and children in the low economic groups have sustained severe nutritional deprivation in utero as well as many being undernourished in infancy and childhood" (Livingston,

Callaway, MacGregor, Fisher, & Hastings, 1975). If this is true, the prognosis for the subsequent development of these individuals to their maximum genetically based potential is not a very positive one.

CHILD ABUSE

Recently, because of now mandatory reporting regulations among health care professionals, increases in frequency, or both, national attention has been focused on child abuse as a significant risk factor for development. The abused child has been defined by Parke and Collmer (1975) as "any child who receives nonaccidental physical injury (or injuries) as a result of acts (or omissions) on the part of his parents or guardians that violates the community standards concerning the treatment of children" (p. 513). This definition, which incorporates the intent of the abuser and prevailing cultural standards (i.e., levels of acceptable aggression), includes physical and sexual abuse and neglect, either actual or psychological.

Current estimates place the overall incidence of child abuse at about 1% of all children; 70% of abused children are likely to be physically abused, 23% neglected, and 7% sexually abused (this latter figure may be especially conservative because of reporting problems; Smith, 1977). Within the population of abused children, a significant proportion are low-birth-weight infants. It is also likely that other (e.g., congenital) problems may characterize abused children. For example, Baldwin and Oliver (1975) found that, of their abused child sample, 21% had been premature and 10% had congenital defects that detracted from their physical appearance. Abused children in this investigation were characterized as displaying fear of adults and as being withdrawn, listless, and hyperactive. Persistent crying and other signs of irritability, as well as poor skin color, were also typical of these abused children, most of whom were less than 1 year old. It appears, then, that many abused children possess certain traits that interfere with the formation of positive social relationships with their caregivers; these traits may actually elicit abuse (Belsky, 1978; Frodi, 1981).

While some children may possess characteristics that predispose others to abuse them, child abuse is not a one-way phenomenon. Certain parental characteristics appear to predispose some parents to abuse their children. As Belsky (1980) notes, the degree of marital conflict between spouses, parental negative interaction styles, parental unemployment, and parental isolation from community and cultural support systems are all significant factors. There is some evidence that certain cultural factors, such as crowding, membership in a large family, or prevailing levels of violence within society at large, also contribute to child abuse. Such findings have led Belsky (1980) to suggest that the causes of child abuse are ecologically nested and that, although certain characteristics of children and adults may predispose them to abuse, social stressors trigger the abusive act. Consequently, abuse is likely to be fairly common in families with little ability to cope with stress. This was certainly the case as reported by Baldwin and Oliver (1975); they found over 225 incidents of abuse among their sample of 38 abused children under age 3.

Regardless of how or why it comes about, child abuse contributes significantly to delayed or retarded mental, physical, and emotional development. Baldwin and Oliver found, for example, a high percentage of brain damage, speech difficulties, and locomotor defects among their sample, all of which were caused by injury. Furthermore, as Wasserman and Gromisch (1981) point out, psychosocial dwarfism or retarded physical development may result from living in a highly emotionally charged situation. Because of its deleterious effects on development and because of its frequency among very young and already potentially at risk infants, child abuse represents not only a major environmental threat to the individual but also a serious problem for the culture. (For a more detailed discussion of this topic, see Belsky, 1980, or Parke & Collmer, 1975.)

CONCLUSION

Children who are born with or who develop some kind of physical disorder obviously will not develop in a "normal" manner because their available modes of interaction with others are altered by the nature of their disorders. Atypical physical development is a collective label, describing a variety of physical handicapping conditions that affect development. It is necessary to understand atypical physical development in order to understand the vital relationships that occur between and among physical, social, and cognitive aspects of human development. Because senses and bodies are used to interact with the world, both to take in and process knowledge and to learn efficient behavior for dealing with the physical and social world, any interference with normal development will have a subsequent effect on both cognitive and social development. If we are to help children with handicaps, we must understand how the nature of the disability can best be used to help the child develop.

REFERENCES

Abel, E.L. Fetal alcohol syndrome: Behavioral teratology. *Psychological Bulletin,* 1980, *87*, 29-50.

Alberman, E., & Creasy, M.R. Factors affecting chromosome abnormalities in human conceptions. In A.J. Boyce (Ed.), *Chromosome variations in human evolution*. London: Taylor & Francis, 1975.

American Psychiatric Association. *Diagnostic and statistical manual (DSM-III)*. Washington, D.C.: Author, 1980.

Anderson, G.F., & Diacumakos, E.G. Genetic engineering in mammalian cells. *Scientific American*, 1981, *245*, 106-121.

Baldwin, J.A., & Oliver, J.E. Epidemiology and family characteristics of severely-abused children. *British Journal of Preventive and Social Medicine,* 1975, *29*, 205-221.

Belsky, J. Three theoretical models of child abuse: A critical review. *International Journal of Child Abuse and Neglect*, 1978, *2*, 37-49.

Belsky, J. Child maltreatment: An ecological integration. *American Psychologist*, 1980, *35*, 320-335.

Bourgeois, B., Schmidt, B., & Bourgeois, R. Some aspects of catecholamines in under-nutrition. In L.L. Gardner & P. Amacker (Eds.), *Endocrine aspects of malnutrition: Symposium of the Kroc Foundation*. Santa Ynez, Calif.: 1973.

Boyce, A.E. (Ed.). *Chromosome variations in human evolution*. London: Taylor & Francis, 1975.

Coursin, D.B. Electrophysiological studies in malnutrition. In J. Cravioto, L. Hambreaus, & B. Vahlquist (Eds.), *Symposia of the Swedish Nutrition Foundation XII*. Uppsala: Almquist & Wiksell, 1974.

Cravioto, J., De Licardie, E.R., & Birch, H.G. Nutrition, growth, and neurointegration development: An experimental and ecologic study. *Pediatrics*, 1966, *38*, 319-372.

Davies, P.A., & Stewart, A.L. Low-birth-weight infants: Neurological sequelae and later intelligence. *British Medical Bulletin*, 1975, *31*, 85-91.

Denhoff, E. Current status of infant stimulation or enrichment programs for children with developmental disabilities. *Pediatrics*, 1981, *67*, 32-37.

Deo, M.G., Bijlani, V., & Ramalingaswami, J. Nutrition and cellular growth and differentiation. In M.A.B. Brazier (Ed.), *Growth and development of the brain*. New York: Raven Press, 1975.

Fancourt, R., Campbell, S., Harvey, D., & Norman, A.P. Follow-up of small-for-dates babies. *British Medical Journal*, 1976, *1*, 1435-1437.

Ferry, P.C. On growing new neurons: Are early intervention programs effective? *Pediatrics*, 1981, *67*, 38-41.

Field, T., Widmayer, S., Stringer, S., & Ignatoff, E. Teenage, lower-class, black mothers and their preterm infants: An intervention and developmental follow-up. *Child Development*, 1980, *51*, 426-436.

Frodi, A.M. Contribution of infant characteristics to child abuse. *American Journal of Mental Deficiency*, 1981, *85*, 341-349.

Garn, S.M., & Clark, D.C. Nutrition, growth, development, and maturation: Findings from the ten-state nutrition survey of 1968-1970. *Pediatrics*, 1975, *56*, 306-319.

Garrod, A.E. *Inborn errors of metabolism*. London: Oxford University Press, 1909.

Hertig, A.T. The overall problem in man. In K. Benirschke (Ed.), *Comparative aspects of reproductive failure*. Berlin: Springer, 1967.

Hertzig, M.E., Birch, H.G., Richardson, S.A., & Tizard, J. Intellectual levels of school children severely malnourished during first two years of life. *Pediatrics*, 1972, *49*, 814-824.

Johnston, F.E. Introduction: The course of malnutrition. In L.S. Greene & F.E. Johnston (Eds.), *Social and biological predictors of nutritional status, physical growth, and neurological development*. New York: Academic Press, 1980.

Lipper, E., Kwang-sun, L., Gartner, L.M., & Grellong, B. Determinants of neurobehavioral outcome in low-birth-weight infants. *Pediatrics*, 1981, *67*, 502-505.

Livingston, R.B., Callaway, D.H., MacGregor, J.S., Fisher, G.J., & Hastings, A.B. U.S. poverty impact on brain development. In M.A.B. Brazier (Ed.), *Growth and development of the brain*. New York: Raven Press, 1975.

Martorell, R. Interrelationship between diet, infectious disease, and nutritional status. In L.S. Greene & F.E. Johnston (Eds.), *Social and biological predictors of nutritional status, physical growth, and neurological development*. New York: Academic Press, 1980.

McClearn, G., & DeFries, J. *Introduction to behavioral genetics*. San Francisco: W.H. Freeman, 1973.

McDavid, J.W., & Garwood, S.G. *Understanding children*. Lexington, Mass.: D.C. Heath, 1978.

Money, J., & Ehrhardt, A. *Man and woman: Boy and girl*. Baltimore: Johns Hopkins Press, 1972.

Moore, K.L. *The developing human*. Philadelphia: Saunders, 1977.

Parke, R., & Collmer, C. Child abuse: An interdisciplinary review. In E.M. Hetherington (Ed.), *Review of child development research* (Vol. 5). Chicago: University of Chicago Press, 1975.

Parkinson, C.E., Wallis, S., & Harvey, D. School achievement and behavior of children who were small-for-dates at birth. *Developmental Medicine and Child Neurology*, 1981, *23*, 41-50.

Phelps, D.L. Retinopathy of prematurity: An estimate of vision loss in the United States—1979. *Pediatrics*, 1981, *67*, 924-925.

Polani, P.E. Chromosomes and chromosomal mechanisms in the genesis of development. In K.J. Connolly & H.R. Prechtl (Eds.), *Maturation and development*. London: Heinemann, 1981.

Pollitt, E. Behavioral correlates of severe malnutrition in man. In W.M. Moore, M.M. Silverberg, & M.S. Read (Eds.), *Nutrition, growth and development of North American Indian children* (DHEW Publication #NIH 72-76). Washington, D.C.: 1972.

Report of the ad hoc committee to define deaf and hard of hearing. *American Annals of the Deaf*, 1975, *120*, 509-512.

Robinson, J.S. Growth of the fetus. *British Medical Bulletin*, 1979, *35*, 137-144.

Sameroff, A.J., & Chandler, M.J. Reproductive risk and the continuum of caretaking causality. In F. Horowitz (Ed.), *Review of child development research* (Vol. 4). Chicago: University of Chicago Press, 1975.

Smith, D.W. *Recognizable patterns of human malformation: Genetic, embryologic, and clinical aspects*. Philadelphia: Saunders, 1976.

Smith, D.W. (Ed.). *Introduction to clinical pediatrics*. Philadelphia: Saunders, 1977.

Warren, D.H. *Blindness and early childhood development*. New York: American Foundation for the Blind, 1977.

Wasserman, E., & Gromisch, D. *Survey of clinical pediatrics*. New York: McGraw-Hill, 1981.

Winick, M., & Noble, A. Cellular responses in rats during malnutrition at various ages. *Journal of Nutrition*, 1966, *89*, 300-306.

Wright, L., Schaefer, A., & Solomons, G. *Encyclopedia of pediatric psychology*. Baltimore: University Park Press, 1979.

Zemenhof, S., van Marthens, E., & Margolis, F. DNA (cell number) and protein in neonatal brains. *Science*, 1968, *160*, 322-323.

Chapter 4

The Implications of Physical Impairments for Early Intervention Strategies

M. Beth Langley

As Connor, Williamson, and Siepp (1978) so aptly point out, the needs of children with physical impairments are as diverse as are the disabilities. Heterogeneous physical conditions, differing life experiences, and the time involved in medically related procedures (Kinnealey & Morse, 1979) necessitate an educational program for each physically impaired child that focuses on the psychological, social, and physiological impediments to the child's achievement of competence and independence. The primary goal of early intervention for physically impaired youngsters is to enable them to function at the top level of their abilities in gaining control over their social and physical environment (Calhoun & Hawisher, 1979; Connor et al., 1978; Myers, Cerone, & Olson, 1981; Sirvis, 1978). Connor and associates stress that "what appears to be called for is careful selection of equipment and materials, so placed for the individual learners as to promote integration of learning" (p. 32).

Norton (1972) explains that cognitive and perceptual motor progress are dependent on integrated feedback from vestibular, proprioceptive, tactual, visual, auditory, olfactory, visceral, and thermal mechanisms. She further emphasizes that "only if movement patterns are sufficiently varied and if feedback is accurate can a child develop a sound basis for more advanced behavior in a stable environment" (p. 142). Clearly, movement with a normal tone base enhances the central nervous system's potential to assimilate and integrate sensory and perceptual feedback to prepare the child for accommodating to the environment.

Special methods of physically handling the child are designed to facilitate sequential patterns of movement and organization of the central nervous system and postural reactions. Norton (1975) provides an excellent description of the specialized effects of appropriate handling:

> Handling provides the sensation of normal movement and posture on the basis of normalized muscle tone. Inhibitory handling is used to alter the

> abnormal gross sensorimotor patterns throughout the body. When sensation has changed as a result of feedback from normalized muscle tone, the child is encouraged to move and experience normal motion. (p. 95)

Therapy approaches advocated by the Bobaths (1972), Ayers (1980), and Heiniger and Randolph (1981) have been preferred over more traditional therapy designs for developmentally disabled children because of their emphasis on active but automatic reactions from the child. The objectives of a neurodevelopmentally oriented educational program as outlined by Bobath (1967) include

- development of normal postural reactions and muscle tone
- facilitation of qualitative movement sequences
- inhibition of abnormal postures and reflex patterns
- prevention of contractures and deformities
- opportunities to develop functional patterns through physical handling and play

Carlsen (1975) added that other essential aspects of a neurodevelopmental program are the development of grasp and release, eye-hand coordination, handedness, perception, and self-help.

Among the greatest developmental needs of physically impaired children are a sense of order, structure and organization, experiences to elicit flexible thought processes and initiative in problem solving, the development of self-discipline, and an awareness of the rights of others. The types of disabilities associated with physically impaired children suggest that a heavy emphasis be focused on visual-perceptual and perceptual-motor learning.

DEFINITION, PREVALENCE, AND CLASSIFICATION

A physical impairment in a child is a neurological, orthopedic, or health-related condition that adversely affects the child's development and educational performance. Such impairments may be due to congenital anomalies, accidents, disease, metabolic dysfunction, birth trauma, toxic reactions, or irradiation. (See Chapter 3, Physical Bases of Handicapping Conditions, for a more complete discussion of many of these causes of physical impairment.)

The terms *impairment, disability,* and *handicap* are frequently used interchangeably, but there are important differences in their meaning: What may be a disability for one child may represent a handicap for another, depending on psychological state and, as the child grows older, the desired occupational goals and directions. Impairment refers to a structural loss or defect, which, in some children, may be artificially restored in some degree (Love & Walthall, 1977). Disability indicates the impairment's impact on daily activities and the resulting lack of, or limitation in, abilities. When a child is unable to adjust and allows the defect to inhibit maximal function, impairment becomes a handicap.

An estimated 5 in 1,000 school-aged children are orthopedically handicapped. Of these approximately 328,000 children, 28% were receiving no special education services in 1975 (Hallahan & Kauffman, 1978; Goldstein, 1978). Safford and Arbitman (1975) reported that 1 in 14 children are born with some form of birth defect.

The degree to which the impairment limits the child's physical interaction with the environment determines whether the impairment is considered mild, moderate, or severe. Love and Walthall (1977) have provided guidelines to severity of impairment that are medically oriented:

1. Mild. Child can ambulate (with or without prostheses or orthoses), use arms, and communicate well enough for own needs.
2. Moderate. Child is handicapped in locomotion, self-help, and communication, but not totally disabled; child requires some special help.
3. Severe. Child is incapacitated and usually confined to a wheelchair; complete rehabilitation may not be possible.

Healey and McAreavey derived levels of severity from the extent to which the impairment influences participation in and modification of instruction:

1. Level I: mild. The impairment does not impinge on day-to-day functioning, and no modification of the program is required. The child is not considered handicapped.
2. Level II: mild to moderate. While there may be occasional crises, the impairment does not affect learning, and no program change is necessary. Personnel should be aware of first aid procedures, and the child may be considered handicapped.
3. Level III: moderate. The child's participation in school is often limited by the impairment, and school activities must be altered to allow the child to be an active participant. First aid knowledge is a must, and the child is considered handicapped.
4. Level IV: severe. Medical attention is required on a regular basis, and the child may not be able to participate in a regular classroom. Extensive class alternatives must be employed, including homebound services. The child is significantly medically and educationally handicapped.

ORTHOPEDIC AND HEALTH IMPAIRMENTS

Cerebral Palsy

Primarily a nonprogressive disorder of posture and movement against gravity (Nelson, Note 1), cerebral palsy results from a brain lesion that occurred either in utero or in early childhood. The lesion affects development of normal tone, integration of early reflexes, and acquisition of righting and equilibrium reactions. Children so affected typically cannot develop normal movement components nor achieve normal movement skills. It is estimated that approximately 1.5 of every 1,000 children born manifest cerebral palsy (Hallahan & Kauffman, 1978). Cerebral-palsied and other physically impaired children are grouped into functional levels, depending on the number and type of limb involvements:

1. diplegia. All limbs are involved, with lower limbs more severely so.
2. quadriplegia. All limbs are involved, but upper limbs are more severely so.
3. hemiplegia. Only one side of the body is involved.
4. paraplegia. Only the lower limbs are involved.

Although cerebral palsy is often difficult to diagnose prior to 6 months of age (Harryman, 1981), there are early diagnostic signs, such as difficulty in sucking and feeding, a weak cry, abnormal muscle tone qualities, and continuation of reflexes past their usual point of integration. In a normal child, primitive reflexes are synthesized, elaborated, and reintegrated into more mature motor patterns. In the cerebral-palsied child, these reflexes remain static and constant, completely dominating the child's motor skill development unless therapeutic intervention is initiated. Diagnosis prior to 9 to 12 months of age provides the greatest opportunity for change in children with cerebral palsy. Magee (Note 2) explains the advantages of beginning therapy prior to 12 months:

1. Muscle tone quality is the most normal it will ever be.
2. There are some normal components of movement on which to build.
3. The child has not practiced abnormal movement.
4. Therapists do not have to deal with secondary deformities.
5. It is more natural to handle a baby.

Motor Development

Functionally, the primary disabilities associated with cerebral-palsied children are a narrow range of postures and a lack of the readiness to move (Nelson, Note 1). Although Magee (Note 2) reports that 90% of brain-damaged children are born with low muscle tone, the type of damage determines whether the child is classified as spastic, athetoid, hypotonic, or ataxic, the primary forms of cerebral palsy. Because many variables affect tone, a child may exhibit components of more than one form. It is not unusual to have two medical reports on one child, each indicating a different form of cerebral palsy.

Spastic children are characterized by high tone (hypertonic) qualities, a lack of dissociated (isolated) movements, a paucity of movement but movement in total patterns, and abnormal sensorimotor sensation. Spasticity is most often associated with tonic neck reflexes. The asymmetrical tonic neck reflex may cause one side of the body to shorten more than the other, and scoliosis may develop. Visually, a high percentage of these children display strabismus and hemianopsia, in which they lack half the visual field in one or both eyes. Spastic children may have difficulty adjusting to changes in posture and righting themselves in space. Retraction of head, neck, and shoulders is a characteristic posture of spastic children.

Initiation of movement requires excessive effort, and movements are uncontrollable; frequently, reactions are seen in limbs other than the one that is being voluntarily moved (referred to as associated movement). Rotation around the body axis is often lacking and flexion is difficult. These children encounter problems with intentional reaching and grasping and often have tightly fisted hands. The restricted range of motion and the hypertonic muscles frequently inhibit the children's ability to support weight on arms and hands. The lower extremities are usually the more involved. Internal rotation, adduction, plantar flexion of toes, and scissoring of the legs at the knees frequently characterize their gait; walking on the toes is not uncommon.

Primary treatment goals include the reduction of tone, normalization of sensory responses, enhancement of differentiated movement and rotation, varied movement in extreme ranges of motion, and facilitation of righting and equilibrium reactions (Bobath, 1967; Bobath & Bobath, 1972).

Athetoid children exhibit fluctuating tone and totally disorganized, asymmetrical movement patterns. Lack of alignment and stability, as well as the presence of extraneous movements, severely interferes with sensory, respiratory, communication, and learning mechanisms. Visually, athetoid children often exhibit nystagmus and encounter difficulty in achieving a vertical gaze. The inability to stabilize the head prevents these children not only from directing their gaze, but also from localizing auditory stimuli in various spatial planes. Because athetoid children with a history of Rh incompatibility often manifest a high-frequency hearing loss, teachers and parents should be alert to hearing problems. Drooling may result from jaw and head instability, and facial grimacing from the fluctuating tone is typical. Oral musculature patterns for feeding and speech are most often severely deficient.

Upper extremity involvement predominates and is manifested in associated reactions, hypersensitivity to touch, and writhing hand movements that preclude maintenance of grasping. Securing the arms beneath a lap tray or between the legs often facilitates stability from which the child can achieve more effective mobility for direction of gaze. This technique may also improve oral musculature functioning.

Athetoid children have very little midline control and move in extreme ranges, unable to control the speed, force, or direction of their movement. They enjoy movement and usually maintain some normal movement components (Magee, Note 2). It is easier for them to initiate movement when they are upright against gravity. Treatment goals revolve around facilitating normal tone, proximal stability, alignment, and midline control. Grading the introduction of sensory input helps the child to control responses to incoming stimuli and to organize movement in preparation for learning and communication.

Hypotonic children retain normal movement patterns but lack the tone to initiate or maintain a change in posture. They are dominated by gravity, and the influence of gravity interferes with weight shifting and the emergence of righting and equilibrium reactions. The terms *floppy* and *ragdoll* have been appropriately applied to hypotonic children. These children frequently manifest a flat affect due to minimal facial tone, and they exhibit hyposensitivity to sensory stimuli. Treatment is focused on increasing tone and facilitating alignment, stability, and a variety of controlled movement experiences. Quick, light touch and handling is suggested because these children tend to sink into a support. Proprioceptive input is invaluable in enhancing normal reactions.

Ataxic involvement results from damage to the cerebellum, the area of the brain that controls balance and posture. The primary identifying characteristic of ataxic children is the gait; because their balance is unstable, they have a high, lurching step. The sense of spatial relationships, especially awareness of body position in space, is often distorted. These children fall frequently and may not even be aware that they are falling; they also tend to overreach, since they have difficulty judging distance. When they are sitting, these children look normal because they learn to stabilize with their heads and fix with their trunks. They exhibit more normal tone quality than children with other forms of cerebral palsy, but sensory functioning may be severely impaired. They cannot focus on close visual stimuli for long periods without becoming nauseated. Treatment methods used with the athetoid child are also indicated for the ataxic child. Figure 4-1 contrasts the various forms of cerebral palsy.

Mental Development

Intellectually, children with cerebral palsy range from profoundly mentally handicapped to gifted and talented, depending on the type of brain damage sustained and experiential opportunities provided at appropriate developmental and maturational levels (Langley, 1980). A concomitant view of cerebral-palsied

Figure 4-1 Postural Characteristics of Spastic and Athetoid Children

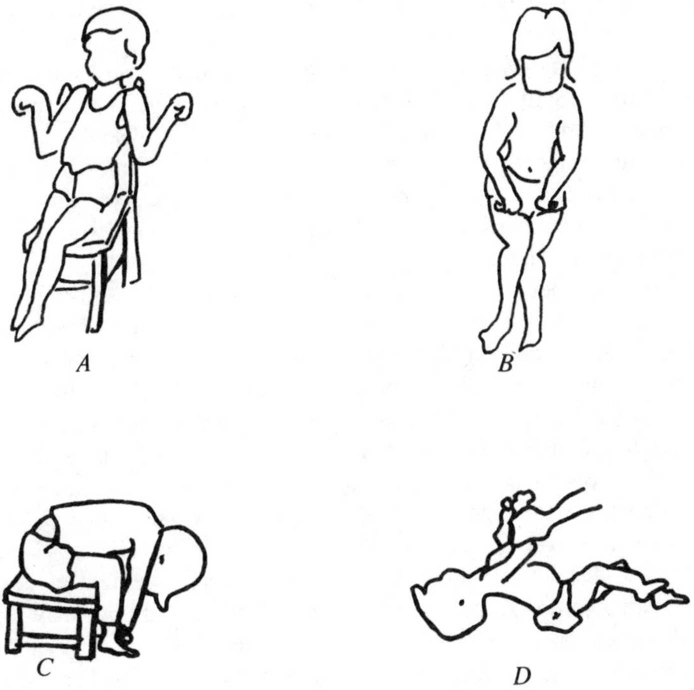

Key: A, problems of an athetoid child with spasticity who tries to sit; *B,* typical standing position of a spastic child; *C,* floppy child sitting, unable to raise the head and straighten the back; *D,* athetoid child being assisted to sit up from a lying position.

Source: From *Handling the Young Cerebral Palsied Child at Home,* Second Edition, by Nancie R. Finnie, F.C.S.P. Copyright © 1974 by Nancie R. Finnie, F.C.S.P. Additions for U.S. edition, copyright © 1975 by E.P. Dutton & Co., Inc. Reprinted by permission of the publisher, E.P. Dutton, Inc.

---

children is that they seem to progress along the normal developmental sequence intellectually, but the central nervous system damage significantly interferes with knowledge acquisition (Campbell, 1974; Fetters, 1981; Norton, 1972; Tessier, 1969). For example, Fetters (1981) and Tessier (1969) have conducted studies with cerebral-palsied children to determine if their development conforms to Piaget's sensorimotor theory. Fetters (1981) concluded that, when motor responses were used to determine whether the children understood the concept of object permanence, cerebral-palsied children lagged two to four stages behind performance expected at their respective chronological age levels. Results improved, however, when visual searching behaviors were the contingent variable rather than upper extremity responses. Tessier (1969) found that cerebral-palsied children paralleled their normal peers in the sequence of stage development but their rate of progression was slower.

Berko (1966) and Marks (1974) have enumerated specific learning problems characteristic of children with neurological dysfunctioning; many of these problems are also found in children with musculoskeletal disorders. Problems of attention are foremost among these learning difficulties. Children with attention span difficulties find it difficult to maintain focus on critical variables. They may begin sorting on the basis of shape but appear to forget what to do and randomly sort the remaining shapes.

Children with inefficient muscular or skeletal systems have difficulty learning to automatize actions and to perform unconsciously a series of related actions. Their physical abilities may be so restricted that they must concentrate on each movement, which produces a continually high anxiety level. Having to plan each move consciously, these children are susceptible to pressure and emotional lability, exhibiting outbursts of temper or laughing and crying inappropriately when the learning context becomes too tense. Perseveration is not uncommon; the children continue to respond with a previously successful behavior when that response is no longer appropriate. The most outstanding learning characteristic that inhibits abstract reasoning is the inability to shift thought processes. For example, after sorting shapes on the basis of color, these children may experience difficulty reorganizing attributes to sort by shape.

Perceptual difficulties are paramount among cerebral-palsied and spina bifida children. Figure-ground discrimination, part-whole relationships, and missing element tasks are extremely difficult for such children to solve. Errors in discrimination and visual closure abilities are frequent. Berko (1966) reported that cerebral-palsied children made 10 times the errors of a normal child on a formboard task.

Speech

Of all physically impaired children, cerebral-palsied children experience the most severe communication disability. Mecham (1966) reported that 70% to 80% of cerebral-palsied children have some speech involvement. The muscles of the face, mouth, diaphragm, and thorax that are responsible for speech production are affected by the injury to the brain. Neurological involvement prevents most cerebral-palsied children from coordinating their muscles for efficient, intelligible speech, and they are said to be dysarthric. It is most important to understand that the child's first sounds occur spontaneously with movement (Davis, 1978). It is little wonder then that children with severe motor impairment lack functional speech and communication patterns.

Articulation errors are frequently misdiagnosed in athetoid children because of their inability to stabilize articulators and to coordinate phonemes with respiration (Davis, Note 3). Ataxic children display neuromuscular speech problems primarily because their feedback mechanisms are disordered by their disorientation in position and direction (Mecham, 1966). One of the most pronounced disabilities associated with the cerebral-palsied child and an underlying inhibitor to speech development is their asynchronous breathing pattern. They frequently lack the thoracic and trunk stability to counteract the force and pull of the diaphragm. Asynchronous breathing is incompatible with efficient inspiration and grading of exhalation for sustaining sound, and these children attempt to talk on vegetative air. Thus, they may manifest a severely depressed sternum; a flattened, flared ribcage; and breathy speech (Davis, Note 4). Associated language disorders include delays in vocalizations, in onset of vocabulary and the combination of words, in verbal recall, and in verbal reasoning. Generally, spastic children demonstrate better automatic language skills, and athetoid children exhibit greater facility in representational skills.

Epilepsy

A convulsive disorder caused by excess firing of electrical discharges in the brain cells, epilepsy is manifested in seizures, that is, loss of control over specific muscles in the body. Epilepsy occurs in 30% of the population before the age of 4 and in 1 of every 50 children. While any form of brain damage is a potential cause of seizure disorders, the exact origin of the imbalance of electrical discharges is unknown. Abnormal brain wave activity, indicative of epilepsy, can be detected and identified by an electroencephalogram (EEG). Three major forms of epileptic seizures include (1) grand mal, (2) petit mal, and (3) psychomotor.

The typical pattern of a grand mal seizure includes loss of consciousness and postural control, with muscle rigidity (tonic phase) that progresses to jerking reactions; suspended breathing, loss of bowel and bladder control, and a frothing of saliva often occur. Lasting from 1 to 10 minutes, a grand mal seizure is often preceded by an aura, a warning sign that a seizure is forthcoming. Auras may take the form of an unusual taste, smell, or sound; dizziness; weakness; sensation of fear; numbness or tingling; unusual color sensation; or headache. After regaining consciousness, a child who has had a seizure is confused and drowsy and needs to sleep for several hours.

A child having a petit mal seizure may appear to be daydreaming. There may be a twitching of the eyelids or minimal head or extremity movements. No warning precedes these ''little'' seizures. The child maintains postural control and may not even be aware of the seizure, although contact with the environment is lost for 5 to 30 seconds. The petit mal seizure is the most common form of epilepsy among children 4 to 10 years of age, and seizures may recur many times during the day, interrupting attention span, memory, and thought processes in general. Petit mal seizures can be detected by observing the repeated occurrence of two or more of the following signs:

1. head dropping
2. daydreaming, lack of attentiveness
3. slight jerky movements of arms or shoulders
4. eyes rolling upward or twitching
5. chewing or swallowing movements
6. rhythmic movements of the head
7. purposeless body movements or sounds.

The teacher should report observations both to parents and to the school nurse.

Kinetic and myoclonic seizures are variant forms of petit mal seizures in which the child experiences sudden loss of muscle tone, falling, and sudden involuntary muscular contractions of the limbs and trunk, in that order. The child does not lose consciousness, and the seizures are brief but frequent. A child performing unusual but apparently purposeful motor behaviors may be exhibiting a psychomotor seizure. Lip smacking, constant chewing, repetitive arm and hand movements, and disrobing attempts are characteristic of such an episode and are frequently mistaken for hysterical or psychotic symptoms. Confusion and dizziness may occur. The child actively resists help during the seizure, which may last from 1 minute to several hours. After the seizure, the child does not generally recall the incident and wants to sleep.

Diphenylhydantoin (Dilantin), phenobarbital, ethosuximide (Zarontin), primidone (Mysoline), or trimethadione (Tridione) can control 80% of seizure activity, but they often produce side-effects, such as hypertrophy (swelling) of the gums, nausea, dizziness, and a decreased state of arousal. Lack of sleep and poor diet can predispose a child to an epileptic seizure, as can blinking lights and vestibular motion.

Status epilepticus is a seizure condition in which the child progresses from one grand mal to another without regaining consciousness. Parents and medical assistance must be sought immediately.

Spina Bifida

An opening in the spinal column caused by the failure of vertebrae to fuse is called spina bifida. It may occur at any point along the spinal cord between the head and lower end of the spine. In some children, the defect may not be at all apparent as the child engages in daily activities. In others, all aspects of development are severely affected. The higher the lesion on the spinal column, the greater the involvement and paralysis of the child.

Spina bifida can take various forms. For example, in spina bifida cystica, the surface of the child's back reveals an underlying formation of cysts, while a protruding mass of tissue is seen above the skin surface. There are two forms: meningocele and myelomeningocele. In the former, the coverings of the spinal column extend through the unfused vertebral arches into a tumorlike sac. In myelomeningocele, the spinal cord and its nerve roots also protrude through the vertebrae into a saclike mass of tissues (Figure 4-2). In both forms, cerebrospinal fluid is usually found in the sac, and some form of paralysis results because of the nerve damage that occurs below the site of the defect. One child in every 300 to 400 births is born with spina bifida, making it one of the most common birth defects to cause a physical impairment (Hallahan & Kauffman, 1978).

Children not treated by surgery are treated with antibiotics and dressings over the lesion. The myelomeningocele is washed, dressed, and protected from pressure each day. Meticulous care of the skin in the perineal area is essential to prevent skin infection. If the legs are weak or paralyzed, active or passive exercises are needed.

Figure 4-2 Myelomeningocele

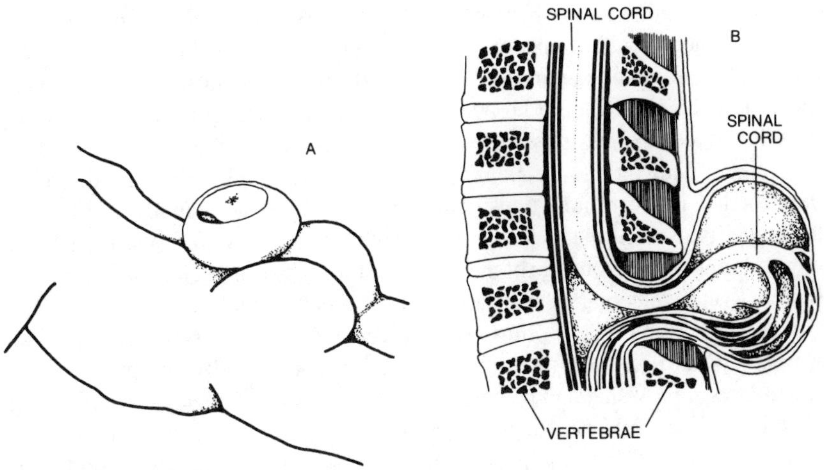

Key: A, the swelling of myelomeningocele as it appears at birth; *B,* a cross section showing that portions of the usually defective spinal cord are contained within the myelomeningocele sac.

Source: From "Child with Chronic Illness" by B.R. Myers. In R.H. Haslam and P.J. Valletutti (Eds.), *Medical Problems in the Classroom.* Baltimore: University Park Press, 1975. Copyright 1975 by University Park Press. Reprinted by permission.

Clinical features of myelomeningocele include flaccid paralysis, muscle wasting and weakness, decreased or absent tendon reflexes and proprioceptive sensation, bowel and bladder incontinence, and hydrocephalus. Secondary and associated features are retarded physical, mental, or emotional development; dislocated hips; scoliosis; talipes equinovarus; cleft lip and palate; soft tissue contractures; and eventual skeletal deformity as a result of unopposed muscle action, gravity, and posture. The child may have no sensation of touch, pain, and temperature below the site of the lesion. The autonomic system may not function properly, and there may be a decrease in perspiration. In addition to the location of the defect, factors such as upper extremity involvement, presence of a shunt, and head size are associated with limitations in mobility.

Incontinence associated with myelomeningocele usually results from damage to the second, third, and fourth sacral nerves that interferes with voluntary control of the sphincter muscles. The genitourinary system is often disturbed in myelomeningocele populations, as the innervation to this region is only partially present, if it exists at all. Neurogenic vesical dysfunction because of the low level of innervation to the bladder (Wilson, 1965) is perhaps the most common neurological deficit associated with myelomeningocele. Although surgical procedures are frequently performed to correct this deficiency, the system is kept intact as long as possible to develop a healthy body image and determine the child's capacity for effective utilization of the bladder's reflex activity. Large intakes of water and cranberry juice should be encouraged to maintain the acidity level of the urine and prevent the growth of bacteria, as well as to flush out the kidneys and the bladder regularly. The child should be put on a scheduled toileting routine, which may include manual expression of urine by firm pressure on the lower abdomen or intermittent catheterization. Some children require surgical construction of an ileal conduit if severe infections persist or the kidneys are damaged. When this technique is used, urine bypasses the bladder on its way from the kidneys via ureters brought to the outside of the abdomen through an artificial opening called a stoma. Urine-collecting devices are selected according to the needs of the individual child. Pekarovic, Robinson, Lister, and Zachary (1968) found that construction of an ileal loop often made the child more socially acceptable.

Mild to severe visual and perceptual motor development delay is characteristic of spina bifida children. In addition, mild to moderate asymmetry of hand preference, posturing in the hands, mild decrease of tone and strength of upper limbs, and decreased range of motion at the shoulders have been among the major deficits observed in spina bifida infants at 12 months. Early visuomotor training activities have been shown to reverse the trend toward poor eye-hand coordination (Rosenbaum, Barnett, & Brand, 1975). Shurtleff (1966) noted considerable delay in reading and writing skills of grade school spina bifida children who had not experienced an upright posture between 3 and 18 months of age. Rosenbloom (1977) found serious delays in the manipulative abilities of spina bifida children who ambulated by means of walkers or wheelchairs; according to Rosenbloom, these children missed critical manual exploration opportunities because they had to depend on their hands as a means of compensatory locomotion (i.e., to maneuver crutches and the wheels on their chairs).

Hydrocephalic and spina bifida children display unique, characteristic language patterns. They converse readily with whoever will listen, but, although they talk fluently, their language reflects disorganized thought processes and weakness in conceptualization. Swisher and Pinsker (1971), Laurence (1971), and Parsons (1968) all reported on the prevalence of the "chatterbox" syndrome or the "cocktail party" syndrome in hydrocephalic children. Their speech is often delayed until 2½ years of age, after which the output increases rapidly. The general consensus is that they are hyperverbal, enjoy imitating, learning, and using new words, but their speech lacks content and their words are illogical.

Physical management of spina bifida children should focus on maintenance of a stable, straight back; stability and alignment of the lower extremities in weight bearing; plantigrade feet; and mobility of hips (Shepard, 1974). The use of standing tables, prone boards, para-podiums, Flexi-stands, rollator walkers, and scooter boards with these children allows upright postures and patterns of extension and weight bearing that improve stability, strengthen lower extremity muscles, facilitate respiration and circulation, and improve bowel and bladder functions. Use of adaptive equipment and aids also affords the child stability for hand use and the opportunity for independent mobility. Extreme caution must be exerted when lifting myelomeningocele children. The midback area and the upper region of the thighs should be supported so that the child's hips are flexed and legs extended. Daily observations of physical status should include the development of any contractures, tissue breakdown, spinal changes, or loss of sensation.

Hydrocephalus

Eighty percent of children with myelomeningocele also manifest hydrocephalus, a condition in which more cerebrospinal fluid is produced than can be absorbed by the cortex and circulatory system. In small infants, this imbalance results in an enlargement of the ventricles with progressive cranial distention (Allen, 1964). The Arnold-Chiari malformation, the most common cause of hydrocephalus in children who have a myelomeningocele, obstructs the flow of cerebrospinal fluid. This congenital anomaly of the hindbrain is characterized by elongation of the brain stem and cerebellum into the cervical portion of the spinal cord (Gold, Hammil, & Carter, 1964).

The child with hydrocephalus is characterized by a greatly enlarged head, thinned scalp, prominent scalp veins, upward retraction of the eyelids, inverted triangle appearance of the face, strabismus because of sixth nerve paralysis, and spastic paraplegia. In more severe cases, neurological deficiencies may include lack of grasp and prehensile actions; inability to sit, stand, or walk; and generalized spasticity. When hydrocephalus appears in older children whose scalps are less pliable, attacks of nausea and vomiting with intermittent head pain occur. Episodes of neck retraction and extensor rigidity of the limbs often occur, and papilledema may be found. With increased cranial pressures, a reduction in the level of consciousness, lethargy and loss of recently acquired motor achievement, drowsiness, and confusion may occur (Allen, 1964).

The excess fluid buildup may be alleviated by the insertion of a shunt to drain the fluid from the brain ventricles into either the abdominal (ventriculoperitoneal) or chest (ventriculoatrial) cavities via the jugular vein in the neck (Figure 4-3). These shunts assist in circulation of the fluid throughout the circulatory system. As the children grow older, shunts must be changed to accommodate growth, necessitating frequent operations.

Figure 4-3 Ventriculoatrial Shunt To Relieve Hydrocephalus

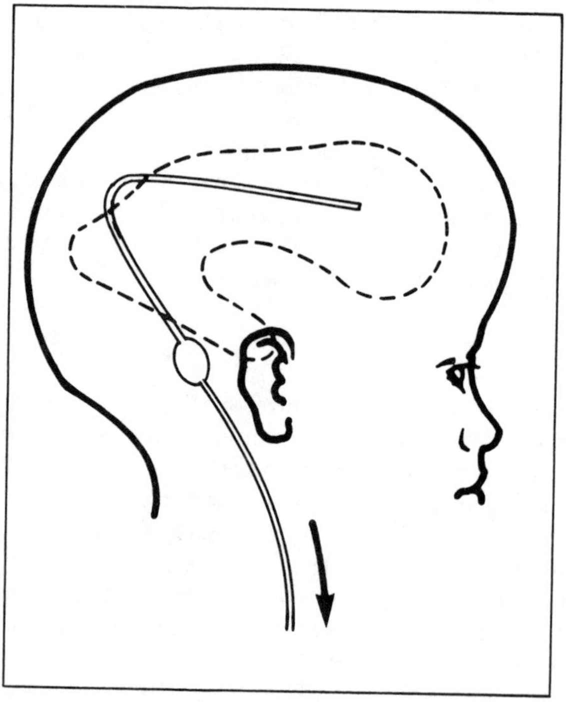

Source: From "Myelomeningocele, Meningocele, Spina Bifida" by E.E. Bleck. In E.E. Bleck and D.A. Nagel (Eds.), *Physically Handicapped Children: A Medical Atlas for Teachers.* New York: Grune & Stratton, 1975. Copyright 1975 by Grune & Stratton. Reprinted by permission.

Shunts may become entangled with brain tissue, resulting in blockage of the shunt that prevents circulation of cerebrospinal fluid. Among the signs of a blocked shunt are irritability, headaches, loss of appetite, nausea, vomiting, seizures, loss of consciousness, drowsiness, and visual problems. If the blockage is not corrected in time, the child can suffer irreversible brain damage and even blindness. Teachers and parents can be taught how to pump the shunt valve to ensure that it is functioning properly and how to facilitate the circulation of cerebral spinal fluid if there is some concern that the shunt is malfunctioning.

Muscular Dystrophy

Occurring in approximately 0.2/1,000 births (Batshaw & Perret, 1981) and in approximately 0.279 of every 1,000 male births, muscular dystrophy is a group of inherited muscle diseases characterized by degeneration of muscle tissue and progressive weakness of the muscles used for moving and maintaining posture (Karagan, 1979). Among the dystrophies, the most common childhood form is Duchenne, which, as are other forms, is inherited from the mother in a sex-linked recessive transmission. A critical sign of this disease, which affects primarily males, is an elevated blood level of a muscle enzyme, creatine phosphokinase (Harris & Cherry, 1974; Bleck, 1975). Because the disease also affects involuntary muscles of the heart and diaphragm, early death is common in this population.

Usually not apparent at birth, muscular dystrophy becomes evident by 3 years of age when these children appear to be clumsy. Children with muscular dystrophy that has not been diagnosed by the time they enter kindergarten may be mistakenly considered learning-disabled or lazy. Prominent among early signs are a waddling gait due to weakness of the pelvic girdle muscles, tiptoeing, frequent falling, and difficulty in running, climbing stairs, and rising from the floor or low chairs (Brink, 1975). As muscle fibers degenerate, deposits of fatty tissue cause the calf muscles to enlarge—a condition called pseudohypertrophy because of the false appearance of increased muscle development. These children soon develop lower lumbar lordosis, in which posture is characterized by a protuberant abdomen as a result of the deterioration of the muscles in the foot, the front thigh, hip, and abdomen. As muscles of the lower extremities weaken, these children develop the most characteristic sign of muscular dystrophy, Gower's sign, when they rise by "walking up" their lower limbs with their hands (Figure 4-4).

Following the weakening of the lower extremity muscles, those of the shoulders and elbows deteriorate. The child has difficulty raising the arms above the head or lifting heavy objects and stands with stooped shoulders. Fractures of the extremities are common because lack of muscle activity results in loss of bone calcium (Brink, 1975). With this weakened musculature, scoliosis and contractures develop.

Figure 4-4 Gower's Sign

Source: From "Muscular Dystrophy" by J.D. Brink. In R.M. Peterson and J.O. Cleveland (Eds.), *Medical Problems in the Classroom: An Educator's Guide.* Springfield, Ill.: Charles C Thomas, 1975. Copyright 1975 by Charles C Thomas. Reprinted by permission.

The primary goal is to maintain ambulation as long as possible; even during periods of illness, the child should ambulate frequently to prevent contractures and to maintain muscle tone and strength. Daily performance of various motion activities sustains good joint position for functional weight bearing. Splinting at night and having the child lie prone with the feet extending over the mattress edge inhibit flexion contractures. Aluminum and plastic orthoses can alleviate scoliosis and prevent contractures.

Intellectual functioning has been reported to be somewhat depressed in children with the Duchenne form of muscular dystrophy. Karagan (1979) reported that the incidence of mental retardation in association with muscular dystrophy has been higher with Duchenne than with any other form, possibly because of the suggested neuropsychological and neurobiological parameters of the disease. Sherwin and McCully (1961) and Florek and Karolak (1977) found that, in general, the IQ of children with muscular dystrophy was shifted downward one standard deviation from that of the normal population. A global trend of lower verbal scores than performance scores on intelligence tests has been recorded (Karagan & Zellweger, 1978). Marsh and Munsat (1974) discovered that a discrepancy in verbal and performance scores emerged as early as 10 years of age in Duchenne children who were still ambulatory. As physical status deteriorated, however, scores on performance items decreased. There has also been some discussion that lower intellectual functioning is associated with more rapid progression of the disease (Karagan, 1979).

Educationally, these children should be engaged in comprehensive programs with special emphasis on counseling and development of hobbies and other outside interests. Occupational therapy can integrate tasks of perception and daily living, as well as fine motor skills, to maintain adaptation and upper extremity function as long as possible. Use of clay, putty, and Theroplast helps to maintain grasp strength and cocontraction of the joints in the hand. Reachers and long-handled combs and toothbrushes can be employed when the range of motion in the upper extremities is limited. Typing skills can be encouraged when pencils can no longer be held. Loop-handled scissors can be substituted for regular scissors. Tearing and pasting art activities and working with Play-Doh are excellent tasks for preschoolers. Rehabilitation programs cannot arrest the progression of the disease, but they can give the child self-confidence, independence, and social responsibility (Brink, 1975).

Osteogenesis Imperfecta

A brittle bone disease, osteogenesis imperfecta is manifested by fragile bones that are repeatedly fractured. The collagen fibers of the bones are loosely woven, and the bones are deficient in protein and bone salts. Lower limbs are more frequently involved than upper extremities; angulation and overriding of bones in the lower limbs causes weakening, loss of stature, and bowing. When broken, bones heal in a deformed, shortened position, but at a normal rate (Twomey, 1977). The bones of the trunk may also be involved, and the chest assumes a beehive shape with protrusions of the breastbone. Kyphosis and scoliosis frequently develop as the child grows, and hypermobile joints and a dislocated patella are often secondary conditions.

Because the sclera of the eyes is also formed from collagen fibers, the eyes have a characteristic blue coloration in the sclera. Triangular in shape, the face has a flat, broad forehead and poor development of teeth. The skin may be thin and almost translucent. Of children with this condition, 25% develop hearing loss as a result of otosclerosis and malformed inner and exterior bone structure of the ears (Twomey, 1977).

Most often, these children are in wheelchairs, and teachers should exert extreme caution in handling them. They should be lifted as a myelomeningocele child is lifted, with support under the buttocks and behind the back of the child. Because of their limited body surface, these children perspire heavily and should wear cool, loose clothing during the summer. The condition stabilizes as the child grows older, and training should emphasize academics and preparation for attendance in a school program with normal children.

Legg-Calve-Perthes Disease

A common hip disorder among children between 3 and 10 years of age, Legg-Calve-Perthes disease is most frequently noticeable at 4 to 5 years of age. It affects four times as many boys as girls. The cause of Legg-Calve-Perthes is a disruption in the blood supply to, and destruction of, the growth center of the hip end of the thigh bone (Nagel, 1975). Throughout a 2-year process, the growth center fragments, degenerates, and then rejuvenates. The onset, which may be gradual or sudden, is characterized by complaints of intermittent pain in the knee, thigh, or hip joint; limitation of motion; a limp in the involved leg; and loss of internal rotation of the hip.

Primary treatment consists of (1) braces and casts that allow weight bearing in an abducted posture and (2) protection of the hip joint while repair is in progress. In the classroom, care should be taken to prevent bumping, stumbling over, or injuring the leg. Swimming is a highly recommended rehabilitative activity.

Juvenile Rheumatoid Arthritis

Each year, approximately 3 of every 100,000 children are affected by juvenile rheumatoid arthritis (Myers, 1975). Miller (1975) suggests that a disorder of the body's immunologic system is a contributing factor in this disease, which usually becomes apparent between the ages of 1 and 4. Half of all children affected show symptoms before the age of 5 (Jacobs & Downey, 1974). The arthritis attacks the joints, causing swelling and tenderness. The swollen joints may cause the surrounding muscles to become stiff and tense. Involvement of the jaw, producing pain and leading to a receding chin, is not uncommon. The heart, liver, and spleen may also be involved. Other clinical manifestations include high fevers, skin rash, and general malaise and fatigue (Kiernan & Connor). Irritability, loss of appetite, and anemia result from chronic pain associated with the swollen joints, particularly early in the day and after long periods of immobility. Children with juvenile rheumatoid arthritis tend to be small for their age, lose range of motion, and may develop joint contractures that permanently interfere with movement. The severity and location of the arthritis vary from child to child and may even vary in the same child from day to day. Inflammation of the iris (uveitis) is frequently associated with juvenile rheumatoid arthritis and, without early detection and treatment, may lead to a change in vision, pain or light sensitivity, or blindness.

Aspirin, gold salts, and cortisone help to reduce the fever and relieve the swelling, but teachers and parents should be alert to the possibility of toxic reactions to salicylate as a result of the large dosages of aspirin. Other side-effects may include high-tone hearing losses, hyperventilation, drowsiness, and gastrointestinal upset (Miller, 1975; Myers, 1975). Physical therapy techniques include full range of motion exercises and activities to maintain and increase joint mobility and muscle strength. Heat enables the joints to move more smoothly, and splints, braces, and plaster casts keep joints from becoming frozen by giving the child stability for movement (Gearheart & Weishahn, 1980).

The child should be encouraged to move frequently in order to prevent stiffening. During naptime, the child should lie face down with the legs extended to inhibit flexion contractures (Jacobs & Downey, 1974). Exercise that jolts the joints, such as jumping and stopping and starting in running games, should be avoided and swimming and bike riding encouraged. Prolonged fine motor activities should be kept to a minimum. The child may need adaptive writing aids and an elevated work surface, as well as assistance with clothes fastenings, doorknobs, and water fountain handles on days when pain and stiffness are heightened.

Spinal Deformities

Any disturbance to the trunk muscles and nerves that results in a weakness of the trunk, lack of muscle support to the trunk, asymmetrical muscle pull, or abnormally fused or partially formed vertebrae may result in spinal deformities (Garrett, 1975). Kyphosis, lordosis, and scoliosis are frequently associated with other chronic health and crippling conditions. Kyphosis is a pronounced outward curvature, usually in the upper thoracic region of the spine and often referred to as humpback; lordosis is an inward curvature of the spine, most frequently seen in the lower lumbar area and often referred to as swayback. The most common and severe of the three major spinal deformities is scoliosis, an s-shaped lateral deviation of the spine, the cause of which is primarily idiopathic. Katz (1974) found that 5.6% of the general population exhibited scoliosis.

Hip Dysplasia

When the head of the femur is pulled from its normal alignment in the pelvis, the hip is dislocated. Etiology of hip dislocation includes hormonal irregularities that affect the fetal pelvic ligaments, intrauterine and extrauterine environmental factors (Katz & Challenor, 1974), and trauma. Dislocation may be unilateral or bilateral and is often associated with cerebral palsy and myelomeningocele. Overt signs of hip displacement are a waddling gait or a limp as the child walks, increased lumbar lordosis when standing, and complaints of pain in the hip joint. Diagnosis can be difficult and is most often made radiographically. The most frequent course of treatment for a unilateral dislocation during the preschool period is a 6- to 8-week period of immobilization, with a body cast if warranted by the degree of the dislocation, followed by 2 to 3 months of restricted activity and physical therapy (Silberstein, 1975). While mobility in the classroom may be impeded, there should be no interruption in regular classroom activities.

Talipes Equinovarus

Often termed clubfoot, talipes equinovarus occurs in 1 to 3 of every 1,000 live births. The primary clinical manifestation is an internally rotated foot; the heel points posteriorly, and the lateral portion of the foot touches the floor. It is a condition to which individuals are genetically predisposed. Talipes equinovarus is frequently associated with myelomeningocele, hydrocephalus, and dwarfism. Corrective techniques include plaster casts, wrapping, and manipulation. Splints are often attached to the child's shoes, and nightsplints may be needed until age 5. Shoes with outersoled wedges maintain the corrected position of the foot. Surgery may be indicated in more severe cases.

The Limb-Deficient Child

Limb deficiencies in children may be of congenital or traumatic origin. Although some drugs (e.g., thalidomide) are known to cause the congenital absence of limbs and metabolic disorders have been suggested as probable causes, origins of this disability are usually unknown. Shepard (1974) reported that the malformation occurs when the limb buds are forming during the 4th to 8th gestational week. The type of deformity is determined by the stage of limb development at which the insult occurs (Swanson, 1981). Genetic and environmental agents, or a combination of both, may be behind limb anomalies or malformations. Environmental causes may include anoxia, irradiation, hormones, chemicals, and viral infections.

Traumatic causes of limb deficiencies include exposure to extremes in temperature, lack of circulation, vascular diseases, thrombi or emboli (blood clots), malignant tumors, accidents, and severe burns.

Limb deficiencies are classified according to the location from which the limb is missing and the degree of limb remaining. Swanson (1981) has provided the most comprehensive monograph to date on the subject of congenital limb defects and discusses seven major categories of classification:

1. failure of formation of parts
2. failure of separation of parts
3. duplication
4. overgrowth
5. undergrowth
6. congenital constriction band syndrome
7. generalized skeletal anomalies

A more functional description of limb absence revolves around the terms *amelia* and *phocomelia*. Amelia refers to the total absence of a limb; phocomelia, used interchangeably with the term *meromelia,* refers to partial absence of limbs.

Because of limited body surface, limb-deficient children perspire heavily. Especially during the summer months, parents and teachers must be alert to excessive heat and the moisture that will collect on the child's clothing. Asymmetry or deformities may distort body image and self-concept. Fear of falling and rejection by others are not uncommon reactions in these children.

Some delay in acquisition of motor skills, obviously, results from lack of a limb. The child without upper limbs has difficulty with the postural control and equilibrium reactions required first for sitting and later for walking. Sitting balance and trunk control are delayed in the child without lower extremities. Children lacking distal upper extremities can learn to manipulate and explore objects with their feet, lips, and tongue at an early age. Swanson (1981) states that use of the feet for prehension develops extraordinary flexibility in hips and legs that allows the preschool child to position the feet for function, even around the head region.

Intellectual function seems to depend on whether the child has normal experiences and whether there are other disabilities (i.e., brain damage). Zelazo (1979) reported that thalidomide children displayed normal cognitive and intellectual functioning. Decarie (cited in Zelazo, 1979) found no relation between intellectual functioning and the severity of the malformation. The most significant information derived from Decarie's study was that time spent in institutional care negatively influenced the test performance of thalidomide children. Independence in self-care and motility via use of prosthetic devices, as well as communication effectiveness, are highly dependent on the child's cognitive abilities. Langley (1980) pointed out the importance of teaching tool use during the child's sensorimotor stage so that the child will later be able to understand and make use of artificial limbs and prostheses.

Depending on the extent of the disability, the site of the anomaly, and the child's psychological adjustment to the disability, the content of the curriculum may require minimal, if any, adaptation. The physical therapist prescribes activities to lengthen soft tissues that surround joints responsible for excessive range of motion. In the preschool setting, the bilateral upper amputee without prostheses should be allowed to use the feet during play and in art activities, whenever necessary. The teacher should be familiar with the basic mechanics, proper fitting, and maintenance of the prosthesis.

Arthrogryposis

A congenital condition in which the child is born with one or more joints contractured and maldeveloped and with weakened musculature, arthrogryposis is complete at birth (i.e., it is nonprogressive). It appears to result from the failure of muscles to function in the developing fetus (Bleck & Nagel, 1975; Eckel, 1970). The joints may be fixed in either flexion or extension, and there is a loss of muscle bulk and strength; shortening is evident. Deep tendon reflexes may be absent, but sensation is intact.

Children with arthrogryposis have been described as having a "wooden doll" appearance (Bleck & Nagel, 1975; Eckel, 1970). The arms are usually medially rotated at the shoulder, while the legs are laterally rotated at the hip joints. The distal joints appear to be involved more often than the proximal ones, and the lower extremities may show greater involvement than the upper limbs. Facial anomalies, body asymmetry, talipes equinovarus, scoliosis, cleft palate, renal aplasia, congenital heart disease, and inguinal hernias are often associated conditions. Although subluxation of the hips, elbows, knees, and thumb may occur, the joints are not painful.

Orthopedic management begins at birth; the best results are obtained with these children if treatment begins before age 1. Surgery is often indicated to correct deformities and to increase function. Bracing, casting, and joint manipulation all are accepted orthopedic procedures. Normal muscle use is not anticipated, although functional use of the extremities is expected with therapy. It may or may not be possible for these children to walk, although they are very mobile in a wheelchair.

Intelligence is usually average to above average. Adaptive aids are important for independence and for cosmetic and psychological reasons. Hall (1979) designed easily constructed eating and toileting aids for children with arthrogryposis;

such devices are beneficial in improving self-concept and establishing a sense of achievement. Electric typewriters, elastic sling mechanisms supported from metal uprights on a wheelchair, and elevated working surfaces are alternatives to the more traditional reading and writing implements. Emphasis on self-care is of primary importance.

CHRONIC HEALTH CONDITIONS

Cystic Fibrosis

The most common fatal hereditary childhood disease is cystic fibrosis; its incidence ranges from 1 in 800 to 1 in 3,000 live births. It is characterized by the widespread presence of abnormally thick, viscid mucus in the respiratory and intestinal tracts, causing continuous respiratory infections, particularly pneumonia. Major treatment involves postural drainage, in which the child is placed in various positions and vibrated vigorously over the chest regions to dislodge and propel the mucus from the lungs.

Sickle Cell Anemia

One of every ten black people is a carrier of sickle cell anemia, an inherited disorder affecting the black population primarily. In this disease, the chemical property of hemoglobin changes so that the red blood cells lose oxygen and their flexibility. As the sickle hemoglobin molecules become rigid and "stacked," the shape of the cell changes from its normal disk shape to that of the sickle shape. This process is referred to as the sickling phenomenon (Bleck & Nagel, 1975; Calhoun & Hawisher, 1979; Pearson & Diamond, 1977).

The most characteristic problems of sickle cell disease are anemia and episodes of blood vessel occlusion. Because the body rejects the abnormal cells, the child is left with one-half to one-third as many red blood cells as the normal child. Bleck and Nagel (1975) reported that the destruction of this number of cells results in anemia and jaundice, especially of the whites of the eyes. When the sickle cells become rigid, they cannot pass easily through the blood vessels, which blocks the distribution of oxygen throughout the body. This vessel occlusion affects the bones, the major organs, and even the brain, subsequently producing severe pain crises.

Asthma

Among the most common chronic childhood diseases, asthma is seen as a difficulty in breathing because narrowed bronchial tubes interfere with normal airflow in and out of the lungs. Occurring in 1.5 million children, asthma accounts for 20% of days lost from school.

Children with asthma have an overabundance of antibodies to substances (antigens) to which they are allergic. Contact between antibody and antigen produces an explosive release of chemicals from body cells that creates reactions known as allergy (Harvey, 1975). Ingestants and inhalants are the two types of antigens that produce asthma. Ingestants that are common antigens in early childhood include milk, eggs, nuts, chocolate, wheat, and citrus fruits. Many children are also allergic to various types of drugs. Among inhalant offenders are grass, tree and weed pollens, house dust, molds, wool, feather, kapok, and animal fur.

Before an asthma attack, the child has a clear-running nose and a characteristic hacking dry cough followed by wheezing. During an attack, the child sits with shoulders hunched forward to facilitate air intake (Harvey, 1975). Breathing is very audible, and a blue tinge may appear on lips and fingertips.

STRUCTURING THE PHYSICALLY IMPAIRED CHILD'S ENVIRONMENT

Kinnealey and Morse (1979) stress that programs for physically impaired children must prepare them to cope effectively with the real world. In essence, this objective is no different from that set for the normal preschool child. The primary programming differences involve the need for specialized personnel and modifications of the environment and instructional material to minimize the handicap and maximize the child's independence and opportunities to participate actively in all learning experiences.

Personnel

The members of a team providing services to physically impaired children include parents; teachers; physical, occupational, and speech therapists; principals; physicians; and nurses. Exhibit 4-1 and Table 4-1 reflect how a team might share the responsibility for helping a physically impaired child accomplish a goal.

A critical team member in any school that serves physically handicapped children is the physical therapist, who administers the various forms of physical therapy prescribed by the physician. Although primarily concerned with the muscle tone, posture, range of motion, and locomotion abilities of these children, the physical therapist also trains teachers and aides in transfer activities, proper positioning techniques, and principles of handling the child in ways that facilitate maximum motor skill development. Scarnati (1976) stresses the importance of the physical therapist in the preschool setting as the person who provides both early

Exhibit 4-1 An Integrated Approach to Programming for the Handicapped Learner

Goal: The learner will develop normalization of oral motor control.

Objective: Positioned in midline with good alignment and support, the learner will actively remove three textures of foods from the spoon with his lips with good closure skills 60% of the time.

Skills to be developed:

1. Postural control
2. Normalization of tone
3. Midline control
4. Lip closure
5. Visual regard
6. Increase in recoil capacity to improve breathing and to strengthen abdominals
7. Normalization of response to tactile stimuli

physical intervention for the child and training for the parents. The physical therapist develops home programs and instructs the parents in therapeutic techniques and their rationale. Denhoff (1981) feels that the primary role of the physical therapist is to enhance mobility while preventing complications of abnormal tone, reflexes, and contractures.

Equally valuable to the team in the preschool setting is the occupational therapist. Often difficult to distinguish from the role of the physical therapist, the occupational therapist's role is to facilitate arm, head, hand, and mouth movements to fit the child's functional developmental level. The occupational therapist helps the child to develop and refine control of the small musculature by ensuring stability of head, shoulder girdle, and scapula, as well as trunk and arm control, on a normal tone base. Using toys and developmental play, the occupational therapist teaches tasks of daily living, the use of adaptive equipment and upper extremity prostheses, reach, grasp and release, and other hand function skills, visual perceptual skills, and sensory integration. Making adaptive feeding and dressing devices and facilitating oral motor and feeding programs are also within the realm of the occupational therapist.

The efforts of the speech therapist working with orthopedically and health-impaired preschool children must be coordinated with those of the physical and the occupational therapists who are developing feeding and positioning techniques so that prespeech behaviors and vocalization will be facilitated. Normalization of oral motor sensitivity, integration of primitive oral reflexes, and facilitation of normal respiration during feeding and speech programs are primary aspects of a speech therapist's role in the preschool setting for physically impaired learners.

Table 4-1 Personnel Roles in an Integrated Programming Approach

Skill Areas	*Class Teacher*	*Speech Therapist*	*Occupational Therapist*	*Physical Therapist*
Postural control	Positions learner in corner chair, prone stander, and sidelyer	Positions learner supine on small wedge with head in midline; maintains midline control in response to auditory stimuli	Supports learner in feeding chair or on elevated wedge; ensures good alignment of shoulders, hips, neck; introduces stability in trunk and jaw area	Introduces righting and equilibrium reaction in supine, prone, sitting, weight bearing to normalize tone; introduces rotation in all positions
Normalization of oral musculature	Has the learner "kiss the baby" (own reflection) in a mirror; offers a variety of toys to the mouth to explore	Uses oral-motor normalization techniques (e.g., pressure to tongue midline, to gums; shaking of cheeks; tapping) to build or reduce tone	Places toys to mouth, hand to mouth; applies pressure tapping to cheeks and tongue; introduces various textured foods; facilitates biting, chewing, swallowing reactions	Normalizes tone in trunk; applies deep pressure to oral area while in various positions
Normalization of tactile stimuli	Exerts deep pressure on squeak toys and other toys that provide motion; tapes rattles to hands and other body points; moves learner's own hands to various body points	Moves child's hands to face of therapist, then to own, particularly during vocalization; moves hands to sound toys	Introduces spoon, cup, other feeding utensils to hands and mouth to explore; facilitates open hand, and graded grasp	Applies deep pressure, cocontraction, weight bearing to joints in all areas on graded textures

Midline control	Gives toys to reach for in midline, to gaze at in midline, and to kick at in midline	Positions learner with wedge, approaches with stimuli for speech in midline; places both hands to lips and face	Facilitates jaw control, approach of spoon to midline with lips closed, graded opening and closure	Practices supine, prone positions, weight shift and control in midranges
Lip closure	Plays kiss the baby; helps learner to imitate /m/ for "good" and to use mirror and straw	Facilitates jaw control; uses motokinesthetic techniques for oral motor stimulation with straw and cup	Stimulates upper lip to remove food, waits for swallow; moves cup to bottom lip with chin tuck	Facilitates sidelying, rolling dissociation of head and trunk, and scapular stability
Increased recoil capacity	Helps blow pinwheels, bubbles; encourages active movement of body parts during music time	Applies pressure to ribs and abdominal area during exhalation; elevates and rotates arms and trunk; sweeps abdominal area upward; vibrates chest upon exhalation	Facilitates cocontraction through scapula to hip region in sidelying; abducts upper extremities; facilitates weight shift in prone position to reach for toy lateral to and above the shoulder	Elevates upper extremities; facilitates trunk rotation in sitting and sidelying; cocontraction through scapular and trunk region in sitting
Visual regard	Places toys and teacher's face to midline, to side and back; dims light in room with exposure to black light materials	Uses puppets, own face, and mirror	Uses direct approach with spoon, therapist's face, food containers to midline; facilitates shift of gaze	Uses therapist's face, mirror, and toys during treatment; facilitates dissociation of head and trunk for freedom of movement of eyes

Concept and vocabulary development supplement meaningful conversation goals for children with spina bifida and hydrocephalus. Designing and selecting augmentative communication modes, such as picture boards, Blissymbols, or electronic communication aids, are the primary responsibility of the speech therapist.

Kinnealey and Morse (1979) found that teachers wanted therapists to help them understand how to (a) interpret therapeutic goals, (b) incorporate therapists' goals into the educational plan and implement them on a daily basis, (c) cope with physical limitations involved in daily functioning, and (d) plan future educational goals based on prognostic information. The classroom teacher often assumes the primary task of coordinating all other professional services. The teacher's role as a member of the multidisciplinary team is to provide adaptive instructional material and to individualize instructional approaches. In a preschool setting, the teacher serves as the environmental engineer by arranging the setting in a way that encourages children to learn how to learn, express ideas, and participate in social and emotional experiences that will develop adaptive and independent living behaviors.

Denhoff (1981) explains that the pediatrician's key role as a member of the team working with the handicapped child is to provide the parents with realistic periodic assessment and to help them differentiate progress accelerated by team efforts from progress provided by time and maturation. The nurse's responsibilities may include administering medication, monitoring nutrition and growth, diapering, catheterizing and assisting with urinary diversion appliances.

Unlike their physically intact peers who abandon crayon, books, and paste at the end of the day, children whose physical impairments necessitate adaptive and specialized equipment cannot leave behind walkers, prostheses, braces, and adapted feeding and writing equipment. Communication boards, urinary devices, artificial limbs, and cuffs to hold spoons and crayons must become an integral part of the child's life if the child is to function as independently as possible. Parents need support and instruction from team personnel in order to be effective in continuing the educational process at home.

Assessment

Regardless of the type of physical impairment, curriculum planning must be based on an up-to-date assessment of the child's cognitive, linguistic, motor, and social-personal development. Since no instrument's norms have been established on a physically handicapped population, the greatest dilemma in the assessment of severely physically impaired children is discovering a functional response mode. The majority of infant scales depend on gross and fine motor, imitative, and vocal responses, all of which penalize the handicapped child and reflect the child's disabilities rather than abilities and potential. Zelazo (1979) notes that "it appears to be an unfortunate accident of psychological and medical history that cognitively intact children with marked neuromotor damage are shortchanged by prevailing assessment procedures'' (p. 50).

Obtaining a valid estimate of the physically impaired child's developmental strengths and weaknesses depends on judiciously selecting assessment scales appropriate for the child's developmental level, handicapping conditions, and available response possibilities; adapting assessment procedures to the available response modes; and positioning the child to facilitate optimal response opportunities.

Existing instruments have been adapted by having the child signal through some predetermined facial, vocal, or body response to a yes-no question or a scanning of response choices and by enlarging pictorial or manipulative test materials. Cruickshank, Hallahan, and Bice (1976) suggest that a child who cannot perform a task occasionally can tell the examiner how to perform it. Langley (1977) cautions examiners to be sensitive to the fact that the content of the test items must be kept intact when adaptations are made. Adaptations of Piagetian sensorimotor tasks for physically handicapped children have been documented by Bower (1974), Decarie (cited in Zelazo, 1979), Fetters (1981), and Tessier (1969). Sattler and Anderson (1973) adapted the Stanford Binet Form L-M to a yes-no/pointing response mode. In a study comparing 80 normal preschoolers with 20 cerebral-palsied preschoolers on the adapted version of the Stanford Binet, they found a significant correlation between performance on the standardized administration and the adapted administration.

Tests and developmental assessment tasks have been designed specifically for physically handicapped youngsters by French (1964); Haeussermann (1958); Jedrysek, Klapper, Pope, and Wortis (1972); and Taylor (1961). The Pictorial Test of Intelligence (French, 1964) is a series of cards, each of which has four response choices positioned at the top and bottom and at either side of the card. Approximately 12 × 12 inches in size, the cards were designed for eye-pointing responses. The test is used to assess the abilities of children aged 3 through 8 years in the following six areas: (1) picture vocabulary, (2) size and number, (3) form discrimination, (4) information and comprehension, (5) immediate recall, and (6) similarities. Before children can perform successfully on this test, they must be functioning cognitively at a minimum age of 42 to 48 months, be able to discriminate visually fine black and white line figures, and demonstrate consistent visual scanning skills. Studies by Coop, Eckel, and Stuck (1975) and Harper and Tanner (1974) found the *Pictorial Test of Intelligence* to be a valid measure to use with physically handicapped children.

Haeussermann (1958) provided the most relevant and practical assessment tool for educational screening of the physically impaired child. Haeussermann's *Developmental Potential for Preschool Children* was designed primarily to help teachers devise educational programs. Innovative and creative, flexible developmental tasks between ages 2 and 6 years developmentally are presented for the assessment of vision, hearing, fine motor abilities, discrimination, classification, numeration, seriation, memory, spatial concepts, and reasoning. Materials for this scale can be found in any classroom, or they can easily be made by the teacher, parent volunteers, or classroom aides. The manual of Jedrysek, Klapper, Pope, and Wortis (1972) is an adaptation of Haeussermann's techniques for preschool children.

The most recent assessment scale developed for severely multihandicapped learners between 1 and 5 years of age is the *Psychological Evaluation for Severely Multiply Handicapped Children* (Mullen, Danella, & Myers, 1977). This test is divided into three major sections: auditory-language, visual motor, and tactile differentiation. In this scale, "the stimulus and response item content is designed to minimize physical aspects of tasks while tapping behaviors which demonstrate acquisition of concepts traditionally associated with levels of intellectual development" (p. 2). The results are reported as a functional age, and the test purports to provide a good understanding of the child's optimal intake channel and most effective response system.

Positioning of the child in a corner chair with a tray, on a prone stander, over a wedge in a sidelyer, or with a combination of inflatables may be viable alternatives for ensuring optimal head and trunk control.

Barrier-Free Architecture

Now that education focuses on serving disabled children in the least restrictive environment, orthopedically and health-impaired children are likely to be integrated into daycare and preschool centers with normal children. If they are to receive this special population, such centers must eliminate architectural barriers, for such barriers make children dependent, limit opportunities for experience, and contribute to lowered self-esteem.

In the classroom, furniture and equipment should be spaced far enough apart to allow passage of a wheelchair, a child on crutches, or a walker. At least 32 inches is needed for the passage of a chair or walker. Loose throw rugs or slick tile flooring should be avoided to prevent slipping and falling. All entrances and exits should have ramps; hallways should have handrails; entrances and doorways should be at least 33 inches wide; and doorknobs, light switches, drinking fountains, and fire alarms all should be within easy reach of the child in a wheelchair (Barnes, Berrigan, & Biklen, 1978). Toilet heights should permit easy transfers, and toilet stalls should be equipped with handrails. The child's wheelchair should fit easily under sinks, working tables, and lunch tables. Windows should be 24 to 28 inches from the ground; mirrors and bookcases, toy shelves, drawing easels, and sand/water tables all should be accessible to any child. Gordon (1969) describes a unique circular table designed to accommodate various-sized wheelchairs and to decrease the possibility of objects falling from the table surface. Shallow steps and curbs facilitate ascent and descent with a minimum of stress and balance requirements.

Learning Environment

The classroom should be physically safe but comfortable. It should be adapted to the cognitive and physical levels of all children, and the atmosphere and structure of the room should promote active and independent learning and exploration. Although accessibility to all areas and equipment is a must, the children should learn that they must solve problems and initiate some adjustments to the environment because the world will not totally adapt to them. Structure is critical, and furniture, bookcases, and even lighting can be used to define activity centers.

The instructional materials themselves should ''shout'' (Cormack, Note 5) to the child what is expected. Multisensory materials and experiences should be abundant, and opportunities should be provided to work with media that offer superficial change possibilities, such as sand and water. These media are invaluable to a child with physical impairments for a variety of reasons. First and foremost, physically handicapped children often experience only extremes of control in their surroundings. A child may have either no control or total control of teachers, parents, and the environment; in either case, the child has limited opportunities to adapt and alter responses according to the feedback inherent in the situation. Substances such as Styrofoam packing ''peanuts,'' rice, beans, water and soap flakes, or liquid bubbles allow the child to create and solve problems. Second, these substances can be used with a wide variety of containers and implements that can be geared to the child's manipulative skills. Finally, the concepts, social skills, and motor skills that can be acquired by means of such media are innumerable. Other variables to consider in the design of the classroom include a choice of seating possibilities, a functional means of mobility, and accessibility.

An ''ongoing curriculum'' is an educational intervention process to integrate the development of motor, cognitive, language, self-care, and social skills into a continuing program for children functioning on a preschool sensory-motor level. While each child engages in activities specifically designed to develop skills in one of the five curriculum areas, the activities are not necessarily carried out independently. For example, head control, a motor activity, may be practiced while the child actively learns to recognize shapes and colors, a cognitive activity. Grasping and hand-to-mouth skills, fine motor activities, may be integrated with self-feeding. The classroom can be sectioned into areas for each curricular aspect so that the child can begin to anticipate and associate the corresponding activities. The teacher must be constantly aware of each child's physical comfort and needs, including positioning and toileting.

This strategy permits the child to continue an activity even when the teacher is working with another child. Thus, while one child may be positioned in the motor area in a flexion box to facilitate hip flexion and counteract extension patterns, the teacher may be working with another child in the language area. Each child is rotated through the various areas and repositioned until all the tasks individualized to that child's needs in all areas have been performed.

Because movement is an essential component of learning, the child needs to experience a variety of movement patterns in all planes: prone, supine, sidelying, sitting, standing, and all transitional positions. The child who cannot change position to one that is more functional for a given activity can be assisted through specialized handling and equipment used to stabilize postures for mobility. Drillien and Drummond (1977) have provided detailed observations and noted precautions of which the teacher needs to be aware in order to ensure good positioning.

POSITIONING AND HANDLING THROUGH ADAPTIVE EQUIPMENT AND MATERIALS

Physically impaired children should always be positioned and handled with the goal in mind of preparing them with sensory cues to assume control of their own posture and movement. Nelson (Note 1) emphasizes that, if handling is to be effective, the teacher must change the type of handling being done. Both positioning and handling of these children are aimed at providing them with a greater amount of postural control to increase the possibility of movement in the extremities. The children must be handled throughout the day, even during play, sleeping, and bathing, if handling is to be beneficial. The manner in which the children are picked up and carried can help to develop head and trunk control, midline orientation, and normalization of tone. Figures 4-5 and 4-6 depict methods of carrying a spastic child and an athetoid child that inhibit abnormal postural patterns and facilitate more normal ones.

Prostheses, Orthoses, and Wheelchairs

A prosthesis is a substitute for a missing body part. The use of a prosthesis may have several benefits. An artificial limb, for example, not only replaces the missing limb, but also encourages the wearer to maintain residual function in the deficient limb. Children are fitted with prostheses as early as possible to facilitate their acceptance of the equipment, promote bilateral activities, incorporate the artificial limb into their body image, and improve balance and posture (Challenor & Katz, 1974). Additionally, use of a prosthesis prevents atrophy of muscles surrounding the residual limb.

Figure 4-5 Method of Carrying a Spastic Child

Source: From *Neurodevelopmental Problems in Early Childhood: Assessment and Management* by C.M. Drillien and M.B. Drummond. Oxford: Blackwell Scientific Publications, 1977. Copyright 1977 by Blackwell Scientific Publications. Reprinted by permission.

Artificial limbs are designed for cosmetic and functional purposes. Fitting should coincide with developmental landmarks to facilitate all possible normal and sequential motor skill development. Children without normal upper limbs are fitted with prostheses when they have sitting balance, usually around 6 to 8 months of age when they are ready to stand (Shepard, 1974). Prosthetic devices are designed to match the maturation of the central nervous system and become more complex as the children develop more control over their movements and as cognitive processes allow more complex movement-planning abilities. Severely retarded children are only rarely fitted with functional prostheses as their level of thinking skills may prevent efficient use. Maximum independence, both with and without prosthetic devices, is an ultimate goal for these children.

Rolling activities prepare children who have no upper limbs for assuming a sitting posture. They are taught to stand by a sequential progression of movements. Facilitation of muscle strength and endurance, as well as of equilibrium reactions and appropriate falling techniques, is included among physical management goals for these children. More specific procedures and techniques are offered by Challenor and Katz (1974), Shepard (1974), and Angliss (1974).

Figure 4-6 Method of Carrying an Athetoid Child

Source: From *Neurodevelopmental Problems in Early Childhood: Assessment and Management* by C.M. Drillien and M.B. Drummond. Oxford: Blackwell Scientific Publications, 1977. Copyright 1977 by Blackwell Scientific Publications. Reprinted by permission.

Should the child experience trouble with or damage to the prosthetic limb while at school, the teacher should take no action other than alerting the prosthetist and the child's parents.

Braces, or orthoses, serve many functions for physically impaired children, but they primarily aid or substitute for weak muscles. Challenor and Katz (1974) name these purposes of bracing:

1. stabilization of joints for weight bearing
2. prevention of contractures
3. alignment and control of the body
4. immobilization of painful joints
5. positioning of proximal limbs for functional hand use
6. facilitation of desired movements for functional use and training

Short leg braces, ankle-foot orthoses or ankle-knee orthoses, have recently been made from a lightweight plastic (polypropylene) material. These braces are neither as heavy nor as hot as the metal ones; require less maintenance; attract less attention, as they can be worn under clothing; and encourage independence in dressing as there are minimal or no buckles or locks to be fastened. Short leg braces are usually worn to provide stability to the foot, to correct foot position, and to prevent shortening of the heel cord. Often, a good, sturdy children's shoe with adaptations is equally effective. The value of short leg braces is a matter of controversy because the foot is held in a fairly static position.

The type of wheelchair that is selected for a child depends on age level, developmental motor level, type and degree of physical impairments, the size of the child, family needs, and cognitive level. Wheelchairs are designed primarily for support and positioning or for locomotion. Within each group, there is a wide variety of types, each with its own form of accessory equipment. A popular type among preschool cerebral-palsied children has been a chair that converts to a carseat. This chair is commercially available in a variety of styles from companies such as Invacare, Orthokinetics, Mullholland, and Safety Travel (Figure 4-7). Wheelchairs should be adjusted to the individual child in order to ensure a proper fit and to accommodate for any spinal deformity. Whenever possible, wheelchairs that can grow with the child and that can be adjusted in angle, height, and weight should be purchased.

Figure 4-7 Wheelchair That Converts to Carseat

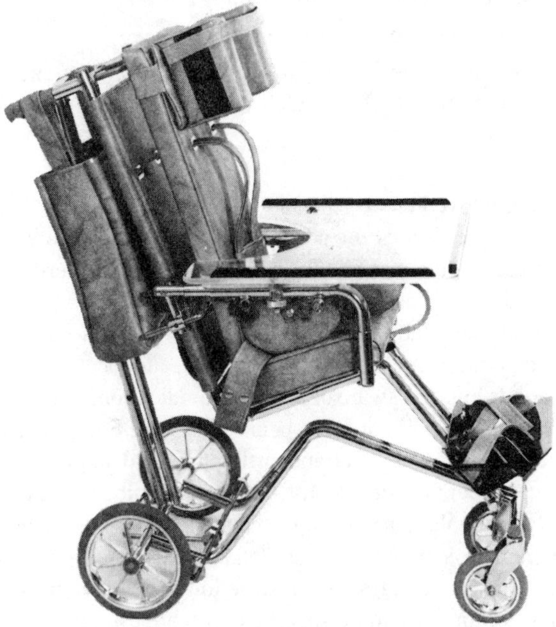

Source: Courtesy of Safety Travel Corporation.

Adaptive Equipment

Any piece of equipment designed to enable physically impaired children to be more independent can be considered adaptive equipment. Such assistive devices typically include a variety of common objects modified for use in the daily living activities of these children. Adaptive equipment facilitates components of movement in a developmental sequence, increases the range of motion, normalizes tone, decreases the tendency toward pathological reflexes, allows maximal function with minimal pathology, eliminates the need for one-to-one assistance, and minimizes abnormal-looking postures. Disadvantages of using such equipment are the immediate identification of the child's impairments; sensitivity about appearance; and limitation of opportunities for sensory feedback, free exploration of space, and physical contact with other children.

The following variables should be considered when adaptive equipment is selected:

- Is it functional in the home in terms of size, appearance, and ease of setting up?
- Can it be adjusted to fit different children, different handicapping conditions, and different functional uses?
- Can it withstand frequent use and cleaning?
- Is it difficult to obtain repair services?
- Can a more normal material or child-sized piece of furniture or equipment from home serve the purpose as well or better?
- Is it expensive?

If the equipment employed can be the same as or resemble that found in homes, neighborhoods, and preschools for normal children, children are more likely to accept it and to use it outside the educational setting. Furthermore, it will not immediately flag the child as different (Nelson, Note 1).

The selection and adaptation of any equipment requires cooperation among parents, teachers, and, especially, the physical and occupational therapists. Teachers and parents must be aware of any contraindications to the use of adaptive equipment with a specific child or for a specific purpose. Equipment and materials designed for use in positioning and transporting the child and for facilitating daily living, cognitive, perceptual-fine motor, and communication skill development are commercially available, but classroom teachers can work with the physical and occupational therapists, school carpenters, and parents to design and construct the same materials. The advantages of construction by school personnel are that adaptations can be tailor-made for a specific child, are usually more creative, and can be constructed for nominal fees—usually, only the cost of the materials.

Guidelines for constructing adaptive equipment have been provided by Bergman (1974); Connor, Williamson, and Siepp (1978); Copeland, Ford, and Solon (1976); Finnie (1975); and Levitt (1977). Barton, Hollobon, and Woods (1980) stress the importance of timing the adaptive aid to match the child's developmental readiness. These authors explain that a "delay of a few months in obtaining an appliance can make its application useless" (p. 211).

Positioning Aids

When planning adaptive equipment to be used in early intervention settings, the teacher must include items that will facilitate movements in prone, supine, sidelying, sitting, and standing positions. Wedges and rolls of varying lengths and heights promote weight shift, midline control, symmetry, head control, extension, eye-hand regard, and weight bearing on knees, hips, forearms and palms when prone; and flexion, eye-foot regard, hand to mouth, reach, and manipulation when supine. Neurodevelopmental balls (made by J.A. Preston Corporation), beach balls, and rolls can facilitate proprioceptive input and weight bearing on palms and soles of the feet. Plastic pool inner tubes and floats can also be used for prone and supine positioning and weight shift, and they have the additional benefit of providing a flexible surface. Mobility in prone positions can be provided by scooter boards, the Jettmobile (Tumble Forms), the developmental sled (made by Achievement Products), and Rifton's prone scooter board.

Sidelyers are available from Preston and from Kaye Products, but they can be constructed easily with wood and L braces or rolled up towels. The inflatables for the pool and beach can also be used to facilitate sidelying. The advantages of this position are that the child can achieve symmetry, midline control, eye-hand integration, and stability for reach and activation of toys. This is a most beneficial position for children who have not integrated the asymmetrical tonic neck reflex or who exhibit strong extension patterns. Placing a small wedge or pillow under the child's head enhances lateral head righting and dissociation of head and trunk.

An infinite number of seating systems can be purchased or can be arranged by using materials that are found in the home. Often, the best seating systems are simple modifications of child-sized chairs and infant seats. Corner chairs, floor sitters, and flexion boxes all enable the child without sitting balance to assume an upright posture and to participate in group activities. Floor sitters and corner chairs appropriate for children whose motor level is below that of a 9-month-old (Barton, Hollobon, & Woods, 1980) facilitate hip flexion with extension of the legs (long leg sitting). A tray can be fitted on a floor sitter at a height indicated by the child's posture. Placed at nipple level, the tray prevents the child from sinking into flexion patterns and facilitates head and trunk control. If the child's posture is dominated by spasticity, shortened hamstrings, and posterior pelvic tilt when long leg sitting, the floor sitter is contraindicated. Although beautiful corner chairs are commercially available from Kaye Products, Preston, and Rifton, ingenuity with cardboard boxes, rubber trashcans, plastic swim rings, and triwall (a triple-thickness cardboard) can produce more individualized and less expensive seats. Bolster seats and rolls provide seating surfaces that inhibit adduction of the legs and W sitting, while they facilitate abduction at the hips and rotation, providing a wide base of support. Small children's stools, infant seats, and inflatable chairs are also excellent seating alternatives.

Prone boards, the Flexistand (made by Maddak), the supine board (made by Rifton), standing tables, and the freedom stander (made by Rifton) all facilitate weight bearing in an upright position and extension patterns, as they inhibit flexion patterns and plantar flexion of the feet.

Various types of positioning aids and other adaptive equipment are shown in Figure 4-8, and a list of the names and addresses of the manufacturers of such equipment is provided in Appendix 4-A.

Daily Living Aids

By preschool age, children should be able to rest crutches or walkers against sinks while they wash their hands, empty urine-collecting bags or use portable urinals with minimal assistance, and manipulate zippers, braces, and cutlery with moderate help. Some children may need more time for eating, toileting, and dressing and should be allowed to begin preparation for such skills earlier than their peers do so as to perform them independently as soon as possible. When helping the child with dressing skills, the teacher should remember that clothing should be removed first from the nonimpaired (lead) limb and first put on the involved limb. Loose-fitting clothes with front openings, elastic waists, and Velcro attachments facilitate independent dressing. Special dressing techniques designed for physically impaired children have been presented in Connor, Williamson, and Siepp (1978); "Dressing Techniques for the Cerebral Palsied Child" (1954); Copeland, Ford, and Solon (1976); Finnie (1975); and Levitt (1977).

Oral motor and prefeeding techniques to offset the influence of primitive oral reflexes, normalize tone, and facilitate sucking and chewing have been described by Davis (1978), Evans-Morris (1977), and Wilson (1977). Cutout cups, spout cups, and cups with handles can be made or readily purchased where infant feeding aids are sold. The Mothercare, Tommee Tippee, and Gerber companies produce plastic feedings spoons that are appropriate for children with oral motor problems. Spoon handles can be built up with plastic Clorox bottle handles, bicycle grip handles, or special washable foam material. Universal cuffs can easily be constructed from Velcro and washcloths or purchased from companies such as Fred Sammons. For children who are beginning to feed themselves with assistance, Nelson (Note 1) suggests a method of control in which the instructor holds

Figure 4-8 Adaptive Equipment

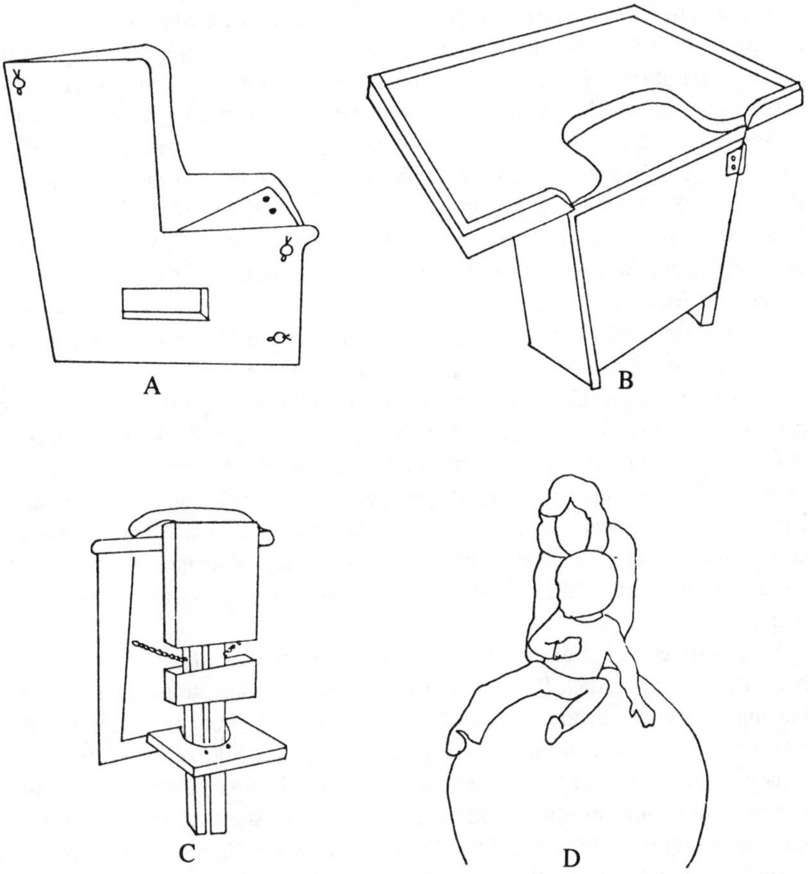

Key: A, flexion box; *B,* standing table; *C,* prone board; *D,* cage ball.

Source: From *Developmental Physical Management for the Multi-disabled Child* by B. Buttram and G. Brown. University, Ala.: University of Alabama. Reprinted by permission.

---

the spoon handle between the index and third fingers. The child's hand is then wrapped around the instructor's fingers holding the spoon, and the instructor's thumb is placed on the dorsal surface of the child's hand. Spoon use and arm control are then introduced. The shape of the eating utensil must not be designed to compensate for and reinforce abnormal patterns, but to facilitate a more normal grasp.

Feeder seats such as those produced by Tumble Forms (made by Preston), wedges, rolled up towels, and swim rings all can serve as support and positioning aids to free the parent's or instructor's hands for oral motor control. Scoop bowls and plates or cake pans can be used when children are learning to scoop, as the higher sides of these bowls assist in the scooping actions, or special plate guards can be purchased. Dycem matting is nonslip material that prevents plates and glasses from sliding; bathtub stickers can serve the same purpose and are less expensive. Feeding techniques for the physically impaired have been described by Finnie (1975), Matheny and Ruby (1963), and Mueller (1972). Cerebral palsy feeders, automatic feeding systems, and ball bearing feeders can be purchased to allow even children with minimal or no upper extremity function to be independent in feeding.

Bathing aids are designed primarily to position the child in the tub. Swim rings and inflatable boats or infant bathing inflatables can be used to support the small child. Older, larger children may require a child-sized plastic lawn chair or commercially available netted bathing aids, such as the bath chair produced by Rifton and those produced by Maddak and Preston. Washcloths sewed into mitts or sponges can be used to facilitate independence in washing. The commercial bathing sponges shaped into cars and animals that fit over the child's hand and contain the soap are excellent for handicapped children. Bath gels applied with the hand may be easier for the child to use and facilitate normalization of hypersensitive tactile systems.

Special toileting systems that position and support the child are available from Kaye Products, Maddak, Preston, and Rifton. Simple adaptations can be made by placing potty chairs inside cardboard boxes or circular laundry baskets from which a section has been cut out, or by placing a small sturdy child's chair with the back turned so that the child can hold on to it. Frames can be made from wood or triwall to be placed around an adult-sized toilet, and boxes or stools can be placed so that the child has support for the feet and flexion at the knee. Plastic swim rings can be placed on the adult toilet to narrow the seat and to facilitate hip flexion.

Learning Aids

Within the perceptual realm, adaptations to material may include fastening handles or spoons to puzzle pieces or attaching Velcro or magnets to blocks for easier manipulation. Magnetic wrist cuffs or Velcro and leather bands may be used to hold paintbrushes, pencils, and spoons for the child with no grasping ability. Multisensory, textured letters and numbers, as well as raised line writing paper, can be fastened on clipboards or secured to tables with masking tape. Pencils and crayons can be fastened to the child's chair or table with long pieces of string so that the child can retrieve them if they are dropped. Spring-handled scissors make cutting less frustrating for the child with an uncoordinated or weak grasp. Cardboard or plastic templates of shapes, numbers, letters, animals, and even the child's name can be used to develop discrimination and visual-motor integration skills. By taping the templates over a tagboard, the child lacking fine motor movements to draw letters and shapes can successfully execute them with a crayon through gross motor movements of the arm.

Placing pencils inside rubber balls, a large textured bead, a universal cuff, a plastic handle from a milk carton, or an adaptive writing device (made by Fred Sammons) enables children without a functional grasp to hold and use writing implements. The teacher can facilitate their writing motions by securing the arm over the elbow joint and abducting the arm at the shoulder. Often, children have a greater mobility of the arm if they sit with rotation (hips facing straight while the truck is turned to the right or left). An elevated writing surface is also very helpful in promoting a good postural pattern for writing. Holding on to a dowel secured vertically to the writing surface with the opposite hand not only provides stability and symmetry but also inhibits the asymmetrical tonic neck reflex. Commercial pencil adaptors are made by Developmental Learning Materials and the Zaner Bloser Company, but pushing the pencil through firm small rubber toys or finger puppets may work equally well. Toy erasers in the shape of miniature cartoon figures, vehicles, monsters, and animals may be used to turn pages and may be more functional for preschool children than an electric page turner.

Papers can be secured by taping them to the table surface or attaching them to a clipboard. A cardboard writing frame can be made by gluing three sides of two sheets of cardboard around the edges. A window is cut into the top piece, and papers can be slipped into the open edge.

Headbands can be adapted to hold paintbrushes, crayons, and pointers. Styrofoam letters and numbers permit children with headbands to hold up letters along with their peers by piercing the Styrofoam with the tip of the pointer. Similarly, colors or shapes can be sorted with cardboard figures, a magnet, paper clips, and a muffin tin. The magnet is attached to a special headstick and the paper clips to the figures. By tapping the colored disks with the headstick, the child can secure and then release them into the appropriate compartment by scraping the disks against the sides of the muffin tin. Such adaptations may be applied to any material.

Materials from Developmental Learning Materials and Teaching Resources are excellent for training in part-whole associations, figure-ground relationships, missing element concepts, and visual and auditory discrimination and association skills. Zedler (1955) developed an innovative multisensory procedure for teaching brain-injured children letter identification, auditory discrimination, and sound-symbol associations in preparation for reading and writing. Cruickshank, Bentzen, Ratzenburg, and Tannhauser (1961) created a wealth of methods for developing perceptual and quantitative abilities in this group. Robinault (1973) and Barry (1961) have designed equipment and procedures to facilitate perceptual, fine motor, and language acquisition in multiply handicapped and aphasic children. Teaching procedures, adaptations of materials, and presentation of concepts and activities to preschool cerebral-palsied children have been extensively discussed by Haeussermann (1969). Electronic learning aids, such as Bell and Howell's Language Master and Texas Instruments' Touch and Tell, Speak and Spell, and Speak and Read, require minimal hand control, have numerous preschool level concept and language programs, and are highly motivational.

Augmentative Communication Aids

Communication Boards

To enable nonverbal children (or children who may be able to verbalize but whose speech is unintelligible) to communicate, conversation or communication boards can be designed. A communication board may be constructed of posterboard, plywood, or Plexiglass; it contains pictures, words, symbols representing ideas, or letters and numbers to which the child points to convey thoughts. Pointing can be accomplished with the eyes, finger, head, mouthstick, or even toes.

Other forms of communication boards may involve notebooks or cards kept in the pocket. One preschooler designed her own "communication board" by having this writer cut out frequently needed representational pictures and pasting them on colored circles. The circles were laminated, hole-punched, and strung on a necklace. Initially, this child rejected a typical communication board, but she was motivated by the necklace to progress to a more conventional form of communication. Other children in this writer's classroom preferred boards on which magnetized inch cubes portraying pictures were positioned. To express responses or initiate requests and immediate needs, the children pushed the block representing their idea into a designated taped area on a board (Figure 4-9). The specific response area on each child's board depended on the child's range-of-motion abilities.

While most communication boards are attached to the wheelchair, they can be placed elsewhere for the ambulatory child. Bigge (1976), McDonald and Shultz (1973), and Vanderheiden and Grilley (1976) all suggest excellent designs for nonverbal communication devices. Usually, communication boards are designed and constructed by the child's parents, teachers, and speech or occupational therapist, but many commercially produced communication machines are available. Vicker (1974) and McDonald (1976) have provided valuable guidelines for developing a communication board:

1. It must be designed to match the child's cognitive and receptive language skills.
2. The child must be able to attend to visual and verbal symbols and have some means of storing and retrieving them.

Figure 4-9 Examples of Communication Boards

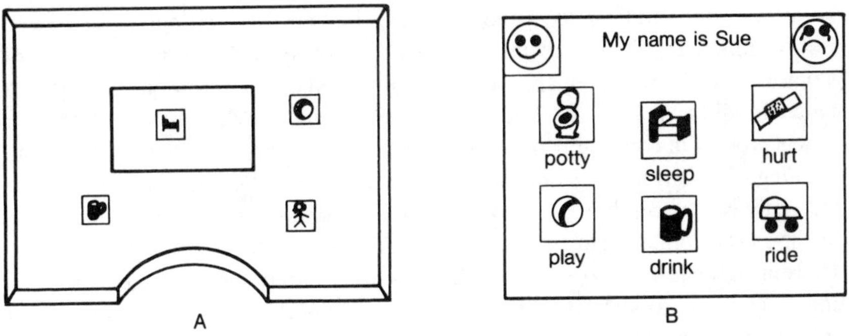

Key: *A,* a magnetized board on which the child responds by pushing the block representing the need into the rectangular space; *B,* a direct selection board on which the child responds by pointing to the picture representing the need or message.

3. The child must consistently be able to indicate responses so that any listener can interpret them.
4. The child's ambulatory, visual, and postural abilities must be evaluated to determine the type, size, and position of the board that will be most functional for the child.
5. The content of the board must reflect the child's needs in varying environments. Always a must is some way for the child to indicate "yes" and "no," feelings, and social amenities.
6. The board must be continually monitored and evaluated so that it can be modified with the child's expanding and changing needs.
7. There must be some motivation for the child to want to communicate.

Blissymbols

An alternative nonverbal communication system advocated for cerebral-palsied and other nonverbal children has been based on Blissymbols, developed by Charles K. Bliss in an effort to create a universal language. This system is based on approximately 100 idiopathic and pictographic symbols that can become quite abstract, requiring integrative cognitive functions. According to Vicker (1974), the pronounced visual-perceptual difficulties of cerebral-palsied children plus the abstraction level of Blissymbols and their altered syntactic pattern must be considered before this communication system is selected for a cerebral-palsied child. For many nonverbal children, however, Bliss has opened up an entirely new avenue for actively controlling and interacting with the environment. Blissymbolics is a system of line drawings that represent a thing, an action, an evaluation, or an abstract meaning.

In 1971, the Ontario Crippled Children's Centre in Toronto, under the direction of Shirley McNaughton, adapted Bliss' symbol system to a communication mode for prereading, handicapped children who exhibited varying degrees of speech dysfunction. The primary advantage of Blissymbols over a picture or word board is that Blissymbols is an open, meaning-referenced communication system from which the child can generate thousands of new meanings (McDonald, 1980). By a logical process of combining basic elements, the child can create new symbols and meanings that may not be available on a board. For example, the symbols for chair and water can be combined to form the symbol for toilet, the symbols for feeling and up can be combined to express happy (Figure 4-10). Each symbol's meaning is determined by its size, position, spacing, and configuration in relation to the basic unit of a square. Any sized square can be used but McDonald (1980) stresses that only symbols based on the same square unit can be used together and that consistency in symbol size is critical to its interpretation.

Figure 4-10 Blissymbols for a Preschool Playground

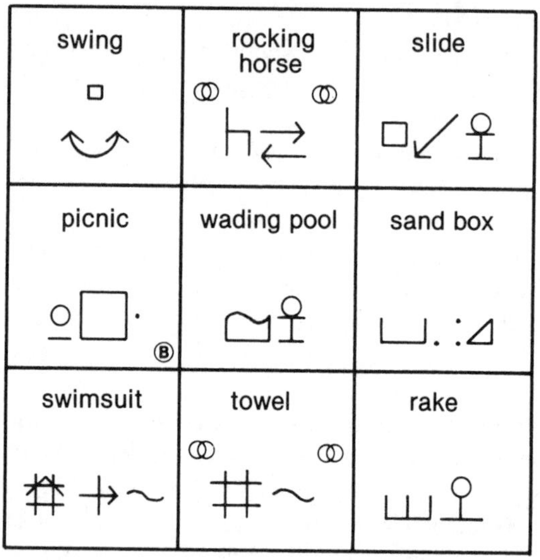

Key: Swing: The two-headed curved arrow represents a swinging motion. *Rocking horse:* something to sit on that moves back and forth. *Slide:* a thing for a child to slide down. *Picnic:* food that is eaten outside. *Wading pool:* a pool for a child. *Sand box:* half of an enclosure for sand (powder and rock). *Swimsuit:* clothing used to move through water. *Towel:* piece of cloth used with water. *Rake:* a comb for the garden.

Source: From *Blissymbols for Preschool Children* by A. Warrick. Toronto: Blissymbolics Communication Institute, 1981. Copyright 1981 by Blissymbolics Communication Institute. Reprinted by permission. Blissymbolics illustrated above are in accordance with BCI approved symbols.

Blissymbols afford a nonverbal child an immediate means of expressing needs and feelings. Furthermore, this system can supplement difficult-to-understand speech, provide communication in a wide variety of settings, and be useful with a variety of ages and functioning levels, including mentally handicapped learners (Harris-Vanderheiden, Brown, McKenzie, Reinen, & Scheibel, 1972). The printed word always accompanies each symbol. Children who are good candidates for Blissymbols have a basic understanding of the relationship between a symbol and the object, person, or feeling it represents, can match objects with pictures, can perform simple classification tasks, and can identify similarities in objects and in pictures. Most importantly, successful Blissymbol users have a need to communicate and supportive listeners with whom to communicate.

Blissymbol vocabularies selected for the preschool child are determined by the child's interests, physical and mental abilities, parent or caregiver recommendations, and environmental and personal needs of the child. Silverman, McNaughton, and Kates (1978) suggest that the preschool child's display board contain symbols for body parts because they promote understanding of verb usage and body awareness, and for greetings because they produce immediate rewards for being used. Additional recommendations include color coding the symbol display, labeling all familiar objects with Blissymbols, and selecting symbols that, initially, are visually dissimilar (Silverman, McNaughton, & Kates, 1978). Numerous activities and games for teaching and reinforcing Blissymbol use have been provided in resources by McDonald (1980); Silverman, McNaughton, and Kates (1978); and Warrick (1981).

The Blissymbol system has been invaluable in developing a means of communication with another individual. It also helps to reduce frustration and emotional lability, increase self-confidence and independence, and encourage initiative in assuming the role as a leader in class activities.

Other Programs

Zygo Communication Systems publishes a program designed to teach the use of a communication board to physically handicapped children and assess its effectiveness (Hall, O'Grady, & Talkington, 1978). The program is intended to be used with the Zygo Model 16C Communication System, but the concepts can be applied to almost any communication board system. An excellent language program for developing organized, functional syntactic generation is a system based on the Fitzgerald Key for the deaf. Designed by Fokes (1977), the *Fokes Sentence Builder* provides visual cues for structuring language into seven different categories. Another language development program beneficial to brain-injured children is Lee's Interactive Language Development System (Lee, Koenigsknecht, & Mulhern, 1975). Particularly useful in a preschool setting in which children work in groups, this program provides specific lessons to elicit spontaneous use of indefinite and personal pronouns, primary and secondary verb forms, negatives, conjunctions, wh-questions, and interrogative reversals. McDonald and Chance (1964) have outlined detailed, practical suggestions that parents may use in the home to develop preverbal skills in their cerebral-palsied preschooler. Crickmay (1966) and Mysak (1980) have described a series of reflex-inhibiting postures and techniques designed to encourage speech production. Young (1962) developed motokinesthetic procedures for teaching children where and how to position their articulators for generating and producing sounds.

CONCLUSIONS

A major responsibility of the preschool program is to help the child develop a healthy self-image. Disfigurements often make it difficult for children to feel good about themselves. Teplin, Howard, and O'Connor (1981) found the self-concept of young cerebral-palsied children to be similar to that of normal children, but somewhat lower. They also reported that handicapped children display a lower self-esteem at school than they do at home. Since physical appearance seems to be critical in social acceptance, a realistic but accepting attitude in these children regarding the appearance of their bodies is essential to the formation of positive peer relationships. Physically impaired youngsters must feel good enough about themselves to take the "risk" of being an active member of "the gang." Figure 4-11 is a fairly accurate self-representation drawn by an osteogenesis imperfecta child who is outgoing, well accepted, and liked by her peers. Children with craniofacial anomalies have also been reported to execute accurate self-images (Teplin et al., 1981). Kiernan and Connor (no date) suggest that children with neuromuscular or skeletal disabilities may not have a complete understanding of their body parts and how they fit together because the messages to and from the senses and muscles are distorted. Spina bifida children often can name even minute body parts, such as eyelashes and ankle, but cannot integrate them to draw a whole person. Similarly, hemiplegic children may draw either a body that is very asymmetrical or one that lacks one side.

Several authors have commented on the behaviors that contribute to a teacher's effectiveness in working with the physically handicapped child. Safford and Arbitman (1975) insist that psychological acceptance of the child's impairment is a precondition for effective coping, realistic planning, and serving the child's best interests. Lubin (1975) advises teachers of physically impaired children to acknowledge their own feelings about stereotypes of children and to try to identify with the child's perception of the world. Furgang and Yerxa (1979) feel that negative teacher attitudes may evoke sterile, insincere interactions that are over-controlled. Such unnatural teacher approaches may foster inaccurate feedback to students that, in turn, may impair the student's role performance. High expectations are beneficial only if the child can meet them. If expectations cannot be met,

Figure 4-11 Self-Representation Drawn by an Osteogenesis Imperfecta Child

the negative stereotype of the physically impaired child is reinforced (Furgang & Yerxa, 1979).

Normal children can be helped to accept and understand their handicapped peers through programs to develop social, affective behaviors. Two outstanding programs are *Developing Understanding of Self and Others* and the *Peabody Early Experiences Kit,* both published by American Guidance Service. Among the numerous children's books that have addressed the circumstances of the handicapped child, *Howie Helps Himself* (Fassler & Lasker, 1975) and *Don't Feel Sorry for Paul* (Wolf, 1974) focus on cerebral-palsied and limb-deficient children, respectively. *A Hospital Story: An Open Family Book for Parents and Children Together* (Stein, 1974) is full of natural pictures of a child progressing through various phases of surgery. Reading this book to the group before a child enters the hospital may alleviate both the child's fears and peers' concern over the separation. Gross motor equipment, such as the Sociobowl (manufactured by Skill Development Equipment), a plastic wading pool, and snack time are excellent facilitators of social interaction. Jointly finger painting a large mural, engaging in a game of picture dominoes, playing catch with soft balls, and other activities that require little fine motor control but do require cooperative efforts are but a few of the ways to encourage interactive play among physically limited preschoolers.

Both parents and children need support and encouragement as they adapt to and accept the effects of a physical or health impairment. The early intervention atmosphere should offer stability and understanding while simultaneously providing opportunities for developing self-awareness and independence.

The role of the educational team serving the preschooler with a physical handicap is that of maximizing the child's ability to interact with the environment, to achieve independence and a sense of self-worth, and to develop a realistic awareness of both the potential and the limitations associated with the specific health or physical impairment. Success in these areas ensures that the physically impaired preschooler will not develop into a handicapped child but will grow to be an individual who is only inconvenienced.

REFERENCE NOTES

1. Nelson, C. Lecture notes from the neurodevelopmental treatment certification course. Washington, D.C.: Georgetown University, June 16-August 6, 1979.

2. Magee, M. Lecture notes: Overview of neurodevelopmental treatment. Cerebral Palsy Institute. Tuscaloosa, Ala.: University of Alabama, June 16-27, 1980.

3. Davis, L.F. Lecture notes. Prespeech and feeding. Cerebral Palsy Institute. Tuscaloosa, Ala.: University of Alabama, June 16-27, 1980.

4. Davis, L.F. Lecture notes from the neurodevelopmental treatment certification course. Washington, D.C.: Georgetown University, June 16-August 6, 1979.

5. Cormack, E. Learning environments for physically handicapped preschoolers. Presentation. Orlando, Florida: Florida Council for Exceptional Children, October, 1981.

REFERENCES

Allen, N. Developmental and degenerative diseases of the brain. In T.W. Farmer (Ed.), *Pediatric neurology*. New York: Harper & Row, Hoeber Medical Division, 1964.

Angliss, V.E. Habilitation of upper limb deficient children. *American Journal of Occupational Therapy*, 1974, *28*(7), 407-414.

Ayers, J. *Sensory integration and the child*. Los Angeles: Western Psychological Services, 1980.

Barnes, E., Berrigan, C., & Biklen, D. *What's the difference? Teaching positive attitudes toward people with disabilities*. Syracuse, N.Y.: Human Policy Press, 1978.

Barry, H. *The young aphasic child: Evaluation and training*. Washington, D.C.: Alexander Graham Bell Association for the Deaf, Inc., 1961.

Barton, E.M., Hollobon, B., & Woods, G.E. Appliances used to help the handicapped under three to follow the normal developmental sequence. *Child: Care Health and Development*, 1980, *6*, 209-232.

Batshaw, M.L., & Perret, Y.M. *Children with handicaps: A medical primer*. Baltimore: Paul H. Brookes, 1981.

Bergman, A. *Selected equipment for pediatric rehabilitation*. Valhalla, N.Y.: Blythedale Children's Hospital, 1974.

Berko, M.J. Psychological and linguistic implications of brain damage in children. In M. Mecham, F.G. Berko, M.F. Berko, & J. Palmer (Eds.), *Communication training in childhood brain damage*. Springfield, Ill.: Charles C Thomas, 1966.

Bigge, J.L., & O'Donnell, P.A. *Teaching individuals with physical and multiple disabilities*. Columbus, Ohio: Charles E. Merrill, 1976.

Bleck, E.E. Muscular dystrophy: Duchenne type. In E.E. Bleck & D.A. Nagel (Eds.), *Physically handicapped children: A medical atlas for teachers*. New York: Grune & Stratton, 1975.

Bleck, E.E., & Nagel, D.A. (Eds.). *Physically handicapped children: A medical atlas for teachers*. New York: Grune & Stratton, 1975.

Bobath, B. The very early treatment of cerebral palsy. *Developmental Medicine and Child Neurology*, 1967, *9*, 373-390.

Bobath, K., & Bobath, B. Cerebral palsy. In P.H. Pearson & C.E. Williams (Eds.), *Physical therapy services in the developmental disabilities*. Springfield, Ill.: Charles C Thomas, 1972.

Bower, T.G.R. *Development in infancy*. San Francisco: W.H. Freeman, 1974.

Brink, J.D. Muscular dystrophy. In R.M. Peterson & J.O. Cleveland (Eds.), *Medical problems in the classroom: An educator's guide*. Springfield, Ill.: Charles C Thomas, 1975.

Calhoun, M.L., & Hawisher, M. *Teaching and learning strategies for physically handicapped students*. Baltimore: University Park Press, 1979.

Campbell, S.K. Facilitation of cognitive and motor development in infants with central nervous system dysfunction. *Physical Therapy*, 1974, *54*, 346-353.

Carlsen, P.N. Comparison of two occupational therapy approaches for treating the young cerebral palsied child. *American Journal of Occupational Therapy*, 1975, *29*, 267-272.

Challenor, Y.B., & Katz, J.F. Limb deficiency in infancy and childhood. In J.A. Downey & L.N. Low (Eds.), *The child with disabling illness: Principles of rehabilitation*. Philadelphia: W.B. Saunders, 1974.

Connor, F.P., Williamson, G.G., & Siepp, J.M. *Program guide for infants and toddlers with neuromotor and other developmental disabilities*. New York: Teachers College Press, 1978.

Coop, R.H., Eckel, E., & Stuck, G. An assessment of the pictorial test of intelligence for use with young cerebral-palsied children. *Developmental Medicine and Child Neurology,* 1975, *17,* 287-292.

Copeland, M., Ford, L., & Solon, N. *Occupational therapy for cerebral palsied children.* Baltimore: University Park Press, 1976.

Crickmay, M.C. *Speech therapy and the Bobath approach to cerebral palsy.* Springfield, Ill.: Charles C Thomas, 1966.

Cruickshank, W., Bentzen, F.A., Ratzenburg, F.H., & Tannhauser, M.T. *A teaching method for brain injured and hyperactive children: A demonstration pilot study.* Syracuse, N.Y.: Syracuse University Press, 1961.

Cruickshank, W.M., Hallahan, D.P., & Bice, H.V. The evaluation of intelligence. In W.M. Cruickshank (Ed.), *Cerebral palsy.* Syracuse, N.Y.: Syracuse University Press, 1976.

Davis, L. Pre-speech. In F.P. Connor, G. Williamson, & J. Siepp (Eds.), *Program guide for infants and toddlers with neuromotor and other developmental disabilities.* New York: Teachers College Press, 1978.

Denhoff, E. Current status of infant stimulation or enrichment programs for children with developmental disabilities. *Pediatrics,* 1981, *67,* 32-37.

Dressing techniques for the cerebral palsied child. *American Journal of Occupational Therapy,* 1954, *8*(1 & 2), 8-10, 37-38, 48-52.

Drillien, C.M., & Drummond, M.B. (Eds.), *Neurodevelopmental problems in early childhood: Assessment and management.* Oxford: Blackwell Scientific Publications, 1977.

Eckel, E.M. Arthrogryposis multiplex congenita. *Physical Therapy,* 1970, *50,* 665-668.

Evans-Morris, S. *Program guidelines for children with feeding problems.* Edison, N.J.: Childcraft, 1977.

Fassler, J., & Lasker, J. *Howie helps himself.* New York: Albert Whitman, 1975.

Fetters, L. Object permanence development in infants with motor handicaps. *Physical Therapy,* 1981, *61,* 327-330.

Finnie, N. *Handling the young cerebral palsied child at home.* New York: E.P. Dutton, 1975.

Florek, M., & Karolak, S. Intelligence level of patients with Duchenne type of progressive muscular dystrophy. *European Journal of Pediatrics,* 1977, *126,* 275-282.

Fokes, J. *The Fokes Sentence Builder.* Boston: Teaching Resources, 1977.

French, J.L. *Pictorial Test of Intelligence.* Boston: Houghton-Mifflin, 1964.

Furgang, N.T., & Yerxa, E.J. Expectations of teachers for physically handicapped and normal first grade students. *American Journal of Occupational Therapy,* 1979, *33,* 697-704.

Garrett, A.L. Orthopedic diseases. In R.M. Peterson & J.O. Cleveland (Eds.), *Medical problems in the classroom: An educator's guide.* Springfield, Ill.: Charles C Thomas, 1975.

Gearheart, B.R., & Weishahn, M.W. *The handicapped student in the regular classroom* (2nd ed.). St. Louis: C.V. Mosby, 1980.

Gold, A.P., Hammil, J.F., & Carter, S. Cerebrovascular diseases. In T.W. Farmer (Ed.), *Pediatric neurology.* New York: Harper & Row, Hoeber Medical Division, 1964.

Goldstein, H. *Readings in physically handicapped education.* Guilford, Conn.: Special Learning Corp., 1978.

Gordon, R. The design of a preschool "learning laboratory" in a rehabilitation center. *Rehabilitation Monograph,* 1969, *39.*

Haeussermann, E. *Developmental potential for preschool children*. New York: Grune & Stratton, 1958.

Haeussermann, E. Evaluating the developmental level of cerebral palsy preschool children. In J.M. Wolfe & R.M. Anderson (Eds.), *The multiply handicapped child*. Springfield, Ill.: Charles C Thomas, 1969.

Hall, K.W., & Hammock, M. Feeding and toileting devices for a child with arthrogryposis. *American Journal of Occupational Therapy*, 1979, *33*, 644-647.

Hall, S., O'Grady, R.S., & Talkington, L. *Communication board training program for the multihandicapped*. Portland, Ore.: Zygo Industries, 1978.

Hallahan, D., & Kauffman, J. *Exceptional children: An introduction to special education*. Englewood Cliffs, N.J.: Prentice-Hall, 1978.

Harper, D.C., & Tanner, H. The French Pictorial Test of Intelligence and the Stanford-Binet, L-M: A concurrent validity study with physically impaired children. *Journal of Clinical Psychology*, 1974, *30*, 178-180.

Harris, S.E., & Cherry, D.B. Childhood progressive muscular dystrophy and the role of the physical therapist. *Physical Therapy*, 1974, *54*, 4-12.

Harris-Vanderheiden, D., Brown, W.P., McKenzie, P., Reinen, S., & Scheibel, C. Symbol communication for the mentally handicapped. *Mental Retardation*, 1975, *13*, 34-37.

Harvey, B. Cystic fibrosis. In E.E. Bleck & D.A. Nagel (Eds.), *Physically handicapped children: A medical atlas for teachers*. New York: Grune & Stratton, 1975.

Healy, A., & McAreavey, P. *Mainstreaming preschoolers: Children with health impairments*. Washington, D.C.: U.S. Department of Health, Education and Welfare.

Heiniger, M.C., & Randolph, S.L. *Neurophysiological concepts in human behavior: The tree of learning*. St. Louis: C.V. Mosby, 1981.

Jacobs, J.C., & Downey, J.A. Juvenile rheumatoid arthritis. In J.A. Downey & N.L. Low (Eds.), *The child with disabling illness: Principles of rehabilitation*. Philadelphia: W.B. Saunders, 1974.

Jedrysek, E., Klapper, Z., Pope, L., & Wortis, J. *Psychoeducational evaluation of the preschool child*. New York: Grune & Stratton, 1972.

Karagan, N.J. Intellectual functioning in Duchenne muscular dystrophy: A Review. *Psychological Bulletin*, 1979, *86*, 250-259.

Karagan, N.J., & Zellweger, H.V. Early verbal disability in Duchenne muscular dystrophy. *Developmental Medicine and Child Neurology*, 1978, *20*, 435-441.

Katz, J.F. Scoliosis. In J.A. Downey & N.L. Low (Eds.), *The child with disabling illness: Principles of rehabilitation*. Philadelphia: W.B. Saunders, 1974.

Katz, J.F., & Challenor, Y.B. Childhood orthopedic syndromes. In J.A. Downey & N.L. Low (Eds.), *The child with disabling illness: Principles of rehabilitation*. Philadelphia: W.B. Saunders, 1974.

Kiernan, S.S., & Connor, F.P. *Mainstreaming preschoolers: Children with orthopedic handicaps*. Washington, D.C.: U.S. Department of Health, Education and Welfare.

Kinnealey, M., & Morse, A.B. Educational mainstreaming of physically handicapped children. *American Journal of Occupational Therapy*, 1979, *33*, 365-372.

Langley, B. Functional assessment of the brain damaged physically handicapped child: Cognitive communication and motor variables, *Diagnostique*, 1977, *2*(2), 31-37.

Langley, M.B. *The teachable moment and the handicapped infant*. Reston, Va.: Council for Exceptional Children, 1980.

Laurence, E.R. Spina bifida children in school: Preliminary report. *Developmental Medicine and Child Neurology*, 1971 (Supplement 25), 44-46.

Lee, L.L., Koenigsknecht, R., & Mulhern, S. *Interactive language development teaching: A clinical presentation of grammatical structure*. Evanston, Ill.: Northwestern University Press, 1975.

Levitt, S. *Treatment of cerebral palsy and motor delay*. Oxford: Blackwell Scientific Publications, 1977.

Love, H.D., & Walthall, J.E. *A handbook of medical, educational, and psychological information for teachers of physically handicapped children*. Springfield, Ill.: Charles C Thomas, 1977.

Lubin, G.I. Emotional implications. In R.M. Peterson & J.O. Cleveland (Eds.), *Medical problems in the classroom: An educator's guide*. Springfield, Ill.: Charles C Thomas, 1975.

Marks, N.C. *Cerebral palsied and learning disabled children: A handbook/guide to treatment rehabilitation and education*. Springfield, Ill.: Charles C Thomas, 1974.

Marsh, G.G., & Munsat, T.L. Evidence of early impairment of verbal intelligence in Duchenne muscular dystrophy. *Archives of Diseases of Children*, 1974, *49*, 118-122.

Matheny, M.M., & Ruby, D.O. A guide for feeding the cerebral palsied child. *Cerebral Palsy Review*, 1963, *24*, 14-16.

McDonald, E.T. Design and application of communication boards. In G.C. Vanderheiden & K. Grilley (Eds.), *Nonvocal communication techniques and aids for the severely physically handicapped*. Baltimore: University Park Press, 1976.

McDonald, E.T. *Teaching and using Blissymbolics*. Toronto: Blissymbolics Communication Institute, 1980.

McDonald, E.T., & Chance, B. *Cerebral palsy*. Englewood Cliffs, N.J.: Prentice-Hall, 1964.

McDonald, E.T., & Shultz, A.R. Communication boards for cerebral palsied children. *Journal of Speech and Hearing Disorders*, 1973, *38*(1), 73-88.

Mecham, M.J. Appraisal of speech and hearing problems. In M.J. Mecham, M.J. Berko, F.G. Berko, & M.F. Palmer (Eds.), *Communication training in childhood brain damage*. Springfield, Ill.: Charles C Thomas, 1966.

Miller, J.J. Juvenile rheumatoid arthritis. In E.E. Bleck & D.A. Nagel (Eds.), *Physically handicapped children: A medical atlas for teachers*. New York: Grune & Stratton, 1975.

Mueller, H.A. Facilitating feeding and prespeech. In P.H. Pearson & C.E. Williams (Eds.), *Physical therapy services in the developmental disabilities*. Springfield, Ill.: Charles C Thomas, 1972.

Mullen, E.M., Danella, E., & Meyers, M. *Manual Meeting Street School psychological S-R, evaluation for severely multiply handicapped children*. East Providence, R.I.: Meeting Street School, 1977.

Myers, B.A. Child with chronic illness. In R.H.A. Haslam & P.J. Valletutti (Eds.), *Medical problems in the classroom: The teacher's role in diagnosis and management*. Baltimore: University Park Press, 1975.

Myers, G.J., Cerone, S.B., & Olson, A.L. *A guide for helping the child with spina bifida*. Springfield, Ill.: Charles C Thomas, 1981.

Mysak, E.D. *Neurospeech therapy for the cerebral palsied: A neuroevolutional approach* (3rd ed.). New York: Teachers College Press, 1980.

Nagel, D.A. Temporary orthopedic disabilities in children. In E.E. Bleck & D.A. Nagel (Eds.), *Physically handicapped children: A medical atlas for children*. New York: Grune & Stratton, 1975.

Norton, Y. Minimal cerebral dysfunctions: II. Modified treatment and evaluation of movement. *American Journal of Occupational Therapy*, 1972, *26*, 186-199.

Norton, Y. Neurodevelopment and sensory integration for the profoundly retarded multiply handicapped child. *American Journal of Occupational Therapy*, 1975, *29*, 93-100.

Parsons, J.G. An investigation into the verbal facility of hydrocephalic children. *Developmental Medicine and Child Neurology,* 1968 (Supplement 16), 108-109.

Pearson, H.A., & Diamond, L.K. Sickle cell disease crises and their management. In C.A. Smith (Ed.), *The critically ill child: Diagnosis and management* (2nd ed.). Philadelphia: W.B. Saunders, 1977.

Pekarovic, E., Robinson, A., Lister, J., & Zachary, R.B. Pressure variations in intestinal loops used for urinary diversion. *Developmental Medicine and Child Neurology,* 1968 (Supplement 16), 87-92.

Robinault, I.P. *Functional aids for the multiply handicapped.* New York: Harper & Row, 1973.

Rosenbaum, P., Barnett, R., & Brand, H.L. A developmental intervention program designed to overcome the effects of impaired movement in spina bifida infants. In K.S. Holt (Ed.), *Movement and child development.* Philadelphia: J.B. Lippincott, 1975.

Rosenbloom, L. The consequences of impaired movement—A hypothesis and review. In K.S. Holt (Ed.), *Movement and child development.* Philadelphia: J.B. Lippincott, 1977.

Safford, P.L., & Arbitman, D.C. *Developmental intervention with young physically handicapped children.* Springfield, Ill.: Charles C Thomas, 1975.

Sattler, J.M., & Anderson, N.E. The Peabody Picture Vocabulary Test, and the modified Stanford Binet with normal and cerebral palsied preschool children. *Journal of Special Education,* 1973, *7,* 119-123.

Scarnati, R.A. The role of the physical therapist in special education. In R. M. Anderson & J.G. Greer (Eds.), *Educating the severely and profoundly retarded.* Baltimore: University Park Press, 1976.

Shepard, R.B. *Physiotherapy in pediatrics.* London: William Heinemann Books, 1974.

Sherwin, A.C., & McCully, R.S. Reactions observed in boys of various ages to a crippling, progressive and fatal illness. *Journal of Chronic Diseases,* 1961, *13,* 59-68.

Shurtleff, D.T. Timing of learning in meningomyelocele patients. *Journal of American Physical Therapy Association,* 1966, *46,* 136-148.

Silberstein, C.E. Orthopedic problems in the classroom. In R.H.A. Haslam & P.J. Valletutti (Eds.), *Medical problems in the classroom: The teacher's role in diagnosis and management.* Baltimore: University Park Press, 1975.

Silverman, H., McNaughton, S., & Kates, B. *Handbook of Blissymbolics.* Toronto: Blissymbolics Communication Institute, 1978.

Sirvis, B. Developing IEP's for physically handicapped students: A transdisciplinary viewpoint. *Teaching Exceptional Children,* 1978, Spring 78-82.

Stein, S.B. *A hospital story: An open family book for parents and children together.* New York: Walker, 1974.

Swanson, A.B. Congenital limb defects: Classification and treatment. *Clinical Symposia,* 1981, *33,* 373-378.

Swisher, L.P., & Pinsker, E.J. The language characteristics of hyperverbal, hydrocephalic children. *Developmental Medicine and Child Neurology,* 1971, *13,* 746-755.

Taylor, E.M. *The psychological appraisal of children with cerebral defects.* Cambridge, Mass.: Harvard University Press, 1961.

Teplin, S.W., Howard, J.A., & O'Connor, M.J. Self-concept of young children with cerebral palsy. *Developmental Medicine and Child Neurology,* 1981, *23,* 730-738.

Tessier, F.A. The development of young cerebral palsied children according to Piaget's sensorimotor theory. *Dissertation Abstracts International,* 1969.

Twomey, M.R. Osteogenesis imperfecta. *Nursing Times,* 1979, *25,* 159-161.

Vanderheiden, G.C., & Grilley, K. (Eds.). *Nonvocal communication techniques and aids for the severely physically handicapped.* Baltimore: University Park Press, 1976.

Vicker, B.A. *University hospital nonoral communication system project.* Ames, Iowa: University of Iowa, 1974.

Warrick, A. *Blissymbols for preschool children.* Toronto: Blissymbolics Communication Institute, 1981.

Wilson, J.M. (Ed.). *Oral-motor function and dysfunction in children.* Chapel Hill, N.C.: University of North Carolina, 1977.

Wilson, M.A. Multidisciplinary problems of myelomeningocele and hydrocephalus. *Journal of the American Physical Therapy Association,* 1965, *45*(12), 1139-1146.

Wolf, B. *Don't feel sorry for Paul.* Philadelphia: J.B. Lippincott, 1974.

Young, E. The moto-kinesthetic method as applied to the cerebral palsied. *Cerebral Palsy Review,* 1962, *23,* 7-8.

Zelazo, P.R. Reactivity to perceptual-cognitive events: Application for infant assessment. In R.B. Kearsley & I.E. Siegel (Eds.), *Infants at risk: Assessment of cognitive functioning.* Hillsdale, N.J.: Lawrence Erlbaum Associates, 1979.

Appendix 4-A

Addresses for Adaptive Equipment

Achievement Products, Inc.
P.O. Box 547
Mineola, New York 11501

Bell & Howell
7100-T McCormick Boulevard
Chicago, Illinois 60645

Fred Sammons
Be-OK Self-help aids
Box 32
Brookfield, Illinois 60513

Invacare Corporation
1200 Taylor Street
Elyria, Ohio 44035

J.A. Preston Corporation
(TumbleForms)
60 Page Road
Clifton, New Jersey 07012

Kaye Products, Inc.
1010 East Pettigrew Street
Durham, North Carolina 27701

Maddak Inc.
Pequannock, New Jersey 07440

Mullholland Corporation
1563 Los Angeles Avenue
Ventura, California 93003

Orthokinetics
W220 N507 Springdale Road
P.O. Box 436
Waukesha, Wisconsin 53187

Rifton Equipment for the
Handicapped
Rifton, New York 12471

Safety Travel Corporation
147 Eady Court
Elyria, Ohio 44035

Texas Instruments
P.O. Box 1444
Houston, Texas 77001

Zaner Bloser Company
612 North Park Street
Columbus, Ohio 43215

Zygo Communication Systems
Zygo Industries Inc.
P.O. Box 1008
Portland, Oregon 97207

Part III

Cognitive Development

Chapter 5

Intelligence and Cognition

S. Gray Garwood

The nature of human intelligence has occupied a key position among scientific concerns about developmental processes, reflecting both the importance attached to the term *intelligence* for describing mental functioning and the importance ascribed to such functioning in humans. Intelligence is a concept used to describe particular qualities of mental behavior, such as the abilities to (1) sense information (stimuli) from the environment (sensory functioning); (2) recognize that information as something that has been experienced in some form previously, which requires selectivity as well as organization (perception); (3) store this information (memory); and (4) retrieve it for use in making decisions. These abilities enable individuals to understand or make sense of the world. Thus, intelligent behavior is also cognitive (from the Latin *cognoscere*, meaning to know or to understand) behavior, and the abilities just described are frequently referred to as cognitive abilities. Binet, credited with developing the first intelligence test, wrote that intelligence consists of acts of judgment, the use of common sense, and the display of initiative and the ability to adapt to the world. "To judge well, understand well, reason well—these are the essentials of intelligence" (Binet & Simon, 1916, p. 42).

THEORIES OF INTELLIGENCE

Factor Theories

Binet proposed a global factor theory of intelligence. Binet assessed intelligence by using a series of tasks that tapped diverse abilities (e.g., tracking a lighted candle, stringing beads, explaining proverbs). The "more intelligent" child was better at all or most of these tasks; hence, the assumption of a common intelligence factor. This approach was continued in Terman's revision of Binet's scale (the Stanford-Binet), as it was in the Wechsler intelligence tests. The Stanford-Binet and the Wechsler tests (e.g., the WISC-R) are currently the most widely used individually administered intelligence scales, and both are based on the assumption that intelligence is global.

Spearman (1904, 1927) believed that a general factor (''g'' factor) was the basis for abstract reasoning and problem solving, but he felt that a variety of specific factors (''s'' factors) accounted for the lack of consistency across all areas of an individual's performance. Thurstone (1938, 1948) proposed a seven-component theory of intelligence, consisting of (1) verbal comprehension, (2) word fluency, (3) numerical ability, (4) space visualization, (5) associative memory, (6) perceptual speed, and (7) reasoning abilities. Thurstone's views are reflected in the Primary Mental Abilities Test (PMAT).

The ultimate in multiple-factor approaches to conceptualizing and assessing intelligence is represented in the work of Guilford (1967), who proposed a three-dimensional model. In this model, intelligence is viewed as particular actions carried out *(operations)* on different entities *(products)* consisting of different kinds of material *(contents)*. Guilford hypothesizes that intelligence can be subdivided into five operations acting on six products consisting of four contents; thus, 120 different aspects or factors of intelligence are possible.

Operations are mental acts involved in the performance of intellectual tasks. Guilford's model contains five: (1) cognition (knowledge about objects or events), (2) convergent production (problem-solving behavior focused toward the correct solution), (3) divergent production (problem-solving behavior that produces a variety of possible solutions), (4) memory, and (5) evaluation.

Products are the types of information upon which mental operations are performed. These classifications include units (basic information, such as the ability to recognize letters), classes (categories of information), relations (correspondences between things), systems (information patterns), transformations (changes in information), and implications (information that suggests a particular outcome is likely).

Content is the type of material upon which intellectual operations are performed. The four categories are (1) figural (sensory information on properties of objects, such as form or texture), (2) symbolic (cultural symbols, such as letters), (3) semantic (meanings attached to symbols or events), and (4) behavioral (social actions).

Fluid and Crystallized Intelligence

A slightly different view of intellectual structure, originally proposed by Cattell (1957), has been expanded by Horn and Cattell (1967). They suggest that intelligence consists of two general classes of abilities, fluid and crystallized. Crystallized intelligence develops from experience with one's culture, especially its educational aspects. Horn (1970) has pointed out that schools focus on particular abilities and, thus, on individuals who possess those abilities. In this selective process, abilities that have survival value but were not initially correlated tend to become so, contributing to the perception of intelligence as global. In addition, the individuals involved, because they remain within the formal educational system for longer periods of time, tend to become more acculturated than individuals who leave the educational system earlier. Crystallized intelligence is therefore reflected best by culturally loaded intelligence test items, such as vocabulary, general information, and knowledge of social situations.

Fluid intelligence, in contrast, describes abilities that are less directly affected by cultural experiences and more related to neurological-physiological functioning. It is defined by performance on such tasks as common word analogies, letter series, rote memory, verbal reasoning with common materials, and matrixes. In other words, fluid intelligence relates to an individual's capacity to perceive complex relations, form concepts, and reason. Guilford (1980) has criticized the fluid-crystallized dichotomy, claiming that the concept of two broad factors is not supported by more methodologically sound factor analysis strategies; Guilford believes that the two factors reflect either test characteristics or aspects of his own multifactorial view of intelligence.

DEVELOPMENTAL CHANGE IN INTELLECTUAL ABILITY

If rates of change in an infant were compared with those in a child or adult, it is obvious that, on most indexes, the infant would show more rapid change. Intellectual development is no exception. An infant is more a reflexive than an intelligent organism at first, and the infant begins to develop intellectually by using reflexive activity to establish initial contact with the environment. These continued interactions help refine skills, which, in turn, generate new interaction patterns and new skills. Thus, "intellectual" behaviors typically show not only marked gains in their efficiency (quantity) but also marked changes in their nature (quality).

Table 5-1 illustrates the nature of such changes across several behavioral domains during the first 2 years. These stages and behavioral domains have been postulated by McCall, Eichorn, and Hogarty (1977) and are based on their analysis of infants' responses to 244 items from the California First Year and California Preschool Scale (Bayley, 1933; Jaffa, 1934). The infants were all subjects in the Berkeley Growth Study, and at any age the number ranged between 49 and 72. As Table 5-1 indicates, intellectual behaviors progress from reliance on reflexive responses (Stage I) to reliance on symbolic means (Stage V). This increasingly mature intellectual functioning is especially apparent in behaviors summarized in the column headed Fundamental Cognitive Attribute. In addition, it can be seen how the infant's increasing sophistication is becoming integrated throughout the several behavioral domains of each stage.

Table 5-1 Hypothesized Stages of Development of Cognitive Behaviors during Infancy and Early Childhood

Stage and General Age Range	*Fundamental Cognitive Attribute*	*Object Concept and Object Permanence*	*Attention/ Exploration Behaviors*	*Imitative Behaviors*	*Language Behaviors*
I: Period of reflexive development (0-2 months)	Exercises built-in structural behavioral dispositions; selectively attends to environment				
II: Period of complete subjectivity (2-7 months)	"Knows" world through own actions but does not distinguish between own actions and actions of external objects or events	Does not separate objects from own actions; does not solve visible displacements but returns to place where action was successful	Attends to readily assimilable information; explores objects that provide responses in response to own actions	Imitates only behaviors in current repertoire	
III: Period of means-ends separation (7-13 months)	Can separate cause and effect; continues to base knowledge on own actions	Separates objects from own action, but strongly associates them; can solve a single visible displacement	Separates others from own actions; recognizes family members, thus separation and stranger distress behaviors begin	Separates means from ends; pursues goals and generalizes means to new ends; can coordinate or differentiate diverse actions to	Can imitate new responses that are close to existing behaviors

				meet demands of simple problem-solving situations	
IV: Period of environmental separation (13-21 months)	Recognizes separate nature of objects and events, enabling infant to compare and associate these objects/ events without having to act on them	Separates objects from own actions; can solve a series of successive visible displacements	Has high social distress responsivity because of ability to generalize more response uncertainty in various situations; recognizes own ability to influence the behavior of others	Deliberately varies actions on objects to identify causal chains; uses environmental feedback to modify actions toward a goal	Truly imitates new behavior because actions are recognized as independent of particular objects or events and because object-object, object-event, and event-event relationships are mentally constructed independent of actions
V: Period of symbolic relations (21 + months)	Begins to understand via symbolic means that relationships exist independent of own actions or specific object or event configurations	Symbolically manipulates objects and their relational configurations; can solve series of successive invisible displacements by inferring outcome	Uses language in goal-directed social influencing of others	Can imitate sequential actions, defer imitation, and selectively imitate; able to generalize imitative activity to new context	

Source: Based on McCall, Eichorn, & Hogarty, 1977.

ASSESSMENT OF INTELLIGENCE

American views of intelligence are directly related to the measuring instruments used for its assessment, so it is important to examine some of the properties of intelligence tests, as well as some assumptions regarding the measurement of intelligence. Intelligence tests may be administered either to an individual or to a group, although individually administered tests are considered more reliable because a wider range of behaviors can be tapped. Also, individual intelligence tests, such as the Bayley Scales of Infant Development (Bayley, 1969), and the Stanford-Binet, do not always rely on the individual's ability to read or write, which is a necessity for successful performance on group tests. Finally, individually administered tests enable the examiner to

1. deal with interfering environmental distractions that could hamper successful test performance
2. consider characteristics of the individual's relationship to the examiner and the test conditions when interpreting the test results
3. identify strategies used by individuals in dealing with particular test items as well as considering the correctness of the answer
4. evaluate other behavioral characteristics (e.g., auditory difficulty, speech problems) that might have a bearing on the outcome

Intelligence test items are based on the assumption that all individuals at a given age have had equivalent exposures, through experiences within a common culture, to the types of information required for the tasks. (This does not mean that all individuals understand this information equally well; they simply must have been equally exposed to opportunities to acquire and make use of it.) Furthermore, in most tests, a commonality of experience (both educationally and culturally) across generations is assumed.

Many items on intelligence tests require verbal ability. On the other hand, performance tasks emphasize nonverbal abilities, such as eye-hand coordination. In order to perform well, individuals must have a fund of conventional knowledge and must be able to remember and apply this knowledge, which includes (1) general information about the words associated with pictures, objects, and behavioral events; (2) definitions of words that stress the essential characteristics of their meaning; (3) appropriate responses to common social situations; (4) symbol systems and arithmetic operations; and (5) the ways objects can appear or that events typically occur. Successful performance also requires the ability to recognize similarities and differences between the units of information or concepts presented, as well as the ability to remember new information. Finally, successful performance requires the ability to work toward a goal and solve problems. All of these abilities are specifically assessed on intelligence tests.

In addition to these primary abilities, several additional skills are typically required. These include the abilities to

1. focus attention
2. hear and understand questions and instructions
3. imitate actions of the examiner
4. make use of input information
5. remember and use information derived from prior experiences effectively
6. communicate ideas appropriately and fluently

Consideration of these prerequisites is important. Even though they are not isolated or specifically evaluated on intelligence tests, their absence on a particular task can interfere with performance. For example, is the failure of a young child to describe the similarity between an apple and an orange caused by a deficit in primary ability to recognize similarity, or could it be due to a failure to understand the instructions (prerequisite 2), to a lack of knowledge of the meaning of the words *alike* or *similar,* or to discomfort in the testing situation (prerequisite 1)?

Structure of Intelligence Tests

Typically, there are four assumptions about abilities measured on intelligence tests:

1. Although items or tasks measuring certain cognitive abilities may change, the basic ability remains essentially unchanged throughout the age span covered by the test.
2. Abilities measured show incremental increases in the person's efficiency and effectiveness for making use of them.
3. Items that assess the same type of ability are arranged in order of increasing complexity or difficulty.
4. Proficiency norms for each ability tested are based on the level of proficiency normally displayed by individuals at a given chronological age.

Most intelligence tests focus on the individual's ability to perform successfully on a selective and limited number of test items. The items generally are selected because of their relationship to other test items. For example, if vocabulary knowledge were highly related to ability to recall a series of numbers (digit span task) and to ability to place a series of pictures depicting a social situation in a logical order, then all three types of items would probably be included. If the digit span task did not show a strong relationship to the other two, however, it would not be included, even though it might require the same level of cognitive activity.

Tests constructed in this way encourage the belief that intelligence is a global entity, because a person who does well on one part of such a test is likely to do well on the test's other components.

Testing Limitations

There are major weaknesses and limitations associated with the use of intelligence test data.

Instability of Performance

It is fairly clear that global measures of infant mental functioning do not predict later intellectual functioning among normally developing infants (Bayley, 1970; McCall, 1976; Stott & Ball, 1965). As Bayley points out, "it is now well established that test scores earned in the first year or two have relatively little predictive validity . . . although they may have a high validity as measures of children's cognitive ability at the time" (p. 1174). Ausubel and Sullivan (1970) cite several reasons why this is so. First, the growth rate in infancy is rapid and the range of individual differences is very narrow; thus, any temporary change in the growth rate of an infant would produce much larger fluctuations in test scores than would occur at a later age when individual variability is greater and growth rate is slower. Second, the overlap of test items between successive age levels is much less in infancy than in later years. Finally, difficulties in testing infants (e.g., interpreting behaviors, establishing rapport, resolving changes in attentional level) lead to maximal errors of measurement.

Confusion of Potential with Performance

The sample of ability revealed by a particular test, given by a particular tester, in a particular place, at a particular time may not reflect the individual's full potential. In fact, any particular sample is more likely to underestimate than overestimate the individual's true ability level. This holds for any individual, regardless of age.

Interaction of Motivation and Performance

All individuals are not equally motivated to perform well on an intelligence test. It is difficult to hold motivational factors constant in intelligence testing. For example, some people are so fearful that they may disappoint themselves, the examiner, or others by failing that they become embarrassed and uncomfortable, which can lead to withdrawal and reluctance to answer when uncertain. Their distress and discomfort is thus heightened and can lead to confusion and deterioration in test performance.

Cultural Bias

Since all test procedures are framed within a particular cultural network of values, beliefs, language, and events, these things are an integral part of the test procedures. This factor is not especially critical when the individuals being tested have a common culture, but it becomes very important when children are compared across different cultures or subcultures.

Socioeconomic Status

Social class groupings are defined on the basis of such factors as education, income, and occupation. Therefore, socioeconomic status or social class is a composite variable describing differences across subcultural groups. Studies generally show a positive relationship between social class and intelligence.

Racial Differences

In Shuey's (1966) review of nearly 400 studies comparing intelligence test performances of blacks and whites, blacks usually scored 1 to 20 points lower than whites, regardless of age, type of test used, or region of the United States. While Shuey interpreted these results from an hereditarian perspective, an alternative interpretation is equally feasible. In the United States, blacks, who comprise the largest minority group, tend to have less education, lower income, and lower status occupations; they are typically overrepresented among the lower class. Because whites tend to have more education, income, and higher status occupations, they are usually overrepresented in the middle class. The result is a confounding of race and social class, which suggests that it is possible to attribute racial differences in intelligence test scores to environmental factors associated with level of education, income, and type of occupation.

In support of this view are data from a study of black children adopted by white families (Scarr and Weinberg, 1976). These researchers postulated that "if black children have genetically limited intellectual potential . . . their IQ performance will fall below that of other children reared in white upper middle-class homes. On the other hand, if black children have a range of reaction similar to [that of] other adoptees, their IQ scores should have a similar distribution" (p. 727). (Range of reaction is a concept indicating that a variety of genotypes exist and can specify a variety of phenotypes, each differing in its potential range of reaction.) Scarr and Weinberg studied 101 families, including 321 children over age 4. Of these, 145 were biological children and 176 were adopted children. Within the adopted group, 130 were black. The mean IQ of black and interracial children who had been adopted by advantaged white families was 106.3; in those children who had been adopted early in life, the mean IQ was even higher (110.4). "This mean represents an increase of 1 standard deviation above the average IQ of 90 usually achieved by black children reared in their own homes in the North Central Region '' (p. 736). These researchers conclude, ''If all black children had environments such as those provided by the adoptive families in this study, we would predict that their IQ scores would be 10-20 points higher than the scores are under current rearing conditions'' (p. 738).

HEREDITY, ENVIRONMENT, AND INTELLIGENCE

It is no accident that intelligence has been given a significant amount of attention over the life of psychology as a science. The roots of this interest go back at least as far as the early Greek philosophers; for example, Plato (428-348 B.C.) believed that rational thought, that is, the ability to reason logically and with dispassion, was the ultimate goal of human development. Plato also set the stage for the later separation of thinking (cognition) from feeling (affect) and the nature-nurture controversy. His ideas were extended by later theological concepts of instantaneous creation, which implied that all knowledge came from God, by Locke's beliefs that all knowledge came from sensation and thus intelligence resulted from environmental conditions that facilitated learning, and by Rousseau's idea that all development was internally regulated (i.e., genetically controlled), to mention only a few.

Indeed, Locke's belief that all knowledge was derived through sensing of the environment became the cornerstone of American political thought when it was translated into the view that ''all men are created equal,'' an idea that follows logically from the belief that all knowledge comes from experience. Today, the issue of human intelligence has brought developmental psychology into the political arena as a tool of social policy and planning, for example, as a means to determine the effectiveness of using federal monies to develop, implement, and maintain early intervention programs for children at risk for intellectual disability.

Nature vs. Nurture

According to the extreme nature position, intelligence is essentially determined by a combination of genetic factors and thus is fixed at the time of conception. Human consistency in the developmental patterns by which many behaviors are acquired lends support to the nature position by suggesting that development is a built-in unfolding process (often called maturation).

Recent expressions of the nature position with respect to intelligence have centered around the work of Jensen. Jensen (1969) discussed racial differences in intelligence, using as a basis his analysis of data from four studies of identical twins who had been raised apart. These studies included 122 such twins, some English (Burt, 1966; Shields, 1962), some American (Newman, Freeman, & Holzinger, 1937), and some Danish (Juel-Nielsen, 1965). The median correlation coefficient for the separated twins was 0.75. Using this figure, plus supporting data from other twin studies, Jensen proposed the now famous 80-20 hypothesis: about 80% of the total variability in intelligence test scores among the general population is attributable to genetic factors, leaving only about 20% associated with environmental factors.

Jensen also pointed out that children from the lower (mostly black) and middle (mostly white) classes did *not* differ in their ability to learn simple associative tasks (e.g., spelling and rote memorization), but they did differ significantly in their ability to master tasks requiring conceptual abilities (e.g., problem solving and abstract reasoning behaviors). Terming the first type as Level I learning and the second Level II learning, Jensen proposed that black children were as skillful as white children at Level I learning tasks, but were genetically inferior to white children on Level II tasks. He suggested that school curriculums be altered to reflect this difference and thus maximize their potential effectiveness.

More recently, Jensen (1977) was unable to find support for his nature views; instead, he found evidence for the environmentalists' position in his analysis of IQ scores of 826 blacks and 653 whites living in rural Georgia. Based on sibling comparisons, this analysis showed a significant decrement in verbal and nonverbal IQ between Kindergarten and Grade 12. These data support the environmentalists' "cumulative deficit" hypothesis, which explains the progressive decline in IQ with age as the result of a continued lack of necessary cognitive stimulation. Despite these findings and the serious charges that the late Cyril Burt, the English psychologist who reported much of the separated twins data discussed earlier, had falsified data (Kamin, 1977), Jensen (1980) has recently published a book aimed at more clearly establishing the validity of his nature position. The new work has received considerably less attention than Jensen's previous works.

The other end of the nature-nurture continuum is, of course, the extreme nurture position. Proponents of this position believe that all behavior, including intelligent behavior, results from environmental effects that "mold" the individual. This position, expressed most clearly in the behaviorism of John Watson and B.F. Skinner, resulted in psychologists' early interest in infant learning. If newborns could be conditioned, then such conditioning could be used to explain all development. To this end, Watson made child psychology the focal point in his efforts to reform psychology in general.

Data to support the environmentalists' position have been available for some time. In studies of children living in the Blue Ridge Mountains, both Wheeler (1932) and Sherman and Key (1932) found the average IQ levels to be lower in culturally isolated villages. Wheeler (1942) also studied children in a Tennessee community that was less isolated after the dam construction program of the Tennessee Valley Authority. Children living in this community now scored higher than had the children living there 10 years earlier. Likewise, Crissey (1937), Goldfarb (1945), Dennis and Najarian (1957), and Spitz (1946; Spitz & Wolff,

1946), among others, provided data showing the deleterious effects of institutionalization on intellectual development.

Just as the data showed negative effects of environmental deprivation on intellectual development, other data began to show the advantages of environmental stimulation. Wellman and her co-workers (1932a, 1932b, 1934, 1937, 1938; Crissey, 1937; Skeels, 1938; Skeels & Fillmore, 1937; Skeels, Updegraff, Wellman, & Williams, 1938; Wellman & Coffey, 1936), through a series of research reports, argued that young children whose environment was enriched (nursery school attendance) showed meaningful gains in measured intelligence. In her first report, Wellman (1932a) noted that the greatest gains in IQ were made by children whose initial IQs were below average (using today's terminology, such children would be termed at risk). Their average gain in IQ was 28 points, whereas the group of children who had been average in intelligence at the beginning gained only an average of 22 points and the children who had been above average in intellectual ability gained only an average of 12 points.

In a time when intelligence was viewed as a fixed trait, it was unlikely that the views of Wellman and others would go unchallenged. The challenges were many and sometimes very acerbic. A representative response was Goodenough's (1940) review of the nursery school studies. Goodenough charged that the gains shown in IQ scores were really not gains at all but rather were artifacts caused by the use of poor statistical methods. Recently, Longstreth (1981) has criticized Skeels' data once again, concluding that Skeels' 1966 follow-up study of the effects of early experience on intelligence is so flawed that nurture interpretation is not tenable.

Current research data seem to support Wellman's original findings. Belsky and Steinberg (1978) reviewed more than 40 well-designed studies of day-care effects. They conclude that attendance at a "good" day-care facility has positive effects for children who are at risk, probably by attenuating the declines in IQ that are typically found to occur in such groups after the 1st year of life. Belsky and Steinberg point out, however, that daycare appears to have neither positive nor negative effects for otherwise "normal" children. This latter conclusion must be qualified because nearly all the day-care facilities studied were well-funded university centers offering high-quality programs with an emphasis on cognitive stimulation. Very little is known about the effects of other types of day-care facilities.

Home Environment

Bloom (1964) reported evidence indicating that a significant amount of the variance in adult intelligence appears in the early years of childhood. In his analyses of longitudinal data, Bloom found no relationship between IQ at age 1 and at age 17. At age 2, the correlation was 0.41; by age 4, 0.71. Finally, by age 11, the correlation was 0.92. Obviously then, as Bloom's data implied, early home experiences are critical to later intellectual development. Since Bloom's initial report, a number of investigators have produced convincing evidence of a linkage between the quality of home stimulation received early in life and later intellectual or cognitive ability (Falender & Heber, 1975; McCall, Appelbaum, & Hogarty, 1973; Walberg & Marjoribanks, 1973).

Caldwell (1968) has compiled a list of environmental features that apparently contribute significantly to intellectual development. This list has been developed, standardized, and named the Inventory of Home Stimulation; it includes 45 items divided into the following subscales:

1. emotional and verbal responsivity of mother
2. avoidance of restriction and punishment
3. organization of the physical and temporal environment
4. provision of appropriate play materials
5. maternal involvement with child
6. opportunities for variety in daily stimulation

When this inventory is used, the items making up these six subscales are marked present or absent by a trained observer who either sees the behavior identified by an item or receives confirming information from the child's parent(s).

This inventory has provided valuable information about the importance of the infant's early home environment in subsequent measures of intelligence. For example, Elardo, Bradley, and Caldwell (1975) reported data on 77 normal infants, both boys and girls, blacks and whites, who were heterogeneous with respect to social class. The home environment of these infants was assessed when they were 6 months of age, and their mental ability was determined at 6 and 12 months (Bayley Scale) and again at 36 months (Stanford-Binet). Correlations were calculated between the Inventory of Home Stimulation scores and intelligence test scores. At 6 and 12 months, the correlations were not significant; by age 3, however, home environment variables appeared to be significant predictors of intelligence.

Bradley and Caldwell (1976) did a follow-up study on 49 of these same infants at 54 months. In this report, home environment scores, taken when the infants were 6 months of age and again when they were 2 years of age, were correlated with Stanford-Binet scores at 4½ years. As expected, the correlation between home environment scores at 2 years and Stanford-Binet scores at 4½ years was higher than the correlation between home environment at 6 months and Stanford-Binet scores at 4½ years. These data offer "evidence of a substantial relationship between the quality of stimulation available to the child during the first 2 years of life and IQ at age 4½" (p. 1173).

Ramey, Farran, and Campbell (1979) pointed out that findings such as those of Bradley and Caldwell are based on samples heterogeneous with respect to social class. In such a situation, the correlational relationship between home environment and child development may be attributable to other factors, such as differences in parental attitudes or home structure and organization. Therefore, these researchers essentially replicated some of the earlier studies, but used only infants from one social class. Their results indicate that "one can look within an apparently homogeneous social class group and predict the child's later intelligence . . . [and] . . . the level of predictability is remarkably high; one can account for between 50% and 65% of the variance in children's 36-month Stanford-Binet scores by knowing only information about their mothers' attitudes, behavior, and at-home interactions with the children when they were toddlers" (p. 812).

Twin Studies

Both environmentalists and nativists have relied on data from twin studies (especially those of identical twins raised apart) as support for their respective positions. Because monozygotic twins result from the splitting of one fertilized ovum, they contain identical genetic material. Dizygotic twins are not genetically identical; they develop from two separately fertilized eggs, but they share a uterine environment. Ordinary siblings share the properties of genetic material as do dizygotic twins, but differences in their environmental circumstances (e.g., changes in the family's composition and economic circumstances) preclude as much environmental similarity as found among dizygotic twins. Finally, unrelated individuals have no genes in common, so any similarities among them must arise from shared environmental influences. These four groups have been studied when reared together and when reared apart.

The correlations between the scores of monozygotic twins are the highest, regardless of type of rearing, followed in order by the correlations for dizygotic twins, siblings, and unrelated individuals. For the nativists, this is just the pattern expected; the greater the genetic similarity of two individuals, the higher the correlation between their IQs. It is not as readily apparent, however, that this is also the pattern predicted by degree of environmental similarity. Thus, environmentalists can use the same data to support their position.

Between these two extremes is the interactionist position. Very few scientists regard intelligent behavior as the product solely of either genetic inheritance or environmental experiences. Most agree that both factors are influential. Some, however, debate the relative contribution of each to development, with estimates of genetic control ranging from 80% to 45%. The former figure is Jensen's; the latter is Jencks' (1972). Jencks, who stresses gene-environment covariation, believes that heredity explains 45% of behavioral variability, environment accounts for 35%, and their covariation explains 20%. Lochlin, Lindzey, and Spuhler (1975) have reanalyzed Jencks' data and report figures of 60%, 25%, and 15% for heredity, environment, and gene-environment covariation, respectively.

CURRENT STATUS OF INTELLIGENCE

Research on intelligence has contributed greatly to current knowledge and understanding of human behavior. For example, a great deal is known about its heritability and modifiability, as well as the effect on it of such variables as social class or subculture membership. Unfortunately, because of the association of the concept with many other issues, the term *intelligence* has acquired an excess of meaning. As Horowitz and Dunn (1978) point out, intelligence has become a "positivistic nightmare." Intelligent behavior is too broad a domain to be adequately summarized by a global index, especially when there is still no agreement about what intelligence is.

One attempt to overcome some of the problems associated with the use of a global measure of human functioning focuses on a relatively new concept, that of competence (Ainsworth & Bell, 1973; Connolly & Bruner, 1973; Harter, 1978). White (1959) originally discussed the concept of competence as an outgrowth of such behaviors as visual exploration, grasping, and exploration and manipulation of the environment. This perspective holds promise, for it permits not only identification of relevant behaviors but also development of appropriate support systems to facilitate the growth of such behaviors.

THE NATURE OF COGNITION

Whereas those interested in intelligence per se focus on the outcome (i.e., the product), cognitive development researchers are more concerned with the processes involved in the acquisition of intelligence. Individuals are constantly demonstrating a variety of complex and interrelated cognitive activity as they attempt to identify and interpret experience. This activity includes the behaviors needed to comprehend, remember, and make "sense" of experiences. Experience, to make sense, must be broken into identifiable, meaningful, and manipulable information units. These information units must be interpreted within the framework of existing knowledge and retained in some retrievable form for later use. Consequently, a system of behaviors that allows the individual to maintain control is needed to coordinate cognitive behaviors to solve problems. For example, memory for a recently acquired piece of information (e.g., an unfamiliar telephone number) is very brief unless the individual makes an effort to retain it. One way to do this is to repeat continuously what was sensed. This rehearsal strategy is a cognitive control process aimed at retaining the telephone number as long as it is needed.

Cognition thus includes a complexly interrelated system of behaviors directed toward identifying, interpreting, organizing, retaining, retrieving, and applying information about experience with objects, words, ideas, and people. Cognitive behaviors determine the application of appropriate strategies to solving problems and attaining goals. Still other behaviors are cognitively relevant because they promote the development and mastery of further cognitive skills. Thus, in a global sense, cognition describes the *processes* associated with learning.

Cognitive Developmental Theory

Piaget has provided a comprehensive theory of cognitive development. He believed that intelligence evolved from simple sensory (e.g., visually tracking an object moving in space or turning toward a sound source) and motor (e.g., grasping or sucking) behaviors in interaction with environmental events. From this perspective, intellectual development is tied to neurological maturation (performance of sensory-motor behaviors) and to physical and social stimulation (environmental events) in which the individual's active exploratory behaviors play a part. Furthermore, intellectual or cognitive development is characterized by increasingly more sophisticated and efficient behavioral interaction. Reflexive physical behaviors become voluntary and give rise to symbolic mental behaviors. These, in turn, become progressively more organized and differentiated as logical mental or cognitive structures that are capable of processing environmental information at both concrete and increasingly more abstract levels are formed. Table 5-2 describes this sequence.

Piaget's observations are derived from his attempts to determine the process by which the ability to reason develops. He divides this process into four major periods of cognitive development. During each of these periods, the ability of a child to interpret, understand, and represent experience differs significantly. These three general classes of behaviors are the essential ingredients of all cognitive activity, which Piaget views as an attempt to adapt to environmental experiences by imposing structure on experience. This imposition of structure, with the help of environmental feedback, leads to comprehension. Consequently, increased knowledge of the world is derived from attempts to modify and refine existing knowledge. Human intelligence is thus seen as active and constructive.

The foundation for this view of intelligence rests in the notion of schemes. To Piaget (1976), schemes are basic cognitive units. They represent "what can be repeated and generalized in an action (e.g., the scheme is what is common in the actions of 'pushing' an object with a stick or any other instrument)" (p. 191). Schemes are thus structures used to interpret experience. Because individuals grow and develop in a variety of ways, so do schemes. Cognitive schemes presumably increase in sophistication and abstractness with age and experience, logically leading to more and more accurate interpretations (constructions) of experience (i.e., to more intelligent behavior).

Schemes emerge in early infancy as biologically programmed behaviors (i.e., reflexes). Reflex interactions with the environment result in the development of

Table 5-2 Piaget's Hierarchical Stages of Cognitive Development

10. PERIOD 4: FORMAL OPERATIONS (11 years on)	10. Able to think abstractly, formulate hypotheses, reason deductively, and evaluate solutions. Thought is organized into systems of knowledge.	
9. PERIOD 3: CONCRETE OPERATIONS (7-11 years)	9. Capable of concrete problem solving. Able to organize and classify information. Thought about real objects and events is logical and reversible.	
8. PERIOD 2: PREOPERATIONAL Intuitive Phase (4-7 years) 7. Preconceptual Phase (2-4 years)	8. Speech becomes more socialized. Reasoning is egocentric. Can solve problems but unable to explain how solution was derived.	7. Verbally expressive; uses repetitious speech patterns; frequent egocentric monologues occur.
6. PERIOD 1: SENSORIMOTOR Symbolic Representation (18-24 months) 5. Tertiary Circular Reactions (12-18 months)	6. Invents new means to solve problems through internal experimentation. Develops ability to represent objects and actions through primary imagery.	5. Begins to alter behavioral repertoire through trial-and-error experimentation. Becomes more sophisticated in locating hidden objects.
4. Coordination of Secondary Schemes (8-12 months) 3. Secondary Circular Reactions (4-8 months)	4. Begins to solve simple problems. Behavior becomes clearly intentional. "Object permanence."	3. Repeats chance behaviors that result in novel stimulation.
2. Primary Circular Reactions (1-4 months) 1. Reflexive (0-1 month)	2. Behaviors (sucking, opening and closing a fist, fingering a blanket) become repetitious.	1. Innate reflexes (unlearned responses) become more efficient.

Source: Adapted from *Understanding Children: Promoting Human Growth* by John W. McDavid & S. Gray Garwood. Copyright © 1978 by D.C. Heath and Company. Reprinted by permission of the publisher.

integrated patterns of sensory and motor responses. Early sensorimotor schemes are believed to be represented by physical, not mental, action. Gradually, in association with both maturational and experiential history, sensorimotor schemes become more mental, more cognitive. Cognitive schemes, then, are abstract mental structures, such as concepts.

Attempts to adapt to environmental experiences are aided by two complementary processes: assimilation and accommodation. Assimilation is the process by which new experiences are incorporated into the individual's fund of existing information. Piaget (1976) writes, "From a biological point of view, assimilation is the integration of external elements into evolving or completed structures of the organism. . . . Thus all the organism's reactions involve an assimilation process. . . . Assimilation is necessary in that it assures the continuity of structures and the integration of new elements to those structures" (pp. 170-171). Just as the assimilation of food involves a chemical transformation to enable the incorporation of this food into physical structures, assimilation of experience requires a psychological transformation to enable its incorporation into mental structures. Accommodation is the process by which accumulated experiences are adjusted to reflect new experiences being assimilated. "Biological assimilation . . . is never present without its counterpart, accommodation. . . . In the field of behavior we shall call accommodation any modification of an assimilatory scheme or structure by the elements it assimilates" (Piaget, 1976, pp. 171-172).

Assimilatory and accommodatory processes are reciprocal and inseparable, and they provide the basic mechanism for cognitive growth. Through their interplay, cognitive adaptation (growth or change) occurs. Piaget (1976) uses the term *equilibration* to describe this interplay: "it seems highly probable that the construction of structures is mainly the work of equilibration, defined not by balance between opposite forces but by self-regulation; that is, equilibration is a set of active reactions of the subject to external disturbances" (p. 200).

The overall direction of cognitive development is defined by a process termed *decentering,* the ability to shift one's point of view while processing information. This ability is the opposite of behaviors summarized by the term egocentrism. The egocentric individual is unable to interpret information from another's frame of reference. As children mature cognitively, they become less and less egocentric, eventually escaping the tendency to be held by their own unique assimilatory framework. This decentering process is important to overall cognitive growth because it leads to new ways of thinking and acting.

Piaget's Stage Theory

Piaget's model of development includes an elaborate account of four major developmental periods: (1) sensorimotor, (2) preoperational, (3) concrete operational, and (4) formal operational. In each of these periods, Piaget identifies particular cognitive structures that accompany thought and distinguish one period of intellectual development from another. At the same time, Piaget describes the overall course of cognitive development across the four periods. The first two periods encompass the preschool years.

The Sensorimotor Period

During the first few years of life, cognitive development is based primarily on physical action. Despite this apparent simplicity, development during the sensorimotor period is sufficiently complex to entail six descriptive substages. Their sequence is considered invariant because the competencies that emerge during each are prerequisites for the next.

Stage One: Reflexive Activity (Birth to about 1 Month). At birth, infants possess a variety of reflex behaviors, including sucking, swallowing, crying, and movements of the body and eyes. Throughout the 1st month, the exercise of these reflexive behaviors organizes them into crude schemes. Their use does not show intelligence, however, as they are used primarily to assimilate experience without making the accommodations necessary for adaptation. This first sensorimotor stage is important because these crude schemes become the foundation for subsequent cognitive development.

Stage Two: Primary Circular Reactions (About 1 to 4 Months). Attempts to adapt to experience are first observed in Stage Two and essentially act as the defining property of this stage. Among the more significant adaptations is the coordination and integration of previously independent schemes, which enables the infant to control actions in order to look at what is heard, suck what is grasped, and eventually to reach for what is seen. This coordination of schemes occurs as a result of circular reactions. In general, these are action sequences that produce interesting stimulation and therefore tend to be repeated. Such repetition leads to scheme differentiation, consolidation, and generalization; cognitive growth follows.

Primary circular reactions are typically more reflexive than voluntary, and the behavioral sequences are focused on the infant's body, such as sucking or grasping behaviors. Bodily actions are more likely to trigger primary circular reactions than are external environmental events. Although infants do indeed notice interesting events in their environment, they usually cannot reproduce them because they do not have the necessary response skills (coordinated schemes such as visually directed reaching).

Stage Three: Secondary Circular Reactions (About 4 to 8 Months). The accomplishment of eye-hand coordination during Stage Two contributes to a major cognitive breakthrough. Infants begin to shift their attention to effects their responses have on their external environment. Stage Three is thus characterized by infants' first attempts to consolidate and coordinate responses to produce interesting environmental effects. As in the previous stage, these effects first occur accidentally and attempts to reproduce them evoke secondary circular reactions, which are voluntarily initiated behavior sequences focused away from the body. Schemes produced in this context represent infants' habitual patterns of responding toward particular events (consolidation of schemes) and are not yet schemes used intentionally to adapt to new experiences.

Stage Four: Coordination of Secondary Schemes (About 8 to 12 Months). Stage Four marks the emergence of intentional, goal-directed behavior. Infants in this stage begin to anticipate external events that occur independently of their own behavior and to adapt more effectively to new and unfamiliar experiences. These accomplishments result from the infant's ability to coordinate the secondary schemes that developed in the previous stage into meaningful combinations for attaining goals, solving problems, and adapting to new experiences.

Stage Five: Tertiary Circular Reactions (About 12 to 18 Months). Tertiary circular reactions occur when familiar responses applied to new objects produce unexpected effects. This event stimulates the infant to explore the new objects. In doing so, the infant repeatedly contacts the objects, varying the form of response each time, and adopts what Flavell (1977) calls a "let's-see-what-would-happen-if" attitude, applying a flexible and varied means-end sequence of behaviors. As a consequence of tertiary circular reactions, infants actively investigate new means; they are more attuned to the properties of objects and accommodate their responses to them more readily.

Stage Six: Invention of New Means through Mental Combinations (About 18 to 24 Months). Stage Six is marked by a dramatic change. Infants begin to represent experiences symbolically, which is necessary for the invention of new schemes through mental combinations. Mental representation liberates infants from the cognitive limitations imposed by the immediate practical experience of objects and events and enables them to use knowledge gained from prior experience even without a direct external referent to the experience.

The advent of symbolic images is facilitated by infants' increased ability to distinguish between environmental signals (signs) contained in immediate experience and their own actions. As a direct consequence, infants show more interest in accommodating to the properties of objects and events as they exist rather than simply extracting sufficient information from this experience to allow the application of a familiar response scheme. This direct attention to objects and events helps infants develop stable perceptual schemes for representing experience, leading ultimately in Stage Six to the ability to evoke images of the objects or events in their absence. In addition, infants in this stage can respond to, manipulate, and transform such images as cognitive contents in their own right. This accomplishment frees infants from the limitations of direct perception; they can now relate knowledge obtained from prior experience to the present with more flexibility. The evolution of this representational ability is paralleled by developments in the areas of imitation and play.

Object Permanence. During the sensorimotor period, several fundamental concepts emerge; one especially important is that of object permanence. Table 5-3 outlines the changes that occur over the six sensorimotor stages as infants come to understand the concept of object permanence. Piaget's observations of infants' reactions to disappearing objects indicates that, before approximately 8 months of age, "out of sight" is literally "out of mind." Not until that time do infants actively search for hidden objects. Even at Stages Four and Five, there are limitations to infants' concept of object permanence. In Piaget's classic experiment, for example, an interesting object (e.g., keys, a watch, a novel toy) is placed before an infant and then, as the child watches, is completely covered by a cloth. Beginning about Stage Four, infants remove the cloth and retrieve the object. If, after hiding the object, the experimentor moves it (in full view of the infant) to a second hiding place (visible displacement), Stage Four infants return to the first hiding place to look for the object. When they discover that the object is not there, they cease their search. Only at Stage Five are infants capable of following visible displacements of the object and looking where it was last hidden.

During Stage Five, the limitations imposed by the object permanence concept can still be observed when an object is hidden through a series of invisible, rather than visible, displacements. If an object is hidden in one place and then moved in such a way that the infants cannot see that it has been moved, infants search for the object only where they actually saw it hidden. Not until Stage Six, when infants are capable of representing an object symbolically, do they maintain the search despite invisible displacement; this persistent search indicates their recognition that the object continues to exist. From Stage Six onward, children possess a mature concept of object permanence. As an additional consequence of their understanding of object permanence, infants begin to see themselves as objects in a world of objects; this differentiation is associated with their subsequent development of a self-concept.

Piaget's ideas about the concept of object permanence have generated considerable research and debate. Support for Piaget has been found in human infants' sensorimotor behavior (Kopp, Sigman, & Parmelee, 1974; Uzgiris & Hunt, 1974) and among lower order animals, such as kittens (Gruber, Girgus, and Banuazizi, 1971), squirrel monkeys (Vaughter, Smotherman, & Ordy, 1972), and rhesus monkeys (Wise, Wise, & Zimmerman, 1974). Bower's (1974) research with 20-, 40-, 80-, and 100-day-old infants offers the strongest counterargument. Bower propped up these infants before a screen that could move to reveal a brightly

Table 5-3 Stages in the Development of Object Permanence Concept

Stage One *(Birth-1 month)*	*Stage Two* *(1-4 months)*	*Stage Three* *(4-8 months)*	*Stage Four* *(8-12 months)*
No sense that objects exist when not immediately perceived; "out of sight, out of mind"; objects are fleeting sensations	Possibly, aborted attempts to preserve or reproduce interesting events (primary circular reactions) by looking, listening, etc.	Movements of objects anticipated, and brief searches made for objects that escape their grasp; deferred circular reaction: infants may abandon activity with an object, then rediscover it soon afterward; reach for partially hidden object (recognize object based on only a small part of it)	Active searches made for hidden objects (initially, only if they are in the process of reaching when it disappears); later, obstacles removed to find hidden objects

Stage Five *(12-18 months)*	*Stage Six* *(18-24 months)*
Hidden objects sought where they were last seen, even though objects were moved through a series of displacements to different hiding places before infants can initiate their search; possible only when these displacements are in full view	Persistence in search for hidden objects that have been displaced invisibly (search sustained although infants do not know where objects were hidden); full notion of object permanence, since they recognize that objects exist somewhere

colored ball. The screen covered the ball for one of several time limits: 1.5, 3, 7.5, and 15 seconds. On one-half the trials, the ball was visible when the screen moved away; on the remaining one-half, it was not visible.

Bower reasoned that infants who possessed some concept of object permanence would not be surprised when the screen moved and the ball was visible again. On the other hand, if the screen moved and the ball had disappeared, these infants' faces would show surprise. The reverse was predicted if the infants lacked an idea of object permanence. Bower's results indicated that age and exposure time are critical. After the 1.5-second time period, all age groups were surprised if the ball had disappeared; none were surprised if it was still there. After 15 seconds, however, the youngest were surprised if the ball reappeared, but the oldest expected the ball to be there. Bower concluded in this study that other factors, such as memory span, affect the display of object permanence in infants.

More recently, Bower (1979) added the lack of motor skills as a limitation on the development of the object permanence concept. Traditional Piagetian assessment approaches (e.g., searching for hidden objects) require motor behavior (e.g., reaching under or inside) that is not effectively in use until the fourth sensorimotor stage. Bower and Wishart (1972) showed babies as young as 4 months of age a toy (held in front of them) but turned out the lights before the infants could reach for it. These babies, even after a 90-second interval, reached for the toy, even though they literally could not see it. Cowan (1978) suggests that turning off the lights reduces an infant's processing load. In darkness, the infant no longer need coordinate present visual perceptions (the object gone) with past representations (the object present); this load reduction may make it easier for the infant to represent the absent object and thus reach for it earlier than predicted by Piaget.

Consensus. In general, psychologists agree with Piaget's description of the sequential nature of sensorimotor developments. When differences occur, they tend to involve mediating factors, such as task characteristics, memory span, processing load, or dependence on other related, but as yet insufficiently developed behaviors. It may be true, as Scarr-Salapatek (1976) notes, that sensorimotor development is nearly universal since the pattern of skills called sensorimotor evolved earlier in our primate past. She writes, "I would agree that the genetic preadaptation in sensorimotor intelligence is a strong bias toward learning the typical schemes of infancy and toward combining them in innovative flexible ways" (p. 186).

The Preoperational Period (About 2 to 7 Years of Age)

Beginning about age 2, children begin to incorporate their new representational skills into efficient patterns of interaction. In order to accomplish this task, they must translate sensorimotor knowledge into an equivalent symbolic mode, as schemes of mental actions, a translation that leads to the acquisition of mental concepts. Concepts provide structure for understanding experience; they make it possible to respond to the common elements within a particular concept. Therefore, knowledge abstracted from experience with specific objects or events can be generalized at a conceptual level to similar objects or events, and this gives mental activity much greater efficiency.

The child's emerging use of symbols to represent experience enables movement to a new level of understanding. Flavell (1977) has detailed the many advantages of symbolic representational intelligence. These are contrasted with the action-based sensorimotor intelligence in the following:

Sensorimotor Intelligence	*Symbolic-Representational Intelligence*
Slow, step by step, one action at a time	Faster, more flexible
Oriented toward actions and concrete, practical results	Interested in knowledge per se, concerned with information and truth
Concrete and earthbound	Potentially abstract, "free to soar"
Present-oriented	Can begin to think about own thoughts
Private, idiosyncratic, uncommunicable	Can make use of socially shared symbol system and can communicate with and become socialized by others

Young children's concepts are usually unstable and inconsistent. For example, they seem to be unable to classify objects or events consistently. When confronted with a task that requires sorting various objects according to shape, size, or color into appropriate groups, young children may instead create pictures with the shapes or may start applying a rule but then forget to use it consistently in the sorting process. This instability is also reflected in their inability to recognize that some properties of objects remain the same even when the objects are changed in outward appearances. For example, a 3-year-old may have trouble recognizing his mother after she has dressed up for a very fancy party. Likewise, some young children may believe that if they dress and act like boys, they are boys, and vice versa. In other words, young children fail to recognize that objects have an inherent identity that is unchanged by perceivable transformations.

Because their perceptual framework is unstable, young children's understanding of their experience is poorly organized, often chaotic, and unstructured. This lack of organization is reflected in their own style of reasoning, transductive reasoning. Because they cannot abstract general principles from particular experiences and thus cannot anticipate particular experiences based on an understanding of general principles, children in the preoperational period cannot reason either inductively or deductively. Instead, they tend to interpret an experience according to their perception of its similarities to other experiences. They assume that, if two experiences are alike in one way, they must be alike in all ways; this results in errors in logical thinking, as is illustrated by the following newspaper story:

> My young grandchildren, dressed in their best, were walking on the beach at Destin, Fla., for the first time. The sand there is extra white and fine.
>
> Beth, intrigued, asked why the sand squeaked under their feet.
>
> "Silly!" responded David, 5, disdainfully, "Don't you know why? It's because the sand is made out of Sunday School shoes."
>
> (*Times-Picayune,* New Orleans, La., May 29, 1977)

David was wearing his white "Sunday School" shoes, which, since rarely worn, probably squeaked. Because the sand at this beach also "squeaked" when he walked on it and was also very white, David's response was logical to him; however, it was just another in a multitude of "cute" sayings by young children as far as most adults are concerned.

These children are characterized by their seemingly endless string of who, what, where, when, and why questions. This behavior makes sense in view of the fact that such children have difficulty understanding and explaining things on their own. Because their abilities to manipulate their experiences mentally are inadequate, they depend on others for explanations. The answers they receive are assimilated if the information is comprehensible to them; in this way, young children gradually accommodate mental schemes that fit closer to reality.

A major characteristic of preoperational thought is its egocentric nature. Piaget believes that a child lacks the ability to recognize that other people differ not only from each other but also from the child in their needs, desires, thoughts, and feelings. This lack of awareness of others' points of view limits the degree of sensitivity with which young children are able to adjust their own actions to correspond effectively with what others are doing, saying, or feeling. According to Brainerd (1978), "any behavior that suggests children are preoccupied with themselves and/or unconcerned with things going on around them may be termed egocentric" (p. 103).

Piaget used the mountain problem, a perspective-taking task, to assess egocentrism. In the original version, there were three mountains of different heights. First, a child stands, observing this display. Next, a doll is placed at various locations around the table, as part of a "game." The child's task is to tell the experimenter what the doll "sees" by selecting from several photographs taken from different perspectives. Piaget's data revealed that children in the preoperational period usually do not select the correct picture if the doll's perspective is different from their own. Consequently, Piaget concluded that these children are not fully capable of understanding that others can have points of view that are different from their own. In other words, they have difficulty taking the role of another.

Piaget calls the first part of the preoperational period (from 2 to 4 years of age) the preconceptual subperiod; the later part (from 4 to 7 years of age), the intuitive subperiod. Piaget believes that children in the intuitive subperiod are so certain of their knowledge that they draw general conclusions, even though they are unaware of how they know what they know and see no need to justify conclusions to themselves or to others. When asked "why," they tend to assume the way things appear is the way things are and thus will usually answer such a question with "just because."

Children in the intuitive phase of preoperational thought are more sophisticated in using concepts. They can apply stable mental schemes to their representations of experience more readily, and their classification of experience into related clusters is now more flexible, as indicated by their ability to classify the same objects or events consecutively into different conceptual clusters. Differences between preconceptual and intuitive thought are summarized in the following:

Preconceptual Thought (Approximately Ages 2 to 4)	*Intuitive Thought (Approximately Ages 4 to 7)*
The child is characteristically self-centered (egocentric) in relating to the world and is typically one-dimensional, simplistic, and egocentric in cognitive functioning.	The child is characterized by greater maturity in categorization (narrower and more refined classification schemes) and decentering (less egocentric and therefore better able mentally to shift consideration from one aspect of an event to another); concepts become more complex, multidimensional, and relative.

Even with advances in conceptualization, however, preoperational intuitive thought is still limited, as indicated by the difficulty these children have in resolving a conflict between their immediate perceptions of an object or event and their understanding of what they experience. Because children in the preoperational period appear to be unable to coordinate mental representations of experience systematically with their concepts for classifying this experience, they tend to be dominated by perceptions, and these perceptions can distort reality so that relevant information goes unnoticed.

In summary, preoperational thought (1) is grounded in the perceived appearance of immediate experience, and perceptions are integrated (often inaccurately so) as a reliable representation of reality; (2) is characterized by attempts to solve problems on the basis of information derived from immediate experience, resulting in a concentration on static end states with little attention to the nature of changes leading to the end state; (3) reflects a lack of flexibility in the deployment of attention; (4) consists of isolated, uncoordinated, and irreversible mental actions; and (5) is considered egocentric and not subject to reflection (i.e., children are not aware of their own thoughts as possible objects of thought and consequently cannot adequately justify their conclusions and interpretations of experience).

Such a view of the child in the preoperational period may, at first, appear fairly negative, for the child appears to be cognitively inept. This is so, however, only in comparison to the relatively more sophisticated child in the later stages of development. When compared with the child in the sensorimotor period, the child in the preoperational period is quite cognitively adept. Consequently, arguments that contemporary research presents a bleak picture of preschool children (Gelman, 1978) would be true only if the acquisition of cognitive skills were an all or none proposition.

Just as the concept of object permanence has been emphasized in sensorimotor research efforts, much preoperational research effort has been focused on Piaget's concept of egocentrism, especially on communicative egocentrism. Piaget (1969, 1926) proposed that, since preoperational thought was characterized by egocentrism, the communicative abilities of children in this period would also be marred by egocentric responding, termed *egocentric speech*. Many investigators have offered research support for Piaget's views. For example, Flavell and his colleagues (Flavell, Botkin, Fry, Wright, & Jarvis, 1968) pointed out that "intellectual egocentrism is fundamentally an inability to take roles; it is an inability . . . to search out the role attributes of others, compare them with one's own, and make effective use of the comparison in any of a variety of adaptations" (p. 17). These investigators, using several role-taking tasks, found general support for the view that both role taking and communicative ability increase with age. In this report, Flavell and co-workers proposed a taxonomy of role-taking behavior by which they attempt to explain the development of children's ability to infer about others. The proposed components include

- existence: general awareness that different perspectives exist
- need: recognition of the usefulness of the awareness of differing perspectives
- prediction: ability to infer others' task-relevant responses
- maintenance: ability to hold such inferences over time
- application: ability to apply this awareness as needed in a given situation

Other researchers (Maratsos, 1973; Menig-Peterson, 1975; Shatz & Gelman, 1973) have reported evidence of substantial role-taking ability in younger children, a finding inconsistent with Piaget's views. Shatz and Gelman, for example, used as a measure of nonegocentric behavior the young child's ability to adjust syntax complexity when talking to younger and older listeners about a familiar item, such as a toy. They found that 4-year-olds used simple and short messages when communicating to 2-year-olds, but relied on longer and more complex messages with older individuals. Likewise, Menig-Peterson found that preschoolers modified their communication behavior to take into account a listener's perspective. If the children were aware that the listener had not been present when the event they were describing occurred, they would include more information, presumably to ensure the listener's understanding.

Such differential outcomes have typically been attributed to differences either in competence or in performance ability. Those who hold a competence view believe that failure of younger children to show nonegocentric behavior is due to the lack of some necessary skill or concept (i.e., lack of object permanence concept explains failure to search for objects removed from sight). Those who hold a performance view, however, explain such a failure by pointing to such factors as task difficulty or lack of experience with relevant task items. Flavell and Wohlwill (1969) have addressed this issue directly by distinguishing between two determinants of a child's performance on a cognitive task. One determinant is the probability that the necessary cognitive operation is fully formed and functioning (competence); the other depends on the task attributes and is the conditional probability that the task will evoke the required cognitive operation (performance).

Research workers are increasingly relying on a performance interpretation (Borke, 1975, 1977; Chandler & Greenspan, 1972; Gelman, 1978; Rubin & Maioni, 1975). For these and other researchers, failure at tasks measuring nonegocentrism is due more to performance factors, such as difficulty level, than to (in this case) presence of the concept. While Piaget argues for a competence view, finding that young children below age 5 consistently fail at such tasks, these performance researchers contend that, when the task difficulty is adjusted, even 3-year-olds show an awareness of others' points of view. As Gelman (1978) has stated,

> It seems that . . . the preschooler can and does take the perspectives of others into account. But how do we reconcile recent findings with the earlier data that suggest the opposite? First, it no longer seems appropriate to characterize the thought of preschoolers as egocentric. Such a global characterization is contradicted by the evidence at hand, evidence which leads me to conclude that the very young child typically attempts to take his listeners' perspectives into account. If the task is simple enough . . . then the young child's nonegocentric abilities will show through. If, on the other hand, the child has to deal with just-learned materials, just-acquired responses, emerging concepts or not-yet-developed concepts, or unavailable strategies, the coordinated demands of this task will surely overload his processing capacities, and, likely as not, lead him to fail. By such a view, perspective-taking abilities become better and better with experience, the acquisition of knowledge in a variety of domains, and sheer practice. It is not an ability that is first absent and then present. It is an ability that continues to develop into adulthood. (p. 319)

Additional support for the performance interpretation has been provided by Ford (1979), who investigated the construct validity of egocentrism. He interprets his data as *not* supporting the validity of egocentrism as a useful behavioral construct. Ford organized measures of egocentrism into three general categories: (1) visual and spatial (e.g., the three mountains task), (2) affective (e.g., judging how others feel in different situations), and (3) cognitive and communicative (e.g., inferring others' thoughts, motives, or intentions). Ford concludes from his analysis:

> Visual/spatial, affective, and cognitive/communicative perspective taking measures do not appear to tap a single unitary dimension of egocentrism. Measures of egocentrism are typically as highly correlated with other constructs (i.e. IQ, conservation, and popularity) as they are with measures of the same construct. . . . For all the measures purporting to measure egocentrism, task specific and response specific characteristics may account for a large proportion of the variance in performance. . . . Taken as a whole, the evidence . . . fails to support the construct validity of egocentrism. (pp. 1183-1184)

Concrete Operational Thought Period (About 7 to 12 Years of Age)

The third period of cognitive development, the concrete operational thought period, is characterized by reliance on more organized and coherent cognitive systems (operations) for acting on the world. "Operations are a continuation of actions; they express . . . forms of coordination which are general to all actions" (Inhelder & Piaget, 1959, p. 172). In the sensorimotor period, the child acted on the world physically. In the preoperational period, physical actions were replaced by internalized actions (thought). Now these internalized actions become integrated into organized and coherent systems of actions, called cognitive or logical operations. Brainerd (1978) has identified the following characteristics of operations.

1. Operations are mental, representing internalized behaviors.
2. Mental operations develop from action, usually according to the following sequence: (a) the child first develops a particular ability, which (b) becomes generalized and stable through use, and ultimately (c) becomes internalized as a mental representation, a cognitive scheme.
3. Operations obey certain logical (and abstract) rules, such as reversibility (the ability to reverse thought mentally). Some systems of operations can be used to reverse the effects of others. Reversibility of operations by negation requires the application of an exactly opposite mental operation; reversibility by compensation requires the application of a completely different mental operation to nullify the action of another mental operation.

4. Operations become organized into integrated *structures d'ensemble* (structures of the whole); logical and coherent mental thought depends on these structures acting in concert.

Operations may be thought of as similar to explanatory concepts or principles; they are integrated systems for mentally representing actions. Operations identify the rules governing relationships between concepts and their application. "A useful rule of thumb," suggests Flavell (1963), "is to say that all the actions implied in common mathematical symbols like $+$, $-$, $\div$, $>$, $<$, etc., belong to, but do not exhaust the domain of what [Piaget] terms *intellectual operations*" (p. 166).

There are two major types of operations: (1) logico-arithmetic, used to act on discrete data, and (2) spatial, used to act on continuous data. Logico-arithmetic operations include conservation, relations, and classification.

Conservation refers to the ability to comprehend that quantitative relationships between two objects are not changed by perceptual transformations of one of the objects. For example, when two pencils of equal length are arranged in parallel form, such as ═══, and then are transformed into ‾‾‾ ___, there has been no change in the length of the two pencils. Children in the preoperational period are likely, however, to focus only on the end state of this transformation and view one pencil as now longer than the other.

Piaget describes three levels in the development of conservation. At first, children do not conserve at all; they are misled by irrelevant perceptual transformations. Next, they sometimes do and sometimes do not conserve. For example, they may conserve if the perceptual transformation is rather slight, but fail to conserve if the transformation becomes greater. Finally, children learn not only to conserve but also to predict conservation before an irrelevant transformation has occurred. Because the first level corresponds to the preoperational period, preschool or kindergarten children would not be expected to conserve. The second level parallels the transition between preoperational and concrete operational functioning. Thus, most children around age 6 are likely to conserve if the transformation is small but not if it is major. Children at the third level of conservation, those in the later elementary grades (ages 7 or 8 and over), would be expected to conserve and to predict conservation. Because reversibility is necessary to solve conservation tasks, the ability to reverse thought mentally is also a characteristic of concrete operational thought.

The cognitive structures required to comprehend asymmetrical relations are seriation, multiple seriation, and transitive inference. To seriate, a child must be able to order a set of objects on the basis of only one asymmetrical transitive relation (e.g., arrange block buildings in order of their increasing height). Multiple seriation involves ordering a set of objects by two symmetrical transitive relations at the same time, forming a matrix. In both examples a transitive inference has occurred when a child understands that A > C, after being given the premise that A > B and B > C. Likewise, transitive inference is required to solve such problems as "If Karen's hair is lighter than Susan's but darker than Lisa's, who has the darkest hair"?

Relational concepts also progress through three levels. In the preoperational period, children are at the first level and are unable to comprehend relational tasks. On a seriation problem, for example, these children may be able to construct a few pairwise sets, but they will fail to order all elements in a series. Again, the second level parallels the transition from preoperational to concrete operational thought; it is characterized by an increasing ability to order along a single dimension, although children at this transitional level are unable to coordinate two dimensions effectively in problem solving. Finally, at the third level, children are able to solve all three relational problems.

Membership in a set is described by classification operations, that is, abilities to sort objects into two or more classes or categories. Classification can vary along dimensions also. One-dimensional classification involves sorting objects into a class or category on the basis of a single dimension, such as color, size, or texture. Multiple classification involves sorting on the basis of two dimensions simultaneously, such as color and size, or size and texture. It is also necessary to recognize the superordinate and subordinate aspects of categories, for example, that green grapes and blue grapes are subordinate sets of the class grape or that chocolate chip cookies and Oreo cookies are members of the general class cookie.

Spatial operations are primarily geometrical, focusing on topological and Euclidean concepts. Topological concepts concern proximity, openness, separation, succession, enclosure, and connectedness, whereas Euclidean concepts are used to relate distances. Spatial operations develop over two invariant stages. The first parallels preoperational thought; the second, concrete thought. Piaget believes that children understand topological concepts during the first stage and master Euclidean concepts during the second.

Concrete operational thought allows children to execute mental actions by identifying in advance the operations needed to solve a problem. More attention is paid to task demands, and appearances are no longer deceptive. At this stage, children are able to see that situations are not always as simple as they seem on the surface; apparent discrepancies in momentary experiences can be accounted for and resolved by new understanding of ways to change experience through overt and mental actions.

Concrete operational thought is based in rules. As children become aware of these rules, they can apply them to new situations and direct their mental actions in conformance with these rules. At the simplest level, rules define the operation of isolated mental actions. Objects and events and their more abstract dimensional properties can now be relegated to functional categories according to these rules. At higher levels, rules describe how categories or concepts can be altered, not only to provide for either more general or more specific concepts, but also to generate a hierarchy of conceptual relationships. For example, at the simplest level, children learn that 1 + 4 = 5, that 2 + 6 = 8, or that 5 − 2 = 3. At higher levels, children learn that adding more elements to a set increases set size, just as abstracting elements decreases set size. Functioning at this higher level is more efficient. Such a rule generalizes to both physical and social situations. Thus, rules contribute to more stable and integrated thought.

In summary, mental actions in concrete operational thought are reversible, and children are less likely to be confused by the perceived appearance of immediate experience. Children in the concrete operational thought period can decenter their attention and, consequently, can more flexibly consider relevant information. Likewise, egocentrism becomes even less pronounced. Despite these advances, however, concrete thought is still grounded in the concrete reality of experience; reasoning about problem situations begins with information derived from experience, although this information is coordinated to produce a general conclusion. Thus, mental actions during this period are restricted to manipulating relationships between concepts or objects and events in immediate experience. Finally, the conclusions and interpretations made by children during this period are justified in terms of their factual relationships to reality. These children state their conclusions in terms of concrete explanatory concepts or propositions that can be verified.

Most of the research in this area has focused on Piaget's claims about conservation, relations, and classification, and the evidence is generally supportive. For example, Uzgiris (1964) studied the acquisition of conservation of quantity, weight, and volume concepts and found evidence to support Piaget's belief regarding invariant sequencing in the acquisition of these concepts. Similar support can be found in the longitudinal investigation of conservation skills by Almy, Chittenden, and Miller (1966) and in the longitudinal investigation of seriation, conservation, and class inclusion tasks by Little (1972). More recently, Tomlinson-Keasey and her colleagues (Tomlinson-Keasey, Eisert, Kahle, Hardy, & Keasey, 1978) have conducted a 4-year longitudinal investigation, tracing the development of concrete thought abilities in 68 children, using the following tasks: seriation, numeration, class inclusion, hierarchical classification, and conservation of mass, weight, and volume. These children were tested five times over the course of 3 years. The researchers found that steady advances in the use of concrete reasoning were made by these children on all tasks over the 3-year period. However, the rate of growth was not very smooth. According to Tomlinson-Keasey and associates,

> As a group, there are rather remarkable increases in the percentage of children who achieve concrete operational skills between Waves 1 and 2 in Conservation of Mass and Conservation of Weight. There are minimal changes on all dimensions from Wave 2 to Wave 3. Between

> Waves 3 and 4 there is another large increase in the percentage of concrete operational responses to all tasks, and this seems to remain relatively unchanged during the last year of the study. (p. 12)

Since, in Piaget's theory, development is considered an upward progression through a series of sequential stages, regression downward over time would place the adequacy of the theory in doubt. Longitudinal data enable the analysis of possible regressive trends. As Tomlinson-Keasey and colleagues (1978) point out,

> Although some vacillation of responses might be predicted during the acquisition period, once subjects have reached a concrete operational level, their responses should stabilize. In . . . three years . . . , subjects regressed only 12 times after they had given a concrete operational response. Overall then, it seems that subjects who show mastery of a skill at the concrete operational level in either classification or conservation seldom regress. (p. 14)

Just as Bower's (1979) work on object permanence calls into question the reliability of the postulated age range within which this concept is acquired, there have been criticisms of conservation theory along similar lines. Elkind (1967) pointed out that the typical conservation of number task, for example, actually requires two different kinds of knowledge: (1) awareness that the number of objects in the transformed row has not been changed by the perceptual illusion (quantitative identity) and (2) awareness that the two rows still contain equal numbers (quantitative equivalence). Since Piaget's theory stresses quantitative identity, Elkind wished to make clear that an understanding of identity was probably necessary for solution of the equivalence portion and that a type of transitive inference must be added to the identity component in order for the child to be correct on this task. ''Given the need for this additional deductive step, it may be that the equivalence task underestimates the child's actual ability to conserve'' (Miller, 1977, p. 181).

A number of studies have been conducted to compare the relative difficulty of identity and equivalence tasks, with mixed results (for a brief review, see Miller, 1977). Miller (1977) points out that there are at least two ways that equivalence and identity tasks differ:

> First, the perceptual pull toward non-conservation is . . . greater for equivalence than for identity. In the former . . . the child is confronted with two perceptually discrepant stimuli at the time of the conservation question, whereas in the latter . . . only one stimulus is present. The nonconservation illusion on an identity trial is dependent on the child's comparison of the transformed stimulus with his *memory* of the stimulus prior to the transformation.

> The other difference . . . concerns the number of questions asked. An identity test requires just one question, after the stimulus has been transformed. An equivalence test typically involves two questions: a pretransformation . . . and a posttransformation question. (p. 182)

Miller has examined the influence of these two variables, using 64 lower middle-class white kindergarten children. Each child was tested for the ability to conserve number and liquid quantity. Within each concept, ability was assessed on an identity problem containing only one stimulus, on one with two perceptually discrepant stimuli, and on an equivalence problem. Also, 50% of the children were asked one question, and 50% were asked two questions. Correct conservation judgments were slightly more frequent in the two-question condition, but this was not statistically significant. There were also no significant differences that could be attributed to type of conservation (number vs. liquid quantity) or to sex. Miller's major finding was that there was no evidence to indicate that identity tasks were easier than equivalence tasks. Thus, Miller rejects the view that "the use of the equivalence paradigm may seriously underestimate the child's ability to conserve" (p. 188).

Research into classification behavior is also generally supportive of Piaget's theory. Using a cross-sectional approach, Hooper and his colleagues (Hooper, Sipple, Goldman, & Swinton, 1974) gave classification, multiple classification, and class inclusion tests to nearly 300 children, aged 4 to 13. These researchers verified Piaget's claims that children first understand classification, then multiple classification and class inclusion. Surprisingly, and counter to theory, they found that an understanding of class inclusion, instead of appearing with multiple classification ability, followed it.

Research examining children's understanding of relations has focused on transitive inference ability. Some years ago, Braine (1959) suggested that Piaget's transitivity tests measured, in addition, children's language ability, memory, and their ability to resist visual illusions. Several studies have since examined Braine's contention and have found that controlling these extra-performance variables reduces the age at which children master transitivity to about age 5, into the intuitive preoperational period (Brainerd & Van Den Heuvel, 1974; Roodin & Gruen, 1970; Toniolo & Hooper, 1975). Thus, some researchers, notably Brainerd (1978), believe that research in this area does not support Piagetian theory. However, these countertheory findings were generated by research efforts that really resulted from a different strategy than was originally applied. It is likely, then, that some of these nonsupportive findings may be due to differences in research strategy (oversimplification) and not necessarily to errors in theory per se. (See Larsen, 1977, for a succinct criticism of such sequencing and simplification efforts.)

While not without its problems or its critics, Piaget's cognitive developmental theory has been and continues to be very useful, not only in furthering the understanding of normal cognitive development, but also in aiding efforts to assess and intervene in development. It has spawned various useful intellectual assessment strategies, e.g., the 1974 Uzgiris-Hunt Scale, curriculum intervention strategies (Dunst, 1981), and intervention models. Recently, Flavell (1982) has reevaluated Piaget's contributions and concludes that Piaget's stage theory of cognitive development should not be abandoned; instead, he argues that probably there "is something general-stage-like about the child's cognitive development, if only we knew how and where to look" (p. 9).

INFORMATION-PROCESSING APPROACHES TO COGNITION

Instead of focusing on the development of cognition, many researchers have focused on the cognitive processes used to translate incoming sensory information into some form of behavior. With this approach, cognitive activity includes those behaviors that enable individuals to attend to sensory stimulation; to transform this stimulation into mental symbols; to store these symbols in memory; to alter, combine and recombine, synthesize, integrate, and otherwise manipulate this stored information together with other information; and ultimately to act on this experience in some way (e.g., by thinking, expressing a thought, showing a preference, moving the body). This information-processing approach to explaining cognitive activity is summarized in Figure 5-1.

Contact with the world is maintained through perceptual systems. People see, hear, feel (or touch), taste, or smell in response to stimulation from the environment. This stimulation is translated into units of information to represent experiences. As Figure 5-1 indicates, several cognitive processes are involved in this activity, including

- attending to selected aspects of the environment (attention)
- identifying and interpreting this information (perception)
- organizing this information for memory
- testing and refining interpretations of this information (problem solving)

Attention

Selectivity of focus is necessary for survival. It is likely impossible even to list all the different stimuli operating at any one given moment, much less try to respond to all of them. Consequently, attention describes selectivity in seeing, hearing, and otherwise experiencing objects and events in the environment.

Figure 5-1 A Scheme for Making Sense of Experience

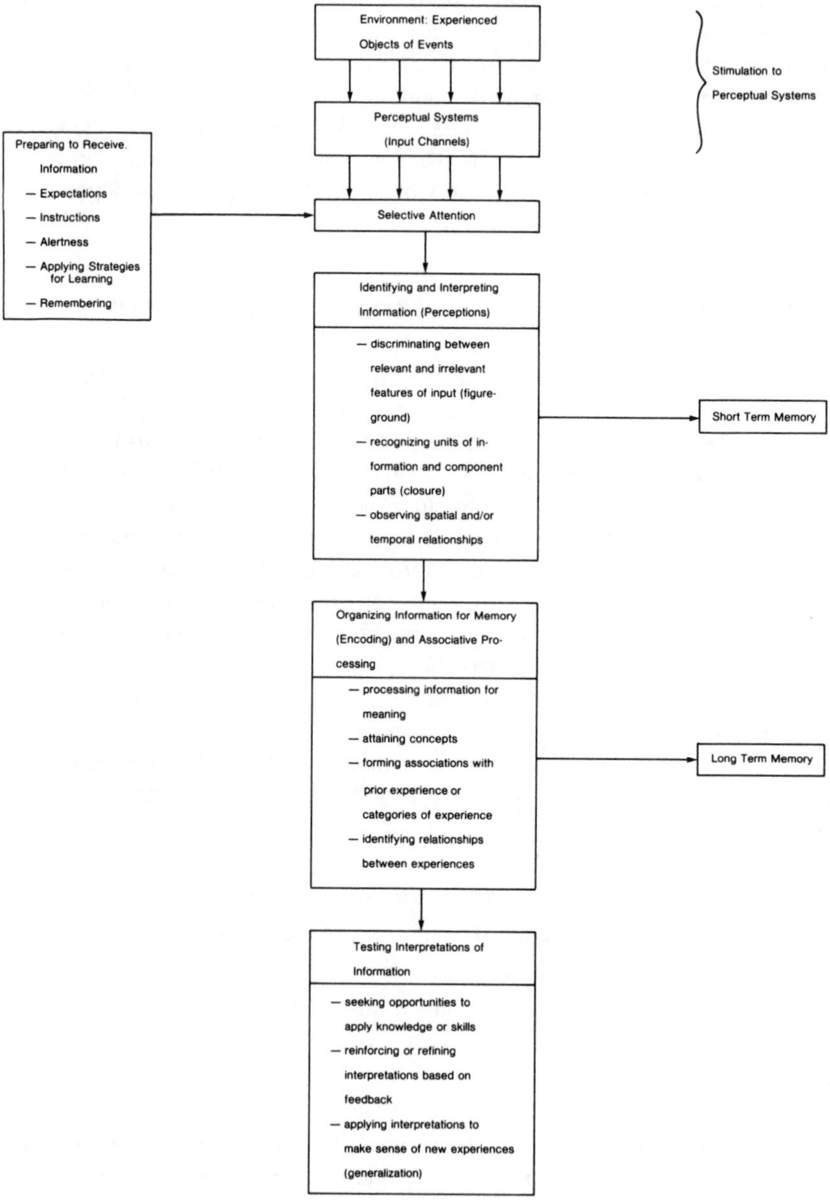

Selectivity in attention is accomplished through the orienting reaction, described as a general "What is it?" reaction that occurs when environmental changes are detected by the sensory systems (Sokolov, 1963). This reaction establishes the optimal conditions for intensive concentration on the source of stimulation. For example, Paden's study (cited in Horowitz, 1975) of 24 infants' visual attending behaviors (viewing a checkerboard pattern) revealed that the addition of an auditory stimulus (a recording of *Switched on Bach*) caused the infants to renew their visual attending behaviors. Paden's data are supported by others (Horowitz, 1975).

Selectivity in attention also results from the use of attentional strategies for organizing input information. Attentional strategies, which are based, at least in part, on prior experience, are information acquisition routines, that is, consistent patterns of focusing on environmental stimuli to extract information systematically. One such strategy is scanning, used as an individual surveys the environment. Studies of scanning strategies used while the individual is attending to objects or pictures show that the eyes follow a consistent pattern, such as along the boundaries of figures, rather than darting haphazardly (Miller, 1962). Searching, another attentional strategy, is systematically selective. It is essentially looking for specific information, with the direction for searching operations provided by prior experiences and perhaps by innate predispositions within the individual. Haith (1980) and his colleagues believe that newborns are inherently equipped with information acquisition routines. Mendelson and Haith (1976), for example, have studied healthy newborns' responses to changes in auditory and visual stimuli and find that

> without qualification, newborns scan in darkness in a prototypical manner which is different from scanning in lights. In darkness . . . [they] . . . open their eyes more widely, scan with better eye control, fixate more centrally but less dispersedly, and make slightly smaller eye movements.
>
> Visual activity in darkness clearly reflects the functioning of an inherent scanning routine that is independent of specific visual input. More so than any other evidence, dark scanning . . . indicates that the newborn is predisposed to interact with the visual world. (p. 53)
>
> It appears that a newborn's response to sound increases the probability of detection of a visual event related to the auditory event. Even when . . . viewing a stable display, sound initiates a scanning routine which enables the infant to find a visual change associated with the auditory change. (p. 55)

Attention may also be considered in relation to those behaviors that direct cognitive activities to a given task. Attention-sustaining activities establish optimal conditions for cognitive processing by providing a period of time that is free from distractions and can be devoted to task-related activities. Thus, attention-sustaining activities are defined in terms of the time an individual devotes to task-related cognitive processing. When no distractions intrude on a task, the length of sustained attention, called attention span, gives a rough index of the complexity of the task and the intensity of cognitive processing activities being devoted to a task.

As measured by resistance to irrelevancy, attention span appears to increase during the childhood years. Flavell and Hill (1969) cite a variety of evidence attesting to this. For example, older children can more accurately reproduce one of two simultaneously presented messages; they can more efficiently focus on the relevant features in a display and can more correctly identify stimuli that have been masked by visual and auditory noise. Older children also examine all stimulus attributes more carefully before determining those that are relevant to problem solving.

Perception

The process by which an individual obtains firsthand information about the world is termed perception (Gibson, 1969). It involves the conversion of sensory data that are registered by visual, auditory, tactile, gustatory, and olfactory mechanisms into meaning. Since the infant's cognitive world is self-constructed, beginning soon after birth, perceptual learning begins almost immediately. It is through the development of increasingly more efficient perceptual processes that children learn to attach meaning to their sensory experiences.

Holmes and Morrison (1979) point out that, since infants are unable to tell others what they see, hear, and feel, psychologists have resorted to studies of infant attending (Horowitz, 1975) as secondary sources. Pick, Frankel, and Hess (1975) argue that the development of attention per se has been studied only indirectly for the same reasons. It is frequently a variable examined as a contributing factor in information-processing behavior, that is, the role of attention in learning (Lorch, Anderson, & Levin, 1979; Yussen, 1974; Zelniker & Jeffrey, 1976). Knowledge of attention as a developmental function is still incomplete, however, and must be extracted from knowledge of developmental change in associated cognitive behaviors, such as memory. There is obviously some circularity here. Unfortunately, it is as much a consequence of the state of the infant (i.e., inability to describe relevant behaviors) as of the state of infant research methodology, which is necessarily hampered by its dependence on such very immature subjects.

Despite the lack of direct measures of early infant behaviors, research does offer some important data. With regard to visual perception, Haith's (1980) research is helpful. He interprets his data to indicate that infants' visual perceptions are guided by "operating" principles that conform to the following rules:

1. If awake and alert, and the light is not too intense, open your eyes.
2. If your visual field is dark, search for shadows or objects.
3. If exposed to an area of light with no observable edges, search broadly.
4. If an edge is located, examine it more closely.

If Haith is correct, infants should show a preference for certain "perceiving" behaviors. Research suggests that this is true. Infants between the ages of 1 and 6 months, when given the choice of looking at a sphere or a disk that are equal in diameter, show a preference for the sphere. Fantz (1961) interprets this data as evidence that the infants detect the sphere's solidarity. Likewise, Walk and Gibson (1961) and Walk (1966) have shown that young infants who are placed on a centerboard between glass surfaces that display different areas of different depths below typically do not crawl out onto the glass over the deep end of the visual cliff; this was true with 90% or more of infants between the ages of 6 and 15 months. Some of these infants could be coaxed to crawl over the deep end, but these infants were usually younger or had had less crawling experience (according to mothers' reports), or the surface beneath the glass was solid rather than checkered.

Bower (1974) reported on a series of investigations in which very young infants had been conditioned to turn their heads when a 30-mm cube was presented to them at a distance of 1 m. The generalization of this learning was then tested by presenting the infants with the initial cube at a 3-m distance and by presenting a larger cube (90-cm) at the 1-m and 3-m distances. Bower found that the most generalization occurred with the 30-m cube at 3 m; next most generalization occurred with the 90-cm cube presented at a 1-m distance; the least generalization occurred when the 90-cm cube was presented at the 3-m distance. Bower concluded that young infants may be aware of size and shape constancy differences as early as 1 month of age.

In addition to perceiving differences in size, shape, depth, and contour, infants are also apparently able to react differently to different colors. Bornstein (1975, 1978) exposed young infants to pairs of equally bright lights that differed in color. He found that, like adults, infants preferred some colors over others and also looked longer at colors near the middle of a color category. As these data indicate, even very young infants respond differentially to different and diverse perceptual cues in their environment.

It is clear from this evidence of early perceptual ability that later cognitive behavior is based on the meaning component supplied by perceptual processes. While these perceptual abilities may dominate early cognitions, as suggested by Piaget, increases in cognitive information-processing behaviors during the early childhood years apparently render null this overreliance on especially salient perceptual cues.

Memory

Information processing was described earlier as a series of cognitive processes used to construct meaning out of sensory experiences that are in themselves meaningless. Memory has traditionally been included, essentially as a storage component, but such categorization is, at best, artificial, intended only to help give meaning to memory. Unfortunately, the effect has been consideration of memory as a unitary phenomenon: memory is where information is stored for later use. Such a passive view is not only inaccurate, but also fails to consider memory as essentially developmental.

Scientists are increasingly viewing memory as a collective label for a series of cognitive processes. Flavell (1977) and his colleagues (Flavell & Wellman, 1977), for example, find it useful to divide memory or mnemonic behavior into four categories of cognitive activity: (1) basic processes, (2) knowledge, (3) strategies, and (4) metamemory.

Basic Processes

Recognition. Ability to recognize that a presently occurring event has been experienced (e.g., seen, felt, heard) at some time in the past appears to be one important memory process. Recognition memory refers to this ability and implies the presence of some stored representation. Kagan (1971) refers to this stored representation as a schema, an abstract, mental image of an object or event that has been constructed by the individual. Once a schema has been established, recognition memory is triggered when an instance of the object or event is encountered.

Kagan has described three stages of infant perceptual development that may help explain development of recognition memory. During the first stage (0 to 2 months), infants begin to form schemata as different objects in the environment capture their attention. Attention to environmental objects, and consequently the formation of subsequent schemata, is a function of the object's rate of change (i.e., perceptual qualities associated with rate of movement, amount of contour, and amount of contrast of the object). Objects with a relatively low rate of change allow for more easily formed schemata and correspondingly are usually looked at less when seen later. Objects with a high change rate do not lend themselves too easily to schemata formation because their complexity makes this difficult. Therefore, such objects are also not usually looked at too long when seen later. Kagan argues that objects with moderate rates of change contribute the most to schemata formation. (See Ruff, 1980, for a review of research pertinent to the development of object perception in young infants.)

The second stage (2 to 12 months) is marked by a major change. The infant's attention to objects now depends on how close the match is between the object and the infant's existing schemata of it. Objects that are slightly discrepant from existing schemata hold more interest for the infant. Thus, infants should show a preference (i.e., look at more) for the moderately novel over the familiar, but this preference should diminish once the novel object has become familiar.

During the third stage (1 year on), the young child moves into the final stage in perceptual development. Now the child begins to think, to determine meaning. Consequently, this stage is marked by beginning attempts to use rules or generate hypotheses to relate new to past experience meaningfully.

As Kagan's theory suggests, recognition memory is a developmental phenomenon. It appears to develop very early, however, since preschoolers and young children differ little from adults in recognition memory accuracy. For example, Daehler and Bukatka (1977) exposed 1½-, 2-, 2½-, and 3-year-olds to 108 stimulus trials, consisting of 12 training trials, 16 fillers, 40 familiarization, and 40 test trials. On the familiarization trials, the children saw the same picture exposed in the two windows of a viewing screen; on the test trials, they saw one familiar and one novel picture exposed in the two viewing windows. These researchers assumed that greater attention to the novel pictures indicated recognition of the familiar pictures. Their results indicated that "children between the ages of 17 and 40 months do attend to novel stimuli longer than familiarized stimuli even when the latter are seen for only brief amounts of time and when there are many familiar stimuli to be recognized" (p. 695). Furthermore, there was an age effect in recognition ability, indicating that the older children were more accurate.

Recall. Because the object to be retrieved is not present, recall requires more than just recognition; the individual is required to initiate a search process. Consequently, more cognitive activity is needed to recall. In addition, recall involves a semantic or meaning component.

Moely (1977) has summarized developmental changes in recall as follows: recall accuracy increases in a linear fashion, from about age 2 until a ceiling is reached in adolescence. Data from a study by Waters and Waters (1979) illustrate this. The average recall memory sources indicated that the older the child, the more accurate the recall. In this study, recall was tested under either a standard set of instructions (Remember these words; you will be asked to recall them later.) as well as under a semantic orienting set (Is this [the word on the list] nice? or Will this [the word on the list] fit into the box?). In addition, the words used were either high or low in meaningfulness, based on established meaningfulness norms. Despite the age differences, no differences occurred in recall due to type of instruction. Older children recalled more high-meaningfulness words under the semantic orienting instructions, but Waters and Waters attribute this increase to the more elaborate encoding that likely occurred under this set of instructions.

Knowledge

What you know determines what you know! This seemingly fatuous statement really implies that a person's past acquired knowledge influences what is stored in, and later retrieved, from memory. Piaget refers to the former type of knowledge as "memory in the wider sense" and to the latter as "memory in the strict sense" (Piaget & Inhelder, 1973).

Piaget believes that knowledge is constructed by the individual through continual active interactions with the environment. The outcome of this continual interaction process is typically reflected by a qualitative progression in how the individual thinks, associated with increasing reliance on logical mental operations. In this vein, Piaget and Inhelder (1973) suggest that memory development is tied to overall knowledge development. More specifically, they argue that improvements should appear in the child's memory as operative schemes develop, if the stimulus that evoked an operative scheme is retained in memory. Furth, Ross, and Youniss (1974) asked 116 children to draw four pictures over five sessions (initial, 2 hours, 2 weeks, 6 months, and then 1 year later). The drawings included a tilted glass, half-filled with liquid (memory for horizontality); the movement of a stick, falling from a tabletop and turning during the fall; a number sequence in a series of dice; and a house with a chimney at right angles with the roof. When the study ended, the children were in Grades 1, 2, 3, and 5. Since Piaget's theory of memory focuses on making operatively correct modifications to the drawings, such changes would be expected to occur over time, and there is evidence of this. "In confirmation of memory changes dependent on operative understanding there was an increase over time in operative correctness of the chimney that was much more marked at older than at younger ages" (p. 69). In addition, there were "20 among the 116 children, aged 5-9, who drew an operatively correct liquid level in the glass at session 4 or 5 after having drawn an incorrectly modified drawing 6 months before" (p. 69).

Liben (1975, 1977) and Liben and Belknap (1981) offer supporting data. After a careful review of both cross-sectional and longitudinal research in this area, Liben (1977) concludes that it is possible to replicate the findings of Piaget and Inhelder (1973). "Studies that included children of different ages have shown that the developmental levels of reproductions and the patterns of memory change correspond to the differing cognitive levels of the age groups tested. Furthermore, in almost all investigations in which memory was studied longitudinally, some long-term memory improvements were found" (p. 327). Liben does, however, caution against uncritical acceptance of these data, since there are discrepancies between group analyses and within subject analyses. Despite such discrepancies, Piaget and Inhelder have suggested a theoretically based approach to the study of memory development in which memory is tied to change in other areas of cognitive behavior.

Strategies

Information that is "remembered" is information that has been somehow stored or retained. To aid in this retention process, individuals frequently (and increasingly so with age) employ mnemonic strategies, deliberate activities to promote more orderly storage and retrieval of information. More simply put, strategies reflect planned, goal-oriented behavior (Flavell, 1977).

Memory has traditionally been described by means of a three-tiered model. Sensory memory is relatively passive; the individual is required to do little more than pay attention to the aspect of information to be stored. Immediate memory results from direct stimulation. For a very brief period of time (about 2 miliseconds), a literal copy of the experience is retained and provides sufficient information to direct attention more selectively to interesting aspects of the stimulus display.

A more permanent residue of immediate experience is termed short-term memory. Selected features of a stimulus pattern are entered into short-term memory as the individual attempts to make sense of current experience. The information retained in short-term memory usually represents the physical characteristics of what was experienced. Both the capacity (four to seven items) and the duration (about 30 seconds) of short-term memory are limited and thus require strategies for efficient operation. Chunking, or grouping, is one such active process that is a means to expand the capacity limitations of short-term memory by redefining the units of information contained there. To illustrate, examine this string of numbers for 1 to 2 seconds: 5048910267. Now close the book and write the sequence of numbers from memory. How correct are you? Now repeat the same exercise with these numbers: 404-755-1246. You probably were more accurate on the second attempt, because the string of numbers was broken into chunks and it could be recognized as a telephone number. Chunking is one application of prior knowledge to aid the retention of new information. As such, chunking is based on the ability to detect regularities, recurrent patterns, or previously learned associations of stimuli and to organize these into more meaningful units of information.

Rehearsal is another retentional activity. If you "cheated" a bit during the memory exercise by repeating the numbers to yourself, you were rehearsing. Whereas chunking expands short-term memory storage limits, rehearsal alters its normal duration by reexposing representations and thus strengthening their sequential associations. Rehearsal may also provide an opportunity to discover subtle consistencies within the stimulus pattern that facilitate chunking.

Young children have a more limited short-term memory (only three or four units of information) than do adults, who average about seven units (Miller, 1956). Although children can learn to rehearse, they often fail to recognize when these skills should be used. Thus, there are developmental changes in understanding what is needed to retain information effectively. Regarding developmental change in use of rehearsal strategies, it seems that, while younger children (5- and 6-year-olds) usually do not rehearse and older (7-year-olds) ones sometimes rehearse, most children begin to be efficient rehearsers by about age ten (Flavell, Beach, & Chinsky, 1966).

Young children are less likely than older children to use strategies deliberately. They also may not use an appropriate strategy spontaneously (Appel, Cooper, McCarrell, Sims-Knight, Yussen, & Flavell, 1972) or as efficiently (Cuvo, 1975); although they can be encouraged to use strategies (Rohwer, 1973), they will not always continue to do so unless continually reminded (Gruenfelder & Borkowski, 1975) or directly trained to do so (Ornstein, Naus, & Stone, 1977). (For a recent review that summarizes all these findings and suggests some educational implications, see Pressley, 1982.)

Meaningful information is more likely to be retained in long-term memory, which has relatively unlimited capacity and duration. Information enters long-term memory by a process called encoding (see Figure 5-1). Encoding, which can take various forms, provides an associative relationship between new information to be remembered and information already stored. Through this process, existing data are refined or altered. Encoding can occur by associative transfer, imagery, verbal elaboration, and mnemonic systems.

Associative transfer occurs when existing verbal mediators, concepts, or principles are used to link new events with previously learned information; these new events become more meaningful, to a degree determined by the number of associations formed. This enhanced meaning facilitates the retention and retrieval of these events. Imagery makes use of visual representations of concrete events or concepts to facilitate encoding. Mental pictures of two or more events can be superimposed upon each other to form an association between them. For example, in order to remember the words *giraffe* and *umbrella* as paired associates, a picture of a giraffe holding an umbrella could be imagined. This imagery would serve as a retrieval cue in recalling both words.

Verbal elaboration is an encoding strategy that associates concepts with word labels by linking the words together in sentence form. By forming a sentence such as "The giraffe carried an umbrella," the individual may be able later to recreate the sentence associated with the word *giraffe* and thus recover the word *umbrella* contained within it. Another encoding strategy, mnemonic systems, is used to mark the location in memory of a particular unit of information. Retrieving the information then becomes a matter of recalling the storage code. For example, "All cows eat grass" is a classic mnemonic device for remembering the notes that fall between the lines of a musical staff, just as "Every good boy does fine" aids in recalling the notes that fall on the lines.

Metamemory

The fourth category of memory phenomena refers broadly to ''the individual's potentially verbalizable knowledge and awareness concerning any aspect of information storage and retrieval'' (Kreutzer, Leonard, & Flavell, 1975, p. 1). In other words, metamemory refers to what individuals know about their memory ability and includes their awareness that some things are harder to remember than others, that sometimes they may forget unless reminded to do so, and that some events are more worthy of remembering than others. Metamemory is obviously not a separate phenomenon from basic memory processes, knowledge, and strategies. As indicated earlier, each of these three categories is developmental in nature; since metamemory is tied to these developmentally oriented memory categories, differences in what younger and older children realize about their memory ability can also be expected.

The developmental aspects of metamemory are illustrated in a study by Kreutzer, Leonard, and Flavell (1975), who attempted to determine what elementary children knew about their memory. To do so, Kreutzer and associates interviewed 80 middle-class children who had been randomly selected from kindergarten and the first-, third-, and fifth-grade classes of a suburban public school. The interview centered around the following memory ability questionnaire, which was orally and individually administered to each child:

> Sometimes I forget things. (1) Do you forget? (2) Do you remember things well—are you a good rememberer? (3) Can you remember better than your friends, or do they remember more than you? For example, if I gave you 10 things to look at quickly and remember and you remembered six of them, how many do you think your friends would remember? (4) Sometimes although a person is a good rememberer, he can still remember some things better than others. Do you remember some kinds of things better than others? (5) Are there some kinds of things that are really hard to remember? (p. 5)

Examination of the resulting data indicated that older children were more knowledgeable about mnemonic activity and ability. In addition, the older children were better able to conceive of memory ability as variable according to the situation.

Flavell and Wellman (1977) proposed a model to account for mnemonic performance. In this model, they conceive of mnemonic performance as an interaction of memory ability, which is itself the outcome of the interaction between the individual's personal attributes that relate to memory and the individual's use of particular strategies, and memory difficulty, which involves item characteristics and task demands in interaction. Personal attributes are those characteristics that influence an individual's ability to retrieve information from memory. One such personal attribute is mnemonic self-concept, self-view as a good or poor rememberer (Kreutzer et al., 1975). Others include the knowledge that some situations call for extra memory effort (Ritter, 1978) and the development of an understanding of the meaning of the verbs *remember* and *forget* (Wellman & Johnson, 1979).

The organizational and retrieval strategies previously discussed are only a few of the strategies available. For example, Wellman, Ritter, and Flavell (1975) performed three different experiments in which 2-, 3-, and 4-year-olds were told several stories about a dog. The experimenter, using a small toy dog to illustrate the story content (e.g., dog looking into several "doghouses" for food) actually moved the toy dog around several paper cups before hiding the dog under one of them. Half the children were then told simply to wait while the experimenter left the room to get something necessary to complete the story; the remaining half were instructed to remember where the dog was. The experimenter left the room for either 40 or 45 seconds, depending on the age of the child. The findings from this study indicate that children as young as 3 engage in deliberate external mnemonic strategies, but only when instructed to remember; these external strategies included peeking under the cup periodically, immediately lifting the cup containing the dog, and holding their hand on the correct cup until the experimenter returned. Children asked to wait did not engage in such strategies.

Particular task characteristics affect storage and retrieval. Some information is obviously more difficult to store and retrieve. For example, recalling a string of digits is, for many, less taxing than recalling a prose passage (Taub, 1975). Likewise, remembering a list of 60 words requires more mnemonic skill than remembering a list that contains only 24 words (Erber, 1974).

Flavell and Wellman's memory performance model seems a reasonable one; it takes into consideration the contribution of each of the four categories of memory and illustrates how these categories interact in a person's actual mnemonic performance. Furthermore, this model is heuristic in that it suggests interesting combinations of person-task variables for future study. Additionally, this model lends itself to such applied fields as educational psychology, curriculum development, as well as diagnostic and intervention efforts, to name a few.

Recently, Cavanaugh and Perlmutter (1982) have strongly criticized the concept of metamemory, arguing that it is a concept without much utility in its present form and that assessment strategies are inadequate. They suggest a reconceptualization that would include the development of more psychometrically valid assessment devices and more consideration of interrelationships among different areas of knowledge. They also believe that multiple assessment of memory knowledge should be standard procedure.

REFERENCES

Ainsworth, M., & Bell, S. Mother-infant interaction and the development of competence. In K. Connolly & J. Bruner (Eds.), *The growth of competence*. New York: Academic Press, 1973.

Almy, M., Chittenden, E., & Miller, P. *Young children's thinking: Studies of some aspects of Piaget's theory*. New York: Columbia University, Teachers College Press, 1966.

Appel, L.F., Cooper, R.G., McCarrell, N., Sims-Knight, J., Yussen, S.R., & Flavell, J.H. The development of the distinction between perceiving and memorizing. *Child Development*, 1972, *43*, 1365-1381.

Ausubel, D.P., & Sullivan, E.V. *Theory and problems of child development*. New York: Grune & Stratton, 1970.

Bayley, N. Mental growth during the first three years: A developmental study of 61 children by repeated tests. *Genetic Psychology Monographs*, 1933, *14*.

Bayley, N. *Bayley scales of infant development*. New York: Psychological Corporation, 1969.

Bayley, N. Development of mental abilities. In P.H. Mussen (Ed.), *Carmichael's manual of child psychology*. New York: Wiley, 1970.

Belsky, J., & Steinberg, L.D. The effects of day care: A critical review. *Child Development*, 1978, *49*, 929-949.

Binet, A., & Simon, T. The development of intelligence in children. Baltimore: Williams & Wilkins, 1916.

Bloom, B. *Stability and change in human characteristics*. New York: Wiley, 1964.

Borke, H. Piaget's mountains revisited: Changes in the egocentric landscape. *Developmental Psychology*, 1975, *11*, 240-243.

Borke, H. Piaget's views on social interaction and the theoretical construct of empathy. In L.S. Siegel & C.J. Brainerd (Eds.), *Alternatives to Piaget: Critical essays on the theory*. New York: Academic Press, 1977.

Bornstein, M. Qualities of color vision in infancy. *Journal of Experimental Child Psychology*, 1975, *19*, 401-419.

Bornstein, M.H. Visual behavior of the young human infant: Relationships between chromatic and spatial perception and the activity of underlying brain mechanisms. *Journal of Experimental Child Psychology*, 1978, *26*, 174-192.

Bower, T.G.R. *Development in infancy*. San Francisco: W.H. Freeman, 1974.

Bower, T.G.R. *Human development*. San Francisco: W.H. Freeman, 1979.

Bower, T.G.R., & Wishart, J. The effects of motor skills on object permanence. *Cognition*, 1972, *1*, 165-172.

Bradley, R.H., & Caldwell, B.M. The relation of infants' home environments to mental test performance at fifty-four months: A follow-up study. *Child Development*, 1976, *47*, 1172-1174.

Braine, M.D. The ontogeny of certain logical operations: Piaget's formulation examined by nonverbal methods. *Psychological Monographs*, 1959, *73*(5, Whole No. 475).

Brainerd, C.J. *Piaget's theory of intelligence*. Englewood Cliffs, N.J.: Prentice-Hall, 1978.

Brainerd, C.J., & Van Den Heuvel, K. Development of geometric imagery in five- to eight-year-olds. *Genetic Psychology Monographs*, 1974, *98*, 89-143.

Burt, C. The genetic determination of differences in intelligence: A study of monozygotic twins reared together and apart. *British Journal of Psychology*, 1966, *57*, 146.

Caldwell, B.M. On designing supplementary environments for early child development. *BAEYC [Boston Association for the Education of Young Children] Reports*, 1968, *10* (No. 1), 1-11.

Cattell, R.B. *Personality and motivation structure and measurement*. New York: World Book, 1957.

Cavanaugh, J.C., & Perlmutter, M. Metamemory: A critical examination. *Child Development*, 1982, *53*, 11-28.

Chandler, M.J., & Greenspan, S. Ersatz egocentrism: A reply to H. Borke. *Developmental Psychology*, 1972, *7*, 104-106.

Connolly, K., & Bruner, J. (Eds.). *The growth of competence*. New York: Academic Press, 1973.

Cowan, P.A. *Piaget: With feeling*. New York: Holt, Rinehart and Winston, 1978.

Crissey, O.L. Mental development as related to institutional residence and educational achievement. *University of Iowa Studies in Child Welfare*, 1937, *13* (No. 1).

Cuvo, A.J. Developmental differences in rehearsal and free recall. *Journal of Experimental Child Psychology*, 1975, *19*, 265-278.

Daehler, M.W., & Bukatka, D. Recognition memory for pictures in very young children: Evidence from attentional preferences using a continuous presentation procedure. *Child Development*, 1977, *48*, 693-696.

Dennis, W., & Najarian, P. Infant development under environmental handicap. *Psychological Monographs*, 1957, *71* (7, Whole No. 436).

Dunst, C.J. *Infant learning: A cognitive-linguistic intervention strategy*. Hingham, Mass.: Teaching Resources, 1981.

Elardo, R., Bradley, R., & Caldwell, B. The relation of infants' home environments and mental test performance from six to thirty-six months: A longitudinal analysis. *Child Development*, 1975, *46*, 71-76.

Elkind, D. Piaget's conservation problems. *Child Development*, 1967, *38*, 15-27.

Erber, J.J. Age differences in recognition memory. *Journal of Gerontology*, 1974, *29*, 177-181.

Falender, C.A., & Heber, R. Mother-child interaction and participation in a longitudinal intervention program. *Developmental Psychology*, 1975, *11*, 830-836.

Fantz, R.L. The origin of form perception. *Scientific American*, 1961, *204*, 66-72.

Flavell, J. *The developmental psychology of Jean Piaget*. Princeton: Van Nostrand, 1963.

Flavell, J. *Cognitive Development*. Englewood Cliffs, N.J.: Prentice-Hall, 1977.

Flavell, J.H. On cognitive development. *Child Development*, 1982, *53*, 1-10.

Flavell, J.H., Beach, D.R., & Chinsky, J.M. Spontaneous verbal rehearsal in a memory task as a function of age. *Child Development*, 1966, *37*, 283-299.

Flavell, J., Botkin, P.T., Fry, C.L., Wright, J.W., & Jarvis, P.E. *The development of role-taking and communication skills*. New York: Wiley, 1968.

Flavell, J., & Hill, J.P. Developmental psychology. *Annual Review of Psychology*, 1969, *20*, 1-56.

Flavell, J.H., & Wellman, H.M. Metamemory. In R.V. Kail & J.W. Hagen (Eds.), *Perspectives on the development of memory and cognition*. Hillsdale, N.J.: Erlbaum, 1977.

Flavell, J.H., & Wohlwill, J.F. Formal and functional aspects of cognitive development. In D. Elkind & J.H. Flavell (Eds.), *Studies in cognitive development*. New York: Oxford University Press, 1969.

Furth, H., Ross, B., & Youniss, J. Operative understanding in reproduction of drawings. *Child Development*, 1974, *45*, 63-70.

Gelman, R. Cognitive development. *Annual Review of Psychology*, 1978, *29*, 297-332.

Gibson, E. *Principles of perceptual learning and development*. New York: Appleton-Century-Crofts, 1969.

Goldfarb, W. Psychological privation in infancy and subsequent adjustment. *American Journal of Orthopsychiatry*, 1945, *15*, 247-255.

Goodenough, F.L. New evidence on environmental influence on intelligence. *39th Yearbook of the National Social Studies Education,* 1940, Part I, 307-365.

Gruber, H.E., Girgus, J.S., & Banuazizi, A. The development of object permanence in the cat. *Developmental Psychology,* 1971, *4,* 9-15.

Gruenfelder, T.M., & Borkowski, J.G. Transfer of cumulative-rehearsal strategies in children's short-term memory. *Child Development,* 1975, *46,* 1019-1024.

Guilford, J.P. *The nature of human intelligence.* New York: McGraw-Hill, 1967.

Haith, M.M. *Rules that babies look by.* Hillsdale, N.J.: Erlbaum, 1980.

Harter, S. Effectance motivation reconsidered. *Human Development,* 1978, *21,* 34-64.

Holmes, D.L., & Morrison, F.J. *The child.* Monterey, Calif.: Brooks/Cole, 1979.

Hooper, F.H., Sipple, T.S., Goldman, J.A., & Swinton, S.S. *A cross-sectional investigation of children's classificatory abilities.* Madison, Wis.: University of Wisconsin, Research and Development Center for Cognitive Learning, 1974. (Technical Report No. 295)

Horn, J.L. Organization of data on life-span development of human abilities. In L.R. Goulet & P.B. Baltes (Eds.), *Life-span developmental psychology: Research and theory.* New York: Academic Press, 1970.

Horn, J.L., & Cattell, R.B. Age differences in fluid and crystallized intelligence. *Acta Psychologica,* 1967, *26,* 107-129.

Horowitz, F.D. (Ed.). Visual attention, auditory stimulation, and language discrimination in young infants. *Monographs of the Society for Research in Child Development,* 1975, *39* (Serial No. 158).

Horowitz, F.D., & Dunn, M. Infant intelligence testing. In F.D. Minifie & L.L. Lloyd (Eds.), *Communicative and cognitive abilities—Early behavioral assessment.* Baltimore: University Park Press, 1978.

Inhelder, B., & Piaget, J. *The early growth of logic in the child.* New York: Norton, 1964 (Originally published, 1959).

Jaffa, A.S. *The California Preschool Scale-Mental Scale* (Syllabus Series No. 251). Berkeley: University of California Press, 1934.

Jencks, C., et al. *Inequality: A reassessment of the effect of family and schooling in America.* New York: Basic Books, 1972.

Jensen, A.R. How much can we boost IQ and scholastic achievement? *Harvard Educational Review,* 1969, *39,* 1-123.

Jensen, A.R. Cumulative deficit in IQ of blacks in the rural south. *Developmental Psychology,* 1977, *13,* 184-191.

Jensen, A.R. *Bias in mental testing.* New York: Free Press, 1980.

Juel-Nielsen, N. Individual and environment: A psychiatric-psychological investigation of monozygotic twins reared apart. *Acta Psychiatrica et Neurologica Scandinavia,* Monograph Supplement 183, 1965.

Kagan, J. *Change and continuity in infancy.* New York: Wiley, 1971.

Kamin, L.J. *The science and politics of I.Q.* New York: Wiley, 1977.

Kopp, C.B., Sigman, M., & Parmelee, A.H. Longitudinal study of sensorimotor development. *Developmental Psychology,* 1974, *10*(5), 687-695.

Kreutzer, M.A., Leonard, S.C., & Flavell, J.H. An interview study of children's knowledge about memory. *Monographs of the Society for Research in Child Development,* 1975, *40* (1, Serial No. 159).

Larsen, G. Methodology in developmental psychology: An examination of research on Piagetian theory. *Child Development,* 1977, *48,* 1160-1166.

Liben, L.S. Long-term memory for pictures related to seriation, horizontality, and verticality concepts. *Developmental Psychology,* 1975, *11,* 795-806.

Liben, L.S. Memory in the context of cognitive development: The Piagetian approach. In R.V. Kail & J. Hagen (Eds.), *Perspectives on the development of memory and cognition.* New York: Wiley, 1977.

Liben, L.S., & Belknap, B. Intellectual realism: Implications for investigation of perceptual perspective taking in young children. *Child Development,* 1981, *52,* 921-924.

Little, A. A longitudinal study of cognitive development in young children. *Child Development,* 1972, *43,* 1124-1134.

Lochlin, J.C., Lindzey, G., & Spuhler, J.N. *Race differences in intelligence.* San Francisco: W.H. Freeman, 1975.

Longstreth, L.E. Revisiting Skeels' final study: A critique. *Developmental Psychology,* 1981, *17,* 620-625.

Lorch, E.P., Anderson, D.R., & Levin, S.R. The relationship of visual attention to children's comprehension of television. *Child Development,* 1979, *50,* 722-727.

Maratsos, M.P. Nonegocentric communication abilities in preschool children. *Child Development,* 1973, *44,* 697-700.

McCall, R.B. Toward an epigenetic conception of mental development in the first three years of life. In M. Lewis (Ed.), *Origins of intelligence.* New York: Plenum, 1976.

McCall, R., Appelbaum, M., & Hogarty, P. Developmental changes in mental performance. *Monographs of the Society for Research in Child Development,* 1973, *38*(3), (Serial No. 150).

McCall, R.B., Eichorn, D.H., & Hogarty, P.S. Transitions in early mental development. *Monographs of the Society for Research in Child Development,* 1977, *42* (Serial No. 171).

Mendelson, M.J., & Haith, M.M. The relation between audition and vision in the human newborn. *Monographs of the Society for Research in Child Development,* 1976, *41* (Serial No. 167).

Menig-Peterson, C.L. The modification of communicative behavior in preschool-aged children as a function of the listener's perspective. *Child Development,* 1975, *46,* 1015-1018.

Miller, G.A. The magical number seven, plus or minus two: Some limits to our capacity for processing information. *Psychological Review,* 1956, *63,* 81-97.

Miller, G.A. *Psychology: The science of mental life.* New York: Harper & Row, 1962.

Miller, S.A. A disconfirmation of the quantitative identity-quantitative equivalence sequence. *Journal of Experimental Child Psychology,* 1977, *24,* 180-189.

Moely, B.E. Organizational factors in the development of memory. In R.V. Kail & J.W. Hagen (Eds.), *Perspectives on the development of memory and cognition.* New York: Wiley, 1977.

Newman, H.H., Freeman, F.N., & Holzinger, K.J. *Twins: A study of heredity and environment.* Chicago: University of Chicago Press, 1937.

Ornstein, P.A., Naus, M.J., & Stone, B.P. Rehearsal training and developmental differences in memory. *Developmental Psychology,* 1977, *13,* 15-24.

Piaget, J. Piaget's theory. In P. Neubauer (Ed.), *The process of child development.* New York: New American Library, 1976.

Piaget, J., & Inhelder, B. *The psychology of the child.* New York: Basic Books, 1969. (Originally published, 1926.)

Piaget, J., & Inhelder, B. *Memory and intelligence.* New York: Basic Books, 1973.

Pick, A.D., Frankel, D.G., & Hess, V.L. Children's attention: The development of selectivity. In M. Hetherington (Ed.), *Review of child development research* (Vol. 5). Chicago: University of Chicago Press, 1975.

Pressley, M. Elaboration and memory development. *Child Development,* 1982, *53,* 296-309.

Ramey, C.T., Farran, D.C., & Campbell, F.A. Predicting IQ from mother-infant interactions. *Child Development,* 1979, *50,* 804-814.

Ritter, K. The development of knowledge of an external retrieval cue strategy. *Child Development,* 1978, *49,* 1227-1230.

Rohwer, W.D., Jr. Elaboration and learning in childhood and adolescence. In H.W. Reese (Ed.), *Advances in child development and behavior* (Vol. 8). New York: Academic Press, 1973.

Roodin, M.L., & Gruen, G.E. The role of memory in making transitive judgments. *Journal of Experimental Child Psychology,* 1970, *10,* 264-275.

Rubin, K.H., & Maioni, T.L. Play preference and its relationships to egocentrism, popularity, and classification skills in preschoolers. *Merrill-Palmer Quarterly,* 1975, *21,* 171-179.

Ruff, H.A. The development of perception and recognition of objects. *Child Development,* 1980, *51,* 981-992.

Scarr, S., & Weinberg, R.A. IQ test performance of black children adopted by white families. *American Psychologist,* 1976, *31,* 726-739.

Scarr-Salapatek, S. An evolutionary perspective on infant intelligence: Species patterns and individual variations. In M. Lewis (Ed.), *The origin of intelligence: Infancy and early childhood.* New York: Plenum, 1976.

Shatz, M., & Gelman, R. The development of communication skills: Modification in the speech of young children as a function of listener. *Monographs of the Society for Research in Child Development,* 1973, *38* (2, Serial No. 152), 1-37.

Sherman, M., & Key, C.B. The intelligence of isolated mountain children. *Child Development,* 1932, *3,* 279-290.

Shields, J. *Monozygotic twins brought up apart and brought up together.* London: Oxford University Press, 1962.

Shuey, A.M. *The testing of Negro intelligence.* New York: Social Science Press, 1966.

Skeels, H.M. Mental development of children in foster homes. *Journal of Consulting Psychology,* 1938, *2,* 33-43.

Skeels, H.M., & Fillmore, E.A. Mental development of children from underprivileged homes. *Journal of Genetic Psychology,* 1937, *50,* 427-439.

Skeels, H.M., Updegraff, R., Wellman, B.L., & Williams, H.M. A study of environmental stimulation: An orphanage preschool project. *University of Iowa Studies in Child Welfare,* 1938, *15*(No. 4).

Sokolov, E.N. *Perception and the conditioned reflex.* New York: Macmillan, 1963.

Spearman, C. General intelligence objectively determined and measured. *American Journal of Psychology,* 1904, *15,* 201-293.

Spearman, C. *The abilities of man.* New York: Macmillan, 1927.

Spitz, R.A. Hospitalism: A follow-up report. *Psychoanalytic Study of Children,* 1946, *2,* 113-117.

Spitz, R., & Wolff, K. Anaclitic depression. *Psychoanalytic Study of Children,* 1946, *2,* 313-342.

Stott, L.H., & Ball, R. Infant and preschool mental tests. *Monographs of the Society for Research in Child Development,* 1965, *30*(No. 3).

Taub, H.A. Mode of presentation, age, and short-term memory. *Journal of Gerontology,* 1975, *30*(1), 56-59.

Thurstone, L.L. *Primary mental abilities.* Chicago: University of Chicago Press, 1938.

Thurstone, L.L. Psychological implication of factor analysis. *American Psychologist,* 1948, *3,* 402-408.

Tomlinson-Keasey, C., Eisert, D., Kahle, L., Hardy, K., & Keasey, B. A longitudinal study of concrete operations. Paper presented at the 86th annual meeting of the American Psychological Association, Toronto, Canada, 1978.

Toniolo, T., & Hooper, F.H. Micro-analysis of logical reasoning relationships: Conservation and transitivity. Madison, Wis.: University of Wisconsin, Research and Development Center for Cognitive Learning, 1975. (Terminal Report No. 326.)

Uzgiris, I.C. Situational generality of conservation. *Child Development,* 1964, *35,* 831-841.

Uzgiris, I.C., & Hunt, J. McV. *Toward ordinal scales of psychological development in infancy.* Urbana, Ill.: University of Illinois Press, 1974.

Vaughter, R.M., Smotherman, N., & Ordy, J.M. Development of object permanence in the infant squirrel monkey. *Developmental Psychology;* 1972, *7,* 34-38.

Walberg, H., & Marjoribanks, K. Differential mental abilities and home environment: A canonical analysis. *Developmental Psychology,* 1973, *9,* 363-368.

Walk, R.D. The development of depth perception in animals and human infants. In H.W. Stephenson (Ed.), Concept of development. *Monographs of the Society for Research in Child Development,* 1966, *31*(Serial No. 107), 82-108.

Walk, R.D., & Gibson, E.J. A comparative and analytic study of visual depth perception. *Psychological Monographs,* 1961, *75* (15, Whole No. 519).

Waters, H.W., & Waters, E. Semantic processing in children's free recall: The effects of context and meaningfulness on encoding variability. *Child Development,* 1979, *50,* 735-746.

Wellman, B.L. Some new bases for interpretation of the I.Q. *Journal of Genetic Psychology,* 1932(a), *41,* 116-126.

Wellman, B.L. The effects of preschool attendance upon the IQ. *Journal of Experimental Education,* 1932(b), *1,* 48-49.

Wellman, B.L. Growth in intelligence under different school environments. *Journal of Experimental Education,* 1934, *3,* 59-83.

Wellman, B.L. Mental growth from the preschool to college. *Journal of Experimental Education,* 1937, *6,* 127-138.

Wellman, B.L. The intelligence of preschool children as measured by the Merrill-Palmer scale of performance tests. *University of Iowa Studies on Child Welfare,* 1938, *15,* No. 3.

Wellman, B.L., & Coffey, H.S. The role of cultural status in intelligence changes for preschool children. *Journal of Experimental Education,* 1936, *5,* 191-202.

Wellman, H.M., & Johnson, C.N. Understanding of mental processes: A developmental study of "remember" and "forget." *Child Development,* 1979, *50,* 79-88.

Wellman, H.M., Ritter, K., & Flavell, J.H. Deliberate memory behavior in the delayed reaction of very young children. *Developmental Psychology,* 1975, *11,* 780-787.

Wheeler, L.R. The intelligence of East Tennessee mountain children. *Journal of Educational Psychology,* 1932, *23,* 351-370.

Wheeler, L.R. A comparative study of the intelligence of East Tennessee mountain children. *Journal of Educational Psychology,* 1942, *33,* 321-334.

White, R. Motivation reconsidered: The concept of competence. *Psychological Review,* 1959, *66,* 297-333.

Wise, K.L., Wise, L.A., & Zimmerman, R.R. Piagetian object permanence in the infant rhesus monkey. *Developmental Psychology,* 1974, *10,* 429-437.

Yussen, S.R. Determinants of visual attention and recall in observational learning by preschoolers and second graders. *Developmental Psychology,* 1974, *10,* 93-100.

Zelniker, T., & Jeffrey, W.E. Reflective and impulsive children: Strategies of information processing underlying differences in problem solving. *Monographs of the Society for Research in Child Development,* 1976, *41*(Serial No. 168).

Chapter 6

Language Development and Language Disorders in Young Children

Kevin Cole and S. Gray Garwood

DEFINITION

Language is such an integral part of life that most people give it very little thought. If it becomes necessary to enhance language acquisition or to intervene with a child who is not developing adequate language, however, then it becomes essential to understand what language is and how it develops. Apart from this practical or applied aspect, language governs behavior and consequently is of interest to scientists who study behavior. Language can be analyzed in a variety of ways—by detecting rules that govern word order (syntax) or rules that determine how units of words and inflections are combined to provide meaning (morphology). The relationship between concepts and words used to code these concepts (semantics) and the system of sounds that form words (phonology) are other bases for linguistic analysis. Furthermore, language can be studied as the way in which these four factors are organized to convey meaning within a social context (pragmatics).

Language has many components, and it is difficult to understand exactly how these components comprise language. The following general definition may be helpful in clarifying the concept of language: in the broadest sense, language can be defined as a system of symbols that is agreed upon by a group of speakers and is used to convey meaning. Thus, there can be many languages. Computer languages (e.g., FORTRAN or BASIC), mathematics, and signing, to name but a few, are all considered a type of language according to this definition. Of special interest to educators and psychologists is verbal language, which is word-based and includes spoken utterances (speech) and writing (graphic language).

Language Is Social

Because language is a common symbol system agreed to by members of a group, it is social in nature. Just as children use language to organize their experiences into cognitive units, so do they learn to regulate these experiences by using language. Since communication is social in nature, language links children to the culture in which they live, acting as a primary vehicle for their socialization into adult society. The child, through acquisition and use of the common language, assimilates a culture's beliefs, customs, and values, all of which provide control for behavior and help the culture maintain stability and continuity.

Language Is Systematic

Every language has a systematic set of rules for ordering words within sentences (syntax). If the word order in the sentence "The dog bites the man" is changed to "The man bites the dog," the message is altered in an important way, even though the words in the sentence are exactly the same. The combining of words and inflections also gives structure to language. A unit of meaning (a morpheme), such as the word *walk*, and the past tense inflection *ed* are combined to form *walked*. A unit of meaning is referred to as a free morpheme if it can occur in isolation and as a bound morpheme if it must be combined with another word. The word *walk* in the example given is obviously a free morpheme since it can stand alone, but the *ed* inflection is a bound morpheme since it has no meaning unless combined with a word.

Structure is also made systematic by the use of rules to arrange sounds into words (phonology). Each language has patterns and restrictions for sequencing sounds. In English, for example, the consonants *s* and *t* are often combined in the beginning of words; the consonants *l* and *k*, however, are never combined at the beginning of a word.

Language Is Symbolic

Language is composed of symbols that are arbitrarily agreed upon by speakers of that language. The word *boy*, for example, is a verbal symbol of the combined characteristics of maleness and youthfulness. The use of a verbal sign to stand for something else allows the speaker to reduce the amount of processing time needed during mental representation and to refer to objects and events that are not physically present or that are remote in time (Bates, 1976). The relationship between the verbal symbols, or words of a language, and the concepts and ideas they represent or encode is referred to as semantics. While syntax and morphology provide the structure of language, semantics involves ideas and concepts; semantics provides the meaning in language.

LANGUAGE AND INFORMATION

Language is a tool used to communicate and must be considered not only in terms of rules for putting words together or words representing ideas and concepts, but also in terms of the social motivation and context that determines how the speaker constructs a particular sentence in order to meet communication needs. The emotionally disturbed child who formulates the sentence "The sun is a bright ball of fire, burning in the sky." is using appropriate syntax, morphology, and phonology, and the meaning of the words (semantics) is appropriate; however, if the sentence is in response to the question "How are you?", it becomes apparent that the child's use of language is deviant. What is lacking in this example is pragmatics, an appropriate relationship between language and the social context in which it occurs. The child is not using language to serve a communicative function. A child's normal use of pragmatic skills can be seen in the use of more than one type of sentence to serve a function, such as requesting. The child can ask directly, "May I have a cookie?" or may use a less direct approach, stating "I'm hungry." Although one sentence has the structure of a question, the other the structure of a statement, both function as a request.

In contrast, the same sentence may have entirely different functions. The mother who asks "Do you know what time it is?" of a child who is standing by the clock in the kitchen has a different function in mind from that of the mother who asks the same question of a child who is arriving home 2 hours late for dinner. Knowledge regarding the use of language within a social context (pragmatics) is necessary in order to communicate effectively.

Language, then, involves the components of meaning (semantic rules for labeling and organizing ideas and concepts), structure (syntactic, morphological, and phonological rules for ordering the semantic elements into sentences), and function (pragmatic rules for the use of language within a social context).

DEFINING LANGUAGE DISORDERS

Disorders in language functioning can involve any or all of the three aspects of language that have been discussed: meaning, structure, and function. Disorders may be manifested as complete mutism (use of no language), or they may be seen in more subtle form, as in the use of inappropriate words or sentence structures, difficulty following directions, and problems in understanding the speech of others. Of course, these manifestations of disordered language must be put into a developmental context as well. Younger children may use words or sentence structures inappropriately, but this is more a function of their developmental status with respect to language acquisition than an index of potential or actual language delay or deficiency. Consequently, judgments about language disorders must always be developmentally based.

A variety of terms have been used to describe language that does not follow a normal pattern of development, including language delay, language/learning disorders, and deviant language. The term *language disorder* describes language that is developing in an abnormal pattern; however, some research suggests that "language disorder" in this sense is rare in children, and the majority of individuals who have difficulty learning language are progressing in the normal sequence of language development, only at a slower rate (Berry, 1976; Yoder & Miller, 1972). Bloom and Lahey (1978) recommend that the term *language disorder* be used to identify language that is different from language behaviors observed in most children of the same chronological age.

Information regarding the incidence of language disorder in preschool children is limited. However, two studies involving 3-year-olds have found that approximately 7% to 8% of children at this age evidence significant delay in receptive or expressive language functioning (Silva, 1980; Stevenson & Richman, 1976).

Language Disorders vs. Speech Disorders

While language involves organizing concepts into semantic and grammatical structures and using these structures for communication, speech is the motor act that encodes language in order to transmit its meaning to someone else. It is possible to encode language by using other systems, such as manual communication (sign language) or writing (graphic language), but speech is the most common method for transmitting language. Speech and language can be disordered individually in a variety of ways, and it is common to find disorders in both language and speech.

Disorders of speech include voice abnormalities, stuttering, and articulation disorders. The most common disorder in young children is disruption of articulation, which involves the positioning of the teeth, tongue, and lips in order to produce the sounds of speech. Kopin (1979) suggests that disorders of articulation in some cases reflect deficiencies in language experience, perhaps as a result of mild hearing loss for even a short period of time during a critical stage of development. Although speech disorders and language disorders do not always occur together, it is prudent to evaluate both systems.

Language Disorders and Later Academic Functioning

Several studies have indicated that early language disorders are associated with later difficulty in academic functioning. Silva (1980) found that 85% of all 3-year-old children identified as delayed in receptive and expressive language functioning performed poorly on intelligence tests in a follow-up study at age 5. Aram and Nation (1980) found similar results; they found that 40% of preschool children with language disorders were not able to function in regular classrooms 4 years later and required special education. King, Jones, and Lasky (1982) followed 50 preschool children in whom some form of communication impairment had been diagnosed and found that 42% of the children identified as "language disordered/delayed speech" were reported to have some difficulty communicating 15 years later. This group received poor grades and required tutoring more frequently than did other children. Clearly, early language disorders do not simply go away with the passage of time. Early intervention is indicated.

Language development is strongly tied to the specific academic skill of reading. Wiig and Semel (1980) suggest that competent readers must have well-developed rules for word order (syntax) and knowledge of the relationship between words and their underlying meaning (semantics). Reading obviously develops from knowledge of the spoken language. Dale (1976), while recognizing that language competence is a prerequisite for the initial development of reading ability, identifies several ways in which reading ability at later stages of development may influence language. Reading may expose the child to new and varied language information, and it may give the child an awareness that language can be analyzed into its components.

LANGUAGE ACQUISITION THEORIES

The impact of language disorders on academic development is clearly recognized, yet the processes that underlie normal language development and disorders of language are not clearly understood. Several theories have been constructed in an effort to provide information that will aid in the treatment of language disorders.

Early theories of language acquisition centered around an operant conditioning paradigm that emphasized imitation of the adult language model and reinforcement of correct language production. Skinner (1957) presented perhaps the most well-developed operant theory to account for children's acquisition of language. The basic characteristics of the operant view include the shaping of behavior by others—the learner playing a passive role in the learning process—and an emphasis on consequences of reinforcement of verbal behavior. However, this model does not account for the fact that children often create sentences they could not possibly have learned from adult models (e.g., "all-gone bye-bye"). In addition, the importance of reinforcement in language learning is seriously questioned by research. Hubbell (1977) found that verbal praise following spontaneous utterances by children tended to reduce the amount of spontaneous talking by the children. This finding is directly contrary to one of the most basic assumptions of an operant model of language learning: children learn to speak because their utterances are followed by positive reinforcement. Nelson (1973) found similar results with 18-month-old children. Children whose mothers reinforced utterances according to the correctness of pronunciation developed their language abilities more slowly than did children whose utterances were not selectively reinforced. In normal parent-child interactions, in fact, the parent tends to respond only to the correctness or incorrectness of the meaning of a child's utterance, not to the appropriateness or inappropriateness of the grammar (Brown, Cazden, & Bellugi, 1969). This suggests that direct reinforcement does not play a major role in acquisition of the rules of language.

Because the behavioral paradigm did not adequately explain language acquisition, an alternative hypothesis was developed. In this theory, often referred to as the nativist theory (Chomsky, 1965; Lenneberg, 1967), the child is considered to be innately endowed with the ability to learn language. This, of course, stands in strong contrast with the behaviorist model, in which learning is attributed to environmental input. Although the behaviorist and nativist theories are at opposite poles regarding the ways in which children learn language, both are based on the assumption that the child is passive in the process. In the one instance, the environment shapes the child's language performance; in the other, biological maturation predisposes the child to acquire language.

Skinner's behavioral model concentrated on the process by which children acquire various functions of communication, such as commanding, labeling, and controlling, while the nativist approach focused on the process by which children acquire the rules of grammar. Neither approach, however, has provided a full explanation of how children acquire linguistic complexity that involves interactions between knowledge and concepts used in language, grammatical forms to code the knowledge, and the sophisticated use of this knowledge and structure within a social context. Current theory attempts to solve this problem by combining the two models and by adding a third important consideration—that the child may be an active participant in language learning.

Miller (1981) has described three theories in which the child is believed to be an active participant in language learning and the environment is believed to influence the learning process to some degree. In the first theory, the "strong cognitive hypothesis," it is suggested that the child's level of cognitive development determines the degree to which that child will learn language. A minimum of exposure to language is sufficient for the child to discover and employ the rules of language. Only severe sensory or motor handicaps would prevent a child from learning language under this model. From this view, it can be concluded that (1) normal children would show normal language patterns, (2) children could not develop language skills beyond their cognitive ability, and (3) it would be unlikely for children to have language skills that lagged behind their cognitive skills.

A second, related theory is the "weak cognitive hypothesis." Proponents of this hypothesis believe that more extensive language experience and a general language learning ability are necessary, in addition to cognitive ability. In this model children are still unable to develop linguistic skills beyond their cognitive level, but they may have difficulty learning language skills despite adequate cognitive ability if they lack adequate exposure to language or experience a disruption in their ability to learn language independent of general cognitive functioning.

The third theory is based on the belief that common maturational or general intelligence factors affect both linguistic performance and cognitive performance. This "correlational hypothesis" suggests that a global factor, such as general intelligence, influences both areas of development and that either language or cognition could develop slightly beyond the other at any given point in time.

Cromer (1981), in a reexamination of current theories regarding the acquisition of language, argues for reconsideration of factors within the child that may account for language development; he suggests that some form of innate ability, coupled with the child's cognitive capacity to explore and understand the environment, provides the basis of language development.

NORMAL LANGUAGE DEVELOPMENT

Children appear to have an interest in language at a very early age. Condon and Sander (1974) observed that infants as young as 12 hours old would synchronize their body movements to an adult's speech, but would not respond in the same manner for isolated vowel sounds or tapping sounds. Eimas, Siqueland, Jusczyk, and Vigorito (1971) also found evidence that infants are likely to attend to important aspects of speech. They found that 1- and 4-month-old infants could discriminate between speech sounds that are very similar, such as "b" and "p" or "g" and "k," suggesting that these infants were able to attend to the same sound categories used by adults.

Cognitive Prerequisites to Language Learning

Although children may show an interest in language at an early age, linguistic development is thought to be an outgrowth of earlier cognitive development (Cromer, 1976; Muma, 1978; Sinclair-deZwart, 1969). Coggins and Carpenter (1979) have identified the cognitive prerequisites of language as object permanence, spatial relations, means-ends, imitation, play, and communicative intentions.

Object Permanence

The concept of object permanence involves the child's understanding that objects in the environment are permanent entities that exist even when they are not directly within sight. Object permanence develops in stages over a period of time, beginning around 6 to 10 months. The child at this age is capable of searching for an object hidden behind a screen if allowed to watch the object being hidden. In the final stage of object permanence development, 18 to 24 months, the child has an internal representation of the object and no longer needs to see it being hidden in order to imagine that it might be found in a given location.

Object permanence is thought to be related to language development in that children must understand the nature of objects in the environment before they can talk about the objects and the events that involve them.

Spatial Relations

A child's understanding of how things are related in space develops with object permanence. At approximately 8 to 12 months of age, children can predict the movement pattern of an object, even though part of the line of travel is obscured. By approximately 18 to 24 months, children can mentally represent their own position in relation to that of other objects and plan the position of objects as they move through space without seeing the actual movement. For example, if a ball goes over the fence, a child at this age can go around the fence and locate the ball according to the direction in which it had been moving.

Spatial relations is thought to be related to language development in the same manner that object permanence is related. Because children's initial linguistic utterances frequently deal with basic relationships between objects and spatial relationships, a basic knowledge of these relationships may be necessary to language development.

Means-Ends

The ability of the infant to act purposefully to obtain a goal begins to develop at approximately 8 to 12 months of age. Movements that had been reflexive, or had been performed because they were intrinsically motivating, are now used to achieve results, such as reaching for objects or pushing objects away. By approximately 18 to 24 months, the child is able to plan the movements needed to obtain a goal and to carry out the plan without trial and error. The child has learned to represent goal-seeking behavior mentally.

The understanding of means-ends relationships is essential to the acquisition of language because language is frequently used by children to control their environment and obtain needs through social interaction.

Imitation

Occurring earlier than the other cognitive prerequisites to language, imitation is generally thought to begin around 8 months of age (Sherrod, Vietze, & Friedman, 1978). Imitation begins with visible movements that are already in the child's repertoire, later developing to a point at which the child can imitate new, complex sequences that are delayed in time from the original model. The child is also able to imitate vocalizations accurately.

Play

The importance of play in relation to language has been examined by McCune-Nicolich and Carroll (1981). The authors define several levels of play, suggesting that "the levels of play reflect the child's gradual transition from the expression of meanings through action, to more abstract forms of expression" (p. 2). Their description of the levels of play, with accompanying language behavior, is as follows:

1. *presymbolic schemes*. Play at this level involves using objects and activities within their normal context. For example, a child presented with a cup might demonstrate how to drink from it. Although no pretending is involved, these actions are important precursors of later symbolic play. Language at this level is also presymbolic, involving vocalizations and gestures to indicate desires and interests. Vocalizations are not clearly referential and are often associated with reaching, pointing, and other gestures.
2. *autosymbolic schemes*. Children are now able to pretend, obviously exaggerating the gesture involved. The actions are less dependent on the presence of the real objects and can be conducted without them. These children, however, incorporate in play only those actions that deal with themselves; they will not, for example, comb a doll's hair. Words are first used at this level, indicating the use of symbols, but the words may not be directly related to the referent of the communication. A child at this level, for instance, may use the words *baby* or *milk* to mean the same thing in order to request a drink.
3. *single-scheme symbolic games*. Children now have the ability to extend their play beyond their own body and beyond their usual routines. They can comb a doll's hair, for example, or pretend to carry out a task normally done by an adult. This decentering of play is accompanied by a more refined use of single-word utterances. Words are no longer used globally, requiring the listener to infer the meaning; they are more specifically related to events in the environment. Secondly, vocabulary, like play, is becoming more differentiated, allowing these children to develop labels for subcategories of objects, such as names of body parts. At this level, children do not yet combine words.
4. *combinatorial symbolic games*. The major advance at this level is the ability to combine two or more of the play behaviors that are already established in a child's repertoire into a sequence. These children may use the same play

activity with several participants or may use several different activities with a single participant. Language, as might be expected, expands to include two-word utterances during this period. The progression from single-word utterances to two-word utterances may involve intermediate steps in which children incorporate presyntactic devices, such as empty forms preceding or following words (e.g., uh more, uh cookie), repetition of the same word (e.g., shoe-shoe), or the combination of two one-word utterances. The latter can be differentiated from true two-word utterances by the intonation used, as well as the word order in which they occur.

5. *internally directed symbolic games*. At this stage, children move away from play activities (brushing a doll's hair, brushing a table, brushing their hair) that are conducted in a similar sequential manner toward play that is planned before performance and involves the coordination of several play schemes. These children can use objects in a symbolic manner, pretending, for instance, that a block is a car. They are able to create play situations that are not necessarily associated with conventional uses of play objects. During this stage, language becomes truly syntactic.

McCune-Nicolich and Carroll (1981) hypothesize that the close correlation between the development of play and language is associated with underlying cognitive development, and they suggest that the close relationship lasts through the first 2 years of development. After the age of 2, "both activities, play and language, continue to be influenced by the child's capacity to symbolize. Thus the characteristics of a child's play may reveal insights concerning language capacity. In addition, as play matures, the role of language in play itself becomes critical" (p. 9).

Although a number of prerequisites to language development have been presented here, the exact relationship of these skills to later language development is not clearly defined at this time. It has been suggested by Ferreiro and Sinclair (1971) that specific cognitive prerequisites may influence specific aspects of language development rather than language development in a global sense.

Beginning of Linguistic Production

A great deal of preparation, in the form of early nonlinguistic communication and cognitive development, goes into that milestone of language development, the first word. Although children may produce wordlike utterances prior to their first meaningful words, consistent use of words usually appears between approximately 1 year and 18 months of age (Bates, Benigni, Bretherton, Camaioni, & Volterra, 1977).

The first words consist primarily of names of objects in the environment, and children appear to learn first the names of objects that can be acted upon easily

(Dale, 1976). The word *key* is more likely to be used by the child than the word *wall,* for example. Children's first words do not always have the same meaning that they have as commonly used by adults, however. Clark (1973) observed that children frequently overgeneralize the use of a word, usually based on such features as shape and size. A child may use the word *dogs* to refer to dogs, horses, or cows, for example. Underextensions are also evident; a child may use the word *dog* to refer only to one dog.

Expressive vocabulary develops at a very rapid rate during the preschool years. Van Hattum (1980) states that vocabulary grows from 22 words at 18 months, to 2,500 words at 6 years of age.

Beginning of Syntactic Production

Around 2 years of age, children begin to combine words in a meaningful manner. Brown (1973) provides a framework for examining early syntactic skills, dividing development into five stages that reflect growth in the average length of sentences that children produce, as well as the increase in complexity of these utterances.

The stages are based on a measure of mean length of utterances (MLU), which is derived from a sample of the child's conversational speech. MLU is based on the average number of morphemes (smallest units of meaning) in the child's utterance rather than the number of words, since this measure has been found to be more representative of the child's level of language development. During the first stage (MLU, 1 to 2 morphemes), children's utterances are composed primarily of one- and two-word utterances. The two-word utterances contain basic semantic and relational functions, which are outlined by Gardiner (1978) and summarized in Table 6-1. First-stage utterances typically lack complexity, being without some elements of adult speech, such as articles, prepositions, and verb inflections.

During the second stage (MLU, 2 to 2.5 morphemes), the major change is that children begin to use noun and verb inflections, prepositions, and articles. The morphemes, which are typically acquired in a consistent order, are described by Brown (1973) and are listed in Table 6-2. The past tense forms of verbs are learned before the regular forms because past tense forms are more widely used in the English language. As children learn the rules of grammar (e.g., verb + *ed* = past tense), they often overgeneralize the newly learned rule and produce verb forms such as "goed" in place of the verb *went,* which they had previously used correctly! This error actually indicates a linguistic advancement, as the child is now applying abstract rules to create word forms.

The use of question forms (i.e., who, what, where, when, why, and negatives begins to occur during the third stage (MLU, 2.5 to 3.25). Prior to this time, questions are indicated primarily by a rising inflection on a declarative sentence (e.g., "You see car?"). Although the form of questions is not perfect in this stage,

Table 6-1 Forms of Sensorimotor Knowledge Implied by the Child's Two-Word Utterances

Type	*Sensorimotor Knowledge Implied*	*Example*
Naming	there exists a world of objects, whose members bear names	it ball there doggie
Recurrence	a substance or activity can be prolonged, made to reappear, added to, or otherwise enriched or lengthened	more ball
Nonexistence	an object can disappear from a situation	all-gone ball no doggie
Agent-action	people do things	Johnny fall
Action-object	objects are acted upon	put truck change diaper
Agent-object	a person can perform actions on an object	Johnny stone me milk
Action-location	an action can occur in a specific place	sit chair fall floor
Object-location	an object occupies a specific place	book table
Possessor and possession	people possess objects	my ball Adam ball
Attribution	objects have characteristics	big ball little story
Demonstrative entity	one of a set of objects can be specified	that ball

Source: Derived by permission of the author and publishers from R. Brown, *A First Language: The Early Stages*. Cambridge, Mass.: Harvard University Press, 1973. Copyright © 1973 by the President and Fellows of Harvard College. Adapted from H. Gardiner, Developmental Psychology, Little-Brown, 1978.

with productions such as "What boy's name?" and "Why not he play?" being somewhat typical, the word order approximates adult grammar. In the fourth stage (MLU, 3.25 to 3.75), children combine simple sentences into more complex embedded sentence forms (i.e., "The girl who ran was fast."). The major feature of the fifth stage (MLU, 3.75 to 4.25) is also increased complexity and coordination of sentences. For example, the child combines two simple sentences to form utterances such as "He is little but smart."

The MLU is a better general indicator of language development than chronological age, since the rate of language development varies a great deal among children. When the MLU of a child exceeds five words, however, it may no longer

Table 6-2 Morphemes and Their Usual Order of Acquisition

Morpheme	*Meanings Expressed or Presupposed*	*Examples*
Present progressive	temporary duration	I walk*ing*
in	containment	*in* basket
on	support	*on* floor
Plural	number	two balls
Past irregular[a]	earlierness[b]	it *broke*
Possessive inflection	possession	Adam's ball
Uncontractible copula[c]	number; earlierness	there it *is*
Articles	specific-nonspecific	that *a* book that *the* dog
Past regular	earlierness	Adam walk*ed*
Third person regular	number; earlierness	he walks
Third person irregular	number; earlierness	he *does* she *has*
Uncontractible progressive auxiliary	temporary duration; number; earlierness	this *is* going
Contractible copula[d]	number; earlierness	that'*s* book
Contractible progressive auxiliary	temporary duration; number; earlierness	I'*m* walk*ing*

[a]Formation of past tense by means other than *-ed.*
[b]Denotes understanding that an action or state may occur before the time of utterance.
[c]Use of the verb *to be* as a main verb without contraction.
[d]Use of the verb *to be* as a main verb with contractions.

Source: Derived by permission of the author and publishers from R. Brown, *A First Language: The Early Stages.* Cambridge, Mass.: Harvard University Press, 1973. Copyright © 1973 by the President and Fellows of Harvard College. Adapted from Gardiner, 1978.

be a valid indicator of language development (Dale, 1976). Past this point, complexity of language, rather than length, is a more sensitive measure of development.

Phonological Development

As their ability to produce longer and more complex sentences increases, children are also developing their system of sounds to transmit language. American English is composed of approximately 50 individual speech sounds, or phonemes (Weiss, Lillywhite, & Gordon, 1980), although the number varies within the dialects spoken in the United States. The phoneme can be defined as an individual sound that identifies differences between words. For example, the words *bat* and *back* are each comprised of three phonemes ("b," "a," "t" and "b," "a," "ck," respectively). The substitution of a single phoneme changes the meaning of the word. It should be noted that the phonemes do not necessarily correspond to the number of letters in a word.

Phonemes can be divided into two major categories, vowels and consonants. Vowels are produced by exhaling air from the lungs in a controlled manner through the vocal folds and letting it pass freely through the mouth. The vocal folds vibrate as the air passes between them, and the positioning of the tongue, jaw, and lips creates the differences among the various vowel sounds. Consonants, on the other hand, are produced by constricting the stream of air.

Although several consonant sounds are used consistently before the age of 2 years, many do not become firmly established in a child's repertoire until well after the age of 6 years. Normal variation among children for acquisition of speech sounds can be as much as 4 years. Prather, Hedrick, and Kern (1975) identified the approximate age at which children used consonant sounds correctly 75% of the time (Table 6-3).

Table 6-3 Acquisition of Consonant Sounds

Age	*Sound*	*Example*
2 years	m	*m*an
	n	*n*ose
	ng	goi*ng*
	p	cu*p*
	h	*h*ow
2 years, 4 months	d	*d*og
	k	duc*k*
	f	*f*ive
2 years, 8 months	b	*b*all
	t	*t*oy
	w	*w*ash
3 years	g	*g*ood
	s[a]	bu*s*
3 years	r[a]	*r*un
	l[a]	fa*ll*
3 years, 8 months	sh	*sh*oe
	ch	*ch*ur*ch*
4 years	v[a]	*v*ote
	th[a]	*th*umb
	j	*j*udge
	zh	vi*s*ion

[a]Children demonstrated an extremely wide variation in the age at which these sounds were acquired. The range of normal acquisition extended up to 8 years of age for some sounds.

Source: Adapted from Prather, Hedrick, & Kern (1975).

The development of speech (i.e., sound production) usually involves several stages. Early vocalizations consist primarily of undistinguished cries. At around 1 month of age, children add variety to their vocalization, making an assortment of consonant and vowel sounds in addition to crying. The term *cooing* is generally applied to these sounds. Between approximately 3 months and 1 year of age, children produce vocalizations that become increasingly speechlike. Consonant sounds are quite frequent, and consonant-vowel combinations are used, sometimes involving repetitions and combinations of sounds (e.g., "mama," "baba"). This is often referred to as the babbling stage and includes the use of adultlike intonation patterns toward the end of the stage.

Children continue to develop the ability to make speech sounds throughout early childhood, usually mastering all sounds by the age of 8 (Winitz, 1969). Although there are similarities among children in phonological development, the process appears to involve both active strategies on the part of each child and maturation. Children abstract rules about the ways in which sounds go together based on the speech models in their environment, sometimes forming patterns of errors that result from their incomplete knowledge (Bloom & Lahey, 1978).

The fact that phonological development involves more than maturation and imitation is important in the treatment of phonological disorders in children. If speech sound errors occur as the result of an impaired system of rules for speech production, rather than a maturational error involving isolated sounds, a different approach to intervention may be required.

Functions of Language: Pragmatic Development

In order to facilitate language development in young children it is necessary to understand the reasons children use language, as well as the structure and meaning of their utterances. Bates (1976) observed children's early communication attempts and identified two categories of purposeful communication: protoimperatives and protodeclaratives. The protoimperative is an intentional signal to another individual through gesture or vocalization to get that individual to meet some goal of the child. The protoimperative evolves from a gesture that the child originally used to obtain the goal, such as reaching for an object. Later in development, the child ritualizes the gesture, reaching for an object in a truncated fashion, looking at the adult, then back to the desired object. In this manner, the child makes a symbolic gesture for the purpose of getting the adult to act as a means to an end. The protodeclarative, like the protoimperative, is a preverbal communication attempt. It involves the effort to direct the adult's attention to some event or object in the environment.

Chapman (1981) suggests that children at 16 to 18 months undergo a major change in relation to speech, or discourse skills. Children generally answer simple questions and acknowledge the responses of others before the age of 2. Past the age of 2, however, a greater variety of discourse functions, such as turn taking, changing topic, and offering the floor, are used by children. When speech is analyzed for communicative function, categories that include discourse functions appear to be necessary if the child whose speech is being analyzed has developed skills beyond the 18-month level. The list of communicative functions outlined by Dore (1978) for preschool-aged children (Table 6-4) would be appropriate for children beyond this level of development.

Communicative functions for 3-year-olds were also examined by Dore, who clearly demonstrated the growth in complexity of functions children are able to use as language develops. These language functions are described in Table 6-5.

To assess language functions adequately, Chapman (1981) suggests that it is necessary to take into account any motor problems that might limit a child's means of expressing certain communicative intents, as well as the child's language environment, which may not provide opportunities for the development of all functions.

NEUROLOGY OF SPEECH AND LANGUAGE

The first person to suggest that specific areas of the brain relate to language and speech functioning was Jean Baptiste Bouillaud, a French professor of medicine. In 1825, Bouillaud suggested that the left hemisphere of the brain is responsible for language functions, and this belief has been confirmed through current research (Eisenson, 1973). While a small percentage of individuals process language in the right hemisphere or in both hemispheres, the majority of people process language on the left side of the brain.

Table 6-4 Early Language Functions

Function	*Example*
Labeling	Child names parts of a doll.
Repeating	Child repeats words spoken by another person.
Answering	Child gives name of object when requested by mother.
Requesting action	Child has difficulty with a task, then vocalizes and looks at adult.
Requesting answer	Child picks up a book and says "book?", looking at parent.
Calling	Child calls parent from some distance away and waits for a response.
Greeting	Child says "hi!" when adult enters room.
Protesting	Child says "no!" or screams to resist parent action.
Practicing	Child says word when referent is not present.

Source: Adapted from Dore, 1975.

Table 6-5 Language Functions of 3-Year-Olds

Category of Language Function	*Example*
Requesting	
Yes-no questions	"Is this an apple?"
Wh- questions	"Where's John?"
Clarification questions	"What did you say?"
Action requests	"Give me some juice."
Permission requests	"May I go?"
Rhetorical questions	"You know what I did?"
Responding	
Yes-no answers	"No."
Wh- answers	"John's here."
Clarifications	"I said no."
Compliance	"Okay, I'll do it."
Descriptions	
Identification	"That's a house."
Events	"I'm making a pizza."
Properties	"That's a red house."
Locations	"The zoo is far away."
Times	"It happened yesterday."
Statements	
Rules	"You have to share things with others."
Evaluations	"That's nice."
Internal reports	"I like to play."
Attributes	"He doesn't know the answer."
Explanations	"It will fall."
Acknowledgments	
Acceptance	"Yes." "Oh."
Approval/agreement	"Right." "Yes."
Disapproval/disagreement	"No." "Wrong."
Returning floor to speaker	"What?" "Really?"
Organization devices	
Boundary markers in conversation to indicate beginning, end, and change points	"Hi." "Bye." "By the way,"
Call for attention	"Hey, John!"
Explicit speaker selection	"John." "You!"
Politeness marker	"Thanks." "Sorry."
Accompaniments to nonverbal context	"Here you are."

Table 6-5 continued

Category of Language Function	*Example*
Performatives	
Protests	"Stop that."
Jokes showing nonbelief toward a proposition	"The doggie says meow."
Claims	"That's mine."
Warnings	"Watch out!"
Teases	"You can't do it, you can't do it."

Source: Adapted from Dore, 1978.

Several areas in the left hemisphere are involved in the comprehension and production of language. Broca's area (Figure 6-1) is often thought to be involved in the ability to plan and execute the rapid coordinated movements involved in speech production (Brookshire, 1978). Damage to this area can make it difficult to produce voluntary speech without great effort, even though reflexive movements that are similar to the speech movements can be made with ease. The problem lies in the inability to preplan voluntary movements, rather than in muscle weakness or paralysis. Errors in comprehension and production of syntax are also common when damage occurs in this region.

Wernicke's area (Figure 6-1), located posterior to Broca's area, is also important for language ability, although it is believed to have quite a different function from that of Broca's area (Geschwind, 1972). Damage to Wernicke's area is thought to result in fluent speech production in which the individual often chooses incorrect words and sounds, and may have trouble repeating information that was heard. Wernicke's area is also believed to be involved in the comprehension of speech, lexical and semantic processing, and occasionally in the comprehension of the written word (Kaplan, 1971).

Studies involving electrical stimulation of the brain have shown that disruption of either Broca's area or Wernicke's area sometimes results in errors that had been previously thought to be associated with disruption of one area specifically (Kolb & Whishaw, 1980). In addition, stimulation of a single area occasionally resulted in disruption of both speech production and auditory reception abilities. It appears that the neural mechanisms of speech and language vary in their location from individual to individual and that specific abilities are not always clearly separated anatomically.

Although the left hemisphere is the most prominent area for language functioning, other areas of the brain also appear to be involved in the process. The right hemisphere is thought to play a part in the pragmatic and semantic functions of language, although it is very seldom involved in the processing of the syntactic or

Figure 6-1 The Brain

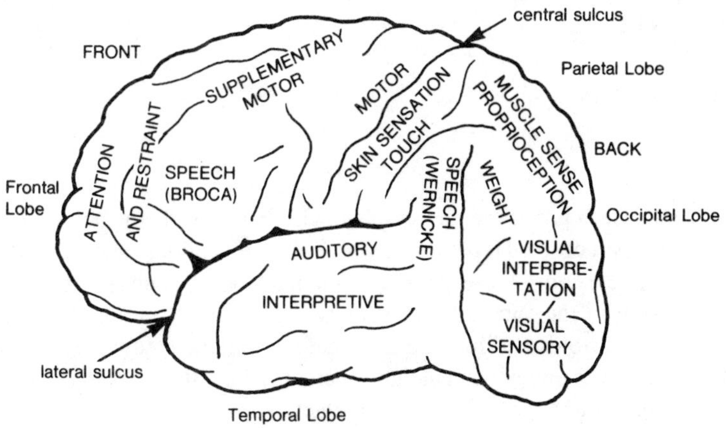

phonological aspects of language. In addition, subcortical structures located deep within the brain, primarily the thalamus, are now known to be involved in language processing. Electrical stimulation to portions of the thalamus have resulted in total arrest of speech, difficulties in naming, perseverative errors, and reduced speed of talking (Ojemann, 1975). The relationship between language functioning and human neurological organization is a complex one that is only beginning to be clearly defined.

DISORDERS OF SPEECH AND LANGUAGE

Communication disorders can be categorized in a number of ways. A distinction is sometimes made between disorders that result from physiological abnormalities (organic disorders) and those that result from environmental circumstances (functional disorders). This distinction is not always useful, however, because the precise origin of the disorder cannot always be determined. In addition, Sameroff and Chandler (1975) have suggested that the physical status of the child and the child's environment interact in the development of some handicapping conditions. Since, under their model, both environmental and physical causal factors must be present before some disorders occur and since both physical and environmental factors may be present in many disorders, a categorical distinction between the two is not always valid.

A more useful distinction can be made between disorders of speech and disorders of language. Speech disorders are disruptions of the motor act of speech, while language disorders are disruptions of (1) the syntactic and phonological rules for language; (2) semantic development, involving formation and coding of concepts; and (3) pragmatic development, whereby language is used appropriately within a social context.

Speech Disorders

Stuttering

Disfluent speech is common in preschool children. The disfluencies frequently heard include part of word repetitions, whole word repetitions, phrase repetitions, interjections, revisions, tense pauses, prolongations of sounds, and excessive muscle tension in the formation of sounds. Yairi (1981) examined disfluency patterns of 2-year-olds and found a great deal of variation; some children in the study were 10 times more disfluent than others. In a later study, Yairi (1982) found 3 years of age to be a peak period of disfluent speech.

Although these disfluencies are common in preschool children, the cause of stuttering, which can be defined as a disruption of verbal expression involving frequently occurring involuntary repetitions or prolongations (Wingate, 1972), is not clearly identified. Studies have been conducted to investigate physiological differences in people who stutter (Hall & Jerger, 1978; Howie, 1981); however, the most parsimonious explanation for stuttering behavior suggests it occurs as a result of operant conditioning (Shames & Sherrick, 1963). It is possible that the normal disfluencies of the preschool child are mistakenly viewed as abnormal behavior by parents, and the negative attention directed toward the child's speech production increases stress and tension on the part of the child. Williams (1978), in a discussion of stuttering, suggests "It is a problem that involves not only a speaker but his listeners as well. Indeed, it may be said with peculiar validity that in the beginning stuttering is not so much a problem for the speaker, who is most often a small child, as it is for his important listeners, who are usually, although not always necessarily, his parents" (p. 284). At the preschool level, effective stuttering treatment sometimes involves counseling parents to influence their attitude toward the child's speech, rather than direct intervention with the child.

Voice Disorders

The majority of voice disorders are due to misuse of the vocal mechanisms (Boone, 1971). Morris and Spriestersbach (1978) identify several descriptive categories of voice disorders, including

- pitch disorders, involving too high or too low a pitch, or a pattern of pitch that is so monotonous that it calls attention to itself

- disorders of loudness, wherein speech is habitually too loud or soft for the setting, or where sporadic bursts or cycles of excessive loudness are observed
- voice quality disorders, involving breathiness, harshness, and nasality.

Excessive nasality results in speech that seems to be coming through the nose (hypernasality). At the other extreme, hyponasal speakers sound as if they have a head cold, with little or no sound coming through the nose.

Before any treatment for voice disorders is initiated, a medical evaluation must be obtained in order to ensure that the problem is due to misuse of the vocal mechanism rather than other more serious causes.

Articulation Disorders

Disorders of articulation are defined by McDonald (1980) as "production of speech sounds which are not adequate acoustic representations of the phonological sequences of the language " (p. 163). In other words, the speech sounds produced by the child are not the same as those used by other speakers. Traditionally, articulation errors have been divided into the following categories:

1. omissions ("ca" for "cake")
2. substitutions ("fum" for "thumb")
3. distortions (producing an "s" sound with the airstream flowing laterally over the sides of the tongue, rather than forward, over the tip of the tongue. This particular distortion is referred to as a lateral lisp.)
4. additions ("aluminumnum" for "aluminum," or "buhlast" for "blast")

The majority of articulation errors produced by young children result from lack of maturational development; however, the cause may be more serious. For example, the disorders of apraxia and the dysarthrias result from a variety of neurological disruptions and are sometimes present in young children.

Apraxia interferes with motor programming of speech, rather than the production of any specific speech sound. The disorder is characterized by difficulty in performing oral nonspeech tasks volitionally (e.g., blowing, coughing, puffing out the cheeks), general clumsiness and awkwardness, difficulty producing rapid speech or polysyllabic words. Errors of distortion and addition are more common in apraxic children than in children who produce developmental articulation errors (Darley, 1978).

The dysarthrias result from damage to the central or peripheral nervous system that disrupts the basic motor processes of speech. Speech movements may be disrupted in their speed, range, strength, or coordination (Wertz, 1978). Muscular movement involved in breath support for speech, phonation (vibration of the vocal folds), articulation, and resonance (altering the size and shape of the speech cavity to produce appropriate sound quality) may be disrupted. Dysarthria is characteristic of the speech of children with cerebral palsy, although it may be present without other accompanying disorders.

Language Disorders

There are several ways to classify language disorders. Two common methods are a categorical approach and a descriptive approach. The categorical approach is based on causal factors, such as autism, mental retardation, hearing impairment, and aphasia. The descriptive approach, on the other hand, is based on language functioning (i.e., syntactic, semantic, pragmatic, and phonological ability), regardless of the medical or educational diagnosis that accompanies the language disorder.

Both the categorical approach and the descriptive approach have value for teachers of language-disordered children. An awareness of the cause of a language disorder may indicate *how* to present materials and instruction to a child. A child with a hearing loss, for instance, may require additional visual cuing and demonstration of tasks, while a mentally retarded child may require more repetition of a task, paired with a detailed task analysis of the behavior.

The descriptive analysis of language skills can provide the teacher with information on *what* to teach, even if the cause of a language disorder is known. Although the components of a language description can be discussed separately, it should be recognized that they may be involved in a language disorder in various combinations. A child may be delayed in all the areas of syntactic, morphological, semantic, and pragmatic functioning or in one or more areas to any degree.

Grammatical Functioning: Syntax and Morphology

Children who have deficits in grammatical functioning may understand the meaning of words (semantics) and may know that language can be used for certain functions (e.g., requesting, describing, acknowledging, controlling), but they have difficulty putting words together correctly in sentences and using the right form of a word to convey a specific meaning. Errors that can be expected from a child with impaired skills in this area include incomplete sentences; use of gestures in place of sentences; omission of word forms that signify important meanings, such as number ("two boy" instead of "two boys") or verb tense ("yesterday I walk" instead of "yesterday I walked"). It is possible for a child to have difficulty in the area of grammatical functioning and still have adequately developed conceptual skills, as well as an understanding of the social rules involved in communicating.

Semantic Functioning: The Relationship between Words and Meaning

In some cases, children may have adequately developed syntactic and morphological rule systems and may understand the social uses of language, but lack basic knowledge regarding objects and events in the environment. The language of these children may be characterized by lack of specificity (i.e., "I found this thing over here."), difficulty elaborating on a topic, or frequent changes in topic in order to guide the conversation into an area where the child has some knowledge. Bloom and Lahey (1978) suggest that blind children and hydrocephalic children sometimes exhibit a disorder of semantic functioning, even though their knowledge of the structure of language and pragmatic use of language are adequate.

Pragmatic Functioning: Language and Social Context

Children who have difficulty with language use may not understand the rules governing what it is appropriate to say and to whom, when, and where it should be said (Carrow-Woolfolk & Lynch, 1982). Speech may be produced, but directed to no one in particular and unrelated to the immediate context. Children who do not use the language to achieve the variety of functions previously discussed (see Tables 6-4 and 6-5) may also fail to use other behaviors related to social interaction, such as maintaining eye contact, turn taking, and acknowledging responses.

Memory Skills: Storage and Recall

Deficient memory skills can impede language learning by inhibiting the child's recall of the adult model, which may be remembered incompletely or inaccurately due to poor short-term memory. Although a child may be able to recall information distant in time (long-term memory), the short-term memory necessary for the processing of messages may be impaired. Children with memory deficits may have difficulty remembering the exact wording of sentences, even though they can recall the general meaning of the message. Because of this, they may have more trouble recalling sentences in which the word order does not match the order of events (e.g., "Before you go outside, wash your hands." as opposed to "Wash your hands, then go outside."). Questions in which word order is reversed and other complex sentence structures are particular problems to these children (Wiig & Semel, 1980).

These children may also have difficulty in recalling words. They may be able to recognize the correct word when it is spoken, but be unable to recall it on demand. Errors often include selection of words that are incorrect but related to the desired word, such as the opposite of the word, a word that sounds the same, or a word from the same semantic class, such as "banana" for "apple."

EXCEPTIONALITIES ASSOCIATED WITH LANGUAGE DISORDER

Hearing Loss

Children who are hearing-impaired generally exhibit some difficulty with speech and language, although there is a great deal of variation because of differences in degree and type of hearing loss, age at onset, amount of early intervention, and ability level of the child. Hearing loss may affect speech and language development in a number of ways, including

- delayed syntactic and morphological development
- delayed speech development
- voice disorders, involving resonance and pitch
- limited oral vocabulary, lacking pronouns, prepositions, and adverbs
- simplified and shortened sentence production

Mental Retardation

Approximately 45% of mentally retarded individuals have some impairment in language functioning (Spreen, 1965). It is difficult to describe general patterns of language development and language disorders in children who are mentally retarded, however, because individual skills vary according to the degree of retardation, the cause of the retardation, and the environment of the child. Miller, Chapman, and MacKenzie (1981) found that some mentally retarded children demonstrated delays in both comprehension and production of language, while others were delayed only in production. In addition, several children had developed language skills *beyond* their mental age. Language characteristics that may be found in mentally retarded children include

- delay in onset of language
- articulation delay
- high incidence of hearing loss
- difficulty generalizing language rules to new situations
- higher than normal incidence of auditory memory, stuttering, and voice problems

Emotional Disturbance

The primary characteristic of emotional disturbances in children is an impairment in the development of relationships with people (Rutter, 1978). Although autism and childhood schizophrenia share this major characteristic, they differ in several ways. Autism present prior to 30 months of age is more likely to be associated with mental retardation and seldom involves delusions and hallucinations, which are common in schizophrenia. Autism is also more common in boys than girls (Carrow-Woolfolk & Lynch, 1982). Language characteristics that may be found in children with emotional disturbances include

- impairment in pragmatic use of language, including inappropriate and noncommunicative language production
- mutism
- echolalia (meaningless repetition of words or phrases)
- difficulty generalizing word meaning
- pronoun reversals (e.g., substitution of *I* for *you*)
- monotone voice

Acquired Aphasia

Existing language skills may be lost as the result of brain injury. Children who suffer head injury, brain tumor, or other neurological insults that disrupt language functioning tend to follow a common pattern of recovery. An initial period of mutism, which may be related to psychological trauma as well as to the neurological injury (Alajouanine & Lhermitte, 1965), is followed by rapid recovery with some, but not all individuals. Younger children appear to recover more completely. Although recovery may appear complete, there is often some subtle residual deficit in linguistic or cognitive functioning (Hecaen, 1976). Characteristics of children with acquired aphasia include

- an initial period of mutism
- generally, greater impairment in production than in comprehension of language
- dysarthria
- telegraphic speech during recovery
- difficulty with math skills

COMMUNICATION DISORDERS: INTERVENTION AND MANAGEMENT

A classroom teacher has two main goals in working with children who have communication disorders: the improvement of communication skills and the effective presentation of other academic tasks to children who have difficulty understanding and producing language. The process of improving a child's ability to communicate is generally referred to as language intervention. Language management, in contrast, is the structuring of the child's environment so that the child can learn despite the communication disorder. Since language is an integral part of academic and social development, a team approach, involving the classroom teacher, the speech/language pathologist, parents, and others, is essential in intervention and management of communication disorders. General considerations include selection of appropriate goals and programs, the establishment of an environment that is conducive to language development, and the use of language-facilitating techniques that enable the child to understand and use language successfully.

Selecting the Program

The development of a program for a child with a language disorder should contain six basic components, according to Carrow-Woolfolk and Lynch (1982):

1. the overall goal of the program and a series of intermediate goals expressed in terms of behavioral objectives or targets
2. selection of content
3. specification of the content in terms of priority and hierarchy of tasks and procedures to reach the objectives
4. specification of instructional and motivational strategies
5. identification of measures for evaluation of progress
6. procedures for stabilization and generalization

From these basic components, it can be clearly seen that the development of a successful language skill program involves analysis of a child's specific communicative needs, detailed planning of intervention procedures, and ongoing assessment to evaluate progress. While commercial programs may be useful, they must be examined in terms of these components to ensure that they meet the needs of each child with whom they are to be used; they cannot be used indiscriminately, as though all language-disordered children had the same needs.

Teaching Functional Skills

Those who are developing a program must decide whether to attempt to remediate underlying processes that are thought to be essential to language development, such as auditory discrimination, memory, and sequencing, or whether to teach specific language behaviors, such as grammatical constructs and word meanings. There is little reason to believe that programs directed toward the facilitation of underlying processes improve language functioning (Rees, 1973; Hammill & Larsen, 1974). It is more useful to include both the process involved and the behavior that is necessary in the language objective. For example, if a child has difficulty following directions in the classroom because of a memory deficit, an appropriate lesson might involve responding to gradually longer and more complex classroom directions, rather than a memory task that is unrelated to the functional needs of the child.

Structuring the Program

Language intervention programs vary considerably in the degree of structure. Highly structured programs incorporate specific directions for presenting stimuli, scheduling reinforcement, and correcting errors that are based on a behavioral paradigm. Other methods, such as the *Interactive Language Development Teaching Program* (Lee, Koenigsknecht, & Mulhern, 1975), involve a more natural, conversational setting, with emphasis on using language structures in a meaningful way. A study by Friedman and Friedman (1980) in which high and low structure programs were compared suggests, not surprisingly, that no one approach is best for all children. The highly structured approach was more successful with children who had limited cognitive ability or who had very poor syntax skills. Conversely, the less structured program was more effective for children who had a higher level of intellectual functioning and who were not so markedly delayed in syntax functioning. While these are very broad guidelines, they emphasize the need to individualize language intervention.

Arranging the Environment To Facilitate Language Use

In order to use language effectively, children must practice their skills in a variety of settings. Children often learn a specific language behavior in a classroom or clinic setting, but fail to generalize the skill to other settings. The involvement of parents, siblings, and school personnel as participants in language training is one method of encouraging carryover of the skill. In addition, Spradlin and Siegel (1982) suggest several other techniques for establishing generalization in language training. They suggest that the teacher

1. arrange the setting so the child is more likely to use language to meet needs
2. be responsive to attempts at communication
3. teach skills that are useful outside the classroom
4. vary the events and objects used in language training
5. use consequences that are varied and are related to the language being taught
6. as skills improve, reduce the rate of reinforcement
7. avoid responding to needs before the child has an opportunity to use communication to achieve needs (give the child time to respond)

As mentioned earlier, Hubbell (1977) suggests that the teacher avoid using verbal praise to reinforce spontaneous language production. He found that children were *less* likely to speak when their utterances were followed by verbal praise (e.g., "Good talking." and "I like the way you said that."). This finding is not particularly surprising, since few people would be willing to carry on a conversation with an individual whose conversational skills consisted primarily of this type of response. The technique should be used cautiously when generalization of spontaneous language is the goal of intervention.

The use of these general techniques, combined with the implementation of an organized individual language intervention plan that involves the teacher, speech/language pathologist, and parents, will help provide an environment in which the language-disordered child can develop greater proficiency in communication skills.

REFERENCES

Alajouanine, T., & Lhermitte, F. Acquired aphasia in children. *Brain,* 1965, *88,* 654-662.

Aram, D., & Nation, J. Preschool language disturbance and subsequent language and academic difficulties. *Journal of Communication Disorders,* 1980, *13,* 159-178.

Bates, E. *Language and context: The acquisition of pragmatics.* New York: Academic Press, 1976.

Bates, E., Benigni, L., Bretherton, I., Camaioni, L., & Volterra, V. From gesture to the first word: On cognitive and social prerequisites. In M. Lewis & L. Rosenblum (Eds.), *Interaction, conversation, and the development of language.* New York: John Wiley, 1977.

Berry, P. (Ed.). *Language and communication in the mentally handicapped.* Baltimore: University Park Press, 1976.

Bloom, L., & Lahey, M. *Language development and language disorders.* New York: John Wiley, 1978.

Boone, D. *The voice and voice therapy.* Englewood Cliffs, N.J.: Prentice-Hall, 1971.

Brookshire, R. *An introduction to aphasia.* Minneapolis: BRK Publishers, 1978.

Brown, R. *A first language: The early stages.* Cambridge, Mass.: Harvard University Press, 1973.

Brown, R., Cazden, C., & Bellugi, U. The child's grammar from I to III. In J.P. Hill (Ed.), *Minnesota symposium on child psychology* (Vol. 2). Minneapolis: University of Michigan Press, 1969.

Carrow-Woolfolk, E., & Lynch, J. *An integrative approach to language disorders in children.* New York: Grune & Stratton, 1982.

Chapman, R. Exploring children's communicative intents. In J. Miller (Ed.), *Assessing language production in children: Experimental procedures.* Baltimore, Md.: University Park Press, 1981.

Chomsky, N. *Aspects of the theory of syntax.* Cambridge, Mass.: M.I.T. Press, 1965.

Clark, E. What's in a word? On the child's acquisition of semantics in his first language. In T. Moore (Ed.), *Cognition and the acquisition of language.* New York: John Wiley, 1973.

Coggins, T., & Carpenter, R. Introduction to the area of language development. In M. Cohen & P. Gross (Eds.), *The developmental resource: Behavioral sequences for assessment and program planning.* New York: Grune & Stratton, 1979.

Condon, W., & Sander, L. Neonate movement is synchronized with adult speech: Interactional participation and language acquisition. *Science,* 1974, *183,* 99-101.

Cromer, R. The cognitive hypothesis of language acquisition and its implications for child language deficiency. In D. Morehead & A. Morehead (Eds.), *Normal and deficient child language*. Baltimore: University Park Press, 1976.

Cromer, R. Reconceptualizing language acquisition and cognitive development. In R. Schiefelbusch & D. Bricker (Eds.), *Early language: Acquisition and intervention*. Baltimore: University Park Press, 1981.

Dale, P. *Language development: Structure and function*. New York: Holt, Rinehart and Winston, 1976.

Darley, F. Differential diagnosis of acquired motor speech disorders. In F. Darley & D. Spriesterbach (Eds.), *Diagnostic methods in speech pathology*. New York: Harper & Row, 1978.

Dore, J. Holophrases, speech acts and language universals. *Journal of Child Language*, 1975, *2*, 21-40.

Dore, J. Requestive systems in nursery school conversations: Analysis of talk in its social context. In R. Campbell & P. Smith (Eds.), *Recent advances in the psychology of language: Language development and mother-child interaction*. New York: Plenum Press, 1978.

Eimas, P., Siqueland, E., Jusczyk, P., & Vigorito, J. Speech perception in infants. *Science*, 1971, *171*, 303-306.

Eisenson, J. *Adult aphasia: Assessment and treatment*. New York: Appleton-Century-Crofts, 1973.

Ferreiro, E., & Sinclair, H. Temporal relationships in language. *International Journal of Psychology*, 1971, *6*, 39-47.

Friedman, P., & Friedman, K. Accounting for individual differences when comparing the effectiveness of remedial language teaching methods. *Applied Psycholinguistics*, 1980, *1*, 153-170.

Gardiner, H. *Developmental Psychology*. Boston: Little-Brown, 1978.

Geschwind, N. Language and the brain. *Scientific American*, 1972, *226*, 76-83.

Hall, J., & Jerger, J. Central auditory function in stutterers. *Journal of Speech and Hearing Research*, 1978, *21*, 324-337.

Hammill, D., & Larsen, S. The effectiveness of psycholinguistic training. *Exceptional Child*, 1974, *9*, 5-13.

Hecaen, H. Acquired aphasia in children and the ontogenesis of hemispheric functional specialization. *Brain and Language*, 1976, *3*, 114-134.

Howie, P. Concordance for stuttering in monozygotic and dizygotic twin pairs. *Journal of Speech and Hearing Research*, 1981, *3*, 317-321.

Hubbell, R. On facilitating spontaneous talking in young children. *Journal of Speech and Hearing Disorders*, 1977, *42*, 216-231.

Kaplan, H. *Anatomy and physiology of speech*. New York: McGraw-Hill, 1971.

King, R., Jones, C., & Lasky, E. In retrospect: A fifteen year follow-up report of speech-language-disordered children. *Language, Speech, and Hearing Services in Schools*, 1982, *13*, 24-32.

Kolb, B., & Whishaw, I. *Fundamentals of human neuropsychology*. San Francisco: W.H. Freeman, 1980.

Kopin, M. Articulation. In M. Filter (Ed.), *Speech/language clinician's handbook*. Springfield, Ill.: Charles C Thomas, 1979.

Lee, L., Koenigsknecht, R., & Mulhern, S. *Interactive language development teaching*. Evanston, Ill.: Northwestern University Press, 1975.

Lenneberg, E. *Biological foundations of language*. New York: John Wiley, 1967.

McCune-Nicolich, L., & Carroll, S. Development of symbolic play: Implications for the language specialist. *Topics in Language Disorders*, 1981, *2*, 1-15.

McDonald, E. Disorders of articulation. In R. Van Hattum (Ed.), *Communication disorders: An introduction*. New York: Macmillan, 1980.

Miller, J. *Assessing language production in children: Experimental procedures*. Baltimore: University Park Press, 1981.

Miller, J., Chapman, R., & MacKenzie, H. *Individual differences in the language acquisition of mentally retarded children*. Paper presented at the Society for Research in Child Development. Boston, 1981.

Morris, H., & Spriestersbach, D. Appraisal of respiration and phonation. In F. Darley & D. Spriestersbach (Eds.), *Diagnostic methods in speech pathology*. New York: Harper & Row, 1978.

Muma, J. *Language handbook: Concepts, assessment, intervention*. Englewood Cliffs, N.J.: Prentice-Hall, 1978.

Nelson, K. Structure and strategy in learning to talk. *Monographs of the Society for Research in Child Development*, 1973, *38*(No. 149).

Ojemann, G. The thalamus and language. *Brain and Language*, 1975, *2*, 1-120.

Prather, E., Hedrick, D., & Kern, C. Articulation development in children aged two to four years. *Journal of Speech and Hearing Disorders*, 1975, *40*, 179-191.

Rees, N. Auditory processing factors in language disorders: The view from Procrustes' bed. *Journal of Speech and Hearing Disorders*, 1973, *38*, 98-110.

Rutter, M. Language disorders and infantile autism. In M. Rutter & E. Schopler (Eds.), *Autism: A reappraisal of concepts and treatments*. New York: Plenum Press, 1978.

Sameroff, A., & Chandler, M. Reproductive risk and the continuum of caretaking causality. In F. Horowitz (Ed.), *Review of child development research* (Vol. 4). Chicago: University of Chicago Press, 1975.

Shames, G., & Sherrick, C. A discussion of nonfluency and stuttering as operant conditioning. *Journal of Speech and Hearing Disorders*, 1963, *28*, 3-18.

Sherrod, K., Vietze, P., & Friedman, S. *Infancy*. Monterey, Calif.: Brooks/Cole Publishing, 1978.

Silva, P. The prevalence, stability and significance of developmental language delay in preschool children. *Developmental Medicine and Child Neurology*, 1980, *22*, 768-777.

Sinclair-deZwart, H. Developmental psycholinguistics. In D. Elkind & J. Flavell (Eds.), *Studies in cognitive development*. New York: Oxford University Press, 1969.

Skinner, B. *Verbal behavior*. New York: Appleton-Century-Crofts, 1957.

Spradlin, J., & Siegel, J. Language training in natural and clinical environments. *Journal of Speech and Hearing Disorders*, 1982, *47*, 2-6.

Spreen, O. Language function in mental retardation. *American Journal of Mental Deficiency*, 1965, *69*, 482-494.

Stevenson, J., & Richman, N. The prevalence of language delay in a population of 3-year-old children and its association with general retardation. *Developmental Medicine and Child Neurology*, 1976, *18*, 431-441.

Van Hattum, R. *Communication disorders: An introduction*. New York: Macmillan, 1980.

Weiss, C., Lillywhite, H., & Gordon, M. *Clinical management of articulation disorders*. St. Louis: C.V. Mosby, 1980.

Wertz, R. Neuropathologies of speech and language: An introduction to patient management. In D. Johns (Ed.), *Clinical management of neurogenic communicative disorders*. Boston: Little, Brown, 1978.

Wiig, E., & Semel, E. *Language assessment and intervention for the learning disabled*. Columbus, Ohio: Charles E. Merrill, 1980.

Williams, D. The problem of stuttering. In F. Darley & D. Spriestersbach (Ed.), *Diagnostic methods in speech pathology*. New York: Harper & Row, 1978.

Wingate, M. A standard definition of stuttering. In L. Emerick & C. Hamre (Eds.), *An analysis of stuttering: Selected readings*. Danville, Ill.: The Interstate Printers, 1972.

Winitz, H. *Articulatory acquisition and behavior*. New York: Appleton-Century-Crofts, 1969.

Yairi, E. Disfluencies of normally speaking two-year-old children. *Journal of Speech and Hearing Research*, 1981, *24*, 490-495.

Yairi, E. Longitudinal studies of disfluencies in two-year-old children. *Journal of Speech and Hearing Research*, 1982, *25*, 155-160.

Yoder, D., & Miller, J. What we may know and what we can do: Input toward a system. In J. McClean, D. Yoder, & R. Schiefelbusch (Eds.), *Language intervention with the retarded: Developing strategies*. Baltimore: University Park Press, 1972.

Chapter 7

Working with Sensorily Impaired Children

Rebecca R. Fewell

Children who are born without vision or hearing must learn about their world in ways that are different from those in which other children learn. These differences affect the mental, physical, and social aspects of development. For example, lack of vision causes delays in certain milestones, such as the acquisition of the object permanence concept and the ability to use and respond to nonverbal communicative acts. During the early years, the impact of blindness or deafness on the developing child can be minimized by means of carefully planned experiences in which the child's parents, siblings, extended family, teachers, neighbors, and other concerned people all have roles.

VISUAL IMPAIRMENTS

There are no consistent procedures for defining visually handicapped populations or for determining inclusive criteria. In order to permit easy classification, definitions and criteria usually reflect units of measurement or particular services that an agency provides. Measurement units typically are expressed in reference to Snellen Chart notations of visual acuity. This chart consists of symbols (numbers or letters) that decrease in size; it is read at a distance of 20 feet. Symbol size corresponds to the standard distance at which a person with normal vision can recognize the symbol.

An acuity of 20/20 means that a person can read the 20-foot-size symbol at a distance of 20 feet, a ratio considered representative of normal vision. If, at this distance, a person can read only the 200-foot-size letter (2-1/2 inches), vision would be considered 20/200. In other words, an object that a person with normal vision (20/20) can see at 200 feet must be brought to 20 feet before the person with 20/200 acuity can read it. When visual acuity is more significantly impaired (20/400 or worse) or when very young or handicapped persons are tested, it is frequently necessary to test vision at distances of less than 20 feet. In these cases, the numerator is less than 20, usually 10 or 5. A reading of 10/200 means that an object distinguished by persons with normal acuity at 200 feet must be brought as close as 10 feet for recognition.

DEFINITION

While early definitions of blindness were stated for legal and economic decisions, the current definition was written into the Social Security Act of 1935, primarily to identify aged persons in need of increased benefits:

> visual acuity for distance vision of 20/200 or less in the better eye, with best correction; or visual acuity of more than 20/200 if the widest diameter of field of vision subtends an angle no greater than 20 degrees. (National Society for the Prevention of Blindness, 1966, p. 10)

In order to identify persons whose vision is sufficiently limited to require special education services (partially seeing children), Hathaway (1959) provided this classification:

> 1. Children having a visual acuity of 20/70 or less in the better eye after all necessary medical or surgical treatment has been given and compensating lenses provided when the need for them is indicated. Such children, must, however, have a residue of sight that makes it possible to use this as the chief avenue of approach to the brain.
> 2. Children with a visual deviation from the normal who, in the opinion of the eye specialist, can benefit from the special educational facilities provided for the partially seeing. (p. 16)

Currently, educators believe that the most important visual consideration is *functional visual efficiency,* or how well children use their vision, rather than the particular measure of visual acuity. Visual efficiency (American Medical Association Committee Report, 1955) includes visual acuity (both distant and near), as well as visual fields, ocular motility, binocular vision, adaptations to light and dark, color vision, and accommodation (Lowenfeld, 1973). Experimental programs for children with severely limited vision have demonstrated that visual training can achieve significant gains in visual efficiency (Ashcroft, Halliday, & Barraga, 1965; Barraga, 1964). Table 7-1 presents the relationship between Snellen measurements of distance acuity and the percentage of visual efficiency.

Functional vision is either central or peripheral. Central vision is used for color discrimination and sharp seeing tasks, such as spotting an M&M on the floor.

Table 7-1 Central Visual Acuity for Distance and Corresponding Percentage of Visual Efficiency

Snellen Measure of Central Visual Acuity	*Percent of Visual Efficiency*
20/20	100
20/40	85
20/50	75
20/80	60
20/100	50
20/200	20

Source: From "*Estimation of Loss of Visual Efficiency,*" *Archives of Industrial Health,* October 1955. Copyright 1955, American Medical Association. Reprinted by permission.

Peripheral vision allows the individual to be aware of movement and to recognize features of the environment under decreased illumination. With peripheral vision, an infant can locate a bottle on one side of the crib and track it 180°. Children with damage in the peripheral areas can see only things directly in front of them: this is called "gun barrel" or "tunnel" vision. For the teacher, functional vision determines where materials are placed, their size, the colors chosen, and the light selected (Langley & DuBose, 1976).

PREVALENCE

Exact figures on the number of visually impaired persons in the United States are difficult to obtain, even though visual defects typically occur in about 20% of the general population. Blind or partially sighted students represent about 0.1% of the school-aged children (Caton, 1981) or about 1 student per 1,000. Only 3 of 10 such children are considered blind for educational purposes (Reynolds & Birch, 1978). Kirchner, Peterson, and Suhr (1979) reported that the estimated number of severely visually impaired children and youth (aged 17 and under) was 36,800 in 1977, although, according to the same authors, a survey of the American Printing House for the Blind showed only 29,400 legally blind persons for that same year. The Office of Special Education and Rehabilitative Services reports that 1,838 visually impaired and 232 deaf-blind children between the ages of 3 and 5 years were served under PL 94-142 and PL 89-313 during 1980-1981. A comparison of the number of children served during later school years with the prevalence rates and the numbers reported served during the preschool years strongly suggests that a large majority of young visually impaired children are not receiving services. (See Fewell, 1982, and Demott, 1982, for more complete discussions of prevalence issues.)

THE EYES: PROBLEMS AND TREATMENTS

Much of what is learned comes through the combined efforts of eyes and brain. For the eyes to receive information, light must fall on the image. As light rays are reflected from the image to the eyes, they pass through the cornea, the clear front window surrounding the eye; the aqueous, the watery liquid behind the cornea; the pupil, the opening in the colored iris; and the lens. The lens bends the light rays, inverting the image and focusing it on the retina, the rear inner lining of the eye. After hitting the retina, which contains rods (black and white receptors) and cones (color receptors), light rays are converted to electrical impulses that are relayed via the optic nerve to the brain. The brain adds meaning to the sensation, and the image is experienced in a form compatible with what is known about it or what it means to the individual in that given moment. (For more complete information on the anatomy of the eye, see Vaughan, Asbury, & Cook, 1971.)

PHYSIOLOGY OF THE EYE

Common Causes of Visual Dysfunction

Refractive errors are the most common eye problems, with one of every two persons having a refractive error. The light rays that enter the eye do not fall exactly on the retina. When the eyeball is too long, the image falls in front of the retina and myopia (nearsightedness) results. Nearsighted persons can see things that are near them, but they cannot distinguish images at a distance. When the eyeball is too short, the image falls in back of the retina and hyperopia (farsightedness) occurs. Farsighted persons see things better at a distance; however, the effort to view things clearly at various distances requires excessive accommodation of the lens curvature and can cause fatigue and restlessness.

If the cornea of the eye has an imperfect curvature, light rays focus separately rather than at a single point and astigmatism (distorted and blurred vision) results. A person can have both astigmatism and nearsightedness or farsightedness.

Many young children have amblyopia, sometimes called "lazy eye," a dimness of vision in one eye that causes them to suppress the weaker eye and use only the stronger one. The condition may be due to eye-muscle imbalance, refractive error, or other defects present when the infant is learning to use vision.

The failure of the eyes to focus together properly is called heterotropia. One eye usually focuses on an object, while the other eye is directed elsewhere. Other terms for this abnormality are squint and strabismus.

A cataract—the leading cause of blindness in the United States—is a cloudy condition or opacity in the lens of the eye. Opacity begins gradually as the light rays are partially blocked and are distorted by the time they fall on the retina.

Cataract surgery, which involves the removal of the lens, is successful in 95% of cases. In young children, cataracts occur most frequently because of an insult during their intrauterine life. Surgery is usually performed when the ophthalmologist considers the cataract "ripe."

Vision loss produced by increased pressure within the globe of the eye is called glaucoma. The watery fluid in the eye fails to drain properly and pressure builds up, damaging the nerve fibers of the optic nerve and impairing vision. Symptoms develop slowly and are very difficult to detect at first. If diagnosed early, however, proper treatment can prevent damage.

Retinitis pigmentosa is an inherited disease caused by changes in the retina. The disease gradually destroys the rods and cones and decreases ability to see at night; night blindness is frequently a first symptom of the disease. Later, retinitis pigmentosa decreases peripheral or side vision, even in the presence of light, and results in tunnel vision.

The separation of the inner layer of the retina from its outer layer is known as retinal detachment. This condition occurs most frequently when a tear or hole develops in the retina and vitreous fluid seeps between the retinal layers and causes the separation. The usual effect is a darkening of one portion of the visual field; other signs are sootlike spots or light flashes. If diagnosed early, surgery can restore vision in 85% of cases.

In some cases, a degeneration is limited to a very small but important area of the retina, called the macula. Located in the central retina, the macula is responsible for perception of fine details. A properly functioning macula is required for reading. Macular degeneration results in a gradual loss of central vision.

Observable signs of visual problems that can be noted by teachers or other caregivers include

- eyes turning in or out at any time
- red or watery eyes
- encrusted eyelids
- frequent styes
- swollen eyes
- frequent head adjustment when looking at distant objects
- focusing difficulties
- tracking difficulties
- frequent rubbing of eyes
- complaints of itchy, scratchy, or stinging eyes
- avoidance of close work
- frequent blinking, frowning, or scowling
- tilting or turning head to focus on objects

- fatigue after visual tasks
- moving head rather than eyes while looking at a page
- frequent confusion of similarly shaped letters, numbers, and words
- covering one eye to see with other eye
- unusual clumsiness or awkwardness
- poor eye-hand coordination
- headaches or nausea after close visual tasks

Visual Aids and Treatments

Corrective lenses (eyeglasses or contacts) are the aids most often used to improve impaired vision. Many preschool children, however, are not being fitted with contact lenses when large refractive errors are found.

Amblyopia is treated by patching the stronger eye, forcing the child to use the amblyopic eye. Cataracts are treated by surgical removal of the damaged lens and implantation of a substitute lens; special eyeglasses or contact lenses may be prescribed. Surgery is also possible to correct retinal detachment. Glaucoma is treated by drugs or, if necessary, surgery to create another outlet for the fluid. Heterotropia is treated with lenses, prisms, occlusion, visual training, drugs, or surgery (Harley & Lawrence, 1977).

In many cases of eye disease, early detection and treatment can mean usable vision for a longer period.

TESTING PRESCHOOL CHILDREN WITH VISUAL IMPAIRMENTS

Routine examinations in daycare centers and preschool settings frequently identify children with severe visual problems. Tests that are useful in vision screening of young children are

- *A Flash-Card Vision Test for Children* (New York Association for the Blind, 1966) was designed for preschool children and has proved successful with children 27 months of age. Three symbols (apple, house, umbrella) are presented, and the children verbally or manually label or match symbols at 10 feet or less to determine visual acuity. The result is given in Snellen acuity notation.
- *The Home Eye Test* (Boyce, 1973) has been successfully used with children as early as the age of 3. It is easy to administer, reliable, and inexpensive. The kit consists of an E chart, with instructions for training and administration. The test is given at a distance of 10 feet.

- *The Symbol Chart* for 20 feet (National Society for the Prevention of Blindness, 1969) contains "E" symbols that are read at a distance of 20 feet. The Snellen E is designed so that the letter subtends an angle of 5 minutes and the space between the bars subtends angles of 1 minute at the designated distance (Harley & Lawrence, 1977).
- *Stycar Vision Tests* (Sheridan, 1973) consist of a battery of screening tests for young children and retardates. One test is the miniature toy test, designed for children with limited verbal and coordination skills. Children are shown a set of 10 familiar toys or objects and asked to name them from a distance of 3 or 10 feet. If they cannot name the toys, the children match them to a duplicate set.

Visual Screening of Handicapped Children

Severely handicapped children may require screening in order to determine their functional vision. In recent years, many centers have received federal support to develop procedures for screening deaf-blind, multihandicapped, and severely and profoundly impaired students. Two procedures have been developed and field tested so far.

Parsons Visual Acuity Test

Spellman, DeBriere, and Cress (1979) designed the Parsons Visual Acuity Test using the theory of errorless learning. The test requires discriminating pictures of a bird, a hand, and a cake, all presented together in a series of cards in mixed order. The authors report that children can be initially trained to make the appropriate discriminations by using a procedure in which the intensity of the stimulus is gradually reduced. Children can respond through pointing, eye blinks, or yes/no responses to indicate the correct picture on both far and near tests of vision.

Functional Vision Inventory for the Multiply and Severely Handicapped

According to Langley (1980), the Functional Vision Inventory for the Multiply and Severely Handicapped helps determine if a visual impairment is interfering with learning and enables educators to determine how to make maximum use of any remaining vision. It is administered by two persons, one interacting with the child and the other recording responses. The examiner uses a variety of stimuli and provides multiple trials to elicit responses that are recorded on the profile, which includes information about structural defects and behavioral abnormalities, reflexive reactions, eye movements, near vision, distant vision, visual field preference, and visual perception.

Adaptations of Tests

Formal tests of children with visual impairments should focus on the same behavioral domains as those assessed in sighted children. Because there are no formal measures designed for visually impaired children, many tests must be adapted or administered in part (DuBose, 1978; DuBose, Langley, Bourgeault, Harley, & Stagg, 1977; DuBose, Langley, & Stagg, 1977; Fewell, 1982; Silberman, 1981; Swallow, 1981). Appendix A contains a list of instruments that can be used or adapted for this population. These tests were selected because of the information they provide about vision use and because they are less likely to penalize those who have poor vision. Three play observational scales for social development are included; no standardized tests are yet available. Play behavior is a new area of assessment that is proving to be valuable as an indicator of both present and future language and cognition.

EFFECTS OF VISUAL IMPAIRMENT ON DEVELOPMENT

Motor Development

Children whose visual impairments are so severe that they have light perception only or are considered blind experience selective lags in the development of certain motor and locomotor behaviors. On the early development of blind infants, information is limited to tabular data provided by Norris, Spaulding, and Brodie (1957) and Fraiberg (1977). Table 7-2 shows developmental milestones of sighted and blind children, using data from Fraiberg (1977).

Items falling within the normal range included rolling, independent sitting, and independent standing behaviors, as well as taking stepping movements when hands were held. Because these motor behaviors required a low and relatively stable center of gravity and did not require leaving the immediate base of support, they could be performed by blind children with little risk or danger.

Lags were reported in behaviors that required the infants to project their bodies into space (elevating upper torso by arm support, raising self to sitting, pulling to stand, crawling, or walking). In an older preschool population, Folio (1974) found that more advanced projectile skills of running, hopping, jumping, and skipping were also delayed.

Prehension Skills

Behaviors that are dependent on prehension, such as holding two objects simultaneously, one in each hand, and the transfer of objects from one hand to the other, are delayed in blind infants. Fraiberg (1977) has poignantly described the dramatic effects of loss of sight on development of prehension in early infancy.

Table 7-2 Gross Motor Items and Age Achieved by Blind (Child Development Project) and Sighted (Bayley)

	Age Range		*Median Age*		*Difference in*
Item	*Sighted*	*Blind*	*Sighted*	*Blind*	*Median Ages*
Elevates self by arms, prone	.07-5.0	4.5-9.5	2.1	8.75	6.65
Sits alone momentarily	4.0-8.0	5.0-8.5	5.3	6.75	1.45
Rolls from back to stomach	4.0-10.0	4.5-9.5	6.4	7.25	.85
Sits alone steadily	5.0-9.0	6.5-9.5	6.6	8.00	1.40
Raises self to sitting position	6.0-11.0	9.5-15.5	8.3	11.00	2.70
Stands up by furniture (pulls up to stand)	6.0-12.0	9.5-15.0	8.6	13.00	4.40
Stepping movements (walks hands held)	6.0-12.0	8.0-11.5	8.8	10.75	1.95
Stands alone	9.0-16.0	9.0-15.5	11.0	13.00	2.00
Walks alone, 3 steps	9.0-17.0	11.5-19.0	11.7	15.25	3.55
Walks alone, across room	11.3-14.3	12.0-20.5	12.1	19.25	7.15

Note: All ages given in months.

Source: From *Insights from the Blind: Comparative Studies of Blind and Sighted Infants* by S. Fraiberg. New York: Basic Books, 1977. Copyright 1977 by Selma Fraiberg. Reprinted by permission.

> The hand unites the infant with a world "out there," in which the purposeful reach gives intentionality to action and a sense of voluntariness in the formative period of the ego. . . . In cruelest irony, these hands quite literally groping in the near void of the blind child's world derailed in their progress by a deficit in the biological plan, must come to serve the blind child as primary perceptual organs—something not "intended," . . . in human biology. (pp. 147-148)

In regard to prehension, the most obvious difference in sightless infants is position of the hands when seated. At 5 months, when sighted infants are becoming proficient in intentional reaching, blind infants maintain their hands at shoulder height in a neonatal posture. If a rattle is placed in their hand, they firmly grasp and retain it; if a second toy is introduced, the first is dropped; if a favorite toy drops, the hands do not search for it.

The blind infant's grasping, while apparently emerging within the age range for sighted infants, is clumsy and unpracticed. When interest wanes or the hands are empty, they return to the shoulder position. Another characteristic is the lack of engagement of the hands at midline; the head has found its midline orientation, but the hands have not. The fingering seen in sighted infants is apparently sustained through the visual spectacle, which is not possible for the sightless infant. Thus, hand reciprocity and coordination of hand and eye in intentional reaching remain in nascent form.

The various forms of grasps, while basically in the blind infant's repertoire, are not always functional. For example, the sighted infant at 9 months may choose to use a neat pincer grasp to secure a piece of dry cereal. The blind child reverts to a raking movement, since it is more adaptive and efficient in locating and securing the small morsel. Sighted infants are able to reach for and obtain an object at approximately 4.6 months, while blind babies who substitute hearing for vision develop this ability at approximately 8.27 months (range, 6.18 to 11.01 months).

The developmental differences in gross motor skills and in prehension are more significant than they may appear. The blind infant's tendency to resort to more primitive responses or to clumsily executed behaviors affects coordination, experimentation with variations, acquisition of problem-solving skills, and other behaviors that are more obvious in the delayed cognitive development of sensorimotor schemes.

Language Development

Unfortunately, few researchers have investigated language development in blind children. Warren's thorough review (1977) concludes that blind children develop the expected language although some interfering factors are noted before 4 and 5 years of age.

In the 1st year of life, there appear to be very few differences between blind and sighted babies in early vocalizations and imitation, since these depend on neurophysiological maturation and performance and are not deterred by blindness. Interestingly, blind babies in Fraiberg's study (1977) imitated words to a degree above the mean for sighted babies. Language, however, is more than mere vocalization and imitation; it also includes facial expressions and bodily gestures. Researchers stress the importance of the mother's role and the dyadic reciprocity between mother and child that accompanies the latter's development of linguistic competency. Because blind infants are unable to read nonverbal language cues, they fail to develop a capacity to exchange language behaviors with their caregivers. Nevertheless, Als, Tronick, and Brazelton (1980) have described the modified interactions made by a blind child's parents that enabled their daughter to acquire excellent interaction skills from birth. These successful experiences are believed to have played an important role in this child's development of advanced language and cognitive skills.

During the early part of the 2nd year, sighted infants begin to utter single words. By 14 months, sighted babies say two words under test conditions, but blind babies cannot do this until 18.5 months. Fraiberg suggests that representational behavior is involved and blind children have a deprived experiential base because they must rely solely on experiences with things touched or heard. Another possible factor is mobility; the sighted 14-month-old infant has been creeping for 7 months and is now walking; the blind child's mobility is significantly delayed, which hinders experiences with objects in the surrounding world and the opportunity to learn names to associate with those objects.

When the Bayley Scale item "uses words to make wants known" was assessed, blind infants' responses were approximately on the same level as those of sighted infants. The wants expressed by babies apparently derive from internal needs, and blindness, therefore, does not impede verbal expression of those needs. A lag of 6 months was noted when assessing "sentences of two words." Putting two words together is a function of concept development and, like the delay in initial single words, the linking of two words is delayed because blind children are not as easily exposed to attributes, actions, and qualities that are readily visible to the sighted youngster.

Wills (1979) described the language development in a blind boy, Boris. He began to repeat words between 12 and 18 months of age and would fill in the omitted words in nursery rhymes. He used words, but he did not always use them appropriately or pronounce them correctly. During his 2nd year, he used the word *no* almost constantly, but it took him much longer to use the word *yes* consistently. During this time, he asked for more things and activities by name; by the end of the year he was using inflection in his voice as a means of communication. Around 3 years of age, he used longer sentences, but they were always exact replicas of what he had heard and learned as whole phrases rather than in the telegraphic patterns that normal children use to expand their speech. It was not uncommon for him to admonish himself with phrases such as "Don't touch it" or "I'll smack you." When compared with norms on the Maxfield-Buchholz Scale of Social Maturity for Preschool Blind Children, his speech at 3 years was below that of sighted peers. However, after 2 years in a nursery school for blind children, his speech at 5 years of age was essentially normal.

An interesting aspect of language, so deeply embedded in self-concept, social relationships, and cognitive behavior that it cannot clearly be distinguished as language development, is the use of the words *me* and *I*. Sighted children begin to represent themselves in their world of play around 2½ years of age. For blind children, these play interactions occur between 3 and 4½ years of age. The use of these pronouns is closely related to the symbolic representation of the self; the delay is a factor of this delay in play behavior.

In summary, language in blind children develops at a different rate from that of unimpaired children in the early years of language acquisition, but these differences typically are overcome by age 5.

Cognitive Development

Piaget traced the origins of cognitive development to the sensorimotor period, during which infants progress from reflexive responses to representational behavior. Table 7-3 indicates the major stages of the sensorimotor period and the effects of blindness at the various stages.

The earliest indications of divergence in the acquisition of sensorimotor skills appear in the third stage when blind infants fail to reach for objects. Lack of sensory stimulation to these infants hinders integration of sensorimotor experiences. Toward the end of the 1st year, blind children begin to use auditory senses actively as visual substitutes, and evidence of their organization of the world begins to emerge. Only after blind infants understand the concept of person and object permanence do they seek objects or people by turning toward the sound.

Perhaps the most obvious delay experienced by blind infants is in object concept, considered by Fraiberg (1968) to emerge between ages 3 and 5 years in blind children, in contrast to age 2 years in the sighted child. The delay in object concept further inhibits acquisition of the concepts of object permanence, spatial relationships, and causality. Once ambulatory, blind children can explore the environment more freely and begin the important construction of mental images (Rapin, 1979).

Delays reduce the amount of information about the surrounding world that reaches blind children and therefore diminish understanding of the relationships of objects to other objects, events, persons, and experiences. These deficiencies, in turn, affect the acquisition of higher level cognitive skills, such as classification and conservation. Piaget and Inhelder (1969) noted:

> The sensory disturbance peculiar to those born blind has, from the outset, hampered the development of sensory-motor schemes and slowed down general coordination . . . action learning is still necessary before these children develop the capacity for operations on a level with that of the normal child. (pp. 88-89)

Fortunately, Brekke, Williams, and Tait (1974) have found evidence that understanding of certain kinds of concepts (e.g., weight conservation) is not delayed in blind children; such evidence reinforces the importance of intervention. There is substantial agreement among vision educators and researchers that blindness itself is not a detriment to academic achievement if favorable educational opportunities are available. There is some evidence, however, that indicates blind children's achievement in mathematics was 20% behind that of sighted peers (Goldberg, 1969).

Social and Emotional Development

Socialization is the process by which skills are acquired to live in harmony with others and to care for one's own physical, mental, and emotional needs. It is a continuous process, starting at birth and continuing throughout life. Blindness affects acquisition of social skills not only because the child cannot see the context in which these skills are normally learned, but also because the persons who interact with the child may not respond in the same way that they respond to sighted children.

Hallenbeck (1954) found that a significant factor associated with emotional stability in a group of residential school blind children was whether a child has established a good relationship with some person before entering the school. Lowenfeld (1964) pinpointed the attitude of parents as more critical to a blind child's development than the particular child-rearing techniques they employed. The role of the blind child's family, especially the mother, in fostering a positive self-concept and establishing an appropriate base from which to develop acceptable interaction and self-care skills cannot be underestimated. "They hold the string of his independence, and they must slowly let it go, giving him all the freedom he can handle at a given time, so that he can develop self-reliance and the ability to function quite apart from them" (DuBose, 1976).

For the first few months of life, blind children typically are quiet and passive, and they are likely to remain so if outside stimulation does not evoke pleasurable experiences. It is critical that these children be cuddled, enjoyed, and placed at the center of family activities. The emotional message that must be conveyed is that they bring pleasure to those around them and that others can provide pleasure for them. (Again, see Als, Tronick, & Brazelton, 1980, for a detailed account of the early social development of a blind infant.)

Table 7-3 Effects of Blindness on Sensorimotor Development

Period	*Expectations*	*Blindness*
I. Reflexes (0 to 1 month)	Behavior is characterized primarily by reflexive responses to infant's own body and to some aspects of external world. Some refinement of reflexive behavior occurs as infant discovers, for example, that some objects are "suckable" and some are not.	No pupillary restrictions to light in some cases.
II. Primary circular reactions (1 to 4 months)	Infant begins to repeat selectively those actions that produce interesting or satisfying effects. These actions are primarily directed to infant's own body rather than to external objects.	No visual tracking. No examination of feet and hands. No intentional grasping of objects.
III. Secondary circular reactions (4 to 9 months)	Behaviors that produce effects in external world that are satisfying or interesting to infant are reproduced. This marks the beginning of the infant's effective orientation to the external world.	Body-centered sensations continued. Failure to follow rapid movements of persons and objects. Failure to understand the cause or source of object activation.
IV. Coordination of secondary circular reactions (9 to 12 months)	Beginnings of intentionality are seen in that infant begins to coordinate own behavior with respect to external world in more complex ways. Use of specific ends demonstrates increasing organization of world. Infant begins to anticipate effects of own actions and those of other people.	Failure to attend visually to objects or persons or imitate movements. Failure to realize similarity in objects; thus, old schema not generalized to new objects. Failure to see a distant goal to attain it. Failure to perceive self in relation to environment. Initiation of interaction with adult to repeat an action less likely.

V. Tertiary circular reactions (12 to 18 months)	Behavior clearly involves active trial-and-error experimentation with world. Behavior becomes more flexible in that infant can systematically vary own actions to obtain a specific goal. Infant seems to seek novelty to learn more about world.	Failure to see relationships between action and solution that can be accomplished to produce activity. Less problem solving in environment. Failure to attack barriers to secure toys. Failure to see the usefulness of tools to assist in securing goals.
VI. Invention of new means through mental combination (18 to 24 months)	Internalized thought begins. Child need no longer engage in overt trial-and-error behavior, but rather can think about possible behaviors and effects that they would have. According to Piaget, this stage frees child from own perceptions and behaviors and child begins to imagine behaviors and their consequences.	Delayed internalization of action schema. Failure to categorize objects by salient dimensions. Previously observed adult behavior not imitated in pretending.

An early sign of appropriate social behavior is smiling. Blind babies smile less frequently and less dramatically. "During the second year, open displays of affection remain induced responses and the child behaves as if he cannot himself be the initiator of a relationship" (Lairy & Harrison-Covello, 1973, p. 5). This is seen in the child's failure to become independent from the mother; hence, separation anxiety intensifies and continues beyond the 2nd year. When separation does occur, the child reacts with helplessness and regression.

Tait (1972) has suggested that play and exploratory behavior are related to the degree of social attachment experienced by blind children. These behaviors move the infants away from themselves and toward the external world where both social independence and social reciprocity with persons other than parents can develop. Fraiberg (1977) reported that blind children are severely delayed in their capacity to play, particularly when it is necessary to pretend. (Educators may find the play assessment scales noted in Appendix A helpful in monitoring play behaviors in blind children.) When caregivers provide experiences that encourage appropriate play and independence, social skills, like those in language, usually resemble those of sighted peers when the blind children enter elementary school.

Development of a positive self-concept is also critical to social competency. Scott (1968) maintains that self-concept is acquired in large part through social interactions and the expectations of others, particularly the parents. These perceptions, transmitted from significant caregivers to these children, can make them *blind* children or can make them *children* who happen to have a visual impairment.

Self-Care Development

The development of independence in caring for their physical needs is critical for blind children. Strategies for teaching independence in eating, toileting, and dressing must be adapted to each child's learning style.

Before they are fed, blind infants must be prepared for the experience, since they cannot anticipate what is going to happen. By placing a hand on the adult's mouth, blind children can begin to associate opening the mouth with food intake. These children also need time to smell food. Finger feeding is very important and should be introduced around the end of the 1st year. Spoon training should likewise be encouraged, once finger feeding has been mastered.

Converting from strained to solid foods is sometimes very difficult for blind babies, and there is a tendency for them to rebel. Frequently, parents give way in the face of this rebellion and fail to move the child from strained foods. The same resistance is seen when chewing is introduced. Again, allowing the child to feel the adult's mouth while the adult imitates chewing and, possibly, manually exercising the child's jaw can facilitate the process. Chewing can be introduced by placing foods, such as peanut butter, on the roof of the mouth or between the back teeth and cheek so that the child will begin to manipulate the mouth. It is usually necessary to introduce a piece of bread as a ''pusher'' in order to ensure that the blind child locates food on the plate. Since this skill requires some degree of hand coordination, it is usually not introduced until the 3rd year. A consistent sequence of procedures should be used to teach blind children to feed themselves, and verbal input is needed to alert them to this experience.

Parents of blind children report greater difficulties in toilet training blind than sighted children. There is no physiological reason for this, and the problems could well be a factor of the environment. It is necessary to explain to blind children what the toilet is and how it is used, since they cannot observe others using it. Otherwise, the general procedures for toilet training blind children vary little from those for training sighted children.

The ability to dress independently is related to development of gross and fine motor skills and of concepts. Because of delays in these areas, delays in dressing skills can be expected. Again, sequencing and consistency are critical in training blind children to dress themselves. Proper orientation of clothing is required, for example, if blind children are to find the various holes in shirts and pants.

Slight delays can be expected in attainment of self-care objectives. The sequence of learning is simply longer, frequently because the caregivers do it for the blind child rather than taking the time to train the child to perform a task. Instruction in new tasks should follow an orderly progression that builds on skills already possessed. Instruction should be

1. concrete, using objects or events being experienced
2. individual, adapted to meet particular needs
3. unified, using prior knowledge or experience
4. structured, introducing concepts or ideas in a logical manner
5. motivational, requiring the child to initiate ways to care for needs and act independently in as many situations as possible

INSTRUCTING INFANTS AND TODDLERS WITH VISUAL IMPAIRMENTS

The frequently heard adage that parents and teachers should ''teach/treat a handicapped child like they do any other child'' has been taken out of context and misused. The content of instruction for the visually impaired is usually the same as that for sighted children; however, materials and procedures may be the same or quite varied. Although, in many respects, caregivers' responses to the handicapped child should be the same as responses to the child's nonimpaired peers, special instruction may be needed to lessen effects of the impairment on the child's developing behavior.

Home Visitor Programs

When an infant's vision is severely limited, caregivers must be aware of the effects this limitation has on the developing child and must begin special instruction in the early weeks of life. The first professional educator is usually a home visitor whose responsibilities can be to

- provide information regarding (a) availability and options for other services, (b) effects the lack of vision will have on development, (c) instructional procedures for minimizing effects of visual loss, and (d) support networks
- work with parents in setting periodic objectives
- provide access to materials needed to facilitate instruction
- demonstrate teaching strategies
- observe and record the child's progress
- provide parents with feedback on the child's progress and on their own progress
- serve as a resource and support to parents as needed
- engage in parent counseling

Several school systems have established some form of home visitor program to serve visually impaired children. For example, in the Seattle, Washington area, two home visitors serve 25 to 30 children (aged from birth to 36 months) with weekly visits. The visitor demonstrates appropriate teaching activities and leaves materials so that the parents can work on these activities. Parents meet one morning a week for a discussion of mutual concerns and support. A group of local volunteers work with the young children during these sessions.

Infant and Preschool Programs

Once major medical problems have been addressed and the child's immediate physical condition permits exposure to other young children, programs for young handicapped children may be undertaken.

In infant programs, caregiver training remains paramount; however, the infant does receive more attention and instruction than is provided in the home visitor model. The programs provide support, frequently from other parents whose children are visually impaired, and direct access to ancillary services and lending libraries that provide books, toys, and materials. The programs are also likely to provide a more precise system for measuring child progress and program effectiveness; thus, caregivers are more likely to have a clearer understanding of a child's current abilities and potential.

Several infant, toddler, and preschool programs that follow a mainstreaming model include visually impaired youngsters. Other programs have been designed specifically for visually impaired children. The very comprehensive manual *Alive . . . Aware . . . A Person* (O'Brien, 1976) describes in detail the program for visually impaired preschool children in the Montgomery County (Maryland) Public Schools. Other valuable resources are *The Oregon Project for Visually Impaired and Blind Preschool Children* (Brown, Simmons, & Methvin, 1979); *Can't Your Child See?* (Scott, Jan, & Freeman, 1977); *Raising the Young Blind Child* (Kastein, Spaulding, & Scharf, 1980); and *Practical Guidance for Parents of the Visually Handicapped Preschooler* (Maloney, 1981).

CURRICULAR CONCERNS FOR PRESCHOOL VISUALLY IMPAIRED CHILDREN

Young visually impaired children need to acquire most of the same basic skills needed by other children. However, the ways in which they acquire skills may be quite different and, therefore, may mandate different curriculums and means of instruction. In considering what and how to teach young visually impaired children, teachers may want to review commercially available curriculums, such as those previously mentioned. They may want to adapt other curriculums to the learning aptitudes of the child or children they teach, or they may wish to plan some activities based on their own ideas. Appendix B includes examples of key instructional targets and suggestions for experiences to foster skill achievement.

HEARING IMPAIRMENTS

Those who care for children with hearing impairments must receive credit for being the first caregivers to stress the importance of intervention services during the preschool years. They were quick to note the negative effects of hearing impairment on the acquisition of basic skills, particularly language development; they were also aware that sounds in the environment attract infants to attend, to associate with people and objects, to discriminate, to imitate, to internalize, and later to formulate sounds into words.

DEFINITION AND PREVALENCE

In June, 1975, the Conference of Executives of American Schools for the Deaf adopted definitions that classify persons according to ability to process auditory input. The definition of hearing impairment was also restated for the field:

> *Hearing Impairment:* A generic term indicating a hearing disability which may range in severity from mild to profound; it includes the subset of deaf and hard of hearing.
>
> A *deaf* person is one whose hearing disability precludes successful processing of linguistic information through audition, with or without a hearing aid.
>
> A *hard of hearing* person is one who, generally with the use of a hearing aid, has residual hearing sufficient to enable successful processing of linguistic information through audition.
>
> (Report of the Ad Hoc Committee to Define Deaf and Hard of Hearing, 1975)

It has been difficult to determine precisely the number of hearing-impaired persons, since degree of loss is a critical factor. It has been estimated that 14 million Americans, including 500,000 to 700,000 children, have impaired hearing (Green, 1981). An estimate prepared by the Deafness Research and Training Center at New York University reports 2 million Americans lack sufficient hearing to understand speech. In its 1980-1981 report, the Office of Special Education and Rehabilitation Services reported 85,126 hearing-impaired and deaf-blind children and youth, aged 1 to 21 years, were being served under PL 94-142 and PL 89-313. Of these children, 5,667 fall in the 3 to 5 age group. The actual number of hearing-impaired preschool children is likely to be very much higher because of delay in early detection.

PHYSIOLOGY OF THE EAR

The ability to communicate orally is a distinctly human trait. The combined efforts of ears and brain make it possible to acquire and use a language system. Sound waves are collected by the outer ear, or pinna, and channeled into the auditory canal where they strike the eardrum, or tympanic membrane. The eardrum is a clear window through which it is possible to see into the middle ear where three small bones, the hammer (malleus), anvil (incus), and stirrup (stapes), transmit the sound waves to the oval window at the far end of the middle ear. Opening into the middle ear from the pharynx is an air passage regulator, the Eustachian tube. Sound waves pass from the middle into the inner ear or labyrinth, containing the cochlea, which is the organ of hearing, and the semicircular canals, which are central to balance. Fluid activated by the movements of the oval window circulates through the labyrinth and stimulates the auditory nerve, which mediates sensations of sound. The brain perceives the sound in the temporal lobe and adds meaning to the vibrations; in this way, the individual understands the meaning of the sound.

SCREENING FOR HEARING IMPAIRMENTS IN CHILDREN

Since there is no system for mass detection of hearing deficits in infants, professional organizations, including the American Academy of Ophthalmology and Otolaryngology (AAOO), the American Academy of Pediatrics (AAP), and the American Speech and Hearing Association (ASHA), jointly recommend use of case histories and identification of physical deficits. One or more of the following characteristics will cause a neonate to be considered at risk:

1. history of hereditary childhood hearing impairment
2. rubella or other nonbacterial intrauterine fetal infection (e.g., cytomegalovirus infection, herpes infection)
3. defects of ear, nose, throat; malformed, low-set or absent pinnae; cleft lip or palate, including submucous cleft; any residual abnormality of the otorhinolaryngeal system
4. birthweight less than 1,500 (approximately 3.3 pounds)
5. bilirubin level greater than 20 mg/100 ml serum

A neonate at risk according to these factors should be given a complete audiologic evaluation during the first 2 months of life.

Teachers and daycare workers must be aware of possible signs of a hearing loss. Table 7-4 contains a list of observable behaviors that could be associated with a hearing impairment.

Types of Audiometry

Behavior Observation Audiometry

The most common neonatal hearing screening procedure is behavior observation audiometry, which is based on observations of the neonate's response to a sound stimulus. Behavior observation audiometry provides sufficient audiological

Table 7-4 Behaviors Indicating Possible Hearing Difficulty

Physical Signs	*Behavioral Signs*
Frequent earaches	Head cocked to one side
Ear discharges	Preference for high- or low-pitched sounds
Mouth breathing	Extreme shyness in speaking
Complaints of buzzing or ringing in ear, noises in head	Delayed or abnormal speech
Frequent problems with tonsils	Frequent unresponsiveness when addressed
	Abnormalities of articulation
	Abnormalities in voice
	Attention difficulties

information to permit a tentative hypothesis and to initiate habilitative procedures (Cox & Lloyd, 1976).

The case history method, physical examinations, and behavior observation procedures have produced a large number of false-positives. Researchers have therefore attempted to find ways to identify more precisely hearing-impaired children between 3 and 12 months of age. By 3 months of age, the developing infant is a more reliable testee, responding less reflexively and more purposely to sound stimuli.

Watrous, McConnell, Sitton, and Fleet (1975) developed a procedure to determine a predictable developmental pattern during the 1st year of life. Subjects were 40 normally developing infants from the Rubella Follow-up Project at Vanderbilt University. Children less than 6 months of age exhibited greater percentages of reflexive responses (e.g., body startle, eye blink, eye widening, eye movement, brow movement, and head movement). Attending responses (e.g., brief cessation of activity, momentary increase in activity, prolonged facial grimace, listening behavior, and searching behavior) were also more common among the younger subjects. Localizing responses were far more prevalent in older infants, particularly after the age of 6 months. Inspection of responses revealed that localization on a horizontal plane with the head was the predominant response for 6- to 8-month olds; although localizing on a vertical plane did not occur at all in the younger group and quite infrequently in the 6- to 8-month-old group, it was the preferred response for the 9- to 12-month-old infants.

In testing several groups of infants, Moore, Thompson, and Thompson (1975) monitored head turns to sound that was introduced through loudspeakers. When correct, head turns were reinforced with sound, light, and movement from an animated toy. The procedure elicited responses from infants as young as 5 months of age, but failed to do so with younger infants.

Behavioral Play Audiometry

Testing becomes more widespread and useful for children 18 to 36 months of age, who are better able to cooperate. Responses to parental questionnaires supplement information from pure tone audiometric procedures, which may take some form of play, such as putting a block in a can or a peg in a pegboard. Children over 3 years of age generally are able to respond to pure tone audiometry and should be tested annually to detect possible middle ear pathology, a major cause of hearing deficits at that age.

Impedance Audiometry

Three tests of impedance are used to evaluate the functioning of the middle ear system. A test of tympanometry gives information about compliance or resistance of the eardrum; the mobility of the middle ear system is examined through a test of static compliance; and stapedial reflex testing measures the response of the stapedial muscle to pure tone signals. None of these tests require responses from the child.

Pure Tone Audiometric Screening

The first formal means of testing hearing is usually pure tone audiometric screening. A pure tone audiometer is used to measure the child's reception of pure tones over a frequency range.

Speech Audiometry

In order to determine how well a child hears and understands speech, speech audiometry is used. The lowest intensity at which a child hears words is the speech reception threshold; it is found by asking the child to repeat two-syllable words. The audiologist reduces the intensity of the words to find the threshold level. Speech understanding, or discrimination, is determined by presenting the child with a list of one-syllable words. The child responds by repeating the words. The number of correct responses is converted to a percentage score called a speech discrimination score. Both the speech reception threshold and the speech discrimination measures are determined through the use of earphones (Green, 1981).

Interpretation of Hearing Loss

An audiometer is an electronic device that measures sharpness and range of hearing. Results are recorded on a graph (called an audiogram) that shows frequency in Hertz (Hz), a measure of cycles per second, across the top. Frequencies are heard as pitch; as frequencies, or Hz, increase in number, pitch becomes higher. Intensity of a sound is a measure of loudness and is expressed in decibels (dB) along the side of the graph. Decibels are scaled by standards of the International Standard Organization (ISO) or American Standard Association (ASA). Normal hearing is defined as 0 dB for each frequency level.

Pure tone audiometry uses signals of known frequencies within the communication range of human audibility (i.e., 250 to 8,000 Hz). These signals are delivered by air conduction (through earphones or sound field speakers) or by bone conduction (through a small oscillator placed on the child's mastoid bone behind the ear or on the forehead).

The degree of handicap is usually classified by the descriptors noted in Table 7-5.

The configuration of responses that are recorded on the audiogram is important both for identifying the kind of hearing loss and for determining the potential

Table 7-5 Relationship of Amount of Hearing Loss to Communicative Efficiency

Loss in Speech Range (ISO dB)	*Degree of Impairment*	*Effects*
15 to 30	Mild	Without awareness of hearing needs, problems in language and speech may emerge.
31 to 50	Moderate	Child has difficulty with whispers and normal speech; understands conversational speech at 3 to 5 feet; needs auditory training, language training, and hearing aid. With sufficient training and no other impairments, child will function in regular classroom with minimum support.
51 to 80	Severe	Conversational speech must be loud; child will experience difficulties with classroom discussions and telephone conversations; will need considerable support in acquiring speech. Some will understand strongly amplified speech, but have difficulty with consonants.
81 to 100	Profound	Maximally amplified speech is not understood by most persons; most will use total communication systems.
Total loss	Anakusis	Total deafness.

usefulness of amplification. If responses are recorded across the frequency spectrum or on a flat configuration, amplification can be very helpful; if hearing is within the speech range (500 to 2,000 Hz), amplification is probably also of benefit. However, if responses are noted outside the speech range, amplification is much less likely to be successful (Larson & Miller, 1978).

TYPES OF HEARING LOSS

Conductive Hearing Loss

A conductive loss results from malformations or problems of the outer or middle ear that prevent clear transmission of sound waves to the inner ear. Sources of such problems are impounded wax; foreign objects, such as beans or candies; or excess fluid in the Eustachian tube. A conductive loss is identified as the loss of air-conducted sounds. Thus, sounds that are transmitted through bone conduction and go directly to the inner ear are heard normally. Most conductive impairments are amenable to medical intervention or amplification.

Sensorineural Loss

Defects in the inner ear or dysfunction of the auditory nerve or the cochlear hair cells result in a sensorineural loss. The outer and middle ear are likely to be normal, air and bone conduction thresholds are likely to be nearly the same, and sensorineural losses are not likely to be corrected surgically or medically. With training, some children with mild sensorineural loss find amplification helpful. Amplification is less successful, however, with children who have greater sensorineural losses, as the amplified sound is distorted and unclear. Common sensorineural impairments include inherited deafness, maternal rubella, or other syndromes associated with deafness.

Mixed Hearing Loss

When both a conductive loss and a sensorineural loss are present, the loss is classified as a mixed loss. There may be a significant gap between air and bone conduction thresholds, but the air conduction component of the loss may be resolved. Many persons with mixed losses can benefit from amplification, although some have problems similar to those of persons with sensorineural losses.

AGE OF ONSET

The age at which an individual becomes hearing impaired affects the degree of the language handicap. If the impairment is a congenital loss, its impact on language acquisition is likely to be more severe. An impairment acquired some time after birth is an adventitious loss; the later it occurs, the less it affects acquisition of language. Adventitiously deaf children are more likely to have (1) knowledge of their native language, (2) clear oral speech, (3) understanding of the oral speech of others, (4) ability to read with speed and comprehension, and (5) understanding of abstract concepts (Reynolds & Birch, 1977).

Hearing loss should be identified as early in life as possible. According to Northern and Downs (1978), a loss as small as 15 dB or even frequent otitis media early in life results in language delays. The reason for this lies in the nature of speech sounds. The most speech energy is in voiced vowels and consonants, and the unvoiced consonants (*s, p, t, k, th, f, sh*) may not be heard because they contain so little speech energy that they fall below even normal hearing thresholds. The infant just learning speech needs to hear all sounds clearly.

CAUSES OF HEARING IMPAIRMENT IN CHILDREN

There are two major causes of deafness: genetic or chromosomal abnormalities, and disease or trauma. Genetic factors account for 40% to 60% of all causes of deafness. The genetically deaf are least likely of all deaf children to be multiply handicapped. The major ancillary handicap among these children is a visual problem. Of the 57 identified forms of genetic deafness, 10 involve both hearing and vision (Larson & Miller, 1978).

The majority of human inherited deafness (about 90%) is recessive rather than dominant, meaning that both parents must be the carriers of the particular gene. The chances of an offspring being deaf are 25% and chances of an offspring being a carrier are 50% (Northern & Downs, 1978).

External agents that result in deafness fall into three major categories: (1) disease, (2) toxicity, or exposure to toxic substances, and (3) physical injuries, malformations, or trauma. The most prevalent diseases that result in deafness are viral infections, such as maternal rubella. Pregnant women who contract the rubella virus during their first 3 months of pregnancy may give birth to a deaf child. Deafness can be the only handicap, or the child might also be visually impaired, mentally retarded, or afflicted with heart or kidney problems.

Meningitis is the cause of deafness for about 10% of all cases. The high fever associated with the illness results in a sensorineural loss.

In young children, serous otitis media is the most common ear disorder. It is generally caused by blockage of the Eustachian tube, which partially closes the middle ear and causes the gases in it to be partially absorbed; the result is a collection of fluid in the middle ear. Treatment usually consists of aspiration of the middle ear by myringotomy (incision of the eardrum), followed by placement of a hollow plastic tube to ensure that the ear remains open.

Toxic drugs taken either by the mother during pregnancy or by the child may produce hearing impairments; in the latter case, however, these impairments may be resolved by discontinuing the drugs.

Blows to the head can cause serious hearing losses. Injury to bones in the ossicular chain or other internal ear parts are likely to affect hearing. Damage can occur in any part of the sound-receiving and sound-processing system. The middle ear is particularly vulnerable to infections that reach it from the throat and nasal passages via the Eustachian tube. Frequent infections can cause scar tissue to form or produce other changes that prevent the concatenate functioning of the bones. The inner ear can be damaged through the lymph system or through prolonged exposure to high-intensity sounds.

Blood incompatibility accounts for 3% to 4% of all deafness. In almost all residential schools, there are children whose deafness can be traced to this factor. Birth complications, such as fetal stress, prolonged labor, or prematurity, are other causes of deafness.

HEARING AIDS

Simply put, hearing aids are tiny amplifiers. They make all sounds louder, including the extraneous noises that most people have learned to ignore. The deaf child with a hearing aid is bombarded with all environmental sounds and must be carefully and laboriously trained to distinguish speech sounds from environmental noises. Because young children are now fitted with aids as early as possible, the number of hearing impaired children in preschool settings is likely to increase.

Although body type aids comprise only about 10% of all hearing aids, they are most likely to be used by young children. These children require an instrument that is sturdy, can deliver high-quality sound, uses a battery with longer life, and is acoustically more flexible (Ross, 1975). The body aid contains microphone and amplifier in the same chassis; wires connect the amplifier to the receiver (or earphones) at the ear (Ross, 1976). A cord can go to a single ear, or a Y cord, with the output split into two channels, can connect with both ears. One disadvantage of body aids is that additional extraneous noise is caused by the microphone rubbing against clothing. A single aid is called a monaural hearing aid system. A binaural hearing aid system consists of two complete monaural hearing aid systems.

Keeping a hearing aid in proper working condition is quite difficult. Ross (1976) states it bluntly: "There are perhaps more hearing aids and auditory trainers gathering dust in school storerooms than serving the purpose for which they were designed" (p. 317). Without a properly functioning instrument, all the theoretical benefits of early intervention are minimized. The following guidelines are helpful in maintaining the proper operation of these instruments:

1. The batteries should be tested for power before the child leaves home each morning. A spare should always be available, both at home and at school.
2. Small controls much like the knobs on a radio regulate the amount of amplification. Since the small child does not have the manual dexterity to manipulate these controls, parents and other caregivers must know how to set them.
3. The sound is received by the small power unit, serving the same function as a person's external ear, and transmitted through a cord or cords attached to an earmold that fits the child's ear or ears. Cords can be defective and should be checked regularly to ensure proper transmission.
4. The earmold must be cleaned to remove ear wax that collects at the mold openings. Small brushes, such as a typist's eraser brush, are very useful in cleaning molds. If the mold is not inserted properly or slips from the snug fitting, a squealing can be detected by others. It should be gently reinserted.
5. As a child develops, the mold should be checked periodically for proper fit; a new fitting is needed if bleeding occurs.
6. An inexpensive battery tester and stethoscope are valuable tools in testing aid functioning.

ASSESSMENT OF THE DEVELOPMENT OF YOUNG HEARING-IMPAIRED CHILDREN

The formal psychoeducational assessment of the development of young hearing-impaired children can be done through a number of formal measures. Some can be administered according to directions in the test manual, while others must be adapted so that the hearing impairment does not handicap the child unduly. Appendix A includes a list of tests to be used or adapted for hearing-impaired preschool children. Extreme caution must be exercised when language tests are used to measure skills in deaf children—the scores from these tests are too frequently and incorrectly interpreted as scores of mental ability.

EFFECTS OF HEARING IMPAIRMENT ON DEVELOPMENT

Motor Development

Schlesinger and Meadow (1972) offer convincing documentation in support of their conviction that a hearing impairment alone will not delay motor development. Table 7-6 shows the relationship among chronological age, motor development, and language development in one deaf child, Ann.

Children with hearing impairments resulting from inner ear damage may have gross motor problems related to balance and equilibrium. These skills should be carefully checked to see if weaknesses do exist. Such problems, if present, are manifested in all motor skills that require static or dynamic balance.

Language Development

The language system that a child acquires depends entirely on the system used by the caregivers, who shape the child's language through modeling and reinforcement. Deaf children who are raised by parents who communicate manually acquire the manual language system quickly (Schlesinger & Meadow, 1972).

Language must be given the highest priority in the deaf child's ongoing education. Through language, the child expresses feelings, understands what others are feeling, and shares experiences with others. Language training is the responsibility of every person in the deaf child's world: the parents, the siblings, the schoolteacher, the swimming instructor, the neighbor, everyone in contact with the child. The concept of shared language training responsibility is based on a particular understanding of what language is and how it is acquired. Clark (1974) stated that "language does not develop 'in vacuo'; it develops with the functions of representing thoughts, percepts, and feelings" (p. 105). DuBose (1976) maintains that "physical attachment and interaction were as necessary for survival before birth as social attachment and interaction are for survival after birth'' (p. 38). Language is the key to interaction.

A hearing impairment's greatest effect on the developing child occurs in regard to language—both the receptive and the expressive systems. During the 1st year of life, the normal child hears thousands of words and soon begins to attach meaning to some of them. Children learn a first language through active participation in the world. For example, they come to associate such experiences as hunger, smell, sounds, caregiver, and satisfaction with their bottle. Gradually, they visually associate their needs with the object and later add phonemes to what already has a semantic meaning. First ''ba-ba'' then ''bottle,'' gradually moving from signal to symbol, enter the children's language repertoire.

Northern and Downs (1978) concluded that the vocalizations of children with hearing impairments are identical to those of children without impaired hearing until the age of 5 or 6 months. Babbling is thus a reflexive, preadaptive behavior. Hearing babies use the auditory feedback loop (which is present at birth) to self-stimulate and monitor their own primitive speech sounds. They begin to use selectively the rhythm, intonations, duration, and range of sounds that they hear from those around them. Hearing-impaired infants fail to progress past babbling because they cannot hear the feedback from the parent, associate it with past auditory experiences, and modify their own production in a meaningful way. Deaf children need a much longer period of input before they can produce meaningful sounds. If language potential is to be maximized, then intervention must be timed to coincide with periods of experience critical to language and speech development. Because the stages through which hearing-impaired infants progress are longer in duration, it is important that efforts be made to maximize critical input during the stage and encourage movement to the next stage (Simmons, 1972).

The impact of deafness becomes more critical in the 2nd year of life when normal children name many more things and put together agents and actions. Simmons-Martin (1981) has provided insights into the development of language in children enrolled in early intervention programs for the hearing impaired. Average 2-year-olds in the Central Institute for the Deaf Early Education Project comprehend and express themselves by demonstrating their awareness that the mouth and voice convey information. Although they cannot understand or spontaneously produce any real words, they are beginning to imitate a few syllables or combinations of phonemes. At 3 years, the children understand words such as ''bye-bye'' or ''mama '' in appropriate situations and can imitate a variety of words fairly easily when they are presented singly. By 4 years, they are beginning to express themselves in one-word utterances, mostly nouns. They can imitate two- to three-word phrases, but not spontaneously. The 5-year-olds understand more than 20 words in almost any context, but they are still dependent on the context for acquiring new words and comprehending their meanings. They can combine two- to three-word phrases in order to express ideas and can also imitate two-word

Table 7-6 Interrelated Patterns in Ann's Motor and Linguistic Development

Age	*Motor Development*	*Language Development*
8 months/ 1 day	Stands holding on; thumb opposition when grasping plastic beads	Blinking in response to sound with hearing aid. "Vocalization and gestures convey emphasis and emotions."
9 months	Playing "peek-a-boo"	
10 months/ 5 days	Claps hands; pulls to standing position; creeps efficiently (S10)	"Beginning to differentiate words by making differential adjustment"; waves "bye-bye." Hits side of head with heel of open hand (like *father*). Hits side of head with fist (like *stupid*). (S10)
10½ months		Hands in loose fist to mouth (like *eat*).
11 months	Secures toy from under cup (C10) Four teeth	Vocalizes negatively after mother gives a mock scolding with "*no*."
12 months	Hits cup with spoon (C10) Marks with pencil (C12) Squeezes doll (C11) Stands alone	Covers face with both hands to avoid mother. Turns to see who is recipient of sign language. SIGNS: *pretty; wrong*. Understands "come here." (S12)
13 months	Takes first steps alone	
14 months		SIGNS: *cat, sleep, bye, sleep.*
14½ months	Unwraps toy (C14) Inserts peg (C14) Holds three cubes (C14)	SIGNS: *hat, eat, no;* imitates mother.
15 months	Drinks from straw	SIGNS: Letter *r, smell, dirty, no smart, mommy, daddy, kitty, dog, pretty, wrong, sleep, eat, milk, bye-bye, good, car, no, Ann* (with letter *a*). SIGN VOCABULARY TOTAL 19 SAYS: "mamma" and "hi" Points to nose and ear upon oral request. (S12)

16 months	Drinks from cup and glass	SIGN: *cow.*
17 months	Sits in regular chair	Joins two words (C22; G21): *Bird wait bird* *water milk* *good finished* *eat cracker* *cookies more* *home car* *girl funny* *sleep up* *dirty dog*
18 months/ 10 days	Throws ball with both hands, gait semi-still (S18)	SIGN VOCABULARY TOTAL: 106 LETTER TOTAL: 3
19 months	Scribbles spontaneously (C18) Builds tower 5 blocks (C20 with 3) Walks upstairs with help (B20.3) Walks downstairs with help (B20.5) Twelve teeth	Points to 3 parts of doll (C20). Attempts to follow directions (C20). Pulls person to show (G21). Echoes by gestures or words (G21). Identifies 2 pictures from name (C22). SIGN VOCABULARY TOTAL: 117 LETTER TOTAL: 5 (fingerspelling)
19½ months		SIGN VOCABULARY TOTAL: 142 LETTER TOTAL: 14 (fingerspelling)
22 months/ 10 days	Runs (S24) Alternates between sitting up and standing (S24)	*Boy girl play* *Me girl* *Hello, thank you food* Language creation and interest (S24)

Key: C, Cattell Score (in months); B, Bayley Score (in months); G, Gesell Score (in months); S, Slobin Score (in months) from Lenneberg, 1967.

Source: From *Sound and Sign: Childhood Deafness and Mental Health* by H.S. Schlesinger & K.P. Meadow. Berkeley: University of California Press, 1972. Reprinted with permission.

utterances. The 6-year-olds put words together in a sentencelike manner spontaneously and are beginning to use a variety of verbs, either preceding or following a variety of nouns.

According to Schlesinger and Meadow (1972), there is a paucity of literature on the language achievement of deaf children between the ages of 9 months and 6 to 7 years. The authors reported results on the Mecham Verbal Language Development Scale (1958) scores for the deaf and hearing subjects in their preschool program (Table 7-7).

With regard to older hearing-impaired children, the results of performance on word meaning and paragraph meaning subtests are significantly below the results for normal children. According to the DiFrancesca *Survey of Hearing Impaired Children and Youth* (1972), the highest reading competence level attained by hearing-impaired students at age 19 was equivalent to Grade 4.36. The reading performance was lowest for students with the most severe hearing loss. Furth (1966) reports only 12% of deaf children achieve true linguistic competency as adults and only 4% are proficient speech readers and speakers.

Cognitive Development

Lenneberg (1972) wrote that the development of cognition is relatively unimpaired (at least up to a certain age level) if only one sensory avenue is blocked. During the infant and toddler years, deaf children are less likely to be penalized by intelligence testing; measures of sensorimotor intelligence include a high percentage of visual and fine motor manipulating tasks. In the measurement of mentation, however, linguistic competence plays a major role in performance—an importance that increases with age; the lack of an obvious linguistic proficiency has caused a number of deaf persons to be erroneously labeled retarded. Therefore,

Table 7-7 Mecham Scores of Deaf and Hearing Children

Language Age in Months (Quartiles)	*Deaf* %	(N)	*Hearing* %	(N)
5-16	35	(14)	—	(0)
17-28	40	(16)	—	(0)
29-52	23	(9)	25	(5)
53-69	3	(1)	75	(15)
Totals	101	(40)	100	(20)
Average Age	43.8		43.7	

Source: From *Sound and Sign: Childhood Deafness and Mental Health* by H.S. Schlesinger and K.P. Meadow. Berkeley: University of California Press, 1972. Reprinted with permission.

psychologists must be extremely cautious in selecting instruments for assessment of the abilities of the deaf.

Macnamara (1972) and Bloom (1970, 1971) suggest that the development of thought precedes and is essential for linguistic development. According to Macnamara (1972), infants learn their language by first determining, independently of the language, the meaning a speaker intends to convey, then working out the relationship between meaning and language. "The infant uses meaning as a clue to language, rather than language as a clue to meaning" (p. 1).

Furth and Youniss (1976) investigated formal operations in deaf and hearing adolescents (mean age for both groups was 16 to 17 years). The subjects were tested in symbolic logic, probability, and combinations. The results demonstrated rather large differences between the groups in symbolic logic, but only small differences in probability and combinations. The researchers concluded that the data "support a view that sees in a special environment, including its verbal aspect, a powerful factor in motivating individuals toward selective formal operatory functioning without, however, making language the determining cause underlying these operations" (p. 407). The study indicated that language facilitated formal operations that were expressed in a symbolic medium, but did not affect other kinds of formal operations.

It must be concluded that cognition as an entity separate from language is not impaired in the young deaf child. In functional mentation and the activities expected of school-aged and adult persons, however, hearing-impaired individuals fall considerably behind their hearing peers. In the Babbidge Report (1965) of an 11-member advisory committee appointed to study the educational opportunities for the deaf, the following statements clearly demonstrate the effects deafness has on achievement. "The average graduate of a public residential school for the deaf—the closest we have to generally available 'high school' for the deaf—has an eighth grade education. . . . Five-sixths of our deaf adults work in manual jobs, as contrasted to only one-half of our hearing population" (p. xv).

Social Development

Levine (1960) stated that the deaf tend to lag behind the hearing in social maturity. Graham and Rutter (1968) have reported that the rate of emotional problems in deaf children is 15.4%, more than twice as high as the rate for nonhandicapped children. Freeman, Malkin, and Hastings (1975), in a much larger study of deaf children in the Greater Vancouver area, found that 22.6% were judged by parents and teachers as having a psychiatric disorder of moderate or severe degree.

The tension and stress experienced by families of deaf children because of their reduced abilities to communicate have been poignantly described by Murphy (1981), Knox and Chrisman (1979), and Ferris (1980). These familial strains are likely to contribute to the increased social and emotional problems of the deaf child. Williams (1970) collected retrospective developmental data on eight deaf children in whom psychosis had been diagnosed. Some of the noted behaviors included excessive sleeping during the 1st year of life, failure to anticipate being picked up, negativism, excessive placidity, indifference, and gaze avoidance.

Freedman, Cannady, and Robinson (1971) observed five congenitally deaf girls and noted that they tended to translate their desires into action more than nonhearing impaired children did. Lesser and Easser (1972) suggested that the impulsivity of deaf children results from the lack of adequate communicative channels for expressing needs and emotions. Because the deaf child lacks a name or label for a feeling, it is more likely to be expressed in a manner that might appear immature or inappropriate. Heider (1948) reported that deaf children had difficulty gaining control of social situations; their reactions in such situations were more diffuse, less structured, and less clearly differentiated than those of hearing children. The parents of deaf children tend to feel helpless when they try to explain complicated events, such as a move to a new city, a trip to a hospital, the death of a family member, or the decision to place a child in a residential program. Parental attitudes contribute to the impact of deafness on a child's social behavior.

EDUCATIONAL SERVICES MODELS FOR YOUNG DEAF CHILDREN

Hearing-impaired preschool children are educated in many kinds of programs, depending on the child's needs, the availability of ongoing programs in the local area, and the parents' wishes. There are six types of common service models (Lowenbraun & Thompson, 1982).

Home intervention programs have been particularly popular in rural areas. These programs are designed to help the family adjust to the problems associated with hearing impairment and to learn to communicate with the child as soon as possible. Training is provided for early aid use, as well as initial instruction in language, speech, and total communication. Instruction takes place in the home, and all family members are included in the sessions. The home-based program usually has some means of connecting parents to parents (e.g., through meetings or newsletters). An example of this type of program is the Ski*Hi Program in Utah (Clark, 1975). In this program, deaf infants gained 16 months of development in 11 months of programming, while 4-year-olds with 21 months of treatment had lower language levels than 2½-year-olds with 13 months of treatment.

Center programs can be located in homelike environments, speech and hearing clinics, or in regular public schools. The John Tracy Clinic in California is an old converted home, while the Mama Lere Home in Nashville was built on a home model for the express purpose of serving young hearing-impaired children and their families. The success of the Early Education Project at the Central Institute for the Deaf, a center-based program conducted in a home demonstration center, has shown that this model (which targets not just the child but the whole family) is a highly effective plan for early intervention (Simmons-Martin, 1981). In some of these programs, the parent attends with the child; in others, the child participates in typical preschool activities that have a particular emphasis on language acquisition. Many of the center-based programs have hearing children as models in the classroom.

Residential schools are operated in most states so that deaf children who have no services available in their local community can have the training they need. The residential program can care for children with various types of hearing losses and specific instructional needs. Most of these schools provide transportation for the child to go home once or twice a month. The environment of the institution offers a good opportunity for socialization and exposure to deaf adults, an experience that is not always available in a child's local community. Of course, there are also disadvantages to the residential programs. The child and family may find it difficult to shift back and forth on weekends between school and home. In addition, the children do not get as much interaction with hearing children and do not have as many opportunities to enter usual family routines, such as helping with chores to learn responsibility.

There are day schools in many communities. In these settings, children live at home, but attend a school for deaf children. These schools are usually located in large metropolitan areas that have enough deaf children to support an environment that (like the residential school) separates them from hearing children for education.

Day classes are classes for preschool deaf children that are self-contained, although they may be in a building with hearing peers. The hearing-impaired children are provided with many opportunities to have instruction and participate in activities with the hearing students, but the emphasis on separated instruction allows teachers to focus specifically on the needs of the hearing-impaired children.

Resource rooms and itinerant services are provided for hearing-impaired students who can function in a classroom for hearing students, but need some special instruction from a trained specialist. For most hearing-impaired students, this arrangement provides the least restrictive environment. Resource rooms are not usually practical for the very young preschool child, however. The younger child needs a program that has a very heavy language orientation, which is not always available in preschool classes for normal children. Parents may choose to send their hearing-impaired youngster to a normal preschool and make private arrangements for special assistance.

Baldwin (1977) reviewed programs for hearing-impaired children and reported six common characteristics of quality programs: (1) leadership, (2) esprit de corps, (3) curriculum centralization, (4) systematic use of amplification, (5) speech and language instruction, and (6) high level of expectation.

CURRICULUMS FOR PRESCHOOL DEAF CHILDREN

Language Instruction

Programs for deaf children emphasize language acquisition, then follow general guidelines of instruction that are appropriate for this particular approach. After a child has been fitted with an appropriate amplification device, a training program must be initiated to make maximal use of residual hearing. Audiologists and programs differ in the ways they train the child to use hearing. Programs that emphasize the auditory input alone use unisensory or aural methods (Pollack, 1970). Programs that emphasize the auditory input but also include visual and contextual cues use aural-oral methods or natural language methods (Groht, 1958).

The aural-oral instruction approach is based on the assumption that hearing-impaired persons should be trained to hear and speak as normally as possible and that manual means of communication should not be used. In this method children are taught (1) to use their remaining hearing to discriminate speech sounds, (2) to read the speech of others, (3) to use taction and kinesthetic feedback to understand sounds that cannot be heard or easily seen, and (4) to speak through special training (e.g., in breathing, pitch).

In manual communication instruction, children use their hands, fingers, and arms to communicate. This approach is represented by several systems, all of which have unique aspects (Table 7-8).

A study by Jordan, Gustafson, and Rosen (1976) revealed that the number of classes reporting the use of total communication instruction as a primary mode is far greater than the number of all other classes combined. This is evidence of a clear trend toward total communication instruction in the education of the deaf. Garretson (1976) states that total communication is neither a method nor a prescribed system of instruction, but an approach that encourages communication flexibility without ambiguity, guesswork, and stress; it includes visual support. Research by Chasen and Zuckerman (1976) and White and Stevenson (1975) offered convincing evidence that children using the total communication approach improved significantly more in academics than did children in oral classes. There are some disadvantages to this approach, however; for example, there is no nationally agreed upon sign system, and it may be difficult to mainstream children who have received this type of instruction.

Verbotonal instruction, developed from a rhythm-based technique for teaching foreign language, uses body movements to establish speech patterns and auditory perception of these patterns. The emphasis is on acoustic memorization of these patterns. Games and play activities are used to teach language, speech, use of residual hearing, and (later) academic skills.

Table 7-8 Elements of Total Communication

American Sign Language (Ameslan or ASL)	Standard signs Non-English language Some fingerspelling one sign = one concept	Unique grammar Unique syntax
Aural/Oral	Amplification Lipreading Cued speech (eight hand configurations, four facial positions) one lipsign = one or more phonemes	Oral gesture Speech
Fingerspelling	Finger rather than hand signs Letters run together as in oral or written production Rochester method (fingerspelling combined with speech) one hand configuration = one letter	
Gestemic	Childrenese Esoteric (localisms) International sign one gesture = one concept	Natural gestures Pantomime
Manual English	Seeing essential English Signed English Signing exact English Linguistics of visual English one sign = one word or affix	Fingerspelling Standard sign often used as root Creation of new signs for inflections, endings, tense, affixes, articles
Siglish (Sign English)	Pidgin sign English Finger spelling Syntax heavily English-oriented one sign = one concept	Standard sign modified on continuum toward English Gear shifting between English and ASL idiom

Source: From "Total Communication" by M.D. Garretson. In R. Frisina (Ed.), *The Volta Review, A Bicentennial Monograph on Hearing Impairment: Trends in the USA,* 1976, *78* (No. 4).

Two methods of instruction have been used to teach language to hearing-impaired students: the grammatical method and the natural method. The grammatical method focuses on teaching specific grammatical rules that students learn to use in order to construct sentences. Fitzgerald (1937) developed a key for arranging words in order according to categories of questions, such as who, what, whose, and when. The deaf child learns to make sentences by combining words from the different categories, e.g., "Philip (who) ate (what) the apple." The natural method is basically the aural-oral method noted earlier. The learning of language and speech occurs in natural, meaningful situations that are carefully constructed but nevertheless provide a functional basis for instruction. Groht (1958) described this method in great detail some years ago.

Motor Instruction

There are no widely recognized motor programs that are designed specifically for hearing-impaired preschool children. Many schools for the deaf have designed their own programs, while a number of teachers have adapted traditional motor programs for their deaf students. The motor area is one of the easier areas in which to integrate deaf children with hearing children. For the most part, deaf children can follow the motor cues of peers and have few delays that are directly related to their hearing loss. For example, even without dependable cues from auditory stimuli in the environment, the hearing-impaired child can profit from refined visual-perceptual skills. The child can sense the auditory stimuli by responding to movements and contextual cues of others, coordinating motor responses in synchrony with the patterns of those who are picking up auditory cues. There are some areas (e.g., visual-motor coordination, static balance, dynamic balance), however, that may prove difficult for the deaf child and some instruction may be required.

To facilitate visual-motor coordination, the child can be taught dance sequences in which cues can be taken from the steps of others in order to perform the sequences with proper timing. The child can be encouraged to engage in ball activities that require a body adjustment after following the trajectory of a ball. On a card or chalkboard, a pattern in different colors or shapes to indicate forward, backward, or side movements can be placed and the child taught to perform these movements according to the visual cues.

Many hearing-impaired children have balance problems. The motor curriculum should, therefore, stress static balance activities. For example, in a supine position, the child imitates movements of the head and shoulders; shoulders and arms; body and trunk; legs, knees, ankles, and feet; and combined movements. The child should also execute these movements while in a prone position. Static balance can also be developed by having the child crawl in place, using either a homolateral or a cross pattern.

Movement of the body in space requires an internal perception of body movement in order to make the adjustments necessary for equilibrium. Dynamic balance is facilitated by crawling activities in both a homolateral and a cross pattern, creeping in the homolateral and cross patterns, imitating various animals, and following obstacle courses. For dynamic balance in a seated position, there are trunk movements, rotations and body extensions, arm movements, and leg and knee exercises. In an upright position, the child can engage in stretching movements, such as running, marching, and jumping in place. Trunk rotation and bends from a standing position are also important for dynamic balance. Walking, running, hopping, trotting, galloping, marching, and combinations of these are more advanced dynamic motor procedures.

Social Instruction

Like motor instruction, little social competency instruction is designed specifically for deaf children. Instruction in this area is less structured and seldom programmed, but it should be taught in the context of the situation at hand; that is, the teacher, parents, and others involved with the child should intervene in the situation and instruct or model the proper behavior.

Like all other children, the deaf child needs to feel that caregivers can be trusted and that the world is a predictable and dependable place. There must be opportunities for trust to grow, in an environment where it can be learned, internalized, and expressed to others. The child must also learn to be trusted, perhaps through interactions with family animals, siblings, or peers who depend on the child for specific actions or responses.

Because deaf children cannot communicate easily with others, they are likely to be more passive than others are, to initiate fewer interactions, and to see themselves as individuals whom others must help and whom others pity. If these feelings persist, these children will act in ways to justify others' responses to them. Parents and teachers must help deaf children to build independence by stressing their strengths and working to overcome problems relating to their sense of worth and self-respect. In addition, these children should be provided with opportunites to do things for others. Showing a friend how to perform a task that has been mastered; playing the mother or father role in play activities; pretending to be professional persons, such as dentists, doctors, teachers, and sportsmen, are ways in which these children can assume an independent and responsible role.

Cognitive Instruction

In innate mental ability, the young deaf child is not different from the hearing child; however, in expressing understanding in measurable ways, the deaf child's facility decreases with increasing language requirements. In addition to specific instruction in language, there are other areas, particularly in the preoperational stage, in which specific instruction can facilitate mental development of the child with a hearing loss.

Labels, Symbols, or Signs for Objects or Events Not Present

It is important to stress representation of things not visually present. This can be done through hide-and-seek games or other activities that require imitation or reasoning. The child can be given objects and told to use them in different ways to convey different meanings:

- Ask the child about current situations and surroundings; encourage a reply.
- Involve the child in many different activities in the home, school, and away; encourage communication by asking questions.
- Use appropriate facial expressions and body gestures to express emotion (e.g., joy, anger, fear, love).

Classification Skills

- Have the child sort objects or pictures using a model.
- Have the child sort objects or pictures without a model.
- Have the child associate pictures or objects that have a direct relationship to one another, such as lamp and light switch.

Time Sequences

- Have the child arrange pictures in the order of naturally occurring events.
- Have the child tell or draw what happened yesterday and what will happen tomorrow.
- Have the child explain the sequence of events that will occur in the classroom, for example, What will come first, a class subject or lunch? Where will recess fit in?
- Have the child explain the sequence of dressing in the morning (i.e., which articles first) and the sequence of events up to school time.
- Have the child sequence his or her activities while playing outdoors or explain sequences to certain tasks that must be accomplished in the classroom.

Distance Sequences

- On a game board or map, lay out routes for movement to and from places. Have the child follow various routes (e.g., a long way, a short way).

- Have the child actually follow different routes to various destinations indoors and out and ask which was shorter, longer, or the same.
- Create mazes and have the child follow the shortest or longest route, with finger or pencil, and find the goal.
- Create mazes using desks, chairs, or other objects present and have the child crawl or walk the shortest or longest route to a place in the classroom.

Size Sequence

- Give the child objects that must be sequenced according to size, such as beads, blocks or cubes, or balls.
- Have the child sequence the chairs or desks in the classroom according to size.
- Have the child sequence the other persons or their body parts, such as legs and arms, according to size.
- While looking from a window, have the child sequence the cars in the parking lot or pedestrians passing by according to size.

Patterned Sequences

- Present a bead pattern with one variable, and have the child replicate. Build a more complicated pattern and ask the child to copy by color and shape. After the child can do this, have the child repeat from memory after brief exposure to the model.
- Line up children in the room and have the child study their positions; have one of the children in the line change position while the observing child turns away; then have the observing child either explain who moved or physically move child back into original position in line.

Number Conservation

- Use comparisons to see if the child can identify more, less, same.
- Use direct correspondence tasks in which the child must match a number to the grouped objects.
- Present a set of objects and have the child arrange an equivalent set.

Missing Elements

- Remove one item from a group and have the child identify the missing element. Have the child identify a whole object on the basis of several of its parts presented as visual cues or in uncompleted drawings.

- Show the child pictures that have missing elements; have the child identify where something is missing and describe what it is. This task can also be done with a group of children: one child removes an item of clothing, such as shoe, socks, hat, glove, or coat, and another must state what is missing.
- Plan sequences with something missing. Show the child possible missing parts; then have the child select correct part.

CONCLUSION

Children with sensory impairments have not only many needs that are the same as those of other children but also needs that are specifically related to the nature of their impairments. To understand the special needs of sensorily impaired children, educators must know how impairments affect development, as well as how environments and experiences can be arranged in order to help these children develop and learn. One cannot assume that time will make a difference or that a child's learning problems need not be addressed until formal schooling begins; the early years are indeed critical for the sensorily impaired infant who is ready to learn. Parents, teachers, and others can begin meeting these special needs from birth and, in doing so, will strengthen both development and learning.

REFERENCES

Als, H., Tronick, E., & Brazelton, T. Affective reciprocity and the development of autonomy: The study of a blind infant. *Journal of the American Academy of Child Psychiatry,* 1980, *19,* 22-40.

American Medical Association committee report. *Estimation of loss of visual efficiency.* A.M.A. Archives of Industrial Health, October 1955.

Ashcroft, S.C., Halliday, C., & Barraga, N. *Study II: Effects of experimental teaching on the visual behavior of children educated as though they had no vision.* Nashville, Tenn.: George Peabody College, 1965.

Babbidge, H. *Education of the deaf in the United States: Report of the Advisory Committee on Education of the Deaf.* Washington, D.C.: U.S. Government Printing Office, 1965.

Baldwin, R.L. Characteristics of quality programs for hearing impaired children. *Volta Review,* 1977, *77,* 436-439.

Barraga, N. *Increased visual behavior in low-vision children.* New York: American Foundation for the Blind, 1964.

Bloom, L. *Language development: Form and function in emerging grammars.* Boston: M.I.T. Press, 1970.

Bloom, L. Why not pivot grammar? *Journal of Speech and Hearing Disorders,* 1971, *36,* 40-51.

Boyce, V.S. The home eye test program. *Sight Saving Review,* 1973, *43,* 43-48.

Brekke, B., Williams, J.E., & Tait, P. The acquisition of conservation of weight by visually impaired children. *Journal of Genetic Psychology,* 1974, *125,* 89-97.

Brown, D., Simmons, V., & Methvin, J. *The Oregon project for visually impaired and blind preschool children* (Rev. ed.). Medford, Oreg.: Jackson County ESD, 1979.

Caton, H.R. Visual impairments. In A.E. Blackhurst & W.H. Berdine (Eds.), *An introduction to special education*. Boston: Little, Brown, 1981.

Chasen, B., & Zuckerman, W. The effects of total communication and oralism on deaf third grade "rubella" students. *American Annals of the Deaf*, 1976, *121*, 394-401.

Clark, E.V. Some aspects of the conceptual basis for first language acquisition. In R.L. Schiefelbusch & L.L. Lloyd (Eds.), *Language perspectives: Acquisition, retardation, and intervention*. Baltimore: University Park Press, 1974.

Clark, T.C. (Ed.). *Project Ski*Hi*. Ogden, Utah: Project Ski*Hi, 1975.

Cox, B.P., & Lloyd, L.L. Audiologic considerations. In L.L. Lloyd (Ed.), *Communication assessment and intervention strategies*. Baltimore: University Park Press, 1976.

Demott, R.M. Visual impairments. In N.G. Haring (Ed.), *Exceptional children and youth* (3rd ed.). Columbus, Ohio: Charles E. Merrill, 1982.

DiFrancesca, S. *Academic achievement test results of a national testing program for hearing impaired students, United States, Spring 1971*. Series D, Number 9. Washington, D.C.: Office of Demographic Studies, Gallaudet College, 1972.

DuBose, R.F. Developmental needs in blind infants. *The New Outlook for the Blind*, 1976, *2*, 49-52.

DuBose, R.F. *Assessment of visually impaired infants*. Paper presented at the Westar/Model Preschool Center for Handicapped Children Topical Conference on Infant Assessment and Intervention. Seattle, June 1978.

DuBose, R.F., Langley, M.B., Bourgeault, S.E., Harley, R.H., & Stagg, V. Assessment and programming for blind children with severely handicapped conditions. *Visual Impairment and Blindness*, 1977, *2*, 49-53.

DuBose, R.F., Langley, M.B., & Stagg, V. Assessing severely handicapped children. *Focus on Exceptional Children*, 1977, *9*(7), 1-13.

Ferris, C. *A hug just isn't enough*. Washington, D.C.: Gallaudet College Press, 1980.

Fewell, R.F. Assessment of visual impairment. In B. Bracken & K. Paget (Eds.), *The psychoeducational assessment of preschool children*. New York: Grune & Stratton, 1982.

Fitzgerald, E. *Straight language for the deaf: A system of instruction for deaf children* (3rd ed.). Houston, Tex.: Steck, 1937.

Folio, M.R. *Assessing motor development in multiply handicapped children*. Paper presented at annual meeting of Council on Exceptional Children, New York, April, 1974.

Fraiberg, S. Parallel and divergent patterns in blind and sighted infants. *Psychoanalytic Study of the Child*, 1968, *23*, 264-300.

Fraiberg, S. *Insights from the Blind*. New York: Basic Books, 1977.

Freedman, D.A., Cannady, C., & Robinson, J.A. Speech and psychic structure: A reconsideration of their relation. *Journal of the American Psychoanalytic Association*, 1971, *19*, 765-779.

Freeman, R.F., Malkin, S.R., & Hastings, J.O. Psychosocial problems of deaf children and their families: A comparative study. *American Annals of the Deaf*, 1975, *120*, 391-405.

Furth, H.G. *Thinking without language: Psychological implications of deafness*. New York: Free Press, 1966.

Furth, H.G., & Youniss, J. Formal operations and language: A comparison of deaf and hearing adolescents. In D.M. Morehead & A.E. Morehead (Eds.), *Normal and deficient child language*. Baltimore: University Park Press, 1976.

Garretson, M.D. Total communication. *The Volta Review*, 1976, *78*, 88-95.

Goldberg, M.H. (Ed.). *Blindness research: The expanding frontiers, a liberal studies perspective*. University Park, Pa.: Pennsylvania State University Press, 1969.

Graham, P., & Rutter, M. Organic brain dysfunction and child psychiatric disorder. *British Medical Journal,* 1968, *3,* 695-700.

Green, W.W. Hearing disorders. In A.E. Blackhurst & W.H. Berdine (Eds.), *An introduction to special education.* Boston: Little, Brown, 1981.

Groht, M. *Natural language for deaf children.* Washington, D.C., Volta Bureau, 1958.

Hallenbeck, J. Two essential factors in the development of young blind children. *New Outlook for the Blind,* 1954, *48,* 308-315.

Harley, R.D., & Lawrence, G.A. *Visual impairment in the schools.* Springfield, Ill.: Charles C Thomas, 1977.

Hathaway, W. *Education and health of the partially seeing child* (4th ed.). New York: Columbia University Press, 1959.

Heider, G.M. Adjustment problems of the deaf child. *Nervous Child,* 1948, *1,* 38-44.

Jordan, I.K., Gustafson, G., & Rosen, R. Current communication trends at programs for the deaf. *American Annals of the Deaf,* 1976, *121,* 527-532.

Kastein, S., Spaulding, I., & Scharf, B. *Raising the young blind child.* New York: Human Sciences Press, 1980.

Kirchner, C., Peterson, R., & Suhr, C. Trends in school enrollment and reading methods among legally blind school children, 1963-1978. *Journal of Visual Impairment and Blindness,* 1979, *73,* 373-379.

Knox, L., & Chrisman, C. *Today is not forever.* Nashville, Tenn.: Intersect, 1979. (Videotape)

Lairy, G.C., & Harrison-Covello, A. The blind child and his parents: Congenital visual defect and the repercussion of family attitudes on the early development of the blind. *Research Bulletin, American Foundation for the Blind,* 1973, *25,* 1-24.

Langley, B., & DuBose, R. Functional vision screening for severely handicapped children. *The New Outlook for the Blind,* 1976, *70*(8), 346-350.

Langley, M.B. *Functional vision inventory for the multiply & severely handicapped.* Chicago: Stoelting, 1980.

Larson, A.D., & Miller, J.B. The hearing impaired. In E.L. Meyen (Ed.), *Exceptional children and youth: An introduction.* Denver: Love Publishing, 1978.

Lenneberg, E.H. Prerequisites for language acquisition by the deaf. In T.J. O'Rourke (Ed.), *Psycholinguistics and total communication: The state of the art.* Washington, D.C.: American Annals of the Deaf, 1972.

Lesser, S.R., & Easser, B.R. Personality differences in the perceptually handicapped. *Journal of the American Academy of Child Psychiatry,* 1972, *11,* 458-466.

Levine, E.S. *Psychology of deafness.* New York: Columbia University Press, 1960.

Lowenbraun, S., & Thompson, M.D. Hearing impairments. In N.G. Haring (Ed.), *Exceptional children and youth* (3rd ed.). Columbus, Ohio: Charles E. Merrill, 1982.

Lowenfeld, B. *Our blind children: Growing and living with them* (2nd ed.). Springfield, Ill.: Charles C Thomas, 1964.

Lowenfeld, B. *The visually handicapped child in school.* New York: John Day, 1973.

Macnamara, J. Cognitive basis of language learning in infants. *Psychological Review,* 1972, *79,* 1-13.

Maloney, P.L. *Practical guidance for parents of the visually handicapped preschooler.* Springfield, Ill.: Charles C Thomas, 1981.

Mecham, M.J. *Verbal language development scale.* Circle Pines, Minn.: American Guidance Services, 1958.

Moore, J.M., Thompson, G., & Thompson, M. Auditory localization of infants as a function of reinforcement conditions. *Journal of Speech and Hearing Disorders,* 1975, *40,* 29-34.

Murphy, A.T. *Special children, special parents.* Englewood Cliffs, N.J.: Prentice-Hall, 1981.

National Society for the Prevention of Blindness. *N.S.P.B. fact book: Estimated statistics on blindness and visual problems.* New York: Author, 1966.

National Society for the Prevention of Blindness. *The symbol chart for 20 feet.* New York: Author, 1969.

New York Association for the Blind. *A flash-card vision test for children.* New York: Author, 1966.

Norris, M., Spaulding, P.J., & Brodie, F.H. *Blindness in children.* Chicago: University of Chicago Press, 1957.

Northern, J.L., & Downs, M.P. *Hearing in children* (2nd ed.). Baltimore: Williams & Wilkins, 1978.

O'Brien, R. *Alive . . . aware . . . a person.* Rockville, Md.: Montgomery County Public Schools, 1976.

Office of Special Education and Rehabilitative Services, U.S. Department of Education, National Summary of Handicapped Children Receiving Special Education and Related Services under PL 94-142 and PL 89-313, 1980-1981.

Piaget, J., & Inhelder, B. *The psychology of the child.* New York: Basic Books, 1969.

Pollack, D. *Educational audiology for the limited hearing infant.* Springfield, Ill.: Charles C Thomas, 1970.

Rapin, I. Effects of early blindness and deafness on cognition. In R. Katzman (Ed.), *Congenital and acquired cognitive disorders.* New York: Raven Press, 1979.

Report of the ad hoc committee to define deaf and hard of hearing. *American Annals of the Deaf,* 1975, *120,* 509-512.

Reynolds, M.C., & Birch, J.W. *Teaching exceptional children in all American schools.* Reston, Va.: Council for Exceptional Children, 1977.

Ross, M. Hearing aid selection for preverbal hearing-impaired children. In M. Pollack (Ed.), *Amplification for the hearing impaired.* New York: Grune & Stratton, 1975.

Ross, M. Amplification systems. In L.L. Lloyd (Ed.), *Communication assessment and intervention strategies.* Baltimore: University Park Press, 1976.

Schlesinger, H.S., & Meadow, K.P. *Sound and sign: Childhood deafness and mental health.* Berkeley: University of California Press, 1972.

Scott, E.P., Jan, J.E., & Freeman, R.D. *Can't your child see?* Baltimore: University Park Press, 1977.

Scott, R. *The making of a blindman.* New York: Russell Sage Foundation, 1968.

Sheridan, M.D. *Manual for the Stycar Vision Tests.* Windsor, Ontario: JFER Publishing, 1973.

Silberman, R.K. Assessment and evaluation of visually handicapped students. *Journal of Vision Impairment and Blindness,* 1981, *75,* 109-114.

Simmons, A.A. The critical stages of language development. Presented at the Council for Exceptional Children Convention, Washington, D.C., March 21, 1972.

Simmons-Martin, A. Efficacy report: Early education project. *Journal of the Division for Early Childhood,* 1981, *4,* 5-10.

Spellman, C., DeBriere, T., & Cress, P. *Parsons visual acuity test. Final Report.* Parsons, Kans.: Parsons Research Center, 1979.

Swallow, R. Fifty assessment instruments commonly used with blind and partially seeing individuals. *Journal of Vision Impairment and Blindness,* 1981, *75,* 65-72.

Tait, P. Play and intellectual development of blind children. *New Outlook for the Blind,* 1972, *66,* 361-369.

Vaughan, D., Asbury, T., & Cook, R. *General ophthalmology.* Los Altos, Calif.: Lange Medical Publications, 1971.

Warren, D. *Blindness and early childhood development.* New York: American Foundation for the Blind, 1977.

Watrous, B.S., McConnell, F., Sitton, A., & Fleet, W. Auditory responses of infants. *Journal of Speech and Hearing Disorders,* 1975, *40*(3), 357-366.

White, A.H., & Stevenson, V.M. The effects of total communication, oral communication, and reading on the learning of factual information in residential school deaf children. *American Annals of the Deaf,* 1975, *120,* 48-87.

Williams, C.E. Some psychiatric observations on a group of maladjusted deaf children. *Journal of Child Psychology and Psychiatry,* 1970, *11,* 1-18.

Wills, D.M. Early speech development in blind children. *Psychoanalytic Study of the Child,* 1979, *34,* 83-117.

Part IV

Social Development

Chapter 8

The Young Mildly Retarded Child

Paul A. Alberto

NATURE OF MENTAL RETARDATION

John is 6 years old. He is able to play in the street with the neighborhood kids and understands the rules of games and of friendship. But, he has an absolute fit when he loses a game. He can communicate his wants and needs, find his way around the neighborhood, and do chores for his mother; if you give him two dimes and a nickel, he can buy a Milky Way at the corner candy store. In school, John has problems pronouncing his words, cannot do take-away problems, and is still trying to memorize the alphabet. The school psychologist says John has an IQ of 61. Is John mentally retarded?

Definition

The mentally retarded have been recognized as an identifiable population subgroup for hundreds of years. Various ways of labeling and educating the retarded have been used. Definitions have gone through numerous revisions, dating as far back as the middle of the thirteenth century, when it was the prerogative of each king to identify ''idiots''—those who had not understanding of their nativity. Around 1500, Sir Anthony Fitzherbert defined a retarded person as one who ''cannot account or number, nor can tell who was his father or mother, nor how old he is, so as it may appear he has not understanding of reason what shall be his profit or his loss'' (Brockett, 1856).

During the middle decades of this century, the prevailing definition of mental retardation was that of Doll (1941), who stated six criteria essential to an ''adequate definition and concept'' of mental retardation: ''(1) social incompetence, (2) due to mental subnormality, (3) which has been developmentally arrested, (4) which obtains at maturity, (5) is of constitutional origin, and (6) is essentially incurable'' (p. 215). This definition of mental retardation has been revised as knowledge of the causes and course of mental retardation increased. Professionals came to understand the potential effect of environment on intelligence, the differentiation between social competence (adaptive behavior) and cognitive competence, and the fact that mental functioning (IQ) is not necessarily a static index.

Since 1959, the generally accepted definition is the one published in the *Manual on Terminology and Classification in Mental Retardation* by the American Association on Mental Deficiency (AAMD). The current definition (1973) is as follows:

> Mental retardation refers to significantly subaverage general intellectual functioning existing concurrently with deficits in adaptive behavior, and manifested during the developmental period. (1977, p. 11)

Significantly Subaverage Intellectual Functioning

The indicator of significantly subaverage intellectual functioning is the child's IQ score. The IQ is determined by an individually administered test of intelligence. Such tests include the Wechsler Intelligence Scale for Children-Revised (WISC-R; 1974), the Stanford-Binet Intelligence Scale (Terman & Merrill, 1960), the Bayley Scales of Infant Development (1969), the Cattell Infant Intelligence Scale (1969), and the Wechsler Preschool and Primary Scale of Intelligence (1967). The test most often selected is the WISC-R, which is divided into two scales, the Verbal Scale and the Performance Scale. Each scale is composed of several subscales designed to assess various aspects of the child's mental functioning at the time when the test is administered. The WISC-R subscales are as follows:

Verbal Scale	*Performance Scale*
Information	Picture Completion
Similarities	Picture Arrangement
Arithmetic	Block Design
Vocabulary	Object Assembly
Comprehension	Coding
(Digit Span)	(Mazes)

If the WISC-R were administered to the general school population, the children's scores would result in a normal distribution, yielding a proportional spread of scores (Figure 8-1). The average IQ score for children in the population would fall between 90 and 110, with a mean score of 100. Scores are grouped in 15-point intervals, because members of the population are said to be statistically signifi-

Figure 8-1 Normal Distribution Curve

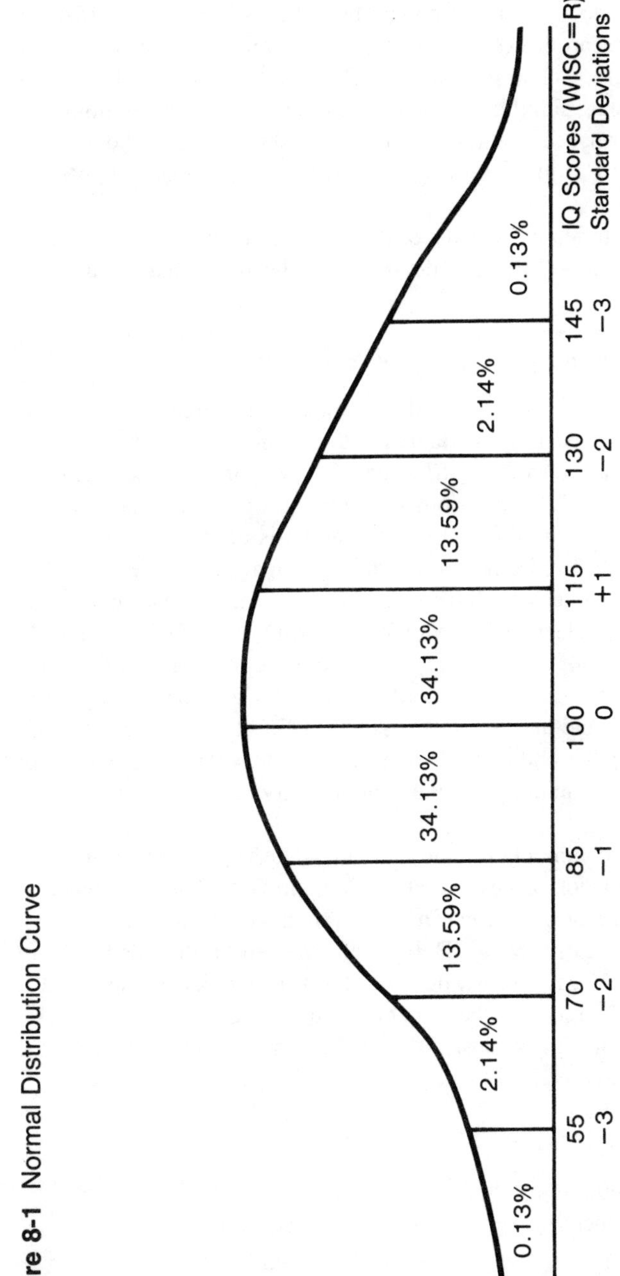

cantly different from one another at a point where their scores vary in 15-point increments from the mean of 100. Each 15 points is referred to as a standard deviation. Operationally, a child with an IQ of 85 (−1 standard deviation below the mean) is considered significantly below average in current abilities and potential school performance; a child with an IQ of 70 (−2 standard deviations below the mean) is still further below average in current abilities and potential school performance.

To meet this first criterion of mental retardation, a child must have a measured IQ equal to or greater than −2 standard deviations below the mean, or an IQ score equal to or less than 70.

Existing Concurrently with Deficits in Adaptive Behavior

Several class action suits have contested the content of intelligence tests on the basis of cultural bias, especially in reference to children of minority groups. Because of cases such as *Larry P. v. Riles*[1] and *Diana v. State Board of Education,*[2] federal law (PL 94-142) and various state laws now prohibit a classification of mental retardation for school placement on the basis of IQ scores alone. In addition, tests must be administered in the child's primary language.

In accordance with these court rulings, it has been determined that a child must demonstrate deficits in adaptive behavior before being classified as mentally retarded. Adaptive behavior is defined as "the effectiveness or degree with which an individual meets the standards of personal independence and social responsibility expected for age and cultural group (Grossman, 1977, p. 11). This definition requires assessment of the child's ability to perform those tasks necessary for functioning within the community and the child's ability to make and be responsible for decisions.

Testing instruments commonly used to measure adaptive behavior include the AAMD Adaptive Behavior Scales (Lambert, Windmiller, Cole, & Figueroa, 1975), the TMR Performance Profile (DiNola, Kaminsky, & Sternfield, 1968), the Vineland Social Maturity Scale (Doll, 1965), and the Balthazar Scales of Adaptive Behavior (1971). A recently developed instrument that attempts to take into account cultural differences is the System of Multicultural Pluralistic Assessment (SOMPA). Typical of the subtests found in these instruments are those of the AAMD Adaptive Behavior Scales:

Part I	*Part II*
Independent Functioning	Destructive Behavior
Physical Development	Antisocial Behavior
Economic Activity	Nonconforming Behavior
Language Development	Untrustworthiness
Number and Time Concepts	Withdrawn Behavior

Vocational Activity	Odd Mannerisms
Self-Direction	Interpersonal Manners
Responsibility	Vocal Habits
Socialization	Eccentric Habits
	Hyperactive Tendencies
	Psychological Disturbances
	Use of Medication

When the possibility of deficits in adaptive behavior is being investigated, two critical variables that must be considered are expectations based on age and expectations based on cultural group. For this purpose, three general age groups are delineated: (1) infancy and early childhood, (2) childhood and early adolescence, and (3) late adolescence and adulthood. When deficits in adaptive behavior during infancy and early childhood are being evaluated, assessment is performed to identify delays in the sequential acquisition patterns of maturation. Assessment focuses on sensorimotor development, speech and language, as well as self-help and socialization skills. Indicators of adaptive behavior deficits commonly found among young children are delays in standing, walking, and fine motor tasks; delayed language expansion; poor understanding of safety rules; inability to use money, and problems in number and word recognition.

During childhood and early adolescence, social skills and the application of basic academic skills, reasoning, and judgment in mastery of the environment are assessed to determine the child's ability to learn as a function of experience. During late adolescence and adulthood, vocational performance and social responsibility are assessed to determine the potential for independence, employment, and conformity to community standards.

Manifested during the Developmental Period

For classification of a child as mentally retarded, the diagnosis must be made when the child is between birth and age 18 years (the developmental period).

Levels of Mental Retardation

Individuals classified as mentally retarded have a wide range of ability and require diverse educational services. In order to meet these varying needs more effectively, mental retardation has been divided into four levels of retardation. The AAMD and the public school system use different schemes of dividing the levels of retardation. Although different labels are used, the demarcation criteria between levels are essentially the same (Table 8-1). It should be noted that the educational system's exact IQ limits for each level of retardation are set by departments of education in each of the states. Therefore, there are minor variations from state to state as to which children fall within each level.

Table 8-1 Two Systems for Classification of the Mentally Retarded

American Association on Mental Deficiency (Adaptive Behavior Not Accounted)			*Public Schools*	
	IQ[a]	*SD*		*IQ*
Mentally retarded	≤70	≥ −2	Mentally handicapped	≤70
Mildly retarded	69-55	−2 to −3	Educable retarded	70-50
Moderately retarded	54-40	−3 to −4	Trainable retarded	50-25
Severely retarded	39-25	−4 to −5	Severely retarded	<25
Profoundly retarded	<24	≥ −5		

[a]WISC-R values.

The highest level—or the least retarded—are the mildly retarded or educable mentally retarded. These children display delays of only 1 to 3 years in school performance and, thus, are capable of learning fundamental academics and personal responsibility. Given this minimal delay, these children are able to function within the traditional grade level curriculum with only minor modifications or assistance. As adults, they should be self-sufficient and live independently as productive members of the community. Until the 1970s, these children were automatically placed in self-contained special education classes; however, judicial decisions (e.g., *LeBanks v. Spears*[3]) and legislation (PL 94-142) have required placement in the "least restrictive educational alternative" *appropriate* to meeting the educational needs of each child. In schools, this has meant implementation of mainstreaming, which has revised the traditional system of service delivery. Most mildly retarded children are now placed within regular classes, and special education support services are provided to maintain reasonable academic and social progress (Ingalls, 1978; MacMillan, 1971, 1977).

The second level of retardation includes the moderately retarded or trainable mentally retarded. These children, with a functioning ability approximately one-half to one-third that expected for their chronological age, are able to master self-care skills, basic language, and cognitive concepts to include functional academics. As adults, with minimal supervision, they will be able to live in community homes and work within supervised workshop facilities. Traditionally, these children have been educated within segregated schools, training centers, or private facilities. Currently, to meet the goal of placement in the "least restrictive educational alternative," classes for the trainable retarded are being integrated into regular public school campuses.

The educational emphasis for children who are severely mentally retarded is on acquisition of self-care, motor, and language skills with emphasis on their ability to function effectively in their various environments (e.g., home, school, vocational placement). Traditionally, these children have been housed in state institutions. With the increasing awareness of the debilitating effects of institutional life and with the advent of the social philosophy of normalization, these individuals are being moved from institutions into community group homes to provide them with routines and experiences of daily living that are representative of normal life styles. As of the 1978 school year, compliance with PL 94-142 requires that classes for the severely retarded be established within the public school systems (Paul, Stedman, & Neufield, 1977; Wolfensberger, 1972).

The most involved individuals are those classified as profoundly mentally retarded. Currently, the majority of these individuals are placed in state institutions. There is growing concern, however, about whether the tests available can differentiate between the two lower levels of retardation and whether there is any merit in such differentiation. It is becoming more apparent that the distinction between the severely and the profoundly retarded may not rest on IQ scores, but on factors such as responsiveness to environmental stimulation, the potential for a means of communicating needs and wants, and the need for continuous medical monitoring.

Prevalence

A demographic statistic, prevalence refers to the percentage of a population that is expected to fall within a given category, classification, or subgroup. The prevalence figure for mental retardation is 3%, which means that an estimated 6.4 million people in a population of 214 million Americans would be classified as mentally retarded. This figure would equal the combined populations of Colorado, Delaware, Kansas, New Hampshire, and South Dakota. As seen in Table 8-2, the greatest proportion of this 3% consists of individuals within the mild range of retardation (85%). As the degree of retardation increases, the percentage of the population decreases.

Several objections have been raised to the use of 3% as the prevalence figure for the retarded, particularly by researchers such as Mercer (1973) and Tarjan, Wright, Eyman, and Keeran (1973). Their primary objections concern assumptions made about the mildly retarded segment of the population; they believe that

Table 8-2 Prevalence of Mental Retardation

Level of Retardation	*Estimate of Total Population (%)*	*Estimate of Mentally Retarded Population (%)*	*Mentally Retarded in Total Population*	*Mentally Retarded in School-Aged Population*
Educable	2.6	85.0	5,564,000	1,391,000
Trainable	0.3	12.0	642,000	160,500
Severe or profound	0.1	3.0	214,000	53,500
Total	3.0	100.0	6,420,000	1,605,000

these assumptions have artificially inflated the prevalence figure. It is estimated that the prevalence of retardation would be closer to 1% if the following objections were taken into account:

1. To date, diagnosis is still made primarily on the basis of IQ scores. If cultural differences were considered, the number of educable mentally retarded children would be significantly reduced.
2. The concept of prevalence assumes a retarded individual can be identified at birth. Such an early diagnosis cannot be made in infants with the potential for mild retardation because later environmental conditions play a critical role.
3. The 3% figure assumes a diagnosis of retardation does not change. Yet classification decisions at any given time should be made in relation to the behavioral standards and norms of the individual's age and cultural group. An individual labeled mentally retarded at one time of life may not be at another if there has been an alteration in intellectual functioning, adaptive behavior, or societal expectations. A diagnosis of retardation does not necessarily imply prognosis; the latter depends on such factors as the presence of secondary handicapping conditions and the effects of training and treatment.
4. Studies (Farber, 1968; Heber & Dever, 1970; Levinson, 1962) have shown that, while the incidence of the more severe levels of retardation remains stable across populations, there is great variability in incidence at the mild level. A higher incidence of mild retardation has been found among racial and ethnic minorities, low socioeconomic groups, and residents of rural, isolated communities and inner-city ghettos. Most noticeably, there are higher figures during the school years than in later life. This discrepancy is probably a function of the testing and certification requirements of the public schools for special education placement. Similar requirements do not exist for service delivery to adults.
5. A 3% figure assumes that the mortality rate of the retarded is similar to that of the general population. While life expectancy of the mildly retarded is similar, the mortality rate among those with the more severe levels of retardation is higher.

Etiology

Despite years of investigation, the cause of mental retardation can be identified in only 6% to 15% of cases (Dunn, 1973). In general terms, it may be determined that a specific case of retardation has a definite organic or physical cause (e.g., brain damage, genetic disorder), or it does not have such a basis and must be attributed to a nonorganic or nonphysical cause (e.g., environmental deprivation).

The preponderance of the 6% to 15% of cases in which a definite cause can be determined are those in which the child's retardation is moderate, severe, or profound. Retardation in the majority of these children has an organic and, therefore, readily diagnosed cause. These identifiable organic causes of retardation have been categorized by the AAMD as the following:

1. infections and intoxications, including both maternal and child infectious diseases and intoxications (e.g., rubella, syphilis, toxoplasmosis, encephalitis, lead poisoning, maternal diabetes, narcotic addiction)
2. trauma or physical agents, including brain injury due to trauma or mechanical or physical agents (e.g., hypoxia, irradiation, instrument injury during the birth process)
3. metabolism and nutrition, including disorders directly due to metabolic, nutritional, endocrine, or growth dysfunction (e.g., Tay-Sachs disease, Hurler's disease, phenylketonuria [PKU], Wilson's disease, brain damage due to marasmus)
4. gross brain disease (postnatal), including disorders due to neoplasms (tumors) (e.g., von Recklinghausen's disease, Sturge-Weber-Dimitri disease, tuberous sclerosis)
5. unknown prenatal influence, including cranial anomalies and congenital defects (e.g., anencephaly, Cornelia de Lange's syndrome, microcephaly, macrocephaly)
6. chromosomal abnormalities, including disorders due to chromosomal aberrations (e.g., Down's syndrome, cri du chat syndrome, Klinefelter's syndrome, Turner's syndrome)
7. gestational disorders, including defects related to atypical gestation (e.g., prematurity, low birth weight)

In approximately 85% of children classified as mildly retarded, there is no demonstrable organic cause of retardation (Zigler, 1967). The retarded development of these children is most often attributed to one of a variety of environmental causes, such as a lack of early "cultural" experiences, malnutrition (as opposed to marasmus), or some form of social deprivation. These children are referred to as the cultural/familial retarded (Zigler, 1967). These nonorganic causes of retardation would be included in the following AAMD categories:

8. following psychiatric disorder, including "retardation following psychosis or other psychiatric disorder when there is no evidence of cerebral pathology" (Grossman, 1977, p. 67).
9. environmental influences, including cases in which there are "indications of adverse environmental conditions and in which there is no evidence of other significant organic disease" (Grossman, 1977, p. 67).

The nonorganic etiology of mental retardation implies nonstability of diagnosis. Provision of extensive compensatory exposure to life experiences, a variety of stimulation activities, and problem-solving opportunities may ameliorate the environmental conditions that induced the retardation. This would support the idea of a fluid rather than stable diagnosis of retardation in the mildly retarded (Bloom, 1964; Hunt, 1961).

Even though there is an organic cause for the condition of most children classified trainable through profoundly retarded, their classification may still be considered fluid. Although the actual organic pathology may not as yet be "curable" and is therefore stable, the manifestations of retardation represented by cognitive competence (IQ) or social competence (adaptive behavior) may be lessened through medical or educational intervention. For example, with alterations in the diet and appropriate educational experiences, the IQs of children with PKU may rise as high as the educable mentally retarded range; their adaptive behavior may come to equal in competence that of children in the mild level of retardation.

NATURE OF THE CHILD

In most cases, children are first recognized and labeled as mildly retarded when they enter a formal learning setting. Earlier developmental delays have usually been so minor that they have been overlooked. Once in school, however, these delays appear as a consistent pattern of low achievement and immature classroom performance.

Mental retardation is characterized by generalized developmental delay. It would be an error in the understanding and identification of mildly retarded children for the teacher to look for a single learning or behavioral deficit in performance, such as in reading or parallel play. The teacher should expect a pattern of development characterized by delays from 1 to 3 years across all the various curriculum domains: cognitive, motor, and social development; self-help skills; language development and use; and academic readiness skills. It is this difference in overall achievement ability that differentiates mildly retarded children in school from their normal peers.

This generalized pattern of delay also differentiates mildly retarded children from learning-disabled children. Whereas mildly retarded children are delayed in all areas of development or achievement owing to their subaverage intelligence, learning-disabled children display "developmental imbalances" (Gallagher, 1966). They have "a specific and significant achievement deficiency in the presence of adequate overall intelligence" (Heward & Orlansky, 1980, p. 83). In learning-disabled children, delay or disability appears in one or two areas of performance rather than in all curriculum areas. The delay is characterized by a discrepancy of 1 to 2 years between their presumed ability based upon intelligence testing and their actual achievement based on a standardized achievement test (Johnson & Myklebust, 1967; Myklebust, 1968). Dunn (1973) coined the terms *general learning disabled* for the mildly retarded and *specific learning disabled* for the learning disabled to characterize this difference between the two groups of children.

Certain overriding characteristics (e.g., deficiency in memory function or language development) may be attributed to most retarded children. However, each child demonstrates a unique degree or pattern of domain-specific development, which is dependent on previous experiences at home and in school where strengths and weaknesses, likes and dislikes have been shaped. Differences in characteristics are referred to as interindividual differences. Therefore, most assumptions professionals bring to the learning situation concerning a child are probably based on a stereotype and not a realistic picture of the child's behavior.

A phenomenon traditionally ascribed to the learning experience of retarded children is that of a cumulative failure effect (MacMillan, 1977). Because of a depressed mental age (MA), retarded children are not ready to begin the traditional school curriculum at the same chronological age (CA) as are normal children. The mental age ($MA = \frac{CA(IQ)}{100}$) indicates a functioning ability equal to one-half to one-third that expected of a normal child of the same chronological age. For example, a child with an IQ of 80 has a mental age of 6.5 years at the chronological age of 8 years; a child with an IQ of 50 has a mental age of 6.5 at the chronological age of 13 years. Therefore, these children begin school at a distinct disadvantage, compared with their normal peers, in age-appropriate ability. Faced with repeated failure and frustration in the classroom, they fall further and further behind academically, thereby increasing their expectancy for failure. Heber (1964) described the circular effect that results:

> Since expectancy is one of the variables mediating behavior potential, the performance of the retarded child should show a further qualitative and quantitative decrement with the acquisition of a low expectancy for success. This reduction in performance efficiency would result in further failure leading to even lower expectancies and so on, in circular fashion. (pp. 165-166)

Parallel to the cumulative effect of academic failure is the cumulative effect of frustration caused by inappropriate expectations and tasks that lead to continuous failure, resulting in a child with behavior problems in class.

The teacher of the young mildly retarded must place major emphasis on prevention. By providing extended periods of readiness and enrichment activities, individualized instruction, and opportunities for success and overlearning, the teacher may prevent cumulative failure. Intelligence develops rapidly during the first few years of life, after which it slows and stabilizes. The earlier the schools and the teacher intervene to prevent the onset of, or interrupt, this failure cycle, the greater the possibility of negating its effects. Environmental variables probably have reduced impact after the age of 8 years.

A number of early intervention projects with the retarded have been undertaken. Notable among these are Heber's Milwaukee Project, Karnes' PEECH Project at the University of Illinois Child Development Center, Bricker's Intervention for Young Developmentally Delayed Children at Miami's Mailman Center, and the Shearers' Portage Project (Tjossem, 1976). Each has dramatically demonstrated the benefits of early intervention for delayed or potentially delayed children and has provided evidence to support the belief that the cognitive competence and the social competence of the mildly retarded child may be increased by appropriate educational intervention.

Learning Readiness Skills

Children must have certain basic skills or abilities before they can receive information through instruction. These learning readiness skills include the ability to discriminate, an understanding of relativity, an understanding of cause-and-effect relationships, the ability to mediate information, and the ability to imitate an instructional model.

Discrimination

One of the foundations of learning is the ability to discriminate between instances and noninstances of an item when presented with an option(s). For example, children must be able to indicate that a given item is an instance of the letter *A* and another is not an instance of the letter *A;* or an instance of something blue and not an instance of something blue. In order to accomplish this fundamental learning, children must be able to attend to the learning task and to the dimensions of the materials being presented. According to the research of Zeaman and House (1963), a deficit in retarded children's ability to attend and thereby correctly identify dimensions upon which to discriminate may be the basis of many of their learning problems.

Instruction brings children to the understanding that objects vary along dimensions and therefore can be discriminated from each other or grouped into sets (classified). This decision on similarity or difference (and identification) is based upon the ability to attend to the presence or absence of dimensions along which the objects vary. Materials may vary on the dimensions of shape (form), color, size, brightness (intensity), and position. Among the various dimensions of each material, children must be able to identify the relevant dimension and use that to discriminate consistently the instance from various noninstances. They must be able to identify that the dimension of form discriminates the letter *A* from other letters and that the dimension of size discriminates a toothbrush from a hairbrush. According to Zeaman and House, the time required for this initial attending to the relevant dimension distinguishes the learning of normal learners from that of retarded learners. Once retarded learners have figured out this puzzle, their learning curve is comparable with that of normal learners.

There are several programs available for structuring instruction in discrimination learning (Mercer & Snell, 1977). Initially, the teacher may present a two-choice option of items in which all dimensions are held constant except the one that will yield the correct answer. For example, the teacher may present a child with two cups that are of the same form, color, brightness, and position, but vary according to their size. In order to help the retarded learner attend more quickly to the relevant dimension, the teacher may use intrastimulus cues. Such cues highlight the relevant dimension, thereby attracting the child's attention; the teacher may outline the shapes of the choice items in order to highlight their difference or exaggerate the relevant dimension difference. If size is relevant, for example, the teacher may demonstrate with items of extreme size difference (1-inch screws and ¼-inch screws) and slowly diminish this exaggerated difference to reach the difference that the child is being taught to recognize (e.g., discrimination between ½-inch screws and ¼-inch screws). An alternative method is the use of oddity. The child is presented with an array of objects from which to select the one that is different. The array might consist of four objects that have all dimensions in common and a fifth that is different (e.g., four blue socks and a red sock, or four cups with handles and one without a handle).

Relativity

During the early stages of cognitive development, children live in a world they have divided into extremes. This dichotomous division soon proves inadequate for making judgments concerning relativity in even the simplest choice decisions, such as selecting the biggest of three balloons. The ability to make relative comparisons along dimensions of size, distance, time, and ordinality (e.g., first, second, third) is the basis for more complex tasks involving measurement, sequencing of events, memory, and the further structuring of the environment into abstract hierarchical classifications.

Cause-and-Effect Relationships

An understanding that certain events cause others to occur enables children to predict events and anticipate consequences. With this understanding, children can be expected to take increasing responsibility for their own actions, and this sets the foundation for reinforcement and corrective feedback as a part of instructional procedure.

A child's progression through much early cognitive growth is a result of maturation and opportunity for interaction with the environment (Piaget, 1963), and it may be facilitated by appropriate instructional activities arranged by the teacher. The development of an understanding of cause-and-effect relationships may be structured as four successive learning steps (Robinson & Robinson, 1978):

1. Systematic repetition for environmental effect ''requires the child to display a variety of different responses, each specific to producing a particular environmental effect'' (p. 134).
2. Development of attached tool use ''requires that the child be able to use a variety of objects (string, pillows, pieces of cloth, box tops, etc.) as tools for bringing desired objects into reach. The child should be able to differentiate when a tool is functional or not functional'' (p. 137).
3. Use of unattached object as a tool requires that the child use ''objects within reach (rakes, sticks, chairs, etc.) in order to obtain objects which are out of reach (toys, cookie jars on counters, etc.)'' (p. 140).
4. Operational causality ''requires that the child search for a means of reproducing a particular spectacle, such as causing a mechanical toy to operate, where there are alternative correct solutions'' (p. 141).

Mediation

Retarded children consistently have more difficulty than do their normal peers in retaining information the teacher has just presented. This deficit in short-term memory is attributed to an inability to use mediation strategies (Borkowski & Wanschura, 1974). In remembering numbers, words, and days of the week, normal children employ the mediation strategy of rehearsal; they repeat information to themselves or aloud. Retarded children do not rehearse new information without being instructed to do so; when they do, however, their memory function improves significantly (Borkowski & Cavanaugh, 1979; Ellis, 1970). Rehearsal may be facilitated by presenting new information in small learning groups. As each group member takes a turn repeating the new information aloud or performing a requested procedure, the other children are afforded several opportunities to rehearse the information simultaneously. Once the information has been secured in their memory, retarded children are equally efficient as their normal peers in retaining that information over longer periods of time (Belmont, 1966; Ellis, 1970).

The teacher may also employ a clustering strategy to overcome the mediation deficit (Gerjuoy & Spitz, 1966; Spitz, 1966). Clustering is the presentation of information in recognizable category or functional groupings that will help the child to make associations among the items and thus to recall them more easily. For example, when presenting new vocabulary, the teacher may present them in category groups, such as people (e.g., man, woman, boy, girl), colors, or animals. Self-help objects would be presented in functional groups, such as eating utensils in one lesson unit, clothing items in another, and play items in another. When presenting a string of numbers, such as a telephone number, the numbers may be grouped in smaller bits of information; for example, 6364539 may be presented for recall as 636 45 39.

Imitation

Often the teacher will say to a child, "Watch me do this. Now you do it." Imitation is a skill normal children develop naturally through play and learning experiences at home and with peers. Retarded children do not necessarily develop this vital learning skill in the same manner. Many retarded children require specific instruction and practice before they can imitate a model (Bandura, 1965).

Imitation skills may be taught in the following sequence (Baer, Peterson, & Sherman, 1967; Striefel, 1974):

1. imitation of gross motor movements (e.g., hands on head, clapping hands, walking two steps
2. imitation of fine motor movements and manipulations (e.g., ringing of a bell, picking up a cup, stacking blocks)
3. vocal imitations

Each component in this sequence begins with the request to imitate actions already in the children's repertoire, followed by the introduction of novel actions for the children to imitate. It is important to remember that the objective is not to teach the specific motor movement being modeled, but the concept of imitation. Therefore, the instructional cue used should not be "Clap hands." or "Ring the bell." but rather "Do this." or "Do as I did."

Speech and Language

Because speech and language are distinct processes, they require separate intervention plans. Speech is the motor process involved in the production of sound. Language is the cognitive process of making object-label associations. Moderate delays in speech and language development are common among the mildly retarded, but they are seldom sufficient by themselves to make it possible to predict retardation in the preschool years.

Speech

Defects in speech are seen in 8% to 37% of mildly retarded children (Keane, 1972), compared with a 3% prevalence in the general population. No single pattern of speech defects can be associated with the mildly retarded, but articulation, voice, and stuttering problems are the most common (Spradlin, 1963).

There are four basic types of articulation errors that the teacher may expect to encounter:

1. Omissions are errors in which only parts of words are pronounced. A particular letter may be consistently omitted as in "__his is my __eddy." or may be consistently omitted except when it appears as an ending sound as in "I __ove my __ittle __o__ __ipop."
2. Substitutions are errors in which the sound of one letter is pronounced in place of another. Examples of common letter sound substitutions are:

   "w" for "r" as in "wed" for red
   "w" for "l" as in "wike" for like
   "b" for "v" as in "bery" for very
   "f" for "th" as in "baf" for bath
   "t" for "k" as in "tite" for kite

3. Additions are inclusions of an extra sound (phoneme) in words, as in "sumber" for summer and "sawr" for saw.
4. Distortions are improper productions or pronunciations of a sound. Completely accurate articulation may not be expected until the child is between the ages of 6 and 8 years. Therefore, the presence of these errors may be age-appropriate. A 2-year-old is expected to say the word "baf," but this may be an articulation error for a 7-year-old. Dialectal differences are not considered articulation errors.

Voice disorders concern the use and modulation of three components of the voice. Disorders of pitch are recognizable by monotone or sing-song production. Disorders of voice quality are recognizable by words that are nasal, hoarse, thin, or rough. Disorders of loudness are demonstrated by continuous yelling or whispering.

Stuttering is sound production disfluency, but not until the disfluency becomes frequent and severe enough to be noticeable and irritating to the speaker is the term *stuttering* applicable (Johnson, Brown, Curtis, Edney, & Keaster, 1967; Perkins, 1980). Stuttering may have three manifestations in speech: (1) repetitions of consonant sounds, vowel sounds, or complete syllables; (2) hesitations in the general speech pattern; or (3) prolongations, usually of the first sound of a word or phrase.

During the preschool years, Bloodstein (1975) suggests that children might be expected to have alternating periods of fluent speech and stuttering. The stuttering generally occurs on the first word of a sentence or on such words as prepositions, conjunctions, and pronouns (Dunn, 1973). It appears to be related to the circumstances under which a child is asked to perform. Heward and Orlansky (1980) suggest "a child may be likely to stutter when called upon to say his name, address, or telephone number, or when speaking in front of the class. He may not stutter at all when singing, reciting in unison with others, or talking to babies or animals. Pressure to communicate appears to increase stuttering" (p. 163).

Language

The language proficiency of mildly retarded children is below that of their normal peers and below that expected for their mental age (Smith, 1974). The most common characteristics of their language are a limited vocabulary pool, short sentence length, and the use of fewer abstract words than their normal peers (McLean, Yoder, & Schiefelbusch, 1972; Miller & Yoder, 1972). Rules of grammar are acquired by most of these children, but at a slower rate. Many educators relate these characteristics to retarded children's limited experience and demand for practice, which restrict their proficiency in expressive and receptive language.

The language development of retarded children is quantitatively, not qualitatively, different from that of their normal peers (Lenneberg, 1967); that is, their stages of language development are the same and occur in the same sequence as those of normal children. Their lower IQ does not result in bizarre language but in longer periods at primitive stages—where they remain without appropriate intervention. Because of this developmental similarity, the basic approaches to language instruction of normal children are applicable to the mildly retarded, given extended readiness activities, exposure, and practice.

Readiness activities that emphasize oral language stimulation appear to be effective with mildly retarded learners. At the preschool and early primary levels, instruction in oral language is more important than instruction in reading and writing. Language instruction should not be considered an isolated curriculum component. Opportunities for verbal expression should be provided throughout the day's activities. Suggested readiness activities for language development include

- auditory discrimination activities
- increased opportunity for describing objects and their functional use, activities that take place in class, and events they have experienced outside the classroom
- imaginary play
- choice situations in which more than a yes or no answer is required
- group activities that require peer communication
- stories read by the teacher, records, dramas, and puppetry

Social Development

The teacher's goal in social and emotional development is to prevent frustration as a result of inappropriate interactions with peers and adults. Although no particular social and emotional behaviors are associated with retardation, the slow maturation of retarded children results in poor social judgment and immaturity. Their social maturity is more directly associated with mental age than with chronological age. The mental age association for social development is related to the ability to make social judgments based on abstract moral or ethical considerations. A 9-year-old with a mental age of 3 is not expected to act in all instances as a 3-year-old. This relationship is mitigated by the additional years of experience the 9-year-old has had that a 3-year-old has yet to experience. With time, as intellectual limitations inhibit the ability to develop and evaluate alternative problem resolutions, the developmental discrepancy becomes more noticeable.

While the findings are mixed, it appears that mildly retarded children placed in segregated special classes tend to become overconfident and unrealistic about their abilities as their self-concepts improve (because of the greater number of success experiences afforded in the segregated class). Mildly retarded children placed in regular classes tend to be more fearful of failure. There is some evidence that the retarded in a partially integrated setting show greater improvements in self-concept over the school year than those in a totally segregated class. Former special class children who returned to a regular class program had more favorable attitudes toward themselves and school, and they believed that other students considered them less deviant than children in a special class (Carroll, 1967; Cegelka & Tyler, 1970; Gottlieb & Budoff, 1972; Kaufman & Alberto, 1976; Meyerowitz, 1962, 1967).

Studies of the educable mentally retarded who have been mainstreamed suggest a correlation between lower intelligence and lower social status in the classroom (Dentler & Mackler, 1962). Retarded children in regular classes tend to be ignored or rejected; however, this has been attributed by their classmates not solely to intellectual status, but to negative behaviors, such as belligerence and aggressiveness. These inappropriate behaviors may result from the social immaturity of retarded children in cooperative play and work situations. Social isolation is also apparent in neighborhood play groups where lack of acceptance is seen independently of class placement.

Efforts to overcome this low social status have met with mixed results. When mildly retarded children and popular students have been paired for academic work, were seated close together, or put on joint projects, the immediate result was a gain in peer acceptance, but this acceptance diminished over time (Rucker & Vincenzo, 1970).

Suggested readiness activities in the area of social development include

- role playing of problem situations and real life encounters (simulation activities)
- assignment of high-status responsibilities in the classroom
- committee assignments within which there are individual assignments and grades, and total group responsibility and a single group grade
- team sports
- joint responsibility for nonacademic class activities, such as planning field trips
- class plays and other presentations for outside audiences

Motor Development

The mildly retarded differ least from their normal peers in motor development. They have no significant physical and motor impairments, and they approach chronological age expectancy in height, weight, and skeletal maturity. They lag behind their peers, however, on measures of gross motor proficiency and physical fitness, showing a marked difference in body coordination, strength, and flexibility—generally described as "clumsiness" (Cratty, 1969; Francis & Rarick, 1960; Kral, 1972; Rarick, Dobbins, & Broadhead, 1976). This deficiency is evident in activities that involve

- body awareness in space
- basic physical abilities (i.e., strength, flexibility, agility, balance, and endurance)
- sequential patterns of movement
- eye-hand coordination
- eye-foot coordination
- fine motor activities that are timed

Mildly retarded children can increase their efficiency in these areas if structured training programs are consistently scheduled as part of their school day (Lillie, 1968). While there are full-range physical fitness programs available (AAHPER, 1968, 1972; Hayden, 1964; I CAN, 1976), classroom teachers can include similar activities outside formal physical education periods. For example, gross motor activities include

- movement exploration to music
- directionality exercises

- ball throwing, bean bag toss (aim)
- running relay races, team sports
- balance beam walking, obstacle course running

Fine motor activities include

- tracing, cutting, pasting
- coloring within lines
- manipulative puzzles, pegboards, geoboards
- clay modeling, sand writing

Self-Help Skills

As in any discussion of early education, a major concern of programming for young retarded children is the acquisition of self-help skills, which provide independence in personal care (Lent, 1975). There are two possible reasons for a child's inability to perform self-help skills: (1) overly helpful parents and siblings create a home environment that inhibits independent performance, and (2) the child has a correlated deficiency in a prerequisite skill, such as an inability to imitate or a deficiency in fine motor capabilities.

In most instances of self-help instruction, the teacher demonstrates the activity (e.g., pushing a button through a hole or zipping a zipper) and then asks the child to do the same (ability to imitate should not be assumed). Along with an assessment of self-help skills, the teacher should evaluate the child's fine motor abilities, such as grasping and releasing, pulling and pushing materials, and picking up small objects. These are necessary prerequisites for pulling clothing on and off, zipping, buttoning, and fastening, and for manipulating items such as shoelaces and toothpaste caps.

Four primary areas of self-help skills are feeding, toileting, grooming, and dressing. Instruction for any of these areas must be designed to show the child how single behaviors are related within an entire matrix of behavior. The teacher should plan lessons for repertoires of behaviors, not for isolated skills. Feeding is not just getting a bit of food off a fork and into the mouth, but rather a matrix of many motor and social abilities. Figure 8-2 is an example of toilet training as a repertoire of related individual skills.

When planning individualized instruction, the teacher should remember that there is no single correct procedure for performing most self-help skills. Any number of alternative procedures can accomplish a desired goal in a socially acceptable manner. For example, a coat may be put on (1) by placing one arm at a time into the sleeves from the back, (2) by placing the arms in the sleeves of a coat laid out on a table in front of the child and lifting it over the head, and (3) by

Figure 8-2 Components of a Total Toileting Repertoire

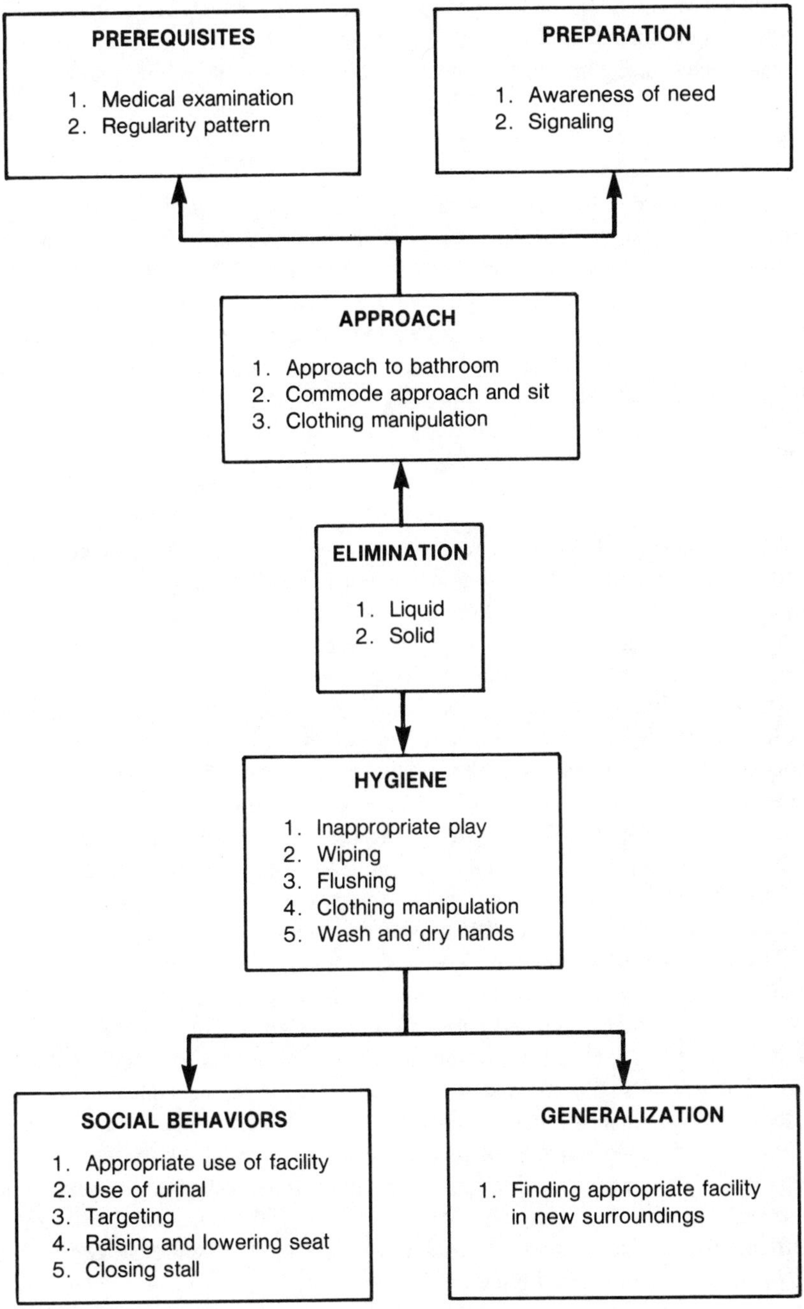

placing both arms into the sleeves of a coat laid out behind the child and then lifting it onto the shoulders. Even though the method that the child is currently capable of performing is considered by the teacher or parent to be "babyish," independence is the actual goal; adult performance can be shaped as the child matures.

Academics

Generally, the mildly retarded fail to begin reading, writing, and doing arithmetic in the first grade. The average child is expected to begin reading at a chronological age of approximately 6 years. Retarded children at that chronological age may have a mental age of 3 to 4 years and may not be ready to read until their mental age approaches the chronological age at which the average child begins to read. The retarded may be 8 to 10 years old before they are ready for traditional reading instruction. Their rate of mastering new skills is slower so, without appropriate intervention, they fall increasingly behind.

Reading

The mildly retarded do not read at the level that may be expected at their chronological age. Generally, they make two-thirds of a year's progress for each year in which only routine attention is given to reading. In classes in which reading is stressed throughout the school day and reading readiness skills are emphasized, they are often brought to mental age expectancy.

In oral reading (recognition), the mildly retarded are inferior in word attack skills, making significantly more vowel sound errors and omissions; the teacher must pronounce more words for them. This relates to the difficulties these children have in oral speech development. In addition, they cannot use context clues as a source for word meaning, as skill in the use of contextual clues relies upon inferential or incidental learning. The ability of the mildly retarded to gain information incidentally to direct instruction tasks has been found to be deficient (Baumeister, 1963; Postman, 1964; Williams, 1970).

The mildly retarded tend to be more deficient in reading comprehension than in oral reading. They are noticeably inferior in locating relevant facts, main ideas, and in drawing inferences and conclusions (Cegelka & Cegelka, 1970).

Research in the variety of approaches to reading instruction has not demonstrated that any single method of teaching reading to the educable mentally retarded is consistently superior to another. The teacher's choice of instructional approach should be related not to the fact that the child has been labeled as retarded, but to the area in which the child demonstrates deficiency. For example, a phonic reading program for a retarded child with pronounced articulation difficulties is probably unwise (Cegelka & Cegelka, 1970; Gillespie & Johnson, 1974; Kirk, Kliebhan, & Lerner, 1978).

Evidence is also very mixed on the effectiveness of teaching machines and programmed instruction (e.g., Distar, Edmark, Rebus, i/t/a). Each of these technologies has produced reading gains, but the usefulness appears to depend on the teacher's proficiency and commitment to the particular program. A teacher of the mildly retarded needs to know and use a variety of methods in order to serve children of different backgrounds and characteristics.

Arithmetic

The arithmetic ability of the mildly retarded is inferior to that of normal peers in all aspects. Retarded children apparently lack the ability to grasp advanced concepts and experience difficulty in making generalizations without specific instruction.

The strongest performance of these children is in the computational and functional areas of arithmetic, where they perform up to mental age expectancy. These areas lend themselves to concrete instruction and practice. The children can master the basic mechanics of addition and subtraction, although they show limited understanding of the process and, therefore, little transfer of their ability across situations. In computation, they become and remain more dependent on crutches, such as counting on their fingers, using chips or numberlines. Their accuracy is hindered by weaknesses in work habits, typified by careless errors, fast pacing, and impulsivity. Some educators are adapting Meichenbaum's (1977) steps of self-instruction (process practice) to reduce these weaknesses. Self-instruction has five basic steps:

1. The teacher performs the task while guiding himself or herself aloud through the steps in the process.
2. The children perform the task while the teacher provides the verbal guidance.
3. The children perform the task while guiding themselves aloud, modeling previous teacher guidance.
4. The children perform the task while guiding themselves in a whisper.
5. The children perform the task while guiding themselves with "private" or silent speech.

Mildly retarded children perform least well in arithmetic reasoning that involves reading and problem solving (Peterson, 1973). Their low arithmetic vocabulary and poor ability to deal with concepts of sequence and temporal relationships make it difficult for them to follow directions and organize material. Poor skills in verbal mediation and an inability to separate irrelevant from important information in a word problem contribute to poor performance.

These children develop quantitative concepts in the same order and stages as normal children do, but at a slower pace. These concepts are acquired through a combination of instruction and maturation. Even when drilled in the performance of more advanced Piagetian quantitative tasks, they appear to have the skills but lack sufficient understanding of the concept for generalization.

Some suggested readiness activities in arithmetic include

- concrete experience in object permanence and conservation of number
- seriation, classification, and equivalence experience
- combinations and identification of sets of various objects
- functional use of objects leading to one-to-one correspondence
- rational counting, leading to rote counting
- number recognition, matching numerals and quantities, and ordination

NATURE OF INSTRUCTION

Service Delivery

Since the middle 1970s, there has been a tendency to group preschool and kindergarten children likely to be labeled mildly retarded, learning-disabled, or behavior-disordered as children at risk. Such grouping is done in an effort to forestall the negative effects of labeling (Mercer, 1973) and to take into account the tentativeness of predictions or classifications based on IQ testing of young children (Dunst & Rheingrover, 1981; McCall, 1979). The term *at risk* is used to refer to children who, given their current functioning and environmental history, may eventually be classified as mentally retarded—in the absence of appropriate educational intervention. In order to prevent such a classification for these children, various programs have been conducted to investigate the content of educational intervention.

Some intervention programs are intended to prevent the debilitating effects of environmental deprivation during infancy. Encouraging results have been reported in several of these early intervention projects. The Milwaukee Project (Heber & Garber, 1975) produced up to a 30-point difference in measured IQ, following stimulation activities and parental training in child care, between those children who were part of their infant intervention program and a control group. Ramey and Campbell (1979) reported that the results of their infant intervention project indicate amelioration of predicted IQ deficits. In an 11-year follow-up of their infant intervention population, Schweinhart and Weikart (1981) reported higher achievement scores and fewer years in special education classes.

In 1968, PL 90-538, The Handicapped Children's Early Education Act, was passed. As part of the implementation of this act, the Bureau of Education for the Handicapped created the Handicapped Children's Early Education Program to fund model/demonstration services to preschool handicapped children. In 1972, the Head Start act was amended to mandate that at least 10% of the children served in these programs have a handicapping condition. Currently, half of the states have enacted legislation mandating that some preschool handicapped children receive needed specialized education services through the public schools (Vincent, Brown, & Getz-Sheftel, 1981).

In an effort to meet the goal of educating children in the least restrictive environment (PL 94-142), the primary model of service delivery in these preschool programs has been to mainstream at risk children into classes with normal peers. Mainstreaming is based on the assumption that normal peers provide the handicapped children with models for appropriate behavior that the handicapped children can, in turn, imitate, rehearse, and make part of their behavioral repertoire. The literature has emphasized, however, that simply placing handicapped and normal children together does not guarantee the desired interactions. Effective interactions must be structured (Dunlop, Stoneman, & Cantrell, 1980). Cooke, Ruskus, Apolloni, and Peck (1981) make the following suggestions for implementation of mainstreamed classes:

1. Emphasis on structured practices that bring handicapped and non-handicapped classmates together. Teachers must assume active responsibility to see that developmentally significant forms of intervention and imitation occur.
2. The need for systemic data collection. Since it is apparent that positive outcomes of integrated preschools do not necessarily occur, but rather must be engineered, data-based accountability is indicated.
3. Interventions conducted under natural conditions that tap into ongoing patterns of behavior and preexisting reinforcement hierarchies are most likely to produce generalized effects.
4. Consideration should be given to integrating handicapped children not necessarily with non-handicapped agemates, but rather with children of a lower CA [chronological age]. This practice would tend to reduce the developmental disparity of the groups and lead to increased opportunities for productive social interactions.
5. When peer models are selected on the basis of their behaviorally indicated propensity for being a "teacher" or a "helper" or showing other children how to do what they do, the positive outcomes should be increased in both directions. (pp. 81-82)

Data from various mainstreaming programs have demonstrated that the integrated placement of handicapped and nonhandicapped children provides considerable benefit to the handicapped children; this is evidenced by increases in the number of appropriate behaviors and decreases in the number of maladaptive behaviors (Bricker & Bricker, 1972; Falvey, 1980). Of equal importance, the data indicate that integration has no detrimental effect on the normal children (Guralnick, 1978). (For thorough reviews of mainstreaming programs see Blacher-Dixon, Leonard, & Turnbull, 1981; Turnbull & Blacher-Dixon, 1981.) In reviewing the literature on mainstreaming for young children, Vincent and associates (1981) conclude that "the current definition of best educational practice must be that integrated programming is always the first choice. Such programs have been shown to result in equal if not greater skill gain for the handicapped students involved than segregated programs" (p. 23).

Structuring Instruction

Principles of good teaching are applicable to all children in a class. Instructional techniques required by the mildly retarded are those required by any child who is having difficulty learning a particular skill. Certain practices and characteristics of learning are known to be of particular importance in instructing the mildly retarded, however.

1. Direct instruction of a skill or concept is absolutely necessary. The teacher cannot assume that these children will acquire important information through inferential or incidental learning while engaged in another learning experience.
2. Complex skills should be presented in small sequential steps to ensure mastery.
3. Opportunities for overlearning or repeated practice must be provided if information is to be retained. Practice of a skill in small increments distributed over time is more effective than concentrated or massed practice within one or two lessons.
4. New concepts or skills should be presented by means of concrete examples of the learning to take place. These children require realistic experience with new learning tasks in order to understand the relationships or process being taught.
5. External sources of motivation provided by the teacher increase the rate at which new learning is acquired. There is no doubt among educators that reinforcement through praise, attention, or stars and classroom privileges increases the probability that the skill or behavior will be repeated. Immediate and continuous feedback provides important guidance to mildly retarded children.
6. Once a skill or behavior has been taught and learned, the teacher should make follow-up checks during the year to ensure that these children maintain that ability.

7. Mildly retarded children are highly susceptible to distractors. The teacher should keep to a minimum excess noise and movement in the classroom, limit the number of irrelevancies found in instructional materials, and keep verbal instructions clear and unencumbered by extraneous words and movement.
8. When planning work activities, the teacher should build in success opportunity, since the frustration of failure may cause retarded children to give up. Work sessions should begin with problems the children can solve and end before long periods occur when they cannot provide any correct answers.

Task Programming

The bridge between assessment, planning, and instruction is the process of task programming, a compound process that combines three elements of instructional technology: statement of behavioral objectives, task analysis, and behavioral programming. The behavioral objectives, which are listed in individualized education programs (IEPs), target the need for particular skill instruction based on assessment information. These should be written for each new learning experience. Task analysis is the process in which the teacher outlines plans for instruction of complex skills in a sequence of constituent components. Behavioral programming is the preparation of a full instructional blueprint for those skills that are of particular difficulty for the child.

Behavioral Objectives

A staffing committee and the teacher must gather specific information concerning a child's functioning level and skill deficiencies in order to select appropriate learning targets for inclusion in the IEP. Sources of this information are numerous:

- standardized assessment instruments
- criterion referent examinations
- curriculum guides
- developmental checklists
- parents
- environmental demands
- functional analysis of behavior
- resource personnel
- last year's teacher

All learning targets cannot be dealt with simultaneously. To manage properly the child's learning and the classroom schedule, the teacher must set priorities, taking these factors into consideration:

1. Are there inappropriate behaviors that must be brought under control before formal instruction can begin?
2. What are the immediate concerns of the parent or primary caretaker(s)?
3. What are the skills the child is lacking for current appropriate functioning in the home and school environments?
4. How functional is the activity for the child, and what skills may be built on it?
5. What are the prerequisites of the skill, and how does it fit into a lattice of skills across content areas?
6. What is the child's history of skill acquisition?
7. What is the amount of instructional time available for the child—within the school day and within the total school experience?
8. What resource personnel are needed and available (e.g., speech therapist, remedial reading teacher, physical therapist)?

A behavioral objective is a statement of an individualized instructional target, such as a proposed change in behavior. A properly written objective guides the teacher in using a curriculum and planning instructional sequences; it also provides criteria for determining when a target has been achieved. In addition, behavioral objectives can be used to keep parents and administrators informed of goals for the child, as well as how and when they are expected to be accomplished.

There are four basic components to a properly written and easily communicated behavioral objective.

The Learner. Identification of the learner in the behavioral objective individualizes the focus of learning and instruction to the specific child.

The Desired Performance. For precise interpretation, the desired performance should be written in observable, measurable, and repeatable terms. To aid in clarity, the verb used within the description of the desired performance must be carefully chosen. A child's ability can be verified only when the teacher sees or hears the behavior or a direct product of the behavior. This ensures identification of the behavior in teaching sessions that follow, accurate data, and instruction or confirmation by a third party. The following are examples of actions that cannot be directly observed and therefore must be inferred from other behaviors, making consistent agreement on their presence or absence difficult (Deno & Jenkins, 1967):

- to appreciate
- to discover
- to know
- to feel

- to become competent
- to distinguish
- to understand
- to learn
- to recognize
- to analyze

The following are examples of verbs that are precise statements of directly observable behavior:

- to circle
- to point to
- to underline
- to fill in
- to remove
- to say
- to name
- to write
- to read (count, repeat) orally
- to place

The Conditions under Which the Child Will Perform. If the learning experience is to be repeated accurately in later teaching sessions and if the child's ability to perform the task across a variety of materials, settings, and cues is to be generalized at a later date, the objective should contain the conditions the teacher has set for this learning to take place:

- when the sign for "drink" is given . . .
- without the aid of . . .
- given an array of materials containing . . .
- when presented with . . .
- with the use of . . .
- when given a pullover sweater . . .

The Criteria. The behavioral objective should include criteria for acceptable performance, that is, to what extent the child will be able to perform the desired behavior, given the conditions specified. The nature of the criteria will vary according to the specific behavior, the level of learning (e.g., acquisition, fluency, generalization), the method of instruction, and the form of data collection. Examples of the variety of criteria include

- 25 of 40 correct responses, in 5 minutes for 3 consecutive days
- all 10 objects labeled within 40 seconds for 2 consecutive days
- 85% accuracy for three consecutive math sessions
- 5 consecutive successful trials on 4 consecutive days
- 4 out of 5 successful trials for three consecutive sessions
- all steps in the handwashing program completed independently for 5 consecutive days
- return within 10 minutes on three consecutive trips to the bathroom

To ensure inclusions of all the elements of a behavioral objective, it is suggested that a standard format be devised for writing objectives. One such format is

condition — learner — behavior — criteria

For example,

> Given the words GO, STOP, MEN, WOMEN, EXIT, written in block letters/Kelly/will orally identify the words/with 100% accuracy within 3 minutes on three consecutive training sessions.

Task Analysis

The key to programming is task analysis; it provides a format in which to plan the best way to bring the child from the current level of functioning to the behavior described in the behavioral objective. Task analysis is the identification of the component abilities or intermediate steps that, when merged, will result in the completion of a complex task. In other words, task analysis is the breaking down of a complex task into its simpler component tasks. Each step is listed in serial order and is a prerequisite for the one that follows.

The format for a task analysis has three basic elements.

Terminal Objective. A restatement of the behavioral objective, the terminal objective includes the same four basic elements: learner, desired performance, conditions, and criteria.

Task Components. The skills that lead to acquisition of the complex task, listed in serial order, are the task components. This breakdown of the task continues until all component skills or steps have been identified. It may take a child from picking up a sock to putting it on, or from identifying a blue block in isolation to identifying it within an array of blocks of different colors.

Components or steps may be identified by doing the task and noting each time a change in body position is required, watching someone else do the task, or listing a new step each time an action verb must be changed to describe the task (e.g., pick up, place, say, push, turn, repeat).

Some complex tasks may involve phases in addition to the listing of steps. For instance, teaching a child to put on a pair of pants may be viewed as having four phases: (1) pulling the pants on to the waist, (2) snapping, (3) zipping, and (4) buckling the belt. Each phase will have its own steps listed.

Prerequisite Skills. Those skills that the child must be capable of before learning the new task are the prerequisite skills. If a review of the first three or four steps in the list of components reveals a particular prerequisite skill that the child cannot perform, that skill should be taught first.

Logical vs. Empirical Task Analysis. The following is an example of a completed task analysis:

> Terminal objective: Given a tube sock with the toe color cued red John will pull on the sock appropriately without assistance while in a sitting position on three of four trials for 5 consecutive days.
>
> Task components:
> 1. John will pick up his sock with either hand.
> 2. John will bend his leg up and bend from the waist.
> 3. John will grasp the sock with both hands, turning the opening up.
> 4. John will place both thumbs inside the opening of the sock.
> 5. John will pull his hands apart to open sock.
> 6. John will put his toes into the opening of the sock.
> 7. John will pull his arms toward his body, pulling the sock to his heel.
> 8. John will pull the sock over the heel and up to the ankle.
>
> Prerequisite skills:
> 1. John must be able to follow one-step directions.
> 2. John must be able to balance in a chair.
> 3. John must have appropriate grasp.
> 4. John must recognize a sock.

The task analysis as written is referred to as a logical task analysis. Each step making up the behavior has been worked out logically, but the analysis is untested.

In trying out the task analysis, the teacher may find that a step has been left out, steps placed in improper order, or a prerequisite skill overlooked. Once the accuracy of the analysis has been verified by using it with a child and any necessary alterations have been made, the analysis is an empirical task analysis.

Whereas a behavioral objective is focused on the individual child, task analysis focuses on the components of a particular skill. A well-written task analysis may be used with any child. After current ability has been assessed, a child may be started on the appropriate step of the task analysis.

Behavioral Programming

A further expansion of task analysis, behavioral programming, returns the focus to the individual child. Although task analysis divides complex instructional objectives into a sequence of less complex components or steps, it is not a statement of how to teach. Behavioral programming adds the steps specific to the instruction that is to occur.

The written format of behavioral programming begins with the three elements of task analysis and includes five additional elements:

1. terminal objective
2. task components
3. prerequisite skills
4. method
5. materials
6. constraints
7. procedure:
    - phase:
        - step:
            - cue—
            - response—
            - criterion—
8. data collection

Method. Selection of the overall method for instructing the particular task should be based on the child's characteristics and the nature of the task. A wide variety of methods are available:

- shaping
- chaining (forward and backward)
- fading
- novelty
- oddity
- imitation
- paired associate
- match to sample
- visual-visual match
- visual-verbal match
- auditory-visual match
- verbal-motor match

Materials. For consistency in instruction from session to session or from teacher to aide, it is important to list the material selected (e.g., objects included in an array, type of numberline, specific vocabulary picture cards, items that have particular adaptations). The reinforcer(s) being used should also be listed.

Constraints. Not only child-specific characteristics to which the teacher must be alert, such as type of child response (verbal, gestural, mechanical), but also physical limitations of the child or limitations of receptive or expressive vocabulary are constraints that should be noted.

Procedure. The teacher must specify the procedure for instruction within each step. The cues to be used (i.e., the exact verbal instruction and material presentation), the exact response the child is to make to the verbal cue, and the criterion for success of the particular step must be listed. The steps are listed in the sequence in which they are to be taught, and a step is taught only after the child has reached the specified criterion of the previous step.

Data Collection. To delineate successes and failures, the teacher must record the child's performance during each training session in order to make adjustments where necessary and to validate performance to criterion. If the data collected on the child's performance indicate that the child is not acquiring the skill or is doing so at an unacceptable rate, the teacher should examine the following points regarding the task program:

1. Is the reinforcer still effective, or has satiation set in?
2. When the criteria were set for each step, was sufficient opportunity provided for overlearning or repeated practice?
3. Are the steps too large, or has one been left out?
4. Would another method be more efficient?
5. Is the definition of the behavior desired specific enough for the same behavior to be sought during each trial or session?
6. Are the materials confusing or distracting to the child?

Interaction between Teacher and Child

When teaching a specific skill involving one-to-one interaction between teacher and child, such as imitation, self-help, or motor skills, the teacher must use a consistent and systematic approach. The child should be given the opportunity to perform the requested response, without interaction overpowering or interfering with the child's attempt at complying with a request. Figure 8-3 shows a five-step sequence of interaction in which the degree of instructional interaction between teacher and child is systematically increased for the facilitation of a response. Within a given teaching trial, the teacher, as necessary, progresses sequentially

Figure 8-3 Model of Instructional Interaction Pattern

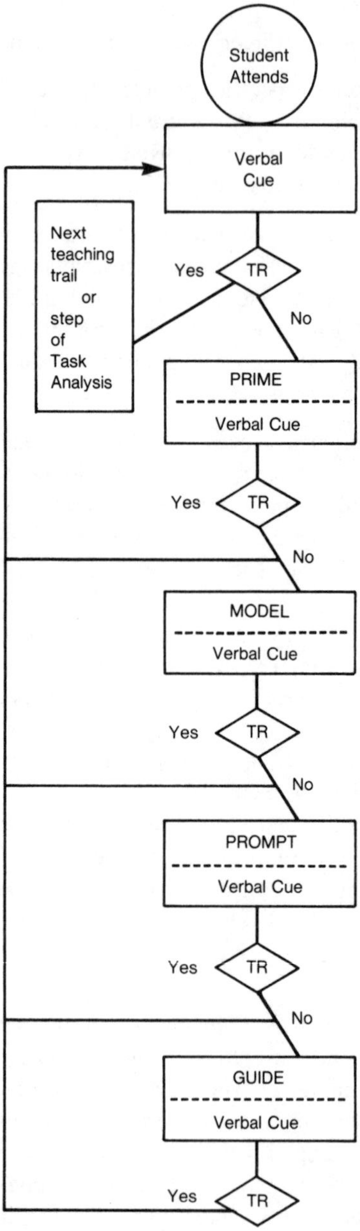

Key: TR, target response.

through each of the five steps, until the child has produced the desired target response.

The goal of most instruction is that a verbal cue or direction become a sufficient interaction for the response to be performed by the child. Thus, the first step in the sequence of instruction is the presentation by the teacher of only the verbal cue. If this is not sufficient to facilitate the response, the teacher repeats the verbal cue with the simultaneous use of a prime. A prime is a signal or gesture to indicate that the child should respond. If this is still not sufficient interaction, the teacher should pair the verbal cue with the use of a model. Modeling is a demonstration of the target response by the teacher so that the child may imitate it. This step may be bypassed in cases such as compliance commands "come" and "stop." The next degree of interaction is the use of a prompt paired with the verbal cue. A prompt is physical assistance by the teacher to initiate the response by the child. The greatest amount of teacher interaction occurs in the final alternative—use of a guide. The teacher acts as a guide, and the teacher and child perform the entire target response together. The teacher physically puts the child through the entire response, while simultaneously presenting the verbal cue. When the child has never performed a similar response before, the use of a guide in the first three or four trials may be necessary before following the normal sequence of steps of this interaction pattern.

When these instructional interactions are sequenced as just outlined, from the least interactive to the most interactive, the type of assistance is referred to as the system of least prompts. With young children who are being instructed in a new skill for the first time, however, the teacher may decide to use this sequence in reverse order, beginning with the most interactive step (guide) and moving to the least interactive step (prime). This reverse sequence provides more aided and, therefore, error-free trials; it is referred to as the system of maximum prompts. When the system of maximum prompts is used, a single type of assistance is used for an entire teaching session; the type of assistance does not change within each trial as it does when the system of least prompts is used.

NOTES

1. *Larry P. v. Riles,* Civil No. C-71-2270, 343 F. Supp. 1306 (N. D. Cal., 1972).
2. *Diana v. State Board of Education,* Civil No. C-70-37 RFP (N. D. Cal., 1970).
3. *LeBanks v. Spears,* 60 F.R.D. 135 (U.S.D. Ct., E.D. La., 1973).

REFERENCES

American Alliance of Health, Physical Education, and Recreation (AAHPER). *A guide for programs in recreation and physical education for the mentally retarded.* Washington, D.C.: Author, 1968.

American Alliance of Health, Physical Education, and Recreation (AAHPER). *Special Olympics instruction manual—From beginners to champions.* Washington, D.C.: Author and the Joseph P. Kennedy Foundation, 1972.

American Association on Mental Deficiency (AAMD). *Manual on terminology and classification in mental retardation,* 1977.

Baer, D., Peterson, R., & Sherman, J. The development of imitation by reinforcing behavioral similarity to a model. *Journal of Experimental Analysis of Behavior,* 1967, *10,* 405.

Balthazar, E.E. *Balthazar scales of adaptive behavior.* Palo Alto, Calif.: Consulting Psychologists Press, 1971-1973.

Bandura, A. Behavior modification through modeling procedures. In L. Ullman & L. Krasner (Eds.), *Research in behavior modification.* New York: Holt, Rinehart, and Winston, 1965.

Baumeister, A. A comparison of normals and retardates with respect to incidental and intentional learning. *American Journal of Mental Deficiency,* 1963, *68,* 404-408.

Bayley, N. *Bayley scales of infant development.* New York: The Psychological Corp., 1969.

Belmont, J. Long term memory in mental retardation. In N.R. Ellis (Ed.), *International review of research in mental retardation.* New York: Academic Press, 1966.

Blacher-Dixon, J., Leonard, J., & Turnbull, A. Mainstreaming at the early childhood level. *Mental Retardation,* 1981, *19,* 235-241.

Bloodstein, O. *A handbook on stuttering.* Chicago: The National Easter Seal Society for Crippled Children and Adults, 1975.

Bloom, B. *Stability and change in human characteristics.* New York: Wiley, 1964.

Borkowski, J., & Cavanaugh, J. Maintenance and generalization of skills and strategies by the retarded. In N.R. Ellis (Ed.), *Handbook of mental deficiency: Psychological theory and research* (2nd ed.). Hillsdale, N.J.: Erlbaum Associates, 1979.

Borkowski, J., & Wanschura, P. Mediational processes in the retarded. In N.R. Ellis (Ed.), *International review of research in mental retardation* (Vol. 7). New York: Academic Press, 1974.

Bricker, D., & Bricker, W. *Toddler research and intervention project report—Year II.* IMRID Behavioral Science Monograph No. 21, George Peabody College, Nashville, Tenn., 1972.

Brockett, L.P. Idiots and the efforts for their improvement. *American Journal of Education,* May, 1856.

Carroll, A. The effects of segregated and partially integrated school programs on self-concept and academic achievement of educable mental retardates. *Exceptional Children,* 1967, *34,* 93-99.

Cattell, P. *Cattell infant intelligence scale.* New York: The Psychological Corp., 1969.

Cegelka, J., & Cegelka, W. A review of research: Reading and the educable mentally retarded. *Exceptional Children,* 1970, *37,* 187-200.

Cegelka, W., & Tyler, J. The efficacy of special class placement for the mentally retarded in proper perspective. *Training School Bulletin,* 1970, *67,* 33-68.

Cooke, T., Ruskus, J., Apolloni, T., & Peck, C. Handicapped preschool children in the mainstream: Background, outcomes, and clinical suggestions. *Topics in Early Childhood Special Education,* 1981, *1,* 73-83.

Cratty, B. *Motor activity and the education of the retarded.* Philadelphia: Lea & Febiger, 1969.

Deno, S., & Jenkins, J. *Evaluating preplanning curriculum objectives.* Philadelphia: Research for Better Schools, 1967.

Dentler, R., & Mackler, R. Ability and sociometric status among normal and retarded children: A review of the literature. *Psychometric Bulletin,* 1962, *59,* 273-283.

DiNola, A., Kaminsky, B., & Sternfield, A. *TMR performance profile for the severely and moderately retarded.* Ridgefield, N.J.: Reporting Service for Children, 1968.

Doll, E.A. The essentials of an inclusive concept of mental deficiency. *American Journal of Mental Deficiency,* 1941, *46,* 214-219.

Doll, E.A. *Vineland social maturity scale*. Circle Pines, Minn.: American Guidance Service, 1965.

Dunlop, K., Stoneman, Z., & Cantrell, M. Social interaction of exceptional and other children in a mainstreamed preschool classroom. *Exceptional Children*, 1980, *47*, 132-141.

Dunn, L. Children with mild general learning disabilities. In L.M. Dunn (Ed.), *Exceptional children in the schools*. New York: Holt, Rinehart and Winston, 1973.

Dunst, C., & Rheingrover, R. Discontinuity and instability in early development: Implications for assessment. *Topics in Special Education*, 1981, *1*, 49-60.

Ellis, N.R. Memory processes in retardates and normals. In N.R. Ellis (Eds.), *International review of research in mental retardation* (Vol. 4). New York: Academic Press, 1970.

Falvey, M. *Changes in academic and social competence of kindergarten aged handicapped children as a result of an integrated classroom*. Unpublished doctoral dissertation, University of Wisconsin-Madison, 1980.

Farber, B. *Mental retardation: Its social context and social consequences*. Boston: Houghton-Mifflin, 1968.

Francis, R., & Rarick, G. *Motor characteristics of the mentally retarded*. Washington, D.C.: AAHPER, 1960.

Gallagher, J.J. Children with developmental imbalances: A psychoeducational definition. In W.M. Cruickshank (Ed.), *The teacher of brain-injured children: A discussion of the bases for competency*. Syracuse: Syracuse University Press, 1966.

Gerjuoy, I., & Spitz, H. Associative clustering in free recall: Intellectual and developmental variables. *American Journal of Mental Deficiency*, 1966, *70*, 918-927.

Gillespie, P., & Johnson, L. *Teaching reading to the mildly retarded child*. Columbus, Ohio: Charles E. Merrill, 1974.

Gottlieb, J., & Budoff, M. Attitudes toward school by segregated and integrated retarded children. *Studies in Learning Potential*, 1972, *2*, 1-10.

Grossman, H. *Manual on terminology and classification in mental retardation*. Washington, D.C.: American Association on Mental Deficiency, 1977.

Guralnick, M. *Early intervention in the integration of handicapped and nonhandicapped children*. Baltimore: University Park Press, 1978.

Hayden, F. *Physical fitness for the mentally retarded*. Toronto: Metropolitan Toronto Association for Retarded Children, 1964.

Heber, R. Personality. In H.A. Stevens & R. Heber (Eds.), *Mental retardation: A review of research*. Chicago: University of Chicago Press, 1964.

Heber, R., & Dever, R. Research on education and habilitation of the mentally retarded. In H.C. Haywood (Ed.), *Social-cultural aspects of mental retardation*. New York: Appleton-Century-Crofts, 1970.

Heber, R., & Garber, H. The Milwaukee Project: A study of the use of family intervention to prevent cultural-familial mental retardation. In B. Friedlander, G. Sterritt, & G. Kirk (Eds.), *Exceptional infant: Assessment and intervention* (Vol. 3). New York: Brunner-Mazel, 1975.

Heward, W., & Orlansky, M. *Exceptional children*. Columbus, Ohio: Charles E. Merrill, 1980.

Hunt, J. McV. *Intelligence and experience*. New York: Ronald Press, 1961.

I CAN: Physical education program. Field Service Unit for Physical Education and Recreation for the Handicapped, Department of Health, Physical Education, and Recreation, Michigan State University. Northbrook, Ill.: Hubbard, 1976.

Ingalls, R. *Mental retardation: The changing outlook*. New York: Wiley, 1978.

Johnson, D., & Myklebust, H. *Learning disabilities: Educational principles and practices*. New York: Grune & Stratton, 1967.

Johnson, W., Brown, S., Curtis, J., Edney, C., & Keaster, J. *Speech handicapped school children.* New York: Harper & Row, 1967.

Kaufman, M., & Alberto, P. Research on efficacy of special education for the mentally retarded. In N.R. Ellis (Ed.), *International review of research in mental retardation* (Vol. 8). New York: Academic Press, 1976.

Keane, V.E. The incidence of speech and language problems in the mentally retarded. *Mental Retardation,* 1972, *10,* 3-8.

Kirk, S., Kliebhan, J., & Lerner, J. *Teaching reading to slow and disabled learners.* Boston: Houghton-Mifflin, 1978.

Kral, P. Motor characteristics and development of retarded children. *Education and Training of the Mentally Retarded,* 1972, *1,* 14-21.

Lambert, N., Windmiller, M., Cole, L., & Figueroa, R. *American Association on Mental Deficiency adaptive behavior scale, public school version.* Washington, D.C.: American Association on Mental Deficiency, 1975.

Lenneberg, E. *Biological foundations of language.* New York: Wiley, 1967.

Lent, J.R. Teaching daily living skills. In J.M. Kauffman & J.S. Payne (Eds.), *Mental retardation: Introduction and personal perspectives.* Columbus, Ohio: Charles E. Merrill, 1975.

Levinson, E. *Retarded children in Maine: A survey and analysis.* Orono, Me.: University of Maine Press, 1962.

Lillie, D. Effects of motor development lessons on mentally retarded children. *American Journal of Mental Deficiency,* 1968, *72,* 803-808.

MacMillan, D. Special education for the mildly retarded: Servant or savant. *Focus on Exceptional Children,* 1971, *2,* 1-11.

MacMillan, D. *Mental retardation in school and society.* Boston: Little, Brown, 1977.

McCall, R. The development of intellectual functioning in infancy and the prediction of later IQ. In J. Osofsky (Ed.), *Handbook of infant development.* New York: Wiley, 1979.

McLean, J., Yoder, D., & Schiefelbusch, R. (Eds.). *Language intervention with the retarded: Developing strategies.* Baltimore: University Park Press, 1972.

Meichenbaum, D. *Cognitive behavior modification.* New York: Plenum Press, 1977.

Mercer, C., & Snell, M. *Learning theory research in mental retardation: Implication for teaching.* Columbus, Ohio: Charles E. Merrill, 1977.

Mercer, J. *Labeling the mentally retarded.* Berkeley, Calif.: University of California Press, 1973.

Meyerowitz, J. Self-derogation in young retardates and special class placement. *Child Development,* 1962, *33,* 443-451.

Meyerowitz, J. Peer groups and special classes. *Mental Retardation,* 1967, *5,* 23-26.

Miller, J., & Yoder, D. On developing the content for a language teaching program. *Mental Retardation,* 1972, *10,* 9-11.

Myklebust, H. Learning disabilities: Definition and overview: In H.R. Myklebust (Ed.), *Progress in learning disabilities.* New York: Grune & Stratton, 1968.

Paul, J., Stedman, D., & Neufield, G. (Eds.). *Deinstitutionalization: Program and policy development.* Syracuse, N.Y.: Syracuse University Press, 1977.

Perkins, W. Disorders of speech flow. In T. Hixon, L. Shriberg, & J. Saxman (Eds.), *Introduction to communication disorders.* Englewood Cliffs, N.J.: Prentice-Hall, 1980.

Peterson, D. *Functional mathematics for the mentally retarded.* Columbus, Ohio: Charles E. Merrill, 1973.

Piaget, J. *The origins of intelligence in children*. New York: W.W. Norton, 1963.

Postman, L. Short-term memory and incidental learning. In A. Melton (Ed.), *Categories of human learning*. New York: Academic Press, 1964.

Ramey, C., & Campbell, F. Early childhood education for psychosocially disadvantaged children: Effects on psychological processes. *American Journal of Mental Deficiency,* 1979, *83,* 645-648.

Rarick, G., Dobbins, D., & Broadhead, G. *The motor domain and its correlation in educationally handicapped children*. Englewood Cliffs, N.J.: Prentice-Hall, 1976.

Robinson, C., & Robinson, J. Sensorimotor functions and cognitive development. In M. Snell (Ed.), *Systematic instruction of the moderately and severely handicapped*. Columbus, Ohio: Charles E. Merrill, 1978.

Rucker, C., & Vincenzo, F. Mainstreaming social acceptance: Gains made by mentally retarded children. *Exceptional Children,* 1970, *36,* 679.

Schweinhart, L., & Weikart, D. Effects of the Perry Preschool Program on youths through age 15. *Journal of the Division for Early Childhood,* 1981, *4,* 29-39.

Smith, R. *Clinical teaching: Methods of teaching for the retarded*. New York: McGraw-Hill, 1974.

Spitz, H. The role of input organization in the learning and memory of mental retardates. In N.R. Ellis (Ed.), *International review of research in mental retardation* (Vol. 2). New York: Academic Press, 1966.

Spradlin, J. Language and communication of mental defectives. In N.R. Ellis (Ed.), *Handbook of mental deficiency: Psychological theory and research*. New York: McGraw-Hill, 1963.

Striefel, S. *Managing behavior: Teaching a child to imitate*. Lawrence, Kans.: H&H Enterprises, 1974.

Tarjan, G., Wright, S., Eyman, R., & Keeran, C. Natural history of mental retardation: Some aspects of epidemiology. *American Journal of Mental Deficiency,* 1973, *77,* 369-379.

Terman, L., & Merrill, M. *Stanford-Binet intelligence scale* (3rd rev.). Boston: Houghton-Mifflin, 1960.

Tjossem, T. (Ed.). *Intervention strategies for high risk infants and young children*. Baltimore: University Park Press, 1976.

Turnbull, A., & Blacher-Dixon, J. Preschool mainstreaming: An empirical and conceptual review. In P. Strain & M.M. Kerr (Eds.), *Mainstreaming of children in schools: Research and programmatic issues*. New York: Academic Press, 1981.

Vincent, L., Brown, L., & Getz-Sheftel, M. Integrating handicapped and typical children during the preschool years: The definition of best educational practice. *Topics in Early Childhood Special Education,* 1981, *1,* 17-24.

Wechsler, D. *Wechsler preschool and primary scale of intelligence*. New York: The Psychological Corp., 1967.

Wechsler, D. *Wechsler intelligence scale for children* (Rev. ed.). New York: The Psychological Corp., 1974.

Williams, E. Effects of readiness on incidental learning in educable mentally retarded, normal and gifted children. *American Journal of Mental Deficiency,* 1970, *75,* 117-119.

Wolfensberger, W. *Normalization: The principle of normalization in human services*. Toronto: National Institute on Mental Retardation (Canada), 1972.

Zeaman, D., & House, B. The role of attention in retardate discrimination learning. In N.R. Ellis (Ed.), *Handbook of mental deficiency*. New York: McGraw-Hill, 1963.

Zigler, E. Familial mental retardation: A continuing dilemma. *Science,* 1967, *155,* 292-298.

Chapter 9

Developments in Social Behavior

David Page and S. Gray Garwood

SOCIAL DEVELOPMENT AND SOCIALIZATION

Our lives are complexly interwoven with the lives of others, beginning at the very moment of birth. It is not likely that infants would survive if it were not for their interactions with others, since infants are not born with sufficient survival skills, but must acquire them through gradual learning. However, infants may be born with a predisposition to develop these varied social abilities, and interaction with others serves as a catalyst and source of information by which such skills develop. Optimum conditions for development are complex, and their absence or variations of them can do much to alter social development.

Social development is the process by which the behaviors necessary to form and sustain interactions with others are acquired; as such, it is largely influenced by cultural socialization processes. Every society seeks to control behavior by establishing conduct rules to stabilize the social system. The process by which new members are taught these rules is called socialization.

When socialization is successful, children learn behaviors that are rewarding and help them to accomplish their goals. Socialization is a very intricate process; children must learn a complex network of clues to determine which actions are appropriate in which situations. For example, they must learn to behave differently in different classrooms and on the playground. They must also learn to react differently to the same people seen in different situations. Children also must learn general rules to guide behaviors in almost all situations. For example, children in our culture usually learn that lying or cheating generally results in disapproval from others; on the other hand, politeness, honesty, and relative independence almost always result in approval.

A variety of social agents (individuals or institutions that present the culture to children) participate in the socialization process. Initially, socialization is controlled by significant individual agents (parents, teachers, or other care-giving agents). With increasing age, collective groups (peer or other social groups) begin to affect socialization. Sometimes superstition, rituals, and the supernatural also influence socialization (e.g., the threat of the bogeyman or the promise that Santa would record good behavior). In many homes, religious beliefs and practices are also utilized as socialization agents.

Socialization is not totally controlled by external forces; children are active participants. For example, the relationship between infant and mother is, in part, due to efforts by the infant to seek and sustain contact with the mother. This maximizes socialization outcomes because, in so doing, the child gradually incorporates standards held by important external socialization agents. Eventually others' standards become the child's personal standards, and the child learns to control and direct his or her own behavior according to culturally defined criteria.

The nature of social development varies according to the child's particular culture or social system. For example, Indian children are socialized to be respectful and obedient. Japanese children are socialized to be submissive and dependent, while American children are socialized to be autonomous and individualistic (Caudill & Weinstein, 1969). These differences seem to result from culture-dependent parental beliefs as to the basic nature of children and how they are to be molded into the ideal adult. Even though the content of social skills can vary across cultural groups, it is assumed that the processes by which these varying skills are acquired are not culture-dependent.

NORMAL AND ATYPICAL SOCIAL DEVELOPMENT

The fact that the products of the socialization process, such as values, expectations, and social skills, vary from culture to culture complicates efforts to define "normal" social development. There is no universal definition of normality. As the voluminous literature in the field of abnormal psychology attests, the distinction between normality and abnormality is often made on the basis of varying criteria that stem from differing concepts of abnormality (Price, 1978). This is an especially critical problem in studying behavior. Unlike physical disorders, which result from specific physiological factors, psychological "disorders" are often so labeled as a consequence of values, expectations, and perceptions of other persons in a particular social environment (Szasz, 1967). This may be less true of those types of exceptionality that reflect genetic anomalies, physical or physiological disorders, or sensory deficits, because socialization problems under these circumstances are more clearly related to processes within the individual. In the case of social or emotional disorders, however, the criteria for abnormality do not necessarily relate to the particular individual, but to others. This is even more likely to apply to children, since children do not label themselves "behaviorally disturbed." The label, along with concomitant intervention, stems from adults in their environment. A child who frequently exhibits aggressive behaviors in environment A may be considered a child with a "conduct disorder," while the same child in environment B might be perceived as completely normal. Research by Thomas, Chess, Sillen, and Mendez (1974) on social class and ethnic differences in parents' reporting of child problems reflects this fact.

The problem is compounded by the fact that even *within* particular social, ethnic, or economic groups there is not necessarily a shared definition of what constitutes normality. Indeed, it could be argued that the perfectly normal or typical individual does not exist. Tremendous individual differences in psychological functioning become evident shortly after birth and become increasingly evident over the course of development. These differences are a product of the complex interaction between an individual and the environment. Personality differences of this sort further complicate efforts to standardize the definition of normality.

It is clear that an acceptable definition of normal or typical social development must be sufficiently general to include the role of environmental considerations and to allow for the great number of adaptive variations in social functioning. For the purposes of this discussion, normal social development is defined as *behaviors and competencies that allow an individual to function within a particular social milieu in a way that contributes to the individual's welfare and does not cause undue alarm on the part of others.*

Adults become concerned about the welfare of children for a variety of reasons related to their interactions with family members, peers, teachers, and others. Most reasons can be fit into one or more of the following categories: (1) conflict with societal expectations, (2) deviations from developmental norms, or (3) sudden changes in the mode of interaction with others. Usually, the child's behavior deviates from that expected by socialization agents. For example, a child may be inappropriately aggressive and disobedient or shy and withdrawn. In this case, the problem can be conceptualized as a behavioral excess or behavioral deficiency. On the other hand, a particular child's behavior may not be in keeping with that of other children in the same age group. The child whose social competencies and behaviors are behind those of peers may be considered immature. The concept of developmental lag is sometimes applied to these cases. Finally, in other circumstances, a child may show sudden remarkable changes in behavior. For example, a preschooler who had been cooperative and gregarious may suddenly become shy, withdrawn, and seemingly depressed. Such rapid changes are usually not indicative of healthy development (see Costello, 1981, for a review of childhood depression).

Specifying the conditions that control normal or atypical development is a significantly more challenging enterprise for child care professionals than simply describing normality and abnormality. Delineating causality is difficult for all sciences, but it is especially difficult in psychology, given the fact that behavior is multidetermined. Social development in both its typical and atypical forms is a product of the complex interaction of a number of factors.

SOURCES OF NORMAL AND ATYPICAL DEVELOPMENT

Conditions that influence the course of social development can be grouped into three major categories: (1) hereditary, (2) maturational, and (3) environmental. Hereditary influences are individual differences in genetic makeup that affect both physical characteristics and, to a certain extent, personality. Genetic contributions to physical characteristics are more easily specified than genetic influences on behavior, since physical characteristics are more easily measured and are relatively less dependent on environmental factors. There is a body of evidence, however, indicating a link between genetic makeup and social behavioral characteristics, such as cuddliness (Schaffer & Emerson, 1964), temperament (Thomas & Chess, 1977), and activity rate (Goldsmith & Gottesman, 1981). In addition, research in psychopathology suggests that predispositions for severe forms of disturbance, such as schizophrenia and manic-depressive psychoses, may be genetically inherited in part (Gottesman & Shields, 1972). Genetic factors can contribute to either adaptive or maladaptive social development, depending on the fit between the phenotypic behavioral pattern and the expectations of the socialization agents in an individual's environment.

Maturation is the genetically determined sequence of development common to all members of a given species. For example, maturation of the human body from conception through adolescence follows a predetermined sequence common to all humans in all societies. Also, motor development, in which individuals gradually attain control over different sets of muscles, follows a specified sequence. Although socialization appears to be primarily a product of social interaction, as many classic theories of social development and socialization maintain (Mead, 1934), recent work in both psychology and sociobiology suggests that maturation influences social development. There is increasing evidence that human beings are born innately social and are predisposed to respond socially to the primary caregiver. The first 2 years of life may be a period of maturational readiness to receive and respond to social stimulation emitted by caregivers. This stimulation in turn aids in developing the social responsiveness of newborn infants (Bowlby, 1969).

The influence of maturation on social development can be extended to cognitive development. A sizeable body of research conducted within the context of Piagetian theory suggests that cognitive development follows a sequence of stages partially under the control of maturational influences (Bruner, Olver, & Greenfield, 1966). These maturationally determined stages denote what types of learning experiences are most likely to be of benefit to the individual at a particular time. In addition, since a child's level of cognitive development influences how a child perceives and interprets others, it follows that maturation has at least an indirect influence on social development (mediated by cognitive development). Research on topics such as sex typing (Kohlberg, 1966), play (Mueller & Brenner,

1977), moral development (Kohlberg, 1973), and role taking (Selman & Byrne, 1974) supports this relationship.

Insofar as developmental norms or expectations reflect a maturational sequence, exceptionality can be considered a deviation from these norms, perhaps as a result of genetically determined individual differences in rate of maturational development. Research by Hill and McCune-Nicolich (1981) on the symbolic play of mentally retarded children supports this view. Most preschool children engage in significant amounts of symbolic play; this behavior is made possible by newly developed cognitive skills that enable these children to construct mental representations (see Garwood, 1982, for a review of this sequence). Hill and McCune-Nicolich found that the symbolic play of Down's syndrome children was more highly correlated with mental age than with chronological age. The social (play) skills of these children may not have been in keeping with chronological age expectations because of maturationally delayed cognitive development.

Environmental effects on social development are manifested in a number of different ways, ranging from global preexisting conditions (e.g., ethnic background and socioeconomic status) to specific behaviors by socialization agents (e.g., styles of parenting). The sum total of an individual's experiences not only exerts profound effects on both typical and atypical social development, but also can influence the expression of maturationally or genetically determined behavioral dispositions. Those environmental effects that contribute to inadequate social development are (1) experiences that foster the development of characteristics inappropriate to the child's cultural milieu, (2) inadequate or excessive stimulation, (3) stimulation inappropriate to a particular child's developmental level.

There is a substantial amount of evidence that an impoverished environment can exert a dramatic impact on both social and nonsocial development. Representative of this work is research on children in minimal care institutions (Dennis, 1960), pioneering investigations with feral children (Singh, 1969), and case studies on "attic children" (Davis, 1940). In addition, there is evidence that overstimulation can have a negative impact on development (Wachs, Uzgiris, & Hunt, 1971). It appears that the quality of stimulation is more important than its quantity. Quality stimulation is characterized by its distinctiveness; that is, it should be contingent on a child's behavior so that the youngster perceives a connection between his or her behavior and variations in the environment (White, 1967).

The timing of particular experiences also seems to affect the course of social development. As indicated previously, children at particular ages may be "primed" to be most sensitive and responsive to certain types of stimulation. For example, the development of the attachment bond between the infant and the primary caregiver during the 1st year of life is partially determined by the maturational readiness of the infant. The young child seems to be predisposed during this time to respond to social stimulation directed by the caregiver (Bowlby, 1969). Because similar periods of readiness may occur in the course of growth, optimum development is most likely to occur if the nature of environmental stimulation corresponds with the child's developmental level. Research that shows child abuse as a failure of the attachment bond and abusive parents as those who hold unrealistically high expectations for their toddlers (Klein & Stern, 1971) underlines the importance of congruity between a child's developmental level and environment.

THE CONCEPT OF DEVELOPMENTAL LAG

Children are usually considered to be in a developmental lag when for some reason (slower than usual biological maturation or inadequacies in the environment) they function at a level below that of other children in their age group. Should this be the case and there is no distinct biological impairment, remedial stimulation often enables such a child to move toward more age-appropriate functioning. Immature social interaction by itself, however, does not indicate a developmental lag. In a young child, performance may differ from competence. Overt behavior is multidetermined; it is a function of a great number of causal factors, only one of which is the underlying ability that enables the child to perform the behavior. A child who possesses a particular ability may not always manifest it behaviorally. Many times, external environmental influences may overcome an underlying ability, and the child will appear to be "immature." The ability continues to exist, however.

The distinction between competence and performance, as well as the relationship between the two, can be seen in the social interaction of hearing-impaired children. Hoemann (1972) found the performance of 11-year-old deaf children on a referential communication task was similar to that of 8-year-old hearing children. Successful performance on tasks of this nature requires somewhat sophisticated role-taking skills and verbal facility, an ability less developed among deaf children. The lack of communication skills inhibits the social interaction of deaf children, and there is considerable evidence that hearing-impaired children show deficits in social skills (Craig, 1975; Myklebust, 1960) and that they find it difficult to be accepted socially by hearing children (Darbyshire, 1977). After reviewing the evidence, Meadow (1975) concluded that deaf children generally lack social maturity and communication skill. A study by Vandell and George (1981), however, indicated that preschool deaf children show considerable interaction and social skill, especially when they interact with other deaf preschoolers. In this study, social effectiveness was analyzed primarily through nonverbal indicators, such as touching or gestures, rather than solely with verbal indicators as in most previous research. Thus, it appears that the detailed interaction analysis used in this study to assess social performance is a more potent indicator of underlying social competence. In addition, the superior social interaction exhibited by deaf children with other deaf children suggests that performance variables related to the presence of hearing children alter the expression of social competencies.

Consequently, in assessing the social competence of a child, particularly that of a handicapped child, it is important to take into account the distinction between competence and performance, the different factors that influence both of these, and the type of behavior used as an index of underlying abilities. A youngster whose social behavior may be immature should not automatically be considered "slow" (in a developmental lag). Immature behavior may simply be a function of a stressful situation or some other performance variable.

THEORETICAL PERSPECTIVES ON SOCIAL DEVELOPMENT

Theories provide conceptual frameworks that organize and explain natural phenomena. Usually, theories include hypotheses as to which factors are determinants or causes of specific events; consequently theories can be classified in terms of the general types of causes considered most important in them. Some emphasize external factors as central causes of behavior (i.e., traditional learning theory). Other theories focus on internal factors, such as drives or instincts (e.g., Freud's psychosexual theory, ethological theories). Still others emphasize the interaction of internal and external factors (e.g., social-cognitive theories, Erikson's psychosocial theory, social learning theory). Each of these theories is based on a unique set of assumptions about humanity and represents a particular viewpoint. Even though they seem to compete, they do not necessarily invalidate each other; they simply illustrate the complexity of the subject matter.

The Hereditary Perspective

Ethology, the study of species-specific behavioral characteristics, has until recently involved almost exclusively the study of nonhuman animals. However, this orientation has lately been applied to human research (Eibl-Eibesfeldt, 1970). For example, extensive work has been done on such human behavioral patterns as mother-infant relationships and children's social interactions with peers.

Ethologists work from an evolutionary perspective to examine the development and functions of behaviors, with an emphasis on the ways in which certain behavior patterns help to ensure the species survival. Consequently, species-specific behaviors are said to be adaptive. Ethologists emphasize the genetic component of behaviors—so long as a behavioral pattern has adaptive or functional significance, the genes responsible are passed to following generations. When the functional significance of a species-specific behavior can be determined, ethologists usually consider members of the species to be predisposed to the particular behavior; hence, organisms are sometimes said to have an instinct to behave in a certain manner.

Ethologists also consider the environment in the analysis of behavior. They maintain that the overt manifestation (phenotype) of an instinctually based behavior (genotype) usually does not occur unless the environment is appropriate. Certain types of environmental stimulation (termed *sign stimuli* or *releasers*) are thought to elicit the phenotypic expression of the genotype. Therefore, it is possible for an organism to have a predisposition to behave in a certain manner, yet, in actuality, not behave accordingly.

In their analysis of human social development, ethologists assume that the human species is fundamentally social. Social behaviors have functional significance; they facilitate a child's acceptance within the social system, thus making it possible for the child to survive and, eventually, reproduce. The process of social development can be understood in terms of genetically preprogrammed social behaviors that are evoked by appropriate environmental stimulation. Intrinsic within this evolutionary perspective is the concept that the child is an active force in socialization; that is, since social behaviors are possibly instinctive, the child also determines the process of social development.

According to this perspective, normal social development proceeds if an infant's environment allows genetically determined predispositions to manifest themselves. Should the environment not be conducive to the expression of these adaptive behavior patterns, undesirable consequences may occur.

The Psychodynamic Perspective

From the psychodynamic viewpoint, human behavior and development are seen in terms of unconscious motivational sources. Accordingly, social development consists of the acquisition of skills and abilities needed to control these motivations in socially acceptable ways. The originator of this viewpoint, Sigmund Freud, formulated a theory of psychosexual development in which he held that human beings are born with a fixed amount of psychic energy (libido), which manifests itself primarily through sexual and aggressive drives. Implicit in this assumption is the belief that, unless discharged, these drives gradually build up and result in discomfort. In the course of development, drives are discharged through various parts of the body. This discharge is thought to be a gratifying and pleasurable experience. The body part that serves as locus for drive discharge at a particular time is determined by the child's developmental status. Freud postulated five stages of development, four of which are differentiated in terms of which part of the body serves as a pleasure zone: (1) oral, (2) anal, (3) phallic, (4) latency, and (5) genital stages.

Of greater import to social development is the structural aspect of Freud's theory. According to Freud, the mature personality is composed of three interdependent components: the id, ego, and superego. The id, present at birth, is the home or source of psychic energy, and it seeks continuous and immediate gratification. Consequently, the human infant at birth is viewed as relatively asocial and hedonistic. During the oral stage, the ego develops and begins to regulate id impulses. Ego development is largely a function of the child's experience with reality. The constant and immediate gratification of urges provided by most parents of a newborn leads the child to view the world as no more than an extension of self. As a result of delays in gratification, plus normally occurring punishments, the child begins to alter this conception of the world. The outcome of this process is the development of the ego, which begins to take control of the expression of id impulses. Consequently, drives are now discharged more in accordance with realistic considerations imposed by the outside world. Accordingly, ego development is the first event in becoming a mature social being.

Although necessary, the ego is not sufficient for mature social functioning, because it is rather immune to the societal standards and morals that should also govern behavior. The internalization of social norms as standards for drive discharge and behavior does not occur until the child reaches the phallic stage of development. At this age, the child is confronted with the Oedipus complex (if male) or the Electra complex (if female). The complex is resolved when the child identifies with the same sex parent and internalizes arbitrary social standards, morals, and values represented by that parent. This results in the formation of the superego, consisting of a conscience and internalized standards, which assumes further control over the expression of id impulses. Superego development is thought to be the hallmark of social development in childhood, since the child is now truly on the path to becoming a mature social being.

As a neo-Freudian, Erikson (1963) proposed a theory of psychosocial development that operates within a psychodynamic framework but differs from Freud's theory on three basic points. First, Erikson rejects the fundamentally sexual nature of human motivation that Freud hypothesized. According to Erikson, development is more than an increasing sophistication in the expression of sexual and aggressive urges; development also involves the creative, adaptive, and reality-oriented aspects of the personality. Basically, Erikson believes that the ego is responsible not only for the control of psychic energies, but also for the development of the individual's overall social competency, including language, thinking, and acquired motivation (e.g., achievement). Second, while Freud viewed social development as complete by adolescence, Erikson considers development a process that extends from birth through old age, with new social abilities and competencies continuously being developed. Third, Freud treated social influences with far less importance than Erikson does. According to Erikson, the social environment is of utmost importance in determining development; it exerts various influences and demands that shape the course of human development. Moreover, Erikson feels that environmental demands change with age and that, because it is necessary to satisfy varying societal demands as a child matures, the child acquires corresponding new social abilities.

According to Erikson, demands of the environment on the individual provoke an emotional crisis. Development thus consists of attempts by the individual to resolve emotional crises by acquiring appropriate capabilities to meet the challenges. If the challenges are met and the abilities are developed, development proceeds in a healthy manner. Each of these newly acquired abilities is considered part of the developing ego.

Inherent in Erikson's theory is a maturational concept that "anything that grows has a ground plan, and out of this ground plan the parts arise, each having its time of special ascendancy, until all parts have arisen to form a functioning whole" (Erikson, 1959, p. 52). Thus, in addition to social factors, Erikson offers a principle of development that is primarily maturational and asserts a timetable of ego development. Not all ego capabilities are present at birth; each has a time or stage in which to develop. During a particular stage, the focus of development is on a particular ability. When the next stage of development is reached, the focus of development is switched to another capability—even though an ego capability associated with the previous stage may not be developed. Thus, in order to become a fully functioning social individual, a child must develop the capabilities inherent in each stage *during that stage of development*.

Psychoanalytic theory, particularly Freud's, has been applied primarily to maladaptive functioning. In fact, some have argued that Freud's approach, which involves analysis of neuroses, prohibits a thorough understanding of the positive adaptive aspects of development (Allport, 1955). According to Freud's perspective, atypical social development can arise for a myriad of reasons, ranging from overgratification or undergratification of libidinal urges to an unresolved Oedipus complex and consequent inability to internalize social standards. Freudian explanations, however complex and compelling, have proved to be of limited usefulness because his loosely defined concepts almost defy empirical assessment, but one of Freud's major contributions was to point out psychological phenomena that deserved further investigation. Much of the research on conscience development during the preschool period can be traced to Freud's contention that the preschool years are important for superego development.

Erikson's theory, since it is less rooted in unconscious dynamics, provides a potentially more fruitful analysis of atypical development. An individual who does not solve a conflict pertaining to a particular stage and thus does not obtain the corresponding ego capability will be less able to solve subsequent conflicts. Even in the case of Erikson's views, however, it is difficult to explain development precisely because there are few agreed upon behavioral definitions for Erikson's ego capabilities. Nevertheless, some of his ideas have been integrated with other theoretical viewpoints in an attempt to provide a comprehensive analysis of development. For example, a successful infant attachment can be conceptualized as the acquisition of a basic sense of trust.

The Learning Perspective

While hereditary and psychodynamic approaches have emphasized internal factors (i.e., instincts, drives, ego capabilities) as primary influences on social development, traditional learning or behavioristic approaches to social development focus heavily on external factors to explain social development. Newer concepts of learning (social learning theory) have recognized the impact of internal factors (attention, cognition) on social development, however.

The traditional behavioristic view of social development virtually excludes cognition and other causal factors within the organism. The process of social development is seen as largely dependent on both antecedent and consequent factors relating to a particular behavioral response. Antecedent factors are customarily stimulus variables; consequent factors are reinforcement variables, including punishment and nonreward. Antecedent factors that bear on social development are usually conceptualized in terms of discriminative stimuli that indicate whether or not a particular social behavior will be rewarded. Thus, socialization involves more than teaching a child required social behaviors; the child must also learn the conditions under which such behaviors are appropriate. In behavioristic terminology, the behavior then comes under stimulus control. This process occurs largely as a result of association; that is, reinforcement and punishments are not isolated from the remaining environment. A particular punishment, for example, becomes associated with stimulus characteristics in the environment, and these stimulus characteristics thus acquire aversive properties. In general, the outcome of the association process is that the presence of positive or aversive stimuli on future occasions may be sufficient to enable the child to behave appropriately.

A relatively new theoretical framework that falls within the learning perspective is social learning theory (Bandura, 1977). Current social learning theory is remarkably different from its original behavioristic orientation, both in its assumptions and its conceptualization of the learning process. The most notable difference is that cognitive processes are now viewed as important to development and stress is placed on the ways in which humans actively process stimulus material and generate meaning. It is assumed that a great deal of learning results from observation of others' behavior and the subsequent imitation of that behavior. Thus, modeling and imitation are considered important to social development.

Modeling influences learning primarily by providing information. As a result of observing a model, children acquire information in the form of symbolic representations of the modeled activities. This learning can be translated into overt behavior. Basic to the overall process of observational learning are four distinct elements: (1) attention, (2) retention, (3) motoric reproduction, and (4) reinforcement history. A number of factors influence attentional and retentional processes, such as the value of the model to the child, the child's sensory capacities, the child's coding (both imagined and verbal), and rehearsal capabilities.

Motoric reproduction is the translation of the symbolic representation of a behavior into overt activity. Motoric reproduction is not necessary for observational learning, but it can help. Its beneficial aspect is reflected in the fact that children can learn via self-observation. By observing themselves as they reproduce the behavior of others, children can assess the accuracy of their learning and modify what has been learned. While reinforcement is not necessary for observational learning, it may enhance learning. Thus, the motivational component in observational learning is viewed in terms of reinforcement and punishment. Direct external reinforcement (or punishment) can serve as an incentive that influences the attentional component of observational learning. Vicarious reinforcement (or punishment), which is that received by a model for some behavior, can affect the likelihood that the child will perform the model's behavior. Bandura (1977) has hypothesized that vicarious reinforcement or punishment may influence learning because it affects the attentional component of observational learning. If a child sees a model being rewarded (punished) for a behavior, the child may perceive the model as more (or less) important and may show increased (decreased) attention to the model's behavior on future occasions. This, in turn, will have a direct influence on the accuracy of the information encoded and learning.

The information learned through observation is not necessarily identical to that supplied by the model; there is an opportunity for originality in the learning process. Thus, social learning theorists assert that, through observation, children can learn not only specific behaviors, but also general abstract rules for behavior. "The evidence accumulated to date suggests that, depending on their complexity and diversity, modeling influences can produce, in addition to mimicry of specific responses, behavior that is generative and innovative in character" (Bandura, 1971, p. 38). Thus, in Bandura's view, children do not merely mimic specific responses, they also abstract productive rules from their diverse observations.

According to the learning theories, the desirability of social development is determined by the nature of a child's experiences. Should children be exposed to socializing agents and concomitant reinforcements (whether direct or vicarious) that teach them socially undesirable modes of conduct, they would have difficulty adapting to society at large. Atypical development could also be a consequence of excessive use of punishment by socialization agents. Punishment can result in conditioned anxiety, the cumulative effect of which is to hamper adaptive ability further. Finally, should children experience some cognitive or attentional deficit, their ability to learn through observation and to generate rules to guide social behavior may decrease, with obvious negative consequences for their functioning.

The Cognitive Perspective

In cognitive theory, a child's level of cognitive development is considered an important determinant of social development. Recent advances in the understanding of cognitive development, plus the inclusion of cognition as a variable in learning theory, have helped to make psychologists and educators more aware of the ways in which social and cognitive development influence each other. Contemporary research on such processes as attachment, sex typing, sharing behavior, and moral development has clearly delineated this relationship and has indicated that the level of cognitive development is a variable that can predict a child's social development. Thus, any attempt at understanding social development must include cognition as an explanatory construct.

As a result of the recent interface of cognitive and social development research, a new research area has emerged—social cognition. This area of investigation concerns what individuals perceive, think, and know about themselves, other people, social organizations, and social institutions (see Flavell & Ross, 1981, for a thorough review of this new area). The scope of social cognition is very wide, as it includes any object of thought that can be considered social: intentions, attitudes, emotions, ideas, personalities, and perceptions of other people or the self.

While social cognition can be distinguished from the traditional concept of cognitive development in terms of the objects of thoughts, it cannot be distinguished in terms of the cognitive abilities involved. Flavell's assertion that "the head that thinks about the social world is the self same head that thinks about the nonsocial world" points out the basis for parallels in the development of social and nonsocial cognition (Flavell, 1977, p. 122).

Flavell (1977) has proposed an information-processing model that delineates three preconditions for an act of social cognition: existence, need, and inference. Children must have a basic knowledge of the existence of social phenomena. For example, they must be aware that others may have thoughts that differ from their own before they can try to infer the others' thoughts. Even though young children may be aware that others possess distinctive feelings or motives, this perception is not sufficient for making a social cognitive act. The children must also perceive the need to make the act happen before they will perform it. While perception of existence and need may ensure that children will attempt to perform an act of social cognition, the correctness and consequent utility of that act is determined by their skill in integrating and interpreting information provided by various cues relevant to the act. The third precondition, inference, refers to the capacity to carry out a given act of social cognition successfully.

Selman (1976, 1981) and his colleague (Selman & Byrne, 1974) have applied the process of cognitive development to social cognition (Table 9-1). In infancy and toddlerhood, the child's major social cognition tasks are, first, to develop a sense of self as a unique object distinct from other living and nonliving objects

Table 9-1 Selman and Byrne's Model of the Development of Social Cognitions

Level and Age Range	*Distinguishing Perspectives*
0: Egocentric role taking; 4 to 6 years	No distinctions are made by child between self-view and others' views of social situations; child can differentiate self from others but does not evidence ability to differentiate various perspectives.
1: Subjective role taking; 6 to 8 years	Child recognizes that he or she may differ from others in their interpretations of social situations, largely due to differences in amount of information available to each.
2: Self-reflective role taking; 8 to 10 years	Child is aware that others can think about him or her; child can reflect on own thinking, on others' thinking, and on others' thinking about him or her.
3: Mutual role taking; 10 to 12 years	Youth can now differentiate personal perspective from generalized or normative perspectives and realizes that self and others can consider each other's perspective simultaneously and mutually.
4: Societal role taking; 12+ years	Adolescent is aware of relativity of perspective and recognizes that culture, history, experience, and other relevant variables mediate interpretations of social cognitions.

and, second, to learn about other people—to distinguish them from nonhuman objects and to develop a crude ranking of their importance. Beginning about age 4, the child's rapidly increasing cognitive, physical, and social skills contribute (interactively) to increasingly more general and extended social cognitions.

Oppenheimer (1978) has incorporated both Flavell's and Selman's models into one model, based on the idea that each of Selman's structured developmental levels could be characterized by a sequential flow of information, as proposed by Flavell.

According to the cognitive perspective, atypical social development is in part a consequence of deficits in cognitive functioning that hamper children's ability to understand others and themselves. The contributions of cognition to social adaptation have been implicated in a number of research areas: attachment (Bell, 1970), self-concept (Lewis & Brooks-Gunn, 1979), person perception (Livesley & Bromley, 1973), friendship formation (Berndt, 1981), moral behavior (Shweder, Turiel, & Much, 1981), and empathy (Hoffman, 1981). Cognitive immaturity can cause children to perform fewer acts of social cognition, which can complicate social adaptability. For example, studies indicate that an individual is more likely to help someone if the potential helper can empathize or understand the need or psychological state of the person who requires assistance (Hoffman, 1977b). An individual who does not possess the cognitive skills necessary for an act of empathic inference (in this case, role-taking skills, decentering) is far less likely to help. Similarly, Vandenberg (1981) reports that preschoolers who were more cognitively mature and less socially egocentric were more likely to involve themselves in social interactions with others (associative play); children who were less cognitively mature and more socially egocentric preferred to play alone.

Intervention Models and Theory

All of these theoretical positions provide a rationale for developing intervention strategies for children whose development is delayed or atypical. As Garwood (1982) and others have noted, it is unwise to develop an intervention strategy without a clear view of the theory on which it is based, since theory determines the methods to be used in trying to alter behavior. MacMillan and Morrison (1979) and Sheehan and Gradel (Chapter 13) discuss various intervention models and their theoretical foundations.

ORIGINS OF SOCIABILITY

Infant-Caregiver Attachments

Traditional learning theory and research failed to explain the origins of sociability from either a drive reduction or a reinforcement framework. Piagetian cognitive psychology and ethology, with its focus on studying behavior in its natural setting, contributed new knowledge. Interest in Piagetian cognitive development theory and in ethological research strategies paralleled a renewed interest in genetic contributions to behavior. As Ainsworth (1972) stated, psychologists were becoming interested "in how that which lies inside the organism contributes to organism-environment interaction" (p. 99). As a consequence of this renewed interest, the scientific perspective shifted from learning theory to concern with the role played by evolution in the development of social behavior.

Bowlby (1958a) introduced the concept of attachment as an alternative explanation for the origins of sociability. Dependency, according to Bowlby (1969), describes the individual's reliance on another for satisfaction of physical needs. Attachment, on the other hand, refers to particular behaviors aimed at maintaining proximity between two individuals. In addition, attachment requires the occurrence of clearly different behaviors toward one or more specific attachment objects than occurs toward other individuals (or objects) in the same setting. Using data collected on mother-infant interaction among the Ganda, Ainsworth (1963, 1967) elaborated and extended Bowlby's original conceptions of attachment. Currently, attachment is regarded as a construct describing a mode of relating to a specific figure (Ainsworth, 1972):

> It has the status of an intervening variable or an organizing construct, to be evaluated in terms of its integrative power. It is not a set of behaviors that are constantly and uniformly operative . . . [thus, attachment may be viewed as] . . . an affective tie between infant and caregiver and to a behavioral system, flexibly operating in terms of set goals, mediated by feelings, and in interaction with other behavioral systems. (Sroufe & Waters, 1977, p. 1185)

From this perspective, attachment behaviors are genetically based and thus serve a biological function—they enhance chances for survival. In other words, infants and mothers are predisposed to form an attachment bond as a way of ensuring the infant's survival during the infant's immature and helpless phase.

From an evolutionary perspective, infants appear predisposed to enact various behaviors that serve as precursors to attachment, such as rooting, sucking, postural adjustment, looking, listening, smiling, vocalizing, crying, grasping, and climbing behaviors. All of these behaviors facilitate the infant's proximity to the primary caregiver. The infant's predisposition for these various behaviors and the mother's responsiveness to them maximize mother-infant interaction.

Formation of the Attachment Bond

The attachment bond does not spring forth fully formed. Instead, it appears to follow a developmental progression over the infant's first 6 to 8 months (Table 9-2). According to Ainsworth's observations (1964, 1969), the infant responds to others in an indiscriminate manner during the first 2 months. Beginning about the 3rd month, the infant begins to respond differently to his or her primary caregiver (usually the mother) and, by the middle of the 1st year, clearly responds differently to this caregiver. An attachment bond between the infant and mother is then said to have occurred.

The formation of this bond between the infant and the primary caregiver is the most notable aspect of social development in infancy. Research by Bowlby, Ainsworth, and others indicates that the attachment bond may be crucial for normal social development. Attachment incorporates two basic components: behavior and affect. The behavioral component is reflected in the infant's tendency to stay near particular people, to be receptive to their care, and to be most comfortable when in their presence. The affective component is seen in the pleasure that the infant and the primary caregivers have in being with each other. The child develops positive feelings toward those who are warm, supportive, and nurturant. Although the infant cannot express these feelings elaborately, they can easily be inferred from the systematic attention, interest, and orientation the infant gives to those who provide care. All subsequent social development is believed to be influenced by the quality of attachment (Ainsworth, 1979), since it determines

Table 9-2 Infant-Caregiver Attachment Behaviors

Attachment Behavior	*Infant's Behavioral Activity*
Differential crying or smiling	Cries when held by someone other than primary caregiver; smiles more often and more readily in interaction with the caregiver than with others
Differential vocalizing	Vocalizes more often and more readily in interaction with the primary caregiver than with others
Visual-motor orientation	Maintains a continuous orientation toward the caregiver when not directly at his or her side
Crying when caregiver leaves room	Cries when caregiver breaks visual contact
Following	When able to crawl, attempts to follow caregiver
Scrambling	Climbs over, explores, and plays with caregiver
Burying the face in caregiver's body	Buries face in caregiver's lap following exploration or while scrambling over caregiver
Using caregiver as a base for exploration	Takes brief excursions away from caregiver
Clinging	Displays excessive holding and grasping, particularly when strangers are present
Lifting arms in greeting	Raises arms, smiles, and vocalizes toward caregiver after a period of absence
Clapping hands in greeting	Claps hands when caregiver appears
Approach through locomotion	When able to crawl, moves toward caregiver as quickly as possible and thus terminates greeting responses

to a significant degree the child's mode of interacting with other people, even perhaps across the entire life span (Kalish & Knudtson, 1976; Troll & Smith, 1976).

The fact that attachments take so long to form suggests that genetic predisposition, while a prerequisite, is not enough for bonding to occur. Other biological and cognitive factors probably contribute to the formation of the attachment bond. For example, Thomas, Chess, and Birch (1970) have identified nine different temperamental characteristics that remain relatively constant over the early years of life:

1. activity level
2. rhythmicity
3. distractibility

4. approach/withdrawal
5. adaptability
6. attention span and persistence
7. intensity of reaction
8. threshold of responsiveness
9. quality of sound

Such temperamental factors govern the quality and quantity of infant-mother interactions; for this reason, they no doubt also affect the bonding process. In support of this inference, Ainsworth, Bell, and Slayton (1972) have identified three distinct patterns of attachment behaviors: Type A babies do not appear strongly attached; Type B babies show classic proximity-maintaining behavior when a stranger is present or after a separation; Type C infants appear uneasy even when their caregiver is present, are anxious for close contact, and avoid exploring the environment.

Research also indicates that the level of cognitive development plays a part in the attachment process. Early social relationships are limited by the infant's primitive information-processing skills, and, in order to form an attachment, the infant must recognize and attend to others (Flavell, 1977; Piaget & Inhelder, 1969; Shantz, 1975). The importance of recognition in forming an attachment has been demonstrated in research tracing the development of the infant's smiling response to familiar faces and ability to recognize familiar people (Zelazo, 1972). The development of memory also appears critical in the formation of early social attachments. Accordingly, the child's recognition of familiar objects or people may depend on the acquisition and development of the object permanence concept. The infant who lacks memory of absent objects can respond only to those people and things that are immediately present; attachments must then necessarily be short-lived and limited to momentary interest or attention. A mature attachment could be formed only when the infant can recall the primary caregiver and recognize that person in memory (Goin-De Carie, 1974). Flavell (1977) agrees with the logic of this position but feels that research support is lacking.

Separation Distress

Once an attachment bond has been formed, separation or the threat of separation can produce negative reactions in some children. A body of evidence indicates that, sometime between the ages of 8 months and 3 years, most young children evidence some form of distress over separation from their primary caregiver—even when the separation is brief (Ainsworth, 1973). Such distress typically begins about the 8th month and peaks about the 18th month. It takes the form of increased crying, decreased exploratory play and movement, following behavior, and calling for the caregiver to return (Weinraub & Lewis, 1977). By about age 3, however, such distress is observed infrequently.

Separation distress may be subdivided into two subcategories: separation protest (attempts to regain proximity with an absent object) and separation anxiety (emotional distress accompanying unsuccessful separation protest behaviors).

The reason that separation distress begins to occur at the age(s) it does has generated some controversy. One hypothesis is that separation distress can occur only when the infant's mnemonic representation of the caregiver, including representation in a variety of places, becomes sufficiently well formed. Another is that the infant's distress is due to a perception of the discrepancy between the present event and the typical scheme (i.e., caregiver usually present). Consequently, a child who experiences the absence of the caregiver in a variety of situations will take a longer period of time to develop this scheme. Until the scheme is fully developed, the perception of a discrepancy is not possible so separation distress will not occur. On the other hand, the infant who experiences few absences from the caregiver will form a scheme earlier and thus is more likely to perceive a discrepancy when the caregiver departs and to experience separation distress.

Another controversy concerns whether separation distress can indicate the strength of the attachment bond. If a 1-year-old infant shows severe anxiety upon the caregiver's departure, is the child strongly attached to the caregiver? On the surface, the answer would seem to be "yes." A finer analysis, however, reveals that this may not be so. Separation distress is influenced by a number of factors, such as temperament and the ability of the infant to make a response in the caregiver's absence. (For a review of this controversy, see Weinraub & Lewis, 1977.)

Stranger Wariness

Another behavior related to attachment is a response termed stranger wariness (Sroufe, 1977). Beginning at approximately 8 months of age (Emde, Baensbauer, & Harmon, 1976), many infants become wary of unfamiliar persons. This occurs shortly after the attachment bond has been formed and the child's response to a stranger is typically to seek out the primary caregiver (Ainsworth & Bell, 1970). Also, the infant is less likely to show a distress response to a strange person when the attachment figure is present (Emde et al., 1976).

Like separation anxiety, stranger anxiety illustrates the relationship between social and cognitive development. Only toward the end of the 1st year of life does the infant develop a complete scheme for the mother and other familiar figures. Once such schemes are formed, a person whose appearance is discrepant may produce a negative reaction in the child. There is also some controversy concerning this phenomenon. Rheingold and Eckerman (1973) found that infants do not always show fear of strangers and may even make friendly overtures to a stranger, provided that the stranger is friendly and gives the child an opportunity to make a response (e.g., play with a toy). Because infants evidence less separation distress when left with attractive and complex toys (Williemsen, Heaton, Flaherty, & Ritchey, 1974) and because they will approach and even touch a stranger in a familiar environment (Tracy, Lamb, & Ainsworth, 1976), environmental cues may play a significant role in the onset of wariness behavior.

Quality Caregiving

Attachment highlights the importance of quality caregiving. Bowlby (1958b) and Ainsworth (1967) stress the importance of quality child-caregiver interactions and maintain that infant-caregiver relationships characterized by mutual delight (as opposed to routine care) are more likely to yield an effective attachment bond. This assertion has generated a certain amount of controversy. Although quantity of interaction is easily measurable and amenable to scientific investigation, quality of interaction is not. There is debate about how quality should be measured and what specific behaviors constitute quality caregiving. More research is needed to identify those behaviors that contribute to a mature attachment and those that inhibit the development of the attachment bond. Once these have been identified, careful observation and experimentation will be necessary to examine how the behaviors influence attachment. Work in this area is already beginning to identify certain behaviors related to effective caregiving (Clarke-Stewart, 1975; White, 1975), such as looking at and talking to the child, responding to distress and social expressions, playing with objects, and expressing positive (and suppressing negative) feelings.

Developments through Attachments

Bowlby (1969) and Ainsworth (1972) have described four general phases in attachment formation over the first 2 years:

1. initial preattachment phase, which begins at birth and extends through the first few weeks. Infants are predisposed to respond to stimuli, within selected ranges, that emanate from other species members. Associated with this predisposition are selected nondiscriminatory and nondifferential behaviors that promote contact with other members of the species (e.g., vocalizations, including distress cries).
2. phase of attachment in the making, which begins as important visual, auditory, and somatic discriminations become learned, leading to differential responsiveness by the infant. This phase usually ends sometime during the last half of the 1st year, with the formation of an identifiable attachment. Closely related to this phase is the onset of locomotor and reaching behaviors that facilitate proximity seeking as well as exploratory behaviors.

3. phase of clear-cut attachments, which is characterized by rapid increases in active proximity-seeking behaviors as the child learns to crawl or walk. This occurs at this stage even if the attachment object is not visible, an accomplishment possibly associated with the child's understanding of object permanence. Much has been made of the quality of infant-caregiver attachments. In general, sensitive, responsive, and accepting caregivers who cooperate, rather than interfere, with their child's efforts are likely to have infants who use them as a secure base from which to explore strange environments and are less likely to be upset over normal daily separations. Consequently, quality caregiving (responsive, sensitive, accepting, and cooperative infant-caregiver behavioral interactions) is likely to result in increased sociability, as well as increased cognitive growth, because the child has more chances for varied contacts with both the social and nonsocial world.
4. phase of a goal-directed partnership, which begins about age 2 and is characterized by the toddler's dawning recognition that it is possible to control others' behavior. With increases in cognitive abilities, the child recognizes that others have different points of view, as well as different feelings and motivations. This knowledge, crude and unsophisticated as it may be at this age, enables the child to begin to influence the caregiver's behavior more directly, possibly resulting in a more complex relationship between the child and caregiver.

Implications for Atypical Development

Several conditions related to attachment may contribute to nondesirable development: the presence or absence of an attachment figure, the nature of postnatal stimulation, and the overall significance of the relationship. Atypical development is likely to follow a failure to develop a secure attachment relationship or exposure to a stimulus-impoverished environment. For example, institutionalized infants do not differ from infants raised in traditional nuclear families until 3 to 4 months of age. At this time, however, institutionalized infants typically vocalize very little, cry very little, and do not adjust their posture when picked up by an adult. By 8 months of age, these infants are less interested in grasping and playing with toys, begin to lose interest in their external environment, and tend to show self-stimulatory behaviors, such as body rocking (Provence & Lipton, 1963).

For a number of reasons, it is difficult to pinpoint the precise factors that contribute to the retarded development of institutionalized children. Not only are the parents absent, but also there is a lack of stimulation in general. Minimal care facilities, by definition, are understaffed, and one attendant may be in charge of many infants. Also, infants placed in institutions may be different in some way from other infants. Consequently, it is difficult to say if the distinctive behavior of institutionalized infants is due to the lack of stimulation in general, the absence of a primary caretaker, or to some other characteristics possessed by such infants.

In his observations of Indian villages in Guatemala where infants are kept continuously with their mothers, Kagan (Kagan & Klein, 1973) found infants showing the same kind of listless and apathetic behavior as institutionalized infants. This suggests that the absence of a single consistent caretaker is not the critical factor. Both the Guatemalan children and institutionalized infants experienced little variety of cognitive and affective stimulation, had little opportunity to explore the environment, and experienced little interaction with adult caretakers. Hence, the critical factor producing nonalertness and general aloofness may be the absence of distinctive stimulation, stimulation intended to attract the infant's attention. There is some research support for this idea. Children who are raised in institutions that provide quality stimulation usually progress along the normal sequence of social development (Dennis, 1960). In fact, the social development of infants raised in good institutions, where the care received may be better than that obtained in the nuclear family, can be advanced (Blackbill, 1962). It appears that distinctive stimulation can be provided by a number of substitute caretakers, and adequate social development is likely to follow.

In evaluating the effects of an impoverished environment and failure of attachment, it is necessary to consider the long-term significance of the attachment bond. According to Bowlby (1969), the attachment relationship is the prototypic relationship upon which subsequent social interaction is based. The social skills and competencies acquired in this context presumably generalize to other relationships and facilitate interaction. A poor adjustment may hamper subsequent social adaptability.

A few current studies support Bowlby's original contention. Sroufe (1978) found that securely attached children were more self-directed and forceful than were insecurely attached children when confronted with a problem; in addition, at 3½ years of age, they seemed to be more generally competent in their social interactions. They readily engaged in social endeavors, were more frequently sought out by others, and were more likely to suggest activities. Similar results were obtained by Lieberman (1977), as well as Main and Weston (1981). The latter study indicated that 12-month-old infants who had close relationships with both parents were more likely to show "friendly responsiveness" in a play session with a strange adult actor; those infants who had insecure relationships were more likely to demonstrate "conflict behavior." Other evidence was obtained in a study by Pastor (1981), who found that securely attached 2-year-olds were more sociable and positively oriented toward peers, while those with resistant attachments (those who seek out, then resist, contact with the caregiver) appeared to be stressed and ignored peer offers. Infants with avoidant attachments (those who do not seek contact with the caregiver) participated actively with others but were rated as negative toward others.

To the degree that a good attachment is predictive of social effectiveness up to 3½ years later, it would seem that a poor attachment would pose long-term disadvantages for the young child. Work by Egeland and Sroufe (1981) indicated that, at 12 and 18 months of age, abused children were far less likely to experience secure attachments. In addition, data collected by Egeland and Sroufe indicated that some infants experienced a secure attachment despite maltreatment. However, these cases were marked either by a supportive family member who may have fostered the attachment or a particularly robust infant. Consequently, it seems that the nature of an attachment, as well as its long-term significance, is a product of the complex interaction of infant characteristics, parenting, and social climate. In this context, Crockenberg (1981) investigated the combined effects of infant irritability, maternal responsiveness, and social support on attachment. Her data indicated that social support (defined in terms of the cooperative activities of family members in regard to infant care) was the best predictor of a good attachment. Social support seems to be most important to mothers of irritable babies. In addition, it may counter the effects on the child of unresponsive mothering.

Taken together, these studies make it clear that a complex web of factors influences attachment. The difficulty of drawing firm conclusions concerning causality and making firm predictions concerning the long-term impact of attachment is compounded by the correlational nature of the evidence. This is a particularly important consideration in evaluating the future consequences of secure or insecure attachments. For example, the finding that children who had secure attachments were socially more effective at the age of 3½ years than those who did not may be explainable in terms of other factors that differentiated between the groups of children, such as their temperament, parenting style, and frequency of peer interaction opportunities.

Infants seem to possess a remarkable capacity for recovery. Retardation in development in the 1st year of life is a poor predictor of future functioning. With age, the effects of a deprived environment diminish, provided the environment does not remain substandard (Kagan, 1972). Hence, even though infants may not be able to reach their genetic potential because of inadequate stimulation during the 1st year of life, their social adaptability is not lost and can emerge later if appropriate stimulation is obtained. The lack of a primary caregiver and distinctive stimulation need not doom children to a life of permanent incompetence.

Individual Differences

The possibility that all children may be predisposed to develop an attachment bond implies that social development during the 1st year of life is fairly consistent among individuals and that there are few individual differences. Individual or personality differences emerge very early in life, however. The similarity of infants in appearance and behavior masks subtle individual differences that can be uncovered through careful observation and research. As early as the first few days in hospital nurseries, observers see apparent variations in fussiness, sleep patterns, and overall activity levels.

The etiology of individual differences so early in life is subject to debate. The fact that differences appear shortly after birth suggests genetic contributions; however, it could be argued that prenatal experiences are causal factors. It is also possible that different experiences shortly after birth are contributing factors. However, data concerning individual differences in sensory responsiveness and motor output gathered before appreciably different postnatal experience could occur seem to reflect congenital differences in neurological functioning (Korner, Kraemer, Hoffner, & Thoman, 1974). Other research has indicated relatively high heritability coefficients for anxiety ratings and persistence of goal-oriented behavior (Gottesman, 1963; Torgeson & Kringlen, 1978).

Also of interest is the long-term stability of these differences found early in life and the contribution of temperament variations to later personality and social development. Klevjord-Rothbart (1981) found evidence of temporal stability between 3 and 12 months in activity level, smiling, and laughter. More impressive is the relative stability between 8 months and 7 years found by Goldsmith and Gottesman (1981). In a longitudinal study of the temperaments of identical twins, these authors obtained evidence of a strong genetic influence on activity level at 8 months of age, on task persistence and irritability at 4 years, and finally on active adjustment and fearfulness at 8 years of age.

One interesting aspect of individual differences investigated by Schaffer and Emerson (1964) is the tendency toward "cuddliness." It appears that some infants enjoy being held in the arms of adults and will readily adjust their posture for the maximum comfort of both infant and adult, while other infants dislike being restrained in this way. They found that cuddliness was not correlated with the degree to which caregivers handled the infant, suggesting that the way in which infants respond to being cuddled is not entirely dependent on the behavior of their caregivers. Moreover, this research indicated a tendency for infants to maintain the same degree of cuddliness over the first 18 months of life. In addition, it was found that noncuddling infants also reacted negatively to "nonsocial" situations that required restraint, such as being clothed or tucked into bed. Finally, it appeared that cuddlers and noncuddlers differed in how long they slept (with noncuddlers sleeping longer) and rate of motor development during the 1st year of life (with noncuddlers developing faster). The interesting consistencies across situations and time, as well as correlations with other behavior patterns, suggests that cuddliness is a dimension of personality at least partially dependent on genetic factors.

In one of the foremost studies on temperament variations, Thomas and Chess (1977) found consistent differences among individuals as infants and young children. This research indicated that children could be divided into three general types according to temperament: (1) the easy child; (2) the difficult child; and (3) the slow-to-warm-up child. Easy children seem to be the happiest; their reactions to stimuli tend to be predictable, and they seem to be quite adaptable. Difficult children are substantially less predictable and react negatively to new stimulus situations. Slow-to-warm-up children do not seem to be quite as negative as difficult children, but they do not adapt as quickly as easy children. Even though their process of adaptation is quite slow, the result is usually positive.

These individual differences found early in life are significant not only because of their temporal stability, but also because of their implications for the course of social development. As previously discussed, social development is a dynamic process involving a complex interaction of genetic, maturational, and environmental factors. Insofar as these variations in makeup are fairly stable across time, they would influence how parents and siblings respond to the young child, which in turn would affect the continued development of the child. Indicative of this is research by Buss, Block, and Block (1980), who found individual stability in activity levels over a number of years and a relationship between activity level and a variety of personality characteristics. Highly active infants were less inhibited, less reserved, less controlled and compliant, and more manipulative, outgoing, and competitive. These personality variations seem to result from the influence of initial temperament variations on the responses of significant others to the child. This possibility is supported in another study by Buss (1981), in which parents of highly active children reported getting into power struggles and competition with their children.

The long-term consequences of others' reactions to a child's temperament could be disadvantageous for the young child. There is evidence that mothers have difficulty forming attachments with infants who seem to be congenitally irritable, and the resulting relationship seems to be detrimental to subsequent social development. Furthermore, if a "handling parent" has a noncuddling infant, the parent may become frustrated and alter approaches to the infant in a way that produces nondesirable effects. Thomas and Chess (1977) found that parents of difficult children either felt threatened or anxious as parents or became resentful of their children. Such a mismatch between an infant's behavioral style and parent preferences is a potential threat to the parent-child relationship and the continued welfare of the child. Indeed, difficult children are more likely to develop behavior disorders later in their development (Thomas & Chess, 1977).

RESPONSIVENESS TO PEERS

The attachment process, which is focused primarily on infant-caregiver interactions, heightens an infant's responsiveness to other members of the same species.

As Suomi and Harlow (1972) point out, however, peer contacts are the "primary vehicle for shaping genetically acquired potential into competent and adaptive social activity" (p. 176). Working with rhesus monkeys, Harlow and his colleagues found that infants who had been raised with their mothers but without peer contact did not develop normal social behaviors. When eventually allowed to interact with peers, those few monkeys who approached a peer exhibited not playfulness, but a high amount of aggression. Likewise, infant rhesus monkeys separated at birth from their mothers and raised only with peers also displayed maladaptive behaviors, although they formed quite strong attachments to their peers.

Involvement with peers contributes not only to "normal" sociability, but also to increases in the complexity of social behaviors. Several studies support such an inference. Mueller and Lucas (1975) describe a turn-taking rhythmicity as characteristic of toddlers' social interactions, suggesting that there are differences between single message-response interactions and sustained interactions. Mueller and Brenner (1977) followed up on this suggestion in a longitudinal study of social interaction patterns that occurred naturally among male infants in two specially formed play groups. In one group, the mean age was 12 months; in the other, 16.5 months. These groups met weekly with two teachers who were instructed not to teach the children how to play. Data for this study came from four separate observations of pairs of children, taken over a 7-month interval.

Central to this study is the distinction that Mueller and Brenner made between socially directed behavior and social interaction. Socially directed behavior was assessed by observing the direction of a child's gaze to infer when an action was directed to another child. Considered essentially a cognitive component of social behavior, a socially directed behavior could consist not only of simple coordinations between looking and one other action (e.g., smiling, waving, vocalizing), but also of more complex combinations (e.g., looking at, vocalizing to, and waving to a peer). This latter type was termed a coordinated socially directed behavior. Social interactions consisted of connected and alternating socially directed behaviors. Consequently, growth of sociability across the 2nd year was viewed "as a progressive series of combinations of formerly separate social behaviors" (p. 857).

Data analysis revealed that prolonged acquaintance with peers was significant only to the development of coordinated socially directed behaviors, which, in turn, enabled sustained and reciprocal social interactions. Mueller and Brenner concluded that development of mechanisms of social interchange with peers is not just the result of maturational processes or generalizations from infant-caregiver interactions; instead, prolonged acquaintance with peers, beginning with object-oriented play, contributes significantly to the development of more complex social interchanges. (For a comprehensive review of the value of peers to social development, see Asher & Gottman, 1981.)

DEVELOPING SOCIAL BEHAVIORS

Social behaviors may be broadly classified as prosocial or antisocial. Prosocial behaviors are commonly viewed as interpersonal unifiers, drawing people closer together and fostering warmth and positive regard between individuals. Prosocial behaviors include play, empathy, altruism (e.g., sharing, helping) and cooperation. As Radke-Yarrow and Zahn-Waxler (1976) point out, prosocial behaviors vary in their appearance, intensity, and duration according to characteristics of the situation. In addition, prosocial responding stems from a variety of different motivational bases, including (1) expectations of approval, (2) prevailing norms of responsibility, and (3) the actor's level of cognitive and social skill. On the other end of this social behavioral continuum, antisocial behaviors, including aggression and competition, tend to increase the psychological distance between individuals and, consequently, do not contribute to the establishment of positive interpersonal relationships.

Play

Children's play behavior is now being recognized as a significant factor in the development of cognitive abilities (Fein, 1981; Ghiaci & Richardson, 1980; Ungerer, Zelazo, Kearsley, & O'Leary, 1981), social behaviors (Guralnick, 1981; Vandenberg, 1981), and perhaps also in language development. In addition, play behavior is coming under increasing scrutiny as a variable to be considered in atypical development (Ungerer & Sigman, 1981; Whittaker, 1980), and as both an assessment (Belsky & Most, 1981) and an intervention strategy (Guralnick, 1981; Pelligrini, 1980). The theories of Jean Piaget are largely responsible for this changing view of the mediating or supportive intellectual function ascribed to play behavior.

During the child's sensorimotor and preoperational years, the development of play appears to be related to developing sociability. Piaget (1952) defines play as an assimilatory function. The infant uses play to incorporate novel experiences into existing modes of action or concepts. Thus, for Piaget, play serves an adaptive function, enabling the young child to increase cognitive functioning. Correspondingly, increases in cognitive sophistication enable more complex social adaptability. During the six sensorimotor stages, Piaget describes the development of play in tandem with the development of the ability to comprehend means-end relationships. Putting means together to achieve a goal is problem-solving behavior; manipulating means solely for the pleasure derived, with no attempt at means-end integration, is play. Thus, play can exist only when the infant begins to understand separation of means from ends. This ability begins to appear during the third sensorimotor stage and shows major changes during the fourth stage, when the infant begins ritual play, that is, the frequent and deliberate repetition of sequences of interesting behaviors. In the fifth stage, the infant can begin to maintain lengthy and repeated back-and-forth interchanges with the environment—the social world of people and objects. Finally, during the sixth stage, the child uses the newly acquired ability to represent experiences symbolically to begin "pretend" play. Table 9-3 shows the changes in both play and imitation during the sensorimotor years. (See Fein, 1981, for a thorough review of pretend play.)

Play during Early Childhood

The symbolic schemes that make their appearance in the sixth stage of the sensorimotor period are, in reality, transitional; they are self-oriented, repeating only the child's own actions. Beginning at approximately age 2, however, these symbolic schemes give way to symbolic games as the character of play becomes less self-oriented and, instead, provides the child with a means to assimilate reality to the ego without the need to accommodate and subsequently adapt too early to a reality not yet well understood.

Piaget divided symbolic games into several levels, ranging over the preoperational period of cognitive development. The first and second stages involve symbolic games that

1. imply representation of an absent object, since the child is making a comparison between a given and an imagined object
2. imply make-believe or pretense, since the comparison being made is distorting assimilation (e.g., a box is a glass)
3. subordinate only the sensorimotor practice element, which, in reality, may continue as a part of play throughout life
4. deviate more and more from mere practice as they acquire additional functions (e.g., compensation, fulfillment of wishes, and resolution of conflicts)

First-stage symbolic games, covering ages 2 to 3 or 4, may be divided into several levels:

1A. projection of symbolic schemes onto new objects. The child, using imitation and now familiar self-oriented schemes, begins to apply these to other objects or people. Consequently, not only is object play increasing in importance, but also such play indicates that the symbol has now become completely disassociated from sensorimotor practice and is used as an independent representation.

Table 9-3 Outline of Sensorimotor Play and Imitation

Stage and General Characteristic	*Imitation*	*Play*
1. Reflexive activity (birth to about 1 month): reflexes more efficient; addition of more voluntary movements	No imitation of new responses; may be stimulated to respond by external events (e.g., may start crying when hears other infants crying)	No evidence of play
2. Primary circular activity (about 1 to 4 months): repetition of interesting body movements	No imitation of new responses; when *others* imitate infants' responses, infants may repeat or intensify own responses	Primary circular reactions repeated for the pleasure of repetition (called functional assimilation)
3. Secondary circular reactions (about 4 to 8 months): repetition of interesting external events	No imitation of new responses; infants imitate model's response if that response is familiar to them but they can imitate in this way only responses that they can see or hear themselves perform	Relaxed repetition of responses distinguished from the serious business of attempting to adapt to new experiences; activity enjoyed for its own sake without need for external reinforcement
4. Coordination of schemes (about 8 to 12 months): schemes combined to obtain a goal	Limitations of stage 3 overcome; infants can imitate simple new responses, even those they cannot see or hear themselves perform	Goal-directed behavior abandoned in favor of playing with obstacle; ritual play
5. Tertiary circular reactions (about 12 to 18 months): repetition varied for novelty effects	More precise imitation of behaviors of a model, including more subtle or complex responses; infants can experiment with different ways of imitating different models	Newly acquired responses rapidly converted to play rituals
6. Representational thought (about 18 to 24 months): thinking prior to acting	Imitation of complex new behaviors; children imitate actions of objects as well as people, begin deferred imitation	Symbolic play (pretense or make-believe)

1B. projection of schemes of imitation onto new objects. The child borrows schemes from models, using imitation, and applies them to others; such schemes do not form part of the child's own activity in the sense that he or she is drawing from already learned self-oriented symbolic schemes.
2A. simple identification of one object with another. For example, the child, seeing Mom's hair, may say (cat) "fur" or, seeing a shell, may say "cup."
2B. games of imitation. The child pretends to be another and carries out the other's activity (e.g., pretending to be mother, the doctor, the cleaning person).
3A. symbolic combinations. The child becomes better able to construct whole scenes and not just isolated fragments, and this enables the child to begin to extend the ability to reproduce reality.
3B. compensatory combinations. This play is still characterized by the use of make-believe to assimilate reality, but the focus is more on correcting reality, doing something through make-believe that is prohibited in reality, or neutralizing something fearful that exists in reality (play as catharsis).
3C. liquidation of combinations. In 3B, a child faced with a difficult situation can either compensate for it or accept it. In 3C, the child tries to relive it by changing it symbolically in order to disassociate it from its unpleasant context.

Second-stage symbolic play, covering years 3 or 4 to approximately 7, is marked by several new characteristics, brought about by the fact that symbolic games begin to lose some of their importance. They do not necessarily become less numerous or less intense, however; instead, the symbol moves closer to reality, thus losing some of its playful aspects. (Thought is also becoming more logical and orderly.) New characteristics of play at this stage include (1) the increasing orderliness of playful constructions, (2) an increasing desire for accuracy and exactness in the child's imitation of reality, and (3) the appearance of collective symbolism that involves the differentiation and adjustment of roles. Hence, social interactions become more important, a finding borne out by Parten's (1932) description of social play among preschool children. (See Garwood, 1982, for a more thorough review of Piaget's views on play and for suggestions regarding its use in assessment and intervention with handicapped children.)

Development of Imitative Ability

As McCall, Parke, and Kavanough (1977) point out, very little research effort has been spent in examining the development of imitative skills—in spite of the role imitation appears to play in learning behavioral standards, information-processing strategies, judgmental orientations, and conceptual schemes (Bandura, 1971).

Piaget (1952) presents the most complete treatment of the development of imitation, which he says begins sometime during the 1st month of life and becomes cognitively functional around the age of 2. Pseudoimitation, which is confined to elementary vocal and visual imitation (repeating a model's sound or looking where the model looks) and to grasping, begins in the second sensorimotor stage and continues into the third. It is characterized by vocal contagion and mutual imitation. In the former, the model stimulates vocal activity in the infant by making different sounds and encouraging the infant to reproduce these sounds. The latter consists of reciprocal imitative behavior; first the model reproduces a sound the infant has just made, then the infant imitates the model imitating the infant. This interaction continues in a gamelike fashion until one or the other tires or loses interest. Apparently, both types of activity serve a social function, encouraging interaction between the infant and others. In addition, such activity probably helps infants to begin differentiating themselves from the surroundings and to begin developing a sense of control over surroundings.

Sometime during the third sensorimotor stage, pseudoimitation becomes true imitation. Infants begin more systematically to imitate the acts of a model—but only if the behaviors are in their repertoires and are visible on their body. Research has placed this last contention in doubt, however. Meltzoff and Moore (1977) have found that infants as young as 2 weeks can imitate lip, mouth, tongue, and finger movements, not all of which are visible on the body. During the fourth and fifth sensorimotor stages, true imitation becomes more efficient as infants become capable of imitating new acts by a model and acts that are not visible on their body. Finally, in the last stage of sensorimotor development (associated with the development of symbolic thought), infants begin to be able to imitate complex new models (even nonhuman and nonliving ones) without extensive trial and error, probably by using newly developed representational abilities to "try out" the behavior mentally before carrying it out physically. In addition to this more sophisticated imitation ability, infants can, for the first time, imitate models who are not actually present (deferred imitation). This new ability is important to the development of play, which, in turn, is important to subsequent cognitive and social development.

Several studies suggest that imitation may be a significant factor in the development of social skills. Being imitated by others helps children to understand how their behavior can influence others' behavior (McCall et al., 1977; Mueller & Lucas, 1975; Thelen, Frautschi, Fehrenbach, & Kirkland, 1978). Also, being imitated may help develop mature social interactions. The social interactions of young children are proximal object oriented; as Mueller and Lucas note, mature social interactions are characterized as distal-relational. When a child is imitated, from a distance and without being touched by another child, the salience of the distance and the relational nature of the interchange may help the imitated child to develop more mature social relations.

The rapid advances in language development during the preoperational years further enable young children to deal with the world symbolically; they are no longer bound by concrete reality and no longer restricted to sensorimotor actions in order to obtain knowledge. This major qualitative change in cognitive development has important implications for social development. The ability to represent experience symbolically and to convey this to others enhances social functioning.

Egocentrism is one aspect of cognitive functioning that can hamper acquisition of new social skills. Children in the preoperational stage are highly self-centered and have difficulty interpreting or assimilating information from others' frames of reference. Many social behaviors require a sensitivity to behaviors and needs of other people. Cooperation, for example, requires the ability to coordinate behavior with the behavior of another person. Egocentric children, who are unable to put themselves in the position of another, are consequently handicapped in the acquisition of social skills.

The progression of developing social skills is one of movement from the self-centered or egocentric to the socially centered or sociocentric, paralleling a child's developing cognitive maturity. As children mature cognitively, their ability to shift focus while interpreting information and to consider alternative frames of reference increases, enhancing the development of social interaction skills. When this happens, new information is available, and a new source of reinforcement comes from children's anticipation of responses to their own actions (Asher & Renshaw, 1981; Flavell & Ross, 1981; Selman, 1981).

Peer influences, increases in cognitive development, and developments of imitative ability affect both friendship formation, one of the more significant aspects of social development, and the nature of the interaction that takes place in social relationships.

Friendships

By approximately age 4, children no longer show much concern over separation from their primary caregivers, either for brief separations, such as leaving home to go to nursery school (Shirley & Payntz, 1941), or for longer ones (Heinicke & Westheimer, 1965). About this same time, the frequency of peer contacts begins to increase (Heathers, 1955). Peer contacts continue to become more frequent, while the frequency of adult contacts diminishes until about age 7, when peer interactions become about as frequent as adult interactions. Friendships begin to develop concomitantly with increasing peer contact.

Friendships are interpersonal social relationships that occur between two individuals and can vary in duration and intensity. Friendships originate from shared activities, values, or goals, as well as from recognition that the needs of one individual can serve, to some extent, the needs of the other, and vice versa.

Friendships also appear to have developmental trends. Bigelow (1977) has tentatively identified three stages of cognitive development in friendships:

1. situational. Friendships are based on common activities and propinquity.
2. contractual. Friendships are based on adherence to socially sanctioned rules governing behavior.
3. empathic. Friendships are based on mutual understanding, intimacy, and self-disclosure.

Similar supportive developmental trends have also been reported by Douvan and Adelson (1966), Livesley and Bromley (1973), and Berndt (1978). Also, both Berndt (1981) and Selman (1981) have proposed models for studying friendship issues. Taken together, these data indicate that friendship behavior, like other sociocognitive variables, undergoes developmental change.

Empathy

Before prosocial interchanges between any two people can be effective, at least one must be aware of the feelings of the other; willing to share, to some extent, those feelings; and willing to act in certain ways as a result of sharing in the other's emotional response. Consequently, empathy includes cognitive components (knowledge of what another is feeling) as well as affective components (sharing in another's emotionality). Empathy may be regarded as a motivational process, since the degree of empathy one feels for another apparently determines, in part, willingness to share, donate, help, and comfort (Hoffman, 1977a; Shantz, 1975).

Empathy is typically measured by one of two different techniques, one based primarily on its cognitive component and one based primarily on its affective component. The cognitive measure, Borke's Interpersonal Perception Test (1971), is used to assess a child's knowledge of four emotional states: happy, sad, fearful, and angry. Borke (1971) studied 200 children between the ages of 3 and 8, and found that 60% of the youngest were able to identify "happy" correctly; these same children, however, failed to identify sad or angry feelings. With increasing age, children became more accurate in identifying affective states.

Borke originally conducted this study to test Piaget's contention that very young children (below age 5) are too egocentric to take the role of another. If role-taking ability is a form of empathy, Borke's younger subjects should not have performed as they did; their egocentrism would have interfered with their ability to infer correctly what another child was feeling. Borke concluded, therefore, that Piaget was probably wrong in his assertion that very young children would not be able to take the role of another. When Chandler and Greenspan (1972) replicated Borke's study, however, they concluded that, although their data supported Borke's age trends, the ability of the younger child to identify correctly what another child was feeling was probably due more to primitive projection or identification mechanisms than to a lack of egocentrism.

To measure affective empathy, Feshbach and Roe (1968) used slides depicting a story sequence and then asked, "How do you feel?" followed by "How does the story child feel?" Feshbach and Roe found that children did not always answer the two questions with the same emotional response and concluded that cognitive empathy may be a precursor of affective empathy, a conclusion subsequently upheld by Mood, Johnson, and Shantz (1974). Such an interpretation is also consistent with Flavell's (1977) belief that social cognitions follow a developmental sequence of existence, need, inference, and application. In support, Shantz (1975) concludes, on the basis of her research review, that "accurate empathy concerning simple emotions is achieved by preschool children when the situation the other person is in is familiar to the child and/or the other person is substantially similar to the child. Accurate understanding of these same emotions is not usually attained until middle or late childhood when the situations and people judged have low similarity and low familiarity to the child" (p. 281). (See Hoffman, 1981, for a review of empathy as a social cognition variable.)

Altruism

Voluntary behaviors that are intended to help others without anticipation of personal gain as a result (Leeds, 1963; Mussen & Eisenberg-Berg, 1977) are termed altruistic or helping. As a class of self-sacrificial and prosocial behaviors, altruism includes behaviors such as sharing with others, donating to others, and offering aid or comfort to others in distress. The reference point is the other person(s); one individual does something for another, something that, strictly speaking, is not required and cost the actor while yielding no reward. As should be immediately apparent, such a behavioral action is inconsistent with the view that humans are essentially hedonistic. For this reason, altruism has been a difficult variable to pinpoint (Katz, 1972).

While various theoretical approaches have been used in attempts to explain altruism, recent efforts have examined the cognitive nature of altruism. Hoffman (1976) has proposed that empathy is the base of altruism. This makes intuitive sense, for acting to help another in distress requires that the actor correctly recognize cues given by others. Hoffman's view has recently received empirical support from Leiman (1978), who exposed 50 kindergarten and first-grade children to a special TV program that was designed to allow children to interact with the actor, whose face revealed his emotional distress over losing his marbles. Children judged to be empathic were subsequently also more altruistic; they donated more of their own marbles to the TV actor than did nonempathic children.

Most research with children reveals a positive correlation between altruism and age, but this correlation does not appear until late childhood (Bryan, 1975). Prior to this time, altruism does not appear to be correlated with age (Buckley, Siegel, & Ness, 1979). Several explanations have been offered for this uneven developmental progression. Bryan offers convincing, research-based arguments for a cognitive developmental viewpoint, one that relates the late childhood increases in altruism to decreases in egocentric responding and to increases in ability to make mature moral judgments (which is, in itself, regarded by many scientists as a cognitive development phenomenon). Bryan's conclusions are further supported by research findings (Iannotti, 1978; Buckley et al., 1979; Raviv, Bar-Tal, & Lewis-Levin, 1980).

Cooperation and Competition

Cooperation has been defined as mutual coordination of individual actions to attain a goal (Nelson & Madsen, 1968). Anthropologists believe it evolved in early humans because it had survival value in a hunter-gatherer culture (Fishbein, 1976). Competition is individually oriented goal seeking, usually at the expense of others; it, too, has cultural origins. McClelland (1961) has traced the rise of individually oriented achievement behavior to the Protestant work ethic: individuals must work hard while on earth, constantly striving for perfection, so that they may be rewarded with a place in heaven. Goal attainment through cooperation usually results in group-shared rewards, but competition typically involves individual reward. Consequently, competition and cooperation behaviors cannot occur simultaneously.

As Bryan's review (1975) indicates, research has traditionally shown developmental progressions in both cooperation and competition; cooperation increases, then decreases, with age while competition increases. For example, Friedrich and Stein (1973) found that cooperative behaviors in children aged 3.8 to 5.5 years correlated significantly with age (0.31 for boys and 0.30 for girls). Parten (1933) reported similar age trends among children aged 2 to 5 years. Both sets of data are based on observations of naturally occurring behaviors. Beginning about school age, however, cooperative behaviors appear to wane while competitive behaviors increase in frequency (Knight & Kagan, 1977).

In contrast to these traditional beliefs, some researchers report opposing developmental trends. McClintock and associates (McClintock & Moskowitz, 1976; McClintock, Moskowitz, & McClintock, 1977), after studying the development of cooperation and competition in nursery school children, report the following developmental trends:

> Very young children are principally own-gain oriented. . . . they "wanna get lots" of whatever . . . is afforded them. As they grow older they learn to make choices in the conflict and coordinative tasks that are consistent with achieving valued own outcomes. The acquisition of appropriate competitive choices occurs earlier, between 4 and 5

> years of age, than the acquisition of cooperative ones, between 6 and 7 years of age. Finally, between the ages of 5 and 6, children begin to make choices in the individualistic task that indicate that children at times are willing to forego their own gain for a competitive advantage. This would imply that competition is achieving the status of an autonomous social motive. (McClintock et al., 1977, p. 1085)

Regardless of the sequence, the outcome appears the same. Apparently, children are initially socialized toward behaving prosocially, but "as the child develops, the socialization emphasis may well change toward greater stress on achievement of individual skills. For older children, when there is an opportunity to compete or cooperate, they compete" (Bryan, 1975, p. 135).

Researchers using different research strategies may be assessing different forms of cooperative and competitive behaviors, leading to conflicts and discrepancies in findings. Furthermore, most developmental research forces a choice between only two types of strategies: cooperation or competition; however, as Knight and Kagan (1977) point out, "These measures have confounded distinct outcomes and leave ambiguous the motivational bases for observed differences" (p. 1386). To correct this, Kagan and his colleagues have devised the social behavior scale, which measures three distinct prosocial motives: altruism (here defined as obtaining absolute gains for another), equality (avoiding disequilibrium between own and other's gains), and group enhancement (obtaining joint gains). This scale also measures two distinct competitive motives: rivalry (avoiding absolute gains for others) and superiority (obtaining relative gains for self).

Kagan and his colleagues have used this approach in studying cultural differences in social motives. In one study, Knight and Kagan (1977) examined age, culture, social class, and sex differences across these social motives. Their subjects were children in two age groups, 5 to 6 and 7 to 9 years: 120 middle-class Anglo-Americans, 39 lower-class Anglo-Americans, and 38 Mexican-Americans. These researchers found the following regarding differential use of social motives:

- Increases with age in rivalry and superiority choices characterized both middle-class and lower-class Anglo-American children's behavior, but not Mexican-American children's behavior. "Both Anglo-American groups are increasingly competitive with age, while with age the Mexican-American group tended to make more prosocial choices. Thus, ethnic background may not be associated with just the magnitude, but also with the direction of developmental trends" (p. 1391).
- Among the four possible response choices (altruism and group enhancement, equality, rivalry, and superiority), the two competitive responses occur more frequently than the two cooperative ones.

Although children may generally become more competitive with age, they still use cooperative strategies. Furthermore, their reasons for selecting one of several available prosocial or antisocial responses over another appear to be tied to differing motivational bases and environmental conditions.

Aggression

The social behavior least conducive to positive interpersonal relationships is aggression; hence, aggressive behavior is regarded as antisocial. Aggressive behaviors are typically harmful (mentally, physically, or both) to those on the receiving end, and the affected individual is likely to respond by fleeing; striking back orally, physically, or both; or submitting.

Aggression is a difficult construct to define. As Johnson (1972) points out, a great deal depends on how the act is interpreted, and this requires further consideration of the context in which the act occurs. A nursery school child who pushes aside a peer while rushing to participate in "juice and cookie time" may not intend to harm the peer. She may be too young (i.e., lack the necessary cognitive skills) to realize that her action could cause the other child to fall and get hurt. Is this an aggressive act? If this same child pushes a peer to keep the peer from obtaining a toy that she wants, is this an aggressive act? Is spanking a child an act of parental aggression or an act designed to help the child learn quickly that certain behaviors can result in painful consequences? Is smiling and calling a good friend a "bastard" when he has just won a coveted prize an act of endearment or an act of verbal aggression?

In an attempt to bridge these interpretation problems, Maccoby and Jacklin (1974) offer a general definition that treats aggression as a "loose cluster of actions and motives that are not necessarily related to one another. The central theme is the intent of one individual to hurt another" (p. 227). Maccoby and Jacklin further qualify aggression as motivated either by the desire to inflict pain on another or by the desire to have power over others. This general definition focuses on the actor's intentions and motivational bases more than on the act itself. Of course, since behavior is not marked by discrete units, determining intent or motive is always difficult, even more so when complex relations generate multiple motives or intentions.

The fact that aggressive behavior is, in part, rooted in biological functioning is clear from studies of animals (Edwards, 1969) and humans (Ehrhardt & Baker, 1974). Consequently, aggression can also be viewed from an evolutionary perspective. Darwin believed that such behavior helped perpetuate the species, for it helped the individual gain access to survival resources. Consistent with this view is Wynne-Edward's position (1962) that aggressive activity helps control population density by determining allotments of scarce resources.

Because aggressive behavior has ties to biological-evolutionary developments, ethologists have also speculated about its functions; they offer perhaps the only positive view of aggressive behavior. Lorenz (1966) believes that aggression is central to group cohesiveness and interpersonal attraction. Aggression is the basis for social behavior because it determines dominance hierarchies that, in turn, facilitate positive interactions between members of a species close together in the dominance hierarchy. This closeness promotes survival by helping group members avoid potentially negative or harmful interactions with those more powerful than they.

Evidence for this interesting ethological perspective is beginning to emerge from studies of children's interactions with peers. Strayer and Strayer (1976) examined agonism and dominance relations among 18 preschoolers observed at free play. The Strayers distinguished agonism, which they defined as a class of dyadic interactions, from aggression, which they felt referred only to an individual's behavior. Initiated agonism was measured by a physical attack category (e.g., pushing, biting, kicking), a threat-gesture category (e.g., gestural intentions to bite or kick), and an object/position category (struggle with or without physical contact). The Strayers also examined five responses to initiated agonism: (1) submission, (2) help seeking, (3) counterattack, (4) object/position loss, and (5) no response. Their results showed that 39% of agonistic episodes among these preschoolers involved some form of physical attack, 33% some form of threat-gesture, and 28% some form of object/position struggle. The dominant response modes were submission (26%) and loss of object or position (26%). As expected, the observed dominance hierarchy within this group predicted the outcome of 96% of the observed initiated agonism interactions. The Strayers concluded that the low incidence of counterattacks suggests that dominance hierarchies in children's groups serve an adaptive function by minimizing aggression within the group; consequently, group or social cohesiveness is maintained.

Further ethological evidence is provided by Shuckin and Smith (1977), who found that not only could the observed hierarchy be used to predict 80% of aggressive incident outcomes, but also preschool children in the group they observed were capable of correctly rank-ordering group members into the existing hierarchy. From another perspective, Camras' (1977) study of facial expressions used by kindergarten children observed in same sex dyadic interaction indicated that an "aggressive face" was associated with attempts by a child to retain his or her access to a disputed object. This face was characterized by "one or more of the following components . . . : (a) lowered brows, (b) stares. . . , (c) face thrust forward, (d) lips pressed together with tightened mouth corners, and (g) nose wrinkle" (p. 1432).

Hartup (1974) has speculated that aggressive behavior is related to level of cognitive development. Hartup bases his argument on the distinction between hostile (person-oriented) and instrumental (behavior aimed at removing a goal block) aggression. Hostile aggression usually occurs in response to threats to self-esteem. Consequently, this form of aggression should show cognitive development trends because its prerequisites include the establishment of a stable self-concept and the development of the ability to infer others' intentions, a social cognition process. Preliminary research data (Garwood & Spera, Note 1) so far support Hartup's views.

Age-Related Changes in Aggressive Behavior

Assessing aggressive behavior is especially difficult in the first 2 years of life because infants and toddlers are not yet sufficiently socialized. Their attempts to get what they want are not yet mediated by appropriate behavior control mechanisms, such as a tolerance of delays or a trust in the future occurrence of desirable events. Therefore, it is difficult to determine if their behavior is really aggressiveness or simply unchecked assertiveness. Goodenough (1931), Bronson (1975), and Mueller and Lucas (1975) all point out that the frequency of disruptive interchanges between peers begins to decline during the 2nd year. This decrease parallels increases in both locomotor and communication skills. Communication is especially critical to the socialization of behavior mechanisms related to the control of aggressive behaviors.

Between ages 2 and 5, physical aggression begins to diminish, but verbal aggression begins to increase (Goodenough, 1931). Hartup's data (1974) are consistent with earlier studies, such as Goodenough's, indicating a general decline in aggression beginning right after early childhood. Hartup conducted a naturalistic observation study of aggressive interchanges in 102 lower-class children, aged 4 through 7 years, over a 10-month period. Aggression was defined as "intentional physical and verbal responses that are directed toward an object or another person and that have the capacity to damage or injure" (p. 339). Hartup's findings reveal that the older children (those over 5) were significantly less aggressive than the younger ones. Of the 102 children, 84 initiated aggressive activity; a significantly higher percentage of aggression among the older children was classed as hostile or person-oriented. The younger children, those under 6 years, however, expressed more instrumental aggressive activity.

> For younger children, when such antecedents elicit hostile outbursts, half (48%) take the form of bodily injury (hitting) and half consist of reciprocated derogation, threats, and tattling (52%). Among the older children, however, derogation shows a decided tendency to produce reciprocal derogation: only 22% of hostile responses to derogation involved hitting while 78% involved some type of insult or reciprocated threat to self-esteem. (p. 340)

Sex Differences in Aggressive Behavior

The absence of sex differences in aggressive behavior during infancy (Van Lieshout, 1975), the emergence of such differences beginning about age 2½ or 3 (Smith & Green, 1975), and the continued presence of such differences thereafter suggest the role played by the larger culture, represented in specific child-rearing practices, in fostering and maintaining differences in the kinds and amounts of aggressive behaviors manifested in the behavior of males and females. Maccoby and Jacklin (1974) and Oetzel (1966) have reviewed research dealing with sex differences in the expression of aggressive behavior, and their reviews document the consistently more aggressive behavior tolerated in males. The Maccoby and Jacklin review attributes these differences, at least in part, to biological differences (e.g., differences in androgen levels). However, Tieger (1980) maintains that differential cultural expectations and reinforcements contribute to such differences, since sex differences are reliably observed only after children reach the age of 5. For example, in a study comparing the behavior of highly aggressive adolescent males with a control group of more normally aggressive males, Bandura and Walters (1959) found that higher levels of aggression were attributable, in part, to parental behaviors. The parents of the highly aggressive boys actively encouraged their sons' aggressiveness significantly more than did the parents of the matched controls.

CONCLUSIONS

One has but to reflect briefly on American life to realize that our culture emphasizes both prosocial and antisocial behaviors in child-rearing. For example, some forms of achievement depend on competition, such as business success, individual sports (e.g., golf or swimming), games (e.g., backgammon or checkers), and education. Others require cooperation for success, such as production line performance, educational group projects, civil service employment, and team sports. Of course, some achievements require both cooperation and competition; for example, cooperation among team players is necessary for successful team competition. Therefore, it appears that group survival depends on the effectiveness of socialization in fostering appropriate levels of both types of behaviors.

Ethologists and other scientists contend that certain social behaviors (e.g., aggression) are genetically based to facilitate species survival. Lorenz (1966), for example, has pointed out that aggression facilitates the formation of personal bonds (interpersonal closeness) between certain members of a particular species. Therefore, without aggression there is no "love." Strayer and Strayer (1976), likewise, argue that the formation of stable dominance hierarchies within groups serves to minimize within-group aggression, for, once learned, adherence to such hierarchies helps group members anticipate and consequently avoid possible harmful encounters with more powerful group members.

There has been considerable debate, however, over the role genes play in both prosocial and antisocial behavior development, particularly in regard to altruism. As summarized by Campbell (1975), the nature position has two different genetic bases. One, focusing on what Wilson (1976) refers to as "soft-core altruism," evolved as a result of selection on the individual level. According to Wilson, soft-core altruism is really disguised selfishness: "(T)he 'altruist' expects reciprocation from society for himself or his relatives. His good behavior is calculating, often in a wholly conscious way, and it is further orchestrated by the excruciatingly intricate sanctions and demands of society" (p. 371). The second genetic position treats altruism as a group-selection trait. Wilson describes this type of altruism as "hard-core altruism," since it refers to "a set of responses relatively unresponsive to reward and punishment beyond childhood. To the extent that . . . [it] . . . exists, it is likely to have evolved through interpopulation and kin selection and hence be directed at the altruist's closest relatives" (p. 371).

Campbell (1975) does not believe altrusim is the result of biological evolution. Instead, he argues the case for social evolution, an essentially nurture position. "By sociocultural evolution we mean, at a minimum, a selective cumulation of skills, technologies, recipes, customs, organizational structures, and the like, retained through purely social modes of transmission, rather than in the genes" (p. 1104). Campbell continues:

> Through social mechanisms of child socialization, reward and punishment, socially restricted learning opportunities, identification, imitation, emulation, indoctrination into tribal ideologies, languages and linguistic meaning systems, conformity pressures, social authority systems, and the like, it seems reasonable to me that sufficient retention machinery exists for a social evolution of adaptive social belief systems and organizational principles to have taken place. (p. 1107)

Kanfer (1979) presents the interactionists' position in this controversy. He states, "Regardless of the extent to which prosocial behaviors are genetically favored, any dispositional trends still need to be channeled towards socially beneficial behaviors. The critical point is that social demands and models can alter the rates and the direction of genetic dispositions that develop" (p. 235). Consequently, although social responding may be biologically based, it is intimately linked to the stability of the environment and of learned behavior control mechanisms that comprise much of what scientists mean when they refer to personality.

REFERENCE NOTE

Garwood, S.G., & Spera, S. Cognition and aggression: The influence of cognition on the display of aggression in young children. Research in progress.

REFERENCES

Ainsworth, M.D.S. The development of infant-mother interactions among the Ganda. In B.M. Foss (Ed.), *Determinants of infant behaviour II*. London: Methuen, 1963.

Ainsworth, M.D.S. Patterns of attachment behavior shown by an infant in interaction with his mother. *Merrill-Palmer Quarterly,* 1964, *10,* 51-58.

Ainsworth, M.D.S. *Infancy in Uganda: Infant care and the growth of love*. Baltimore: Johns Hopkins Press, 1967.

Ainsworth, M.D.S. Object relations, dependency, and attachment: A theoretical review of the infant-mother relationship. *Child Development,* 1969, *40,* 965-1025.

Ainsworth, M.D.S. Attachment and dependency: A comparison. In J.L. Gewirtz (Ed.), *Attachment and dependency*. New York: Wiley, 1972.

Ainsworth, M.D.S. *Anxious attachment and defensive reactions in a strange situation and relationship to behavior at home*. Paper presented at the meeting of the Society for Research in Child Development, Philadelphia, March 1973.

Ainsworth, M.D.S. *Attachment: Retrospect and prospect*. Presidential address given to the Society for Research in Child Development, San Francisco, 1979.

Ainsworth, M.D.S., & Bell, S.M. Attachment, exploration, and separation: Illustrated by the behavior of one-year-olds in a strange situation. *Child Development,* 1970, *41,* 49-67.

Ainsworth, M.D.S., Bell, S.M., & Slayton, D.J. Individual differences in the development of some attachment behaviors. *Merrill-Palmer Quarterly,* 1972, *18,* 123-143.

Allport, G. *Becoming: Basic considerations for a psychology of personality*. New Haven, Conn.: Yale University Press, 1955.

Asher, S.R., & Gottman J.M. (Eds.). *The development of children's friendships*. Cambridge: Cambridge University Press, 1981.

Asher, S.R., & Renshaw, P.D. Children without friends: Social knowledge and social skill training. In S.R. Asher & J.M. Gottman (Eds.), *The development of children's friendships*. Cambridge: Cambridge University Press, 1981.

Bandura, A. *Social learning theory*. Morristown, N.J.: General Learning Press, 1971.

Bandura, A. *Social learning theory* Englewood Cliffs, N.J.: Prentice-Hall, 1977.

Bandura, A., & Walters, R.H. *Adolescent aggression*. New York: Roland, 1959.

Bell, S.M. The development of the concept of object as related to infant-mother attachment. *Child Development,* 1970, *41,* 291-311.

Belsky, J., & Most, R.K. From exploration to play: A cross-sectional study of infant free play behavior. *Developmental Psychology,* 1981, *17,* 630-639.

Berndt, T.J. *Children's conception of friendship and the behavior expected of friends*. Paper given at the annual meeting of the American Psychological Association, Toronto, 1978.

Berndt, T.J. Relations between social cognition, nonsocial cognition, and social behavior: The case of friendship. In J.H. Flavell & L. Ross (Eds.), *Social cognitive development*. Cambridge: Cambridge University Press, 1981.

Bigelow, B.J. Children's friendship expectations: A cognitive-development study. *Child Development,* 1977, *48,* 246-253.

Blackbill, Y. *Research and clinical work with children*. Washington, D.C.: American Psychological Association, 1962.

Borke, H. Interpersonal perception of young children: Egocentrism or empathy. *Developmental Psychology,* 1971, *5,* 363-369.

Bowlby, J. The nature of the child's tie to his mother. *International Journal of Psycho-Analysis,* 1958, *39,* 350-373.(a)

Bowlby, J. Psychoanalysis and child care. In J.D. Sutherland (Ed.), *Psychoanalysis and contemporary theory*. London: Hogarth, 1958.(b)

Bowlby, J. *Attachment and loss* (Vol. 1). New York: Basic Books, 1969.

Bronson, W.C. Developments in behavior with age-mates during the second year of life. In M. Lewis & L.H. Rosenblum (Eds.), *Friendships and peer relations: The origins of behavior* (Vol. 4). New York: Wiley, 1975.

Bruner, J.S., Olver, R.R., & Greenfield, D.M. (Eds.). *Studies in cognitive growth*. New York: Wiley, 1966.

Bryan, J.H. Children's cooperation and helping behavior. In E.M. Hetherington (Ed.), *Review of child development research* (Vol. 5). Chicago: University of Chicago Press, 1975.

Buckley, N., Siegel, L.S., & Ness, S. Egocentrism, empathy, and altruistic behavior in young children. *Developmental Psychology,* 1979, *15,* 329-330.

Buss, D.M. Predicting parent-child interactions from children's activity level. *Developmental Psychology,* 1981, *12*(1), 59-65.

Buss, D.M., Block, J.H., & Block, J. Preschool activity level: Personality correlates and developmental implications. *Child Development,* 1980, *51,* 401-408.

Campbell, D.T. On the conflicts between biological and social evolution and between psychology and moral tradition. *American Psychologist,* 1975, *30,* 1103-1126.

Camras, L.A. Facial expressions used by children in a conflict situation. *Child Development,* 1977, *48,* 1431-1435.

Caudill, W., & Weinstein, H. Maternal care and infant behavior in Japan and America. *Psychiatry,* 1969, *32,* 12-43.

Chandler, M.J., & Greenspan, S. Ersatz egocentrism: A reply to H. Borke. *Developmental Psychology,* 1972, *7,* 104-106.

Clarke-Stewart, A. Dealing with the complexity of mother-child interaction. Paper presented at the Society for Research in Child Development. Denver, 1975.

Costello, C.G. Childhood depression. In E.J. Mash & L.G. Terdal (Eds.), *Behavioral assessment of childhood disorders*. New York: The Guilford Press, 1981.

Craig, H.B. A sociometric investigation of self-concept of the deaf child. *American Annals of the Deaf,* 1975, *110,* 456-478.

Crockenberg, S.B. Infant irritability, mother responsiveness, and social support influences on the security of infant-mother attachment. *Child Development,* 1981, *52,* 857-865.

Darbyshire, J.O. Play patterns in young children with impaired hearing. *Volta Review,* 1977, *79,* 19-26.

Davis, K. Extreme social isolation of a child. *American Journal of Sociology,* 1940, *45,* 554-565.

Dennis, W. Causes of retardation among institutional children: Iran. *Journal of Genetic Psychology,* 1960, *96,* 47-59.

Douvan, E., & Adelson, J. *The adolescent experience*. New York: Wiley, 1966.

Edwards, D.A. Early androgen stimulation and aggressive behavior in male and female mice. *Physiology and Behavior,* 1969, *4,* 333-338.

Egeland, B., & Sroufe, L.A. Attachment and early maltreatment. *Child Development,* 1981, *52,* 44-52.

Ehrhardt, A.A., & Baker, S.W. Fetal androgens, human central nervous system differentiation, and sex differences. In R.C. Friedman, R.M. Richart, & R.L. Vande Wiele (Eds.), *Sex differences in behavior*. New York: Wiley, 1974.

Eibl-Eibesfeldt. *Ethology: The biology of behavior*. New York: Holt, Rinehart and Winston, 1970.

Emde, R.N., Baensbauer, T.J., & Harmon, R.J. Emotional expression in infancy: A biobehavioral study. *Psychological Issues,* 1976, *10*(1), 37.

Erikson, E.H. Identity and the life cycle. *Psychological Issues,* 1959, *1,* 18-164.

Erikson, E.H. *Childhood and society* (2nd ed.). New York: Norton, 1963.

Fein, G.G. Pretend play in childhood: An integrative review. *Child Development,* 1981, *52,* 1095-1118.

Feshbach, N.D., & Roe, K. Empathy in six and seven-year olds. *Child Development,* 1968, *39,* 133-145.

Fishbein, H.D. *Evolution, development, and children's learning*. Santa Monica, Calif.: Goodyear Publishing, 1976.

Flavell, J. *Cognitive development*. New York: Prentice-Hall, 1977.

Flavell, J.H., & Ross, L. (Eds.). *Social cognitive development*. Cambridge: Cambridge University Press, 1981.

Friedrich, L.K., & Stein, A.H. Aggression and prosocial television programs and the natural behavior of preschool children. *Monographs of the Society for Research in Child Development,* 1973, *38*(4), 1-64.

Garwood, S.G. Piaget and play: Translating theory into practice. *Topics in Early Childhood Special Education,* 1982, *2*(3), 1.

Ghiaci, G., & Richardson, J.T. The effects of dramatic play upon cognitive development and structure. *The Journal of Genetic Psychology,* 1980, *136,* 77-83.

Goin-De Carie, T. Manifestations, hypotheses, data.. In T. Goin-De Carie (Ed.), *The infant's reaction to strangers*. New York: International Universities Press, 1974.

Goldsmith, H.H., & Gottesman, I.I. Origins of variation in behavior style: A longitudinal study in young twins. *Child Development,* 1981, *52,* 91-103.

Goodenough, F. *Anger in young children*. Minneapolis: University of Minnesota Press, 1931.

Gottesman, I.I. Heritability of personality: A demonstration. *Psychological Monographs,* 1963, *77*(9, Whole No. 572).

Gottesman, I., & Shields, J. *Schizophrenia and genetics: A twin study vantage point*. New York: Academic Press, 1972.

Guralnick, M.J. The social behavior of preschool children at different developmental levels: Effects of group composition. *Journal of Experimental Child Psychology,* 1981, *31,* 115-130.

Hartup, W.W. Aggression in childhood: Developmental perspectives. *American Psychologist,* 1974, *29,* 336-341.

Heathers, G. Emotional dependence and independence in nursery school play. *Journal of Genetic Psychology,* 1955, *87,* 37-58.

Heinicke, C.M., & Westheimer, I. *Brief separations*. New York: International Universities Press, 1965.

Hill, P.M., & McCune-Nicolich, L. Pretend play and patterns of cognition in Down's syndrome children. *Child Development,* 1981, *52,* 611-617.

Hoemann, H.W. The development of communication skills in deaf and hearing children. *Child Development,* 1972, *43,* 990-1003.

Hoffman, M.L. Empathy, role-taking, guilt, and development of altruistic motives. In T. Lickona (Ed.), *Moral development and behavior.* New York: Holt, Rinehart and Winston, 1976.

Hoffman, M.L. *A three component model of empathy.* Paper presented at the biennial meeting of the Society for Research in Child Development, New Orleans, 1977. (a)

Hoffman, M.L. Empathy, its development and prosocial implications. In C.B. Keaser (Ed.), *Nebraska symposium on motivation.* Lincoln, Nebr.: University of Nebraska Press, 1977. (b)

Hoffman, M.L. Perspectives on the difference between understanding people and understanding things: The role of affect. In J.H. Flavell & L. Ross (Eds.), *Social cognitive development.* Cambridge: Cambridge University Press, 1981.

Iannotti, R.J. Effect of role-taking experiences on role-taking, empathy, altruism, and aggression. *Developmental Psychology,* 1978, *14,* 119-124.

Johnson, J. *Aggression in man and animals.* Philadelphia: Saunders, 1972.

Kagan, J. *The plasticity of early intellectual development.* Paper presented at the meeting of the Association for the Advancement of Science, Washington, D.C., 1972.

Kagan, J., & Klein, R.E. Cross-cultural perspectives on early development. *American Psychologist,* 1973, *28,* 947-961.

Kalish, R.A., & Knudtson, F.W. Attachment versus disengagement: A lifespan conceptualization. *Human Development,* 1976, *19,* 171-181.

Kanfer, F.H. Personal control, social control, and altruism. *American Psychologist,* 1979, *34,* 231-239.

Katz, J. Altruism and sympathy: Their history in philosophy and some implications for psychology. *Journal of Social Issues,* 1972, *28,* 59-69.

Klein, M., & Stern, L. Low birth weight and the battered child syndrome. *American Journal of Diseases of Childhood,* 1971, *122,* 15-18.

Klevjord-Rothbart, M. Measure of temperament in infancy. *Child Development,* 1981, *52,* 569-578.

Knight, G.P., & Kagan, S. Development of prosocial and competitive behaviors in Anglo-American and Mexican-American children. *Child Development,* 1977, *48,* 1385-1394.

Kohlberg, L. A cognitive-developmental analysis of children's sex-role concepts and attitudes. In E.E. Maccoby (Ed.), *The development of sex differences.* Stanford, Calif.: Stanford University Press, 1966.

Kohlberg, L. Stages and aging in moral development: Some speculations. *Gerontologist,* 1973, *13,* 497-502.

Korner, A.F., Kraemer, H.D., Hoffner, M.E., & Thoman, E.B. Characteristics of crying and non-crying activity in normal full-term newborns. *Child Development,* 1974, *45,* 953-958.

Leeds, R. Altruism and the norm of giving. *Merrill-Palmer Quarterly,* 1963, *9,* 229-240.

Leiman, B. *Affective empathy and subsequent altruism in kindergartners and first graders.* Paper presented at the annual meeting of the American Psychological Association, Toronto, 1978.

Lewis, M., & Brooks-Gunn, J. *Social cognition and the acquisition of self.* New York: Plenum Press, 1979.

Lieberman, A.F. Preschoolers' competence with a peer: Relations with attachment and peer experience. *Child Development,* 1977, *48,* 1277-1287.

Livesley, W.J., & Bromley, D.B. *Person perception in childhood and adolescence*. London: Wiley, 1973.

Lorenz, K. *On aggression*. New York: Harcourt Brace and World, 1966.

Maccoby, E.E., & Jacklin, C. *The psychology of sex differences*. Stanford, Calif.: Stanford University Press, 1974.

MacMillan, D.L., & Morrison, G.M. Educational programming. In H.C. Quay & J.S. Werry (Eds.), *Psychopathological disorders of childhood*. New York: Wiley, 1979.

Main, M., & Weston, D.R. The quality of the toddler's relationship to mother and to father: Related to conflict behavior and the readiness to establish new relationships. *Child Development*, 1981, *52*, 932-940.

McCall, R.B., Parke, R.D., & Kavanough, R.D. Imitation of live and televised models by children one to three years of age. *Monographs of the Society for Research in Child Development*, 1977, *42*(5, Serial No. 173).

McClelland, D. *The achieving society*. New York: The Free Press, 1961.

McClintock, C.G., & Moskowitz, J.M. Children's preference for individualistic cooperative and competitive outcomes. *Journal of Personality and Social Psychology*, 1976, *4*, 543-555.

McClintock, C.G., Moskowitz, J.M., & McClintock, E. Variations in preferences for individualistic, competitive, and cooperative outcomes as a function of age, game class, and task in nursery school children. *Child Development*, 1977, *48*, 1080-1085.

Mead, G.H. *Mind, self and society from the standpoint of a social behaviorist*. Chicago: University of Chicago Press, 1934.

Meadow, K.P. The development of deaf children. In M. Hetherington (Ed.), *Review of Child Development Research* (Vol. 5). Chicago: University of Chicago Press, 1975.

Meltzoff, A.N., & Moore, M.K. Imitations of facial and manual gestures by human neonates. *Science*, 1977, *198*, 75-78.

Mood, D., Johnson, J., & Shantz, C. *Affective and cognition components of empathy in young children*. Paper presented at the Southeast Region of the Society for Research in Child Development, Chapel Hill, N.C., 1974.

Mueller, E., & Brenner, J. The origins of social skills and interaction among playgroup toddlers. *Child Development*, 1977, *48*, 854-861.

Mueller, E., & Lucas, T.A. A developmental analysis of peer interaction among toddlers. In M. Lewis & L.A. Rosenblum (Eds.), *Friendship and peer relations*. New York: Wiley, 1975.

Mussen, P., & Eisenberg-Berg, N. *Roots of caring, sharing, and helping*. San Francisco: W.H. Freeman, 1977.

Myklebust, H.R. *The psychology of deafness, sensory deprivation, learning and adjustment*. New York: Grune & Stratton, 1960.

Nelson, L., & Madsen, M.C. Cooperation and competition in four-year-olds as a function of reward contingency and subculture. Developmental Psychology, 1968, *1*, 340-344.

Oetzel, R.M. Classified summary of research in sex differences. In E.E. Maccoby (Ed.), *The development of sex differences*. Stanford, Calif.: Stanford University Press, 1966.

Oppenheimer, L. The development of the processing of social perspectives: A cognitive model. *International Journal of Behavior Development*, 1978, *1*, 144-171.

Parten, M.B. Social participation among preschool children. *Journal of Abnormal and Social Psychology*, 1932, *27*, 243-269.

Parten, M.B. Social play among preschool children. *Journal of Abnormal and Social Psychology*, 1933, *28*, 136-147.

Pastor, D. The quality of mother-infant attachment and its relationship to toddler's imitation of sociability with peers. *Developmental Psychology,* 1981, *17*(3), 326-335.

Pelligrini, A.D. The relationship between kindergarteners' play and achievement in prereading, language, and writing. *Psychology in the Schools,* 1980, *17,* 530-535.

Piaget, J. *Play, dreams and imitation in childhood.* New York: Norton, 1952.

Piaget, J., & Inhelder, B. *The psychology of the child.* New York: Basic Books, 1969.

Price, R.H. *Abnormal behavior: Perspectives in conflict.* New York: Holt, Rinehart and Winston, 1978.

Provence, S., & Lipton, R.D. *Infants in institutions.* New York: International Universities Press, 1963.

Radke-Yarrow, M., & Zahn-Waxler, C. Dimensions and correlates of prosocial behavior in young children. *Child Development,* 1976, *47,* 118-125.

Raviv, A., Bar-Tal, D., & Lewis-Levin, T. Motivations for donation behavior by boys of three different ages. *Child Development,* 1980, *51,* 610-613.

Rheingold, H., & Eckerman, G.O. Fear of the stranger: A critical examination. In H. Reese (Ed.), *Advances in child development and behavior* (Vol. 7). New York: Academic Press, 1973.

Schaffer, H., & Emerson, P.E. Patterns of response to physical contact in early human development. *Journal of Child Psychology and Psychiatry,* 1964, *5,* 1-13.

Selman, R.L. Towards structural analysis of developing interpersonal relations concepts. In A. Pick (Ed.), *Minnesota symposium on child psychology* (Vol. 10). Minneapolis: University of Minnesota Press, 1976.

Selman, R.L. The child as a friendship philosopher. In S.R. Asher & J.M. Gottman (Ed.), *The development of children's friendships.* Cambridge: Cambridge University Press, 1981.

Selman, R.L., & Byrne, D.F. A structural developmental analysis of role taking in middle childhood. *Child Development,* 1974, *45,* 803-806.

Shantz, C.U. The development of social cognition. In E.M. Heatherington (Ed.), *Review of child development research* (Vol. 5). Chicago: University of Chicago Press, 1975.

Shirley, M., & Payntz, L. The influence of separation from the mother on children's emotional responses. Journal of Psychology, 1941, *12,* 251-282.

Shuckin, A.M., & Smith, P.K. Two approaches to the concept of dominance in preschool children. *Child Development,* 1977, *48,* 917-923.

Shweder, R.A., Turiel, E., & Much, N.C. The moral intuitions of the child. In J.H. Flavell & L. Ross (Eds.), *Social cognitive development.* Cambridge: Cambridge University Press, 1981.

Singh, S.D. Urban monkeys. *Scientific American,* 1969, *221,* 108-115.

Smith, P.K., & Green, M. Aggressive behavior in English nurseries and play groups: Sex differences and responses of adults. *Child Development,* 1975, *46,* 211-214.

Sroufe, L.A., & Waters, E. Attachment as an organizational construct. *Child Development,* 1977, *48,* 1184-1199.

Sroufe, L.A. Attachment and the roots of competence. *Human Nature,* 1978, *1*(10), 50-56.

Sroufe, L.A. Wariness of strangers and the study of infant development. *Child Development,* 1977, *48,* 731-746.

Strayer, F.F., & Strayer, J. An ethological analysis of social agonism and dominance relations among preschool children. *Child Development,* 1976, *47,* 980-989.

Suomi, S.J., & Harlow, H.F. Social rehabilitation of isolate-reared monkeys. *Developmental Psychology,* 1972, *6,* 487-496.

Szasz, T.S. *The myth of mental illness.* New York: Dell, 1967.

Thelen, M.H., Frautschi, N.M., Fehrenbach, P.A., & Kirkland, K.D. Imitation in the interest of social influence. *Journal of Personality,* 1978, *14,* 429-430.

Thomas, A., & Chess, S. *Temperament and development.* New York: Brunner, Mazel, 1977.

Thomas, A., Chess, S., & Birch, H.G. The origin of personality. *Scientific American,* 1970, *223,* 102-109.

Thomas, A., Chess, S., Sillen, J., & Mendez, O. Cross-cultural study of behavior in children and special vulnerabilities to stress. In D.F. Ricks, A. Thomas, & M. Roff (Eds.), *Life history research in psychopathology.* Minneapolis: University of Minnesota Press, 1974, *3,* 53-67.

Tieger, T. On the biological basis of sex differences in aggression. *Child Development,* 1980, *51,* 943-963.

Torgeson, A.E., & Kringlen, E. Genetic aspects of temperament differences in infants. *Journal of the American Academy of Child Psychiatry,* 1978, *17,* 443-449.

Tracy, R.L., Lamb, M., & Ainsworth, M.D.S. Infant approach behavior as related to attachment. *Child Development,* 1976, *47,* 571-578.

Troll, L.E., & Smith, J. Attachment through the life-span: Some questions about dyadic bonds among adults. *Human Development,* 1976, *19,* 156-170.

Ungerer, J.A., & Sigman, M. Symbolic play and language comprehension in autistic children. *Journal of Child Psychiatry,* 1981, *20,* 318-337.

Ungerer, J.A., Zelazo, P.R., Kearsley, R.B., & O'Leary, K. Developmental changes in the representation of objects in symbolic play from 18 to 34 months of age. *Child Development,* 1981, *52,* 186-195.

Vandell, D.L., & George, L.B. Social interaction in learning and deaf preschoolers: Successes and failures in imitations. *Child Development,* 1981, *52,* 627-635.

Vandenberg, B. Environmental and cognitive factors in social play. *Journal of Experimental Child Psychology,* 1981, *31,* 169-175.

Van Lieshout, C.F.M. Young children's reactions to barriers placed by their mothers. *Child Development,* 1975, *46,* 879-886.

Wachs, T.W., Uzgiris, I., & Hunt, J. McV. Cognitive development in infants of different age levels and from different environmental backgrounds: An explanatory investigation. *Merrill-Palmer Quarterly,* 1971, *17,* 283-318.

Weinraub, M., & Lewis, M. The determinants of children's responses to separation. *Monographs of the Society for Research in Child Development,* 1977, *42*(4).

White, B.L. An experimental approach to the effects of experience on early human behavior. In J.P. Hill (Ed.), *Minnesota symposia on child psychology* (Vol. 1). Minneapolis: University of Minnesota Press, 1967.

White, B.L. Critical influences on the origins of competence. *Merrill-Palmer Quarterly,* 1975, *21,* 243-266.

Whittaker, C.A. A note on developmental trends in the symbolic play of hospitalized profoundly retarded children. *Journal of Child Psychology and Psychiatry,* 1980, *21,* 253-261.

Williemsen, E.W., Heaton, C., Flaherty, D., & Ritchey, G. Attachment behavior in one-year-olds as a function of mother vs. father, sex of child, session, and toys. *Genetic Psychology Monographs,* 1974, *96,* 305-324.

Wilson, E.O. A contributor to the war between the words. *American Psychologist,* 1976, *31,* 341-384. (Note: This article represents selected letters written in response to D.T. Campbell's 1975 American

Psychological Association presidential address cited in this chapter. Wilson's contribution appears on pages 370-371.)

Wynne-Edward, V.C. *Animal dispersion in relation to social behavior*. Edinburgh: Oliver and Boyd, 1962.

Zahn-Waxler, C., Radke-Yarrow, M., & King, R.A. *Child rearing and the development of children's altruism*. Presented at the annual meeting of the American Psychological Association, Toronto, 1978.

Zelazo, P.R. Smiling and vocalizing: A cognitive emphasis. *Merrill-Palmer Quarterly*, 1972, *18*, 349-365.

Chapter 10

Emotional Disturbance

James M. Kauffman

Many students considering careers in special education believe that most emotionally disturbed children, especially young ones, are simply the victims of parental mismanagement, social cruelties, or biological defects. Many of these students also believe that most disturbed children are very bright and will make dramatic changes in the way they behave if only they are given proper medical care and are treated kindly, permissively, and with insight into the subtle or hidden symbolic meanings of their behavior. These oversimplified and mostly erroneous notions of the causes and cures of disturbed behavior are fostered by popular books, magazine articles, movies, and TV programs, many of which portray dramatic incidents in play therapy, psychotherapy, medical treatment, or special education.

In contrast, current scientific research reveals that most disturbed children are intellectually below average (some, in fact, are severely retarded), that the causes of their disabilities are seldom known, that they are victimizers as well as victims in social relationships, that there is often no effective medical treatment for their problems, and that they usually respond much better to firm direction and control than to permissiveness. Clearly, helping disturbed children change their behavior for the better is an arduous task at which even the most experienced and competent professional will sometimes fail.

DEFINITION

Emotional disturbance in children has been recognized as a problem in psychiatry and special education for well over a century (Kauffman, 1976, 1981). "Seriously emotionally disturbed" is a category of handicapped children included in PL 94-142 and federal regulations. Nevertheless, the definition of emotional disturbance for purposes of special education remains a peculiarly difficult and unresolved problem (Bower, 1982; Kauffman, 1980, 1982; Kauffman & Kneedler, 1981; Wood & Lakin, 1979). While many definitions have been suggested over the years, none has been accepted as adequate or as the standard among the professionals serving disturbed children. The definition proposed by Bower (1969) is probably the one most useful in special education, since it is based on extensive research in schools and written with the concerns of teachers in mind. Bower stated that a child could be considered emotionally disturbed if he or she exhibited one or more of the following to a marked extent and over a long period of time:

> 1. inability to learn that cannot be explained by intellectual, sensory, or health factors.
> 2. inability to build or maintain satisfactory interpersonal relationships with peers and teachers.
> 3. inappropriate types of behavior or feelings under normal conditions.
> 4. a general, pervasive mood of unhappiness or depression.
> 5. a tendency to develop physical symptoms, pains, or fears associated with personal or school problems. (pp. 22-23)

This definition has gained wide acceptance among educators and comes close to being "official" because it is used (in a seriously flawed form) in federal regulations regarding special education services.

In very young children, developmental norms and parental expectations must be considered. Often, the first signs of serious emotional disturbance are seen as difficulties with basic biological functions or early social responses (e.g., eating, sleeping, eliminating, responding to parents' attempts to comfort, or "molding" to the parent's body when being held). At the toddler stage, slowness in learning to walk or talk is a sign of potential emotional difficulty. In short, failure to pass ordinary developmental milestones within a normal age range is a danger signal in the case of emotional development, just as in cognitive development. In fact, cognitive and emotional development tend to be closely linked, and neither aspect of a young child's life can be considered in isolation from the other. Rutter (1978) and Wing (1981) point out that, while many severely disturbed children are mentally retarded and while retarded and disturbed young children show some of the same characteristics, emotionally disturbed children lack social responses that are in keeping with their mental age.

Definition and classification of emotional disturbance are necessarily quite different for children than for adults. With children, the developmental changes in behavior normally seen from year to year must be kept in mind. Furthermore, children do not refer themselves for psychiatric treatment (as adults do) or special education but are selected by adults to receive services. The behavior of school-aged children can be compared with that of a substantial number of peers, and it is easily scrutinized by quite a few different adults. Preschool children are typically seen by fewer adults and in smaller groups of children the same age, however, meaning that reliance must be placed primarily on parental judgment (Achenbach & Edelbrock, 1981).

Other factors complicate the picture for very young children: (1) the developmental tasks for young children are fewer and simpler, which restricts the range of normal behaviors that can be sampled; (2) there is great variability in child-rearing practices of parents and parental expectations for their young children's behavior, which makes it necessary to guard against inappropriate comparisons; (3) normal development in this period of life is rapid and often uneven, which means that it is difficult to judge the prospects for "spontaneous" improvement and that deviations from the norm must be extreme before they can be considered abnormal; and (4) the most profound emotional disorders generally make their appearance in the early months of life, making it difficult many times to distinguish emotional disturbance from mental retardation or deafness.

An important point to remember is that normal children exhibit, at some time during their development, nearly every behavior that is characteristic of emotionally disturbed children. Crying, tantrums, fear of strangers, repetitive behavior involving objects, refusal to obey reasonable requests, negativism, fighting, masturbating—these characteristics can be observed in almost every normal child as well as in many disturbed children; however, disturbed children do such things much more frequently, persistently, or at an age when normal children have "outgrown" them. Disturbed children's behavior upsets adults and handicaps the children themselves because it is developmentally inappropriate and persistent.

PROBLEMS WITH THE FEDERAL DEFINITION

Although the federal definition of emotionally disturbed children contains logical absurdities and inconsistencies, and excludes two groups of children—socially maladjusted and autistic children—it is important because it is the regulation under which special education and related services are provided. Studies of special education for disturbed children (Grosenick & Huntze, 1979; U.S. General Accounting Office, 1981) show that many, probably *most,* disturbed children are not receiving special education. One significant contributing factor in the startling neglect of disturbed children may be the inadequacy of the federal definition (Kauffman, 1980, 1981, 1982).

The federal definition[1] includes the five characteristics Bower (1969) listed, but there are several additions to it. First, the category described by the definition is "seriously emotionally disturbed," not just "emotionally disturbed." Second, it is stated that the child's "educational performance" must be "adversely affected" by the emotional disturbance if the child is to be considered emotionally disturbed. Third, the definition specifically includes children who are schizophrenic but excludes children who are autistic; autistic children are now considered by federal regulation to be "other health impaired" (see Bower, 1982, for comment). "Socially maladjusted" children are also specifically excluded, "unless it is determined that they are seriously emotionally disturbed."

The "Seriously" Qualification

The reason that the qualifier "seriously" was attached to the description of emotionally disturbed children is not clear. Granted, the emotional upsets and behavior problems that children exhibit are sometimes transient and not serious enough to warrant special education or any other special intervention; however, it seems inappropriate to make such an intimation part of the federal regulatory definition for special education purposes. Federal regulations do not refer to the "actually" mentally retarded, the "obviously" physically handicapped, or the "truly" visually impaired, although every handicap may vary from a trivial or almost imperceptible level to a profound or total level. "Seriously" in the federal regulations clearly does not mean only severely as that term is used in the professional literature of psychology and psychiatry. Whatever the reason for the "seriously" qualifier, there is a danger that children in need of help will not receive it because school administrators can determine that, although they are emotionally disturbed, they are not "seriously" so.

The "Educational Performance" Criterion

It is difficult to imagine that a child could exhibit one or more of the five characteristics listed by Bower to a marked extent and over a long period of time without adverse effects on educational performance. If educational performance is always adversely affected when a child is seriously emotionally disturbed, then the stated criterion is meaningless, a redundancy. Of course, "educational performance" can have various interpretations. If the term refers only to academic achievement, children who exhibit extreme, persistent problem behavior (e.g., inability to build or maintain satisfactory relationships, a pervasive mood of unhappiness or depression) but are not academically underachieving would not be considered emotionally disturbed for special education purposes. Obviously, the "educational performance" criterion is open to an interpretation that excludes some children who would be considered seriously emotionally disturbed by any reasonable definition.

The "Socially Maladjusted" and "Autistic" Exclusions

Perhaps the most glaring absurdity in the federal definition is the exclusion of "socially maladjusted" and "autistic" children. As Bower (1982) and others have noted, the distinction between emotional disturbance and social maladjustment is simply not one that can be made rationally, at least not in terms of Bower's definition.

The exclusion of "socially maladjusted children" who are not also "seriously emotionally disturbed" is nonsense, but it is not harmless nonsense. It denies special education services to many children and youth who need help because of their disturbed emotions and behavior but who can be labeled maladjusted for administrative purposes. Bower (1982) has noted also the logical absurdity of excluding autistic children, a group who certainly exhibit one or more of the characteristics listed in his definition to a marked extent and over a long period of time (and with obvious adverse effects on educational performance). Although some psychiatrists and psychologists may consider autistic children "developmentally disabled" rather than "emotionally disturbed," it is obvious that these children are of concern to professionals primarily because of their behavior problems, not because of any known medical condition or physiological defect (O'Leary & Carr, 1982; Werry, 1979).

The "Schizophrenic" Inclusion

The definition specifically includes children identified as schizophrenic. It is quite inconceivable that a child who is schizophrenic would not exhibit one or more of the behavioral characteristics listed in the definition, particularly inappropriate behavior or feelings under normal conditions. Thus the clause including schizophrenic children appears to be unnecessary. Moreover, if any child who is labeled schizophrenic does not exhibit one or more of the five behavioral characteristics to a marked extent and over a long period of time, then that child could be considered to carry an inappropriate label—or at least a label that has no relevance for special education. That is, a child who is "schizophrenic" but whose behavior does not qualify him/her under Bower's definition could be considered mislabeled or deviant in a way that does not have implications for education.

Thus, the federal definition seems to increase confusion about emotional disturbance and to have the potential for inhibiting rather than improving special education services for disturbed children. It is to be hoped that the definition soon will be revised.[2]

ASSESSMENT

The assessment of children's emotional disorders has three major components: (1) screening or surveying a large and heterogeneous group of children in order to detect those who may be disturbed and need more careful evaluation, (2) classification of children who are in fact disturbed so that their problems can be managed effectively, and (3) formulation and evaluation of an intervention plan based on information derived from tests, interviews, and observations. Each of these is important, but assessment related to intervention is most critical to the welfare of disturbed children.

Screening

Although PL 94-142 demands that efforts be made to identify all handicapped children, including all emotionally disturbed children, few school systems have developed systematic and effective methods of screening. One reason is that most school systems have neither the money nor the personnel to do the screening or to serve the additional children who would be identified. Under such circumstances, screening may not be desirable because identification of children for whom services cannot be made available promptly can be extremely damaging both to the children and to their parents (Hobbs, 1975; Keogh & Becker, 1973).

Screening tests are available for use with children in kindergarten and first grade (Bower & Lambert, 1962; Lambert, Hartsough, & Bower, 1979; Pate & Webb, 1967). The Bower and Lambert test has several different forms appropriate for different age groups, including elementary, middle-school, and high-school students (see Wallace & Kauffman, 1978, for brief descriptions of several screening tests and lists of potential problem behaviors). A screening test usually samples several different abilities considered crucial for success in school. For example, the child might be asked to identify pictures when named (a picture-vocabulary task included in some IQ tests), draw objects (a task to sample perceptual-motor skills or self-concept), or judge emotions expressed by drawings of faces. The instrument constructed by Lambert and associates (1979) requires young children to judge whether they themselves or their classmates often act like children shown in various pictures.

Teachers' observations and ratings are generally effective in screening (Bower, 1969, 1982). In the case of young children or infants, teachers or parents usually refer the child to a specialist for assessment when they observe what they perceive to be problem behavior. Screening very young children is fraught with problems because young children's behavior and parental expectations are highly variable. Except in the case of severe early disorders (e.g., autism), it is very difficult to predict how a young child's behavior is likely to change; for any given behavior problem, the parents' expectations and their management of the child must be considered (Chess & Thomas, 1977).

In recent years, researchers have turned to studies of factors that seem to increase the likelihood that a child will become handicapped or that a handicap will be exacerbated (Field, Goldberg, Stern, & Sostek, 1980). In a sense, studies of children "at risk" for emotional disturbance or other disorders are an attempt to make screening procedures more effective by making them more sensitive to causal factors and to the earliest signs of emotional problems. While several obvious factors contribute to risk (e.g., brain injury, maternal deprivation, malnutrition, illness requiring hospitalization, chaotic home life, abuse by parents), relatively little is known about how to predict the influence of these factors on an individual child (Field et al., 1980; Hetherington & Martin, 1979; Rutter, 1979). When several risk factors occur together, the chance that a child will develop a disorder is greatly increased. Some children are more vulnerable than others under the same conditions, however, and the reason for this is not known (Rutter, 1979).

Classification

Special educators have no standard system of their own for classifying disordered behavior; they use classifications borrowed from psychiatry and psychology. Psychiatric systems of classification have tended to be unreliable and of rather little value to special educators (Achenbach & Edelbrock, 1978; S.L. Harris, 1979; Hobbs, 1975; Quay, 1979); classifications established by the research of behavioral psychologists have proved to be somewhat more reliable and useful (Achenbach & Edelbrock, 1981; Quay, 1979). Psychiatric classifications are often referred to in children's school or clinic records, however.

Psychiatric Classifications

Although psychiatrists may use several alternative classification schemes, the most widely adopted is known as DSM-III, the third edition of the *Diagnostic and Statistical Manual of the American Psychiatric Association* (1980). The manual is very detailed, including many subcategories and diagnostic criteria described in highly technical language. It contains a section on disorders usually first evident in infancy, childhood, or adolescence. In simplified form, the major types of disorders discussed in this section are

1. intellectual: mental retardation
2. behavioral (overt): attention deficit disorder, conduct disorder
3. emotional: anxiety disorders, other disorders
4. physical: eating disorders, stereotyped movement disorders, other disorders with physical manifestations
5. developmental: pervasive developmental disorders, specific developmental disorders

DSM-III is recognized as an improvement over earlier editions (S.L. Harris, 1979). Still, it is not a system that is likely to help educators communicate effectively about disturbed children.

Behavioral Classification

Many professionals who work with disturbed children recognize that behaviors can be fairly reliably and usefully classified, even though children can not. Types of behaviors can be grouped into clusters statistically; a child who exhibits one behavior in a cluster is likely to exhibit others in that cluster as well. Quay (1979), for example, found four major clusters of behavior:

1. conduct disorder, which includes disobedience, disruptiveness, fighting, destructiveness, temper tantrums, irresponsibility, impertinence, jealousy, anger, bossiness, profanity, attention seeking, and boisterousness. These behaviors are displayed by the child who assaults others, defies authority, is irritable and quarrelsome, and strikes out with hostile aggression.
2. anxiety-withdrawal, which includes feelings of inferiority, self-consciousness, social withdrawal, anxiety, crying, hypersensitivity, chewing fingernails, infrequent smiling, depression, chronic sadness, and shyness. The child worries a great deal and is timid, shy, seclusive, and sensitive.
3. immaturity, which includes a short attention span, preoccupation, clumsiness, passivity, daydreaming, sluggishness, drowsiness, masturbation, giggling, preference for younger playmates, chewing objects, and a feeling of being "picked on" by others. These are characteristics of a child who is not competent to deal with complex situations and demands for age-appropriate behavior.
4. socialized aggression, which includes association with bad companions or gangs, truancy, stealing, and delinquency. The child relates to others in a social group, but in the context of aggressive, socially disapproved, or delinquent behavior.

Mild-to-Moderate Disorders. As Von Isser, Quay, and Love (1980) report, the behavioral dimensions just described have been found quite consistently in many different samples of children (Quay, 1979). Most of these children exhibited mild-to-moderate emotional disturbance; that is, although the children showed behavioral characteristics that were serious enough to require intervention, they were not typically psychotic (i.e., severely or profoundly disturbed, out of touch with reality). They fell into the nonpsychotic category that has traditionally been referred to as neurotic or psychoneurotic.

Severe-to-Profound Disorders. A small percentage of disturbed children are severely or profoundly disturbed. They are typically referred to as autistic, psychotic, or schizophrenic. Their behavior is bizarre, and many (not all) of them are mentally retarded as well as emotionally disturbed (Rutter, 1978). If their bizarre behavior begins before they are 2½ years old, they are likely to be considered "autistic;" if it begins after the age of 2½ years, they will probably be labeled "childhood schizophrenic."

Autistic children begin before they are 2½ to show a pervasive lack of social responsiveness, peculiar patterns or deficits in speech and language, and bizarre behavior, such as preoccupation with objects, an insistence on maintaining sameness in their surroundings, or excessive self-stimulation. Their behavior tends to be consistently deviant (i.e., not episodically normal and deviant), and they do not show evidence of hallucinations or delusions.

Relatively few children develop severely disturbed patterns of behavior between the ages of 2½ and 13. Those who do, and those who become psychotic during adolescence, may exhibit some of the same types of behavior shown by autistic children. In addition, however, these childhood schizophrenics tend to have intermittent periods of normal or near-normal behavior and to show signs of distorted thinking, such as inappropriate language and speech; sudden, excessive anxiety; catastrophic reactions to everyday situations; inappropriate and highly changeable moods; and, sometimes, delusions or hallucinations.

Rutter (1978) and others have discussed the similarities and differences between autism and other disorders, such as childhood schizophrenia and mental retardation. Research suggests that the characteristics of autistic children as a group set them apart from children with other severe disorders, but autistic children are a very heterogeneous group. A given child does not usually exhibit all the characteristics of the autistic group, and many of the criteria for labeling a child autistic are not well established or highly reliable. Furthermore, identifying a child as autistic does not lead to a specific plan for intervention (Koegel, Rincover, & Egel, 1982; O'Leary & Carr, 1982).

Plan for Intervention

Adequate assessment of disordered behavior includes obtaining information to be used in designing, implementing, and evaluating an intervention plan. No single assessment technique can yield all the necessary information, since information must be obtained not only about the child's behavior but also about the social context in which the behavior occurs and about the child's development in all major areas of functioning. For example, the child should undergo a thorough physical examination, the possibility of sensory deficits should be investigated, and speech and language abilities should be appraised. Assessment by a competent special educator or psychologist invariably involves at least these three methods: tests, interviews, and observations.

Tests

Standardized tests make it possible to compare the child's performance under specified conditions with that of a large normative population under the same conditions. In some cases, standardized instruments may also point to the child's relative areas of strength or weakness.

The social-emotional development of young children is so inseparably tied to cognitive and physical development that any competent assessment of the status of a young emotionally disturbed child includes an IQ test. In order to know what to expect behaviorally from a child, it is necessary to know how well the child responds to tasks requiring conceptual (reasoning, thinking) skills. There are dangers in using IQ test results inappropriately, however. For example, it must not be assumed that a child who scores low on an IQ test cannot or will not learn. Because performance on IQ tests is correlated substantially with how a child performs in many important areas of development and because IQ scores are moderately good predictors of how fast and successfully a child will develop, such tests often provide information to guide professionals in deciding whether a child needs special help. An IQ score is merely a comparison of a child's performance on selected tasks with the performance of many other children of the same chronological age; it does not *cause* a child to behave in any particular way, nor does it reveal what the child's *potential* is for learning.

Intelligence and emotional health are not the same thing by any means, but there is a positive relationship between the two. Numerous studies have shown that mentally bright children tend to have fewer emotional difficulties than do children of dull intellect. Certainly, it is absurd to believe that mental retardation somehow prevents emotional disturbance. In fact, mental retardation increases the risk of emotional disturbance (Balthazaar & Stevens, 1975). (This does not imply a causal relationship between intelligence and emotional disturbance; children are not necessarily disturbed because they are retarded or retarded because they are disturbed.) Some emotionally disturbed children are extremely bright, but the vast majority are not. Most are somewhat below average in IQ, and the more severely disturbed tend to have lower IQs. As a group, severely disturbed (i.e., psychotic or autistic) children have IQs in the moderately to severely retarded range (Kauffman, 1981; Rutter, 1978).

For children who have been in school for several years, tests of academic achievement are useful. One of the most important indications of emotional problems in school-aged children is failure to learn basic academic skills. Does school failure cause emotional disturbance, or do children fail at school because they are disturbed? It is seldom possible to answer this question; school failure and emotional disturbance seem to feed each other.

Academic achievement is an important aspect of child development from the first school years onward, and standardized achievement tests reveal to what extent children are keeping up with normal expectations for someone of the same chronological age. Research indicates that most disturbed children are academically retarded (Kauffman, 1981). Mildly and moderately disturbed children typically need remedial instruction in basic academic skills; severely and profoundly disturbed children, especially young ones, often require instruction in self-care, basic communication, and daily living skills (Koegel et al., 1982).

Relatively few standardized tests are available for very young (prekindergarten) children. Furthermore, because of the deviant response patterns of disturbed children, it may be unfair to compare them with the normal children who were used to standardized tests; the disturbed children cannot show their best performance on IQ and achievement tests because of their maladaptive behavior in the testing situation. Some severely disturbed children cannot be tested by means of standard procedures, and tests must often be adapted especially for them.

Adequate testing of any disturbed child requires particular sensitivity and skill on the part of the examiner (DeMyer, Barton, Alpern, Kimberlin, Allen, Young, & Steele, 1974). It is important to remember that IQ and achievement tests do not tap potential—their purpose is to find out what children can do now, the way they are, in order to make a reasonable guess about what they will be able to do in the future, the way they will be, unless something special is done to change their progress. The fact that disturbed children do poorly on standardized tests and show interfering social behavior should be interpreted to mean that intervention is necessary, not that they have no potential for improvement.

Interviews

An adequate assessment of an emotional disorder in a child cannot be made without interviewing the adults responsible for that child. If the child has language skills, the assessment should include an interview with the child as well. It is sometimes desirable to interview the child's siblings or peers, who may contribute to the problem or its solution. The purpose of any interview is to get the clearest picture possible of the interviewed person's perceptions of the problem, its history, and the solutions that have been attempted.

Parents, teachers, and children are not always accurate, reliable, and unbiased, so unquestioning faith must not be placed in their reports. However, getting their views of the situation is always useful; and, in some cases, their reports may lead to a swift, straightforward solution to a seemingly complex behavioral problem (Evans & Nelson, 1977; O'Leary & Johnson, 1979). For example, a child who cried loudly and almost incessantly in the classroom stopped crying almost immediately after his teacher, by discussing the problem with him and his classmates, found that one of his greatest desires was to be called Sam instead of Sammy. Sam and his classmates agreed that when he cried he would be called Sammy, but that when he was not crying he would be addressed as Sam (Kaufhold & Kauffman, 1974).

Interviewing sounds simpler than it really is. Getting adults (particularly parents) and children (especially disturbed children) to talk openly and sincerely about their problem requires more than good intentions; it requires a great deal of sensitivity and interviewing skill. By the time disturbed children come to the attention of child care specialists, their behavior has generally become such an irritant to others and such a negative mark of distinction for the children themselves that everyone involved is on the defensive. It is not easy to win the confidence of the interviewees, put them at ease, and obtain unbiased information.

Observation

Although testing and interviews are useful, they are poor substitutes for actually watching what happens in the problem situation. Granted, it may sometimes be impossible for observers to visit the home or to avoid influencing behavior just by their presence, but the most helpful assessment data can usually be obtained by direct observation and measurement of behavior. Because the child's behavior is the problem, it is crucial to determine objectively and reliably how often the child behaves in certain ways; behavior must be assessed as it is embedded in other events, that is, its antecedents and consequences (Alberto & Troutman, 1982; Evans & Nelson, 1977; O'Leary & Johnson, 1979).

When a child exhibits a problem behavior (e.g., cries), it is helpful to consider the behavior's relation to a sequence of events, usually to what typically happens just before (its antecedents) and to what typically happens just afterward (its consequences). Antecedents and consequences usually have a great deal of control over the behavior in question; if they are the controlling variables, they can be changed to modify the behavior. Thus, analysis of the behavior (B), its antecedents (A), and its consequences (C) represents an assessment strategy (an "ABC analysis") that should lead directly to an effective intervention. For example, direct observation might indicate that, when a child cries (B), it is usually in response to having been teased by another child (A) and that the crying child then receives attention from an adult (C) in the form of comforting, distraction (encouraging participation in another activity), or mild reprimand. Reasonable intervention strategies, then, would be (1) to reduce or prevent teasing and (2) to shift adult attention from crying to noncrying behavior. Either strategy alone or the two in combination may quickly break up the tease-cry-attention sequence that is troublesome (Kerr & Nelson, in press).

Observation of young children at play may be an extremely helpful means of assessment, not because of what the play may reveal about their unconscious motivations or hidden feelings, but because learning to play is a crucial developmental task. A great deal can be learned about children's cognitive and social competence by watching how they use toys and play materials (e.g., how appropriate, imaginative, and spontaneous their play is) and how they respond to other children and adults.

If it is possible for observers to enter the typical environment in which the child is having difficulty, there is no need for them to guess about exactly what happens in those situations. Obviously, this is ideal, even if it requires extra time, effort, and training on the part of the observers. Naturalistic observation is almost always best when the object is service to the child and the adult caregivers; it serves well for many research projects as well. There are circumstances, however, in which laboratory observation is preferable to observation in the natural environment: (1) when the presence of observers or equipment has too many unwanted effects on the targets of observation, (2) when it is not feasible to move experimental equipment into the natural environment, (3) when the natural environment cannot be controlled adequately, or (4) when the data of interest can best be obtained in a contrived or somewhat standardized laboratory setting, such as a standard play situation.

CHARACTERISTIC BEHAVIORS

There are many hundreds of ways disturbed children can experience difficulty and cause grief to others. Although it is impossible to list all the specific behavioral characteristics of disturbed children, it is possible to describe some general types of behavior that tend to attract the attention and concern of adults and that, if not corrected, are likely to handicap the child seriously: hyperactivity and related problems, aggression, withdrawal, and inadequacy/immaturity.

Boys, far more often than girls (by a ratio of 4 or 5 to 1), exhibit characteristics that cause them to be labeled emotionally disturbed. Whether this sex difference is a result of biological factors, cultural expectations and biases, or a combination of these factors is unknown. The percentage of the child population that is emotionally disturbed cannot be determined precisely, since the definition of emotional disturbance is arbitrary and subjective; however, 6% to 8% seems to be a reasonable estimate based on research of children's problems (Achenbach & Edelbrock, 1981; Rubin & Balow, 1978; see also Graham, 1979; and Kauffman, 1981, for reviews). U.S. government agencies have used a prevalence estimate of 2% for the past two decades, and current government figures show that about 0.7% of the school-aged population is being served by special education under the category "seriously emotionally disturbed" (U.S. General Accounting Office, 1981).

Hyperactivity and Related Problems

Hyperactivity is characteristic of many learning-disabled and mentally retarded children, as well as many emotionally disturbed children. The term refers to a high rate of socially inappropriate activity, not simply to overactivity or a high rate of movement per se (Ross & Ross, 1976). The behavior of hyperactive children—fidgeting, failure to follow instructions, failure to complete tasks, tantrums, clumsiness, fighting, and recklessness, for example—makes them not only an object of concern for adults but unpopular with their peers. Hyperactive children usually do not get along well with other children. They, their peers, and their parents usually realize that they have problems in social relations (Campbell & Paulauskas, 1979).

Hyperactive children often are also impulsive. They frequently respond quickly and without considering alternatives in social situations and on academic tasks. Typically, their impulses lead them to the wrong response, and they make socially unacceptable or academically incorrect responses, causing them to become pariahs in their neighborhoods and schools. Many hyperactive children are also distractible, unable to pay attention to a task long enough or selectively enough to learn efficiently or complete their work (Hallahan & Kauffman, 1976). Moreover, many such children are unable to see alternative ways of behaving in situations involving interpersonal problems (Kneedler, 1980; Spivack & Shure, 1974).

Aggression

Hyperactive, impulsive children may also be aggressive, but they are not necessarily so; furthermore, children who are not impulsive or hyperactive may perform aggressive acts. Aggression can be defined in many different ways (Bandura, 1973), but for purposes here it is considered to be behavior intended to cause injury or pain (physical or psychological) or to destroy property. Nearly all children, especially young ones, exhibit aggressive behavior, but many disturbed children perform aggressive acts much more frequently than do normal children (Patterson, Reid, Jones, & Conger, 1975). Hyperaggressive children also tend to exhibit aggression fairly consistently, in many different settings or circumstances (A. Harris, 1979).

Aggression may involve hitting, biting, scratching, teasing, cursing, name calling, and a variety of other specific behaviors. Children may direct aggressive behaviors toward others or toward themselves. Self-injurious behavior is a fairly common characteristic of severely and profoundly disturbed children. Such children may bang their heads, bite or scratch themselves, or hurt themselves intentionally in a variety of other ways. Sometimes their self-inflicted injuries are minor; sometimes they are serious enough to threaten loss of limb or life (Bachman, 1972; Lovaas, 1982a).

Withdrawal

Withdrawn children keep others at a distance both physically and emotionally. They may lack social approach responses, responsiveness to others' social initiations, or both. The withdrawn child does not engage in the social reciprocity, the mutually satisfying exchange of social reinforcement by pairs of individuals, that characterizes normal social development (Combs & Slaby, 1977). Some withdrawn children lack social skills and are socially isolated because of these behavioral deficits; others may have learned the necessary social skills, but retreat from social interactions into fantasy or self-stimulation (repetitive, stereotyped behaviors that seem to provide only sensory feedback). The social withdrawal of some disturbed children is not extreme, but that of others is so pronounced and persistent as to be considered autistic. Autistic withdrawal, which begins at a very early age, is characterized by unresponsiveness to social stimuli, avoidance of eye-to-eye gaze, language disorders (including muteness and echolalia), and excessive self-stimulation and fantasy.

Inadequacy/Immaturity

Immature children may behave in ways that are characteristic of much younger normal children, or they may fail to meet reasonable demands for performance. For example, they may unexpectedly cry or have temper tantrums, act helpless, regress to primitive behavior, become extremely negative, or show irrational fears. Some disturbed children use their negativism and tantrums to become little tyrants, manipulating their parents into complying with their every whim (Bernal, Duryee, Pruett, & Burns, 1968; Williams, 1959). Others display a picture of helplessness and demand constant adult attendance just to get them through the activities of daily living (Kaufhold & Kauffman, 1974). Still others are prisoners of their own extreme, irrational fears (e.g., of school, of dogs, of tall buildings) and lead lives of seeming desperation in which avoidance of the feared object or situation is a constant concern (Johnson & Melamed, 1979).

Special Considerations for Infants and Young Children

As mentioned earlier, normal children do nearly everything disturbed children do, but not so frequently or persistently. Disturbed children's behavior is not *developmentally* appropriate. It is understandable and normal for a 15-month-old to cling to his mother and hide his face from an approaching stranger; not so for a 6-year-old. The helplessness of a 3-year-old who cannot tie her shoes is not cause for concern; it is not normal for a 9-year-old to be unable to tie her shoes. Two-year-old normal children frequently engage in self-stimulation (e.g., thumb-sucking, blanket-stroking) and have temper tantrums; such behavior is aberrant for 10-year-olds. Normal 2- and 3-year-olds exhibit behavior that would be considered hyperactive in an 8-year-old. Moreover, children's development is characterized by spurts and lapses, and temporary regression is to be expected under stressful circumstances.

Because families differ greatly in the way they respond to child behavior, behavioral characteristics that cause some parents extreme concern cause other parents no anxiety at all (Thomas, Chess, & Birch, 1968). Thus, specific behaviors per se cannot be considered indicative of emotional disturbance in infants and young children. Chronological age, general developmental level, parents' expectations, level of stress, and sociocultural background must be considered in judging any child's behavior.

CAUSAL FACTORS

The reasoning of most professionals who seek the causes of children's emotional disturbances is that discovery of the cause will lead to cure and even prevention. However, this reasoning cannot always be applied to children's behavior problems because it is based on an analogy to physical diseases. The first professionals to deal with disorders of behavior were physicians, and they tended to see problems in thinking, feelings, and socializing as diseases of the mind. It is now apparent that the vast majority of emotional disturbances are not diseases in any usual sense of the word, yet it is common to speak of "mental illness" and "mental health."

In the realm of behavior, it is extremely seldom that the cause of a problem can be pinpointed and verified; even so, effective help can be provided. The fact that a cure has been found for a particular child (i.e., the child's behavior has been made indistinguishable from that of peers) does not indicate that the cause has been identified, however. For example, it would be a mistake to assume that, because a disturbed child began behaving appropriately when his parents changed the consequences for his behavior, his misbehavior was caused by the consequences his parents had provided.

Several different events or conditions may work together to cause a behavioral problem, and it may be the combination of these contributing factors, not any one in isolation, that is the cause. For example, a combination of genetic factors, physical disease, parental mismanagement, and school failure may result in a child's maladaptive behavior. Some contributing factors, perhaps genetic factors, increase a child's susceptibility to disorders and are said to give the child a predisposition to develop problems. Other contributing factors may trigger, or precipitate, a behavior problem. Precipitating factors may be events, such as parents' divorce, teasing by peers, failure on an examination, or injury. Stressful situations can be expected to result in temporary behavior problems even in normal children. Disturbed children do not rebound quickly from situational stress; their behavioral difficulties are chronic.

Until recent years, disturbed children were seen primarily as being acted upon by others, primarily as being the victims of others' behaviors. Now, social scientists are recognizing that children affect their parents and other adults as much as they are affected by adults (Bell & Harper, 1977; Patterson, 1980; Sameroff & Chandler, 1975). Children, by their appearance and behavior, contribute to their own treatment and can make adults their victims. Behavior problems arise in the interactions and transactions among disturbed children and other individuals in their environment. For example, an irritable, whiny infant should be viewed not just as the product of parental caregiving that produces irritable, whiny behavior but as a source of concern to the parents and an infant likely to elicit less than optimum caregiving responses from most adults.

Children and adults appear to influence each other reciprocally. A mother's responsiveness to and stimulation of her young child may increase the child's cognitive development, while the child's positive social and emotional responses to the mother reciprocally increase her responsiveness and sensitivity to the child's needs (Clarke-Stewart, 1973).

An interactional model of influence does not apply only to parent-child relations. Interactive effects are obvious among siblings, schoolmates, and playmates, as well as in teacher-child relations (Whalen, Henker, & Dotemoto, 1981). Even the child's physical and emotional conditions may reciprocally affect each other; illness may increase the probability that the child will exhibit undesirable behavior, and depression or anxiety may increase the probability that the child will become ill.

Biological Factors

Numerous hypotheses have been advanced over the years to explain disordered emotions and behavior in terms of physical origins. It has been suggested that emotional disturbances in children are the result of genetic anomalies, brain dysfunction, biochemical defects, or faulty nutrition, for example. In spite of all the hypotheses, research, and medical advances of the past 40 years, only very rarely is it proved that a specific disturbance is connected to a biological cause or that a biological factor caused a given child's aberrant behavior. When all the facts have been sifted, it must be concluded that there is little, if any, consistent suggestive evidence, much less empirical proof, of a biological cause for the vast majority of children's disordered behavior (Ross, 1980; Werry, 1979). The types of childhood disorders most frequently linked with suspected biological causes are hyperactivity and childhood psychoses (autism and childhood schizophrenia).

Hyperactivity

Perhaps the most common notion regarding the biological cause of hyperactivity is that it is the result of "minimal brain damage"—minimal because the damage cannot be confirmed directly and must be inferred from the child's behavior. This concept has not proved useful to psychologists or educators; indeed, the hypothesis remains unproved (Kauffman & Hallahan, 1979; Werry, 1979). As Werry (1979) points out, diagnosis of brain damage in other than obvious cases of injury is nothing more than an enlightened guess. Even when it is known that the brain has been damaged, there is usually no way of proving that the brain injury causes disordered behavior.

Other suspicions that hyperactivity results from biological misfortune, such as genetic anomalies or the ingestion of food additives or food allergens, have not been confirmed by research (Kauffman, 1981). In short, except in a very few unusual cases, hyperactivity and related disorders have not been demonstrated to have an identifiable biological cause. The failure to identify biological causes does not imply, of course, that psychological causes are known. It is also important to recognize that treatments having high rates of success in reducing hyperactivity—stimulant medication, for example (Gadow, 1981; Whalen et al., 1981)—do not necessarily shed light on the cause of the disorder.

Autism and Childhood Schizophrenia

There is good reason to suspect biological causes of the severe disorders known as autism and childhood schizophrenia. Still, there is no *proof* of a specific genetic, neuropathological, or other biological cause. Research suggests a genetic contribution to childhood schizophrenia (Hanson & Gottesman, 1976) and a neuropathological component in autism (Rutter, 1978), but the specific genetic and neuropathological factors involved are unknown (Werry, 1979). The research evidence indicates, for example, that having close blood relatives who are schizophrenic increases a child's chances of becoming schizophrenic and that autistic children develop seizures in early adolescence far more often than do nonautistic children. However, the specific genes and physiological processes they control, and the manner of their transmission (in the case of schizophrenia) are not known; and the specific location and nature of brain damage or dysfunction (in the case of autism) have not been identified.

Family Socialization Factors

Because parents so obviously influence their children's conduct and are responsible for controlling and teaching their young children, many have construed disturbed children's behavior simply as an outcome of inadequate parenting. Knowledge of the ways in which children respond to various styles and techniques of behavior management does, indeed, suggest that emotional disturbance in children represents family socialization gone awry.

Studies of interaction in disturbed and normal families have not revealed consistent differences that would explain the origin of children's disturbance, however (Goldstein & Rodnick, 1975; Jacob, 1975). Even direct observations of disturbed children's families, although they have yielded information about how family interactions can be improved, have not identified parental behavior as the cause of the trouble (Patterson et al., 1975). Certainly, the behavior of parents toward their child may contribute to that child's difficulty; but having a disturbed child in the family is a highly stressful experience, and parental behavior toward a disturbed child may be as much or more a function of the child's disturbance as a cause of it. In the case of autism, research has effectively destroyed the myth that autistic children are a product of cold, rejecting, upper-middle-class parents (Schopler & Dalldorf, 1980; Wing, 1980). Behavioral researchers are demonstrating that, regardless of the presumed origins of a child's emotional disturbance, parents can be helped to teach and manage their child effectively (Blechman, Kotanchik, & Taylor, 1981; Koegel et al., 1982).

Other Socialization Factors

Children's behavioral development obviously is affected by a wide range of experiences, including interactions with peers, television viewing, and schooling.

Peers

Recently, there has been a great deal of interest in the ways in which peer interactions, from infancy on, are involved in normal and deviant development (Field, 1981; Fundis, 1981). Opportunities to interact with peers are known to be important for normal behavioral development, but relatively little is known about how much and what kind of interaction is necessary or how young children's peer relations may be a cause of disordered behavior. It might be expected that children learn inappropriate behavior from their peers, but peer relations also hold great potential for behavioral therapy. For example, peers may effectively improve disturbed children's behavior through play, tutoring, modeling (providing examples that the disturbed child may imitate), or by giving prompts or reinforcers for desirable behavior as directed by an adult therapist (Strain, 1981a, 1981b).

Television

Many emotional words have been spoken and written regarding the influence of television on young children (Murray, 1980). Aside from any cognitive influences it may exert, its effect on children's social behavior, particularly their aggression and prosocial acts, is a matter of debate. Most researchers agree that many or most young children watch a great deal of TV. Some children probably watch too much TV, and there is some evidence to suggest that restricting the viewing of young children has beneficial effects on their intelligence and behavior (Gadverry, 1980). Watching prosocial programs (e.g., Mister Rogers' Neighborhood, Captain Kangaroo) does not appear to lead to undesirable behavior and may increase prosocial responses, such as helping, cooperating, and sharing (Ahammer &

Murray, 1979). On the other hand, a considerable amount of research suggests that watching TV violence encourages young children's aggressive behavior and decreases desirable responses, such as imaginative play (Huston-Stein, Fox, Greer, Watkins, & Whitaker, 1981; Stein & Friedrich, 1975).

School

It is possible that experiences at school contribute to emotional disturbance, even though the school is supposed to be a major socializing institution. A child encounters many new demands and stresses at school. Parents' and teachers' expectations for performance may be far too high or far too low, making the child feel inadequate, undesirable, or just bored. There are schools in which discipline is too lax or too rigid for the child's previous experience and temperament. It is also possible that the child might be ignored when not causing trouble but be given a great deal of attention when misbehaving, a situation almost certain to teach the child that the way to "be somebody" is to be disruptive.

In reviewing research regarding the school's possible contributions to emotional disturbances, Kauffman (1981) found that school administrators and teachers may demand mindless conformity to rules and routines, unnecessarily squelching children's individuality. Teachers may hold inappropriate expectations for children or may be inconsistent in managing their behavior. Finally, what is taught may have no real meaning or relevance for the children's lives.

CONCEPTUAL MODELS

Psychiatrists, psychologists, special educators, and social workers are likely to suggest different ways to help disturbed children, partly because each group is likely to be guided by a different conceptual model. Such a model is a way of viewing the nature of the problem, and based on that theoretical view, designing techniques of dealing with the problem. Today's professionals may choose from several different conceptual models (Table 10-1). Although a competent professional may be guided primarily by the basic assumptions and strategies of a single conceptual model, few people are so dogmatic as to reject completely everything about competing points of view; most recognize that there are useful insights and valuable practices associated with each of the conceptual models presented in Table 10-1, and perhaps other points of view as well (McDowell, Adamson, & Wood, 1982; Rhodes & Paul, 1978). All conceptual models do not enjoy the same amount of support from empirical research. Probably there is much more scientific support for the behavioral approach or model than for any competing view (Cullinan, Epstein, & Kauffman, 1982).

Table 10-1 Approaches to Educating Disturbed Children

	PSYCHOANALYTIC APPROACH	*PSYCHO-EDUCATIONAL APPROACH*	*HUMANISTIC APPROACH*	*ECOLOGICAL APPROACH*	*BEHAVIORAL APPROACH*
The problem	A pathological imbalance among the dynamic parts of the mind (id, superego, ego).	Involves both underlying psychiatric disorders and the readily observable misbehavior and underachievement of the child.	The disturbed child is out of touch with his own feelings and can't find self-fulfillment in traditional educational settings.	The child interacts poorly with his environment; child and environment affect each other reciprocally and negatively.	The child has learned inappropriate responses and failed to learn appropriate ones.
Purpose of Educational Practices	Use of psychoanalytic principles to help uncover underlying mental pathology.	Concern for unconscious motivation/underlying conflicts *and* academic achievement/positive surface behavior.	Emphasis on enhancing child's self-direction, self-evaluation, and emotional involvement in learning.	Attempt to alter entire social system so that it will support desirable behavior in child when it is withdrawn.	Manipulation of child's immediate environment and the consequences of his behavior.
Characteristics of Teaching Methods	Reliance on individual psychotherapy for child and parents; little emphasis on academic achievement; highly permissive atmosphere.	Emphasis on meeting individual needs of the child; reliance on projects and creative arts.	Use of nontraditional educational settings in which teacher serves as resource and catalyst rather than as director of activities; nonauthoritarian, open, affective, personal atmosphere.	Involves all aspects of a child's life, including classroom, family, neighborhood, and community, in teaching the child useful life and educational skills.	Involves measurement of responses and subsequent analyses of behaviors in order to change them; emphasis on reward for appropriate behavior.

Source: Daniel P. Hallahan and James M. Kauffman, *Exceptional Children: Introduction to Special Education,* © 1978, p. 209. Reprinted by permission of Prentice-Hall, Inc., Englewood Cliffs, New Jersey.

BEHAVIORAL INTERVENTION

A great deal has been written during the past 10 years about behavior modification, its philosophy, techniques, successes, and problems (Morris & Kratochwill, in press; O'Leary & Carr, 1982). It should be noted that the behavioral approach involves direct observation and measurement of behavior as an assessment strategy. The child's problem behavior is defined in measurable terms so that a reliable, objective, daily record of its occurrence can be kept. The direct daily measurement of behavior is useful both in assessing the extent of the problem and in judging the success of the methods used to modify it.

The fundamental assumption underlying the behavioral approach is that the most important factor controlling behavior is its consequence—what happens immediately after the behavior occurs. Therefore, the majority of intervention techniques involve changing the consequences of certain behaviors. Consequences may be changed not just to decrease the occurrence of inappropriate behavior but to increase appropriate behavior as well. Consequences are used to teach new behavior patterns to the disturbed child.

Three basic techniques for changing behavior are extinction, time out, and reinforcement. Extinction and time out are ways of decreasing inappropriate behavior. Reinforcement can be used to increase desirable behavior and, occasionally, to decrease undesirable behavior as well (e.g., when an alternative behavior to the undesirable one is reinforced).

Extinction

A behaviorist assumes that people repeat behaviors because of reinforcing consequences. Therefore, if the reinforcing consequences can be prevented, the behavior will stop. The idea behind extinction is to find the reinforcers for behavior and put an end to them, as illustrated in a case described by Williams (1959). The parents of a 21-month-old boy were seriously troubled by their son's tyrannical behavior at bedtime. At night and at his afternoon nap, he would insist that an adult sit vigilantly by his bed until he fell asleep. This required an hour or two of an adult's time each time the child was put to bed. If his parent tried to read or do something other than give complete attention to him or if his parent tried to leave the room when he appeared to be asleep, he would throw a temper fit. Williams worked from the assumption that the parents' acquiescence to the child's demands was a reinforcer for his tantrums and that, if his tantrums were no longer reinforced by the parents' compliance with his bratty ultimatums, his tantrums would end. Therefore, the parents were instructed to put their son to bed in a pleasant, relaxed manner (making sure before putting him to bed that he was not hungry, wet, or without a nightlight), leave the room, close the door, and not return regardless of how he might rage and scream. After a 45-minute tantrum the first time he was put to bed in this way, the child quickly learned to go to bed without demanding unreasonable attention (i.e., extinction worked).

Time Out

When no single reinforcer for a problem behavior can be identified or there is no way of keeping the reinforcing consequence from happening except by removing the child from the situation, time out might be a useful technique. As a consequence for a specific undesirable behavior, the individual is confronted with a situation in which the behavior cannot be reinforced—it is time out from reinforcement. (Time out is a very useful technique, but it is open to abuses; see Gast & Nelson, 1977; Nelson & Rutherford, in press).

Often, time out means removing the child from ongoing activities for a short while—in effect, isolating the child briefly from the situation in which the misbehavior occurs. Such was the case reported by Wolf, Risley, and Mees (1964), who were called upon to deal with the behavior of Dicky, a 3½-year-old autistic boy. Dicky had severe tantrums, frequently injured himself, and threw his glasses during his tantrums. It was extremely important for him to wear his glasses because he had cataracts, and his vision would deteriorate without his glasses. So Dicky was placed in his room—isolated from social contact, given a time out—immediately, whenever he started a tantrum. He was kept in time out for 10 minutes or until he was quiet (if his tantrum continued during time out). The time out consequence successfully rid Dicky of his undesirable, dangerous tantrums.

Reinforcement

Wolf and associates did not stop with halting Dicky's tantrums, important as that task was. They realized that extinction and time out for inappropriate behaviors are "dead end" techniques unless accompanied by positive teaching of some appropriate behaviors. With reinforcement, the therapist makes sure that a desirable behavior is followed immediately and consistently by consequences the child sees as desirable. It begins with what the child already does, some step in the right direction; the behavior required for a reward is then gradually broadened (a process called behavior shaping).

Wolf and his fellow behavior therapists wanted Dicky to wear his glasses. Since he would not tolerate having the glasses on his face, they began by rewarding him with little bits of food and praise for just holding empty frames. After he became accustomed to that, they rewarded him for putting empty frames up to his eyes, then for holding plain lenses up to his eyes, next for looking through prescription lenses, and so on until step by step they taught him to wear prescription lenses.

Sometimes, reinforcing desirable behavior reduces problem behavior, especially when the reinforced behavior is the opposite of the problem behavior (Dietz & Repp, in press). Kauffman and Hallahan (1973) worked with a 6-year-old boy who was extremely hyperactive and aggressive. This budding Hun would pummel anyone who got in his way (child or adult) and had habits of throwing, banging, stomping, or otherwise abusing play materials. Since extinction and time out were not reasonable alternatives in the preschool class the boy was attending, the teacher was cued to reinforce the boy with praise and a small extrinsic reward if he had been nonviolent for a little while (as short a time as 20 seconds in the beginning). In this case, the problem (rough physical behavior) was greatly reduced by offering reinforcement for gradually longer periods during which he exhibited the opposite type of behavior.

Management of Hyperactivity and Related Problems

Perhaps the intervention that most frequently comes to mind when hyperactivity is mentioned is medication, or the use of stimulant drugs (e.g., methylphenidate [Ritalin] or dextroamphetamine [Dexedrine]). Although such drugs have real value in the control and learning of many hyperactive children (Gadow, 1981; Whalen et al., 1981), it is clear that behavioral interventions can be effective without drugs in many cases and can enhance the effects of drugs in other cases (Kauffman & Hallahan, 1979). Indeed, drugs alone are unlikely to improve the child's ability to learn important skills.

Behavioral techniques include making the environment (classroom or home) very predictable and highly structured. These children must know the rules for behavior, and the consequences for their actions must be consistent. Social and tangible rewards may be given for desirable behavior (e.g., following instructions, staying in seat, completing tasks). Sometimes, mild punishment (time out or loss of rewards) is also necessary. Care must be taken to make the academic work presented to such children interesting and useful and to keep tasks (whether they are academic tasks, social tasks, or chores at home) within their capacity but challenging.

Within the past few years behavior therapists have become interested in using concepts from cognitive psychology to enhance behavioral interventions (O'Leary & Carr, 1982). Strategies called "cognitive behavior modification" have been devised to try to integrate cognitive and affective components into behavioral approaches (Hallahan, 1980; Mahoney, 1974; Meichenbaum, 1977). For example, children may be taught to monitor or record their own behavior, give self-instructions, administer self-reward, or plan strategies for self-control. The underlying idea is to make children more aware of their own thoughts and feelings and to involve these children actively in the management of their own behavior and emotions. These cognitive-behavioral interventions seem to hold promise, especially in the remediation of academic problems, but it is important to note that they have often failed (Hallahan, 1980; Hallahan, Lloyd, Kauffman, & Loper, in press; O'Leary & Carr, 1982).

Management of Aggression

Many of the same techniques used in the management of hyperactivity, distractibility, and impulsivity are effective in managing aggression. Fagen, Long, and Stevens (1974) have devised a self-control curriculum that emphasizes affective and cognitive abilities. Spivack and Shure (1974) describe a program for teaching aggressive, impulsive young children problem-solving skills in real life situations. A great deal of behavioral research has been done, leading to recommendation of the following techniques (Kauffman, 1981; Kerr & Nelson, in press):

1. Provide models (live or filmed examples) of nonaggressive responses to aggression-provoking situations.
2. Guide the child in practicing (role playing and rehearsal) nonaggressive behaviors for real life situations.
3. Reinforce nonaggressive behaviors by giving rewards for specific alternative, nonaggressive behaviors.
4. Extinguish aggression by withholding rewards for aggressive behavior.
5. Give consistent and appropriate punishment for aggressive behavior.

Punishment is a controversial topic and an easily abused method of control (Polsgrove, in press). Kauffman (1981) has suggested the following guidelines for the effective, humane use of punishment to control aggression:

1. Use it only when positive methods fail and the aggressive behavior is worse than the punishment.
2. Make sure the punisher is a warm, loving person who gives the child lots of positive reinforcement for nonaggressive behavior.
3. Administer punishment fairly, consistently, matter of factly, and without anger, threats, or moralizing. Punish immediately and only for behaviors the child has been told are punishable.
4. Make the punishment reasonable in intensity and, whenever possible, related to the offense (e.g., cleaning floors for throwing food).
5. Use loss of rewards rather than infliction of pain whenever possible.
6. Use self-control techniques (e.g., self-monitoring, self-instruction) in conjunction with punishment, if possible.
7. Remember that the objective of punishment is to help the child gain self-control.

Management of Withdrawal, Inadequacy, and Immaturity

Behavior therapists have devised a variety of effective techniques for the management of withdrawn, inadequate, and immature behaviors (Gelfand, 1978;

Johnson & Melamed, 1979; O'Leary & Carr, 1982; Strain, 1981a, 1981b). Such behaviors include a wide range of problems, from fears and phobias to enuresis, social isolation, sexual problems, developmental regression, self-stimulation, and ritualistic behavior. The following general suggestions for management of social withdrawal, social inadequacy, and fears are derived from behavioral research:

1. Show the child examples (live or televised) of children who are having fun playing with others or overcoming their fear of an object, place, activity, or situation.
2. Give children practice, through role playing and rehearsal, in using specific social skills.
3. Arrange play conditions and materials that are conducive to social interaction.
4. Offer rewards for approximations of appropriate social behavior.
5. Allow fearful children to approach feared situations gradually while experiencing pleasurable activities.
6. Prompt the child's peers to approach the child and initiate desirable social interaction.

These are not revolutionary new techniques; they are common-sense methods supported by empirical research. Perhaps it should not be surprising that behavioral science is confirming the correctness of many "old-fashioned" ideas about child management.

Special Considerations for Autism and Related Disabilities

As Koegel and associates (1982) indicate, autistic children as a group can be differentiated from other groups of handicapped youngsters (e.g., schizophrenic, aphasic, deaf, retarded), yet the specific behavioral characteristics of individual autistic children and the teaching procedures appropriate for them are extremely varied. Furthermore, the appropriate intervention techniques for autistic youngsters may be the same as those used for children who have other disorders; appropriate intervention is determined by behavioral characteristics, not by diagnostic label.

Because the characteristics of autistic children are extremely debilitating, the issues in their education are not only *how* to teach them but *what* to teach them and *who* should teach them. Research clearly indicates that a highly structured, directive, intrusive, and explicitly behavioral approach is the intervention of choice (Clark & Rutter, 1981; Koegel et al., 1982; O'Leary & Carr, 1982). Placed in a permissive, nondirective environment or left to their own devices, these children are unlikely to make significant progress. Carefully designed and precisely implemented teaching procedures are necessary to deal effectively with their language deficits, self-stimulation, self-injury, attentional problems, and lack of social responsiveness (see Koegel et al., 1982, for a description of these procedures).

Researchers are coming to realize that teachers of autistic children should concentrate on behaviors that are age-appropriate and likely to contribute to the ability of these children to function independently in as normal an environment as possible; that is, the behaviors that are taught must be useful in meeting the demands of everyday living. Given the severity of autistic children's disabilities and the prospects for their adult level of functioning, it is important that parents be taught to serve as teachers of their autistic children. Teachers at school can make an extremely valuable and necessary contribution to the progress of these children, but, unless the parents are taught to continue the instructional program at home, it seems unlikely that gains at school will be maintained (Lovaas, Koegel, Simmons, & Long, 1973).

PROGNOSIS

What is the long-term outcome for emotionally disturbed children, and what types of children are likely to have the most serious problems in later years? These are difficult questions, especially in regard to young children. The younger the child, the more difficult it is to predict later behavior; moreover, research and early intervention may prove today's prediction wrong. In addition, predictions can become self-fulfilling prophesies for those who take them as inherent limitations of the child rather than as intelligent guesses based on past experience. Nevertheless, research does provide some tentative answers.

The prognosis for nonpsychotic emotionally disturbed young children who receive behavioral intervention is generally quite good, as behavior therapists have developed techniques that are effective in most cases (O'Leary & Carr, 1982). In fact, early behavioral intervention might be expected to make most mildly disturbed children indistinguishable from their peers (Strain, Steele, Ellis, & Timm, 1982). The children likely to have the most long-standing and serious problems are those who show a great deal of hostile aggression (Robins, 1979). Coupled with low intelligence and school failure, a high level of aggression suggests a particularly gloomy prognosis.

The long-term prospects for psychotic children, especially those labeled autistic, is not very good (Eggers, 1978; Lotter, 1978). Although behavioral intervention can produce significant changes in such children's behavior, most of them do not become "normal." Some behavioral researchers may be on the verge of effecting a "cure" rate of 50% or more when they begin intervention very early, however (Lovaas, 1982b; O'Leary & Carr, 1982). The prognosis is poorest for those children who are both psychotic and mentally retarded. Even with today's most effective intervention methods, a high proportion of retarded psychotic children are likely to be institutionalized or, at best, semiindependent.

CURRENT PROBLEMS AND FUTURE DIRECTIONS

As mentioned previously, there is currently a great deal of interest in integrating the child's cognition and affect into behavioral interventions. While it is true that the ultimate goal of any intervention with disturbed children is self-control and that cognitive-behavioral interventions stress self-control procedures, it is important to remember that intervention should seldom *begin* with self-control procedures. It is best to start with a high degree of external control (teacher or parent direction) and move gradually to self-control only after the child has responded to the externally determined structure (Hallahan et al., in press; O'Leary & Carr, 1982).

Another trend in current programming for emotionally disturbed children is family and community intervention. It has become clear that, if behavioral intervention is to be effective in the long run, parents must be trained to continue the program designed at school or to devise their own intervention techniques. This may be especially true for psychotic children, but it applies to aggressive and hyperactive children as well (Koegel et al., 1982; Lovaas, 1982b; Lovaas et al., 1973; O'Leary & Carr, 1982; Patterson & Fleischman, 1979; Patterson et al., 1975). Under the law, parents have a right to be involved in educational decision making about their handicapped children (Turnbull & Turnbull, 1982); effective intervention requires that they also be involved in implementing the intervention plan.

In past years, many psychotic children were placed in residential institutions; if kept at home, they were often excluded from the public schools. Currently, there is movement toward the integration of such children into their communities, including public school classes. With effective intervention, some psychotic children can be included in regular classes (Koegel et al., 1982; Lovaas, 1982b).

One issue almost certain to become increasingly critical and controversial in future years is the definition of emotional disturbance. Because the current federal definition is so clearly flawed, and because so few children are being served in comparison with the estimated number of children who are disturbed, it will be necessary to reexamine the meaning of the term *emotional disturbance*. Some may take the position that prevalence estimates are far too high, that most of the children who are disturbed are now receiving special education, and that the concept of disturbed behavior must be revised to reflect the characteristics of those children now served under the law. According to this view, there is too little tolerance for behavioral difference in children, and many children have been labeled deviant when they are not. Others may take the position that most disturbed children are not currently receiving special education, that the prevalence estimates of the past 20 years are essentially correct, and that the real problem is how to obtain services for the majority of disturbed children who are now neglected.

Obviously, an "emotional disturbance" is not an objective, invariant reality, but a social convention constructed to suit societal purposes. Individuals and professional groups may have different opinions regarding what emotional disturbance is or should be, but the definition in the law and federal regulations will be the single most important factor in determining which children receive special education.

NOTES

1. *Federal Register,* Vol. 42, No. 163, August 23, 1977, p. 42478.
2. Proposed revisions of the definitions are currently being considered (Federal Register, Vol. 47, No. 150, August 4, 1982, p. 33846). Revisions include elimination of the "educational performance" criterion and the "social maladjustment" exclusion.

REFERENCES

Achenbach, T.M., & Edelbrock, C.S. The classification of child psychopathology: A review and analysis of empirical efforts. *Psychological Bulletin,* 1978, *85,* 1275-1301.

Achenbach, T.M., & Edelbrock, C.S. Behavioral problems and competencies reported by parents of normal and disturbed children aged four through sixteen. *Monographs of the Society for Research in Child Development,* 1981, *46*(1, Whole No. 188).

Ahammer, I.M., & Murray, J.P. Kindness in the kindergarten: The relative influence of role playing and prosocial television in facilitating altruism. *International Journal of Behavioral Development,* 1979, *2,* 133-157.

Alberto, P.A., & Troutman, A.C. *Applied behavior analysis for teachers.* Columbus, Ohio: Charles E. Merrill, 1982.

American Psychiatric Association. *Diagnostic and statistical manual of mental disorders* (3rd ed.). Washington, D.C.: Author, 1980.

Bachman, J.A. Self-injurious behavior: A behavioral analysis. *Journal of Abnormal Psychology,* 1972, *80,* 211-224.

Balthazaar, E., & Stevens, H. *The emotionally disturbed mentally retarded.* Englewood Cliffs, N.J.: Prentice-Hall, 1975.

Bandura, A. *Aggression: A social learning analysis.* Englewood Cliffs, N.J.: Prentice-Hall, 1973.

Bell, R.Q., & Harper, L.V. *Child effects on adults.* Hillsdale, N.J.: Erlbaum, 1977.

Bernal, M.E., Duryee, J.S., Pruett, H.L., & Burns, B.J. Behavior modification and the brat syndrome. *Journal of Consulting and Clinical Psychology,* 1968, *32,* 447-455.

Blechman, E.A., Kotanchik, N.L., & Taylor, C.J. Families and schools together: Early behavioral intervention with high risk children. *Behavior Therapy,* 1981, *12,* 308-319.

Bower, E.M. *Early identification of emotionally handicapped children in school* (2nd ed.). Springfield, Ill.: Charles C Thomas, 1969.

Bower, E.M. Defining emotional disturbance: Public policy and research. *Psychology in the Schools,* 1982, *19,* 55-60.

Bower, E.M., & Lambert, N.M. *A process for in-school screening of children with emotional handicaps*. Princeton, N.J.: Educational Testing Service, 1962.

Campbell, S.B., & Paulauskas, S. Peer relations in hyperactive children. *Journal of Child Psychology and Psychiatry,* 1979, *20,* 233-246.

Chess, S., & Thomas, A. Temperamental individuality from childhood to adolescence. *Journal of the American Academy of Child Psychiatry,* 1977, *16,* 218-226.

Clark, P., & Rutter, M. Autistic children's responses to structure and to interpersonal demands. *Journal of Autism and Developmental Disorders,* 1981, *11,* 201-217.

Clarke-Stewart, A.K. Interactions between mothers and their young children: Characteristics and consequences. *Monographs of the Society for Research in Child Development,* 1973, *38*(Nos. 6-7, Serial No. 153).

Combs, M.L., & Slaby, D. Social-skills training with children. In B.B. Lahey & A.E. Kazdin (Eds.), *Advances in clinical child psychology* (Vol. 1). New York: Plenum Press, 1977.

Cullinan, D., Epstein, M.H., & Kauffman, J.M. The behavioral model and children's behavior disorders: Foundations and evaluations. In R.L. McDowell, G.W. Adamson, & F.H. Wood (Eds.), *Teaching emotionally disturbed children*. Boston: Little, Brown, 1982.

Deitz, D., & Repp, A. Reducing behavior through reinforcement. *Exceptional Education Quarterly,* in press.

DeMyer, M.K., Barton, S., Alpern, G.D., Kimberlin, C., Allen, J., Young, E., & Steele, R. The measured intelligence of autistic children. *Journal of Autism and Childhood Schizophrenia,* 1974, *4,* 42-60.

Eggers, C. Course and prognosis of childhood schizophrenia. *Journal of Autism and Childhood Schizophrenia,* 1978, *8,* 21-36.

Evans, I.M., & Nelson, R.O. Assessment of child behavior problems. In A.R. Ciminero, K.S. Calhoun, & H.E. Adams (Eds.), *Handbook of behavioral assessment*. New York: Wiley, 1977.

Fagen, S.A., Long, N.J., & Stevens, D.J. *Teaching children self-control*. Columbus, Ohio: Charles E. Merrill, 1974.

Field, T. Early peer relations. In P.S. Strain (Ed.), *The utilization of classroom peers as behavior change agents*. New York: Plenum Press, 1981.

Field, T.M., Goldberg, S., Stern, D., & Sostek, A.M. (Eds.). *High-risk infants and children: Adult and peer interactions*. New York: Academic Press, 1980.

Fundis, A.T. Social interaction with peers: A developmental perspective on exceptional children's social isolation. *Exceptional Education Quarterly,* 1981, *1*(4), 1-11.

Gadow, K.D. Effects of stimulant drugs on attention and cognitive deficits. *Exceptional Education Quarterly,* 1981, *2*(3), 83-93.

Gadverry, S. Effects of restricting first graders' TV-viewing on leisure time use, IQ change, and cognitive style. *Journal of Applied Developmental Psychology,* 1980, *1,* 45-57.

Gast, D.L., & Nelson, C.M. Legal and ethical considerations for the use of timeout in special education settings. *Journal of Special Education,* 1977, *11,* 457-467.

Gelfand, D.M. Social withdrawal and negative emotional states: Behavior therapy. In B.B. Wolman (Ed.), *Handbook of treatment of mental disorders in childhood and adolescence*. Englewood Cliffs, N.J.: Prentice-Hall, 1978.

Goldstein, J.J., & Rodnick, E.H. The family's contribution to the etiology of schizophrenia. Current status. *Schizophrenia Bulletin,* 1975, *14,* 48-63.

Graham, P.J. Epidemiological studies. In H.C. Quay & J.S. Werry (Eds.), *Psychopathological disorders of childhood* (2nd ed.). New York: Wiley, 1979.

Grosenick, J.K., & Huntze, S.L. *National needs analysis in behavior disorders*. Columbia, Mo.: University of Missouri, Department of Special Education, 1979.

Hallahan, D.P. (Ed.). Teaching exceptional children to use cognitive strategies. *Exceptional Education Quarterly,* 1980, *1*(Whole No. 1).

Hallahan, D.P., & Kauffman, J.M. *Introduction to learning disabilities: A psycho-behavioral approach*. Englewood Cliffs, N.J.: Prentice-Hall, 1976.

Hallahan, D.P., & Kauffman, J.M. *Exceptional children: Introduction to special education*. Englewood Cliffs, N.J.: Prentice-Hall, 1978.

Hallahan, D.P., Lloyd, J.W., Kauffman, J.M., & Loper, A.B. Behavior therapy methods for academic problems. In R.D. Morris & T.R. Kratochwill (Eds.), *Practice of child therapy: A textbook of methods*. New York: Pergamon Press, in press.

Hanson, D.R., & Gottesman, I.I. The genetics, if any, of infantile autism and childhood schizophrenia. *Journal of Autism and Childhood Schizophrenia,* 1976, *6,* 209-234.

Harris, A. An empirical test of the situation specificity/consistency of aggressive behavior. *Child Behavior Therapy,* 1979, *1,* 257-270.

Harris, S.L. DSM-III—Its implications for children. *Child Behavior Therapy,* 1979, *1,* 37-46.

Hetherington, E.M., & Martin, B. Family interaction. In H.C. Quay & J.S. Werry (Eds.), *Psychopathological disorders of childhood* (2nd ed.). New York: Wiley, 1979.

Hobbs, N. *The futures of children*. San Francisco: Jossey-Bass, 1975.

Huston-Stein, A., Fox, S., Greer, D., Watkins, B.A., & Whitaker, J. The effects of TV action and violence on children's social behavior. *Journal of Genetic Psychology,* 1981, *138,* 183-191.

Jacob, T. Family interaction in disturbed and normal families: A methodological and substantive review. *Psychological Bulletin,* 1975, *82,* 33-65.

Johnson, S.B., & Melamed, B.G. The assessment and treatment of children's fears. In B.B. Lahey & A.E. Kazdin (Eds.), *Advances in clinical child psychology* (Vol. 2). New York: Plenum Press, 1979.

Kauffman, J.M. Nineteenth century views of children's behavior disorders: Historical contributions and continuing issues. *Journal of Special Education,* 1976, *10,* 335-349.

Kauffman, J.M. Where special education for disturbed children is going: A personal view. *Exceptional Children,* 1980, *48,* 522-527.

Kauffman, J.M. *Characteristics of children's behavior disorders* (2nd ed.). Columbus, Ohio: Charles E. Merrill, 1981.

Kauffman, J.M. Social policy issues in definition. In M.M. Noel & N.G. Haring (Eds.), *Issues in the education of seriously emotionally disturbed children*. Seattle: University of Washington, Program Development Assistance System, 1982.

Kauffman, J.M., & Hallahan, D.P. Control of rough physical behavior using novel contingencies and directive teaching. *Perceptual and Motor Skills,* 1973, *36,* 1225-1226.

Kauffman, J.M., & Hallahan, D.P. Learning disability and hyperactivity (with comments on minimal brain dysfunction). In B.B. Lahey & A.E. Kazdin (Eds.), *Advances in clinical child psychology* (Vol. 2). New York: Plenum Press, 1979.

Kauffman, J.M., & Kneedler, R.D. Behavior disorders. In J.M. Kauffman & D.P. Hallahan (Eds.), *Handbook of special education*. Englewood Cliffs, N.J.: Prentice-Hall, 1981.

Kaufhold, S., & Kauffman, J.M. Sammy: Frequent crying spells. In J. Worell & C.M. Nelson (Eds.), *Managing instructional problems*. New York: McGraw-Hill, 1974.

Keogh, B.K., & Becker, L.D. Early detection of learning problems: Questions, cautions, and guidelines. *Exceptional Children,* 1973, *40,* 5-11.

Kerr, M.M., & Nelson, C.M. *Strategies for managing behavior problems*. Columbus, Ohio: Charles E. Merrill, in press.

Kneedler, R.D. The use of cognitive training to change social behaviors. *Exceptional Education Quarterly*, 1980, *1*(1), 65-73.

Koegel, R.L., Rincover, A., & Egel, A.L. *Educating and understanding autistic children*. San Diego: College-Hill Press, 1982.

Lambert, N.M., Hartsough, C.S., & Bower, E.M. *A process for the assessment of effective student functioning: Administration and use manual*. Monterey, Calif.: Publishers Test Service, 1979.

Lotter, V. Follow-up studies. In M. Rutter & E. Schopler (Eds.), *Autism: A reappraisal of concepts and treatment*. New York: Plenum Press, 1978.

Lovaas, O.I. Comments on self-destructive behaviors. *Analysis and Intervention in Developmental Disabilities*, 1982, *2*, 115-124. (a)

Lovaas, O.I. *An overview of the young autism project*. Paper presented at the annual conference of the American Psychological Association, Washington, D.C., September, 1982. (b)

Lovaas, O.I., Koegel, R.L., Simmons, J.Q., & Long, J.S. Some generalization and follow-up measures of autistic children in behavior therapy. *Journal of Applied Behavior Analysis*, 1973, *6*, 131-165.

Mahoney, M.J. *Cognition and behavior modification*. Cambridge, Mass.: Ballinger, 1974.

McDowell, R.L., Adamson, G.W., & Wood, F.H. (Eds.). *Teaching emotionally disturbed children*. Boston: Little, Brown, 1982.

Meichenbaum, D. *Cognitive-behavior modification: An integrative approach*. New York: Plenum Press, 1977.

Morris, R.D., & Kratochwill, T.R. (Eds.). *Practice of child therapy: A textbook of methods*. New York: Pergamon Press, in press.

Murray, J.P. *Television and youth: 25 years of research and controversy*. Boys Town, Nebr.: Boys Town Center for the Study of Youth Development, 1980.

Nelson, C.M., & Rutherford, R.B. Time-out revisited: Guidelines for its use in special education. *Exceptional Education Quarterly*, in press.

O'Leary, K.D., & Carr, E.G. Behavior therapy with children: Outcome and evaluation. In G.T. Wilson & C.M. Franks (Eds.), *Contemporary behavior therapy: Conceptual foundations of clinical practice*. New York: Guilford Press, 1982.

O'Leary, K.D., & Johnson, S.B. Psychological assessment. In H.C. Quay & J.S. Werry (Eds.), *Psychopathological disorders of childhood* (2nd ed.). New York: Wiley, 1979.

Pate, J.E., & Webb, W.W. *First grade screening test manual*. Circle Pines, Minn.: American Guidance Service, 1967.

Patterson, G.R. Mothers: The unacknowledged victims. *Monographs of the Society for Research in Child Development*, 1980, *45*(No. 5, Serial No. 186).

Patterson, G.R., & Fleischman, M.J. Maintenance of treatment effects: Some considerations concerning family systems and follow-up data. *Behavior Therapy*, 1979, *10*, 168-185.

Patterson, G.R., Reid, J.B., Jones, R.R., & Conger, R.E. *A social learning approach to family intervention: Families with aggressive children*. Eugene, Oreg.: Castalia Press, 1975.

Polsgrove, L. (Ed.). Aversive control of exceptional children's behavior. *Exceptional Education Quarterly*, in press.

Quay, H.C. Classification. In H.C. Quay & J.S. Werry (Eds.), *Psychopathological disorders of childhood* (2nd ed.). New York: Wiley, 1979.

Rhodes, W.C., & Paul, J.L. *Emotionally disturbed and deviant children: New views and approaches*. Englewood Cliffs, N.J.: Prentice-Hall, 1978.

Robins, L.N. Follow-up studies. In H.C. Quay & J.S. Werry (Eds.), *Psychopathological disorders of childhood* (2nd ed.). New York: Wiley, 1979.

Ross, A.O. *Psychological disorders of children* (2nd ed.). New York: McGraw-Hill, 1980.

Ross, D.M., & Ross, S.A. *Hyperactivity: Research, theory, action*. New York: Wiley, 1976.

Rubin, R.A., & Balow, B. Prevalence of teacher identified behavior problems: A longitudinal study. *Exceptional Children,* 1978, *45,* 102-111.

Rutter, M. Diagnosis and definition of childhood autism. *Journal of Autism and Childhood Schizophrenia,* 1978, *8,* 137-161.

Rutter, M. Maternal deprivation, 1972-1978: New findings, new concepts, new approaches. *Child Development,* 1979, *50,* 283-305.

Sameroff, A.J., & Chandler, M.J. Reproductive risk and the continuum of caretaking causality. In F.D. Horowitz (Ed.), *Review of child development research* (Vol. 4). Chicago: University of Chicago Press, 1975.

Schopler, E., & Dalldorf, J. Autism: Definition, diagnosis, and management. *Hospital Practice,* 1980, *15,* 64-73.

Spivack, G., & Shure, M.B. *Social adjustment of young children*. San Francisco: Jossey-Bass, 1974.

Stein, A.H., & Friedrich, L.K. Impact of television on children and youth. In E.M. Hetherington (Ed.), *Review of child development research* (Vol. 5). Chicago: University of Chicago Press, 1975.

Strain, P.S. (Ed.). *The utilization of classroom peers as behavior change agents*. New York: Plenum Press, 1981. (a)

Strain, P.S. (Ed.). Peer relations of exceptional children and youth. *Exceptional Education Quarterly,* 1981, *1*(Whole No. 4). (b)

Strain, P.S., Steele, P., Ellis, T., & Timm, M.A. Long-term effects of opposition child treatment with mothers as therapists and therapist trainers. *Journal of Applied Behavior Analysis,* 1982, *15,* 163-169.

Thomas, A., Chess, S., & Birch, H. *Temperament and behavior disorders in children*. New York: New York University Press, 1968.

Turnbull, H.R., & Turnbull, A. (Eds.). Parent participation in the education of exceptional children. *Exceptional Education Quarterly,* 1982, *3*(Whole No. 2).

U.S. General Accounting Office. *Disparities still exist in who gets special education*. Washington, D.C.: U.S. Government Printing Office, 1981.

Von Isser, A., Quay, H.C., & Love, C.T. Interrelationships among three measures of deviant behavior. *Exceptional Children,* 1980, *46,* 272-276.

Wallace, G., & Kauffman, J.M. *Teaching children with learning problems* (2nd ed.). Columbus, Ohio: Charles E. Merrill, 1978.

Werry, J.S. Organic factors. In H.C. Quay & J.S. Werry (Eds.), *Psychopathological disorders of childhood* (2nd ed.). New York: Wiley, 1979.

Whalen, C.K., Henker, B., & Dotemoto, S. Teacher response to methylphenidate (Ritalin) versus placebo status of hyperactive boys in the classroom. *Child Development,* 1981, *52,* 1005-1014.

Williams, C.D. The elimination of tantrum behavior by extinction procedures. *Journal of Abnormal and Social Psychology,* 1959, *59,* 269.

Wing, L. Childhood autism and social class: A question of selection? *British Journal of Psychiatry,* 1980, *137,* 410-417.

Wing, L. Language, social, and cognitive impairments in autism and severe mental retardation. *Journal of Autism and Developmental Disorders,* 1981, *11,* 31-44.

Wolf, M.M., Risley, T.R., & Mees, M. Application of operant conditioning procedures to the behavior problems of an autistic child. *Behaviour Research and Therapy,* 1964, *1,* 305-312.

Wood, F.H., & Lakin, K.C. (Eds.). *Disturbing, disordered, or disturbed: Perspectives on the definition of problem behavior in educational settings.* Minneapolis: University of Minnesota, Department of Psychoeducational Studies, Advanced Institute for Trainers of Teachers for Seriously Emotionally Disturbed Children and Youth, 1979.

Chapter 11

Curriculums for Young Handicapped Children

Rebecca R. Fewell and Jean F. Kelly

There is much latitude in the way educators define *curriculum*. Piaget's concept of development (1963, 1973) forms the basis for a broad view of curriculum. He describes development as a process of adaptation whereby children grow through their active engagement with people and objects, observing, operating, inventing, and effecting changes on both the persons and places around them. Olds (1979) defines curriculum from the perspective of a child intrinsically motivated to interact with the environment, limited only by the environment's restrictions. In Olds' opinion, "the environment is the curriculum and the physical parameters of classrooms, as much as books, toys, and work sheets, must be manipulated by teachers as essential aspects of the educational process" (p. 91). It is our opinion, based on the ecological research of Belsky and Tolan (1981), that the child, the teacher, other adults and children, and the features of the environment interact in a complex organism-environment reciprocity that must be considered in developing curriculums.

Not only theoretical perspectives, but also the needs of individual children can have significant impact on curriculum development. Educators have developed special curriculum and instruction practices and models both for preschool children whose needs emanate primarily from the social and economic conditions of their early years and for those whose needs emanate from deficiencies of a biological or medical character. Although curriculum and instruction models developed for different populations (e.g., normal, deaf, retarded, infant, young adult) have common features, some strategies may be more effective with one group than with another.

CURRICULUM DEVELOPMENT

There are at least three reasons to develop a well-defined, written curriculum. First, the identification of program theory, activities, and intended outcomes enables all staff members to adhere to the same teaching approach. Daily program planning, decision making, and resolution of problems take place within a specified framework. Second, program effectiveness can be evaluated. Evans (1975) points out that a program may be evaluated according to (1) the degree to which it meets its own stated goals and (2) its effectiveness in comparison with that of one or more similar programs. Thus, evaluation may serve both as a basis for individual program decision making and improvement and as a means for obtaining empirical evidence in support of adopting one curriculum over another. Third, a written curriculum allows for the replication of exemplary programs.

Authors prepare curriculum materials to transmit knowledge that they have identified as critical for a particular target population. Teachers and school administrators select a curriculum on the basis of their perceptions of their students' needs, their agreement with an author's approach to teaching and learning, their estimation of the quality of the curriculum, as well as other factors, such as cost, availability, and flexibility. Because of the diverse concerns of producers and consumers, there is no organized framework within which to examine the development of various curriculums. Nevertheless, some points for comparison are needed.

Tyler (1949) proposes four central questions to be considered when designing a curriculum:

1. What educational purposes are being sought?
2. What educational experiences can be provided that are likely to attain these purposes?
3. How can these educational experiences be effectively organized?
4. How can we determine whether these purposes are being attained? (p. 1)

Gammage (1980) sees curriculum development hinging on four interrelated questions:

1. What is the content of the program?
2. When is the appropriate time for presentation of activities?
3. How are the activities presented?
4. Why these approaches rather than others?

Answers to these and similar sets of questions provide curriculum designers with a framework for curriculum construction, and also illustrate the major sources of conflict in curriculum design.

Curriculum Goals and Objectives

Evans (1975) discusses two points of view about goals for early childhood education: (1) child development and (2) preparation for scholastic success. Those who adhere to the first perspective design curriculum objectives and activities based on the immediate needs and interests of the children. Opposing this view are those who believe that a curriculum should be designed to meet society's requirements for an individual's future success.

These differing viewpoints highlight the schism between the cognitive-developmental and behavioristic approaches to early education in regard to goals, content, and instructional strategies. In a developmental approach, objectives and strategies allow for maximum child-environment interaction. The teacher does not directly *instruct* the children, but rather the children *construct* their own learning environment according to their individual interests and motivation. In the behavioral approach, teachers instruct the children; they define the learning behavior, correct the behavior, institute reinforcement procedures for changing behavior, and measure the change.

Perhaps the contributions of both perspectives are beginning to be recognized. Spradlin and Siegel (1982) joined together to examine the literature, listen to clinicians, and talk with program developers in order to present both sides of the schism within a single framework for the acquisition of language skills. In addition, Dunst (1981) clearly used contributions of both positions in his curriculum *Infant Learning*.

Dunst advocates the identification of intervention strategies and instructional targets by applying assessment data from the Uzgiris and Hunt Scales of Infant Psychological Development (Uzgiris & Hunt, 1975) to a matrix (Figure 11-1). In Phase I of the intervention:

> It is recommended that (a) at least three to five different behaviors within each *response-contingency category* (manual, social, vocal, etc.) be fostered, (b) the same behavior (e.g., visually directed reaching) be used in different categories (e.g., manually swiping at a mobile and touching an adult's mouth to be kissed) to foster generalization of the responses, and (c) whenever possible, the activities be implemented during ongoing, naturalistic encounters between the child and objects and persons in the environment, rather than under highly structured, artificial learning conditions. The latter is designed to increase the probability that the behaviors facilitated become functional and adaptive. (p. 48)

Figure 11-1 Object Permanence Matrix

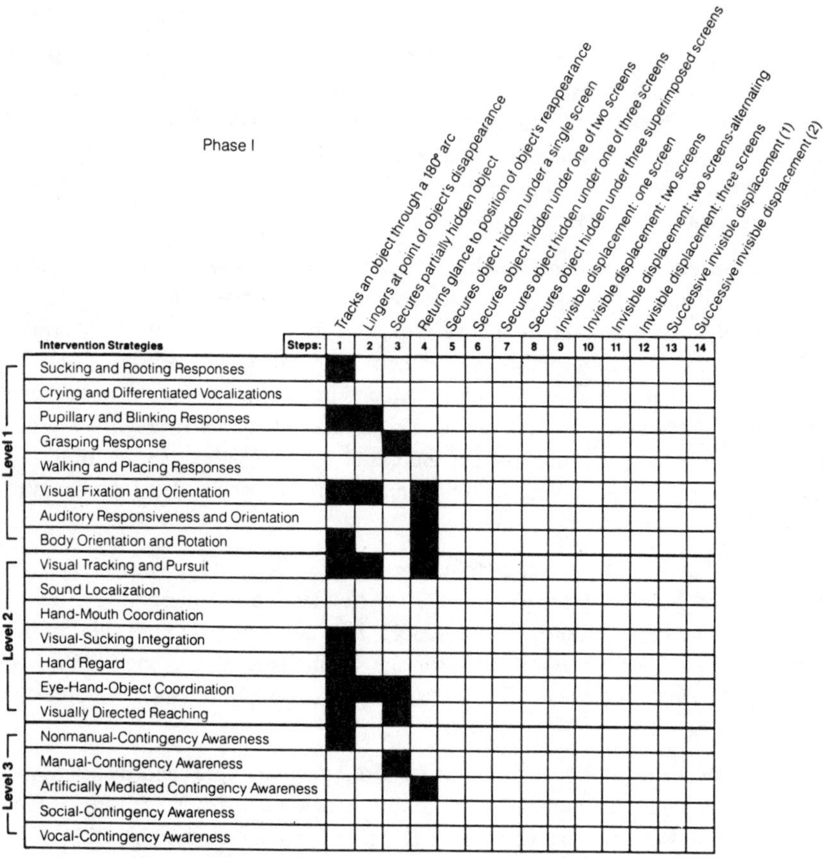

Source: From Dunst, C.J. *Infant Learning: A Cognitive-Linguistic Intervention Strategy.* Copyright 1981 by Teaching Resources Corporation. Reproduced by permission. All rights reserved.

The objectives of the intervention procedures for strategy 4, Grasping Response (Figure 11-1), are as follows:

- to ensure that infants are afforded experiences that will transform the grasping response from a reflexive to a learned (instrumental) behavior.
- to facilitate the adaptive and exploratory use of the grasping response.
- to enhance arm flexion and extension through facilitation of the grasping response.

- to facilitate the grasping response as a response-contingent behavior. (p. 70)

For each intervention strategy, Dunst explains the basic behavior in an introductory paragraph. This is followed, in the example of Grasping Response, by nine key points. Four of the nine points are as follows:

- The natural tendency to resist the removal of objects held in the hands is used to facilitate and strengthen the grasping behavior. Elongated objects about three inches in length (e.g., clothes pins, pegs, etc.) have been used with success. An object is first placed in the child's hand. If grasping does not spontaneously occur, the child's fingers are hand-shaped around the object. The object is then moved in different directions to identify in what positions resistance to withdrawal occurs best. In all instances, it is important to be cognizant of the fact that withdrawal of the object should cause the child to flex rather than extend his or her arm. If the latter occurs, the hand will tend to open and drop the object.
- Active exploration can be facilitated by placing the infant prone on a surface that provides tactile reinforcement for grasping. This can be a rug, blanket, soft toys to be grasped, etc.
- The key to success in facilitating grasping as a response-contingent behavior is finding objects the infant finds particularly reinforcing.
- Particularly salient and potent elicitors of the grasping response are caregiver's fingers. Facilitation of the grasping response using one's fingers as elicitors is highly recommended since the manifestation of the targeted behavior occurs within the context of social interactions, and social reinforcers can be used to sustain the occurrence of the behavior. (pp. 70-71)

Tyler (1949) proposes that the purposes of education be decided by consulting three data sources: society, learners, and subject matter specialists. Goodlad and Richter (1966) suggest turning to recognized societal values first, pointing out that such values influence the examination of the three data sources that Tyler lists. Drawing on Tyler's work, Sparling (1974) presents five sources for synthesizing educational objectives:

1. consumer opinions (parents and children)
2. developmental theory (e.g., Piaget, Skinner)
3. developmental facts ordered and arranged in broad areas, such as language, motor, social/emotional and cognitive/perceptive

4. adaptive sets (those behaviors that generate age-appropriate success)
5. high-risk indicators (the opposite of adaptive sets)

In summary, the selection of curriculum goals and objectives is dependent on the developers' underlying philosophy about education and on the data sources they consult in specifying the purposes of educational activity.

Selection, Organization, and Implementation of Learning Activities

Perhaps the major issue in selecting learning activities in a curriculum is whether primary importance should be assigned to the process or the product of learning. Karnes, Zehrbach, and Teska (1972) define process as the ability to obtain, organize, manipulate, synthesize, integrate, and communicate information. Programs that focus on process, therefore, focus on the way in which children think, evaluate, and seek out new information. Teachers observe the spontaneous strategies that students adopt to solve problems, then teach new strategies and provide opportunities for the students to apply and generalize the new strategies. For example, Cahoon (1974) describes the following task for teaching preschool children skill in predicting the size and weight of objects:

Suggested items for comparison:
- 2 bars of hand soap in original wrappers (one whose contents have been altered by carving out its center and filling it with tissue, then replacing it in the original wrapper)
- 2 cardboard tubes with taped ends (one filled with tissue paper, one filled with small rocks or sand)
- 2 jelly jars of equal size (one filled with water)
- 1 larger jelly jar

Foil-covered items:
- 2 baseballs
- 4 books (two identical, one light-weight loose-leaf binder, and one heavy encyclopedia)
- 2 golf balls (one plastic)
- 2 identical wooden blocks
- 2 plastic blocks
- 1 marble
- 1 tissue paper ball (marble size)
- 2 flashlight batteries

1. First present the cardboard tubes, one filled with tissue paper and one filled with sand. Inform the children that they are to use their hands

and judge which of the two weighs more. Ask them to predict or make a judgment without the aid of balance scales or water. Ask:

What happens to your hand when something heavy is placed in it?

Establish that the hand goes down when something heavy is placed in it, but when something light is placed there, the hand does not go down quite so far. The children will acknowledge that a person can tell by the pressure of an object against his hand whether it is heavier or lighter than another object.

2. Compare a wooden block to a plastic block, both of which are concealed inside aluminum foil and appear to be equal. Encourage the children to feel them and judge which is lighter, which is heavier, or if they are the same weight.
3. Present two foil-wrapped baseballs and encourage the children to judge and compare their weight. Each pair of objects may be passed among the children. They are encouraged to make weight judgments by use of the objects' push against their hands.
4. Next, place a matched pair of objects in a child's hands and ask:

   Which weighs more or do they weigh the same?

   Let each child participate in the weight measurement activity.
5. Present two identical wooden blocks for the children to handle, and ask them to explain why the blocks feel the same weight. Present the golf balls, identical in size and shape but of differing weight. Compare the two identical books by the above procedure, and then two books of unequal size and weight, one larger but lighter, one smaller and heavier. Inform the children that sometimes two objects may appear to be equal, or one may be larger and would seem to weigh more; but to judge weight more accurately, the objects must be handled or weighed on a scale.
6. Compare two bars of soap—one hollowed and filled with paper—and the children will discover that things which appear to be equal are sometimes not. Compare the jelly jars, one empty and one filled with water. Then the water-filled jelly jar may be compared to the larger jelly jar.
7. After the children have handled the objects and completed the comparisons, reveal the contents of the foil-wrapped packages to the children and explain what caused the weight differences in those items which appeared to be equal.[1]

In a product or content approach to instruction, activities are highly structured, both in the way tasks are presented and in the way responses are made. The following example from the Distar Language 1 program by Engelmann and Osborn (1976) illustrates a direct instruction approach to teaching.

Task 10 Same-Different
Look at this picture.

a. Point to each ball and ask: What is this? Touch. The children are to answer, a ball.
b. I know why these things are the same. Because they are balls. Everybody, why are these things the same? Touch. Because they are balls. Yes, they are the same because they are balls.
c. Say the whole thing about why they are the same. Touch. They are the same because they are balls.
d. Repeat a through c until all children's responses are firm. (p. 56)

The organization of learning activities depends on the curriculum planners' theory of learning. In developmental theory, based on the work of Piaget, it is assumed that children move through developmental stages and that mastery of the skills in one stage is a prerequisite for achievement of skills at the next higher level. The curriculum resulting from this approach is organized in clusters of interrelated skills, each cluster built on a previous stage of learning. Any attempt to omit a stage can hinder later learning; each learned concept serves as a foundation for higher order concepts.

In contrast, in operant theory, children are believed to learn by experiencing repeated reinforcement for responses to environmental stimuli. Curriculums developed according to this philosophy often minimize interdependency between skills, as it is believed that behaviors can be taught separately from one another according to behavioral principles.

Regardless of the theoretical perspective that determines the order of learning activities, teachers may vary the stimuli used in the activity or change the level of difficulty, depending on the individual child's capability.

Bissell (1970) incorporated Tyler's questions into operational definitions of objectives, strategies, and structure, three elements that provide a workable framework for comparing curriculum models. Objectives are the ends toward which a curriculum is directed; they are explicit statements of the student behaviors that are to be acquired during the instructional process as a given curriculum is followed. The objectives are stated in measurable terms that permit the users to determine whether the student has acquired the information. In most currently used curriculums, objectives are predetermined in the instructional package.

Strategies are the procedures and processes that the teacher will use to facilitate learning. Stake (1967) referred to these as "transactions," all the activities or processes of engagement that go on during the program. The strategies can include the conditions of instruction, such as where it will occur, or they can be viewed in terms of learning experiences. Tyler (1949) defined the term *learning experience* as "the interaction between the learner and the external condition in the environment to which he can react'' (p. 63). Tyler saw the teacher as controller of the learning experience, responsible for manipulating the environment in order to set up stimulating situations—situations that evoke the desired behavior.

Structure is the degree of a model's external organization in regard to teacher behaviors, student behaviors, expected transactions, and expected outcomes. The degree of structure influences both objectives and strategies of a curriculum.

Programs may be highly structured in some areas and not in others. For example, in the Montessori method, space and materials are highly structured, while teacher and child roles are not. The Bank Street approach is low in structure in all respects; in contrast, the Bereiter-Englemann program is high in structure in all respects. Students of Goodwin and Driscoll (1980) labeled early childhood models with high structure as ''pricklies'' and those with low structure as ''gooeys.'' The prickly approaches, according to the authors,

> tend to incorporate active measurement and testing, more rigid scheduling and drill, limited opportunity for children to follow their interests, external reinforcers, less active home-school relationships and relatively less emphasis on affective outcomes. The gooey models, by contrast, are distinguished by the avoidance of formal testing, less rigid scheduling and no drill, extensive freedom for children to explore their interests, intrinsic motivation, more active home-school partnerships and relatively more emphasis on affective outcomes. (Goodwin & Driscoll, 1980, pp. 435-436)

Admittedly a bit overstated, these terms do distinguish between two very different approaches to teaching children.

Case (1975) presents a method of selecting learning activities and teaching strategies based on developmental theory. He initially describes Gagne's model of learning, in which the instructional designer maps out the hierarchical structure of skills underlying the objective to be attained, determines the learner's prerequisite skills, and plans a set of activities to guide the learner from the present skill level to the objective. Case believes that Gagne's task analysis model must be expanded to take into account the fact that children's cognitive capacities develop with age.

He presents examples to show that children's difficulties in acquiring skills cannot be traced simply to inadequate learning of prerequisite skills, but rather to either an inability to overcome their spontaneity when responding to a situation or an inability to coordinate all the relevant information. Therefore, when a particular skill proves difficult to teach he suggests developing a task analysis from the ''learner's point of view.''

Case (1978) outlines in more detail the development of this type of instructional design. First, before instruction, the educator develops a step-by-step description not only of the strategy to be taught, but also of the strategies that children apply spontaneously in performing instructional tasks. Case points out that children approach tasks with oversimplified strategies dependent on their developmental age. Second, the teacher designs the instruction so that the limitations of the spontaneous strategies will be apparent, and therefore the need for the strategy to be taught will be clear. Thus, the child learns to discriminate the incorrect response from the correct response and to understand the relationship between them. Third, in selecting the strategies and learning activities, the instructor reduces the memory requirements of the learning situation to a bare minimum. Research shows that, when curriculums are based on these procedures, the improvement in children's performance can be dramatic (Case, 1978). Furthermore, Case points out that the cost-effectiveness of applying these procedures is likely to be greatest for groups of learners who would not be expected to show spontaneous improvement.

Research has not yet shown one type of curriculum approach to be significantly superior to another. Weikart's (1981) review of summaries of the various consortium programs caused him to conclude "Various philosophical positions would have us believe that they have direct access to the whole child in ways that are educationally productive and different. These data fail to support that position" (p. 33). Moreover, after reviewing the results of a large number of preschool programs, Palmer and Andersen (1981) concluded that "with existing evidence no clear case can be made for one type of program over another. Almost certainly the characteristics of the sample treated will influence what type of program is best, and even within a given sample, the characteristics of a given child are the relevant variables for determining which program will benefit him most" (p. 65).

MODELS FOR EARLY CHILDHOOD CURRICULUMS

The evolution of early childhood curriculums from the early 1900s to the present relates directly to changing trends in early education during that same period. Several program models have had a direct bearing on the curriculums used in programs for young handicapped children.

Curriculums in Traditional Nursery Schools

Sears and Dowley (1963) examined the proliferation of nursery school programs from the 1920s to the 1960s. Initially, preschools were generally affiliated with colleges and universities and had as their major objective the discovery of better ways to "care" for children. Federal legislation, under the Works Progress Administration Program of the 1930s and the Lanham Act during World War II, was instrumental in providing funds for the spread of preschools beyond the university communities. During the postwar years, cooperatives became popular, as more and more parents recognized the value of group experiences and parent education. Sears and Dowley described the instructional strategies in these traditional preschools as watching and waiting for the children's needs to emerge so that different activities can be timed appropriately. Thus, specific or formal structure is minimal. Teachers are clinical observers, learning from the children and fostering change and development as they feel it is needed.

Traditional nursery school approaches emphasize social-emotional needs, basic health needs, and play to promote sensorimotor and emotional development. Good teacher-child rapport and a free, nonrestrictive environment are essential elements. Program activities are guided by the expressed interests of the children, and the teacher independently interprets their needs within the program rather than following a specified curriculum. Efforts are evaluated through satisfaction of parents, staff, and the children. The progress of the children in meeting the adaptive expectations of their peer group is also considered an outcome variable for purposes of evaluation.

Enrichment Curriculums

Education was one of the areas of concern when the War on Poverty was begun in 1964, and the young disadvantaged child became a prime target. It was widely believed that many disadvantaged children performed poorly in school because they lacked the experiences that advantaged families provided their offspring. To remedy this situation, educators proposed programs for disadvantaged children that would provide learning opportunities similar to those already provided for advantaged middle-class children.

With an emphasis on educating the whole child and improving the child's self-concept, the enrichment curriculum model programs approach child development as an unfolding process that occurs in a supportive environment. The children determine many of their own goals, and the teacher arranges opportunities for actualization. Brophy, Good, and Nedler (1975) viewed this as a permissive-environmental model and identified the Bank Street Program and the Weikart Traditional or Unit Program as examples. Goodwin and Driscoll (1980) describe the Education Development Center (EDC) Open Education Model in much the same manner. DeVries (1974) saw far more of the Freudian psychoanalytic perspective (S. Freud, 1924; A. Freud, 1935) and, later, the neo-Freudian perspective (Ekstein & Motto, 1969; Erikson, 1950) in the enrichment models, exemplified by the Bank Street Program and the Erikson Institute Program.

The objectives of the enrichment curriculum models are global in nature. The well-being of the whole child is the target, and emphasis is placed on global changes. There are no finely specified measurable objectives. The Bank Street model aimed to promote cognitive and affective development "through developing coping skills, using language to express ideas and feelings, experiencing creativity, and establishing a positive self-image'' (Goodwin & Driscoll, 1980, p. 435). The instructional strategies are to determine the children's needs through informal observations as the children interact with the teacher and other children in areas of the classroom designed to engage them in building, art, music, housekeeping, or academic pursuits. Children are free to choose activities and develop their own projects. The teacher's instructional role is to question and extend, through suggestion, the children's investigations in an effort to foster development. The structure of enrichment models is low. The schedule is flexible, the objectives can change at any time as the children move to new interests. There are no lists of measurable objectives by which to evaluate change. Children structure their own learning targets, and the teacher determines the meaning of the children's interactions and arranges the environment to facilitate growth and development.

Evaluation focuses primarily on the demonstration of global changes in the whole child. Testing is usually based upon a pre-post test design. Because of the state of the art, mental development measures are used to determine summative data. Evaluation rating forms have been used by several centers; teachers use very global rating scales to evaluate children's progress, and supervisors evaluate teachers in much the same way. With greater emphasis on process and procedures than on outcomes, evaluation is difficult, however. There are no tests to capture such things as changes in independence, imagination, initiative, community awareness, and self-concept.

In the EDC, for example, process and development are emphasized. Its formative evaluation was based on the observations of its goals, plans, and procedures by an advisory team that visited the site and afterward discussed its findings with EDC staff (Goodwin, 1974). The staff of programs serving under the direction of the EDC Follow Through Programs lamented the inappropriateness of current evaluative instruments to measure the effectiveness of their program. Goodwin (1974) stated their position well: ''EDC staff do not seem to be against evaluation per se, but are against evaluation in terms of A, B, and C when it appears that A, B, and C were selected because they are the most easily measured behaviors'' (p. 211).

Cognitive Curriculums

Researchers at several universities were interested in providing more than enrichment for young disadvantaged children. They saw a need to address more directly the low achievement and progressive retardation of low-income or otherwise disadvantaged children. Assuming that children entered the program already behind middle-class advantaged children, staff of cognitively oriented curriculum programs targeted certain skills as major concerns and designed programs to remediate deficits already noted. They trained children to use cognitive processing skills that would increase their likelihood of performing successfully during the elementary school years. Fortunately, several of these researchers used group designs to investigate the effectiveness of their efforts and have provided data that are still being analyzed some 20 years later (Begab, Haywood, & Garber, 1981) to provide important information on the impact of early intervention.

Several of these programs emphasized the modification of children's cognitive and language skills, and instigated structured programs to accomplish this purpose. The objective of the Early Training Project (Klaus & Gray, 1968), for example, was to reduce the cognitive deficit usually observed in low-income children as they enter public schools. Materials that would help develop cognitive skills were provided, and mothers were trained to instruct their children in how to play with the materials. Furthermore, some mothers received a weekly visit from a staff member when the children were not attending the summer preschool program. In this project, children met in small groups for half-days over the summer only, and home training visits were made weekly during a 9-month period. The goals, strategies, materials, and organization reflected a moderate degree of structure (Brophy, Good, & Nedler, 1975). Teachers carefully monitored child progress on cognitive and language objectives prior to, during, and following intervention.

The cognitive curriculums used in these programs were evaluated in various ways. Some programs were evaluated through control group designs, while others were evaluated only through measurement of progress made by children within their program. Because of the emphasis on cognition and language, researchers relied heavily on measures of mental development and achievement to determine the effectiveness of these programs. Only much later, through post hoc analysis, did researchers analyze factors (e.g., motivation, self-concept, positive attitudes, and parent perceptions and aspirations), that now appear to be critical clues to what actually happened during these early years in the lives of young disadvantaged children.

Direct Instruction Curriculums

In 1966, Bereiter and Engelmann published *Teaching Disadvantaged Children in the Preschool,* in which they described a program designed to raise the linguistic and cognitive levels of disadvantaged children to those of advantaged children through a highly structured direct teaching curriculum. The philosophy followed by Bereiter and Engelmann and (later) Becker and Engelmann is aligned most closely with the theories espoused by B.F. Skinner, who stressed the use of systematic and objective empirical techniques to modify behavior. The theory is simple and transferable, and the results can be dramatic and quickly apparent.

Bereiter and Engelmann contend that disadvantaged children have a severe language deficit in thinking about and describing experiences. They do not address the issues of developmental planning or assessment of individual differences. Their view focuses on the process and the product, not the child. All children in their target group were "equated" and taught as though all needed the same skills.

These predominantly lower class black children did not have time to discover knowledge; time was short, and they needed to catch up with their peers before entering the first grade. The learning of verbal rules was foremost, and specific responses were learned by systematic drill. Bereiter and Englemann thought that learning would occur most rapidly when teachers selected the materials and carefully structured the teacher-child exchanges. The teacher, the key to this instructional model, was expected to bring about child gains in a very short period of time by using a highly structured, direct instructional model that emphasized rewards and punishments.

The original Bereiter and Engelmann model focused almost entirely on language; more recently, however, the Distar curriculum has been expanded to include reading and arithmetic in addition to the language emphasis.

Under the direct instruction curriculum, goals and objectives are stated in precise, measurable terms. Student responses are either correct or incorrect, and the criterion of acceptable behavior is always known. Reinforcement of correct responses increases the likelihood of subsequent correct responses.

In much of the original Bereiter and Engelmann program, strategies were limited to facilitate the acquisition of a simple verbal rule. For example, teachers used the verbal rule "It will float because it's lighter than a piece of water the same size" to teach kindergarten children about conservation of substance, weight, and volume; speed; and specific gravity. Teachers instructed children in groups, with children learning oral responses in unison. The teacher's guide for the Distar program tells the teacher exactly what to say; how to say it; how to signal, point, and use the hands.

The structure of the direct instruction curriculum programs was very high, as reflected in precisely stated objectives that were predetermined by the curriculum package. Timing was an important factor and the schedule always the same. Pupils had a place to be at all times, and these places were assigned by the teacher.

The effectiveness of direct instruction curriculums has been evaluated by measuring the daily and long-term results of the instruction on children. The daily measurement of skill acquisition permits the teacher to determine when program changes are needed and to make them quickly. The long-term measures have enabled researchers to look at skill maintenance over time and to compare the results of this model with those of others. More specifically, Englemann and Becker developed a procedure for rapid uniform handling and analysis of child progress data called the CARDS (collect, analyze, retrieve, disseminate, and store) system (Mahan, 1971). This formative evaluation measure permits ongoing, data-based intervention changes at any point in a child's program.

THE IMPACT OF SPECIAL EDUCATION ON CURRICULUMS

The major thrust in the area of early childhood special education began when Congress passed the Handicapped Children's Early Childhood Assistance Act in 1968. Since that time, hundreds of federally funded, state-funded, and community-supported programs have been developed throughout the United States. The general goal of these programs is to ameliorate the effects of handicapping conditions on each child's potential. Several factors that are uniquely related to educating the handicapped population have had an impact on the development of special curriculums.

Researchers have devoted much time to examining the unique learning process of the handicapped (Borkowski & Wanschura, 1974; Heal & Johnson, 1970; Zeaman, 1973; Zeaman & House, 1963). Robinson and Robinson (1976) summarized the results of these and many other research efforts related to mental retardation, concluding that retarded subjects

1. are not as alert to available environmental cues that would help them solve problems
2. do not attend as readily to relevant dimensions in discrimination learning
3. do not ask strategic questions to gain needed information
4. do not learn as readily from previous trials
5. are less prone to use active strategies in learning
6. do not generalize the effects of learning

The degree to which these learning deficiencies occur is dependent on the extent of the child's handicapping condition.

These findings illustrate the need for special consideration in designing curriculums for the handicapped. Guess, Horner, Utley, Holvoet, Maxon, Tucker, and Warren (1978) describe three models of curriculums that respond to the special needs of this population. The first model, based on developmental logic, draws heavily from the cognitive theories of learning. Clusters of interrelated skills are taught on the assumption that specific behaviors should not be taught independent of the various developmental levels. Guess and associates describe this as horizontal program sequencing and list the following examples of developmental programs: Bricker, Dennison, and Bricker, 1975; Myers, Sinco, and Stalma, 1973; Shearer, Billingsley, Frohman, Hilliard, Johnson, and Shearer, 1972.

A major advantage of programs with horizontal sequencing is that, because they teach clusters of interdependent skills, they encourage generalization of skills—something research has shown to be difficult for handicapped children. Many professionals criticize this approach, however, claiming that "readiness" skills are overemphasized and that failure to learn may be blamed on a child's low developmental level instead of the design and implementation of the curriculum.

In curriculums based on remedial logic, interdependency of skills is minimized. Curriculum content does not depend on the order of learning, but rather on the specific skills handicapped children need to improve their ability to interact with the environment. It is assumed that many skills can be taught independently of one another. Instead of horizontal sequencing, vertical sequencing is employed. Tasks are described in behavioral terms, and criteria for student progress are precisely defined. Examples of this approach are Anderson, Hodson, and Jones, 1975; Brody and Smilovitz, 1974; Fredericks, Riggs, Furey, Grove, Moore, McDonnell, Jordan, Hanson, Baldwin, and Wadlow, 1976.

A third model, the functional curriculum, is designed to bring together the best features of the developmental and remedial approaches. A functional response is defined as one that produces an intermediate consequence, is reinforcing, and is natural to the child's interaction with the environment. The functional model is based on response generalization; it is assumed that responses of similar functional components can best be taught within behavior classes and that generalization of one response to the other is most likely to occur within that class. This functional type of clustering is similar to horizontal sequencing in that it attempts to teach interrelated behaviors. As it is in the remedial approach, however, the emphasis is on identifying and teaching behaviors that are relevant to a child's present or future environment. This is especially crucial for a handicapped population. Curriculums should be designed to teach those skills that are immediately functional for the child and those that will permit the child to interact successfully and productively with the environment in the future.

Williams and Gotts (1977) categorize these different approaches in another way. They distinguish between cognitive sequences and skill sequences. Cognitive sequences, they explain, are constructed on the basis of a cognitive theoretical framework; skill sequences, on the basis of a logical analysis of the complexity of the skills without reference to theory. Cognitive sequences involve generalized plans or the coordinated use of skills, whereas skill sequences may not. Cognitive sequences may not specify the observable behaviors students must perform to demonstrate that they can generalize the skill to new tasks, whereas a skill sequence specifies the skills and tasks a student should perform to demonstrate mastery.

Williams and Gotts also discuss task analysis, a strategy for developing the proper sequence of skills that will facilitate student mastery of the objective:

> The product of task analysis is a *skill* sequence, i.e., a precise delineation of a behavioral objective, the objective's component skills, and an appropriate sequencing of the component skills. . . . A task analysis can usually be accomplished in seven steps: 1) Delineate the behavioral objective. 2) Review instructionally relevant resources. 3) Derive and sequence the component skills of the objective. 4) Eliminate unneces-

> sary component skills. 5) Eliminate redundant component skills. 6) Determine prerequisite skills. 7) Monitor student performance and revise the sequence accordingly. (p. 229)

Williams and Gotts emphasize that a sequence is not a statement of how to teach, but rather a statement of what is to be taught and in what order.

Proponents of applied behavior analysis maintain that behavioral techniques are the most appropriate strategies for *how* to teach handicapped children. This conclusion is based on the premise that the skills must be taught directly, with the use of reinforcement procedures, because handicapped children do not learn spontaneously with the help of environmental cues, appropriate questioning, environmental feedback, and appropriate learning strategies.

Haring (1974) believes that behavior techniques make it possible to:

1. pinpoint the exact behavior of concern
2. observe probable reinforcing events that can be used contingently to maintain, increase, or decrease behavior
3. measure objectively the implementation of an effective intervention, using the environment-behavior relationships to promote substantial behavioral change

Reinforcement of small successive approximations of the task may be necessary, dependent on the abilities of the learner. It is often necessary for the teacher to break the task down into very small increments and use reinforcement to bring about the desired response in the finely sliced sequence.

In contrast to those who adhere to the behavioral viewpoint, Meisels (1979) believes that a developmental perspective is most advantageous for young handicapped children. He argues that, in the behavioral approach, children are not allowed to interact freely with their environment, which inhibits cognitive and emotional growth. Implementation strategies that follow Meisels' approach are designed to enhance interactivity and, hence, developmental advancement. The teacher interacts with the children and guides them to competence, instead of assuming the directive teacher role as in the behavioral approach.

Kiernan (1977) relates the degree of structured learning to the skill level of the children. In describing a curriculum for severely handicapped children, Kiernan suggests that the basis for programming should be an analysis of their ability to operate on and find out about the environment. When a child lacks skills, highly structured teaching techniques are necessary; as skills are acquired, the structure is relaxed.

MacMillan and Morrison (1980) suggest that attention be given to the issue of matching *what* is to be learned with *how* it can most efficiently be taught. Their review of the evolution of behavioral practices led them to predict that behavior modification will be preferred for learning behaviors that consist of well-defined response sequences, but not for learning abstract conceptual material.

Anastasiow (1981) urges educators to recognize that handicapped children have much in common with normal children in terms of basic needs. He discusses a recent shift in special education from the behavioral perspective to a perspective that is more cognitive in orientation. This orientation, he explains, not only draws on the cognitive and perceptual theorists' ideas of how humans learn, but also takes into account behavioral principles in the organization of the learning environment. Cognitive learning programs such as Bricker's (1978), Guralnick's (1978), and Dunst's (1981) illustrate the impact of this trend on early education. Behavioral analysis can be used as a technology of implementation, while cognitive theories can be used to describe human behavior.

EVALUATION

Early childhood programs can be evaluated in many areas (e.g., child progress, parent involvement, cost effectiveness, curriculum impact, program impact). Invariably these areas overlap. (For an extensive discussion of educational evaluation, see Berk, 1981; Garwood, 1982; Goodwin & Driscoll, 1980; and Ruttman, 1980.) Goodwin (1974) defines evaluation as "a systematic process by which judgments are made about the relative desirability, adequacy, effectiveness, or worth of something, often according to a definite criterion or standard, for a specified purpose" (p. 201).

Assessment of Child Progress

Invariably, the effectiveness of a program, particularly one that includes young handicapped children, is measured by the skill gains effected by the intervention. It would be virtually impossible in the 1980s to obtain and continue to obtain program funding if child change data were not an integral part of a program's evaluation design. The support for early intervention for handicapped children has been heavily based on such data.

Assessment of child progress has followed two basic monitoring systems, each with variations as required by characteristics of the population (e.g., test adaptations for blind children), theoretical perspective of staff (e.g., behavioral, enrichment), and curriculum package (e.g., Portage Guide to Early Education Checklist, Developmental Therapy, Peabody Developmental Motor Scales and Programmed Activities). A norm-referenced assessment system is traditionally included in nearly all programs for young handicapped children, although very few such instruments are available for populations of young handicapped children (Bricker, Sheehan, & Littman, 1981). While widespread use of norm-referenced assessment measures in special education is a carryover from regular education, criterion-referenced assessment has been used far more extensively in special education.

Norm-Referenced Assessment

Designed to identify individual differences, norm-referenced assessment involves testing persons on a group of items that discriminate among persons and comparing their performance with that of others who have similar characteristics. The items are not likely to be those included in an instructional program, so the results have little relevance for the educator. Measurement is twice a year for purposes of determining pre-post differences, less frequent if these data are not required. A psychologist or educational diagnostician is more likely than the teacher to administer these tests, thus making this assessment even less relevant for curriculum and intervention.

Early childhood educators have used norm-referenced testing to measure child progress. Achievement tests have been widely used in measuring gains in school-aged populations; however, there are no equivalent measures for infants, toddlers, or preschool children. Several forms of testing have emerged to fill this gap. Standardized mental ability tests for infants and preschool children have become common pre-post test measures of child gains resulting from intervention and have been used for program evaluation purposes. The Bayley Scales of Infant Development (Bayley, 1977) and the McCarthy Scales of Children's Abilities (McCarthy, 1972) are commonly used instruments (Bricker, Sheehan, & Littman, 1981; Sheehan & Gallagher, 1983).

In addition to mental age equivalency comparisons, researchers (Rosen-Morris & Sitkei, 1981) are using raw data pre-post test comparisons to show child progress. A further technique suggested by Abt Associates (1977) and Tallmadge (1977) and used by Bricker, Sheehan, and Littman (1981) is to analyze normative test data in order to determine educationally significant differences. The educational significance index measures the extent to which intervention shifts the distribution of posttest scores from that of pretest scores. If the comparison exceeds 0.25 of the pooled standard deviation, the gains are considered educationally significant (Abt, 1977). This procedure has been used by some program personnel to demonstrate significant change from pretest to posttest scores on developmental measures in moderately and severely handicapped children that, measured otherwise, would not be significant. (For a discussion of the misuse of developmental measures in preschool program evaluation, see Garwood, 1982.)

Criterion-Referenced Assessment

Not only is criterion-referenced assessment more closely tied to curriculum than norm-referenced assessment, it may even be synonymous with curriculum if a prescribed instructional program accompanies the criterion test. The Uniform Performance Assessment System (White, Edgar, Haring, Affleck, Hayden & Bendersky, 1980), the Student Progress Record (Oregon State Mental Health Division, 1977), and the Pennsylvania Training Model (Somerton-Fair & Turner, 1979) are comprehensive assessment systems that list literally hundreds of tasks. Although many teachers who give these tests take the failed items as objectives and design instructional programs to meet the objectives, the test developers have not provided such plans. On the other hand, curriculum-referenced tests provide instructional plans for teaching each task noted in the measure. The West Virginia Assessment and Tracking System (Cone, 1981) and the Hawaii Early Learning Profile (Furuno, O'Reilly, Hosaka, Inatsuka, Allman, & Zeisloft, 1979) are examples of curriculum-referenced measures.

Criterion-referenced instruments, whether the curriculum is included or not, provide information for the instructional program. The skills of each child are assessed, and progress is measured by a comparison only with the child's prior performance. Progress on criterion measures is usually charted daily for immediate feedback. Thus, these measures provide formative evaluation data to program managers. Gain scores are expressed in terms of percentage of skills gained or the raw number of skills achieved on pretests and posttests.

The Teaching Research Handicapped Children's Program of Monmouth, Oregon (Fredericks, undated) was the first program permitted by the Joint Dissemination and Review Panel to present child progress data that were based on the accomplishment of objectives selected from a set curriculum. (The panel is responsible for the evaluation of educational programs.) Although this type of measurement system had been widely practiced in programs for the handicapped, it had never before been approved as a viable means for documenting effectiveness. This action represented a landmark decision in the evaluation history of programs for handicapped children and provided a model for the measurement of child progress and program effectiveness. It is anticipated that other programs serving severely impaired children will pursue this procedure to document accountability.

Curriculum Evaluation

Although broadly defined, two types of evaluation activities, formative and summative, are the areas of most concern to educators of preschool children. Formative evaluation is generally conducted by inside staff or evaluators during program development and implementation in order to improve the curriculum model. Summative evaluation is generally conducted by outside evaluators at the completion of the program in order to determine the overall worth of the project.

Evaluators have developed two different methods of evaluating curriculum models: empirical verification and conceptual analysis. The purpose of empirical verification is to determine curriculum impact by making quantified statements of observable phenomena. There are four primary issues to resolve in an empirical investigation (Messick & Barrows, 1972):

1. What variables are to serve as evaluation criteria?
2. How adequately can these criterion variables be measured?
3. To what degree can observed changes be attributed to the curriculum (internal validity)?
4. How well can the results be generalized (external validity)?

The impact of a curriculum may not be measured most appropriately through child outcomes. For example, use of teacher time, cost of implementation, staff satisfaction, and skill generalization to other settings and conditions may be more appropriate variables in evaluating the effects of a curriculum.

The adequacy with which these variables can be measured affects the quality of any evaluation effort. If curriculum outcomes are clearly stated, the statements can be tested by using a curriculum-referenced or criterion-referenced model for evaluation. In such cases, an arbitrary mastery level is established, usually based on the projected learning of individual students. Criterion variables that are not tied to specific skill competencies are far more difficult to measure. For example, a goal of the Open Learning in Early Childhood (Day, 1975) is "To find success in working with the materials on [the child's] interest and developmental level" (p. 51). While one teacher might know exactly what "success" means in terms of acceptable performance, another teacher may have an entirely different criterion in mind.

In order to determine whether the changes in pupil performance can be attributed to the curriculum, it is necessary to evaluate the children's knowledge of curriculum content both prior to and following instruction. Other measures, such as control or contrast groups, may be required to ensure that content is based solely on the curriculum.

The most desirable focal point for evaluation is the pupil's ability to generalize the skills and knowledge gained from the curriculum. This ability is frequently very difficult to ascertain through observation procedures, however. Some external evaluation can occur, but the time and cost of this process is far more than most programs can afford.

Conceptual analysis involves the application of certain criteria to describing, analyzing, and making judgments of a curriculum's worth. Similarities and differences among curriculums are specified, and the resulting increased understanding about the outcomes for children and parents may lead to the selection of one curriculum over another. It is a subjective evaluation based on rationalized standards.

GUIDELINES FOR CURRICULUM SELECTION

Several educators have raised questions that can be used as guidelines for curriculum selection (Elliot, 1971; Gordon, 1972; Hayden, 1977; Mayer, 1971; Parker & Day, 1972). Parker and Day (1972) proposed a five-dimensional schema for analyzing and evaluating early childhood curriculums. Although quite comprehensive, this schema was not designed to assess the appropriateness of curriculums for handicapped children. Hayden (1977) was particularly concerned about organically impaired infants and posed a valuable set of seven critical questions to use in curriculum selection. Drawing heavily from these two sources and incorporating some of the concerns previously discussed, we propose the following set of questions as guidelines for staff personnel to use in selecting curriculums for young handicapped children. These questions may also be used as criteria for a conceptual analysis of early childhood curriculums.

1. Is the curriculum based on a theory of early development and learning? If a particular theoretical perspective has not been identified and, instead, an eclectic approach has been used, are the various perspectives openly acknowledged? If an eclectic approach has been used, it is essential to include specific guidelines (e.g., for instructional strategies, teachers' roles), so that staff understand why they are to respond in certain ways and how they can generalize behavior to situations not described.
2. Do the goals of the curriculum complement the existing goals of the program? For example, if one of the program's major goals is facilitation of parent-child interaction, how are parents included in the curriculum?
3. Can the goals and objectives be assessed? Entry and exit levels must be determined so that programs can be individualized and child progress can be measured.
4. Are the objectives designed to accomplish the terminal goals of the curriculum? Evans (1975) points out that a rationale for coordinating immediate and long-term goals is often missing, making empirical evaluation difficult. This question, therefore, is an important one for program evaluators to consider in assessing program validity.
5. Does the curriculum focus on the skill domain that is most critical for the target population? If, for example, the children to be served are deaf or language-delayed, a curriculum that carefully addresses communication needs should be selected. This would not preclude inclusion of other skill domains, but strategies for facilitating language while addressing other target skills should be reviewed.
6. Are the instructional objectives and activities broken down into small workable statements appropriate for use with the target population? If the

children are severely handicapped, a finely sliced curriculum with several activities for each objective might be appropriate. If the children are not handicapped or only mildly delayed, fewer items might be required for each domain. A program that serves children with several types of delays (e.g., deaf, blind, communication-delayed) might require a variety of curriculums to develop individualized programs.

7. Are the items developmentally relevant and logically sequenced? A current emphasis in assessment and curriculum materials for handicapped children is the inclusion of only those items that are functional (skills that enable a child to perform in the environment).
8. Does the curriculum include techniques for attracting and sustaining a young child's attention? These techniques are likely to include methods for reinforcing attention and responses, then gradually fading reinforcement as the child acquires the skill and exercises it freely in several settings.
9. Does the curriculum include ways to build and maintain appropriate social interactions between the adult and the child? Whether the child is mildly or severely handicapped, learning should be as enjoyable for the child and parent or teacher/therapist as possible. This requires a curriculum that fosters reciprocity, permitting the child and adult to form a natural and enduring relationship.
10. Does the curriculum allow for skill generalization? As early as 1962, Taba emphasized that generalization occurs through either content or methods used in learning. Does the curriculum address how learning is to be generalized? More recently, Brown, Nietupski, and Hamre-Nietupski (1976) suggested that skills be taught in reaction to or in the presence of at least three different persons, in three natural settings, in response to three different appropriate language cues.
11. Has the curriculum been tested on the population it was designed to serve? For example, if the curriculum is designed for blind children, has its success been documented with this population? Empirical evidence of curriculum validity and reliability are critical if staff are to be accountable for designing and implementing appropriate educational plans.
12. Does the curriculum include procedures for collecting and recording data as the curriculum is implemented? Is the system described in a way that would allow paraprofessionals to use it?
13. Have the authors drawn on the expertise of different kinds of specialists in preparing the curriculum or suggested guidelines for deciding when to turn to specific professionals?
14. Is the curriculum easy to implement and export? This requires written instructions that are easy to follow, as well as clearly defined parent, teacher, and child expectations.

15. Does the curriculum allow for formative and summative evaluation of the child's performance and of the curriculum's impact on the entire program? As a critical element in any program, the impact of the curriculum must be measured to determine its contribution to the program's success.

NOTES

1. From Cahoon, O.W., *A Teacher's Guide to Cognitive Tasks,* pp. 43-45. Copyright 1974 by Brigham Young University Press. Reprinted by permission.

REFERENCES

Abt Associates. *Education as experimentation: A planned variation model* (Vol. 4A). Cambridge, Mass.: Abt Books, 1977.

Anastasiow, N.J. Early childhood education for the handicapped in the 1980s: Recommendations. *Exceptional Children,* 1981, *47*(4), 276-282.

Anderson, D.R., Hodson, G.R., & Jones, W.G. (Eds.). *Instructional programs for the severely handicapped student.* Springfield, Ill.: Charles C Thomas, 1975.

Bayley, N. *Bayley scales of infant development.* New York: The Psychological Corp., 1977.

Begab, M.J., Haywood, H.C., & Garber, H.L. *Psychosocial influences in retarded performance: Strategies for improving competence* (Vol. 2). Baltimore: University Park Press, 1981.

Belsky, J., & Tolan, W.J. Infants as producers of their own development: An ecological analysis. In R.M. Lerner & N.A. Busch-Rossnagel (Eds.), *Individuals as producers of their development: A life-span perspective.* New York: Academic Press, 1981.

Bereiter, C., & Engelmann, S. *Teaching disadvantaged children in the preschool.* Englewood Cliffs, N.J.: Prentice-Hall, 1966.

Berk, R. *Educational evaluation methodology: The state of the art.* Baltimore: Johns Hopkins University Press, 1981.

Bissell, J. *The cognitive effects of preschool programs for disadvantaged children.* Washington, D.C.: National Institute of Child Health and Development, 1970.

Borkowski, J.G., & Wanschura, P.B. Mediational processes in the retarded. In N.R. Ellis (Ed.), *International review of research in mental retardation* (Vol. 7). New York: Academic Press, 1974.

Bricker, D. Early intervention: The criteria of success. *Allied Health and Behavior Sciences Journal,* 1978, *1,* 567-582.

Bricker, D., Dennison, L., & Bricker, W. *Constructive-interaction-adaptation approach to language training* (Mailman Center for Child Development Monograph Series #7). Unpublished manuscript, University of Miami, 1975.

Bricker, D., Sheehan, R., & Littman, D. *Early intervention: A plan for evaluating program impact.* Westar Series Paper #10. Monmouth, Oreg.: Western Technical Assistance Resource, 1981.

Brody, J.F., & Smilovitz, R. *APT: A training program for citizens with severely or profoundly retarded behavior.* Spring City, Pa.: Pennhurst State School, 1974.

Brophy, J.E., Good, T.L., & Nedler, S.E. *Teaching in the preschool.* New York: Harper & Row, 1975.

Brown, L., Nietupski, J., & Hamre-Nietupski, S. Criterion of ultimate functioning. In M.A. Thomas (Ed.), *Hey, don't forget about me!* Reston, Va.: Council for Exceptional Children, 1976.

Cahoon, O.W. *A teacher's guide to cognitive tasks for preschool.* Provo, Utah: Brigham Young University Press, 1974.

Case, R. Gearing the demands of instruction to the developmental capacities of the learner. *Review of Educational Research,* 1975, *45,* 59-87.

Case, R. A developmentally based theory and technology of instruction. *Review of Educational Research,* 1978, *48,* 439-463.

Cone, J.D. *The West Virginia assessment and tracking system* (Rev. ed.). Morgantown, W. Va.: West Virginia University, 1981.

Day, B. *Open learning in early childhood.* New York: Macmillan, 1975.

DeVries, R. Theory in educational practice. In R.W. Colvin & E.M. Zaffiro (Eds.), *Preschool education.* New York: Springer, 1974.

Dunst, C.J. *Infant learning: A cognitive-linguistic intervention strategy.* Hingham, Mass.: Teaching Resources, 1981.

Ekstein, R., & Motto, R. *From learning for love to love of learning.* New York: Brunner/Mazel, 1969.

Elliot, D. Guidelines for the analysis and description of early childhood education programs. *Educational Leadership,* 1971, *28*(8), 812-820.

Engelmann, S., & Osborn, J. *Distar language 1: An instructional system* (2nd ed.). Chicago: Science Research Associates, 1976.

Erikson, E.H. *Childhood and society.* New York: Norton, 1950.

Evans, E.D. *Contemporary influences in early childhood education.* New York: Holt, Rinehart, and Winston, 1975.

Fredericks, H. Joint Dissemination Review Panel Submission, Monmouth, Oreg.: Data based classroom for preschool handicapped children. Teaching Research Infant and Child Center, undated.

Fredericks, H., Riggs, C., Furey, T., Grove, D., Moore, W., McDonnell, J., Jordan, E., Hanson, W., Baldwin, V., & Wadlow, M. *The teaching research curriculum for moderately and severely handicapped.* Springfield, Ill.: Charles C Thomas, 1976.

Freud, A. *Psychoanalysis for teachers and parents.* Boston: Beacon Press, 1935.

Freud, S. *A general introduction to psychoanalysis.* New York: Washington Square Press, 1924.

Furuno, S., O'Reilly, K.A., Hosaka, C.M., Inatsuka, T.T., Allman, T.L., & Zeisloft, B. *Hawaii early learning profile.* Palo Alto: Vort Corporation, 1979.

Gammage, P. School curricula—A social-psychological view. In L.G. Katz (Ed.), *Current topics in early childhood education* (Vol. 3). Norwood, N.J.: Ablex, 1980.

Garwood, S.G. (Mis)use of developmental scales in program evaluation. *Topics in Early Childhood Special Education,* 1982, *1*(4), 61-69.

Goodlad, J.I., & Richter, M.N. *The development of a conceptual system for dealing with problems of curriculum and instruction* (Contract No. SAE-8024, Project No. 454). The Cooperative Research Program of the Office of Education. 1966.

Goodwin, W.L. Evaluation in early childhood education. In R.W. Colvin & E.M. Zaffiro (Eds.), *Preschool education.* New York: Springer, 1974.

Goodwin, W.L., & Driscoll, L.A. *Handbook for measurement and evaluation in early childhood education.* San Francisco: Jossey-Bass, 1980.

Gordon, I.J. An instructional theory approach to the analysis of selected early childhood education programs. In I.J. Gordon (Ed.), *Early childhood education.* Chicago: University of Chicago Press, 1972.

Guess, D., Horner, R., Utley, B., Holvoet, J., Maxon, D., Tucker, D., & Warren, S. A functional curriculum sequencing model for teaching the severely handicapped. *AAESPH Review,* 1978, *3*(4), 202-215.

Guralnick, M.J. (Ed.). *Early intervention and the integration of handicapped and nonhandicapped children.* Baltimore: University Park Press, 1978.

Haring, N.G. Perspectives in special education. In N.G. Haring (Ed.), *Behavior of exceptional children: An introduction to special education.* Columbus, Ohio: Charles E. Merrill, 1974.

Hayden, A.H. *The implications of infant intervention research.* Paper presented at the conference on Early Intervention with Infants and Young Children, Milwaukee, Wisconsin, June 1977.

Heal, L.W., & Johnson, J.T., Jr. Inhibition deficits in retardate learning and attention. In N.R. Ellis (Ed.), *International review of research in mental retardation* (Vol. 4). New York: Academic Press, 1970.

Karnes, M.B., Zehrbach, R.R., & Teska, J.A. The conceptualization of the ameliorative curriculum. In R.K. Parker (Ed.), *The preschool in action.* Boston: Allyn & Bacon, 1972.

Kiernan, C. Toward a curriculum for the profoundly retarded, multiply handicapped child. *Child: Care, Health, and Development,* 1977, *3,* 229-239.

Klaus, R., & Gray, S.W. The early training project for disadvantaged children: A report after five years. *Monographs of the Society for Research in Child Development,* 1968, Vol. 33, No. 4 (Serial No. 120).

MacMillan, P.L., & Morrison, G.M. Evolution of behaviorism from the laboratory to special education settings. In B. Keogh (Ed.), *Advances in special education* (Vol. 2). Greenwich, Conn.: JAI Press, 1980.

Mahan, J.M. *Description of the CARDS data systems for the Engelmann-Becker Follow Through Project.* Research Memorandum No. 14. Eugene, Oreg.: Engelmann-Becker Follow Through Project, University of Oregon, 1971.

Mayer, R.S. A comparative analysis of preschool curriculum models. In R.H. Anderson & H.G. Shane (Eds.), *As the twig is bent: Readings in early childhood education.* Boston: Houghton-Mifflin, 1971.

McCarthy, D. *McCarthy scales of children's abilities.* New York: The Psychological Corp., 1972.

Meisels, S.J. *Special education and development.* Baltimore: University Park Press, 1979.

Messick, S., & Barrows, T. Strategies for research and evaluation in early childhood education. In I.J. Gordon (Ed.), *Early childhood education.* Chicago: University of Chicago Press, 1972.

Myers, D.G., Sinco, M.E., & Stalma, E.S. *The right-to-education child (a curriculum for the severely and profoundly mentally retarded).* Springfield, Ill.: Charles C Thomas, 1973.

Olds, A. Designing developmentally optimal classrooms for children with special needs. In S.J. Meisels (Ed.), *Special education and development.* Baltimore: University Park Press, 1979.

Oregon State Mental Health Division. *The student progress record.* Salem, Oreg.: Oregon State Mental Health Division, 1977.

Palmer, F., & Andersen, L.W. Early intervention treatments that have been tried, documented, and assessed. In M. Begab, H.C. Haywood, & H.L. Garber (Eds.), *Psychosocial influences in retarded performance* (Vol. 2). Baltimore: University Park Press, 1981.

Parker, R.K., & Day, M.C. Comparisons of preschool curricula. In R.K. Parker (Ed.), *The preschool in action.* Boston: Allyn & Bacon, 1972.

Piaget, J. *The origins of intelligence in children.* New York: Norton, 1963.

Piaget, J. Foreword. In M. Schwebel & J. Raph (Eds.), *Piaget in the classroom.* New York: Basic Books, 1973.

Robinson, N.M., & Robinson, H.B. *The mentally retarded child.* New York: McGraw-Hill, 1976.

Rosen-Morris, D., & Sitkei, E.G. Strategies for teaching severely/profoundly handicapped infants and young children. *Journal of the Division for Early Childhood,* 1981, *4,* 81-93.

Ruttman, L. *Planning useful evaluations: Evaluability assessment*. New York: Sage, 1980.

Sears, P., & Dowley, E. Research on training in the nursery school. In N. Gage (Ed.), *Handbook of research on teaching*. Skokie, Ill.: Rand McNally, 1963.

Shearer, D., Billingsley, J., Frohman, A., Hilliard, J., Johnson, F., & Shearer, M. *The portage guide to early education: Instructions and checklist*. Portage, Wis.: Cooperative Education Service Agency, No. 12, 1972.

Sheehan, R., & Gallagher, R.J. Conducting evaluations of infant intervention programs. In S.G. Garwood & R.R. Fewell (Eds.), *Educating handicapped infants: Issues in development and intervention*. Rockville, Md.: Aspen Systems Corporation, 1983.

Somerton-Fair, E., & Turner, K.D. *Pennsylvania training model: Individual assessment guide* (Rev. ed.). Harrisburg, Pa.: Pennsylvania Department of Education, 1979.

Sparling, J.J. *Synthesizing educational objectives for infant curricula* (ERIC Document Reproduction Service No. ED 097 997) Chapel Hill, N.C.: University of North Carolina at Chapel Hill, 1974.

Spradlin, J.E., & Siegel, G.M. Language training in natural and clinical environments. *Journal of Speech and Hearing Disorders,* 1982, *47,* 2-6.

Stake, R.E. The countenance of educational evaluation. *Teachers College Record,* 1967, *68*(7), 523-540.

Taba, H. *Curriculum development, theory, and practice*. New York: Harcourt, Brace and World, 1962.

Tallmadge, K. *The joint dissemination review panel IDEABOOK*. Washington, D.C.: U.S. Government Printing Office, 1977.

Tyler, R.W. *Basic principles of curriculum and instruction*. Chicago: University of Chicago Press, 1949.

Uzgiris, I.C., & Hunt, J.M. *Assessment in infancy*. Urbana, Ill.: University of Illinois Press, 1975.

Weikart, D.P. Effects of different curricula in early childhood intervention. *Educational Evaluation and Policy Analysis,* 1981, *3*(6), 25-35.

White, O., Edgar, E., Haring, N.G., Affleck, J., Hayden, A., & Bendersky, M. *UPAS: Uniform performance assessment system*. Columbus, Ohio: Charles E. Merrill, 1980.

Williams, W., & Gotts, E. Selected considerations on developing curriculum for severely handicapped students. In E. Sontag, J. Smith, & N. Certo (Eds.), *Educational programming for the severely and profoundly handicapped*. Reston, Va.: CEC Division of Mental Retardation, 1977.

Zeaman, D. One programmatic approach to retardation. In D.K. Routh (Ed.), *The experimental psychology of mental retardation*. Chicago: Aldine, 1973.

Zeaman, D., & House, B.J. The role of attention in retardate discrimination learning. In N.R. Ellis (Ed.), *Handbook of mental deficiency*. New York: McGraw-Hill, 1963.

Chapter 12

Understanding and Communicating with Families of Handicapped Children

Milton Seligman

Because of the burdens of parenting a handicapped child and the challenges of teaching a handicapped child, along with added responsibilities, parents and teachers often find themselves at odds with each other. Although this unfortunate situation has improved somewhat since the early 1970s, the relationship between parents and professionals is still too often adversarial. Strickland (in press) notes that the advent of due process hearings, designed to ensure the proper implementation of PL 94-142, has increased stress between parents and the schools. Efforts to secure appropriate educational placements for handicapped youngsters, ironically, have strained relationships between parents and school personnel—certainly an unintended outcome of this landmark legislation.

In order to ameliorate negative parent-school relationships, it is essential that teachers become more knowledgeable about parents of handicapped children—about their hopes, joys, sorrows, and frustrations. It is imperative for teachers to have an awareness and appreciation of the circumstances caused by the presence of a handicapped child in the family, of the dynamics operating both within the family and between family and community, and of the roles of professionals who work with these families. There are both positive and adversarial relationships between parents of handicapped children and professionals who work under the broad human services umbrella. Nurses, counselors, occupational and physical therapists, speech therapists, and others who work with parents play an important role in their perceptions of professionals in general.

UNDERSTANDING EXCEPTIONAL FAMILIES

Insights into exceptional families help teachers make a more realistic appraisal of an exceptional child's family, their enormous burdens, their coping mechanisms, and the strengths that sustain them through crises. Also, such knowledge helps the teacher understand parental reactions that might otherwise appear to be unreasonable and, at times, incomprehensible.

The Family as an Interacting Unit

Just as a physical insult to the body or a severe psychological shock can impede an individual's development, an event of major proportions can have a similar effect on a family. Like individuals, families progress through various stages, and the interaction of many factors fashions a family's response to life events that may interfere with normal family development. Also, the family unit is not a singular entity that reacts as one to external stimuli, but an interacting, interdependent group of individuals. An event that affects one member also either directly or indirectly affects the others. Moreover, the family is not a closed group, existing in isolation, but an open system related to other systems, such as friends, colleagues, institutions/agencies, schools, and the like.

An important aspect of family dynamics is the concept of social roles, defined as goal-directed patterns or sequences of acts tailored by the cultural process for the transactions individuals may carry out in their social group or situation (Spiegel, 1957). Each individual's role relative to the roles of others in the network is determined by cultural expectations and values. For example, a mother enacts certain roles and holds certain role expectations from her children and husband. The fluidity of roles that increasingly characterizes society today makes role expectations more difficult to predict.

Social roles do not exist in isolation but tend to complement the role of someone else or fit into the role structure of a group (or family).

> As long as the role each family member occupies is complementary with and conforms to the role expectations other members have for him, the family lives in dynamic equilibrium. As soon as a discrepancy occurs, however, that is, when two or more family members have conflicting or incompatible notions on how to play their reciprocal roles, complementarity fails and the role system moves toward disequilibrium. Such disequilibrium is experienced by the family members in the form of tension, anxiety, hostility, or self-consciousness and individuals will try to deal with these reactions in a variety of ways. (Ross, 1964, p. 7)

Family interaction in contemporary society cannot be addressed without discussing the rapidly changing nature of family life, changes that may add to or lighten the burdens of parents of handicapped children. Lillie (1981) believes that the following factors account for recent changes in family interaction:

1. Mothers and fathers are striving for self-fulfillment and self-esteem which seem to them to be more obtainable outside the home than inside the home.

2. The role identity of a father or a mother is unclear and vague.
3. Professional careers of mother and father, particularly in the early years of a marriage, may cause high family stress.
4. What today's generation of parents learned about being a parent from their parents is difficult to apply in today's world. (p. 92)

Change is often viewed as negative, and change in the structure of families may add to existing stress. It is true that change frequently increases stress, yet certain changes can reduce it. For example, since the father's role is more flexible now than it was in the past, he may be more available to help care for a handicapped child. As Lamb (in press) notes, the father's lack of availability in the past was an important factor in family conflict involving a handicapped child.

Coping Mechanisms

The presence of an exceptional child in the family often produces anxiety among family members. In reacting to anxiety-producing situations, human beings generally develop coping (or defense) mechanisms that help reduce anxiety.

The source of situations that generate anxiety is sometimes perceived as outside the self. The transfer of blame to an external source, such as another person, group, or institution, is called projection. Ross (1964) explains that the use of this coping mechanism by parents of an exceptional child, thrusting blame for the child's condition onto sources outside the self, is a defense against unconscious guilt. This guilt may be based on realistic or less realistic factors that the parents believe are related to the child's handicap. The physician may be the object of the projection, or the parents may blame something less tangible, such as heredity or poverty. Because it may be impossible to pin a child's exceptionality on a particular cause, parents may ascribe it to a host of causes and may fantasize about the probable cause or whether it could have been prevented (Hollingsworth & Pasnaw, 1977).

In looking for someone to blame for their child's condition, parents may blame each other, the school, or the teacher; doctors make convenient scapegoats during the infant years. Because of unconscious guilt for not spending more time with the child or not helping with schoolwork, parents may blame teachers for a child's slow progress. Teachers who sense that parents may be projecting blame on them might try to help parents understand that a teacher's main interest is not in why a child is not learning but in how to help the child overcome and cope with the handicap to the extent possible.

Bibring and associates (Bibring, Dwyer, Huntingdon, & Vatenstein, 1961) define denial as "literally seeing but refusing to acknowledge what one sees, or hearing and negating what is actually heard" (p. 65). Ross (1964) adds:

> Denial is one of the more primitive defenses against the threatening recognition of the discrepancy between the hoped-for healthy baby and the reality of the defective child. Parents will try to establish the myth that there is nothing wrong with the child and since this pretense serves to protect them from anxiety, they must try to maintain the myth against great odds. (pp. 62-63)

The parents' denial of their child's handicap is often reinforced by professionals. Because of the professionals' own anxieties and their own use of defense mechanisms, they may fail to communicate accurately the severity of the problem, may be unrealistically hopeful, or may promise unattainable cures. Parents, encouraged by such well-meaning but misguided professionals, secretly hold on to the magical belief that the problem will somehow go away or that the child will "grow out of it." Shopping around for a favorable diagnosis may be the result of parent denial.

From the perspective of the child's development, denial has two counterproductive consequences. On the one hand, parents may become overprotective, keeping their child out of situations that would help in the normalization process. On the other hand, parents may exert tremendous pressures for achievement on the child, leading to frustration for both child and parents. Such pressure may subsequently produce emotional problems that further complicate the child's condition.

Sometimes, apparent denial reflects the parents' accurate perceptions. Because of their closeness to their child and their opportunities for observation, parents may perceive factors contributing to their child's problem that should be seriously considered. Therefore, careful, nondefensive listening by the teacher is essential. By the same token, if convinced that parents must be more aware of an aspect of their child's exceptionality, the teacher might consider inviting them to visit the classroom to observe their child in that social context.

Rationalization means "justification, or making a thing appear reasonable, when otherwise its irrationality would be evident. It is said that a person 'covers up,' justifies, rationalizes an act or an idea that is unreasonable and illogical" (Hensie & Campbell, 1970, p. 645). Tied into the mechanisms of projection and denial, rationalization provides the "solution" for an undesirable situation; for example, parents may inform the teacher that their son is behind in his classwork because he is going through a developmental stage, when the evidence clearly points to mental retardation.

Bibring and associates (1961) define intellectualization as "a systematic overdoing of thinking, deprived of its affect, in order to defend against anxiety attributable to an unacceptable impulse" (p. 68). Anxiety is warded off by verbal excesses, especially in situations that arouse strong emotions. There is a qualitative difference between intellectualization and intelligence; the former is a coping mechanism, and the latter is intellectual capacity.

Strong impulses, generally of an aggressive nature, that are considered unacceptable to society are unconsciously deflected into socially acceptable, constructive activities. Gratification of an objectional impulse in a socially valued outlet characterizes this coping mechanism, sublimation. For example, wanting to strike back aggressively at the perceived sources of a child's lack of academic, therapeutic, or recreational resources in the community, a parent of an exceptional child may help form a citizens' group dedicated to the orderly and legal pursuit of expanded opportunities for exceptional children.

Ross (1964) defines repression as

> the mechanism through which unacceptable and threatening psychological content is kept from conscious awareness. Repressed activities, impulses, and conflicts which are thus excluded from consciousness are not eliminated and they continue to cause stress which may become expressed in various indirect symptoms. Because of the continuing threat posed by repressed material, other defense mechanisms are called into play, making repression the mechanism which is central to many other psychic operations. (p. 53)

Thus, repression keeps impulses and events that cause excessive anxiety essentially hidden (unconscious); yet, according to psychoanalytic theory, content that falls into the unconscious is manifested in some way (e.g., through projection, denial, or sublimation).

The terms *repression* and *suppression* are often used interchangeably, even though they are significantly different. Suppression is the act of consciously inhibiting an impulse, idea, or emotion—a deliberate attempt to forget something. In talking with a parent who wishes to suppress an uncomfortable thought, a teacher might hear, "I realize that Tommy won't ever be able to walk like other children. I find this so upsetting that I don't want to think or talk about it."

Kicking the family dog after an unnerving day at the office is the popular characterization of displacement, the shifting of an impulse from one source to another in order to resolve a conflict and avoid anxiety. The impulse (e.g., feeling angry and acting aggressively) does not change, but the direction of the impulse is deflected (e.g., kicking the dog instead of becoming assertive with the boss, the real source of anger). Deflected impulses are not always directed to an external source; they are sometimes turned inward. Ross (1964) notes that impulses turned inward find expression through bodily symptoms (e.g., ulcers) by a mechanism called somatization.

Another response, albeit generally a temporary one, to an uncomfortable situation is to withdraw. If withdrawal, a fairly common and normal reaction to a threatening situation, becomes a characteristic way of responding, professional help is needed. In order to avoid facing a painful evaluation of their child's status, for example, parents may fail to attend parent-teacher conferences. Chronic withdrawal indicates excessive anxiety and/or depression.

The Birth of a Handicapped Child

Those who are about to become parents have a host of expectations, not the least of which is that their child will be normal and able to assume all the roles generally ascribed by society. Although expectations vary, parents tend to expect that their child will achieve at least as much as they have been able to achieve in their lifetime. Writing of parental reactions to children born with severe brain defects, Baum (1962) cites Kozier in observing that

> In many ways, a child represents to the parent an extension of his own self. . . . When the baby is born the mother's wish to be loved is partially transferred from her own person to that of the baby. To the father, a normal child is often an affirmation, at least in part, of his sense of success. The capacity to produce unimpaired offspring is psychologically and culturally important for the parents' sense of personal adequacy. (p. 385)

The ritual performed shortly after birth of counting fingers and toes reflects the underlying fear of most parents that their infant may have been born defective. Although this fear is expressed in subtle and camouflaged ways, the counterbelief that "it can't happen to me" is also present. When the parents' expectations of a healthy, normal child are contradicted by the birth of a handicapped one, their coping mechanisms are put to a severe test.

The more immediate biological role of the mother in the birth process may endow the discrepancy between expectation and reality with greater psychological meaning for her than for the father. After all, it is the mother who "produced" the infant, and, therefore, it is the mother who may experience severe feelings of guilt, remorse, and lowered self-esteem.

Although it is not clear whether or how the birth of a handicapped infant affects the mother and the father differently, the shock renders both parents physically and psychologically vulnerable (Londsdale, Elfer, & Ballard, 1979). During this period, their ability to recognize, evaluate, and adapt to reality is often significantly impaired. Of course, some handicaps are not detectable at birth and become manifest only as a child fails to complete expected developmental tasks. After discovering their child's exceptionality months or even years after birth, mothers often report that they suspected rather early that their child was "different."

Although the mother seems to be involved more deeply with the child at the time of birth, the feelings and reactions of the father should not be ignored. Unfortunately, research on early child development and investigations of families with handicapped children have focused on the mother; research related to the feelings and reactions of the father is regrettably sparse (Lamb, in press). Nevertheless, educated speculations about the father's reactions may be useful.

Because of his secondary role in the birth process, the father is or feels more removed, less emotionally involved. In this regard, Wunderlich (1977) notes that the father's reactions to the birth of a handicapped child are more reserved initially. He tends to use such coping mechanisms as intellectualization or withdrawal. It is only when he sees that his ideas and plans for the future cannot be realized that his emotions are strongly aroused. By the same token, it is difficult to assess the father's reactions, as males have often been characterized as less expressive. This phenomenon is generally considered to reflect a need to project a masculine image, an image of the all-powerful male, undaunted by the vicissitudes of life. Since the father is a partner in the conception and subsequent development of a child, however, there is little reason to assume that his feelings of guilt, remorse, and loss of self-esteem are significantly different from those often attributed to the mother; yet, our understanding of the father's reactions is limited.

It can be hypothesized that the father's fantasies of a normal baby are initially crushed as feelings of disappointment and confusion grow, accompanied by anxiety over the tremendous psychological, physical, and financial burden the family must bear. The dream of playing games with a strong, physically agile child is snuffed out, and instead he sees years of hardship ahead.

Levine's (1966) study should alert professionals to the role fathers play in exceptional families. His research indicates that fathers are more affected by a mentally retarded son than by a mentally retarded daughter, a factor perhaps attributable to the different expectations fathers have for sons. Levine encourages the active involvement of fathers in counseling, especially if the child is male. This study points to the importance of studying fathers as well as mothers, especially as the parent's sex interacts with the sex of the child. Peck and Stephens (1960) showed a high correlation between a father's acceptance or rejection of his mentally retarded child and the family's acceptance or rejection, indicating that the father's feelings are related to (or set) the general tone in the family.

In his review of fathers of exceptional children, Lamb (in press) notes that the literature in this area is sparse, yet speculations can be made on the limited evidence. He concludes that

> it seems that fathers tend to react adversely and rejectingly toward retarded children, and this is likely to set an emotional distance between them, reducing the likelihood of positive effects on child development while increasing the likelihood of deleterious ones. Likewise, rejection and withdrawal by the fathers of retarded children serve to increase the burden borne by their wives. This has the effect of straining the marriage

> and adversely affecting the personal satisfaction of the mothers, which may in turn have harmful effects, not only on the retarded children, but on other children in their families as well. An harrassed, unhappy, overextended, and isolated mother is likely to be an impoverished mother of all her children, not only of the retarded child who is the unwitting cause of the family strain.

Siblings

To understand fully the circumstances faced by exceptional families, it is necessary to understand the impact that a handicapped child has on normal siblings. Some believe that a handicapped child contaminates the family and generates great psychological burdens, especially on normal siblings. A handicapped child does have an effect on normal siblings, but its nature is mediated by a number of factors.

The extent to which siblings are held responsible for a handicapped brother or sister bears a strong relationship to the perception and feelings siblings have toward their handicapped sibling *and* their parents. Available research suggests that a child (especially a female child) who has been given excessive caretaking responsibility for a handicapped sibling may develop anger, resentment, guilt, and, quite possibly, subsequent psychological disturbance (Farber, 1959; Grossman, 1972; Seligman, in press). A handicapped child absorbs a great deal of the family's time, energy, money, and emotional resources, and siblings may be pressed into parental roles they are ill-prepared to assume. The assumption of such roles before a child is emotionally ready may too rapidly move the child through the developmental stages so necessary for normal growth.

Family size seems to affect the extent to which a sibling is asked to assume inordinate caretaking responsibilities. Grossman (1972) reports that college students from two-child families with a retarded sibling found life more stressful than did those who had normal siblings as well. It may be that a "spread of responsibility" effect operates in larger families in which more siblings are available to help.

Females tend to be more burdened by a handicapped brother or sister, presumably because of sex role expectations. This fact should alert professionals to the excessive responsibility females often experience when they reside with a handicapped sibling.

Socioeconomic status also appears to be related to the amount of responsibility a normal sibling assumes for a handicapped brother or sister. The more financially able a family, the better prepared they are to secure needed help from sources outside the family. The relationship between sibling stress and socioeconomic status is somewhat unclear, however. Functional retardation may exist among normal siblings in lower socioeconomic status families, and a retarded youngster may blend imperceptibly into the family tapestry.

Travis (1976) has made a number of observations concerning families with physically handicapped children. According to Travis, siblings who have been excessively burdened with the physical care of chronically, physically ill children leave home at age 16 or 17. Signs of mounting resentment can be seen in the provision of hasty or unkind physical care. Travis also points out that some chronically ill children enslave their physically normal siblings, verbally and even physically abusing their brothers or sisters.

Siblings may also be burdened by excessively high parental aspirations to compensate for parental disappointments and frustrations about a handicapped child. The responsibility for high achievement may fall to the normal siblings, some of whom may not be intellectually or psychologically able to attain in a manner compatible with parental expectations.

In regard to schooling, Michaelis (1980) observes that a handicapped child's education may fall to normal siblings. She properly cautions, "It is important that siblings are not expected to be their 'brother's keeper' to the extent that their own social and academic learning is hampered by the responsibility" (p. 102).

Siblings may worry about the extent to which they must care for a handicapped brother or sister when the parents are unable to do so. They may wonder whether they can cope with the decisions that need to be made in future years and whether they can physically and psychologically manage to care for their handicapped sibling. They may doubt that their present or future spouse will be able to cope with their handicapped brother or sister.

The effect of handicapped children on their siblings is an extremely complex and important area of concern to educators. (For a more comprehensive treatment of the topic, see Seligman, in press.) Our understanding of the relationship between siblings and handicapped children would be incomplete, however, if the benefits of living with a handicapped brother or sister are not explored. In her research, Grossman (1972) reports that a number of the college students who reported on their relationship with their retarded brother or sister "appeared to have benefitted from their growing up with handicapped siblings. The ones who benefitted appeared to us to be more tolerant, more compassionate, more knowing about prejudice" (p. 84). In support of Grossman's findings, Miller (1974) found a number of normal siblings who had expressed a sense of pride in their involvement in the growth and development of retarded siblings. For example, Diane, a normal sibling, said the following in her interview with Klein (1972):

> I always felt there was something very different about our family. Of course, you know, Cathy being that difference. Because of her difference there was a degree of specialness or closeness about us that, I do not know, it was sort of a bond that made us all very, very close. We all pitched in and helped each other out. (p. 25)

Another sister of a mentally retarded, cerebral-palsied, and epileptic brother puts her retrospective thoughts as follows:

> I do not mean to imply that life with Robin has been all goodness and light. I have seen the strain that the responsibility of his constant care has placed upon my parents. I worry about the increasing frequency of his seizures and about what would happen to him should my parents become unable to care for him. Robin, himself, like all brothers I suppose, can be truly aggravating. It makes me angry to see him try to weasel his way out of doing things that I know he is capable of doing. Just the other day, I was scolding him for not clearing his place at the table. I guess my sisterly bossing was too much for him. He pointed at me and angrily made the sign for handcuffs—his way of indicating that I should be put in jail.
>
> All in all, though, I feel that Robin has brought much good into the lives of my family. He has taught us a great deal about acceptance, patience, individual worth, but most of all about love. (Turnbull & Turnbull, 1978, pp. 112-113)

After a lengthy discussion of brothers and sisters of handicapped youngsters and their adaptation to this special circumstance, Featherstone (1980) remarks:

> I have focused, up until now, on the difficulties that the able-bodied child faces. These problems are real enough, and assume major importance in the lives of some children. Nonetheless, the sheer length of my discussion creates a misleadingly gloomy impression. It may suggest that for the brothers and sisters of the disabled the developmental path is strewn with frightful hazards, that all but the most skillful parents can expect to see their "normal" children bruised, irreparably by the experience of family living. The truth is quite otherwise. (p. 163)

THE PARENT SQUEEZE

In order to project an image of success so important in their efforts to obtain funding support, schools and organizations may engage in cruel ploys against exceptional parents. For example, Schleifer (1971) offers the following illustration of how a child's lack of "progress" may jeopardize that child's eligibility for some programs:

> Failing to find an appropriate public school placement the family finds a special program for their child. The child has just finished his third year.

> The family has been called in by the school director to discuss their child's progress. The director tells the family that the child cannot return in the fall. There has been so little progress during the course of the past year that it is not worth the family's money or the school's time to continue the child in this program. The parent is asked to accept the twofold assumption that continuous progress is necessary every year and the lack of it is part of their child's disability. (p. 4)

Parents may feel vulnerable in working with the schools and agencies that have accepted their child for educational or other services. For example, parents may not comment on program deficiencies they perceive in order to avoid the risk of being labeled troublemakers and jeopardizing their child's eligibility. It appears that much more (often negative) attention is given to vocal or truly unreasonable parents than to cooperative parents deeply concerned about their child. Some professionals appear to have given little thought to what Gorham (1975) refers to as a "lost generation of parents," who live lives of enforced silence and acquiescence.

Facilities are expanding, but not fast enough to accommodate all the people who need them. The resulting competitive atmosphere, played to the hilt by some agencies and schools, forces exceptional families to examine what they must do to make themselves acceptable for services.

> They often find themselves trying new things, whether they are suitable or not, in order to cross the agency threshold. Trapped in this fruitless, and often painful, mutual encounter, family and agency unnecessarily expend a great deal of energy criticizing each other. (Schleifer, 1971, p. 4)

Because they want to be accepted, primarily for their child's welfare but also for their own sense of self-esteem, parents are often at a loss as to how they should behave. As if they were taking a psychological test in which it is impossible to escape some stigmatizing label or diagnosis, there is simply no way for them to avoid some (usually derogatory or "sick") label or category.

> If the parent is militantly aggressive in seeking to obtain therapeutic services for his child he may be accused of not realistically accepting the child's limitations. If he does not concern himself with efforts to improve or obtain services he may be accused of apathetic rejection of this child. If he questions too much he has a "reaction formation" and may be overprotective and oversolicitous. If he questions too little he is branded as disinterested and insensitive. (In short, parents tend to be classified if they . . . failed to match up to the expectation of the school or clinic.) (Barsch, 1968, pp. 8-9)

In addition, other barriers stand in the way of a child's acceptance. The child might be too young, too old, too bright, too retarded; or the parent might have too high or too low an income, or live in the wrong geographical area.

Gorham and associates (Gorham, Des Jardinas, Page, Pettis, & Scheiber, 1975) believe that parents are unduly grateful to principals or school directors for merely accepting their children in their programs: "The spectre of 24 hours a day, 7 days a week care at home, with the state institution as an alternative, has made us too humbly thankful" (p. 552). Children are often referred elsewhere because school personnel want only those children who will make their program succeed; however, to parents, another referral can be a devastating blow. Ironically, the assistance provided by social service delivery systems works in inverse ratio to the help needed by parents; the more crisis-laden the child and the family, the less likely they are to find help (Gorham et al., 1975). It is hoped that in future years professionals will vigorously oppose these practices. The disturbing trend noted by Feldman, Byalick, and Rosedale (1975), that parents have learned that minimal contact with their child's school is best, needs to be reversed.

Professional Helpers: Allies or Foes?

In interviewing physicians who treat handicapped children, medical sociologist Darling (1979) discovered that a number of them held negative feelings about treating such children and working with their parents. In a related observation (Fox, 1975), parents of handicapped children were found to believe that professionals did not want to become involved with them. Parents appear to sense such attitudes and are frequently dissatisfied with their experiences with professionals. Telford and Sawrey (1977) quote a mother who characterized her conferences as "a masterful combination of dishonesty, condescension, misinformation and bad manners" (p. 143).

Among the problems faced by exceptional parents, Murray (undated) lists that of receiving inept, inaccurate, and ill-timed professional advice. She further notes that parents' reactions to their child depend to a large degree on the maturity of the professional with whom they consult. According to Anderson and Garner (1973), parents complain about professionals who provide information in highly technical jargon or convey their impressions in purely pejorative terms.

Some professionals hold negative views of certain handicapping conditions and tend to see parents as "disturbed" (Gur, 1976). Roos (1977) points out that professionals view exceptional parents as having such problems as (1) the inability to accept the fact that their child is handicapped; (2) manifest pathological depression; (3) excessive overprotection of their child; (4) irrational hostility, which is usually focused on the professional; and (5) tenuous marital relationships. According to Roos, destructive stereotypes and a general lack of understanding of handicapping conditions result in much professional mishandling of parents.

Gorham and associates (1975) and Hobbs (1975) vigorously attack the negative effect labels have on children and their parents. In their attempt to adjust to the system, some parents learn to manipulate their child's diagnosis to get the best program available (Gorham et al., 1975). The professionals' propensity to rely on labels in lieu of descriptive statements of strengths and weaknesses must be abandoned.

Professionals have a tendency to discount what parents say about their child, as professionals believe that their own perceptions are the only valid ones and that parents' observations are colored by subjectivity, denial, or distortions of reality (Seligman & Seligman, 1980). At times, this might be true, but there is often more than a kernel of truth in what parents report. It makes sense for professionals to treat parents as intelligent, and to treat their observations and child-rearing practices as worthy of consideration and not a reflection of their neurotic behavior. "Again and again we have heard the plea from parents that the diagnostician respect the occupation of parenting, that he not only listen to the parent but hear what he or she says" (Gorham et al., 1975, p. 163). Baxter (1977) puts it clearly:

> The next time you are faced with a handicapped child and his or her family, don't be so ready to make judgments. If the child has only one visible handicap, don't automatically assume that that is all you have to deal with. If a parent comes across as very verbal and competent, don't assume that they have everything under control, or that they are cold and unfeeling. Listen for the little clues that tell you that intellectualizing is their way of handling feelings that are too painful to surface easily. Don't be easily misled if the child is pretty and has a winning smile and seems very docile in your presence. Listen, really listen, to what the parents tell you about the child at home. And, perhaps most importantly of all, help parents to admit to feelings of grief, and shame, and anger, and tiredness, and despair. If you do that, you will not only help parents to seek the fulfillment of their own personal lives, but you will have helped immeasurably to make the child's personal burden much lighter. (pp. 7-8)

Parents find the practice of keeping confidential information from them disturbing. Information about clients or patients must be kept confidential from people who are not professionally involved in a particular case, but keeping such information from parents adds to their sense of distrust and contributes to poor rapport. Also, some information is recorded in such highly technical terms that only other professionals can decipher it, or it is recorded in a form of professional shorthand so that only the person making the entry is able to interpret it. Confidential records must remain available not only to involved professionals (e.g., consultants), but also to parents, who have the right to see what has been recorded about them and their children.

The professional's own anxiety accounts for some of the discomfort and hostile reactions parents experience, but the lack of adequate training in interpersonal skills and the lack of knowledge about the potential social and psychological impact a handicapped child may have on the family are contributing factors. Much of the criticism leveled at inadequate professional training is aimed at physicians, although educators and social service workers are not exempt (Fox, 1975; Gur, 1976). As a consequence of this criticism, attempts have been made to identify the characteristics of professionals that lead to successful helping. Most agree that the most important is honesty. Open, candid responses within the context of a caring relationship are essential. Parents find little value in abrupt or evasive answers to their questions.

Ross (1964) also regards as essential the human qualities of acceptance, understanding, and warmth, as well as the professional attributes of objectivity, confidence, and knowledge. Professionals should also have a familiarity with available community resources, the sensitivity to recognize the need for consultation, and a realistic appraisal of their own limitations. Finally, professionals working with parents of exceptional children should be competent in the technical skill of interviewing.

Parent-Teacher Interactions

The study of young children in isolation from significant others (e.g., their parents) would hardly seem sufficient, since each child lives in a social network that interacts in complex ways. In order to understand exceptional children, it is necessary to view their circumstances from a broad perspective, namely, a family perspective; in order to understand exceptional families, it is necessary to have some familiarity with family structure, theory, and interaction. One conceptual framework, the developmental view, is based on the theory that families need to master successfully a series of tasks or stages to ensure good family relationships. Professionals must also be cognizant of the changing family structures and roles, as well as contemporary values. For teachers who interact with exceptional families, an awareness of the unique characteristics of families with a handicapped child is essential.

Teachers who work with handicapped children must be knowledgeable about families with a handicapped child because, as teachers, they are required to work with the parents as well as with the children in order to maximize education. Historically, teachers have worked with parents (Cartwright, 1981), yet legislation (namely, PL 94-142) has encouraged increased collaboration between parents and school personnel (Reynolds & Birch, 1982). Collaborative efforts between teachers and parents have not always been successful, however, as parents and teachers sometimes view each other as adversaries rather than allies. This is a fact of contemporary life evidenced by the spate of recent publications designed to improve parent-teacher relationships, but it was also observed as early as 1899 in the Harper Report, in which it was concluded that the lack of cooperation between parents and teachers caused school dropouts, insubordination, and vagrancy (Paul, 1981).

Generally, when child care professionals (e.g., teachers, nurses, physical therapists) have difficulty relating to parents of handicapped children, there are two primary reasons: (1) an inadequate understanding of exceptional parents, their problems, triumphs, and coping mechanisms; and (2) a lack of effective communication skills.

Teachers As Facilitators

Teachers are not often well prepared in communication skills. Justifiably, considerable effort is expended in training teachers to teach children, but there appears to be little interest in training teachers to conduct productive parent conferences. The following observations by two educators illustrate the lack of preparedness to confer with parents often found among teachers. These educators also comment on the potential value of such preparation:

> Unfortunately, many teacher training programs do not provide an opportunity to students to learn the skills and techniques of conferring with parents. The importance of effective teacher/parent relationships cannot be overemphasized. Teachers who understand the children in their environment can make appropriate educational plans in the classroom. Parents who are provided with information about the school setting and their child's progress can be strong supporters and assistants in the child's educational growth and development. Parents and teachers who recognize each other's capabilities can join together in successful problem solving. (Kroth, 1975, p. 155)

Barsch (1968) made the following observations regarding teachers' lack of expertise in working effectively with parents of exceptional children:

> One may look hard and long before any listing of courses devoted to understanding parenthood of a handicapped child is found to be a formal part of the professional preparation. Not only do professionals from hundreds of university programs holding varying and differing orientations enter the fields of rehabilitation and special education each year but they also enter the fields with little or no preparation for their encounters with parents. (p. 15)

McWilliams (1976) builds a convincing case that all professionals who work with children and their parents should be well versed in counseling skills; Schmid, Moneypenny, and Johnston (1977) note that teachers cannot avoid some aspects of guidance work and urge teachers to become familiar with the rudiments of counseling. Receptivity to parents, combined with facilitative communication skills, will resolve the problem expressed by Feldman, Byalick, and Rosedale (1975): "It is imperative that something be done to alter the negative conditions that have traditionally been present when parents and school officials are together" (p. 551). Reynolds and Birch (1977) place the responsibility for improved home-school relationships on the teacher:

> Communicating with and guiding parents is now an integral part of the teacher's responsibility. Other school staff members (counselors, social workers, principals, psychologists, supervisors) may assume some of the responsibility, but in the final analysis it is the teacher-parent interaction that is essential. (p. 183)

Reynolds and Birch (1982) note that teachers are presently asked to assume a number of roles in relation to parents, and Buscaglia (1975) believes that a gold mine remains untapped when teachers of exceptional children fail to work with parents: "Teachers . . . who do not use parents as at least one-third of the learning team are utilizing only two-thirds of their potential effectiveness" (p. 298).

In regard to parent-teacher conferences, Barsch (1969) correctly observes that "what would at first glance appear to be a relatively mechanical, simple encounter is in truth a very complex situation" (p. 12). The problematic circumstances lead to considerable frustration and anxiety on the part of both teachers and parents. The relationship is affected, in part, by how parents and teachers view each other. A constructive, candid, focused meeting with a facilitative teacher (supportive, open, nonjudgmental, interested, and sensitive) can maximize parent-teacher rapport, and such positive encounters will, in most cases, ultimately lessen anxiety and frustration for both parties. The variables that affect the parent-teacher relationship are many and interactive. They include

- personality of the parent(s)
- personality of the teacher
- problems presented by the nature of the child's handicap
- parental reactions to their handicapped child
- relationship between the parents of the handicapped child, and between the parents and the child
- stereotypes teachers may have of parents of exceptional children

- anxieties teachers experience (often related to stereotypes)
- the treatment parents have received from other professionals

Teacher Effectiveness

Some years ago when there was a widespread effort to evaluate counseling effectiveness, many were shocked to learn that counseling was less effective than was once thought (Bergin, 1963; Carkhuff, 1968; Eysenck, 1955). One major conclusion derived from the research is that counseling may be "for better or for worse"; some clients improved, some did not change, *while still others actually were worse* after counseling.

Branan (1972) presents some compelling evidence that teachers must be aware of relationships they establish with students. Branan asked 150 college-aged students to describe in detail what they considered to be the two most negative experiences in their lives. Negative experiences were defined as those that the respondents felt made their lives worse or had a negative effect on their development. Responses were divided into two categories: interpersonal and nonpersonal experiences. Of the 300 responses, 257 involved interpersonal relationships, and the largest subcategory was interaction with teachers.

The time at which the experiences occurred (i.e., whether they were recent) was not an important variable; more negative experiences were reported to have occurred in high school than in college, more in elementary than in junior high school. Teachers were involved more often than any other group in the most negative experiences reported, with parents a poor second. Individual situations included humiliation in front of the class, unfairness in evaluation, destruction of self-confidence, personality conflicts, and embarrassment. Branan concludes that "human relations training and skill should be as important a prerequisite for teachers as any other requirement. Human relations knowledge and skill should become a prerequisite to teacher credentials at any level. The damage resulting from sarcastic, insensitive, and noncaring teachers at any level must be decreased" (p. 82).

Teachers generally recognize the importance of being a helping person, but few are capable of putting theory into practice (Wittmer & Myrick, 1974). Research conducted by Wittmer and Myrick (1974); by Combs, Blume, Newman, and Wass (1974); and by Aspy and his associates (Aspy, 1969, 1971, 1972; Aspy & Roebuck, 1967) shows that *effective* teachers

1. see other people as being worthy rather than unworthy
2. do not regard others as threatening but rather as essentially well intentioned
3. regard people as important sources of satisfaction rather than as sources of frustration and suspicion
4. are good listeners

5. have empathy (ability to truly comprehend someone else's circumstances)
6. show care and concern
7. are genuine (not phony)
8. are knowledgeable

Wittmer and Myrick found that ineffective teachers are

1. insensitive
2. cold, disinterested
3. authoritarian
4. ridiculing
5. arbitrary
6. sarcastic
7. punitive

Finally, Lyon (1971), quoting the prominent educator and psychologist, Carl Rogers, on his view of education, makes a most important point:

> Better courses, better curricula, better coverage, better teaching machines will never resolve our dilemma in a basic way. Only persons acting like persons in their relationships with their students (and parents) can even begin to make a dent on this most urgent problem of modern education. (p. 251)

Not unlike counselors, teachers are attracted to education because it enables them to feel helpful, needed, and appreciated by others. Like most people, teachers enjoy not only being viewed as knowledgeable and likeable, but also having status and influence. Relatively few in the helping professions are what some refer to as "gifted" or "natural" helpers. Only a minority of professionals who work with people have a naturally warm, understanding, and generally easygoing (yet productive) manner. Such people, although they can profit by further sharpening of their interpersonal skills, have little need for extensive training. On the other hand, most of us have to work conscientiously to function optimally during interpersonal encounters. This need is particularly critical for teachers, who must work effectively with their classes of children, some of whom are handicapped, and the parents of these children.

In general, in order to work effectively with exceptional children and their parents, teachers need (1) a thorough understanding of the dynamics of families with a handicapped child; (2) a good cognitive understanding of the dimensions of effective interpersonal relationships, combined with opportunities to practice different interpersonal styles; and (3) extensive experience working with parents of handicapped children.

PARENTS AND PROFESSIONALS: RECIPROCAL VIEWS

Although parent-teacher relationships benefit parents, teachers, and, ultimately, the children involved, they are potential sources of conflict. To understand potential impasses, it may be useful to become better acquainted with the perceptions parents and teachers have of each other.

Teachers' Perceptions of Parents

Teachers' attitudes toward parents vary, but they tend to be more negative than positive. Lortie (1975) notes the vulnerable position of teachers. According to him, teachers have discernible reasons to distrust and even fear parents. Parents enjoy considerable rights in regard to the education of their children. Parents sometimes complain to teachers or to administrators about a teacher's performance, and repeated or serious complaints can weaken the teacher's standing within the school system. Teachers have the license to discipline children, but only under certain conditions. Teachers who give vent to anger may fear parental sanctions, not the least of which is a lawsuit. As a consequence, then, of real or perceived threats, teachers have a sense of vulnerability that has its roots in reality.

Teachers must maintain a social order of democracy and fairness, as well as a viable instructional group, often under difficult circumstances. Lortie points out that parents who ask for special treatment for their child make it difficult for the teacher to maintain an atmosphere of fairness, a difficulty compounded when several parents make contradictory requests. A barrage of parental requests makes the teacher fear that the social order is beginning to unravel. The problem of special requests is particularly relevant when the needs of exceptional children are involved.

Teachers are also dependent on parents; they rely on parents to influence their children in ways the teacher values, namely, to infuse a positive attitude toward school. Parental influence can range from support to indifference and open hostility. The way in which parents choose to influence their children has an important effect on the students' behavior in the classroom. Furthermore, when the values of the family and the school are contradictory, the pupils' schoolwork suffers.

Lortie (1975) asked teachers what they see as an ideal parent-teacher relationship. He found that teachers often depict parent-teacher conferences as a "waste of time" or as interpersonally awkward. The teachers wanted more contact with parents, but only with those whose children were having trouble in school. In regard to parent socioeconomic status and teacher conferences, parents in lower status groups often failed to respond to teacher requests for a conference, whereas parents in higher status groups often arrived without invitation, a situation generally not to the liking of teachers. From his analysis, Lortie concluded that teachers prefer a relationship in which they are in the superordinate role and define occasions that justify parental involvement. Chronic, spontaneous visitors were characterized by teachers as "academic hypochondriacs worrying and fussing without cause." In other words, teacher-initiated conferences were looked upon favorably, but other parent visits were considered "interruptions."

When teachers were asked to describe the "good parent," Lortie reported that two central themes were reflected in the responses: (1) parents should not intervene, and (2) parents should support teacher efforts. "Good parents" were characterized as "distant assistants," who imbued their children with a positive attitude toward school, cooperating with the teacher yet not interfering, and taking the lead from the teacher.

From Lortie's research and analysis, some insight can be gained into the underlying causes of tension between parents and teachers. Teachers wish to interact with parents only under certain conditions and, in general, do not view parent contact positively. Barsch (1969), a special educator, concurs with the latter point when he writes that "clinical experience with over 12,000 sets of parents and wide professional experience with many teachers confirm a belief that the parent is more favorable to the teacher than the teacher is to the parent" (p. 8). Bailard and Strang (1964) and Shapiro (1975) agree that parents are appreciative of teachers' efforts. This paradox—where the teacher is negatively predisposed toward the parent and the parent is positively predisposed toward the teacher—is, according to Barsch, at the root of many of the problems reflected in negative parent-school encounters.

Bissell (1976) adds that, because teachers frequently view parents from a pathological perspective, they seldom consider parents desirable or competent full-fledged members of the educational team. Further, teachers may see the emergence of parent groups as a threat; these groups may be seen as enemies having tremendous resources and presenting realistic dangers. Finally, Hetznecker, Arnold, and Phillips (1978) contend that parents may be seen as an added pressure, consuming inordinate amounts of time and energy that teachers feel they can ill afford.

> Educators find themselves in a psychological squeeze. They are required to be more "accountable" for the effectiveness of programs; they are subject to pressures by local communities and by state and federal attempts to establish standards of quality and equality. At the same time, they find themselves increasingly burdened with responsibility for basic socialization for children, and experience frustration, discouragement and anger over what they view as an abdication of responsibility by parents. (p. 364)

Parents' Perceptions of Teachers

As noted earlier, teachers view parents much more negatively than parents view teachers. Teachers tend to be exempted from the widely held negative attitudes exceptional parents have toward other professionals, yet these parents may experience some difficulties relating to teachers.

Some parents view the teacher as a parent figure and may, during conferences, take the role of the dependent child by trying to please the teacher. On the other hand, this same perception of teachers may produce a rebellious or hostile attitude that is really an expression of unresolved feelings for their own parents.

The perceptions of some parents are colored by unfortunate encounters with professionals in the past. Parents who have had such encounters approach a teacher with caution to see if these prior experiences will be repeated. Such parents will feel relieved and will change their preconceived attitudes in the company of a facilitative ally.

Parents who have bitter memories of their own educational experiences may communicate their negative views of teachers and schooling in general to their children. Such experiences have adverse effects on a child's perceptions and subsequent adjustment to school (Rainwater, Coleman, & Handel, 1959).

Unrealistic views of teachers' capabilities could result in parental demands and expectations that the teachers are unprepared and unable to fulfill. For example, teachers may be perceived as psychotherapists, capable of dispensing advice about significant psychological problems (Meadow & Meadow, 1971). In such instances, teachers are well-advised to stay within the boundaries of their competencies.

Teachers and parents may differ in their philosophy of interaction with children, especially around disciplinary methods. Methods of discipline that the parents practice at home will probably be the ones the parents wish teachers to use in school. In addition, parents may see teachers as competitors when the values they emphasize do not coincide with the parents' own. In such an instance, parents feel undercut in their efforts to raise their child, and they envy the teacher who excites the child's affection and respect. Philosophical differences, then, may be one source of tension during parent-teacher conferences.

Parents may have a negative reaction to a teacher because of an inadvertent comment that touched a particularly sensitive area. Also, parents may misconstrue a teacher's comments, and misunderstandings may result. The teacher who senses a parent reaction to a comment may wish to make a sensitive probe, such as "I believe I detected a slight reaction to what I just said. If I'm right I wonder if you'd be willing to share your reaction with me." The purpose of such a probe is to demonstrate sensitivity to the parent's feelings and reactions and to reinforce the value of open communication.

Negative parental attitudes may not be directed toward the teacher but may instead reflect what the conference means to the parent. As noted previously, negative encounters with other professionals predispose parents to view subsequent conferences with apprehension. A sensitive "reading" of the uncomfortable parent is required to determine the source of discomfort—a sense or skill that develops over time.

Parents may feel concerned that the conference will deal only with the child's weaknesses—deficiencies that are painfully apparent and that the parent does not wish to have validated by still another professional. The teacher should not bombard parents of significantly impaired children with a laundry list of their child's problems; such conferences can have a devastating effect on the parent psychologically and can destroy whatever rapport the parent and teacher may have developed. Cooperation and rapport with parents will improve if conferences are balanced to reflect both strengths and weaknesses.

A difference in educational level or age may produce other negative attitudes seemingly directed toward teachers. When parents feel intimidated by the educational discrepancy between them and the teacher, for example, they may approach the conference with a feeling of inferiority. Barsch (1969) believes that this factor may cause the parent to be less open during conferences. Also, a recently graduated young teacher conferring with older parents may cause some consternation during the first few sessions. The teacher's rapport with the parents, as well as the demonstration of expertise, will reduce their preoccupation with age differences, however.

Parents' perceptions of teachers, the school, or schooling constitute a varied tapestry of attitudes and expectations. On the whole, parents tend to value their child's teacher as one who is generally knowledgeable, as a specialist in working with children, and as a source of encouragement and support. With the exception of a few parents, who may be difficult to work with under any circumstances, parents constitute a formidable ally for the teacher.

PARENT CONFERENCES

A number of books can help professionals develop their interviewing and conferencing skills (Benjamin, 1974; Brenner, 1982; Egan, 1975; Seligman, 1979; Zaro, Barach, Nedelman, & Dreiblatt, 1977). Some time ago, McGowan (1956) noted that new behaviors should be compatible with one's natural style of response. In other words, new skills should be incorporated into one's natural way of interacting with others. The behavior, not the characteristic style of response, is subject to modification. This notion should be borne in mind while one attempts to develop interpersonal skills.

Parent-Teacher Values

Conferences between parents and teachers could be described as encounters of two unique sets of values. Strong feelings about certain issues (e.g., politics) are generally not discussed in a parent-teacher conference, yet they are not *always* absent. For example, a parent may openly support a political candidate who is opposed to improved job conditions for teachers. In such instances, the teacher must remember that the purpose of the conference is to discuss issues that will ultimately benefit the child. A heated discussion over political views has no place in a helping interview.

To the extent possible, the teacher should adopt a philosophy of neutrality—even though the teacher may privately and, it is hoped, temporarily respond with anger or resentment. Parents have as much right to their point of view as does the teacher. This is a reality that requires a considerable degree of acceptance, as expressed by Benjamin (1974) in the following observation:

> Basically, to me acceptance means treating the interviewee as an equal and regarding his thoughts and feelings with sincere respect. It does not mean agreeing; it does not mean thinking or feeling the way he does; it does not mean valuing what he values. It is, rather, the attitude that the interviewee has as much right to his ideas, feelings, and values as I have to mine and that I want to do my utmost to understand his life space in terms of his ideas, feelings, and values rather than in terms of my own. Such an attitude is difficult to maintain and even more difficult to communicate to the interviewee. At times it may be misunderstood and interpreted as agreement, consent, or reassurance. And yet we have no choice but to attempt to be accepting. Otherwise, the interviewee will suspect that we are judging him, asking him to feel and think as we do or, even worse, to think and feel as we believe he ought to be thinking and feeling (p. 39).

It is equally important to avoid the imposition of a teacher's values in a parent-teacher conference:

> The hazard lies in an imposition of values by the counselor [teacher]. The danger is great because the counselor may not consciously intend for this to happen. But when it does happen, the counselee [parent] feels somewhat pushed down as a person. An implied denial of the worth of his own views and experiences is given to him, and he senses the disapproval and rejection of himself as he is at the moment. (Johnson & Vestermark, 1970, p. 78)

The Conference Setting

The setting of a parent-teacher conference is important because it helps to create the parent's first impressions of the teacher and general feeling about the meeting. The conference should be held in a room where there are no external distractions and where the conversation cannot be overheard. Classrooms should suffice if these conditions are met.

The teacher should not sit behind a desk because physical objects of any size are felt to represent barriers to a comfortable interpersonal exchange. The most desirable seating arrangement for an interview consists of two chairs placed comfortably close to each other, at a 90° angle. This arrangement allows the parent to look either at the teacher or straight ahead, whichever makes the parent feel more comfortable during the conference. It also allows the teacher to gaze in different directions.

Conferences should be planned so that parents need not wait much beyond their scheduled appointment and interruptions are minimal. In addition to being an inconvenience, a protracted wait may be considered rude and generate feelings of frustration, anger, and a general sense of the teacher's lack of interest and concern. Interruptions, such as telephone calls, people who want "just a word with you," or secretaries who must have something signed immediately, distract from the conference. Arrangements can be made to complete any administrative details prior to the conference, and secretaries and others who might inadvertently "pop in" should be advised that the teacher will be occupied for a specific period of time.

It is sometimes helpful to make a few notes about certain parental concerns or to record some information or data about the child. Continuous note taking during a conference is to be avoided, however, unless it is essential. Not only is continuous note taking rude, but also it conveys a sense of disinterest and an overconcern with cold facts. The teacher can, at leisure, jot down certain pieces of information or the gist of the conference for future reference after the parent leaves.

Conference Goals

Conferences normally begin with a certain amount of small talk about the weather, inflation, or an event in the news. This conversation is to be expected and functions as a warm-up before more serious business is pursued. Abrupt, discourteous interruptions of this kind of talk are to be discouraged, because such an interruption generally signals feelings of nervousness, impatience, or, more seriously, insensitivity. Sooner or later, one of the parties will gradually begin to discuss the (usually) anticipated content of the meeting. People tend to sense when the time has arrived to begin to address more serious concerns.

Whatever the objectives of a conference are, Losen and Diament (1978) believe it is important to keep the following principles in mind:

1. Working objectives should be clear.
2. Objectives should be mutually agreed upon.
3. There should be a specific timetable established for their accomplishments. (p. 61)

When unanticipated topics arise, the most productive approach for the teacher is to remain calm and try not to become defensive. The conference purpose may shift from that originally set by the teacher to one of thoughtful listening, understanding, and responding. Interpersonal interactions are not programmed, mechanical meetings, where the content and outcome is always predictable. As Lisbe (1978) notes,

> The realities of ''people work'' require a presence unlike other fields where processes are replicable. Carpenters follow blueprints, automobile manufacturers use molds, accountants work from forms, and pilots read instrument panels. There are no such guidelines when one human being faces another, when the uniqueness of each encounter requires uncompromising intensity. (p. 242)

During the course of a conference with a general goal, for example, the semiannual parent-teacher conference about a child's performance at school, the parents may mention a family event, such as an impending divorce, that may have serious implications for their child's future. Generally, such an event is mentioned to alert the teacher to anticipated changes in the child's environment that may affect the child's schoolwork and behavior. Possibly the disclosure also serves a cathartic purpose, that is, it provides the parents with a chance to talk about an emotion-filled event. In either case, empathic and supportive listening is all that is called for in most instances of this nature. Parents in difficult situations are often bombarded with well-intentioned but mostly unnecessary advice from a variety of sources and welcome the presence of an interested listener.

Listening

Everyone has encountered other people who heard but did not listen. More often than not, the reaction to this inattention is to feel hurt, ignored, or even angry. Frequently, the reaction to a nonlistener is to change the subject, physically move away from the situation, or uncomfortably continue with the fragmented, superficial chatter.

Listening is not a mechanical activity. It is hard work and requires deep concentration, patience, and practice. It involves hearing the way things are being said and the tone used; observing the speaker's gestures; and paying attention to what is not said, what is only hinted at, what is held back, or what lies beneath the surface. We must learn to listen with our third ear (Reik, 1972); or, to put it more concretely, we hear with our ears, but we listen with our eyes and mind and heart and skin and guts as well (Ekman, 1964).

The interviewer should become as physically relaxed as possible. Schulman (1974) believes this step is so critical to good listening that she proposes a set of relaxation exercises for interviewers who find it difficult to feel physically at ease. Perhaps most important to listening at parent-teacher conferences is the teacher's desire to understand parents and to gain experience. There is much to be said for experience. Teachers teach with greater ease over time, and conferencing skills are no different in that respect; good listening becomes an easier task over time and, in fact, can become a quite natural activity.

There are a number of potential barriers to effective interpersonal communication. Being aware of possible pitfalls is the first step in minimizing these barriers. One major barrier to the acquisition of effective conferencing skills lies not with teachers but with the institutions that train them. Training programs in education place little emphasis on the development of facilitative skills. This is unfortunate, because teachers are required to confer periodically with the parents of the children they teach. Clearly, the acquisition of facilitative interpersonal skills must be given higher priority in teacher education programs.

Another barrier to the development of facilitative interpersonal skills may arise from the personalities and skills of those supervisors and professors who educate teachers. It is not unusual for matriculated students to emulate the practices and behaviors of their mentors. Yalom (1975) observed that "pipe-smoking therapists often beget pipe-smoking patients. Patients during psychotherapy may sit, walk, talk, and even think like their therapists" (p. 17). This behavior is as true in teacher education as it is in psychotherapy. Teacher educators and supervisors are not always the most effective social models for their charges, however. Teaching, whether in college, in elementary school, or elsewhere, is an influencing process, and teacher educators and supervisors are often remarkably naive about the impact their social-interpersonal conduct has on those they teach and train. In discussing the effects of social modeling in counselor training, Jakubowski-Spector, Dustin, and George (1971) observed the following:

> What a counselor educator does may be more influential than what he says; our role as a model may be more important than our role as an instructor. If a counselor educator is trying to teach genuine communication, the educator's interpersonal dealings with his students should reflect or model the kind of behavior he endorses. Through our

> dealings with students, we show them what we are and what we expect from people. Too often, a counselor educator verbalizes the importance of genuineness and self-disclosure while his students do not find these behaviors in their interaction with him as an advisor, practicum instructor, or professor. As models, counselor educators could more effectively facilitate learning through striving to consistently act out the behaviors they are trying to teach. This may lead to a more consistent behavior in counseling students. (pp. 248-249)

Dealing with children for several hours a day is work, hard work, and teachers are often fatigued at the end of a typical day. It is most difficult to be an attentive listener at this time, but inattention due to fatigue conveys a lack of interest and concern. Teachers should be aware of their tolerance levels and regulate their working day to ensure that they are alert when conferring with parents.

It is often difficult to distinguish physical fatigue from boredom. It is not an easy task to uncover the reason for a teacher's boredom at a parent-teacher conference, but disinterest in listening to the problems of others, hearing essentially the same story for the sixth time, or preoccupation might be considered. Different action is required according to the causal factor(s).

Preoccupation with personal circumstances can be a barrier to effective interviewing. Also, novice interviewers may be thinking about their responses while the parent is talking. Transitory preoccupation is common and is to be expected, but teachers who experience chronic preoccupation must examine their tendency to become distracted.

Strong feelings about the parent is another barrier to effective listening. Anger or anxiety directed at the parent cannot help but interfere with the interview. Here again it is helpful to consider the source of the anger or anxiety before taking action. Often such awareness defuses the situation to such an extent that little else is required; the negative emotions decline in intensity, and attentive listening can resume.

Professional roles can be inhibiting, although how they interfere is unclear. Johnson and Vestermark (1970), who believe that some distancing is necessary, feel that professionals should allow for the required sense of objectivity or perspective; others contend that professional roles, with their inevitable distancing, are responsible for the ineffective interpersonal skills of many people in the helping professions. Carkhuff (1968) marshalls a considerable amount of evidence to support the conclusion that paraprofessionals (peers with some training in human relations) perform considerably better than professionals in this area. Paraprofessionals, he argues, are perceived as friends who understand and genuinely care, rather than as authority figures (professionals) who are removed from a client's environment and presumably pretend to care because they receive remuneration for doing so.

Defensive Behavior

Either the parent or the teacher may exhibit defensive behavior, and defensiveness by one party probably will result in some type of reciprocal defensive communication. It is a basic rule that whenever such discernible resistance disrupts or impedes parent-teacher conferences, such roadblocks must be explored immediately—before proceeding to another topic. When a parent appears uncharacteristically quiet (or closed), the teacher should inquire about this behavior; sensitivity and appropriate pacing are necessary for effective intervention.

Silence is one of the most common manifestations of resistance, especially when it is preceded or followed by other cues of avoidance. Carrying on a superficial conversation (or intellectualizing) over a considerable time period, changing the subject, ignoring the teacher's comments, arriving late for appointments, and forgetting conferences altogether are other indications that a parent may feel resistant. Filibustering, excessive questioning, challenging the teacher about his or her shortcomings or flaws are other ways defensiveness is shown.

It is imperative that teachers understand what lies behind defensive behavior. Parents may, for example, be very reluctant to become involved in conferences, which they feel highlight their child's shortcomings and, by association, their own inadequacies. Parents who have attended several conferences that were liberally laced with their child's problems develop a generalized dread of all conferences. Misconceptions of the purpose of parent-teacher conferences could result in negative attitudes; a parent may see them, for example, as a time to exchange social amenities. On the other hand, parents may fear that heavy demands will be placed on them—demands that will be overwhelming. Anger at the school, the school system, or, perhaps, at the teacher may account for resistance, as some parents fear that involvement with the teacher will require some sort of change in the relationship between parent and child. Finally, a parent's defensiveness during conferences may actually be a reflection of ambivalent feelings toward or rejection of the child.

Defensive behavior by parents is to be expected at times, and it is the teacher's task to deal with it effectively. Defensive behavior by teachers is a serious matter, but it is not subject to modification by parents. Teachers are the professional helpers, and the parents are the recipients of a service. Should teachers find themselves feeling or acting defensively toward parents, they would be well-advised to think about the underlying reasons. Discussing the situation with an understanding friend, colleague, or supervisor often can provide fresh insights.

There is nothing wrong with being professional. It implies exercising good judgment and behaving in a responsible and ethical manner. Unfortunately, some professional helpers equate being professional with being aloof, distant, and even arrogant. This is a form of defensiveness that maintains psychological distance. Such behavior makes the teacher appear to be a cold and uncaring person. Feelings of dislike, anger, or fear can lead to defensive or protective maneuvers by the teacher. Here again, self-awareness is an invaluable asset.

Lecturing or moralizing has no place in helping relationships, and it is of questionable value in other interpersonal situations as well. Although teachers are generally viewed as knowledgeable and helpful people, those who lecture or moralize in interpersonal situations may be seen as intellectual or moral superiors, not to be questioned (at best), or uncaring (at worst). Parents who are treated in this way will act with surprise or even shock; they will feel and act defensively (revolt and argue) or feel guilty and ashamed (become passive). Neither attitude leads to healthy and productive interpersonal relationships, positive self-concepts, and personal growth.

Silences

Western cultures, unlike Eastern ones, find silence between people barely tolerable. Because it is viewed as empty and meaningless, silence makes people feel uncomfortable. For people who conduct interviews, however, silences should be considered a positive form of communication.

Beginning interviewers often feel they must talk when pauses or silences occur, and an uneasy sense of wasting time or not doing a good job causes them to make inappropriate comments or ask unnecessary questions. Unfortunately, it takes experience to recognize the value of silence. There are no rules about how long is too long for a period of silence; each situation has to be assessed on its own merit. Silence is worthwhile only as long as it is communicating something or is serving some function. It can best be understood if the meaning of the pause and the context in which it occurs are clear. A high degree of sensitivity is required to know when to remain quiet and when to make an appropriate remark.

Overtalk

Teachers are trained to convey information, to put across ideas, to answer questions, and to ask them. In order to engage in such activities, teachers must talk more, and appropriately so, than the children they teach—although good teachers also listen.

In conferring with parents, teachers must listen more and talk less. As teachers are more accustomed to talking than listening, they must make a concerted effort during parent-teacher conferences to control their own speech and concentrate on what others are saying. Also, Langden and Stout (1954) urge teachers to abandon "teacherish" speech when conferring with parents. Hetznecker and associates (1978) believe that overtalk can best be unlearned in simulated conferences in which role playing is emphasized. This change is critical, the authors feel, because both parent and teacher in their respective roles vis-à-vis the child are accustomed to talk more than to listen.

> Advice, correction, admonishment, persuasion, information giving, and questioning are the adult techniques both parent and teacher direct at children. When relating to parents, a teacher needs to shift to a more receptive, attentive mode which emphasizes listening. (p. 366)

Nonverbal Behavior

General body movements, gestures, and facial expressions are manifestations of nonverbal behavior. Paralinguistic behavior is manifested in tone of voice, inflection, spacing of words, emphasis, and pauses. Body language, another dimension of nonverbal behavior, includes the distance maintained between people and the orientation or direction of the body (proxemics), as well as its motion (kinesics).

The idea that speech is often intended to obscure a true feeling or a particular meaning has gone beyond hypothesis; it has been substantiated that nonverbal cues do, in fact, more accurately reflect a person's inner life than what that person says (Hansen, Stevic, & Warner, 1982). Therefore, it is reasonable for those in the helping professions to become knowledgeable about and sensitive to nonverbal behavior.

The ability to "read" nonverbal cues would be enormously useful for teachers. These cues either augment what teachers are hearing or provide some insight into a feeling or attitude that is hidden. Teachers should be cautious in their interpretation of nonverbal cues, however. The same behavior may have vastly different meanings if manifested by two different people. Interviewers often make a "perception check" on what they think they are perceiving. For example, a teacher may comment to a parent: "I hear you saying that you are pleased with George's progress, but your facial expression leads me to believe that you are not entirely satisfied. Am I reading you right, or am I off-base?" This type of check enables the parent to say what he or she is, in fact, feeling and either to agree with or to refute the teacher's observation. As the teacher gains experience and becomes more aware of nonverbal behavior, the teacher's abilities to interpret and respond to these cues appropriately will grow.

Minimal Encouragement To Talk

A teacher may impede what a parent wishes to convey by saying too much or by intervening inappropriately. Particularly during initial meetings or during the first few minutes of a particular session, it is the teacher's task to stay out of the parent's way and, at the same time, to convey attentiveness. Minimal encouragement to talk, by providing limited structure, reinforces the parent's desire to communicate as well as indicating that the teacher is listening. For example,

- "Could you tell me more?"
- "Where would you like to begin today?"
- "Oh?"
- "So?"
- "Then?"
- "And?"
- "Mm-hm"
- "Uh-huh."
- repetition of one or two key words
- simple restatement of the parent's last comment

Timing

In an interview, timing is a combination of experience and good judgment. Responses to parents are based on the teacher's generalized knowledge of people, as well as knowledge of the specific situation. For example, if parents are anxious and excessively concerned about their child's social behavior, a teacher would certainly not initiate a discussion of the child's academic progress.

Some believe that timing in interpersonal situations can make the difference between acceptance or rejection of an opinion or idea. When parents are in a projecting (blaming others) stage or mood, simple listening and responding (paraphrasing) may be the best course of action. When the same parents begin to adjust to their handicapped child and appear to be ready to take on responsibility, the teacher might include ideas and suggestions as to how the parents can help. Conversely, parents who are coping well and who wish to learn a specific teaching strategy to work with their child require a more active relationship with the teacher and less of a supportive one.

Teachers concerned about proper timing may become excessively self-conscious, especially beginners. The self-consciousness decreases as teachers learn to trust their own intuitive sense of timing. Those who seem to have problems in timing, however, need good supervision.

Questions

It is a foregone conclusion that questions should constitute a large portion of the interview—or is it? Benjamin (1974) believes that interviewers ask too many questions and that the questions are often meaningless and impossible to answer. Questions are often posed that actually confuse or interrupt the interviewee or that the interviewer does not really want answered. By asking questions and getting answers, asking more questions and getting more answers, a teacher may be setting up a pattern from which neither parent nor teacher can be extricated.

Open vs. Closed Questions

According to Benjamin, open questions tend to be broad, allowing the interviewee full scope; widening the perceptual field; soliciting views, opinions, thoughts, and feelings; and deepening the relationship. For example,

- "Jerry appears to be quite active these days. He seems to be at an age where there is much to stimulate him. What do you think?"
- "You don't seem to be your usual self today. Anything happen?"
- "Some kids really like school and others are turned off by it. How do you think Jerry feels about school?"

In contrast, closed questions are narrow, restricting the respondent to a specific answer, limiting the perceptual field, demanding cold facts, and circumscribing the contact. Closed questions include

- "How old is Lori?"
- "Does Lori like school?"
- "When is Lori going to camp?"

Another type of closed question includes the answer, or at least strongly implies that the respondent should agree:

- "Lisa has been acting up in school, and I'm sure at home, too; isn't that so?"
- "I think that the best place for Lisa next year is in a special education setting; isn't that your feeling also?"

Direct vs. Indirect Questions

Direct questions are obvious queries, whereas indirect questions inquire without seeming to do so and are more open. Indirect questions do not end in a question mark, yet it is evident that a question is being asked.

Direct: "Isn't it rough working with such unmotivated kids?"
Indirect: "It must be rough working with kids who have trouble motivating themselves."

Direct: "How do you like your new teaching job?"
Indirect: "I wonder how the new teaching job seems to you."

Direct: "What do you think of the new token economy system we're using?"

Indirect: ''You must have some thoughts about our new token economy system.''

Direct: ''How does it feel to be in your new school today?''
Indirect: ''I'd sure like to know how you feel about your new school.''

Even more than open questions, indirect questions allow for a variety of responses.

Double Questions

At times, double questions, which limit the interviewee to one choice out of two, serve an important purpose:

- ''Do you want to set up an appointment for two or three weeks?''
- ''Would you like to have coffee or tea?''
- ''Do you want Jimmy to be a teacher or social worker?''
- ''Do you want to sit near Darrel or Kevin?''

Simple double questions like these curtail a parent's perceptual field and response, however, and they should be avoided when there are other alternatives. Of course, when only two possibilities are available, it should not be implied that more exist.

Examples of more elaborate double questions, which tend to confuse, are

- ''Have we covered everything we wanted to today, and what do you think about scheduling an appointment for our next conference?''
- ''Is Jimmy more controllable now at home, and how is his toilet training coming along?''
- ''Did you get a chance to see an orthopedic surgeon about Karen's hip, and what did the eye doctor say about her vision?''

A simple solution to this problem is to ask each question singly.

Why Questions

Benjamin views why questions as the most useless and potentially destructive type because they often connote disapproval or displeasure. Thus, someone who hears the word *why* may become defensive, may withdraw and avoid the situation, or may go on the offensive. This type of reaction is generally less likely, however, when rapport has been established between two people and they trust and respect each other.

Examples of why questions that are often perceived in a negative way include

- "Why don't you have your Halloween bulletin boards in black and orange?"
- "Why are you late to our conference today?"
- "Why doesn't Bruce wear warmer clothing during the winter months?"
- "Why doesn't Rita read better than before after we discussed her home reading program last time?"

These questions can be framed so that they will have less bite:

- "I noticed that Bruce seems to be cold during class and I was wondering if there might be something he could wear so that he would feel more comfortable."
- "I noticed that Rita hasn't improved her reading very much since our last conference. I wonder what we could do that would motivate her to read more often."
- "You must have run into that terrible downtown traffic on your way here."

Termination

For some interviewers, beginners in particular, closing is not easy. The teacher may be fearful of giving the impression that the parent is being dismissed; depending on how termination is handled, a parent may indeed have this feeling.

Benjamin (1974) believes that the closing phase of an interview is critical and that two basic factors should be kept in mind: (1) both people in the interview should be aware of the fact that the interview is closing and accept it, and (2) during termination, no new material should be discussed. If fresh information or concerns emerge during closing, another interview should be scheduled.

The termination of a parent-teacher conference should not be taken lightly, as it is likely to determine the parents' experience of the interview as a whole. Teachers should have enough time for closing so that they need not rush, since this might create the impression that the parent is being evicted. In general, the task of ending an interview becomes easier with experience.

Referrals

For some professionals (e.g., physicians, social workers), referrals are made rather easily because they are frequently needed and expected. Parents may be less likely to expect a referral from a teacher, however. Referrals for psychological reasons are particularly sensitive issues, as both parties must deal with what such a referral implies to them.

Barsch (1969) considers three options available to teachers who have concluded that psychological intervention is needed. The first is to discuss the problem with the principal, school psychologist, or social worker in hope that they will either modify the parents' behavior through their own efforts or discuss appropriate community referral with the parent. The second option is to adopt the role of a psychotherapist or counselor and assume the responsibility for positive change. The third and most pessimistic alternative is to regard the situation as unchangeable and, therefore, to do nothing.

Although not addressed by Barsch, there is a fourth possibility: the teacher may make an appropriate referral. If the parent is having obvious difficulties, teachers can do more harm than good by not making an appropriate referral. In doing so, however, teachers should be sure that the community has the necessary resources to accomplish the goals of the referral. Discretion is essential, and the subject should be introduced to a parent in a warm, caring manner. The justification for the referral must be communicated unambiguously to the parent. Finally, it is most helpful if the parent personally recognizes the need for a referral and has the time and means for carrying out the recommendation.

Potentially rich referral sources for teachers are self-help groups. Lieberman and Borman (1979) define peer self-help groups as assemblages of people who are largely self-governing and who are composed of members who share a common condition, situation, heritage, symptom, affliction, or experience. In writing about self-help organizations for parents of exceptional children, Wirtz (1977) notes that

> one of the most important aspects of program development in the United States in recent years has been the development of parent associations. By and large these are truly organizations of parents helping parents. The schools serving handicapped children should capitalize on the existence of these organizations and if they are not there, should establish some of their own. (pp. 63-64)

Referrals can also be made to appropriate reading sources.

BIBLIOTHERAPY

A fancy word for a rather simple technique, bibliotherapy is the use of reading material to help someone better understand a condition or situation or to provide support, encouragement, and a sense of universality (i.e., a feeling that others have similar problems). Parents of exceptional children, especially those who like to read or those who desire information about their child's condition, can benefit from the judicious referral to reading material. Some parents, as well as children, achieve insights and encouragement by reading biographies and classical literature involving a handicap. However, the teacher should remember that, although for some people such books are inspiring, for others they may symbolize unattainable achievements. Mullins (in press) presents a thorough discussion of bibliotherapy and how it can be used with parents.

REFERENCES

Anderson, K.A., & Garner, A.M. Mothers of retarded children: Satisfaction with visits to professional people. *Mental Retardation*, 1973, *1*, 36-39.

Aspy, D.N. The effect of teacher deferred conditions of empathy, congruence, and positive regard upon student achievement. *Florida Journal of Educational Research*, 1969, *11*, 39-48.

Aspy, D.N. Toward a technology which helps teachers humanize their classrooms. *Educational Leadership*, March 1971.

Aspy, D.N. *Toward a technology for humanizing education*. Champaign, Ill.: Research Press, 1972.

Aspy, D.N., & Roebuck, F.N. An investigation of the relationship between levels of cognitive functioning and the teacher's classroom behavior. *Journal of Educational Research*, May, 1967.

Bailard, V., & Strang, R. *Parent-teacher conferences*. New York: McGraw-Hill, 1964.

Barsch, R.H. *The parent of the handicapped child: A study of child rearing practices*. Springfield, Ill.: Charles C Thomas, 1968.

Barsch, R.H. *The teacher-parent partnership*. Reston, Va.: Council for Exceptional Children, 1969.

Baum, M.H. Some dynamic factors affecting family adjustment to the handicapped child. *Exceptional Children*, 1962, *28*, 387-392.

Baxter, D. An open letter to those who counsel parents of the handicapped. *Journal of Rehabilitation of the Deaf*, 1977, *10*, 1-8.

Benjamin, A. *The helping interview*. Boston: Houghton Mifflin, 1974.

Bergin, A.E. The effects of psychotherapy: Negative results revisited. *Journal of Counseling Psychology*, 1963, *10*, 244-255.

Bibring, G.L., Dwyer, T.F., Huntingdon, D.S., & Vatenstein, A.F. A study of the psychological processes in pregnancy and the earliest mother-child relationships. *Psychoanalytic Study of the Child*, 1961, *16*, 9-72.

Bissell, N.E. Communicating with the parents of exceptional children. In E.J. Webster (Ed.), *Professional approaches with parents of handicapped children*. Springfield, Ill.: Charles C Thomas, 1976.

Branan, J.M. Negative human interaction. *Journal of Counseling Psychology*, 1972, *19*, 81-82.

Brenner, D. *The effective psychotherapist*. New York: Pergamon Press, 1982.

Buscaglia, L. *The disabled and their children: A counseling challenge*. Thorofare, N.J.: C.B. Slack, 1975.

Carkhuff, R.R. Differential functioning of lay and professional helpers. *Journal of Counseling Psychology*, 1968, *15*, 117-126.

Cartwright, C.A. Effective programs for parents of young handicapped children. *Topics in Early Childhood Special Education*, 1981, *1*, 1-9.

Combs, A.W., Blume, R.A., Newman, A.J., & Wass, H.L. *The professional education of teachers: A humanistic approach to teacher preparation*. Boston: Allyn and Bacon, 1974.

Darling, R.B. *Families against society: A study of reactions to children with birth defects.* Beverly Hills: Sage, 1979.

Egan, G. *The skilled helper.* Monterey, Calif.: Brooks/Cole, 1975.

Ekman, P. Body position, facial expression, and verbal behavior during interviews. *Journal of Abnormal and Social Psychology,* 1964, *68,* 295-301.

Eysenck, H.J. The effects of psychotherapy: A reply. *Journal of Abnormal and Social Psychology,* 1955, *50,* 147-148.

Farber, B. Effect of a severely retarded child on family integration. *Monograph of the Society for Research in Child Development,* 1959, *24.*

Featherstone, H. *A difference in the family.* New York: Basic Books, 1980.

Feldman, M.A., Byalick, R., & Rosedale, M.P. Parents and professionals: A partnership in special education. *Exceptional Children,* 1975, *41,* 551-554.

Fox, M.A. The handicapped family. *Lancet,* 1975, *2,* 400-401.

Gorham, K.A. A lost generation of parents. *Exceptional Children,* 1975, *41,* 521-525.

Gorham, K.A., Des Jardinas, C., Page, R., Pettis, E., Scheiber, B. Effect on parents. In N. Hobbs (Ed.), *Issues in the classifications of children.* San Francisco: Jossey-Bass, 1975.

Grossman, F.K. *Brothers and sisters of retarded children.* Syracuse: Syracuse University Press, 1972.

Gur, T. *Problems of counseling parents of retarded children.* Unpublished manuscript, University of Pittsburgh, 1976.

Hansen, J.C., Stevic, R.G., & Warner, R.W. *Counseling: Theory and practice* (3rd ed.). Boston: Allyn and Bacon, 1982.

Hensie, L.E., & Campbell, R.J. *Psychiatric dictionary* (4th ed.). London: Oxford University Press, 1970.

Hetznecker, W., Arnold, L.E., & Phillips, A. Teachers, principals, and parents: Guidance by educators. In L.E. Arnold (Ed.), *Helping parents help their children.* New York: Brunner/Mazel, 1978.

Hobbs, N. *Issues in the classification of children.* San Francisco: Jossey-Bass, 1975.

Hollingsworth, C.E., & Pasnaw, R.G. *The family in mourning: A guide for health professionals.* New York: Grune & Stratton, 1977.

Jakubowski-Spector, P., Dustin, R., & George, R. Toward developing a behavioral counselor education model. *Counselor Education and Supervision,* 1971, *10,* 242-250.

Johnson, D.E., & Vestermark, M.J. *Barriers and hazards in counseling.* Boston: Houghton Mifflin, 1970.

Klein, S.D. Brother to sister: Sister to brother. *The Exceptional Parent,* 1972, *2,* 10-15.

Kroth, R.L. *Communicating with parents of exceptional children.* Denver: Love, 1975.

Lamb, M.E. Fathers of exceptional children. In M. Seligman (Ed.), *A guide to understanding and treating the family with a handicapped child.* New York: Grune & Stratton, in press.

Langden, G., & Stout, I.W. *Teacher-parent interviews.* Englewood Cliffs, N.J.: Prentice-Hall, 1954.

Levine, S. Sex-role identification and parental perceptions of social competence. *American Journal of Mental Deficiency,* 1966, *70,* 907-1012.

Lieberman, M.A., & Borman, L.D. Overview: The nature of self-help groups. In M.A. Kieberman & L.D. Borman (Ed.), *Self-help groups for helping with crisis.* San Francisco: Jossey-Bass, 1979.

Lillie, D. Educational and psychological strategies for working with parents. In J.L. Paul (Ed.), *Understanding and working with parents of children with special needs.* New York: Holt, Rinehart & Winston, 1981.

Lisbe, E.R. Professionals in the public schools. In J.S. Mearig (Ed.), *In working for children: Ethical issues beyond professional guidelines*. San Francisco: Jossey-Bass, 1978.

Londsdale, G., Elfer, P., & Ballard, R. *Children, grief, and social work*. Oxford: Basil Blackwell, 1979.

Lortie, D.C. *Schoolteacher: A sociological study*. Chicago: University of Chicago Press, 1975.

Losen, S., & Diament, B. *Parent conferences in the schools*. Boston: Allyn and Bacon, 1978.

Lyon, H.C. *Learning to feel: Feeling to learn*. Columbus, Ohio: Merrill, 1971.

McGowan, J.F. Developing a natural response style. *Education*, 1956, *4*, 246-249.

McWilliams, B.J. Various aspects of parent counseling. In E.J. Webster (Ed.), *Professional approaches with parents of handicapped children*. Springfield, Ill.: Charles C Thomas, 1976.

Meadow, K.P., & Meadow, L. Changing role perceptions for parents of handicapped children. *Exceptional Children*, 1971, *38*, 21-27.

Michaelis, C.T. *Home and school partnerships in exceptional children*. Rockville, Md.: Aspen Systems Corporation, 1980.

Miller, S. *Exploration study of sibling relationships in families with retarded children*. Unpublished dissertation, Columbia University, 1974.

Mullins, J.B. The uses of bibliotherapy in counseling families confronted with handicaps. In M. Seligman (Ed.), *A guide to understanding and treating the family with a handicapped child*. New York: Grune & Stratton, in press.

Murray, M.A. *Needs of parents of mentally retarded children*. Arlington, Tex.: National Association for Retarded Citizens (undated).

Paul, J.L. *Understanding and working with parents of children with special needs*. New York: Holt, Rinehart, & Winston, 1981.

Peck, J.R., & Stephens, W.B. A study of the relationship between the attitudes and behaviors of parents and that of their mentally defective child. *American Journal of Mental Deficiency*, 1960, *64*, 839-844.

Rainwater, L., Coleman, R.P., & Handel, G.H. *Workingman's wife: Her personality, world, and life style*. New York: Oceana, 1959.

Reik, T. *Listening with the third ear*. New York: Farrar, Strauss, & Giroux, 1972.

Reynolds, M.C., & Birch, J.W. *Teaching exceptional children in all America's schools*. Reston, Va.: Council for Exceptional Children, 1977.

Reynolds, M.C., & Birch. J.W. *Teaching exceptional children in all America's schools* (2nd ed.). Reston, Va.: Council for Exceptional Children, 1982.

Roos, P. Parents of mentally retarded people. *International Journal of Mental Health*, 1977, *6*, 96-119.

Ross, A.O. *The exceptional child in the family*. New York: Grune & Stratton, 1964.

Schleifer, M.J. Let us all stop blaming the parents. *The Exceptional Parent*. Aug./Sept. 1971, 3-5.

Schmid, R.E., Moneypenny, J., & Johnston, R. *Contemporary issues in special education*. New York: McGraw-Hill, 1977.

Schulman, E.D. *Interventions in human services*. St. Louis, Mo.: Mosby, 1974.

Seligman, M. *Strategies for helping parents of exceptional children*. New York: The Free Press, 1979.

Seligman, M. Siblings of handicapped children. In M. Seligman (Ed.), *A guide to understanding and treating the family with a handicapped child*. New York: Grune & Stratton, in press.

Seligman, M., & Seligman, P.A. The professional's dilemma: Learning to work with parents. *The Exceptional Parent*, October, 1980, 11-13.

Shapiro, L.J. Teachers and schools, don't be afraid—parents love you (A survey). *Journal of Teacher Education*, 1975, *26*, 269-273.

Spiegel, J.P. The revolution of role conflict within the family. *Psychiatry*, 1957, *20*, 1-16.

Strickland, B. Legal issues which affect parents. In M. Seligman (Ed.), *A guide to understanding and treating the family with a handicapped child.* New York: Grune & Stratton, in press.

Telford, C.W., & Sawrey, J.M. *The exceptional individual* (3rd ed.). Englewood Cliffs, N.J.: Prentice-Hall, 1977.

Travis, G. *Chronic illness in children: Its impact on child and family*. Stanford: Stanford University Press, 1976.

Turnbull, A.P., & Turnbull, H.R. *Parents speak out*. Columbus, Ohio: Merrill, 1978.

Wirtz, M.A. *An administrator's handbook of special education*. Springfield, Ill.: Charles C Thomas, 1977.

Wittmer, J., & Myrick, R.D. *Facilitative teachings: Theory and practice*. Pacific Palisades, Calif.: Goodyear, 1974.

Wunderlich, C. *The mongoloid child: Recognition and care*. Tucson: University of Arizona Press, 1977.

Yalom, I. *The theory and practice of group psychotherapy*. New York: Basic Books, 1975.

Zaro, J.S., Barach, R., Nedelman, D.J., & Dreiblatt, I.S. *A guide for beginning psychotherapists*. London: Cambridge University Press, 1977.

Chapter 13

Intervention Models in Early Childhood Special Education

Robert Sheehan and Kathleen Gradel

The characteristics of successful programs for young handicapped children provide a useful starting point for any discussion of models in early childhood special education. McDaniels (1977) identified these characteristics in a cogent, empirically based argument in support of models in educational intervention. McDaniels' found that successful intervention programs for young children include clear specific goals, careful consideration of timing, and highly specific training for intervention staff. These characteristics are the natural product or outcome of the model development and testing process. Furthermore, evidence from two decades of early intervention efforts indicates that the staff of an intervention program must engage in a continual process of model development and refinement in order to have a lasting positive effect on handicapped children and their families.

Efforts have long been made to translate psychological and educational theory into practice. Intervention models in existence today are heavily rooted in a tradition of theory development and testing that originated in psychology and philosophy. The early 1900s witnessed the development of several schools of thought regarding the nature of learning and behavior in humans. The three most predominant were the behavioral school, the psychoanalytic shool, and the cognitive school. A number of other schools represented combinations or subsets of these three major orientations. In time, the natural desire of these theorists to put their theories into practice led to the development of very rudimentary models in psychology and, eventually, the application and continued development of such models in education.

The term *model* is used loosely and liberally by professionals in early childhood education. Hodges (1973) suggested that "the word model refers to that finite number of varying approaches to early childhood education which are used to guide the development of some portion or all of a program for young children" (p. 275). Such a definition relies heavily upon two vague concepts: approach and program. Clearly, not all approaches are models, nor should all programs be considered models. It is suggested here that *an early intervention model consists of a clearly explicated rationale, set of objectives, and identification of practices and evaluation criteria used in early intervention with an identified population of children, families, and others.*

A HISTORICAL REVIEW OF MODELS IN EARLY CHILDHOOD EDUCATION

Models for Disadvantaged Children

Intervention models for handicapped children are heavily based on earlier models developed for low-income preschool and primary grade children and their families during the late 1950s and early 1960s. The Institute for Developmental Disabilities, conceived in 1958 by Cynthia and Martin Deutsch, examined the effects of a specially developed curriculum with low-income children. Shortly thereafter, early intervention models were proposed by a number of individuals. The models proposed during this time varied greatly in their depth and specificity, although few would meet McDaniels' (1977) criteria for success.

Follow Through Planned Variation

During the late 1960s and early 1970s, many intervention models for disadvantaged children were tested in national experiments funded by the federal government. The first of these experiments, Follow Through Planned Variation, was begun in 1967; eventually, 22 models were implemented and tested in primary grades throughout the United States (Haney, 1977; Hodges & Sheehan, 1978). These models were designed with intentional variations in mind, hence the title Planned Variation. As of 1982, federal support for the Follow Through program continued, although funding had been reduced.

The intervention models tested in the Follow Through experiment represented a number of differing theoretical views (e.g., behavioral, psychodynamic, cognitive) as well as a number of differing structural arrangements (e.g., strictly classroom-based programs, programs with heavy parent involvement, programs with heavy community involvement). Results of the Follow Through experiment are still being published. St. Pierre (1982) published an analysis of the Follow Through study, identifying a number of sources of Follow Through conclusions.

Follow Through models differed greatly in their educational orientation, although each model had these common features:

1. an educational component
2. training of professional and nonprofessional staff

3. extensive parent involvement in the form of parent advisory committees
4. comprehensive medical, dental, and nutritional services for children, as well as social and psychological services for family members

Head Start Planned Variation

The second national experiment in education for disadvantaged children was Head Start Planned Variation, begun in 1967 by the federal government and completed in 1975. This program was designed for disadvantaged children of preschool age. Head Start Planned Variation was distinctly different from the Head Start program. Head Start, begun in 1965, was a national service program with no planned variation; in contrast, Head Start Planned Variation was a research effort to test the relative value of a number of early intervention approaches. Models developed in Head Start Planned Variation included the same components as did models in Follow Through.

Outcomes of Planned Variation

The best reference on the outcomes of the planned variation is Rivlin and Timpane's text (1975), appropriately titled *Planned Variation in Education: Should We Give Up or Try Harder?* As the title suggests, the national experiments of intervention models for disadvantaged children yielded a mixed bag of successes and failures. The Follow Through and Head Start Planned Variation programs were hindered by the fact that, at the time of their conception, little was known about successful model development and testing. Weikart and Banet (1975) describe their impression of the initiation of the experiments:

> The idea of planned variation may have been totally logical at the national level, but at the sponsor level it was mystifying. The meeting in Washington of prospective sponsors to present their various orientations toward curriculum, the idea that evaluation could be done by a third agency, the meeting in a hotel room to add Head Start Planned Variation, and the assumption that each sponsor had a complete package to present—all created a feeling of bewilderment and even madness. (p. 61)

As these comments indicate, at the time that Follow Through Planned Variation and Head Start Planned Variation were initiated, models were viewed as packaged approaches to curriculum that were to be evaluated and compared. Since that time, the concept of models has broadened considerably, and the complexity of model development and testing has been recognized.

Models for Handicapped Children

The Legislative Backdrop

In recent years, the federal government initiated several programs for educational, social, and related services for young disabled children and their families. Four legislative acts have had a particular impact on the field and thus have had most relevance to model developers.

Elementary and Secondary Education Act. Enacted in 1965 as PL 89-10, the Elementary and Secondary Education Act has had an impact on preschool education in several areas, through its various amendments. This act has established the mechanisms for funding at least some individualized approaches to improving the educational opportunities of the preschooler, including the following:

1. Title I monies legislated through PL 89-313 have been used to finance compensatory programs in school districts serving low-income families. Since individual families are not means-tested, all children attending schools in districts that receive such funding are eligible for services. This source of funding is intended for the entire school-aged population. Since few preschoolers are served in public schools, this kind of remedial education has not had a significant impact on this group.
2. PL 89-313, as amended by PL 91-230 (1969) and by PL 95-561 (1978), provides for grant distribution of funds to handicapped children residing in and being educated in state institutions for handicapped children. Per-pupil allocations can be used (a) for improvement of institutional educational programs (e.g., by increasing staff-to-student ratio via teacher's aides), (b) in deinstitutionalization efforts, and (c) in activities designed to maintain students in programs outside state-operated institutions.
3. Title VI-B of the Elementary and Secondary Education Act, as amended by PL 91-230 (1969), authorizes the Department of Education to award monies to state education agencies initiating demonstration programs, regardless of state mandates for preschool education. Funds have typically been provided to meet identified direct service and dissemination needs. These monies are awarded regardless of the age at which educational services are mandated in a state. Because of the focus on public school programs, most of the funded services are targeted for the more traditional preschool group, ages 4 to 6 (Ackerman & Moore, 1976).
4. The Preschool Partnership Act (PL 95-561, §325, 1978) authorizes the funding of educational services for 3- and 4-year-olds and their families as they make the transition from home to school. The target group is the Head Start population, but, as noted by Mallory (1981), "funds can also be used

> for other families in order to identify potential barriers to learning, provide child development and parenting information to families, and support home-based early childhood and family education programs'' (p. 84).

Although these various entitlements have undoubtedly had some impact on the service delivery mechanisms and available resources, appropriations have not resulted in dramatic advances. In addition, evaluation of the changes in service delivery has not yet progressed to the point that the components that—separately or together—comprise model practices can be selected.

The Handicapped Children's Early Education Assistance Act. PL 90-538, The Handicapped Children's Early Education Assistance Act, was signed into law in 1968, authorizing the funding of 70 to 100 model educational programs for young handicapped children. It provided $1 million for the 1969 fiscal year and $10 million for 1970. Congress' obvious intent was to provide seed money for educational programs that would demonstrate to the American public both the feasibility and the impact of exemplary services to handicapped children from birth to age 8, as well as to their families (Ackerman & Moore, 1976; DeWeerd & Cole, 1976). Although there was some overlap of models for disadvantaged and handicapped children, this new program for the handicapped provided an opportunity for rapid expansion of new early intervention models.

Programs funded under this act were to demonstrate the following features:

1. provision of exemplary services that would stimulate children's cognitive, language, motor, social, and emotional development
2. training of professional and nonprofessional staff
3. significant parent involvement
4. coordination with local public school districts and other related agencies
5. dissemination of information on model practices to assist in development of new preschool programs and to illustrate to professionals and the wider community excellent practices and the benefits of early intervention
6. evaluation of model practices (DeWeerd, Note 1; Perkins, Note 2)

Administration of the new program was delegated to the Bureau of Education for the Handicapped (currently, Special Education Programs). From the outset, the major emphasis was on demonstration—not service or research—although each funded project was required to have strong service components and evaluation plans. After a group of approximately 60 professional consultants had developed guidelines, 24 projects were funded in July, 1969, with approximately $1 million. From 1969 to 1979, financial support increased to $22 million, which funded 214 grants and contracts.

The emphasis of the demonstration projects providing service to young disabled children has been to develop models of excellence that can be replicated by others and continued through local and state funding. Over a 3-year period, the early education programs were expected to demonstrate that the target population received services that were significantly better than those received previously. In many cases, this required designing models of service delivery where none had existed. Early in the program's funding history, lack of services to handicapped infants and preschoolers was the rule rather than the exception; demonstration of *need* for funding was rarely an issue. Many projects were involved in documenting for local and state agencies that were in the process of making application for federal dollars just what the needs were in a given geographical region. From the point of view of the administration of the new program, this situation served as an ongoing rationale for its existence. Although the legislated mandate was to fund exemplary models that provided service, there was, during these "days of plenty," an acknowledged emphasis on needs in service-poor areas.

Economic Opportunity Amendments of 1972. The Head Start Handicapped Mandate, provided under PL 92-424, §3(b), required that no less than 10% of the enrollment in the national Head Start program be comprised of handicapped students, ages 3 to 6. Although the act did not authorize additional funds, it required that handicapped students receive adequate services in Head Start programs. Conservative estimates suggest that approximately 30,000 handicapped children were served annually (Ackerman & Moore, 1976).

Early reports regarding implementation of the mandate indicated that many of the students identified as handicapped in the program did not meet the criteria of the demonstrably handicapped in the amendments (Cahn, 1972; Nazzaro, 1974). The Office of Child Development policy statement specifies that

> while children with milder handicapping conditions (e.g., children with visual problems corrected with eyeglasses) will continue to be identified and receive appropriate Head Start services, they fall outside the scope of this issuance. The intent is rather to insure that Head Start serves more fully children who have severe vision and hearing impairment, who are severely physically and mentally handicapped, and who otherwise meet the legislative definition of handicapped children in terms of their need for special services. (1973, p. 3)

The 10% "pocket" appeared to be filled largely by counting children who normally would have been served prior to 1972—those exhibiting mild vision, hearing, and especially speech problems (Cahn, 1972; Ensher, Blatt, & Winschel, 1977; Nazzaro, 1974).

Ensher and associates (1977) suggested that the apparent practice of "overlabeling" might be explained in part by the recruiting procedures employed.

Standard recruitment activities, with some participation by relevant local community agencies, were not particularly effective in locating or recruiting children who were not typical candidates for the Head Start population, especially in light of obstacles such as ''an uninformed populace, misguided parental resistance, and the self-serving competition of community agencies protecting imaginary domains'' (Ensher et al., 1977, p. 206). Given current federal and state funding patterns in preschool handicapped education, it is perhaps even more likely that agencies serving the handicapped will be reluctant to refer identified children (and their tuition) to other agencies, including Head Start.

The inclusion of handicapped children in Head Start prompted several efforts to increase programmatic specificity and disseminate information. Projects included large-scale dissemination by the Council for Exceptional Children Head Start Information Project (Nazzaro, 1974), third party evaluation through Syracuse University (Ensher et al., 1977; Nazzaro, 1974), technical assistance through the Technical Assistance Development System at the University of North Carolina, and personnel training through monies awarded to regional Offices of Child Development (Ackerman & Moore, 1976). In addition the Office of Child Development and Bureau of Education for the Handicapped jointly funded 14 experimental projects designed to evaluate the effectiveness of alternative approaches. These projects enrolled more students with moderate and severe handicaps than did typical Head Start programs (Ensher et al., 1977).

Project staff's reliance on special education and contacts with related community agencies increased as a result of these activities, as did training specifically for personnel working with the handicapped students. However, although the level of services increased modestly over regular Head Start programming, ''only a few programs provided genuinely innovative instruction,'' and ''they just never quite lived up to expectations'' (Ensher et al., 1977, pp. 207-208). Head Start's efforts in providing integrated services to low-income and handicapped children have not had a significant impact on our knowledge or practice base in designing programs for the young disabled child.

The Education for All Handicapped Children Act. PL 94-142 was enacted to protect the rights of handicapped children and their families in regard to school placement and the provision of a free, appropriate public education. PL 94-142 required states to provide educational services to handicapped children aged 3 to 18 no later than September, 1978, and for students aged 3 to 21 no later than September, 1980. In addition, PL 94-142 provided some funding in the form of incentive grants to states that chose to provide services to preschool handicapped children.

The impact of the mandate was weakened, however, as reflected in the following excerpt from the regulations:

> A free appropriate public education will be available for all handicapped children between the ages of three and eighteen within the state not later than September 1, 1978, and for all handicapped children between the ages of three and twenty-one within the state not later than September 1, 1980, except that with respect to handicapped children aged three to five and aged eighteen to twenty-one inclusive, the requirements of this clause shall not be applied in any state if the application of such requirements would be inconsistent with State law or practice, or the order of any court, respecting public education within such age groups in the state. (PL 94-142, 1975, §612 (2) (B))

The effect of this statement is that states in which state law or regulations disallow educational services to youngsters below age 5 are not required to educate handicapped students in that age range.

A study of the impact of age eligibility provisions of PL 94-142 between 1973 and 1980 (Smith, 1980) showed that changes in eligibility of the students on the outer ranges of the federal mandate (below age 6 and above age 18) were made in 28 states (Changes, 1980). In 10 states, the effect was an increase in services to the students. As indicated in Table 13-1, 8 states have mandated eligibility from birth on for at least some handicapped children (e.g., those with visual or hearing impairments), and 8 states have permissive legislation for children from birth to 3 years of age. Many more states—29—have mandated eligibility at age 5 or 6; while 18 require that services be initiated at age 3 or 4.

Because federal regulations allowed all states to adopt regulations consistent with less restrictive state regulations, they in effect *raised* the age at which services are mandated in at least 12 states. In each case, the state had previously lowered mandated eligibility for delivery of services (Smith, 1980). Anastasiow (1981) suggested that the requirements of PL 94-142 may be too strict as states try to generate services for the entire birth to 21 population, especially those in the extreme age groups. This may be particularly true in the case of the birth to age 3 group, which certainly requires more creative models than are typical of traditional education for school-aged handicapped students.

Section 619 of PL 94-142 established the Preschool Incentive Grant program to provide special monetary benefits to states with approved plans that expand services to 3-, 4-, and 5-year-olds. The amendment authorizes a grant to each state of up to $300 for each child in the 3- to 5-year-old range receiving a free appropriate public education, but annual appropriations have averaged only one-third of the amount available. The program is complicated by the fact that, although monies are to be expended on children from birth to age 5, the amount of the grant is determined by the number of children in the 3- to 5-year age range. Because of these disincentives, it is doubtful that this program has enhanced either the quality or the amount of services available.

Table 13-1 Permissive and Mandated Age Limits for Special Education Eligibility

STATE	LAW		REGULATION	
	Ages of Eligibility	*Permissive Ages*	*Ages of Eligibility*	*Permissive Ages*
Alabama	Between 6 and 21			Preschool
Alaska	At least 3		Legal school age 3 to 19	
Arizona	Lawful school age[1]			
Arkansas	Between 6 and 21 if K-5	Below 6 if SHC		
California	Between 3 and 21 C	Younger than 3	4.9 to 21 C	Birth to 4.9[2,3]
Colorado	Between 5 and 21	Under 5		
Connecticut	Over 5 under 21	Under 5	School age and preschool	
Delaware	4 through 20 inclusive		Between 4 and 21 HI & VH — 0 to 21	
Florida*	5	Exceptional children-3 Below 5 D,B Severely PH TMR		
Georgia	6 to C if K-5[4]	0-5 if SHC necessitates early intervention	Between 5 and 18	0-4 If enrolled can continue 19-21
Hawaii	Under 20			
Idaho	School age[5]	To 21	School age Between 5 and 21	
Illinois*	Between 3 and 21	0 to 2	Between 3 and 21	
Indiana	Over 6 and under 18	0-6 mo. 3-5 18 to 21	6 to 18	3 through 5 HI — 18 through 21-6 mo.
Iowa	Under 21		Between birth and 21	
Kansas	Subject to regulations school age[6]		If K then 5 through 21 C, otherwise 6 through 21 C	

Table 13-1 continued

STATE	LAW		REGULATION	
	Ages of Eligibility	*Permissive Ages*	*Ages of Eligibility*	*Permissive Ages*
Kentucky	Under 21		School attendance age pursuant to law	
Louisiana	3 to 21[7]	Below 3 — Seriously handicapping condition	3rd birthday to 22nd birthday	
Maine	5 to school year student reaches 20. If 2-year K, 4		5 to school year student reaches 20	
Maryland	As soon as child can benefit and under 21[8]		Birth through 20 — children under 5 will be phased in as required by law	
Massachusetts	3 through 21		3 through 21 — 3 and 4 year olds must have substantial disabilities[9]	
Michigan	Under 26		Not more than 25 — if turns 26 after enrollment, may complete year	
Minnesota	4 to 21	TMR-through school yr. student is 25, if attended public school	4 to 21	
Mississippi	6 and under 21	Under 6	Under 21	
Missouri	5 and under 21	Under 5	School age	3 and 4
Montana	9/1/80 between 3 and 21	9/1/80 0 to 2	9/80 between 3 and 21	
Nebraska	From diagnosis to 21		5 to 21 (school age) MH-birth to 21 C	

Nevada	5 and under 18	MR-3 G-4 D & VH-under 5		
New Hampshire	3 to 21 C		Up to 21	
New Jersey	Between 5 and 20	Under 5 and over 20	Between 5 and 20	Under 5 and over 20
New Mexico	School age[10]		Legal entry age until age 18	Over 18
New York	Over 5 and under 21		Under 21[11]	
North Carolina	Between 5 and 18		5 through 17	Birth through 4 18 through 21
North Dakota	6 and under 21	3 to 6	6 to 21	
Ohio*	Between 6 and 18 If K-5	Other ages	Legal school age	
Oklahoma	4		4 eligible for a minimum of 12 years[12]	
Oregon	Superintendent establishes eligibility		6 to 21 inclusive If K 5 to 21	
Pennsylvania	6 to 21	Below 6	6 to 21 below 6 if regular programs below age 6	
Rhode Island	3 to 21		3 to 21 C	
South Carolina	Lawful school age[13]			
South Dakota	Under 21		Under 21[14]	
Tennessee	Between 4 and 21	D-3	4 through 21 D-3	
Texas	Between 3 and 21		Between 3 and 21 inclusive. Auditorily, visually handicapped-between birth and 22	
Utah	Over 5 (if K) under 21		5 through 21	

Table 13-1 continued

STATE	*LAW*		*REGULATION*	
	Ages of Eligibility	*Permissive Ages*	*Ages of Eligibility*	*Permissive Ages*
Vermont	Under 21	Over 21 to C	Under 21	
Virginia	2 and under 21 VH-birth to 21		2 to 21	
Washington	Common school age[15]	Preschool	5 to 21[16,17]	
West Virginia	Between 5 and 23	3-5	Between 5 and 23	
Wisconsin	3 under 21	Under 3	3 to 21	
Wyoming	Over 6 and under 21 If 5-K		School age	
District of Columbia			Between 3 and 21	

KEY

K — Kindergarten
C — Completion of Course
D — Deaf
B — Blind

PH — Physically Handicapped
TMR — Trainable Mentally Retarded
HI — Hearing Impaired
VH — Visually Handicapped

MH — Multiple Handicap
MR — Mentally Retarded
G — Gifted
SHC — Serious Handicapping Condition

FOOTNOTES

[1]Arizona — Lawful school age is between 6 and 21.
[2]California — 3-4.9 identified as requiring intensive special education.
[3]California — Exceptions include: 3-4.9 for those identified as requiring intensive services; 19-21 if enrolled before 19 and have not yet completed a course.

[4]Georgia — 3 and 4 year old children who are physically, mentally, or emotionally handicapped or perceptually or linguistically deficient are eligible.
[5]Idaho — Services of public schools are extended to any acceptable person of school age (defined as between 5 and 21).
[6]Kansas — School age is 6 or 5 if kindergarten is available.
[7]Louisiana — Legislation has been passed extending eligibility to 25 in certain circumstances.
[8]Maryland — Effective 7/1/80 Senate Bill No. 734 provides for compensatory education over 21 in certain circumstances.
[9]Massachusetts — Substantial disabilities are defined as intellectual, sensory, emotional or physical factors, cerebral disfunctions, perceptual factors or other specific learning impairments or any combination thereof.
[10]New Mexico — School age is at least 5 and for children in special education a maximum of 21 years of age.
[11]New York — Blind, deaf, or severely physically handicapped children in state schools between 3 and 21; deaf children less than 3 years of age in approved educational facilities.
[12]Oklahoma — No set minimum is specified for blind and partially blind, deaf, hard of hearing, or low incidence severely multiple handicapped children.
[13]South Carolina — Lawful school age is over 5 and under 21.
[14]South Dakota — Programs for children under age of 1 year shall be provided only to those children who are in need of prolonged assistance.
[15]Washington — Common school age is between 5 and 21.
[16]Washington — 0 to 1 and 1 and 2 year old children with multiple handicaps, gross motor impairment, sensory impairment, moderate or severe mental retardation are eligible for services.
[17]Washington — Services are permissive for children 0-2 if they have a multiple handicap, gross motor impairment, sensory impairment, or moderate or severe mental retardation.

COMMENTS

*Florida — According to Florida State Department of Education officials, there is no maximum school age.
*Illinois — Permissive ages are listed in § 10-22-38 rather than in Special Education Law.
*Ohio — According to Ohio State Department of Education officials, Ohio's mandated age range is 5 through 21.

Source: From *Division of Early Childhood position statement on services to handicapped children birth through five.* Reston, Va.: The Council for Exceptional Children, 1980. Reprinted by permission.

While who should be responsible for funding basic early intervention services is a continuing debate (Gallagher, 1979; Mallory, 1981), it is clear that model development, clarification, and evaluation is an ongoing need. PL 94-142 and parallel state regulations have at least touched the outer age ranges of the group for whom some of the handicapped children's model preschool programs were designed. Federal agencies have had few worries about supplanting programs already funded with state and local dollars, largely because of the continuing paucity of services to the preschool group. Although there appears to be a general movement to focus on funding programs for children below age 3, model program monies continue to be awarded to agencies serving children from birth to age 8.

Beyond the provision of service issue, PL 94-142 has had a largely undocumented effect on the quality of educational services to handicapped infants and preschoolers. One of the basic practical requirements of PL 94-142 is that "to the maximum extent appropriate, handicapped children, including children in public or private institutions or other care facilities, are educated with children who are not handicapped" (PL 94-142, 1975, 45 CFR Part 121a. 550-556). States that do not have publicly funded preschool programs for nonhandicapped students have interpreted this statement in various ways. In some cases, programs for handicapped preschoolers have been housed in public schools, which typically involves some interface with regular educational opportunities. Many states, however, have responded by contracting for programs with private agencies and institutions, many of which provided services for handicapped preschoolers prior to the passage of PL 94-142. Programs of this type have been operated by universities, private agencies founded to help those with a specific handicap (e.g., United Cerebral Palsy Association, the Association for Retarded Citizens), and privately operated schools (both residential and day). In some cases, public schools and agencies have cooperated to build shared programs (Cohen, Semmes, & Guralnick, 1979). In a few cases, states have opted to use existing nurseries, preschools, and daycare centers that serve nonhandicapped children as the early education environments for identified handicapped children (Guralnick, 1978). The Head Start mandate to include handicapped preschoolers has had some additional impact on the provision of services in more typical early childhood settings.

Given the range of potential settings in which services can be delivered to handicapped preschool children, it is not surprising that the least restrictive environment principle is broadly interpreted. Although public school-based programs are supported as the option of choice (Martin, Note 3), such programs often involve activities integrated with those of older children and carried out in settings that may be more conducive to typical educational programming, rather than the wide array of services needed by infants and their families. Public schools do, however, imply a closer fit with the least restrictive environment idea than do disability-specific schools. Other variations, involving integrated university "lab" type schools, as well as preschool and daycare centers, tend to offer a positive alternative to segregated situations.

Integration of handicapped preschoolers is viewed philosophically (Wolfensberger, 1972), socially (Bricker, 1978), educationally (Guralnick, 1978; Guralnick & Paul-Brown, 1980), and legally as "the first choice" for best educational practice (Vincent, Brown, & Getz-Sheftel, 1981). Some model programs and research efforts have demonstrated that individually determined, carefully implemented integration can have positive effects on both handicapped and nonhandicapped age peers (Allen, Benning, & Drummond, 1972; Bricker & Bricker, 1972; Cooke, Apolloni, & Cooke, 1977; Guralnick, 1976). Unfortunately, segregated service delivery remains the norm. Large-scale efforts have not been evident either (a) to change patterns of local service delivery or (b) to improve the programs for individual handicapped students served in integrated settings. With the exception of the Head Start mandate, few constraints have been imposed to require the system changes that appear to be necessary (Safford & Rosen, 1981). Furthermore, the handicapped children early education models have been "specialized" to meet the needs of selected handicapped groups. This specialization includes segregated settings and the use of training strategies that typify special education, such as one-to-one training, and ongoing child assessment, rather than early education approaches (Safford & Rosen, 1981; Swan, 1980).

In addition to the least restrictive environment emphasis in PL 94-142, preschool programs that are jointly mandated by the state and federal governments have been affected by the increasing requirements for accountability. These by now relatively familiar practices include

- the involvement of parents in developing educational programs for their children
- specific statements of long- and short-term goals in children's Individualized Education Programs (IEPs)
- the availability of parent counseling and educational services
- the provision of a variety of due process rights to students and their guardians

These practices had—in some form—become familiar in handicapped children early education models even before the passage of PL 94-142 and parallel state legislation. There were, then, some precedents in the design and implementation of these practices with young children, particularly with respect to parent involvement.

Although it is difficult to assess to what extent "nonmodels" solicit information on such practices from model projects, compliance problems are not new. Mallory (1981) cited these four major areas as continuing problems:

1. the lack of efficient systems for assigning qualified surrogate parents to children in residential placements outside of their natural homes
2. the continuing failure of school districts and other agencies to inform parents of their rights and options
3. the lack of adequate related services, including therapies and transportation
4. the minimal services typically afforded children in institutional care outside of their natural homes

In other words, model programs have been in evidence since 1969—models in which practices such as those mandated in PL 94-142 were implemented earlier and with more sophistication than is typical of many private and public school programs today.

PL 94-142 appears to have decreased or minimized the development of intervention models for handicapped children and infants in many locations. As states moved toward provision of services for handicapped youngsters, interest in the comprehensive approach to intervention suggested by the Handicapped Children's Early Education Program appears to have lessened. Common features of these programs appear less frequently in intervention efforts funded by state and local agencies.

Handicapped Children's Early Education Program: A Review

As mentioned earlier, the Handicapped Children's Early Education Assistance Act was designed as a seed money program to build a core group of projects that would be models of exemplary practice to both the professional and lay community (Swan, 1980). Since that time, changes have been made both in increased specificity of the expected outcome of its projects and in the variety of specialized components funded.

Model Demonstration Projects

The first emphasis and primary activity of the Handicapped Children's Early Education Program is generating model demonstration projects. These "First Chance" projects are intended to be examples of excellent practice to the community at large, and the model practices developed through each grant have been disseminated to foster their replication in both existing and yet to be developed preschool projects.

The child-centered nature of the First Chance projects is clear in the following excerpt from the regulations:

> Model programs should be child centered and the outcome of the services directed towards a reduction of dependency on the part of the

> handicapped child by helping him attain his full potential for social, emotional, physical, and cognitive growth. After receiving services in these model programs, many handicapped children should be able to enter regular educational systems or require less intensive levels of special education. Each program should have as its aim, demonstrating the provisions of high quality services for young handicapped children which emphasize assisting the child to overcome his handicaps and attain his highest potential functioning level. (Sec. 623, PL 91-230, 84 Stat. 183, 20 U.S.C. 1423, 45 CFR 121 d. 3)

The obvious intent of these guidelines is that the service effort be specifically directed to remediation of the child's deficits. The optimistic implication is that an increase in independence will result in a concurrent decrease in the need for continuing levels of intensive educational and related services.

Applicants for demonstration grants are expected to detail in their proposals—and, over a 3-year period, to implement—activities in five project components: (1) services to children, (2) services to parents, (3) staff development and training, (4) evaluation, and (5) demonstration and dissemination. Proposals are examined by professional field readers, professional panels, and Department of Education personnel for their adherence to regulations and guidelines; the demonstrated need for the project; the estimated "practice stretching" evident in the project's design, organization, and impact; and the overall potential for being an exemplary program.

Services to Children. Child-related services are, by virtue of federal regulations, expected to be (a) specified in terms of behaviorally formulated progress objectives and (b) built into the program's activities, which should fit a central curricular design (Section 623, PL 91-230, 84 Stat. 183, 20 U.S.C. 1423; 45 CFR, 100 a. 16, 100 a. 26, 121 d. 14, 111 d. 16). The procedures for identifying the target population must be detailed. Related or supplementary services must also be described, including their relationship to services provided or otherwise mandated by relevant cooperative agencies (e.g., public schools). Funded projects are expected to demonstrate, by way of the programmatic intervention, (1) the appropriateness of the intervention activities, (2) the sufficiency (e.g., in duration, frequency, and scope) of the intervention, and (3) the adequacy of the program to meet stated objectives.

The most critical child-centered portion of the proposal is the description of the content of the intervention. Although the service delivery model is important and will certainly have an effect on the child, a clear description of the content of instruction is one of the primary characteristics of good work plans. The child-based intervention plans must be focused, they must have a strong rationale, and it must be possible to accomplish them. For example, a variety of projects have used parent-mediated home-based instruction as the primary mode of service delivery (Soeffing, 1974). For many reasons, given a specific population and locality (e.g., infants living in rural areas), such an approach can be justified. Furthermore, several projects (e.g., Portage) have demonstrated that this approach can be implemented and replicated. Early in the history of the Handicapped Children's Early Education Program, a well thought out operational plan paired with demonstrated need and this innovative means of service delivery would have been more likely to yield funding than it is today. Over the past several years, professional reviewers and federal personnel have, in general, seen that most reasonable service delivery strategies can work (Karnes & Zehrbach, 1977) if their management is adequate. It has not been equally clear, however, that programs can provide comprehensive services before the content of their interventions—their curricular design—has been focused and tested.

In line with this thought is the growing tendency in the field to reject a new developmental checklist as an innovative or particularly valid approach to curricular design (LeBlanc, Etzel, & Domash, 1978; Vincent, Salisbury, Walter, Brown, Gruenewald, & Powers, 1980). Pefley and Smith (1976), in their review of 25 model projects, noted that assessment of a child's status by means of either normative or informal developmental checklists comprised each project's pool of effectiveness data. The logical assumption is that the intervention involved training the children in the specific skills listed on these checklists. As Vincent et al. (1980) pointed out, "while it is true that the more severely handicapped child is recognizable because of a lack of acquisition of major developmental milestones, the teaching of these isolated milestones may not make the child nonhandicapped" (p. 306). Instead, they made a strong case for building curriculums based on the "survival skills" needed by handicapped children to function to the maximum extent possible in the same environment in which nonhandicapped children live and play (Vincent et al., 1980). By extension, this requires teachers to determine and teach behaviors that will allow handicapped children to function in the less restrictive (natural) settings in which they may find themselves. Developing curricular approaches to parallel this evolving notion in the field will surely require more than the generation of checklists.

Services to Parents and Families. Although detailed plans for parent and family participation specific to each project are required, the federal regulations list several recommended services that should be available as needed:

1. Assistance in understanding and coping with the child's handicaps;
2. Psychological or social work services;
3. Information on child growth and development;
4. Information on special education techniques;
5. Observation of the children in the project;

6. Carry-over activities to the home; and
7. An opportunity to participate in planning and evaluation of the program. (Section 623 PL 91-230, 84 Stat. 183, 20 U.S.C. 1423, 1231 d; 45 CFR 121d. 16, 121d. 14)

Model programs are typically seen as primarily center-based, home-based, media-based, or combined home-center arrangements. Cartwright's review (1981) of the parent and family involvement components of model projects suggested that the following are characteristics of successful programs:

1. Structure is obvious in the program; objectives for parents and children are clear, and procedures and responsibilities are described precisely.
2. The decision about who will intervene has been resolved by using parents, teachers, paraprofessionals, and community volunteers.
3. The intervention occurs early and is coordinated; parents need help to coordinate the intervention package.
4. Programs are individualized, most often for the children but often for the parents as well.
5. Planning emphasizes the reciprocity between parent and child and deals with the family as a unit.
6. Ultimate goals for parents involve participation in decision-making and policy discussions to prepare them to become advocates on behalf of their child throughout the child's life span. (p. 7)

Basically, then, projects must build and modify demonstrated strategies to design individually appropriate, meaningful parent programs, including parent involvement in assessment (Gradel, Thompson, & Sheehan, 1981; Vincent, Laten, Salisbury, Brown, & Baumgart, 1980), selection of intervention goals (Roos, 1977; Vincent et al., 1980), and direct child intervention (Bricker & Caruso, 1979; Cartwright, 1981).

In reality, however, parent participation may be limited. In their survey of model infant projects, Karnes, Linnemeyer, and Schwedel (1981) found that very real problems inhibited parent involvement, including job commitment, transportation, and babysitting arrangements. It is apparent that solutions for common interferences to meaningful parent participation must be individualized. Stile, Cole, and Garner (1979) cited several specific strategies that have been reported to be successful by a variety of model projects. These strategies range from individual to group involvement, and possible parent roles range from passive receiver of services to active policy maker. The following appear to be general basic necessities for an adequate parent program:

1. Have a ''menu'' of relevant parent involvement activities, of which any single approach (or combination) is a satisfactory choice for both staff and parents.
2. Determine parent involvement individually; do not predetermine which are the activities of choice for parents.
3. Be willing and able to involve meaningfully all types of parents, including those who are extremely competent, critical consumers and those who may be seen as massive service consumers or as being handicapped themselves (Pomerantz, Colca, & Pomerantz, Note 4).

Staff Development and Training. Although demonstration of services to children is the primary focus of the model projects, each one is expected to provide adequate preservice orientation and in-service training activities for all staff members. As cited in the regulations, ''These activities may include formal and informal staff meetings, workshops, national, regional and state institutes, retreats, demonstrations, work conferences, laboratory and clinical experiences, training in the use of media, and cooperative enterprises with nearby programs'' (Section 623, PL 91-230, 1184 Stat. 183, 20 U.S.C. 1423; 45 CFR 100a. 26, 121 e. 4). Each project is rated, during the review process, for the adequacy of its personnel training program, as well as for the entry level expertise of staff members.

The multiple role descriptors of the preschool educator have been itemized by Karnes (1975) and others. As Hirshoren and Umansky (1977) concluded, a generic certification in special education or elementary education is rarely indicative of adequate preparation for teaching handicapped infants or preschool children. At this time, however, certification in the education of handicapped preschool children is available in only 12 states. Although preparation programs emphasizing preschool handicaps are more common now than they were a decade ago, they are not always translated into personnel hiring. Therefore, individual programs may continue to need ongoing, substantive in-service training.

Unfortunately, although all funded projects are required to provide staff training, there has been little documentation of the relative effectiveness of various training strategies or content. Interproject linkage may be helpful, but it must generally be assumed that programs ''re-create the wheel'' in each case. Those projects that have close associations with university or college personnel preparation programs may be more likely to derive relevant training packages.

Evaluation. The regulations regarding the required evaluation of programs are not specific. When proposals are reviewed, at least two questions are relevant, above and beyond questions related to the project's apparent capability of meeting stated objectives:

1. Are provisions made for adequate evaluation of the effectiveness of the project?
2. Do the evaluation design and procedures adequately provide for assessing the effective use of program resources to attain objectives?

Unfortunately, as Pefley and Smith (1976) and Garwood (1982) concluded, it appears that developmental scales are the instruments most commonly used to measure program effectiveness. Although these measures may be of some assistance in describing an individual student's achievement of normative developmental milestones, Garwood (1982) pointed out that "using existing developmental scales for evaluating program effects will probably not reflect the actual or true gains occurring as a result of participation in such programs" (p. 67). As a result, Garwood (1982) suggested some alternatives for model programs, including the use of:

- a limited number of scales that have been selected by the Office of Special Education for use in a possible national norming effort
- ordinal scales (e.g., Escalona & Corman, 1969; Uzgiris & Hunt, 1975) for some models, in which the emphasis is developmental/cognitive
- ratio scaling techniques (Hashway, 1978)
- detailed case studies
- anthropological field investigations

Wang (1980) reported on the field test of an approach designed to include measures of the degree to which model components were implemented. Bricker, Sheehan, and Littman (1981) described two additional options, including (1) the statistical prediction or norm-referenced model, in which the children's predicted progress is compared with their actual progress; and (2) the model in which children in one program are compared with children enrolled in another program. White (1980) demonstrated the use of the single-subject multiple baseline design for evaluation purposes. These and other strategies have demonstrated at least limited utility in measuring the impact of model programs.

As indicated by Sheehan and Keogh (1982), "Pressures to evaluate are real, although the tools to evaluate are inadequate" (p. 87). Model programs' documentation of their interventions, the degree to which plans are actually implemented, and the patterns of change exhibited by children, parents, and staff as a result of interventions continues to be inadequate. Given this state of affairs and the heterogeneity exhibited in target child, staff, and parent populations across projects, few outcome data can be relied upon completely.

Demonstration and Dissemination. The emphasis on demonstration and dissemination in model programs coincides with the original intent of the Handicapped Children's Early Education Assistance Act. The regulations demand that projects show the means by which (a) model practices will be demonstrated to lay and professional on-site visitors and (b) information on the project will be provided to professionals interested in replication. The primary measurable behavior on the part of disseminators is the "packaging" of their project activities.

This component is probably the most difficult to delineate. Certainly, the travel funds allotted to each project are used to present descriptive or quantitative data at local, state, and national meetings. There are few ways to determine the impact of dissemination activity, however, unless project staff members actually establish replication sites themselves. Perhaps a clearer measure of project dissemination is the extent to which projects obtain continuation funding from nonfederal services. As Swan (1980) reported, of the first cohort of 21 funded demonstration projects, 18 (86%) had maintained operation, drawing from 16 different sources of funding.

Although the results are not always clear, the impact of dissemination efforts can be assessed by examining the packaged products of the various projects. Some of the curriculums and assessment instruments developed have become widely circulated (e.g., Portage), but most have relatively limited use, for example, only by local agencies and replication sites. One of the problems for the consumer is access to the products. Although technical assistance centers have recently begun to collect and disseminate more project information in monograph or bibliographical form, the bulk of the products remain at individual project sites and on shelves in federal offices. Contacting the more than 300 projects funded since 1969 is often seen as more burdensome to new projects than "starting from scratch." The other obvious, related problem is that a majority of the projects have not been mentioned in generally available journals.

Technical Assistance

The Handicapped Children's Early Education Program also developed an organized means of delivering technical assistance to funded projects. Two contracts were awarded—one to the Technical Assistance Development System (TADS) and the other to the Western States Technical Assistance Resource (WESTAR). Their function is to assist demonstration and outreach projects, as well as state implementation programs, as they pursue their objectives. TADS provides assistance to projects located east of the Mississippi River, excluding Illinois, Mississippi, and Wisconsin; WESTAR serves the remainder of the United States, including Illinois, Mississippi, and Wisconsin.

With project directors, personnel from TADS and WESTAR design individual technical assistance plans. Assistance is provided in various ways, including on-site consultation, topical workshops, visitation to other project sites, and information searches. Over the past 10 years, both TADS and WESTAR have developed several publications, particularly collections of papers generated by model developers (available directly from TADS and WESTAR). These materials, including books, monographs, bibliographies, and manuals, are systematically distributed to currently funded projects.

As was pointed out earlier, one of the problems with dissemination of project practices is that the personnel and products of one project are not always readily available to other projects. Both formally and informally, TADS and WESTAR have attempted to minimize this problem, at least among projects funded during any given time period. Topical workshops, regardless of the topic, allow projects in their first, second, and third funding years to interact about issues and practices of common concern. Small-group sessions provide similar services, but perhaps in a more specific way. These and other types of contact (e.g., on-site consultation visits) often result in more meaningful, individualized problem solving as well.

It is difficult to assess the extent to which the formal interproject linkage arrangements have generated innovative approaches in the field. Although the topical workshops, consultations, and other services are evaluated by projects on written feedback forms, these satisfaction and self-report impact data are used primarily for internal review purposes. Obviously, it is impossible to ascertain to what extent projects would have been capable of meeting their own technical assistance needs without large-scale agencies designed for that purpose. It is possible, however, to hazard two non-data-based, pessimistic estimates with respect to the impact of a generic technical assistance approach:

1. Funded projects that have a specific innovative focus, a reasonable management plan, and skilled practitioners will be successful in their model implementation—regardless of the technical assistance provided.
2. Funded projects that lack specificity in their intervention plan, even those with a well-articulated management plan and skilled practitioners, will not be successful in implementing an innovative model—again, regardless of the technical assistance provided.

Outreach Projects

A third component was added to the Handicapped Children's Early Education Program in the 1972-1973 funding year: outreach projects. The general purposes of outreach funding are to stimulate the increase of quality services to handicapped infants and children and to develop efficient outreach models. Previously funded demonstration projects that have met their objectives in providing exemplary services to children are used as the mechanism. Swan (Note 5) presented three major points as the rationale for outreach:

1. It is likely to be most cost-effective to train others to use a given model than to develop a new, similar model.
2. More handicapped children and their families can be served in a shorter period of time.
3. Local and state education agencies are more likely to support new and continued services to handicapped children and their families based on already demonstrated effective models.

Typical activities during the 3-year award period include

- dissemination
- product development and distribution beyond the scope of accomplishments during demonstration funding
- training of additional personnel, especially those in replication sites
- consultation
- coordination with state and local agencies to stimulate the development of additional services

Although projects are required to maintain, in some form, the direct services to children and families provided during demonstration funding, outreach funds do not support these activities. A recent review of outreach projects indicated that nearly one-third of the surveyed projects receive state or local monies to support 75% of their operating costs (Assael & Walstein, 1981).

The Battelle Institute third party evaluation (Stock, Wnek, Newborg, Schenck, Gabel, Spurgeon, & Ray, 1976) of the Handicapped Children's Early Education Program included an investigation of both dissemination and replication efforts by outreach projects. Dissemination activities of outreach projects were characterized by the use of a range of activities not atypical of third year demonstration projects; a focus on intrastate efforts, without particular emphasis on the type of agency; and contact of outreach staff by replication sites largely as a result of third party recommendations (Swan, Note 5). Replication efforts by outreach projects were typified by the following:

1. Of the reported replication sites, 29% were *not* replications.
2. Many of the "substantiated replications" were funded by state and local education agencies and Head Start.
3. The frequency of outreach staff contacts with replication sites ranged from one to four, with a possible variation in duration of from 2 hours to 1 to 1½ weeks per contact.
4. In terms of service delivery, reported replication sites corresponded with outreach projects "moderately on educational programs, well in child populations served, and little on child-staff ratios" (Swan, Note 5, p. 10).

Outreach projects operate without the benefit of technical assistance to refine dissemination and replication efforts or evaluation plans. Many of the outreach projects have documented the amount and kinds of assistance provided to agencies by type and target population. Unfortunately, there has been little measurement of the real impact of outreach activities on the quality of services provided to handicapped youngsters and their families (Swan, Note 5).

State Implementation Grants

Initiated in 1976, state implementation grants are awarded for 1- or 2-year renewable periods and are designed to assist states in planning and implementing new or increased statewide early intervention services. Funds are intended to be used for administrative purposes, not for direct service to children and families. Grants are made regardless of the age at which mandated state services are available to preschool handicapped children.

A primary emphasis of state implementation grants is personnel development. For example, in 1981, 89% of the 18 projects funded by these grants planned in-service education activities in early childhood special education. An interesting parallel figure that may substantiate this focus on training is that only 6 of these 18 states have early childhood special education teacher certification standards (Assael & Walstein, 1981). Training typically is extended to professional and paraprofessional direct service staff, as well as parents, in a variety of ways, such as institutes, seminars, credit-earning practica and coursework, and workshops. Additional activities that form the typical core of planning under state implementation/management/evaluation, dissemination, and interagency coordination (Assael & Walstein, 1981). Despite the general lack of state-mandated services for handicapped children below age 3, there appears to be a movement to include this group in plans under these grants (Swan, 1981).

Documentation data indicate that state implementation grants have supported some system-wide change in service delivery patterns since the initiation of the program in 1976. Again, however, resolution of the basic service delivery issues is not sufficient to meet the field's model development and implementation needs.

Early Childhood Research Institutes

Begun in 1977, the Early Childhood Research Institutes are jointly funded by the Handicapped Children's Early Education Program and the Research Projects Branch. The first cohort has been funded from 1977 to 1982. Overall, the goal of these institutes is to perform and apply research on specific questions related to providing services to young handicapped children and their families. The provision of longer term funding for purposes of in-depth research on several critical questions is a significant departure from the typical 3-year funding pattern evident in the other handicapped children's programs. Whether this precedent will have significant impact remains to be seen. The four institutes that have been funded are

1. Research on Early Abilities of Children with Handicaps (REACH), University of California, Los Angeles. REACH is designed to investigate the longitudinal competence of young handicapped children. The emphasis for infants is on attention and self-control. The preschool studies are focused on temperament, attention, emotional-social development, attribution, and motivation. The target group consists of children between 1 and 6 years of age.
2. Kansas Research Institute for the Early Education of the Handicapped, University of Kansas, Lawrence. Research at the Kansas Institute is focused on the following areas: (a) developmental and environmental correlates to sensorimotor and language skill acquisition, (b) analyses of child-other interactions in intervention, and (c) assessment-based intervention.
3. Early Childhood Research Institute for the Study of Exceptional Children, Educational Testing Services (ETS), Princeton, New Jersey/Roosevelt Hospital, New York City. Major objectives of this institute include (a) design and testing of assessment tools sensitive enough for early identification and broad enough for use with known handicapped infants and children; (b) longitudinal analysis of infants with low birth weights and other handicaps that may affect their cognitive and social development, and parallel intervention programs; and (c) development of media materials, assessment guides, and curriculum modules on handicapped and at-risk children for use by pediatricians, educators, and parents.
4. Carolina Institute for Research on Early Education for the Handicapped (CIREEH), University of North Carolina, Chapel Hill. CIREEH's major objectives include (a) design of a curriculum for severely handicapped infants, from birth to 24 months of age; (b) assessment of new approaches for determining developmental programs in infants; (c) assessment of the effectiveness of home education vs. daycare intervention for at-risk children; and (d) investigation of factors that can assist families in facilitating their handicapped children's education.

COMPONENTS OF INTERVENTION MODELS

It was suggested earlier that an intervention model should consist of the following components:

1. a clearly explicated rationale
2. a set of objectives

3. identification of practices
4. identification of evaluation criteria
5. a clearly identified population of children, families, and others

These components were derived from a number of sources, including reviews, such as those of McDaniels (1977) and Karnes and Zehrbach (1977), discussions of the nature of theories in education and psychology (Crain, 1980), and observations of early intervention programs for the past decade. Whether intervenors are developing, selecting, or adapting a model, these five components must be present to ensure the greatest enduring benefits of implementing the model in an early education setting.

A Clearly Explicated Rationale

Several trends are evident in the evolution of rationales for early intervention. The intervention models developed during the 1960s and early 1970s were largely drawn from psychology and educational psychology. Maturational theories of child development formed the basis for much of the early education provided to middle-class and upper-class children in nursery schools and preschools throughout the United States. As educators began to respond to the plight of disadvantaged and developmentally disabled children, they began to draw on cognitive theories and cognitive development theories for early intervention.

The 1960s and early 1970s also witnessed the emergence of intervention efforts based on behavioral theory and remergence of intervention based upon Montessorian theory. During this period, early intervention was heavily based on clearly explicated rationales.

Decreasing Emphasis on Clearly Explicated Rationales

Recently, there has been a decreasing emphasis on the development of clearly explicated rationales in early intervention programs. Although there are notable exceptions to this trend (Bricker & Dow, 1980), it appears that early childhood educators have become less interested in the why of intervention and more interested in the how or what of intervention. For example, the discussion of models for early intervention found in Karnes and Zehrbach (1977) provides almost no indication of their theoretical rationales. The reader is left with the impression that the model developers have placed similar minimal emphasis on theoretical support for their intervention.

Reasons for the decline in emphasis on clearly explicated rationales in early intervention programs are not difficult to identify. The lack of clear research findings from Follow Through Planned Variation and Head Start Planned Variation may have left the educational community with the feeling that theoretical and philosophical orientations fail to contribute to the relative success or failure of intervention models. Educators may be asking, "If a behavioral approach is as effective as a cognitive approach, why bother with either approach?" In view of decreasing budgets and inflationary costs of providing intervention, educators may simply be making choices as to where they will put their energies in model development—choices that preclude the development and articulation of theoretical rationales. Finally, many current intervention programs are based on infant and preschool assessment measures. Programs such as the Portage Project (Shearer & Shearer, 1972, 1977) and the Chapel Hill Training Outreach Project (Sanford, 1974) are based largely on a collection of developmental items with little or no theoretical structure other than regularity of behavioral emergence in children and infants (Sheehan, 1982).

The long-term effects of intervention in the absence of rationale are cause for some concern. McDaniels' (1977) analysis of model development and experiences with a number of diverse intervention programs indicate that, while one specific theoretical rationale may be as useful as others, presence of a theoretical rationale is critical; the absence of such a rationale ultimately leads to ineffective intervention, teacher and staff burnout, inadequate sense of professionalism, and a host of other problems. Furthermore, early educators must be committed to their theoretical rationale for intervention.

Increasing Complexity in Stated Rationales

The rationales for intervention in early childhood special education that *are* being developed are becoming more complex and systemic. They are beginning to consider handicapped children as individuals within a system, a family system and a social system—and intervention is being designed with those systems in mind. The work of Foster and Berger (1979), as well as Foster, Berger, and McLean (1981), is an excellent example of this systems approach. Drawing heavily on structural and strategic schools of therapy, Foster and her colleagues have incorporated concerns about families and other systems into a highly viable model of early intervention with a sound theoretical base. As Foster, Berger, and McLean (1981) noted, "In summary, systems theory requires attending to structure, hierarchy, and life cycle differences among families when assessing needs and planning interventions" (p. 63). When confronted with rather linear theories of child development that were inappropriate for their population, Foster and colleagues turned to other well-developed theories for guidance rather than developing a model without an adequate rationale. Such an approach is a good example for all those engaged in model development in early intervention.

A Set of Objectives

In contrast to the current minimal concern for clearly articulated rationales, early intervention programs have shown an increasing commitment to specified objectives. The role that increased specificity in requests for proposals may have on this effect, especially in light of budgetary constraints, must be acknowledged.

A review of the proposals and dissemination products for Handicapped Children's Early Education Program demonstration projects over the past 5 years shows an increasing sophistication in the field of early intervention related to child objectives. A number of models have developed and disseminated objectives for intervention with young children. The Portage Project (Bluma, Shearer, Frohman, & Hilliard, 1976), Teaching Research (Fredericks, Riggs, Furey, Grove, Moore, McDonnell, Jordan, Hanson, Baldwin, & Wadl, 1977), the Chapel Hill Training-Outreach Project (Sanford, 1974), and others have each developed a listing of intervention objectives, sequenced in an approximation of a developmental continuum. In the area of parent objectives and parent-child objectives, increasing sophistication is less evident, although it may soon be seen as a result of recently funded projects.

A validated set of objectives is critical for any early intervention model that engages in demonstration and dissemination. Such objectives ensure consistency among staff, facilitate staff training, and provide a basis for involvement of parents, grandparents, and siblings in the instructional process. However, intervenors must beware of developing simplistic lists of intervention objectives from existing developmental measures. Developmental objectives differ considerably from educational objectives. Developmental objectives represent those developmental milestones against which the developmental progress of individual children is measured. The Bayley Scales (Bayley, 1969) represent such a listing of objectives, as do certain portions of the Learning Accomplishment Profile (Sanford, 1974). Many items contained within such scales or lists of developmental objectives (e.g., motor items such as skipping on one foot or walking up and down stairs or neurological items such as infant reflex tests) are not appropriate objectives for educational intervention. Few listings contain objectives that are all appropriate for educational intervention across the heterogeneous groups comprising the preschool handicapped population. In particular, the immediate and longitudinal contextual variables that are critical to determining individual goals typically are not implicit in the generally available lists of instructional objectives.

Intervenors must also ensure that specified objectives do not become the tail that wags the intervention dog. In some infant intervention programs devoted to sensorimotor development, for example, the items of the Uzgiris-Hunt Scales (Uzgiris & Hunt, 1975) appear to be more dominant and to have more influence on intervention than do major concepts in Piagetian theory, such as interactional learning and maturation. A rationale must guide objectives; if the resultant objectives are changed, the rationale must be carefully reconsidered to ensure that it supports such changes.

Identification of Practices

The teaching strategies employed by early intervenors must be carefully thought out and identified. Because one purpose of a model is to demonstrate successful ways of working with children and families, intervenors must be able to specify the ways in which educational objectives were attained. All too often data are presented for an intervention program with little information specifying the actual intervention on which the data are based:

- What reinforcers were used by teachers?
- How many parent meetings did parents attend and for how long?
- What occurred during the conduct of home visits?
- How were classrooms arranged?
- How much actual contact time did intervenors spend with children and families?
- What materials were used during intervention?
- What were patterns of children's attendance at classroom sessions?

The answers to these questions have a direct impact on the effects of the intervention. With inadequate documentation of these and other variables, replication efforts are likely to go awry. Obviously, intervention variables such as these must be consistent with a model's rationale and its objectives.

Unfortunately, many researchers who become model developers have had limited experience documenting intervention practices and conveying those practices to others. Research journals rarely publish actual specifications for treatments, on the assumption that anyone wishing to replicate a study or obtain more information about a study will contact authors directly. Such contact occurs only infrequently, however; as a consequence, little description of actual intervention is available in the published literature.

Early intervention model development differs considerably from basic research in that the strategies of intervention and the outcome of intervention are equally important. Such an equal emphasis is necessary if model development is to be successful. Obviously, identification of practices is not sufficient for model development; evaluation data describing the efficacy of those practices are also necessary. The first step in generating such data is to identify evaluation criteria, specifying the desired outcomes of early intervention.

Identification of Evaluation Criteria

Most early intervention models specify individual child or family objectives, yet few models indicate standards against which the overall worth of the model should be judged. A major lesson to be learned from the Head Start Planned Variation and Follow Through Variation experiments was that model developers must indicate the variables that best represent their intervention goals (Hodges & Sheehan, 1978). Model developers failed to do so in those two federally funded experiments; as a result, criticism about their evaluations continues to the present day.

For the greater part of a decade, early intervention models were considered less than successful because gains shown by children on standard achievement measures tended to decline following intervention. When those who had developed such models formed a consortium (Darlington, 1981) to examine the long-term effects of intervention, they identified outcome variables that approximated the goals of their intervention more closely than achievement measures. These variables, special education placement and grade retention, proved to be extremely sensitive to intervention, demonstrating intervention effectiveness 8, 9, and in some cases, 10 years after intervention had ended.

The need to specify evaluation criteria appears particularly critical in early intervention programs designed to have their primary effect on parents and families. Cross and Sheehan (Note 6) recently discussed a parent education experience that reveals the complexity and subtlety of desired outcomes in such intervention:

> When I began this course I was a tired, worried, and frequently unhappy parent. I had been doing my best for three and a half years, but I still had a large reserve of fear . . . fear that I would do something wrong and irrevocably damage my child; hinder her from achieving her full potential, and spoil her chances for obtaining happiness. I had done a lot of thinking, planning many of our activities to provide her with what I thought to be the right kinds of exposure and stimulation. But I began to feel stale and burnt out, out of ideas and not sure where to look for them; uncomfortable and unsure whether my efforts were good. And as my daughter was growing into a more complex individual, my vision was blurring . . . I felt unable to see things clearly.
>
> So I sought out your course not just because I had a number of specific questions, but because I hoped to become revitalized, to find some insight, reassurance, and inspiration. And I hoped that in the process I would learn something that would enhance my relationship with my child.

> As I have already said, I acquired a good deal of specific knowledge of child development theory and measurements. But the "by-products" of all our discussions have the greatest importance for me. These "by-products" are the changes which have occurred to me; changes in perception, feeling, attitude and living.
>
> I feel that I can now perceive "right" and "wrong" ways . . . or "better" and "worse" ways . . . of disciplining, working with and living with (parenting) my daughter. This is not to say that there is only one good way of discipline for all parents and children or even one family; but now I feel better able to determine what ways will be comfortable and work best for my family. (pp. 9-10)

Attitudinal changes such as this one are at least as important as gains in child development knowledge. In some models of parent education, such attitudinal changes must be stated as desired outcomes to ensure an adequate evaluation and accurate dissemination.

In many instances, model developers can specify instruments that adequately represent their evaluation criteria. Such instruments may be child measures (e.g., intelligence or achievement measures), parent-child interaction measures (Bromwich, 1981), or measures assessing other aspects of parenting and family functioning. If such measures do not exist during the model development process, the desired content and structure of such measures should be specified to guide others who test the model. It is also reasonable for model developers to indicate measures that they consider inappropriate as evaluation criteria.

Clearly Identified Population of Children, Families, and Others

When model developers begin to specify objectives, strategies, and evaluation criteria, they must always indicate the population of children and families for whom the models are appropriate. Is an early intervention model developed in an urban area appropriate for a rural population? Can a model developed for deaf or blind children also be used for autistic children? If definitions of developmental delay vary from one region to the next, should an intervention model note such variations? Can a model that has been proved effective for middle-class families be assumed to be effective for low-income families? These are questions that must be answered by early intervention model developers.

Identification of appropriate populations of children, families, and others for an early intervention model is essential if the model is to meet the needs of its clients. For example, families living in urban areas have differing transportation needs than those living in rural areas. Furthermore, early intervenors have been required to redesign their models completely because they discovered that home visitors and therapists were unwilling to travel alone in certain inner city areas. Similarly, intervenors have had to redesign their parent involvement components when they discovered that 100% of the parents worked full-time outside of the home. Developers of one intervention program designed an extensive parent involvement component only to discover on the 1st day that none of the parents spoke English and the staff spoke nothing else. Such problems will not arise if the model developers carefully specify appropriate populations of clients and develop population-specific intervention strategies.

Identification of populations is also an important element of any evaluation plan. Sheehan and Krakow (1981) made the point that noncategorical early education does not mean noncategorical evaluation. They advocated the use of subset analyses to examine the variation in evaluation results so often found in intervention programs. For example, the involvement of parents with transportation might be compared with that of other parents to determine if lack of transportation caused absenteeism and thereby influenced the amount of intervention experienced by the two groups of families. Once again, many researchers are familiar with the relatively short amount of space devoted to description of subject populations in journals and research reports. Such brevity is extremely limiting for model development.

LIMITATIONS OF MODELS IN EARLY CHILDHOOD

In early childhood special education, models can and have made significant contributions to the services provided to handicapped children, infants, and their families. They have added to our knowledge base about programming for early intervention. In addition, model development activities have provided training and experience for many undergraduate and graduate students—students who have gone on to make their own significant contributions to early childhood special education.

What then are the limitations of a commitment to model development in early childhood special education? Although not fatal, these limitations are serious and must be kept in mind by model developers in early childhood. The limitations are

1. dialogue or monologue? Does discussion really occur among model developers?
2. replication or haphazard sampling? Is replication possible?
3. guided change or chiseling in stone? Do models change over time?

Dialogue or Monologue?

During the years when funding for Follow Through Planned Variation was plentiful, the Follow Through sponsors would meet annually at High/Scope Camp in Michigan. Discussion among model developers would frequently occur at those meetings—debates regarding behavioral approaches vs. cognitive strategies, cognitive vs. open education, parent education vs. classroom-based instruction, and so forth. Such debates rarely appear to have changed anyone's perspectives at the conferences, however, and no one ever really won a debate. Furthermore, 10 years after the Bank Street open education approach and the direct instruction behavioral approach were developed, the model developers of both approaches were still unwilling to admit that children were receiving appropriate education in the classrooms of the other model. While debates occurred during that time, they seemed to be dual monologues rather than dialogues.

The developers of models for young handicapped children appear to be more open to dialogue, although that may be due to a somewhat lessened commitment to theoretical rationales and a greater acceptance of pragmatism. With the Handicapped Children's Early Education Program, the federal government may have consciously or unconsciously encouraged dialogue by refusing to authorize funds for any program similar to those funded in Follow Through Planned Variation and Head Start Planned Variation. By encouraging all qualified model projects to present their claims of effectiveness to the Joint Dissemination Review Panel (Tallmadge, 1977) and by encouraging all projects to collaborate rather than compete, the dialogue among model developers was probably facilitated.

Early intervention model developers spent countless hours demonstrating their approaches and disseminating their materials and findings to intervenors in education. Yet some model developers attend a conference only to present their model and then leave, or they appear on a panel with other model developers for the purpose of dissemination and engage in little interaction with other model developers.

In the context of model development, dialogue can alter attitudes or practices. Model developers must make a continual effort to ensure that this dialogue occurs and they must be open to the possibility that alternative approaches to early intervention can be equally efficacious.

Replication or Haphazard Sampling?

During the past decade, the federal government has funded a number of model projects to engage in outreach and dissemination efforts. One goal of these projects has been to establish "replication sites," and these sites have sometimes been geographically distant and different from the original model. Such an approach can and does lead to a number of problems. For example, if a new project purchases a set of curriculum materials from the Portage Project, should the new site be considered a replication site? What if the materials are used differently than intended or with a different population of children and families?

In the area of research methodology, replication has a particular meaning. Lykken (1968) identified "literal replication" as an exact duplication of a previous research study, while "operational replication" is a duplication of essential conditions and controls. In "constructive replication," a researcher consciously avoids imitation and designs a study based on another author's conclusions. Many of the early intervention "replication sites" may be engaging in operational replication, although few early intervention outreach programs specify essential conditions and controls.

There is some concern that early intervenors may simply "sample the wares" of model developers rather than adopt models for replication purposes. Such a sampling process may be haphazard and may lead to ineffective intervention. To guard against this limitation, early intervention model developers must demonstrate and disseminate all components of their models (rationale, objectives, practices, criteria, and relevant population) and must further specify minimum conditions under which a model operates effectively.

Guided Change or Chiseling in Stone?

How much do early intervention models really change over time? What should be the tenure of an endorsement by the Joint Dissemination Review Panel? If a model was considered an exemplary practice approach 10 years ago, should it still be considered exemplary? What if it has changed during those 10 years? Even more pertinent, what if it has *not* changed during those 10 years? There are as yet no answers to these questions.

During the years of Follow Through Planned Variation, change was evident in models for disadvantaged primary grade children. Models that began without significant involvement of parents as teachers were modified to include parents in classrooms. Models that began with little regard for regular classroom assessment soon added highly sophisticated evaluation systems based on classroom data. Yet these changes were not encouraged by the funding agencies and were considered threats to the research and evaluation design of the Planned Variation experiments.

The Handicapped Children's Early Education Program has not initiated a planned variation experiment, but it has strongly endorsed outreach activities by model projects and has promoted the validation granted by the Joint Dissemination Review Panel for demonstration projects with proved effectiveness. The first such models to receive endorsement did so approximately 7 years ago. Are their models still valid?

At the least, model developers must document changes that have occurred in their models during the process of model development and dissemination. Model developers could also establish a personally regulated timetable to review, revise, or possibly abandon their intervention models. Intervention models cannot become fixed in stone, nor should they be subject to continuous and inconsistent change.

CONCLUSION

The expectations of federal funding agents and leaders in early childhood special education have not been met to date by model service delivery strategies, either in terms of pervasive systems change or in the evolution of discrete model approaches. However, certain funded projects have individually provided models of "good practice," minimally to their specific locales and in selected cases to at least "partial replications." The demonstration of "good practice" has become more a reality than ever, across widely diverse child and family populations, modes of service delivery, and regions of the United States.

REFERENCE NOTES

1. DeWeerd, J. *Handicapped Children's Early Education Program: A retrospective*. Paper presented at the Handicapped Children's Early Education Conference, Washington, D.C., December 1979.
2. Perkins, C. Committee on Education and Labor, Report No. 1793, 90th Congress, 2nd Session, to accompany H.R. 18763, with W.H. Rommel, to the President, September, 1968. Reports on Legislation, Box 52, 9/20/68-10/4/68, Lyndon Baines Johnson Library.
3. Martin, E.W. *A look at the 80's*. Paper presented at the Handicapped Children's Early Education Program Project Directors' Meeting, Washington, D.C., 1979.
4. Pomerantz, D., Colca, L., & Pomerantz, P. *Can disabled adults parent? A case study*. Manuscript submitted for publication, 1982.
5. Swan, W.W. *An overview of the goals and parameters of outreach*. Paper presented at the Outreach Project Directors' Conference, Washington, D.C., September 1977.
6. Cross, C., & Sheehan, R. *An evaluation of parent education: Lessons for educators and evaluators*. Manuscript submitted for publication, 1982.

REFERENCES

Ackerman, P.R., & Moore, M.G. Delivery of educational services to preschool handicapped children. In T.D. Tjossem (Ed.), *Intervention strategies for high risk infants and young children*. Baltimore: University Park Press, 1976.

Allen, K.E., Benning, P.M., & Drummond, T.W. Integration of normal and handicapped children in a behavior modification preschool: A case study. In G. Semb (Ed.), *Behavior analysis and education*. Lawrence, Kans.: University of Kansas Support and Development Center, 1972.

Anastasiow, N.J. The needs of early childhood education for the handicapped: A Song for the 80's. *Journal of the Division for Early Childhood,* 1981, *2,* 1-7.

Assael, D., & Walstein, A. (Eds.). *Handicapped Children's Early Education Program: 1981-82 overview and directory*. Washington, D.C.: U.S. Department of Education, Special Education Programs, Division of Innovation and Development, 1981.

Bayley, N. *Bayley Scales of Infant Development*. New York: Psychological Corporation, 1969.

Bluma, S., Shearer, M., Frohman, A., & Hilliard, J. *Portage guide to early education manual*. Portage, Wis.: Portage Project, 1976.

Bricker, D.D. A rationale for the integration of handicapped and nonhandicapped preschool children. In M. Guralnick (Ed.), *Early intervention and the integration of handicapped and nonhandicapped children*. Baltimore: University Park Press, 1978.

Bricker, D.D., & Bricker, W.A. Toddler research and intervention project report—Year II. *IMRID Behavioral Science Monographs,* 1972, *21.*

Bricker, D., & Caruso, V. Family involvement: A critical component of early intervention. *Exceptional Children,* 1979, *46,* 108-117.

Bricker, D., & Dow, M. Early intervention with the young severely handicapped child. *Journal of the Association for the Severely Handicapped,* 1980, *5,* 130-142.

Bricker, D., Sheehan, R., & Littman, D. *Early intervention: A plan for evaluating program impact.* Seattle, Wash.: WESTAR Publications, 1981.

Bromwich, R. *Working with parents and infants: An interactional approach.* Baltimore: University Park Press, 1981.

Cahn, J. *Preliminary survey: Head Start services to handicapped children.* Washington, D.C.: U.S. Department of Health, Education and Welfare, Office of Child Development, 1972.

Cartwright, C.A. Effective programs for parents of young handicapped children. *Topics in Early Childhood Special Education,* 1981, *1*(3), 1-10.

Changes found in states' ages of eligibility. *Insight,* 1980, *11*(6), 1.

Cohen, S., Semmes, M., & Guralnick, M. Public Law 94-142 and the education of preschool handicapped children. *Exceptional Children,* 1979, *45,* 279-285.

Cooke, T.P., Apolloni, T., & Cooke, S.A. Normal preschool children as behavioral models for retarded peers. *Exceptional Children,* 1977, *43,* 531-532.

Crain, W. *Theories of development: Concepts and applications.* Englewood Cliffs, N.J.: Prentice-Hall, 1980.

Darlington, R. The consortium for longitudinal studies. *Topics in Early Childhood Special Education,* 1981, *3*(6), 37-46.

DeWeerd, J., & Cole, A. Handicapped Children's Early Education Program. *Exceptional Children,* 1976, *43,* 155-157.

Ensher, G.L., Blatt, B., & Winschel, J.F. Head Start for the handicapped: Congressional mandate audit. *Exceptional Children,* 1977, *43,* 202-210.

Escalona, S.K., & Corman, H. *Albert Einstein Scales of Sensorimotor Development.* New York: Albert Einstein College of Medicine of Yeshiva University, 1969.

Foster, M., & Berger, M. Structural family therapy: Applications in programs for preschool handicapped children. *Journal of the Division for Early Childhood,* 1979, *1,* 52-58.

Foster, M., Berger, M., & McLean, M. Rethinking a good idea: A reassessment of parent involvement. *Topics in Early Childhood Special Education,* 1981, *1*(3), 55-66.

Fredericks, H.D., Riggs, C., Furey, T., Grove, D., Moore, W., McDonnell, J., Jordan, E., Hanson, W., Baldwin, V., & Wadl, W.M. *A data based classroom for the moderately and severely handicapped.* Monmouth, Oreg.: Instructional Development Corporation, 1977.

Gallagher, J. Rights of the next generation of children. *Exceptional Children,* 1979, *46,* 98-105.

Garwood, S.G. (Mis)use of developmental scales in program evaluation. *Topics in Early Childhood Special Education,* 1982, *1*(4), 61-69.

Gradel, K., Thompson, M., & Sheehan, R. Parental and professional agreement in early childhood assessment. *Topics in Early Childhood Special Education,* 1981, *1*(2), 31-40.

Guralnick, M.J. The value of integrating handicapped and nonhandicapped preschool children. *American Journal of Orthopsychiatry,* 1976, *46,* 236-245.

Guralnick, M.J. *Early intervention and the integration of handicapped and nonhandicapped children.* Baltimore: University Park Press, 1978.

Guralnick, M.J., & Paul-Brown, D. Functional discourse analysis of nonhandicapped preschool children's speech to handicapped children. *American Journal of Mental Deficiency,* 1980, *84,* 444-454.

Haney, W. *A technical history of the national Follow Through evaluation.* Cambridge, Mass.: Huson Institute, 1977.

Hashway, R.M. *Objective mental measurement.* New York: Praeger, 1978.

Hirshoren, A., & Umansky, W. Certification for teachers of preschool handicapped children. *Exceptional Children,* 1977, *44,* 191-193.

Hodges, W. The implications of design and model selection for the evaluation of programs for the disadvantaged child. *Merrill-Palmer Quarterly of Behavior and Development,* 1973, *4,* 275-288.

Hodges, W., & Sheehan, R. Follow Through as ten years of experimentation: What have we learned? *Young Children,* 1978, *34*(1), 4-14.

Karnes, M.B. Education of pre-school age handicapped children. In W.P. McLure, R.A. Burnham, & R.A. Henderson (Eds.), *Special education: Needs, costs, methods of financing. Report of a study.* Urbana, Ill.: University of Illinois, Bureau of Educational Research, College of Education, 1975.

Karnes, M.B., Linnemeyer, S.A., & Schwedel, A.M. A survey of federally-funded model programs for handicapped infants: Implications for research and practice. *Journal of the Division of Early Childhood,* 1981, *2,* 25-39.

Karnes, M.B., & Zehrbach, R.R. Alternative models for delivering services to young handicapped children. In J. Jordan, A. Hayden, M.B. Karnes, & M.M. Wood (Eds.), *Early childhood education for exceptional children: A handbook of ideas and exemplary practices.* Reston, Va.: Council for Exceptional Children, 1977.

LeBlanc, J.M., Etzel, B.C., & Domash, M.A. A functional curriculum for early intervention. In K.E. Allen, V.A. Holm, & R.L. Schiefelbusch (Eds.), *Early intervention—A team approach.* Baltimore: University Park Press, 1978.

Lykken, D. Statistical significance in psychological research. *Psychological Bulletin,* 1968, *70*(3), 151-159.

Mallory, B.L. The impact of public policies on families with young handicapped children. *Topics in Early Childhood Special Education,* 1981, *1*(3), 77-86.

McDaniels, G.L. Successful programs for young handicapped children. *Educational Horizons,* 1977, *56*(1), 26-33.

Nazzaro, J. Head Start for the handicapped—What's been accomplished? *Exceptional Children,* 1974, *41,* 103-107.

Office of Child Development. *Head Start policy manual* (OCD Notice N-30-333-1-00). Washington, D.C.: U.S. Department of Health, Education and Welfare, 1973.

Pefley, D., & Smith, H. *It's Monday morning.* Chapel Hill, N.C.: Technical Assistance Development System/University of North Carolina, 1976.

Rivlin, A., & Timpane, P.M. (Eds.). *Planned variation in education: Should we give up or try harder?* Washington, D.C.: Brookings Institute, 1975.

Roos, P. A parent's view of what public education should accomplish. In E. Sontag, J. Smith, & N. Certo (Eds.), *Educational programming for the severely and profoundly handicapped.* Reston, Va.: Council for Exceptional Children, Division on Mental Retardation, 1977.

Safford, P.L., & Rosen, L.A. Mainstreaming: Application of a philosophical perspective in an integrated kindergarten program. *Topics in Early Childhood Special Education,* 1981, *1,* 1-10.

Sanford, A. (Ed.). *A manual for use of the Learning Accomplishment Profile.* Winston-Salem, N.C.: Kaplan Press, 1974.

Shearer, M., & Shearer, D. The Portage Project: A model for early childhood education. *Exceptional Children,* 1972, *39,* 210-217.

Shearer, M., & Shearer, D. Parent involvement. In J. Jordan, A. Hayden, M.B. Karnes, & M.M. Wood (Eds.), *Early childhood education for exceptional children: A handbook of ideas and exemplary practices.* Reston, Va.: Council for Exceptional Children, 1977.

Sheehan, R. Infant assessment: A review and identification of emergent trends. In D. Bricker (Ed.), *Intervention with at-risk and handicapped infants: From research to application.* Baltimore: University Park Press, 1982, 47-62.

Sheehan, R., & Keogh, B.K. Design and analysis in the evaluation of early childhood special education programs. *Topics in Early Childhood Special Education,* 1982, *1*(4), 81-88.

Sheehan, R., & Krakow, J. Describing and comparing infant progress during intervention. *Diagnostique,* 1981, *7*(2), 76-90.

Smith, B.J. *Policy issues related to the provision of appropriate early intervention services for very young exceptional children and their families.* Reston, Va.: Council for Exceptional Children, 1980.

Soeffing, M.Y. Early Childhood Program funds varied models to demonstrate successful preschool services. *Exceptional Children,* 1974, *40,* 441-442.

St. Pierre, R. Follow Through: A case study in meta-evaluation research. *Educational Evaluation and Policy Analysis,* 1982, *1*(4), 47-56.

Stile, S., Cole, J., & Garner, A. Maximizing parental involvement in programs for exceptional children. *Journal of the Division for Early Childhood,* 1979, *1,* 69-82.

Stock, J.R., Wnek, L., Newborg, J., Schenck, E., Gabel, J., Spurgeon, M., & Ray, H. *Evaluation of Handicapped Children's Early Education Program (HCEEP): Final report* (Contract No. OEC-0-74-0402). Columbus, Ohio: Battelle Center for Improved Education, 1976.

Swan, W.W. The Handicapped Children's Early Education Program. *Exceptional Children,* 1980, *47,* 12-16.

Swan, W.W. Programs for handicapped infants and their families supported by the Office of Special Education: An overview. *DEC Communicator,* 1981, *7*(2), 1-15.

Tallmadge, K. *The Joint Dissemination Review Panel ideabook* (Contract # NIE-IA-7706). Washington, D.C.: U.S. Department of Health, Education and Welfare, National Institute of Education, U.S. Office of Education, 1977.

Uzgiris, I.C., & Hunt, J.McV. *Assessment in infancy: Ordinal scales of infant development.* Urbana, Ill.: University of Illinois Press, 1975.

Vincent, L.J., Brown, L., & Getz-Sheftel, M. Integrating handicapped and typical children during the preschool years: The definition of best educational practice. *Topics in Early Childhood Special Education,* 1981, *1,* 17-24.

Vincent, L.J., Laten, S., Salisbury, C., Brown, L., & Baumgart, D. Family involvement in the educational processes of severely handicapped students—State of the art and directions for the future. In B. Wilcox & R. York (Eds.), *Quality education for the severely handicapped—The federal investment.* Washington, D.C.: U.S. Department of Education, Office of Special Education, 1980.

Vincent, L.J., Salisbury, C., Walter, B., Brown, L., Gruenewald, L.J., & Powers, M. Program evaluation and curriculum development in early childhood/special education. In W. Sailor, B. Wilcox, & L. Brown (Eds.), *Methods of instruction for severely handicapped students.* Baltimore: Paul H. Brookes, 1980.

Wang, M.C. *Some design considerations in the documentation of program implementation and effects: A working paper.* Pittsburgh, Pa.: University of Pittsburgh, Learning Research and Development Center, 1980.

Weikart, D., & Banet, B. Model design problems in Follow Through. In A. Rivline & P.M. Timpane (Eds.), *Planned variation in education: Should we give up or try harder?* Washington, D.C.: Brookings Institute, 1975.

White, O. Adaptive performance objectives: Form versus function. In W. Sailor, B. Wilcox, & L. Brown (Eds.), *Methods of instruction for severely handicapped students*. Baltimore: Paul H. Brookes, 1980.

Wolfensberger, W. *The principle of normalization in human services*. Toronto: National Institute on Mental Retardation, 1972.

Appendix A

Tests for Use in Assessing Sensorily Impaired Children

Table A-1 Tests for Use with Preschool Visually Impaired Children

Test	*Age Range*	*Domain*	*Skills Assessed/Adaptations*
Developmental Activities Screening Inventory (DASI) Teaching Resources 50 Pond Park Road Hingham, MA 02043	6-60 months	Screening of cognitive development	A teacher-administered screening instrument to determine general cognitive-adaptive functioning levels, accompanied by developmental activities suggestions. This instrument includes specific instructions on how to adapt materials for use with visually impaired children.
Maxfield-Buchholz Scale of Social Maturity for Preschool Blind Children American Foundation for the Blind, Inc. 15 West 16th Street New York, NY 10011	0-72 months	Screening of social maturity	Adaptation of the Vineland Social Maturity Scale for Blind Children. This scale of social development evaluates areas of general motor development, dressing, eating, locomotion, and occupation.
Callier Azusa Scale Council for Exceptional Children 1920 Association Drive Reston, VA 22090	0-84 months	Screening of general development	Assessment of socialization, daily living skills, motor development, perceptual abilities, and language development. An observation model is used. Developed specifically for sensorily impaired children.
The Oregon Project for Visually Impaired and Blind Preschool Children (Rev. Ed.)	0-72 months	Screening of general development	An observational checklist covering cognitive, language, gross motor, fine motor, self-help, and socialization behaviors. This test was developed especially for target population.

Jackson County Education Service District Medford, OR 97501			
Adaptive Performance Inventory University of Idaho Department of Special Education Moscow, ID 83843	0-24 months	General development	8 subtests for examining behavior. Instructions include specific adaptations for blind, deaf, and physically impaired children. A criterion-referenced measure.
Ordinal Scales of Psychological Development Uzgiris, I.C., & Hunt, J.M. *Assessment in infancy: Ordinal scales of psychological development.* Urbana, IL: University of Illinois Press, 1975.	0-24 months	Cognitive development	Series of 6 ordinal scales, based on Piagetian observations of sensorimotor schemas. Six scales include visual pursuit and permanence of objects, development of means for obtaining desired environmental events. Examiner will need to plan tasks and materials for blind children.
Bayley Scales of Infant Development Psychological Corp. 757 3rd Avenue New York, NY 10017	0-30 months	Cognitive development	Similar to Cattell. It includes a separate motor scale and a social record form in addition to a mental scale. This test will need to be adapted by examiner to meet vision requirements of young children.

Table A-1 continued

Test	*Age Range*	*Domain*	*Skills Assessed/Adaptations*
Infant Intelligence Scale (Cattell) Psychological Corp. 757 3rd Avenue New York, NY 10017	0-30 months	Cognitive development	Manipulative tasks for determining sensorimotor development, including imitation, problem solving, and a few language items. This test will need to be adapted by examiner to meet vision requirements of young children.
Merrill-Palmer Scales of Mental Development Stoelting Co. 1350 S. Kostner Avenue Chicago, IL 60623	18-71 months	Cognitive development	Scales to assess not only child's cognitive abilities, but expressive and receptive language and fine and gross motor skills. Comprised largely of performance items, some of which are timed. Provision is made for a child's refusal of an item. Timed items may be a disadvantage for some children.
McCarthy Scales of Children's Abilities Psychological Corp. 757 3rd Avenue New York, NY 10017	30-102 months	Cognitive development	An instrument to measure general cognitive functioning, as well as child's strengths and weaknesses in verbal and perceptual performances. Quantitative, memory, motor development, and lateral skills also are examined.
Wechsler Preschool and Primary Scale of Intelligence (WPPSI) Psychological Corp. 757 3rd Avenue New York, NY 10017	48-78 months	Cognitive development	Verbal subtests usually given to blind children: information, comprehension, similarities, arithmetic, and vocabulary. Supplementary subtest of sentences is also useful with this population.

Cognitive Skills Assessment Battery Teachers College Press 1234 Amsterdam Avenue New York, NY 10027			Assessment of cognitive and physical-motor areas, including orientation toward one's environment, discrimination of similarities and differences, comprehension and concept formation, coordination, immediate and delayed memory. Sets no criterion levels and no total score obtained. Will need to be adapted for blind.
Woodcock-Johnson Psychoeducational Battery Teaching Resources 50 Pond Park Road Hingham, MA 02043	30 months to adult	Cognitive development	For preschool children, 6 tests of part one; 3 can be administered to blind children and the other 3 can be administered to partially sighted children.
Sequenced Inventory of Communication Development University of Washington Press Seattle, WA 98105	4-48 months	Language development	Receptive and expressive scales that permit examiner to work with the child in an informal play atmosphere. Some items will need to be adapted if child is totally blind but most tasks use manipulatives.
Receptive Expressive Language Assessment for the Visually Impaired Shirley Graham Ingham Intermediate School Dist. 2630 Howell Road Mason, MI 48854	0-72 months	Language development	An adaptation of the REEL for preschool blind children.

Table A-1 continued

Test	*Age Range*	*Domain*	*Skills Assessed/Adaptations*
Developmental Sentence Analysis Lee, L.L. *Developmental sentence analysis.* Evanston, IL: Northwestern University Press, 1974.	24-96 months	Language development	Analyzes children's spontaneous speech samples into 8 major syntactic categories to derive a sentence score comparable to normal language development.
Laura Lee's Developmental Sentence Types Lee, L.L. *Developmental sentence analysis.* Evanston, IL: Northwestern University Press, 1974.	Presyntactic formations	Language development	Analyzes children's spontaneous speech into the early developing presyntactic structures based on single- and two-word combinations, and elaborated constructions.
Environmental Prelanguage Battery Charles E. Merrill Publishing Co. 1300 Alum Creek Drive Box 508 Columbus, OH 43216	Early communication stages	Language development	A series of diagnostic procedures for nonverbal client. Assesses semantic and cognitive requirements for language through attention, gestures, imitation, play, comprehension, and single words.

Environmental Language Inventory Charles E. Merrill Publishing Co. 1300 Alum Creek Drive Box 508 Columbus, OH 43216	One and two-word utterance level	Language development	A diagnostic and treatment model that assesses early semantics-based grammar through imitation, conversation, and play. Provides extensive data on early experimental parent-based programs using the ELI design and adaptations to total communication, later language and classroom use.
Peabody Developmental Motor Scales Teaching Resources 50 Pond Park Road Hingham, MA 02043	0-84 months	Motor development	An instrument for use in assessing gross and fine motor development. Scoring section allows child credit for minimum success rather than a pass or failure. Scales are accompanied by developmental activities for each area assessed.
Peabody Mobility Scale Stoelting Co. 1350 S. Kostner Avenue Chicago, IL 60623	48-167 months	Motor development	Scales and intervention materials for multiply handicapped blind children in areas of basic motor, sensory, conceptual and mobility skills.
Kraner Preschool Math Inventory Teaching Resources 50 Pond Park Road Hingham, MA 02043	36-78 months	Math readiness	Criterion-referenced test to assess math concepts such as counting, serialization, etc.

Table A-1 continued

Test	*Age Range*	*Domain*	*Skills Assessed/Adaptations*
Carrow Auditory and Visual Abilities Test Teaching Resources 50 Pond Park Road Hingham, MA 02043	48-120 months	Auditory perception, visual perception	An individually administered norm-referenced test of auditory and visual perceptual, motor, and memory skills. Five visual and nine auditory tests.
Boehm Test of Basic Concepts and the Psychological Corporation Tactile Test of Basic Concepts American Printing House for the Blind	60-96 months	Concept development	Criterion-referenced test of concepts necessary for first-grade success, including spatial, temporal, and qualitative reasoning. Available in tactile edition.
Developmental Progression in Play Behavior Largo, R.H., & Howard, J.A. Developmental progression in play behavior of children between nine and thirty months. I. Spontaneous play and imitation.	9-30 months	Play development	A procedure for involving children in play and scoring responses with regard to exploration, functional, and spatial characteristics in spontaneous and imitation play.

Developmental Medicine Child Neurology, 1979, *21*, 299-310.			
Symbolic Play Scale Checklist (Westby, 1980)	9-60 months	Play development	An observational checklist that permits examination of play as it parallels language development.
Symbolic Play Levels	9-30 months	Play development	Observational schema for play behavior with comparisons to Piagetian stages of development.
McCune-Nicolich, L. & Carroll, S. Development of symbolic play: Implications for the language specialist. *Topics in Language Disorders*, 1981, *2*(1), 1-15.			

Table A-2 Tests for Use with Preschool Hearing-Impaired Children

Test	*Age Range*	*Domain*	*Skills Assessed/Adaptations*
Development Activities Screening Inventory Teaching Resources 50 Pond Park Road Hingham, MA 02043	6-60 months	Screening of cognitive/adaptive development	A teacher-administered nonverbal tool for determining behavior using manipulative tasks of discrimination, seriation, associations, etc. Specifically designed for hearing-impaired and visually impaired children.
Callier Azusa Scale Council for Exceptional Children 1920 Association Drive Reston, VA 22090	0-84 months	Screening of general development	Assessment of socialization, daily living skills, motor development, perceptual abilities, and language. Was designed specifically for deaf-blind children.
Early Intervention Developmental Profile The University of Michigan Press Ann Arbor, MI 48109	0-60 months	General development	Prepared for use by team members trained in 6 areas: perceptual-fine motor, cognition, language, social/emotional, self-care, and gross motor. Accompanying curriculum has adaptations for hearing impaired.
Bayley Scales of Infant Development Psychological Corp. 757 Third Avenue New York, NY 10017	0-2.5 years	Cognitive development, motor development, social development	Three separate scales to assess aspects of early child development. A well-standardized infant scale. Some items will need to be adapted for hearing-impaired children.

Uzgiris-Hunt Ordinal Scales of Psychological Development I.C. Uzgiris and J.M. Hunt University of Illinois Press Urbana, IL 61820	0-2 years	Sensorimotor development	Assessment of object permanence, causality displacement, imitation, means-end relationships, object concepts.
McCarthy Scales of Children's Abilities Psychological Corp. 757 Third Avenue New York, NY 10017	2.5-8.5 years	Cognitive development	Assessment of cognitive skills, such as memory, object concept, problem solving, means-end relationships. There are some subtests that will definitely be difficult for deaf children; thus, one must adapt this test to fit child's communication means.
Smith-Johnson Non-Verbal Performance Scale Western Psychological Service Los Angeles, CA	2-4 years	Cognitive development	Designed for hearing and hearing-impaired children. Instructions are presented in pantomime and cover 14 categories, such as knot tying, paper folding, completion items, and form discrimination.
Merrill-Palmer Scale of Mental Tests Stoelting Company 1350 S. Kostner Avenue Chicago, IL 60623	1.5-6 years	Cognitive development	Large number of manipulative items, thus does not penalize deaf child as much as some other cognitive measures. It taps object concept, visual discrimination, spatial relationships, motor planning, means-end relationships.

Table A-2 continued

Test	*Age Range*	*Domain*	*Skills Assessed/Adaptations*
Hiskey Nebraska Test of Learning Aptitude Marshall Hiskey 5640 Baldwin Lincoln, NE 68508	2.5-17.5 years	Cognitive development	One of few tests that provide norms for deaf children. Among skills assessed are imitation, sequencing, memory, picture identification, association, manipulation, visual attention span, discrimination.
Leiter International Performance Scale Stoelting Company 1350 S. Kostner Avenue Chicago, IL 60623	2-18 years	Cognitive development	Nonverbal test to assess association, sequencing, discrimination, and other nonverbal learning processes.
Columbia Mental Maturity Scale Psychological Corp. 757 Third Avenue New York, NY 10017	3-9 years	Cognitive development	Nonverbal test that requires only a pointing response. Concepts of visual discrimination, association, spatial relations are tapped.
Developmental Potential of Preschool Children, 1968 Grune & Stratton, Inc. 757 Third Avenue New York, NY 10017	2-6 years	Cognitive development	Particularly good test for children with language problems. It covers physical development, sensory skills, mentation, and general social development.

Pictorial Test of Intelligence Houghton-Mifflin 666 Mianie Circle, NE Atlanta, GA 30324	3-8 years	Cognitive development	May require adaptation to communicate questions to the child. Child responds by indicating picture choice. Subtests cover areas of picture vocabulary, form discrimination, information and comprehension, similarities, size and number, and immediate recall.
Basic Concepts Inventory Follett Educational Corp. Department DM, PO Box 5705 1011 West Washington Blvd. Chicago, IL 60607	4-10 years	Concept development, language development	Three parts: (1) basic concepts, (2) statement repetition and comprehension, and (3) pattern awareness.
BOEHM Test of Basic Concepts Psychological Corp. 757 Third Avenue New York, NY 10017	5-8 years	Concept development, language development	Assessment of child's knowledge of concepts considered necessary in the first years of school.
Carrow Auditory and Visual Abilities Test Teaching Resources 50 Pond Park Road Hingham, MA 02043		Auditory perception, visual perception	

Table A-2 continued

Test	*Age Range*	*Domain*	*Skills Assessed/Adaptations*
Motor-Free Vision Perception Test Academic Therapy Publication 1539 - 4th Street San Rafael, CA 94901	4-8 years	Visual perception	Assessment of spatial relationships, visual discrimination, figure ground, visual closure, and visual memory.
Sequenced Inventory of Communication Development University of Washington Press Box 5569 Seattle, WA 98105	4 months-4 years	Language development	Assessment of both receptive and expressive language using both parents' report and child's play with objects.
Environmental Pre-language Battery Charles E. Merrill 1300 Alum Creek Drive Box 508 Columbus, OH 43216	½-2 years	Language development	Can be used with nonverbal children; assesses semantic and cognitive requirements for language through attention, gestures, imitation, play, comprehension, and single words.
SKI*HI Receptive Language Test SKI*HI Outreach Project Utah State University	2-4 years	Language development	Designed specifically for hearing-impaired children. Requires a pointing response to pictures to test comprehension of 5 elements of language: agent, action, object, attribute, and relation.

UN C-10 Logan, UT 84322			
Test for Auditory Comprehension of Language Teaching Resources 50 Pond Park Road Hingham, MA 02043	3-7 years	Language comprehension	Measure of comprehension of different nouns, adjectives, verbs, adverbs, grammatical constructions, and syntax using a picture-pointing paradigm.
Porch Index of Communicative Ability in Children Consulting Psychologist Press, Inc. 577 College Avenue Palo Alto, CA 94306	3-5 years	Language development	Assessment of general communication ability in terms of certain verbal, gestural, and graphic skills.
Peabody Developmental Motor Scales Teaching Resources 50 Pond Park Road Hingham, MA 02043	0-7 years	Motor development	Assessment of gross and fine motor skills using both a developmental and a criterion-referenced measurement system. Skills are programmed for training in accompanying activities section.
California Preschool Social Competency Scale Consulting Psychologist Press, Inc. 577 College Avenue Palo Alto, CA 94306	2.5-5.5 years	Social development	Measure of the adequacy of child's interpersonal behavior and the degree to which child assumes social responsibility.

Appendix B

Curricular Approaches for Working with Visually Impaired Children

SENSORY DEVELOPMENT

Development and refinement of the remaining senses are critical to the young blind child's knowledge of the surrounding world. The child should receive instruction that fosters the goal-directed use of the nonimpaired sensory channels or the visual channel if any vision remains.

1. Kinesthetic Modality. The seeing child learns about body expression by mimicking others. The blind child must learn the body movements and must be told that they express feelings and convey messages to others. The teacher should

a. physically and orally prompt appropriate body responses, such as nodding yes and no, head turns, waving, happy faces, sad faces, winking, directing head movements at persons who are communicating with the child.
b. relate body actions to language; teach all prepositions by physically directing the child in the movements (e.g., under, over, into, beside).
c. permit the child to experience as many physical movements as possible. Crawling, pivoting, tiptoeing, galloping, jumping, stretching, running, throwing, and catching are all important skills for the blind child.

2. Tactual. The sense of touch plays a major role in the child's development. Through the fingertips, the child explores, labels, classifies, compares, and eventually reads. The refinement of the tactual sense is critical to the child's exploratory behavior and eventual learning about the world. The teacher should

a. physically prompt the child to touch surfaces that differ; stress labeling and comparisons. Some examples are coarse, damp, furry, dry, rough, soft, smooth, wet, sharp, hard, oily.

b. encourage the child to experience different surfaces with many parts of the body; have the child walk, run, and jump, for example, on grass, gravel, concrete, dirt; have the child roll on mats, hardwood, grass, up and down hills.
c. present the whole object to the child. The blind child is frequently exposed to only parts of large objects, yet learns the label for the object itself. Let the child feel the entire object, move the various parts, then feel miniature replicas of the whole object for a global understanding of how the parts fit together. Check the child's understanding of whole objects by having the child describe the total object.

3. Auditory. The auditory modality is the major channel for the blind child's learning. The modality will not be keener of its own accord; it must be trained. The teacher should

a. help the child learn to identify sounds that are high, low, loud, soft, close by, far away, slow, fast, rhythmic, moving, stationary.
b. lengthen auditory attention span through games, sequenced instructions, citations of important information such as name, address, telephone number.
c. use music, television, radio, citizens' radio to help the child develop listening and attention skills; ask the child questions to check for comprehension and organization of auditory memory (e.g., "Today is Wednesday, what programs can we listen to tonight?").

4. Olfactory. The sense of smell will alert the blind child to danger or pleasure, and the child must be encouraged to develop the olfactory sense and learn to label experience and the meaning carried by the labels. The teacher should

a. let the child associate smells with different family members.
b. help the child identify foods, places, and events by smell (e.g., the gas station, bakery, shoe store, fish market, hospital).
c. encourage the child to smell many more things than one would introduce to the sighted child through smell: clothes, furniture, foods, kitchen cleansers, seasonings, paper products, bathroom creams.

5. Gustatory. The sense of taste will also serve the blind child as a receptive channel. The child must be encouraged to sample a broad array of foods and other edibles. The teacher should

a. emphasize the differences between hot (temperature) and hot (spicy).

b. expose the child to foods that are sweet, sour, salty, mild, rich, bland, cold, lukewarm, acidic, starchy, raw, cooked. Label each, then have the child label the food.
c. provide all the cues available so that the child knows what is being tasted and develops preferences; encourage the child to eat a very broad selection of foods; explain what the various foods do for the body.

6. Vision. Any remaining light perception should be trained to be as efficient as possible; using it will not harm the remaining vision, but failure to use it will make it even less functional; training will not improve the acuity, but it will improve functional efficiency. The teacher should

a. introduce high contrast items (e.g., yellow on black).
b. emphasize heavy outlines of objects, pictures, letters.
c. use the overhead projector to teach identification of objects by shape.
d. gradually decrease size and intensity of objects as the child becomes more proficient in identification.

GROSS MOTOR DEVELOPMENT

1. Reaching. Not knowing that an interesting spectacle is before him or her, the blind child is not likely to reach for objects. To facilitate reaching, let the blind child touch a noisy object; gradually withdraw the object, but sound it as the child searches. Let the child again grasp the object when arms are outstretched in an exploratory manner. Inform the child that exploration is required in order to find the object.

2. Transferring. The blind child perseverates in unilateral handling of objects. To encourage transference from hand to hand, let the child play with a small car on a table, rolling it from hand to hand. After the child has one object in hand, present another to the same hand. Present a bottle or favorite toy to the nonpreferred hand.

3. Midline skills. The blind child needs to use both hands when handling a single object, with each hand performing a different task. Present the child with a toy drum that must be held with one hand while being hit with the other hand. Present a pot into which the child can drop kitchen utensils such as measuring spoon, jar lids, small cups. Present toys that must be activated by turning handles, for example, while the toy is held.

4. Throwing. Without visual judgment of distance, the blind child does not develop propulsion skills. Have the child drop balls through a suspended hoop. Tie a yarn ball on a string to the child's wrist and physically guide a release through the hoop or just in space. Use auditory balls and have the child throw against walls or to another person.

5. Head control. When the child is in prone position with arms elevated on adult's thigh, dangle sound toys above the child's head.

6. Crawling and creeping. Use human voices and sounds of favorite toys to encourage the child to become mobile. Use an infant scooter board or make a diaper sling and lift the child's abdomen off the floor in a physically prompted crawl.

7. Walking. Support the child around the waist in walking exercises. Walk the child with each foot on top of an adult's foot. Walk the child through a ladder on the floor so that the feet must be lifted.

FINE MOTOR DEVELOPMENT

1. Grasping. Without sight to identify objects in space, the blind child uses the hands to locate things. Because more space can be covered in sweeping, palmar motions, the child resorts to these to accommodate searching behavior. To facilitate higher forms of grasps, provide cradle gyms, busy boxes, small toys to squeak, formboards with holes to finger, and other toys with small areas to explore and manipulate. The child can also benefit from squeezing small pieces of dough between hand and fingers.

2. Locating objects. Provide a play table with raised edges so toys will not be out of reach. Place assorted objects at various places for the child to find and explore. Turn on a radio or phonograph at various positions in the room and have the child locate; this can also be done with a rattle, squeeze toy, or other sound source. Drop an object that creates a sound, such as keys, rattle, and have the child locate. The child can also drop or throw an object and retrieve it. Through these procedures, the child is developing an awareness that objects lost can be found with the aid of the sound they emit.

3. Body sensitivity to objects. Use objects of various shapes, textures, and temperatures, then play games with the child by rolling them across various body parts. Have the child identify the object and the body part; for example, the child might respond, "You drove my truck up my back and it stopped on my neck." After brushing the object over the child, have the child pick it up from a group of objects nearby. Using a paint brush, brush parts of body and have child say when and where.

4. Handcrafts. Encourage activities with dough, clay, finger paints, paper and cloth weaving, painting on an easel, making mosaics, using glue and various materials, stringing.

5. Spatial orientation. Provide experiences in block building, peg and pegboards, Lego blocks, nesting cups and blocks, puzzles, model building, Tinker Toys, construction sets.

6. Cutting. Begin with scissors with four finger holes so that the adult can guide the activity. Progress from straight lines heavily marked to curved lines, then zig-zag lines, to encourage eye-hand coordination. If vision is very limited, glue string or yarn to paper in various designs and have child cut around yarn or string. Make raised-line designs on paper with seamstress tracing wheel. Place pressure on the wheel on one side of heavy Manila or construction paper, and the design will be inverted on the other side.

7. Touch identification. Begin with common objects that must be briefly touched, then identified. Move to raised outlines of the pictures of the objects.

8. Marking and drawing. Teach the child to follow lines between edges of hard liquid glue. Use templates of various shapes, and let the child experience the continuity of movement and shape.

9. Tracing. With tracing paper over first flat objects, then raised picture outlines, let child locate and then trace shapes. Move to more abstract designs, letters, numbers.

10. Reproduction. Use pairs of peg boards and rubber band-nail boards. Have the child reproduce on a board the design felt on another board. Provide two pegboards and have child create identical designs. Present child with design made from toothpicks and let child create an identical design. Do the same with parquetry designs.

11. Sequencing. Begin with simple discriminations on one dimension with two sizes. Move to more items that must be arranged in a continuum of large to small, left to right. Increase difficulty by adding dimensions, such as shape, color, texture, and have child reproduce a model of the sequence (bead stringing using various shapes is a good way to apply this concept). Move to raised outlines of shapes and vary, depending on child's vision and ability.

12. Pre-Braille. For totally blind children, begin teaching the shape of the basic Braille cell, and expose the child to numbers and name in Braille after teaching scanning skills. Have the child match Braille letters and numbers to similar Braille letters and numbers, and then match whole words from two- or three-letter words to more complex ones.

RECEPTIVE LANGUAGE DEVELOPMENT

An understanding of the meaning of sounds will come from listening and experiencing; therefore, provide opportunities for these to coincide.

1. Attending to sound. Call attention to sounds; physically prompt the child to stop and listen.

2. Localization of sound. Prompt the child to turn ear, then nose, in the direction of the sound source. Turn on a radio, phonograph, or shake a sound toy momentarily and ask the child from where the sound was being emitted.

3. Discrimination of sounds. After the child can attend, localize, and identify, encourage the child to note sameness and differences along several dimensions and at several distances. Shake, roll, or squeeze toys, then ask the child what object emits the sound heard. Later ask the child to identify the names with the noises of others in the immediate environment or sounds that animals or other situations (weather, door opening) make. These sounds may be reproduced from records. Move from object sounds to oral sounds.

4. Sound-symbol association. As the child develops sound-symbol association, say object words and have the child locate the object, then later perform acts with the object, such as "Put the spoon in the bowl."

5. Vocabulary comprehension. Have the child respond in different ways (such as raise left or right hand, hit drum or table different number of times) when you name objects that are classified differently, for example, people vs. actions; places vs. descriptive words; physical attributes vs. location (prepositions).

6. Laterality. Emphasize identity of left and right sides and parts of body, and of objects. For example, place your left hand on the table, lift your right foot, or place your left hand on your right shoulder.

7. Directionality. Have the child place things according to directions, permit the child to move in space according to simply stated commands. Emphasize actions such as number of steps as skills develop. Play "Simon Says" to incorporate this into a game. Move from simple one-stage commands to more complex stages, for example, "Pick up the ball." to "Pick up the ball and place it on the table."

8. Listening for sequences. Provide the child with proper sequences that have omissions and errors, and let the child spot the error.

9. Auditory overload. Blind children can be oversaturated with radio input. Encourage selectivity in radio and phonograph input, and do not let this take the place of human contact. Encourage the child to seek out peers for information and socialization.

EXPRESSIVE LANGUAGE DEVELOPMENT

1. Expressions of feeling. Identify cries and sounds with the appropriate emotions, saying to the child, "Oh, you are sad" or "You are happy." Repeat the sound as the child realizes the meaning conveyed.

2. Babbling. Repeat sounds as one would with any child. Let the child feel the sound through your mouth, nose, and throat.

3. Vocabulary building. As words emerge, be sure to attach as much meaning as possible to words so that concept relations develop along with labeling. Keep examples as concrete as possible; if teaching the word "ball," for example, give the child a ball to explore tactually. Give as many different examples as possible

until the child really understands what the object is. Expand the meaning of "ball" with examples that vary on dimensions, such as size and texture.

4. Self-image. Encourage self-awareness by early identification of body parts and properties on self and others. Stress use of "I," "me," "mine," and other personal pronouns applied correctly to others.

5. Concept statements. Provide experiences that are meaningful, then cautiously expand the abstract statements that can be applied so that language maintains its symbolic representation purpose for the child. Provide many different experiences, objects, and events that will facilitate transfer between statements.

COGNITIVE DEVELOPMENT

1. Causality. Provide experiences that enable the child to understand that a motor act causes something to happen. Give the child toys that vibrate or continue moving after the child pushes or hits them to initiate movement, such as a roly-poly toy, a toy secured by suction on a tray, or a pound-around. Make sure that the child feels the effects.

Encourage the child to move about freely in a safe environment in which many objects have been placed so that the child experiences the causality of objects and events as they will occur naturally as mobility develops. This will negate some fears as the child travels into more unfamiliar environments.

2. Means-end. Provide experiences similar to those for causality; however, the effects should be auditory or tactile. For example, the child shakes a toy and it continues to make noise; he activates a music box that plays a tune; he turns a handle and feels the water run.

3. Object Permanence. The blind child is unable to solve simple problems such as finding a toy that might be slightly out of reach or hidden under another object. Play hide and seek games, telling the child that the toy is hiding and he or she must search for it. Model and physically prompt the searching behavior.

4. Problem solving. The blind child is slow to realize that objects in the environment can be used in multiple ways, particularly to solve problems that might exist separately from the object itself. Encourage multiple use of objects, and association of the object with other things. For example, let the child find out that climbing on a footstool makes it possible to reach the sofa without help; or that agitating detergent in a pan of water produces bubbles.

5. Classification. The ability to classify is very important in the developing blind child. Stress qualities that make objects the same or different. Let the child feel and describe these characteristics. Play games in which the child must classify objects according to a specified dimension, or give the child a series of objects that must be classified, for example, beads, blocks, or other objects that must be sorted

into separate containers. Stress shape, size, texture, and weight; do not stress one without the others.

6. Environmental structure. The ability to order one's environment or to understand the order others have imposed is a most important skill. Always maintain furniture and objects in their same and appropriate place. Help the child to identify the objects and tell where they belong. Provide opportunities for the child to manipulate the environment, such as moving a chair closer to the open window in order to feel cooler on a hot day. This will help the child to understand that objects can be manipulated to satisfy needs or achieve personal comfort.

7. Reasoning. Play simple games that encourage reasoning, with assumptions that can be checked against reality. For example, say "If we open the refrigerator door, we will ____ ____ ____ (feel cold air)." "If we turn on the left hand faucet in the sink, we will ____ ____ ____ (get hot water)." Provide the child with concrete examples that will lead to proper reasoning about events. While asking the questions or having the child fill in the blanks, allow the child to experience what will actually happen and later repeat the questions to see if the child has grasped what occurred.

8. Concept development. Distorted concepts of real objects are quite common in blind children, because their tactual experiences have been with small replications of life size objects. Provide comparisons and let the child tactually experience real dimensions when possible. Check verbal understanding by having the child describe size, shape, etc. Whenever possible, provide concrete examples in their real context because removing examples from their context may distort the child's grasp of what the object is and what function it serves.

9. Generalization. It is common for blind children to center on one object or behavior, thus resulting in stereotyped play. Provide experiences that broaden the child's interest in people, events, and objects. For example, if the child develops an attachment for keys, provide many sets of keys, then move to other objects on a chain or string.

10. Conservation. Provide opportunities for the child to handle the same materials under different circumstances, as a prerequisite to an understanding of conservation. For example, let the child roll the same mass of dough into various shapes, pour the same can of water into containers of varying sizes, feel two cups of dried corn that are the same, then feel them when they are in two very different-sized containers.

SOCIAL DEVELOPMENT

1. Emotional responses. Blind babies should be reinforced for showing appropriate emotional responses. Their faces must express feelings; therefore, they should make happy or smiling faces, sad faces, etc., and feel others with these faces. Say, "Oh, your face says you are happy when you hear Daddy's voice."

2. Separation. Separation anxiety can be extended for a longer period when a child cannot sense that the adult is still present at a distance or that other sources of comfort are still nearby. While working at various distances in the child's proximity, say that you are still present although not directly in front of the child.

3. Fear of strangers. The blind child may experience negative reactions whenever strangers appear. Carefully prepare the child for a new person; let the child be touched by the new person while a familiar person is present, then gradually release the child to the new person.

4. Parental influence. Social problems in young blind children are frequently created by parents who are having a very difficult time adjusting to a handicapped child. Parent counseling is critical; it is particularly valuable to introduce such parents to other parents who have been through similar experiences. Try to understand the parent-child relationship, and foster the positive aspects of both the parents' responses to the child and the child's responses to the parents.

A major factor in appropriate social development seems to be in the child's development of a close emotional bond with a significant other. Stress this aspect to the parents, and help the child realize he or she is important to the parents.

5. Development of independence. Foster all the independence possible for a child at any given time. Remove all extremely dangerous obstacles, but do not prevent the child by overprotection from coming into contact with situations that will teach lessons about objects or events to be encountered in later life. For example, the blind child who comes into contact with a footstool and falls will learn, as a consequence, to be aware that one can trip over objects. Be very careful, however, that the first experiences in exploring the child's environment are manipulated so as to provide excitement and joy when traveling. Do not provide an environment that frightens the child and stops further exploration. The child must be allowed and encouraged to act even if performances are not always correct. The child must take independent steps.

SELF-CARE DEVELOPMENT

General Principles

a. Before beginning a new activity with a blind child, simply say what is going to happen. "I am going to help you put on your shirt," "It's time to have a drink of milk." This prepares the child for slight changes that otherwise cannot be anticipated.
b. Establish a place for everything and make sure objects are always in the same place; the spoon is always on the right hand side of the plate, the hairbrush on the dresser at the same place.

c. Mark objects that are difficult to distinguish. The child's toothbrush, comb, brush, bath towels, for example, should bear tactile identification so the child can quickly determine whether it is a personal object.
d. In teaching new behaviors, work from behind the child if possible. Slowly provide less and less help, requiring the child to perform the task independently.
e. Call attention to the sounds associated with self-care events. "I can hear Daddy shaving with his electric razor," "We can hear Mom stirring the iced tea."

2. *Eating*

a. Emphasize the identification of foods by smell. While holding a spoon of peas before the child's mouth, say, "Now you are ready for your peas; can you smell them?"
b. Use bowls or plates with raised edges when teaching the beginning stages of self-feeding.
c. Encourage the blind child to use bread as a pusher when securing food.
d. Before beginning the self-feeding task, tell the child where certain foods are on the plate. For children who have a sense of time, use a clock as a good model for reference (e.g., "Your meat is at six o'clock, your peas are at three o'clock.").
e. When teaching the child to fill glasses, train the child to use the finger of the hand holding the glass to measure the amount of fluid in the glass. The child pours until the finger is wet, signifying the glass is full.
f. Encourage the child, as soon as possible, to ask, receive, and serve himself or herself from the containers being passed. The child should also be encouraged to pass the containers to others.
g. The proper manners that most children observe and imitate are not so easily accessible for the blind child. The child must be told, "We chew with our mouths closed," "We do not eat with our elbows on the table," etc.

3. *Dressing*

a. Be sure there are identification marks that permit the child to distinguish the fronts of garments from the backs.
b. Have shoes, gloves, socks carefully marked to distinguish left from right.
c. Be extremely consistent in how the child is to wear garments: always to wear certain shirt tails tucked in, for example. This permits the child to know when he or she is properly dressed.

d. Teach buttoning, zipping, buckling, snapping, etc., using the child's own garments when dressing so that familiar hand and tactile impressions can be easily reinforced. If garments cause difficulties, adaptations may sometimes prove rewarding, such as a piece of string attached to the zipper which can later be removed as the task proves easier.
e. The child should attempt to dress alone at the appropriate time and in the context of the situation. Do not dress a child in the morning and have him attempt to dress alone later during the day. The child should be encouraged to dress independently when awakening and, if necessary, be corrected. Also, if the child is to go outside during the day, encourage the child to seek out and put on his or her own outside garments. Teach the child what type of clothing should be worn in different types of weather situations.

4. *Toileting*

a. The sequence, the verbal commands, and timing should remain very consistent in teaching toileting skills. Instructions should be short and to the point. "Sit on the toilet," "Flush the toilet," "Wash your hands."
b. Stress tactile awareness as a key to needs. Frequently ask, "Are you dry?" If the child answers, "yes" and is dry, reinforce with "Good, you have dry pants!" If pants are wet say, "No, your pants are wet." Change pants in the bathroom (have the child remove them alone, if possible), and do not talk to the child during the process.
c. Let the blind child accompany other family members to the bathroom so there will be more experiences to imitate.
d. Tie down a toy to the toilet seat or chair for the child to play with while sitting on the toilet.
e. Limit time on the toilet to 8 to 10 minutes. A cue to prerequisite toilet behavior is the ability to remain dry for two hours.

5. *Grooming*

a. Bathing skills should be taught as to any other child. Have faucets marked hot and cold.
b. Teach child as many ways as possible to check appearance: feeling hair, buttons, zippers, checking shoes for paper or trash stuck on the bottom.
c. Find short cuts and alternative ways to accomplish grooming tasks. Squirt toothpaste on teeth rather than on brush bristles; teach frequent use of napkins and handkerchiefs.
d. Discuss with the child the necessity of grooming and when grooming occurs during the day, such as when awakening, after meals, after playtime, before retiring.

e. Have the blind child initiate feedback from others rather than wait to be told something is not right. For example, the child might say "Is my hat on straight?"
f. Stress appropriate dress. It is important that the blind child be dressed comfortably, in manageable clothes that are clean and in keeping with those of sighted peers.

6. *Peer Interaction*

a. Encourage appropriate peer interaction. The blind child cannot see the toy the other is enjoying and thus misses out on modeling behavior. Circumvent this through verbal comment, close parallel play, cueing in to sound-play identification.

7. *Understanding the Body*

a. Encourage as much appropriate bodily exploratory behavior as is acceptable. The child needs to feel physical body differences in parents and sameness of one's self to siblings, as well as to understand why one cannot always explore the entire bodies of everyone contacted. Ask relatives always to wear a certain watch, ring, or bracelet when near the blind child and teach the child to associate those objects with the voice, etc.

8. *Self-Concept*

a. Self-concept is a critical factor in any child's development, but even more important in the development of a handicapped child. Stress human differences, but particularly emphasize the attributes of the handicapped child. It is important for the professional to state the traits he or she values in the blind child in the presence of the child and parents.

9. *Helping Others*

a. The ability to do things for others is particularly important for handicapped children, since many people feel sorry for them and want to "help" them. Provide opportunities for the blind child to assist others, to serve others, to be on the receiving end of "thank you."

Index

A

B

C

D

F

G

H

I

J

K

L

N

O

P

Q

R

S

T

U

V

W

X

Y

Z